I0114863

AN

English Dictionary:

EXPLAINING

The difficult Terms that are used in

Divinity, Husbandry, Physick, Phylosophy, Law, Navigation, Mathematicks, and other Arts and Sciences.

CONTAINING

Many Thousands of Hard Words

(and proper names of Places) more than are in any other English Dictionary or Expositor.

TOGETHER WITH

The Etymological Derivation of them from their proper Fountains, whether Hebrew, Greek, Latin, French, or any other Language.

In a Method more comprehensive, than any that is extant.

By E. Coles, School-Master and Teacher of the Tongue to Forreigners.

Ben. Johnson.

Much phrase that now is dead, shall be reviv'd;
And much shall dye, that now is nobly liv'd,
If Custom please; at whose disposing Will
The pow'r and Rule of Speaking resteth still.

Hor. de Arte Poet.

THE LAWBOOK EXCHANGE, LTD.
Clark, New Jersey

ISBN 978-1-58477-595-9

Lawbook Exchange edition 2006, 2019

The quality of this reprint is equivalent to the quality of the original work.

THE LAWBOOK EXCHANGE, LTD.
33 Terminal Avenue
Clark, New Jersey 07066-1321

Please see our website for a selection of our other publications and fine facsimile reprints of classic works of legal history:
www.lawbookexchange.com

Library of Congress Cataloging-in-Publication Data

Coles, Elisha, 1640?-1680.
An English dictionary : explaining the difficult terms that are used ... / Elisha Coles.
p. cm.
Includes index.
Originally published: London : S. Crouch, 1676.
ISBN 1-58477-595-5 (alk. paper)
1. English language--Dictionaries--Early works to 1800. I. Title.
PE1620.C7 2005
423--dc22

2005000817

Printed in the United States of America on acid-free paper

AN

English Dictionary:

EXPLAINING

The difficult Terms that are used in Divinity, Husbandry, Physick, Phylosophy, Law, Navigation, Mathematicks, and other Arts and Sciences.

CONTAINING

Many Thousands of Hard Words (and proper names of Places) more than are in any other English Dictionary or Expositor.

TOGETHER WITH

The Etymological Derivation of them from their proper Fountains, whether Hebrew, Greek, Latin, French, or any other Language.

In a Method more comprehensive, than any that is extant.

By *E. Coles*, School-Master and Teacher of the Tongue to Foreigners.

Ben. Johnson.

Much phrase that now is dead, shall be reviv'd;
And much shall dye, that now is nobly liv'd,
If Custom please; at whose disposing Will
The pow'r and Rule of Speaking resteth still.

Hor. de Arte Poet.

LONDON, Printed for *Samuel Crouch*, at the Corner Shop of *Popes-head* Al y, on the right hand next *Cornhill* 1676.

TO THE

READER.

THE ſeveral Climates of the World, have influenced the Inhabitants with Natures very different from one another. And their ſeveral ſpeeches bear ſome proportion of Analogy with their Natures. The *Spaniſh* and the *Spaniard* both are Grave, the *Italian* and th' *Italians* Amourous, the *Dutch* as boiſterous as the *Germans*, and the *French* as light as they themſelves are. But the moderate Clime of *England* has indifferently temper'd us as to both: and what exceſs there is in either, muſt be attributed to the acceſſion of ſomething Foreign. Our changes are all profeſſedly owing to the Conqueſts, eſpecially of *Sax* and *Normandy*.

The firſt was far the greater, and by virtue of That the body of our Language is ſtill Teutonick: But the Laſt is that which more nearly concerneth us; becauſe, though its firſt irruption was not a violent Inundation, yet it forced us to ſuch a Communication with *France*, that our Genius is wrought into ſome reſemblance of theirs: and (to imitate them) we bring home faſhions, terms and phraſes from every Nation and Language under Heaven. Thus we ſhould fill one another with Confuſion and Barbarity, were it not for ſome ſuch faithful Interpreter as is here preſented to the Prince of Iſles.

Not that I am ignorant of what's already done. I know the whole Succeſſion from Dr. *Bulloker*, to Dr. *Skinner*, from the ſmalleſt volume to the largeſt Folio. I know their difference and their Defects. Some are too little, ſome are too big; ſome are too plain (ſtufft with obſcenity not to be named) and ſome ſo obſcure, that (inſtead of expounding others) they have need themſelves of an Expoſitor. The method of ſome is fooliſh, and ſuppoſes things to be known before they are explained. For

 when

when the Terms of Art are reduced to their ſeveral Heads, you muſt know (in general) what your word is, before you can poſſibly tell where to ſeek it; or elſe (as they ſay) you muſt look a needle in a bottle of Hay.

Suppoſe you want the meaning of *Belperopis* or *Dulcarnon*, they are not in the Common herd; where will you look them? In the Law-terms? they are not there. Sure then they are proper Names; But they are not there neither.- What's to be done? Why, look till you find and you will not loſe your labour.

Some that pretend to correction and exactneſs, tranſcribe out of others (hand over head) their very faults and all.

Hear how ſeverely Doctor *Skinner* taxes one of them,---*Solens ballucinatur*: and again, ---*Ridicule ut ſolet omnia:* and in another place, ----*ubi notare eſt miſerrimam Authoris ignorantiam*, &c.

But that Man had but a little work, and ſo was bound to have done it well. It is excuſable in a *World of Words* to ſay that Contemptible and Contemptuous, Ingenious and Ingenuous are all one: that *Decompoſit* ſignifies Compounded of two other words: Emberweek is the week next before Lent: Froiſe, a pancake or tanſie: Gallon, a meaſure of two quarts: Gomer, nine gallons (inſtead of one.) *Limbus Patrum*, where the Saints reſide till the Reſurrection: *Nazareth*, the place where Chriſt was born, *Redſtert*, a Robin Red-breaſt, &c.

And a thouſand more ſuch, which ſimple Children would be apt to contradict, but Men of Judgement (for whom they were not writ) know where the miſtake might lie. Yet ſure 't would have made his worſhip ſmile, to have readd, how that *Argus* King of *P*. for his ſingular wiſdom and circumſpection, was feigned by the Poets to have had no eyes.

Cuſtode admittendo, a writ for the removing of a Guardian.

Ejaculation, a yelling.

Eviration, a yielding.

Fidicula, a falling vulture.

Ichidian, the Motto of the Princes Arms.

Iopæna, a ſong of rejoicing.

Lungis, a tall ſlim m n that has no length to his height.

Mayweed, like Cammomile in ſmell, but of a ſtinking ſaour, &c.

So

So many there are of this Nature and ſo groſs, that (let the reaſon be what it will) they are altogether intolerable.

In that which I have done, I do not warrant abſolute perfection. The pains that are taken in it, will appear at firſt ſight. The addition that is made to the number of words in former Authors of this kind, is almoſt incredible (conſidering the bulk) being raiſed from ſeven in th' Expoſitor to almoſt thirty thouſand here; which is ſome thouſands more than are in Mr. *Blunts Gloſſographia* or Mr. *Philips World of Words*. The order I obſerve is altogether Alphabetical; for that beſt anſwers the deſign of Informing others. If any would have the proper Names, Terms of Law, Navigation (or any other Art) by themſelves, they may go through the whole and (with delight and profit) reduce them all to their particular Heads.

I am no friend to vain and tedious repetitions. Therefore you will often meet with words explain'd in their dependance and relation to one another, and the fence compleated by taking them together: as for example,

Lupa, a She-wolf that nouriſhed *Romulus* in the
Lupercal, a place near *Rome*, where were celebrated the
Lupercalia, Feaſts in honour of *Pan*, performed by the
Luperci, Prieſts of *Pan*----.

Poetical expreſſions may be allowed to Poetical Relations and Fictions; yet here and there I give a hint, to let you know, that I take them not for real verities.

The hiſtory of the Bible I ſuppoſe to be ſo well known, as that I only give the plain Engliſh of the *Hebrew*, *Chaldee*, *Syriack* and *Greek* Names.

Here is a large addition of many words and phraſes that belong to our Engliſh Dialects in the ſeveral Counties, and where the particular Shire is not expreſt, the diſtinction (according to the uſe) is more general into North and South-Country words.

Here are alſo added all the Market-Towns (and other conſiderable places) in *England*, with all the places of note in other Countries, eſpecially the Neighbour Nations. Where it is to be obſerved, that (as Dr. *Heylin* ſaies of *Hungary*) it were infinite labour to expreſſe every little place which the ſeat of a war

gives

gives occaſion for Hiſtory to mention.

'Tis no diſparagement to underſtand the Canting Terms. It may chance to ſave your throat from being cut, or (at leaſt) your Pocket from being pickt.

I have not only retain'd, but very much augmented the number of Old Words. For though Mr. *Blount* (as he ſaies expreſsly) ſhunn'd them, becauſe they grew obſolete; yet doubtleſs their uſe is very great: not only for the unfolding thoſe Authors that did uſe them, but alſo for giving a great deal of light to other words that are ſtill in uſe. Thoſe that I call Old Words are generally ſuch as occurr in *Chaucer*, *Gower*, *Pierce Ploughman* and *Julian Barns*.

And whoſoever has a mind, inſtead of them (or other vulgar terms) to uſe expreſſions that are more polite; he ſees what words are markt for Latin, Greek or French, and may himſelf make ſuch Collections as will be far more advantageous, than if they had been gathered to his hand.

Finally, that I might be the more comprehenſive (for here is very much in very little room) I have ſignified the derivation of the words from their ſeveral Originals, and the Names of the Counties in which they are uſed, by one or two of their initial letters; the meaning of which is expreſt in the following Table.

A Table explaining the Abbreviations made uſe of in this Book.

A. *Arabick,*	Ga. *Gallick, old French.*	P. *Perſian.*
Br. *Brittiſh.*	H. *Hebrew.*	Sa. *Saxon.*
C. *Canting.*	I. *Italian.*	Sc. *Scotch.*
Ch. *Chaldee.*	Ir. *Iriſh.*	Sla. *Slavonian.*
Che. *Cheſhire.*	K. *Kentiſh.*	So. *South-Countrey.*
Cu. *Cumberland.*	L. *Latin.*	Sp. *Spaniſh.*
D. *Dutch.*	La. *Lancaſhire.*	Sf. *Suffolk,*
Da. *Daniſh.*	Li. *Lincolnſhire.*	Sſ. *Suſſex.*
De. *Devonſhire.*	No. *North-Countrey*	Sy. *Syriack,*
Der. *Derbyſhire.*	Nf. *Norfolk,*	T. *Tuſcan.*
E. *Eſſex.*	Not. *Nottinghamſhire.*	Tu. *Turkiſh.*
F. *French.*	O. *Old Word.*	W. *Wiltſhire.*
G. *Greek,*		We. *Weſt-Countrey,*
Ge. *German.*		Y. *Yorkſhire.*

To prevent a vacancy, I thought good here to prefix a Catalogue of the most usual words, whose sound is the same, but their sense and Orthography very different.

Altar, for sacrifice.
Alter, change.
Are, be.
Air, Element.
Heir, to an estate.
Assent, consent.
Ascent, of a hill.
Ax, to hew with.
Acts, Deeds.
Baal, an Idol.
Ball, for play.
Bawl, cry out.
Bare, naked, or did [a bear.
Bear, carry
Beer, drink.
Bier, for a Corps.
Barbara, womans name.
Barbary, the Country.
Berberry, a tree.
Base, vile.
Bass-viol.
Bows, bends.
Boughs, branches.
Bouze, quaff.
Buy, with money.
By and by, anon.
Berry, that grows.
Bury, the dead.
Call, by name.
Cawl, like a net.
Cellar, under ground.
Seller, of wares.
Chare, a work.
Chair, to sit in.
Cheer or *Chear*, food.
Clark, a mans name.
Clerk, a Clergy man.
Collar, neck-band.
Choler, anger.
Currents, streams.
Corants, a fruit.
Dam, stop up.
Damn, condemn.
Dear, costly.
Deer, Venison.
Doe, a Female.
Dough, paste.
Done, acted.
Dun, colour.
Due, debt.
Dew, of heaven.
Ear, of the head.
Year, 12 months.
Eaten, devoured.
Eaton, a proper name.
Fain, earnestly.
Feign, counterfeit.
Fillip, on the forehead.
Philip, a Name.
Foul, filthy.
Fowl, a bird.
Fair, comely.
Fare, diet.
Furr-gown.
Fir-tree.
Forth, abroad.
Fourth, day, &c.
Groan, in spirit.
Grown, in stature.
Guilt, conscience.
Gilt, with gold.
Hare, and hound.
Hair, of the head.
Hear, harken.
Here, in this place.
Heard, for heared.
Hard, as a stone.
Herd, of Swine.
Hart, a deer.
Heart, and Soul.
Hallow, sanctifie.
Hollow, with holes.
Hire, wages.
Higher, than you.
Hole, a hollowness.
Whole, entire.
Holy, sacred.
Wholly, altogether.
Home, house.
Whom? what man?
Holm, holly.
Hue, a colour.
Hew, to cut.
Hugh, a mans name.
Hymn, a Song.
Him, that man.
Her, that woman.
Hur, a mans name.
I, my self.
Eye, to see with.
Ile, a walk, or I will.
Isle, an Island.
Kill, destroy.
Kiln, of bricks.
Kiss, with the mouth.
Ciss, *Sauls* Father.
Latin, Roman.
Latten, Tin.
Leper, a Leprous man.
Leaper, a jumper.
Lessen, make less.
Lesson, a Lecture.
Lo, behold.
Low, not high.
Lose, forgoe.
Loose, release.
Manner, fashion.
Manour,-house.
Marten, a bird.
Martin, a mans name.
Meat, food.
Mete, measure.
Mite, small coyn.
Might, Power.
Moat, a broad ditch.
Mote, in the Sun.

Mote,

More, than they.
Moor, a Black.
Mues, *Mews*, for hawks.
Muse to meditate.
Nay, no.
Neigh, as a horse,
Nigh, near.
Nid, a nest.
Nye, a mans name.
Naught, bad.
Nought, nothing.
Nether, lower.
Neither, this nor that.
O, oh, alas!
Ow, to be indebted.
Oat, Corn.
Ought, any thing.
One, first number.
Own, proper.
Our, belonging to us.
Hour, 60 minutes.
Pare, take off.
Pair, a couple.
Pear, a Fruit.
Parson, of the Parish.
Person, any Man.
Place, room.
Plaise, a Fish.
Pole, for hops.
Poll, the head.
Pore, little hole.
Poor, needy.
Pray, beseech.
Prey, booty.
Profit, gain.
Prophet, foreteller.
Rain, water.
Rein, of a bridle.
Reign, of a King.
Rice, Corn.
Rise, advancement.
Room, space.
Rome, in *Italy*.
Red, in colour.
Readd, for readed.
Roe, of fishes.
Row, the boat.
Rew, of Trees.

Ruff, a double-band.
Rough, rugged.
Rung, the bells.
Wrung, his hands.
Rie, Corn.
Wry, crooked.
Rime, a mist.
Rythm, in verse.
Rite, a custom.
Right, not wrong.
Write, with pen.
Wright, work-man.
Reed, that grows.
Read, a book.
Road, highway.
Rode, did ride.
Rhode, proper name.
By Rote, by heart.
Wrote, writ.
Wrought, did work.
Sheep, a Beast.
Ship, at Sea.
Sight, view.
Site, situation.
Cite, summon.
Sink-down.
Cinque, five.
Sloe, a fruit.
Slow, tardy.
Slough, old skin.
So, thus.
Sow, seed.
Sew, cloth.
Some, part.
Sum, of money.
Sole, or *Soal*, a fish.
Sole, of a shoe, or alone.
Soul, spirit.
Sore, painful.
Soar, aloft.
Swore, did swear.
Sound, whole.
Swoon, faint away.
Succour, help.
Sucker, young plant.
Sun, that shines.
Son, of a Father.
Stair, a step.

Stare, with the eyes, &c.
Slight, despise, &c.
Sleight, of hand.
Then, at that time.
Than, in comparison.
Tame, not wild.
Thame, a Towns name.
Tongs, for the fire.
Tongues, languages.
Time, and tide.
Tyme, *Thyme*, the herb.
There, in that place.
Their, of them.
To, the preposition.
Toe, of the foot.
Tow, to spin.
Towe, hale the Ship.
Too, also.
Two, in number.
Throw, hurl.
Through, thorow.
Use, enjoy.
Ews, not Rams.
Ure, practice.
Ewr, and bason.
Your, of you.
Vain, idle
Vein, of bloud, &c.
Vial, a glass.
Viol, for Musick.
Ware, Merchandize.
Were, was.
Wear, Cloaths.
Wast, thou.
Waste, spend.
Waist, the middle.
Wait, expect.
Weight, burden.
Way, passage.
Weigh, in scales.
You, ye.
Ewe, Sheep.
Yew-tree.
Ye, yee, you.
Yea, yes.

E. Coles.

A*A*, The name of a River dividing *Picardy* from *Flanders*.

Aacius, The name of a man.

Aalac, A hill in *Syria*.

Aarassus, A City in *Pisidia*.

Aaron h. Teacher, or Mountain of strength.

Aba, A Tyrant of *Hungary*.

Abaction l. Driving away.

Abacted, l. Driven away.

Abactors, l. Stealers of Cattel.

Abacus, l A flat foursquare piece in Architecture.

Abaddon, h. A Destroyer.

Abæ, A Town in *Greece*, never guilty of Sacriledge.

Abagus Can, a king of the *Tartars*, who ate the *Turk Parvana*

Abaisance, f. Stooping down.

Abalus, An Isle in the *German* Ocean.

Abandon, f S.F. Forsake.

Abannition -ation l. Banishment for a year.

Abantias, An Isle in the Mediterranean Sea.

Abarim, h. Passage.

Abarimon, A Country in *Scythia*, their feet reverted.

Abarstick, o. Insatiable.

Abas, The son of *Metanira*, whom *Ceres* turned into a Lizard.

Abase, l. Bring low.

Abash, Make ashamed.

Abaft, toward the stern or hinder part of the Ship.

Abate A Writ, Destroy it for a time through some defect.

Abatement, Entring on an inheritance before the right Heir, to keep him out.

Abatos, An Island in *Egypt*.

Abawed, o. Daunted, ashamed.

Abba, Sy. Father.

Abbas or *Abbot*, The same to his;

Abbacy or *Abbathy*, as a Bishop to his Bishoprick.

Abbord, l. Draw near the shore, or grapple with a ship.

Abbreviate, l. Shorten.

Abbreviation, l. Shortning.

Abbreviature, short draught.

Abbreviator, He that shortens.

Abbrochment, Ingrossing, buying up wholewares to sell by retail.

Abbuttals, The buttings or boundings of any land.

Abdals, Religious *Persians* vowing poverty.

Abdalmatalis, *Mahomets* Grandfather.

Abdelmonus, King of *Africa*.

Abdera, A City in *Thrace*.

Abderite, *Democritus* who lived there.

Abderian Laughter, foolish, incessant laughter.

Abdevinam. Head of the twelfth Mansion in Astrology.

Abdi, h. My servant, Father of Kish.

Abdicate, l. Renounce, refuse, contrary to adopt.

Abdication, Dis-inheriting.

Abdiel, h. Servant of God, or Cloud of Gods store.

Abdolonymus, A Gardiner, made King of *Sydon*.

Abdomen, l. The fat which is about the belly.

Abdominous, Unwildy, panch-bellyed.

Abduce, l. Lead or entice away.

Abduction, Taking away.

Abecedary, l. Belonging to the letters, *A, B, C*, &c.

Abecedarian, which teaches or learns the *A, B, C*, &c.

Abedge, o. Abide.

Abel, h. Vanity.

In *Abeiance, f.* void, not in any mans present possession.

Abent, o. Steep place.

Abequitate, l. Ride away.

Aberconway, A Town in *Carnarvonshire*.

Aberfraw, A Town in *Anglesey*.

Abergevenny, or,

Abergenny, A Town in *Wales*.

Aberration, l. Going astray.

Aberrancy, the same.

Abesse, o. cast down, humbled.

Abet, Encourage or uphold in evil.

Abettor, or,

Abettator, He that encourages, &c.

Abgregate, l. to disperse or separate (from the flock.)

Abhorrency, l. Loathing, hating.

Abib, h. Ripening [month.]

Abidst, o. Suffered.

Abia, Hercules daughter.

Abiah, h. The will of the Lord.

Abiathar, h. Father of the remnant, or of contemplation, or Excellent Father.

Abject, l. Vile, base, cast-away.

Abiezer, h. The Fathers help

Abigail, h. Fathers joy.

Abii, Rude people of *Scythia*.

Ability, l. power.

Abimelech, h. My Father the King, a common name of Kings.

Abington, A Town in *Berkshire*, and others in *Cambridge*.

Abintestate, l Without a will.

Abinoam, h. The fathers error

Abishai, h. The fathers reward.

Abishering, Mish. Freedom from Amercements.

Abit, o. Dwelleth.

Abition, l. Going away.

Abjudicate, l. Give away by judgement.

Abjure, l. Forswear, renounce, forsake the Realm for ever.

Ablactation, l. Weaning, also grafting & keeping the Cyon for a while on its own stock.

Ablaqueate, l. To uncover the roots of Trees.

Ablation, l. Taking away.

Ablative, l. Belonging thereto.

Ablectick, l. Adorned for sale.

Ablegation, l. sending away
Ablepsy, gr. Blindness.
Ablocation, l. Letting out to hire.
Ablution, l. Washing away,
Abnegation, l. Stiff denying.
Abner, h. The fathers candle,
Abnodation, l. Untying of knots, also pruning of trees.
Aboocrites, A Captain of the *Bœotians*.
Abogen, o. Bowed.
Abolition, l. Destroying, putting out of memory.
Abominate, l. Hate, loath.
Abone, f. Make good, ripen.
Aboord, Within the Ship.
Aborigines, l. The oldest people of *Italy*, also people born where they live.
Abortion, l. Miscarrying in women.
Abortive, Belonging thereto
Abradacaba, A Charm against Agues.
Abraham, h. Father of many
Abram, High Father.
Abrahams baum, An *Italian* willow that bears
Agnus Castus, Like Pepper.
Abracamins, Enchanters among the *Indians*.
Abram-Cove, c. Naked or poor man.
Abrasion, l. Shaving away
Abravanus, A River in *Scotland*.
Abrenunciation, l. Forsaking.
Abric, Sulphur in Chymistry.
Abricot, f. or rather.
Apricock, f. A plum ripened in the Sun.
Abridge, f. Shorten.
Abrodietical, g. Curious in diet.
Abrogate, l. Make void.
Abrotanum, g. *Themistocles* Mother, also the Herb *Southernwood*.
Abrupt, l. Suddenly broken off.
Absalom, or
Abishelom, h. Fathers peace.
Absalonism, The practice of *Absalom*, viz. Rebellion.
Abscession, l. Going away.
Abscission, l. Cutting off.
Absconding, l. or
Absconsion Hiding.

Absentaneous, l. Belonging to Absence.
Absentees, A Parliament at *Dublin* so called.
Absis, The highest or lowest pitch of the Planets.
Absolve, l. Pardon, acquit.
Absolute, l. Perfect.
Absolution, l. A pardon.
Absonant, or
Absonous, l. Disagreeing [in sound]
Absorb, l. Sup up all.
Absorpt, Devoured.
Absoris, A Town in *Minervae's* Isle, built by the *Colchians*.
Abstemious, l. Sober, temperate.
Abstention, l. Keeping the Heir from possession.
Absterge l. Cleanse, wipe off.
Abstersion, l. A Cleansing.
Abstersive, Cleansing.
Abstinence, l. Temperance.
Abstorted, l. Wrested by force.
Abstract, l. Separate, also a small draught of a greater work, also a quality divided from the subject.
Abstraction, l. Taking away.
Abstrude, l. Thrust away.
Abstruse, or
Abstrusive, l. Hid, secret, dark.
Abstrusity, Darkness, &c.
Absurd, l. Foolish, harsh.
Absurdity, Foolishness.
Abvolate, l. Fly away.
Abvolation, Flying away.
Abus, The River *Humber* in *York shire*.
Abism, or,
Abyss, g. Bottomless pit.
Abysmal, Botomless.
Abyssines, *Æthiopians* under the Emperour *Prester John*.
Acacalis, One of *Apolloes* Mistresses, by whom he had *Philarides* and *Philander*.
Acacia, A shrub, and the binding gum thereof.
Academia, g. A place near *Athens* where *Plato* was born.
Academy, g. Publick School or University.
Academic, *Platonic* Philosopher, or
Academical, belonging thereto.

Acadinus, A fountain in *Sicily* wherein all false oathes writ on tables used to sink.
Acaid, Vineger (in Chymistry.)
Acaire, g. The mad-mens Saint.
Acarnon, The bright star of *Eridanus*.
Acastus, The son of *Peleus* King of *Thessaly*.
Acatalepsie, g. Incomprehensibleness, impossibility of being comprehended.
Accedas ad Curiam, l. A writ commanding the Sheriff to make record of such or such a suit.
Accedas ad Vicecomitem. l. A writ commanding the *Coroner* to deliver a writ to the *Sheriff*
Accelerate, l. Hasten.
Accelerator, The Muscle that opens the passage of the seed and Urine.
Accension, l. setting on fire.
Accent, l. The tone or mark directing the lifting up the sound of any syllable.
Acceptance, or
Acceptation, l. Allowing, or receiving kindly.
Acceptilation, l. An acquittance by word of mouth.
Accerse, l. Call forth, provoke.
Access, l. Coming, passage, also [the fit of an] Ague.
Accession, Addition.
Accessor, l. Comer.
Accessible, Easie to come to.
Accessary, or
Accessory, l. Partaking in the guilt of a fault.
Accidalia, Venus.
Accident, l. That which happens.
Accidental, By chance.
Accidence, or
Accidents, The first instructions for the Latin Tongue.
Accements, g. Monks of *Constantinople*, that slept by turns.
Acolastick, g. Riotous, lawless
Acolyte, g. A Young Minister, that serves the Altar with water, wine, and light.
Aconick, Belonging to

Aconite,

Aconite, l. Wolfs-bane, an herb.

Acorus, A sweet-smelling plant, very medicinal.

Acontius, A young man of *Cea*, suiter to *Cydippe*.

Acousti k, g. Belonging to or helping the hearing.

Acquests, or *Acquists*, f. Purchases, [by or for only one.]

Acquiesce, l. Rest satisfied.

Acquietandis plegiis, a writ for the getting an acquittance.

Acquisition, l. Getting.

Acquittal, A discharge.

Acre, 40 Perches length of land and four in breadth.

Acrimony, l. sharpness, sourness.

Acrisius, Son of *Abas* King of *Argos*, and father of *Danae*.

Acroamatick, g. That gives or requires much attention, musical.

Acroatick, g. The subtilest of *Aristotles* Philosophy.

Acrocomick, g. Having long hair.

Acrostick, g. Verses beginning with the letters of ones name

Acroteria, g. Sharp and spiry battlements upon flat buildings.

Achronychal, g. Belonging to those stars that rise in the twilight.

Acsab, b. Adorned, wantonness.

Acteon, Turned into a stag by *Diana*, and torn in pieces by his dogs.

Acteoned, Horned.

Actifs, Fryars that feed on roots.

Action, l. Deed, also a suit at law.

Actisanes, King of *Æthiopia*.

Actitation, .. Debating of Law-suits.

Active, l. Nimble.

Active voice, The way of forming verbs in *o*.

Activity, l. Nimbleness.

Actium, Promontory of *Epirus*, whence Blackcherries are supposed to come.

Actius Nævius, Cutt a whetstone in two with a Razor.

Acton burnel, A Castle in *Shropshire*

Actor, l. Doer, Stage-player

Actual, l. Belonging to Action.

Actuality, Perfection of being

Actuary, l. The Register of a Convocation.

Actuate, l. Bring into act.

Aculeate, l. with a sting.

Acuminate, l. Sharpen.

Acuminous, Sharp-edged, pointed, subtile.

Acupictor, l. Embroiderer, needle-worker.

Acute diseases grow quickly to a height, and so kill or decay. Sharp, witty.

Acyrology, g. Improper speech.

Accius Tullius, Prince of the *Volsci*, warring against *Rome*.

Acclamation, l. Crying out.

Acclivity, l. Steepness.

Acco, Fell mad at her own deformity.

Accolade, f. Clipping about the neck.

Accodrinc. sa. Drink made of Acorns.

Accommodate, l. Fit, apply.

Accommodatitious, Proper, fit.

Accomplish, f. Fulfill.

Accomptable, f. Lyable to give an account.

Accordant, f. Agreeable.

Accordance, f. Agreement.

Accort, f. Wary.

Accost, f. To set upon [in discourse,] to draw near to.

Accoutred, f. Dressed.

Accoutrement, Dressing.

Accoy, o. Asswage.

Accretion, l. growing to.

Accrew, f. Grow, arise.

Accroche, f. To hook unto.

Accumb, l. Sit or lye down.

Accumulate, l. Heap up.

Accurate, l. Exact.

Accusation, l. Blaming.

Accusative, l. Belonging to accusing.

Ace, f. One in the Dice.

Acephalic, g. Without head.

Acephalists, g. Hereticks without an Author.

Acerbity, l. Sharpness or soureness.

Acerate, l. Coarse, full of chaffe.

Acersecomick, g. Whose hair was never cutt.

Acervate, l. Heap up.

Acetars, l. Sallets and Vinegar.

Acetosity, l. Soureness.

Achæmenes, first King of the *Persians*.

Achamech, Silver-dross.

Achan, b. Troubling or Gnashing.

Achat, or *Achapt*, f. To buy, also a bargain.

Achates, g. A stone of divers colours like a Lions skin.

Achelous, Son of *Oceanus* and *Terra*, also a River in *Epirus*.

Acheron, Son of *Ceres*, turned into a River of Hell.

Acherontick, belonging thereto, comfortless.

Acherusia, a River taken for the entrance of Hell.

Acherusian, Belonging thereto.

Achieve, f. Perform.

Achilles, Son of *Peleus* and *Thetis*, he slew *Hector*.

Achior, b. Brothers light, or Brother of Fire.

Achish, b. Sure it is.

Achor, Scald in the head.

Acid, l. Sharp in taste.

Acidity, Sharpness.

Acis, The Son of *Faunus*.

Akele, o. To cool.

Adacted, l. Driven by force.

Adage, l. Proverb.

Adagial, Proverbial.

Adah, b. Assembly of people.

Adam, b. Red earth.

Adamites, l. *Bohemian* Hereticks that went naked.

Adamical, Belonging to *Adam*.

Adamant, l. Diamond.

Adamantine, l. Of or like Diamonds.

Adamate, l. Love dearly.

Adapt, l. Make fit.

Adarige, Salt Armoniac.

Adashed, o. Ashamed.

Adawed, o. Awaked.

Adcorporate, l. Joyn body to body.

Addecimate, l. Take Tithes.

Adderbourn, A River in *Wiltshire*.

Adders-tongue, An herb of one leaf, with ſuch a ſtalk upon it

Addice, A Coopers Ax.

Addict, *l.* give up, encline.

Addiction, *l.* deliverance of goods.

Additament, *l.* A ſupply or

Addition, adding one thing to another.

Additional, Added to.

Addomeſtique, *f.* Tamed.

Addoulce, *f.* Sweeten.

Addreſs, *f.* Apply; alſo application, direction.

Adelantado, *Sp.* the Kings deputy; the General, or his deputy.

Adeling, *Sa.* A Kings Son.

Adelrad or *Ethelred*, *Sa.* Noble advice.

Adelman or *Ed-*, *Sa*, Gentleman.

Ademption, *l.* Taking away.

Adecatiſt, *g.* One againſt Tythes.

Adent, *o.* Faſten.

Adeption, *l.* Getting.

Adeptiſt, That hath got the art of tranſmitting metals.

Adequate, *l.* Even, equal.

Adequitation, *l.* Riding towards.

Ades, King of the *Moloſſians*, *Cara's* father.

Adfiliation, *l.* Adoption.

Adhamate, *l.* Catch (with hook or net.)

Adhere, *l.* Stick to.

Adheſion, Sticking to.

Adjacent, *l.* lying near.

Adiaphory, *g.* Indifferency.

Adiaphorous, Indifferent.

Adjective, *l* Which is joyn'd to a ſubſtantive.

Adjourn, *f*, Put off to a certain day.

Ad inquirendum, *l.* A writ for enquiry, &c.

Adipal, *l.* Fat, groſs.

Adit, *l.* Entrance.

Adjudication, *l.* Determining,

Adjument, *l.* Help.

Adjunct, *l.* Joyned to a quality joyn'd to its ſubject.

Adjure, *l.* Command in Gods name, ſwear or make another ſwear.

Adjuration, *l.* earneſt charging, &c.

Adiutant, *l.* Helping, helper.

Adjuſt, *f.* Set in order.

Adjutory, *l.* Helping.

Adiuvate, *l.* Aſsiſt.

Adle, *o.* Empty; alſo to earn.

Admeaſurement, *f.* A writ to moderate ones ſhare.

Admetas, King of *Theſſaly*, *Apollo* kept his ſheep nine years.

Adminicle, *l.* Help.

Adminicular, Helpful.

Adminiſter, *l.* Diſpoſe, order.

Adminiſtration, *l.* Diſpoſeing his eſtate that dies inteſtate.

Adminiſtrator He,

Adminiſtratrix, She that ſo diſpoſeth, &c.

Admirable, *l.* Wonderful.

Admiration, Wondering.

Admiral, *f.* Chief Commander at Sea.

Admit, *l.* Allow.

Admittendo Clerico, *l.* A writ for preſentation.

Admiſsion, bringing in, entrance.

Admixtion, *l.* Mingling together.

Admonition, *l* Warning.

Adnihiled, made void.

Adnihilation, *l.* A bringing or reducing to nothing.

Ad octo, *&* *octo*. *l.* The higheſt degree (in Philoſophy.)

Adoleſcency, *l.* Youth.

Adolph, *Sa.* Happy help.

Adonai, *h.* Lord.

Adoniah, *h.* Ruling Lord.

Adonibezek, *h.* Lord of *Bezek*, or of thunder.

Adonick verſe, Conſiſts only of a Dactyl and a Spondey.

Adonis, Son of *Cinaras* King of *Cyprus*, turned into a flower,

Adonizedeck, *h.* The Lords juſtice.

Adopt, *l.* Make a ſtranger ones child.

Adoption, Making, &c.

Adore, *l.* Worſhip.

Adorable, Worſhipful.

Adornation, *l.* Decking, trimming.

Adorat, Four pound weight.

Adoxy, *g*, Shame, diſgrace.

Ad quod damnum, *l.* A writ to enquire what hurt would be to grant a fair, &c.

Adramelek, *h.* Kings Cloak or greatneſs.

Adraming, *o.* Churliſh.

Adraſtia, *Nemeſis*, Daughter of *Iupiter* and Neceſsity.

Adrian or *Adriatique* Sea, *Gulph* of *Venice*, parts *Italy* from *Dalmatia*.

Aſcititious or *Adſci-* Falſely taken to ones ſelf, counterfeit

Ad terminum qui præteriit, *l.* A Writ of Entry.

Advancement, *f.* Promotion.

Advantageous, *f.* Profitable.

Advectitious, *l.* Brought from another place.

Advent-Sunday is the neareſt to the feaſt of St. *Andrew*, coming (of Chriſt.)

Advenqtale, Coat of defence

Adventitious, *l.* Adventive or

Adventual, *l.* Coming by chance.

Adventure, *f.* Chance.

Adverbs, *l.* Undeclined words joyned to Verbs for perfection and explanation.

Adverſe, *l.* Contrary.

Adverſative, *l.* Belonging to ſomething that is contrary.

Advertency, *l.* Heed, carefulneſs.

Advertiſe, *l.* Give notice.

Advertiſement, giving notice

Adveſperate, *l.* Grow towards night.

Advigilate, *l.* Watch diligently.

Adulation, *l.* Flatery, fawning.

Adulatory, pertaining thereto

Adult, *l.* Com'n to full age

Adulted, The ſame.

Adulterate, *l.* To corrupt.

Adumbrate, *l.* To ſhadow:

Adumbration, Rude draught; In Heraldry, the bare proportion of outward lineaments, Tranſparency,

Ad unguem, *l.* At his fingers ends.

Aduncity, *l.* Crookedneſs.

Adunque or *Aduncous*, hooked,

Advocate, *l.* Defender of Cauſes.

Advowzen, or

Advouſon, *f.* Reverſion of

A Be,

a Benefice, or a Right to present thereto.

Advowce paramount, the King or highest patron.

Advoutry, Adultery.

Adure, *l.* Roast, burn.

Adust, *Adusted*, *l.* Burnt, parched.

Adustible, Burnable.

Adustion, Burning.

Adynamous, *g.* Weak.

Ædile, *l.* A *Roman* Officer that look'd to Reparations.

Æacus, Son of *Jupiter*, Judg of hell.

Ædone, turn'd into a thistle.

Æeta, King of *Colchos*.

Æga, *Jupiters* Nurse.

Ægæon, One of *Jupiters* giant enemies, who threw at him a 100 rocks at once.

Ægæum or *Ægean*, Sea, called commonly *Archipelago*, from

Ægeus, King of *Athens*, *Theseus's* father, who drowned himself therein.

Ægiale, The wife of *Diomedes* an adulteress.

Ægilops, *g.* A swelling in the great corner of the eye.

Ægina, *Jupiters* Mistress in the shape of fire.

Ægipanes, *g.* Woody deities with Goats feet.

Aegisthus, Son of *Thyestes*.

Aegle, Daughter of *Hesperus* King of *Italy*.

Aegles, A great wrestler.

Aegrimony, or

Aegritude, *l.* Sickness.

Aegroting, Counterfeit sickness.

Aegyptus, The Son of *Belus*, and brother of *Danaus*.

Aelia, Jerusalem rebuilt by *Ælius Adrianus*.

Aelmsfoh, or

Almsfoh, Peter-pence, which used to be paid the Pope.

Æneas, Son to *Anchises* and *Venus*, he came from *Troy* to *Italy*.

Aeneator, *l.* Trumpeter.

Aenigmatical, *g.* full of *Aenigmaes* or dark riddles.

Aeolipile, Hermetical bellows, to try if there be a Vacuum in nature.

Aeolus, God of the winds.

Aepalius, A King restored by *Hercules*; who adopted *Hercules's* son his Successor.

Aequanimity, *l.* Equalness or evenness of temper.

Aequator, A Circle on the Globe, equally distant from the two Poles.

Aequilateral, *l.* Of equal sides.

Aequilibrity, *l.* equal weighing or

Aequilibrium, Gold weight.

Aequipollence, *l.* equal power

Aequiponderancy, *l.* even poysing.

Aequivocal, *l.* Of like sound

Aera, The term from whence men reckon, as we from Christs nativity.

Aëreal, *l.* belonging to the air.

Aëry, *f.* A nest [of Hawks]

Aëromancy, *g.* divining by the air.

Aeromantick, Pertaining thereto.

Aeruginous, *l.* Rusty.

Aerumnous, *l.* Full of troubles.

Aesacus, Son to *Priamus*, turn'd into a dive-dapper.

Aesculapius, The God-physician, *Apollo's* son.

Aesia, The *French* River *Oyse*.

Aesica, A City of *Northumberland* upon the River *Esk*.

Aestuate, *l.* rage like the Sea.

Aestivate, *l.* spend the summer.

Aetate probanda, *l.* A Writ to prove the age of a Kings tenant.

Aeternales domus, *l.* Eternal habitations, sepulchres.

Aethalis, *Mercury's* Son.

Aetherial, *l.* Pertaining to the sky.

Aethiopia, A Country in *Africa*, so called from

Aethiops, *Vulcans* Son.

Aethon, One of the Suns horses, also a great farter.

Aetiologia, *g.* Shewing the reason of a thing.

Aetna, *Mongebel*, The burning Hill in *Sicily*.

Aetolia, Part of *Greece*.

Affable, *l.* Courteous in speaking to and hearing others.

Affability, Such Courtesie.

Affaires, *f.* Business.

Affectation, *l.* Over-curious imitation.

Affectionate, *l.* Bearing good will, full of affection.

Affeerors, They that fine the offenders in Court-Leets

Affiance, *f.* Trust, confidence; also to make sure, betroth.

Affidatus, A Tenant by fealty.

Affidavit, Deposition upon Oath.

Affinage, *f* refining of Metals.

Affinity, *l.* Likeness, kinred by marriage.

Affirmation, *l.* Saying it is so.

Affirmative, Belonging thereto.

Affix, *l.* Fasten to.

Affluence, *l.* Plenty.

Afflux, *l.* Flowing together.

Afforest, To turn ground into forest.

Affray, *f.* Fright, fighting, tumult.

Affri, or *Affra*, Bullocks or plow-beasts.

Affrication, *l.* rubbing.

Affront, *f.* wrong.

Affrontedness, Impudence.

Affusion, *l.* Pouring, sprinkling.

Afgodness, *Sa.* Ungodliness.

Africa, *g.* One of the four parts of the world.

Africk, *African*, Belonging thereto.

Aft, as *Abaft*.

Aga, Captain of the *Turkish Janizaries*.

Agabus, *h.* Grashopper.

Agag, *h.* Garret or upper room.

Agamemnon King of *Argos*

Agamist, *g.* Unmaried.

Aganippe, Fountain in *Bœotia*, sacred to *Apollo*, &c.

Aganippides, The Muses.

Agarick, A root that helps digestion, a mushrom good against flegm.

Agast, *o*. Amazed.

Agate, *Che*. Just a going.

Agate, *g*. A precious stone for hafts of knives.

Agatha, *g*. Good, a womans name.

Agathocles, A Tyrant of *Sicily*, a Potters Son.

Agathonian, Lascivious, from *Agathon*, A wanton fidler.

Agave, daughter to *Cadmus*.

Age, ones life-time, also a hundred years.

Age prier, *f*. Petition of one in minority, to stop the suit till he come of Age.

Agelastick, *g*. Morose, one which never laughs.

Agelastus only laughed when he saw a mare eat thistles.

Agemoglans, or *Agiam Oglans*, Christian Children taken for the service of the *Turk*.

Agent, *l*. Doer, also a dealer for another.

Agesilaus, King of *Lacedemon*: also an *Athenian*.

Aggerate, *l*. Heap up.

Aggested, Heaped up.

Agglomerate, *l*. Rowl together.

Agglutinate, *l*. Glue together.

Aggrandize, *l*. make great.

Aggravate, *l*. To load, heighten, make heavy or worse.

Aggregate, *l*. Meet together, or gather together.

Aggressor, *l*. He that begins, sets upon, or strikes the first blow.

Aggression, Setting upon.

Agility, *l*. Nimbleness.

Agilt, *o*. Committed.

Aginatour, *l*. Retailer of small wares, from

Agina the Ballance-beam.

Agiograph, *g*. Holy writing.

Agipe, *o*. A Coat full of plaits.

Agis, King of *Lacedemonia*, kild in prison.

Agist, To take strangers Cattel into the Kings Forest, and their mony.

Agitate, *l*. toss up and down, discuss.

Agitable, That may be moved.

Agitation, Frequent motion.

Agitators, Men chosen to manage any business.

Aglaia, One of the graces.

Aglais, A very great Sheeater, *Megacle's* daughter.

Aglet, *f*. Tag of a point.

Agnail, *Sa*. Sore under the nail.

Agnation, Kindred by the Father.

Agnes, *g*. Chast, A womans name.

Agnition, *l*. Acknowledging.

Agnize, *l*. To own.

Agnodice, A Maid-physitian.

Agnominate, *l*. To Nickname.

Agnomination, A Surname.

Agnus Castus, *l*. Seeds preserving Chastity. See *Abrahams baum*.

Agnus dei *l*. The holy lamb, with a Cross.

Agonal feasts, kept at *Rome* the ninth of *January*.

Agonarch or *Agonothete*, *g*. Master of the Revels.

Agonism, *g*. Reward of Victory.

Agonist, *g*. Champion.

Agonistic, or *Agonistical*, Belonging thereto, warlike.

Agonizants, Friars in *Italy* assisting such as are in an

Agony, *g*. Extream anguish of mind or death.

Agramed, *o*. Aggrieved.

Agrarian Laws, for dividing Lands among the *Romans*.

Agreat, *Sa*. By the great or lump.

Agredge, *o*. Aggravate.

Agrestical, *l*. Rustical.

Agricole, *l*. Farmer.

Agricolation, *f*. or

Agriculture, Husbandry.

Agrimony, An herb like tansy.

Agrippa, (born with feet formost) a mans name.

Agrise, *o*. Afraid.

Agrose, *o*. Grieved.

Agroied, *o*. Cloyed.

Agryse, *o*. Make one quake.

Abab, *b*. Brothers Father.

Abaz, *b*. Taking, possessing.

Abaziah, *b*. Apprehension, or sight of the Lord.

Abiezer, *b*. Brothers help.

Abimelech, *b*. Kings brother, or of the Kings Council.

Abitophel, *b*. Brother forsaken, he hanged himself.

Aboliab, *b*. Lords Tabernacle, or brightness of the Lord.

Abolibamah, *b*. My tent, or famous Mansion.

Ajax, A Stout *Grecian*.

Aidoneus, King of the *Molossi*, *Proserpina's* father.

Ailesbury, A Town in *Buckinghamshire*.

Ailesford, A Town in *Kent*.

Airy, A nest of Hawks.

Ait, A little Island in a river.

Akmanchester (City of sick folk) *Bath*.

Alabandic, A kind of Rose, not very sweet.

Alabandical, Barbarous, sottish.

Alabandine, or *Amandine*, A blue stone provoking blood.

Alabaster, Clear white Marble.

Alacrity, *l*. Cheerfulness.

Alabab, *Ar*. The Scorpions heart, a star.

Alamac, *Ar*. The left foot of *Andromeda*.

Alamode, *f*. After the fashion.

Alan, *Sla*. (Grey-hound) a mans name, or as

Aelian, Sun bright.

Alary, *l*. Wingy.

Alarme, *f*. to your arms.

Alastor, One of the Suns Horses.

Alata Castra, Edenborough.

Ala volée, *f*. hastily.

Ality,

Alay, A sending fresh Dogs into the cry.

Alba Julia, Weslenburgh in Germany.

Alba Regalis, Stolwissenbergh in Hungary.

Albania, Scotland, also a Country between *Illyricum* and *Macedonia*.

Albanus, a River in *Armenia*, also the first British Martyr.

St. Albans, Verulam so cal'd from him.

Albe, *l.* the Mass-Priests old white Garment.

Albcito, *Ar.* the Swans-mouth, a Star.

Albert, *sa.* all bright; a proper name.

Albion, the oldest name of this our happy Island.

In Albis, *l.* in quires.

Albor, *l.* whiteness.

Albricias, *sp.* reward of good news.

Albuginous, *l.* belonging to white.

Albumazar, a famous *Arabian* Astronomer.

Albutinus beat his servants before the fault, to be sure of leisure.

Alcan, Verses have two dactyles and two trochees.

Alcali, A Spanish University.

Alcalde, *sp.* Sheriff.

Alcals, Salts extracted from ashes.

Alcander, Servant to *Lycurgus*, very respectful.

Alcanna, Ichthyocolla, Isinglass.

Alcathous, the Son of *Pelops*, adopted by *Megareus*.

Alcatraie, a Fowl like a Heron.

Alce, a wild Beast like a Deer.

Alceste, Admetus's wife.

Alchabest, Mercury prepared.

Alchedi, *ar.* a star in the goat.

Archenit, *ar.* a star in *Perseus*.

Alchimilla, *l.* the Herb Ladies mantle.

Alcibiades, a Noble man of *Athens* reclaim'd by *Socrates*

Alchobel, *ar.* Reception.

Alchoodon, *ar.* Giver of years.

Alchorad, *ar.* a contrariety of the light of the Planets.

Alchymist, *g.* He that use the Art of metals.

Alcides, *g.* Hercules.

Alcithoe, turn'd into a Bat, for her slighting *Bacchus*

Alcmaeon, Son to *Amphiaraus*, he kild his mother.

Alchols, Chymical Spirits.

Alcoholization, reducing solid matter into very fine powder.

Alconor, a certain Grecian, against the *Lacedaemon*.

Alcoran, (Scripture) the Turks Bible.

Alcove, *sp.* a close bed-room.

Alcyone, Neptunes daughter, turn'd into a King-fisher.

Alduas-dubis, a River in Helvetia or *Suitserland*.

Aldebaran, *ar.* the Bulls south eye.

Alderanainim; Cepheus's right shoulder, a star.

Aldingham, a Town in Lancashire.

Alevromancy, *g.* Divining by Barly and Wheat.

Alecoast, the herb Coast-mary.

Alecto, *f.* One of the Furies of Hell.

Alectryomachy, *g.* Cock-Fighting.

Alectryomancy, *g.* Cock-Divination.

Alectorius, a precious stone in a Capons maw.

Alectryon, Mars's pimp, turned into a Cock.

Ale-conner, Searcher of Alepots.

Alehoof, Ground-Ivy.

Alegator, a *Jamaica* Crocodile.

Aleger, Sowre Ale.

Alemlick, *Ar.* A Still.

Aleph, the first [*Hebrew* letter,] also a thousand.

Aleppo, A City in *Syria*.

Ale-silver, Paid yearly to the Lord Mayor.

Alestake, *o.* May-pole.

Alet, The true *Peru*-falcon.

Ale-taster, He is to look to the goodness of Bread and Ale.

Aletheia, *g.* Truth.

Aleuromancy, *g.* Cake-divination.

Alexander, Conquered the world, and was poysoned.

Alexanders, An opening herb.

Alexandria, *No.* A Port-Town of *Egypt*.

Alexipharmacal, good against poison.

Alexiteria, *g.* Medicines against poison.

Aletude, *l.* Fatness of Body.

Alferes, *Sp.* Ensign bearer.

Alfred, *Sa.* (all peace) King of *England*.

Alfreton, A Town in *Darbyshire*.

Algareb, *Ar.* The star in the right wing of the Crow.

Algarfe, *a.* Head of the 15 Mansion.

Algate, *o.* Altogether, if so be, notwithstanding.

Algates, *o.* Ever, even now.

Algebar, *ar.* The left foot of *Orion*, a star.

Algebbe, *a.* The head of the 10 Mansion.

Algebra, *a.* The art of Figurative Numbers.

Algebraical, pertaining thereto.

Algebraist, One skil'd therein.

Algerub, *a.* The right wing of *Pegasus*, a star.

Algid, *l.* Chill, cold,

Algidity, *Algor*, Chilness.

Algifical, making chill.

Algerines, People or pirats belonging to.

Algier, A Town in *Affrica*.

Algomeista, *a.* The little Dog-star.

Algon, The head of *Medusa*.

Algorism, *Algorithme*, or *Algrim*, the same as *Algebra*.

Algorift, as *Algebraift*.

Algum, or *Almug*-trees, of excellent wood in *Lebanon*.

Alguze, *a.* *Orions* left foot.

Alhabar, *a.* A ftar in the great Dog.

Albidade, A ruler on an inftrument, to take heights and depths.

Alias, *l.* otherwife.

Alicante, A Town in *Spain*, whence comes wine of Mul berries.

Alible, *l.* Nourifhing.

Alice, (*Adilize*, noble) a Womans name.

Alien, *l.* Foreigner, ftranger.

Alienate, to eftrange.

Aliety, othernefs.

Alif. d. o. allowed.

Aliment, *l.* Nourifhment.

Alimentation, Nourifhing.

Alimony, *l.* The wives allowance when parted from her Husband.

Alimental, or *Alimentary*, *l.* belonging to nourifhment.

Aliath, *a.* A ftar in the bear.

Alkakengi, Winter-Cherry.

Alkali, The herb *Kali* or *Saltwort*.

Alkanet, *Spanifh* Buglofs.

Alkermes, Confection of *Kermes*.

Allaborate, *l.* Labour vehemently.

All-a-bone, *o.* a made requeft.

Allantoides, *g.* The skin that covers the chief parts of a birth.

Allabanny, *Albany*, the Highlands, in *Scotland*.

Allar, Alder-tree.

Alland, *l.* To praife.

Allay, Affwage. Alfo tempering metal with a bafer fort, Alloy.

Allective, *l.* Alluring.

Allectation, An alluring.

Allegation, *l.* Proving.

Allegorical, *g.* belonging to an

Allegory, Myftical fpeech different from the literal fenfe.

Allelujah, *h.* Praife ye the Lord; alfo the herb Woodforrel.

Aller fans jour, *f.* To be difmift the Court.

Allevate, *l.* Lift up.

Alleviate, *l.* Lighten, diminifh.

All-good, Herb Mercury, Good *Henry*.

All-heal, Clowns Woundwort.

All-hallows, All-Saints.

Alliant, *Allie*, *f.* One that is in

Alliance, *f.* Relation, league.

Alliciency, *l.* An enticing.

Alligation, *l.* A binding to.

Allington, A town in *Hampfhire*.

Allifion, *l.* Dafhing againft.

Alliteration, *l.* Repeating and Playing upon the fame Letter.

Allobrogical, belonging to the

Allobroges, *Savoiards* in *France*.

Allocamel, *g.* an *Indian* Camel with a Males head.

Allocation, *l.* Placing, alfo Officers allowance from Superiors.

Allocution, or

Alloquy, *l.* Talking with one.

Alnager, *Alnageor*, *Aulnager*, *f.* Meafurer of woollen [by the Elle] Now Collector of that Subfidy.

Allodial, [Lands] free from fines and fervice.

Allot, Lay out, appoint.

Allude, *l.* Speak in reference to another thing.

Allufion, Speaking in reference, &c.

Alluminor, *f.* (enlightener) who paints on Paper, or parchment.

Alluvion, *l.* Floud, flowing.

Almain, A German, alfo a flow aire in Mufick.

Almaine Rivets, Light armour.

Almanack, *ar.* (the courfe of the year) a Calendar.

Almaner, *a.* A Planets Epicycle.

Almantica, Zodiack.

Almanzer, *a.* Defender.

Almericus, A Chriftian King of *Jerufalem*.

Almadarats, *Almicantharats* *ar.* Lines drawn through the Meridian, Parallel with the Horizon.

Almner, *Almoner*, *Amner*, *f.* Diftributer of alms.

Almnery, *Aumry*, *f.* Almshoufe, alfo a Buttery or Pantry.

Almugia, *ar.* Planets facing one another in the Zodiack.

Almuten, The Planet of moft Power, or Dignities.

Alnath, A ftar in *Aries* horns.

Alnwick, *Alanwick* *Anwick*, A Town in *Northumberland*.

Alody, *o.* Lands of Inheritance.

Aloes, Juice of Sea-horfleek, or Bitterwort.

Aloe Cicotrina, *Succatrina*, or *Zocatrina*, brought from the *African* Ifle *Zocatara*.

Alogick, *g.* Unreafonable.

Alogy, Unreafonablenefs.

Aloof, Keep the fhip near the wind, alfo far off.

Alopecian, Belonging to

Alopecy, *g.* (Foxes evil) fhedding of the hair.

Alosha, a Summer *Spanifh*-drink of Water and Honey.

Alpha, The first Greek letter; the beginning.

Alphabetical, Belonging to the

Alphabet, *g.* The letters of the Greek, or any Language.

Alpharaiz, *a.* *Pegafus's* right Shoulder, a ftar.

Alpheta, The bright ftar of the Crow.

Alpheus, an *Arcadian* River; alfo a mans name.

Alphitomancy, *g.* Divination by barley meal.

Alphonsin-Tables of *Aftronomy* devifed by

Alphonfus King of *Aragon*.

Alphrada, *a.* The Bright ftar in *Hydra*.

Alps, High frozen hills between *France* and *Italy*.

Alp, *Nope*, Bulfinch, *Sf.*

Alrameh, a ftar in *Bootes*.

Aliacaba, *ar.* The Pole-ftar

Alresford, a Town in *Hamp* fhire.

Altahest Paracelfi; a Body educed to its firft Principles.

Altarage,

Altarage, Altar-profit.
Alteration, *l.* Changing.
Altercation, *l.* Contentious dispute.
Alternal, the same as
Alternate, *Alternative*, *l.* that which is done by
Alternation, *Alternity*, Changing by turns.
Altiloquent, *l.* Speaking high.
Altometrical, measuring of
Altitudes, *l.* heights.
Altisonant, *l.* high-sounding.
Altitonant, *l.* high-thundring [Jupiter.]
Altivolant, *l.* high-flying, soaring.
Alto & Basso, High and low, all kind of [differences.]
Alveary, *l.* Bee-hives.
Alveated, *l.* Chanelled or trenched.
Aluminous, *l.* like, or full of
Alume, a binding mineral.
Alumbrado, *sp.* Phanatick, Enthusiast.
Alumnate, *l.* Nourish, feed.
Alumnation, Fostering, feeding.
Alutation, *l.* Tanning of Leather.
Alytarch, *g.* Keeper of order at publick sports.
Amaine, Yield your ship.
Amainable, *f.* Tractable.
Amalagmation,
Amalgamation, or
Amalgaminge, softening metals with Quick-silver.
Amalekites, *Esau's* posterity by his Grand-son
Amalek, *h.* Licking people
Amalthean, belonging to
Amalthea, Jupiters nurse.
Amand, *f.* send away.
Amanuensis, *l.* Secretary or Clerk.
Amaranthus, *g.* Flower gentle.
Amaritude, *l.* bitterness.
Amarous, *l.* bitter, froward.
Amarulent, *l.* the same.
Amaryllis, *g.* shining.
Amasa, *h.* Sparing the people.
Amasiah, *h.* Burden of the Lord.
Amassement, *f.* heaping up.
Amate, *o.* Discourage.

Amatory, *l.* Belonging to love.
Amaurosis, a decay of the eye-sight and no fault seen.
Amazons, *g.* Warlike Women of *Scythia.*
Ambacti, Servants to the *Gaullish* Nobility.
Ambages, *l.* Far-fetch'd circumstance of words.
Ambagious, Full of far &c.
Amber, Hard yellow gum.
Ambergreece, *greese*, or *-grise*, *f.* a sweet clammy perfume, found by the Sea-side.
Ambia, A thick Indian liquor.
Ambianum, *Amiens* in *Picardy.*
Ambidexter, *l.* that useth both hands alike, or plaies on both sides [for gain.]
Ambidexterous, belonging thereto.
Ambient, *l.* Compassing about.
Ambifarious, Having a double meaning.
Ambiguity, *l.* doubtfulness.
Ambiguous, doubtful.
Ambilevous, *l.* Left-handed.
Ambiloge, *Ambilogy*, *g.* a doubtful speech.
Ambiloquent, *l.* Double tongu'd.
Ambition, *l.* An eager desire or thirst after honour.
Ambitude, *l.* Compassing round.
Amblotbridium, A medecine provoking travel before time.
Amblygone, *g.* a blunt angled triangle.
Amboina, An East-India Island.
Amboise a Principal building in *France.*
Ambosexous, Male and Female.
Ambracia, *Lacta* in *Epirus.*
Ambresbury, A Town in *Wilt-shire.*
Ambrey, Cup-board.
Ambrose, *g.* Immortal.
Ambrosia, Wood-sage, also the meat of the Gods.
Ambrosiack, *Ambrosial*, or
Ambrosian, Thereto belonging.

Ambulatory, *l.* A walk, also walking.
Amburbial, [Sacrifices, *l.* which went first] about the City.
Ambuscado, *sp.* Ambuscade, *f.* an
Ambush, laying in wait.
Ambustion, *l.* A burning about.
Amæbean, [Verses] Dialogue-wise.
Amell, *Amel'd* Among, betwixt.
Amen, *h.* Verily, so let it be.
Amenable, *f.* Tractable.
Amendment, Correction of an errour in a process.
Amenity, *l.* Pleasantness.
Amenused, *o.* Diminished.
Ameos, Bishops-weed.
Amercement, or *Amerciament*, *f.* (at mercy) a fine at will.
America, The fourth part of the World [last discover'd]
American disease, the *Great*, *Spanish*, *Naples* or *French* Pox.
Amery, (*gr.* alway rich) proper name.
Amesse, *f.* A Priest's hood or cap in the Quire, See *Amict.*
Amethyst, *g.* (against drunkenness) a precious stone.
Amfractuous, *l.* Belonging to
Amfractuosity, Intricacy, much turning and winding.
Amiable, *l.* Lovely.
Amicable, *l.* Friendly.
Amict, *Amice*, *l.* The Priests first linnen vestment.
Amicted, *l.* Clothed.
Amie, *f.* Beloved.
Aminadab, *h.* free or vowing people, or Prince of people.
Ammishaddai, *h.* the People of the Almighty.
Amission, *l.* Losing.
Amit, To lose or pardon.
Ammodite, A sandy insect with black spots.
Ammon, *Ammonites*, people descended from *Ben-ammi*, *h.* the son of my people.
Ammoniack, a *Lybian* gum, and *Affrican*-Salt.
Ammunition, *f.* Provision store.

Amnesty, g. Oblivion.

Amnick, l. Belonging to a River.

Amnios, The skin that wraps the birth all over.

Amnon, h. True, or Artificer, or School-Master.

Amomum, g. A pleasant seed like Cardamoms.

Amorets, f. Love-toys.

Amorist, Lover.

Amorosity, Lovingness.

Amoroso, I. Lover.

Amort, f. Dead.

Amortize, to kill, also to alien Lands.

Amos, h. Burden.

Amotion, l. Removing away.

Amoz, h. Strong.

Ampelite, g. Black earth to kill worms in Vines.

Ampelusia, A place in *Mauritania*.

Amper, Sf. A flaw in Cloth. E. a swelling.

Amphiaraus, was swallow'd up alive at *Thebes*.

Amphibion, *Amphibious*, g. which lives both by water and land.

Amphibolous, *Amphibolical*, or *Amphibological*, g. Belonging to

Amphibology, Doubtful speech.

Amphictions, The chief Councellors of *Greece*.

Amphion, An Excellent Musician, who built the walls of *Thebes*.

Amphionize, To do like him.

Amphipolis, g. a City compassed round.

Amphiscians g. Who living under the *Equator* have shadows both wayes.

Amphitheater, or -tre, g. A perfect round Theatre.

Amphitrite, g. *Neptunes* Queen.

Amphitrio, *Alcmena*'s Husband.

Amphiction, King of *Athens*

Amphidromical, g. Belonging to the fifth day after birth when the Child was purifi'd and named.

Amphoral, Belonging to the

Amphora, contained (if Italick) five gallons, (if Attick) seven and a half.

Ampliation, l. Enlargement, also deferring the trial.

Amplification, l. An enlarging.

Amplitude, l. Largeness, also dignity.

Amplivagant, l. Far-stretching.

Ampullous, l. Swelling [like a bottle] proud.

Amputation, l. Cutting off.

Amram, h. High people.

Amraphel, h. Speaking Judgement.

Amsanctus, a noisome fen in *Italy*.

Amstelodamum, *Amsterdam* in *Holland*.

Amulet, l. a Ball about the neck to keep from poison or Witchcraft.

Amulius, King of the Latins.

Amuse, f. Put one in a dump.

Amycus, King of the *Bebrycii*.

Amylum, g. white stuff like starch made of *German* wheat.

Amymone, One of *Danaüs*'s 50 Daughters, Mother of *Nauplius* by *Neptune*.

Amyris. One of *Sybaris* in *Italy*, who foretelling its ruine fled from thence.

Ana, g. Of each alike.

Anabaptists, g. [Baptizers-again] they Baptize none, till they can give an account of their Faith.

Anabathrum, g. Any place to which we go up by steps.

Anabrochism, g. Binding with Cords.

Anacardium, g. A *Malacca*-bean, like a little birds heart

Anachoretal, *Anachoretical*, g. belonging to

Anachorite, *Anchoret*, g. A Monk.

Anacephalize, g. To repeat the heads of a matter.

Anachronism, *Anachronitism*, g. False computation or reckoning of time.

Anacoenosis, g. Arguing the case with others.

Anacreontick, Belonging to

Anacreon, a Greek Lyrick Poet, choakt with a Raisonhusk.

Anacrisis, g. Questioning, or racking of Offenders.

Anadem, g. Garland.

Anadesm g. A swathe.

Anadiplosis, g. When a verse begins with the last word of the former.

Anaetis, a *Lydian* Goddess.

Anaglyphick, *Anagleptick*, g. belonging to Carving, &c.

Anagnostick, *Anagnostian*, g. A Reader.

Anagogick, g. or

Anagogical, Deep-learned.

Anagrammatism, g. The art of making

Anagrams, Transposing the letters of a name into something else.

Anagraph, g. A Register, or an Inventory.

Anagrif, -*greph*, Fornication

Anah, h. Answering, singing or poor.

Anak, h. Gyant.

Analects, g. Scraps, Collections.

Analemme, g. an instrument to find the height.

Analeptick, g. Restorative.

Analogical, *Analogous*, g. belonging to

Analogie, Agreement, proportion.

Analogism, g. An unanswerable argument, from the cause to the effect.

Analogists, g. Tutors not accountable for their Wards

Analphabetical, g. unlearned.

Analytick, -*cal*, belonging to

Analysis. g. resolution, unfolding.

Analyze, to unfold [doubts.]

Anamnesis, g. Calling to mind.

Ananiah, *Ananias*, g. The Grace, cloud, or divination of the Lord.

Anapestick, g. belonging to

Anapest, a verse of two short syllables and one long.

Anaphora,

Anaphora, g. The same beginning of several verses or sentences.

Anapologetical, g. Inexcusable.

Anarchick, g. Belonging to

Anarchism, The Doctrine of

Anarchy, Confusion, without Governor.

Anarand, *Honoratus*, br. proper name.

Anastomosis, g. an opening the mouth of the Veins.

Anastrophe, g. preposterous placing of words.

Anathêma, g. any consecrated thing.

Anathema, g. excommunicated-ation.

Anathematize, g. to excommunicate.

Anatiferous, l. bringing the age of old Women.

Anatocism, g. yearly taking usury, and interest upon interest.

Anatomical, belonging to

Anatomy, g. cutting up a body.

Anatomize, to cut up, &c.

Anauntrins, if so be.

Anaxerete, a hard-hearted virgin, turn'd into a stone.

Anaximander, a *Milesian* Philosopher.

Ancæus, *Neptunes* Son kil'd by a wild-Boar.

Ancaster, a Town in *Lincolnshire*.

Ancestrel, done by the

Ancestor, l. fore-runner.

Anchises, *Æneas*'s Father.

Anchoral, l. belonging to an Anchor.

Anchovy, a small Spanish Fish.

Anchoress, a Nun.

Anchurus, rode alive into the gaping Earth.

Ancient, Ensign.

Anciently, Eldership.

Ancile, l. a short shield like a decrescent moon.

Ancona, a City in *Italy*.

Anchorage, duty for anchoring in Port.

Ancus Martius, fourth King of the *Romans*.

Andena, l. a swath in mowing.

Andaluzia, a Country in *Spain*.

Andover, a Town in *Bucks*.

Andradswald, a wood in *Sussex*, once 120 miles long.

Andrago, g. a manly woman.

Andrastes, *Andate*, Goddess of victory among the *Britans*.

Andrew, g. Manly.

Andromant, g. a precious stone.

Androgynal, belonging to

Androgyne, g. Male and Female.

Andromache, g. [manly fight] *Hectors* Wife.

Andromachus, g. [fighting man] *Nero*'s Physician, who added viper's flesh to Mithridate.

Andromeda, *Cepheus*'s Daughter.

Androna, g. a place only for men [in ships.]

Andronicus, g. victorious man.

Anelace, a wood-knife.

Anemone, wind-flower.

Anent, sc. over against, concerning.

Anewst, su. almost.

Anfractuosity, l. intricate turning and winding.

Angel, ten shillings.

Angelica, an herb.

Angelical, belonging to an

Angel, g. Messenger.

Angelot, small french cheese.

Angularity, the being

Angular, having

Angles, l. corners.

Anglicism, l. Speech proper to

Anglia, *England*.

Anglesey, an Island in *Wales*

Angole, a Kingdom of *Æthiopia*.

Angor, l. anguish, grief.

Anguineous, l. Snaky.

Angus, part of North-*Scotland*.

Angust, l. narrow.

Anhelation, l. shortness of breath.

Anheled, l. broken-winded.

Aniented, f. made void.

Anity, *Anility*, l. Womens old age.

Animable, l. which may have life.

Animadversion, l. attention, observation, correction.

Animality, the being of an

Animal, l. a living creature.

Animalio, sp. a little one.

Anima Saturni, l. extract of

Animate, l. give life. (lead

Anime, a West-Indy-Gum.

Animosity, l. stoutness, wilfulness, heart-burning.

Anlace, o. dudgeon-haft-dagger.

Annalist, l. he that writes

Annals, yearly Chronicles.

Annaldale, part of South-*Scotland*.

Annarian Law, l. concerning the age or year of bearing Office.

Annates, l. first-fruits of Spiritual Livings.

Anna, *Anne*, h. Gracious.

Annas, h. as *Anah*.

Anneile, *Anneal*, a *Barbary* Commodity for Diers.

Anneiling of glass, baking the colours quite thorow.

Annexation, l. uniting, joyning.

Annibal, a *Carthaginian* Captain.

Annicrians, Philosophers, Disciples of *Anniceris*, *Paræbates*'s Disciple.

Anniferous, l. bearing [fruit] every year.

Annihilate, l. reduce to nothing.

Annihilation, reducing, &c.

Annise, an herb like smallage.

Anniversary, l. yearly.

Anno Domini, l. In the year of our Lord [Christ.]

Annon, A *Carthaginian* that Taught birds to say, *Annon* is a God.

Annosity, l. agedness.

Annotation, l. marking, observing.

Annoy, f. to hurt.

Annueler, o. secular.

Annual, l. yearly.

Annuity, l. yearly pension.

Annul, l. make void, frustrate.

Annulais, l. the ring finger

Annulated, l. ringed,
Annulet, l. little ring
Annunciate, l. to bring
Annunciation, news, message.
Anodynous, belonging to
Anodynes, g. medicines to asswage pain,
Anoisance, f. damage,
Anomalous, belonging to
Anomaly, g. irregularity.
Anonymal, or
Anonymous, g. nameless.
Anopsy, g. want of sight.
Anorexy, g. want of appetite,
Ansulary, l. belonging to a small handle.
Ant, Pismire.
Antæus, Son to *Neptune* and *Terra*,
Antagonist, g. adversary.
Antal, a small Sea shel-fish
Antalope, *Antilope*, a Beast begotten between a Hart and a Goat.
Antanaclasis, g. (beating back) repeating the like word in a different sense,
Antarchy, g. opposition to Government.
Antartick, g. South, contrary to Artick [pole, circle, &c,]
Antares, The Scorpions heart, a star.
Anteacts, l. by-past acts.
Anteambulate, l. walk before.
Anteambulation, such walking.
Antecedaneous, the same as
Antecedent. l. foregoing.
Antecede, l. go before, excel
Antecession, going before, &c.
Antecessours, l. Fore-fathers.
Antecursor, l. fore-runner.
Antedate, l. date before the time.
Antediluvian, l. being before the flood.
Antefact, l. former action.
Antegenital, l. born before.
Antegressi n, l. a going before.
Anteloquy, l. preface, also the Players Cue.
Antemeridian, l. before noon,

Antenor, a *Trojan*, founder of *Padua* in *Italy*.
Anteoccupation, l. preventing or seising first.
Antepone, l. set before, prefer,
Anterior, l. foremost.
Antevene, l. prevent, come before.
Anthem, g. a Divine song.
Anthima, *Anthine*, g. made of flowers.
Anthologie, g. Treatise of flowers, choice Collections.
Anthologick, belonging thereto.
Anthony, g. flourishing.
Anthera, a medicine for sore mouths.
Anthora, *Antithora*, g. a counterpoison to *Thora* or *Wolfs-bane*.
Anthrax, g. a Carbuncle-sore.
Anthropologie, g. a discourse of Men.
Anthropomorphites, g. Hereticks holding that God hath a corporeal shape.
Anthropomorphitical, thereto belonging.
Anthropopathy, g. having the passions of men, or speaking after the manner of men
Anthropophagy, g. Eating of Mans flesh,
Anthropophagi, g. Men-eaters.
Anthropophagize, to eat Mans flesh.
Antiaxiomatism, g. that which is against any known axiom.
Anti-Camera, g. *Anti-chamber*, f. an outer-chamber.
Anti-Christ, g. Opposer of Christ.
Antichronism, g. false Chronicling.
Antichthones, g. the same as
Antipodes, g. who's feet are directly against ours.
Antipodal, thereto belonging.
Anticipated, l. prevented.
Anticlea, g. the Mother of *Ulysses*.
Antidate, as *Antedate*.
Antidic marians, Hereticks against the Virgin *Mary*.

Antidote, g. medicine against poyson.
Antigonize, to play
Antigonus, one of *Alexanders* Captains, and King of *Macedonia*.
Antigrapher, who keeps the
Antigraphy, g. Copies, Counterpanes of Deeds.
Antick, l. old, strange, confused,
Antilogie, g. *Antiloquy*, l. a speaking against.
Antimetabole, g. turning of words upside-down.
Antimetrical, g. against the rules of verse.
Antimony, a purging stone found in silver Mines.
Antinomians, g. Hereticks against observing the Law.
Antioch, g. a City in *Syria*.
Antiochus, g. King of *Syria*.
Antiæci, g. North and South dwellers under half the Meridian, and parrallels equally distant from the *Equator*.
Antipagments, g. garnishings in posts or doors, or stone.
Antipas, a Contraction of
Antipater, g. against the Father,
Antipast, the first part of a meal.
Antipathetical, belonging to
Antipathy, g. a secret and natural contrariety.
Antipelargy, g. requital of kindness.
Antipendium, the cloth before the Altar,
Antiperistasis, g. the strengthening of a quality against its contrary.
Antiphrastical, belonging to
Antiphrasis, -sie, g. when words have a meaning contrary to their Etymology.
Antiphonary, a Book of
Antiphones, g. Anthems.
Antipilanes, *Antipilani*, l. Soldiers in the front of the Roman Army.
Antipileptical, against the falling sickness.
Antiptosis, g. putting one case for another.

Anti-

Antipreſtigiation, *l.* contrary juggling.

Antiquate, *l.* aboliſh.

Antiquated, out of date.

Antique, *l*, out of faſhion.

Antiquary, *l.* skil'd in Antiquity.

Antiſabbatarians, Hereticks againſt the Sabbath.

Antiſcions, degrees beholding one another equally diſtant from the two *Tropicks*.

Antiſtrophe, *g.* when ſeveral parts of a ſentence end with the ſame word.

Antiſtæchon, *g.* putting of one letter or word for another.

Antitheſis, *g.* the ſame; alſo an oppoſition of contraries.

Antithets, *g.* contraries.

Anti-Trinitarians, Hereticks againſt the Holy Trinity.

Antitype, *g.* an example like the pattern.

Antiveſtæum Penwith, our utmoſt Weſtern Promontory.

Antlier, the lower branch of an Harts horn,

Antonians, Monks of the Order of St. *Anthony* an *Egyptian*.

Antonius, a Romar name.

Antonomaſtically, by the figure

Antonomaſia, *g.* putting another name for a proper name.

Antrim, a County in *Ireland*.

Antwerp, a City in *Brabant*.

Anubis, *Mercury*, worſhip'd in *Egypt* in the ſhape of a dog.

Anweald, *ſa.* Authority.

Anxiferous, *l.* bringing

Anxiety, *l.* grief of mind.

Anyger, a *Theſſalian* River.

Anzigues, *Cannibals* that eat their own friends.

Antromancy, *g.* Divination by conſulting the dead.

Aonian, belonging to

Aonides, *g.* the Muſes, having a well in

Aonia, part of *Beotia*.

Aoriſt, *g.* indefinite.

Aornus, the Lake in *Italy*, into which *Phaeton* fell.

Aorta, the great Artery.

Apamia, a Town in *Bythinia*.

Apathy, *g.* want of paſſions.

Apelby, a Town in *Weſtmorland*.

Apellean, belonging to

Apelles, a famous Painter.

Apennage, *Appennage*, *f.* a Childs portion.

Appennine, a Great hill in *Italy*.

Apepſy, *g.* bad digeſtion.

Aperient, *Aperitive*, *l.* opening.

Apertion, *Aperture*, an opening.

Apertly, openly.

Aphæreſis, *g.* taking away [from the beginning of a word]

Aphelium, *g.* the point wherein the Earth [or any Planet] is moſt diſtant from the Sun.

Aphetical, belonging to the Planet that is diſpoſer of life in a Nativity.

Aphoriſtical, belonging to

Aphoriſm, *g.* a choiſe ſhort ſentence.

Aphrodite, *g.* *Venus*.

Aphtha, an exulceration in the mouth.

Apina and *Trica*, two trifling Towns of *Apulia*.

Apian, *l.* belonging to Bees or Honey.

Apis, *Oſiris*, King of *Egypt*.

Apocalyptical, belonging to

Apocalypſe, *g.* Revelation.

Apocope, *g.* cutting off [from the end of a word,]

Apocryphal, belonging to

Apocrypha, *g.* hidden, doubtfull.

Apocynon, a ſmall bone in a Frogs left ſide.

Apodictical, *g.* demonſtrable, eaſie to be made plain.

Apodioxis, *g.* rejection [of an abſurd argument].

Apogeon, *Apogeum*, as *Apogee*, *g.* the fartheſt diſtance of a Planet from the Earth's Centre.

Apograph, *g.* a Copy, an Inventory.

Apolactize, *g.* kick, deſpiſe.

Apollinean, belonging to

Apollo, the Sun, God of Phyſick and Muſick.

Apollyon, *g.* deſtroyer, the Devil.

Apologetical, or

Apological, belonging to

Apology, *Apologiſm*, *g.* defence, excuſe.

Apologize, *g.* to make ones defence.

Apologue, *g.* Fable.

Apomel, *g.* drink of water and honey.

Apopheret, -*phoret*, *g.* a preſent.

Apophlegmatiſm, *g.* a Medicine to purge plegme.

Apophthegm, *g.* a ſhort witty ſentence.

Apoplectical, belonging to

Apoplexy, *g.* the dead Palſey

Aporetique, belonging to

Aporia, *g.* doubting.

Apoſiopeſis, *g.* holding ones peace.

Apoſtacy, *g.* revolting, falling away.

Apoſtate, he that revolts, &c.

Apoſtatize, to revolt, &c.

Apoſtata capiendo, *l.* a writ to ſeize a Fryar wandring from the Houſe and Orders

Apoſteme, *Apoſtume*, *g.* Impoſtume.

Apoſtolick, *Apoſtolical*, belonging to an

Apoſtle, *g.* Meſſenger.

Apoſtolians, Hereticks pretending to more than Apoſtolick gifts.

Apoſtraph, -*phe*, -*phus*, *g.* the mark of a vowel cut off

Apotheke, *g.* a ſhop, ware houſe.

Apotomy, *g.* cutting off [part of a line.]

Apozeme, *g.* a decoction of Herbs and Spices almoſt to a Syrrup.

Appall, *f.* aſtoniſhed.

Apparition, *l.* wonderful sight.

Apparel, *Appareil*, *f.* preparation, also the summe which remains charged upon the house or Colledge.

Apparent, *l.* clear, plain.

Apparitour, *l.* who summons people to appear.

Apparlement, *f.* appearance, likelyhood.

Appartment, *l.* division, part of a great house.

Appeach, impeach, accuse.

Appellant, *l.* he that makes an

Appeal, *f.* removing a cause from an Inferior to a higher Judge.

Appellation, *l.* the same, also calling.

Appellative, *l.* common to all of that kind.

Appellour, *Approver*, *f.* who confessing himself guilty accuseth another.

Appendant, *l.* belonging. to an

Appendix, *l.* addition, that depends on another.

Appensor, *l.* he that weighs.

Appertenances, *f.* things belonging to another more principal thing.

Appetency, *l.* earnest desire.

Appeteth, *o.* desireth.

Appetible, *l.* desirable.

Appetition, *l.* as Appetency.

Appetite, desire, stomach.

Appian-way, the high-way from *Rome* to *Brundusium*.

Appii forum, *l.* *Appius's* Market, a Town one dayes journey from *Rome*.

Apping'd, *l.* joyn'd, also painted.

Applaud *l.* clap the hands, rejoyce, commend,

Applauds, *Applause*, *l.* such expressions of joy or praise.

Application, *l.* applying, address.

Applumbature, *l.* soldering with lead.

Appertionment, dividing of Rent in two parts.

Apposite, *l.* added, fit.

Apposition, *l.* putting to-

Appostile, *f.* a small addition to a writing.

Apprehension, *l.* understanding.

Apprentice, *f.* learner.

Appretiation, *l.* high-valuing.

Appretiatively, according to the value.

Approbation, *l.* liking.

Approperate, *l.* hasten.

Appropinquate, *l.* draw nigh.

Appropriate, *l.* take to ones self.

Appropriation, *l.* taking the profits of a Benefice and maintaining a Vicar.

Approve, *l.* improve, make the best of.

Approximation, *l.* bringing near.

Appuyed, *f.* propped, also rested on.

Aprique, *l.* Sunny.

Aprication, basking in the Sun.

Apricity, warmth in the Sun

Aprize, *o.* adventure.

Absonus, the City where *Medea* slew her brother.

Aptate, *l.* to fit, prepare.

Aptitude, *l.* fitness.

Ap-thanes, the best of the Scot'sh Nobility.

Aptote, *g.* without case.

Apulia, *Puglia* in *Italy*.

Apyrexy, *g.* the remission of a Fever.

Aqua Cœlestis, *l.* Chymical rectify'd wine.

Aqua fortis, *l.* strong poyson, made of Allum, Vitriol and Salt-petre.

Aqua Tetrachymagogon, purging the four humours of the body.

Aquarians, Hereticks using only water in the Communion.

Aquarius, *l.* the watery sign which the Sun enters in *January*.

Aquatical, *Aquatile*, *l.* belonging to the water.

Aquation, *l.* a watering.

Aqueduct, *l.* a Conduit.

Aqueous, *l.* waterish.

Aquiline, *l.* belonging to

Aquila, *l.* an Eagle.

Aquila Philosophorum, *l.* reducing metals to the first matter.

Aquileia, a City in *Italy*.

Aquiliferous, *l.* the Roman Ensign bearing an Eagle.

Aquisgrane, the City *Aix-covit* in *Gulick*.

Aquitania, *Guien*, the third part of *France*.

Aquite, *o.* to match.

Aquiler, *o.* neeedle-case.

Aquosity, *l.* waterishness.

Arabant, they that hold by tenure of tillage.

Arabella *l.* fair Altar.

Arabesque, *f.* flourishing work in paint or Tapestry.

Arabian belonging to *Arabia*, part of *Asia*.

Arabidi, reformed *Franciscans* of

Arabida, a hill in *Portugal*.

Arable, *l.* plowable.

Arace, *b.* deface pluck up.

Arain, *nota* [large] Spider.

Aramites, *Syrians*, Sons of *Aram*, *h.* highness, deceiving, or their curse.

Araneous, *l.* full of Cobwebs.

Aratrate, *l.* to Plow.

Arausia, *Orange* in *France*.

Aray, *f.* Order.

Arbalist, *Arcubalist*, *l.* a large Crosse-bow.

Arbela, a Town of *Cilicia*.

Arbitrement, *f.* the Judgement of an

Arbitratour, *l.* Umpire, Judge between party and party.

Arblasters, or *Arbalist*.

Arborancy, *l.* belonging to Trees or Arbours.

Aborator, *l.* a lopper of Trees.

Arborist, *l.* one skil'd in Trees.

Arbor Maris, *l.* (Sea-Tree) Coral.

Arbor vitæ, *l.* (Tree of life) it smels like bread and cheese.

Arbustine, *Arbustive*, *l.* shrubby.

Arcubuzier, *Sp.* one that serves with an

Arcabuz, hand-gun.

Arcadian, belonging to

Ar-

Arcadia, a Country famous for Shepherds.

Arcade, *f.* an Arch.

Arcane, *l.* secret.

Archaism, *g.* an old way of speaking.

Archal, *Darbyshire* Liverwort.

Arche, *g.* chief.

Arch-angel, *g.* Prince of Angels, also a weed like dead Netles.

Arch-Dapifer, Chief Sewer of the Empire, Count *Palatine* of *Rhene*.

Arch-Duke, Duke of *Austria*.

Arch-flamines, among the heathens the same as

Arch-Bishops, among Christians.

Archiepiscopal, *l.* belonging thereto.

Archelaus, *g.* Prince of the people.

Arches, a Court of the Arch-Bishop of *Canterbury*, kept in *Bow-Church*.

Archetype, *g.* the Original Copy.

Archeus Paracelsi, the vital air in Chymistry.

Archiatre *g.* chief Physician.

Archigrapher, *g.* cheif Secretary.

Archiloquy, the beginning of speech.

Archimandrite, the chief of an Hermitage.

Archimimick, *g.* chief Player.

Archidiaconal, belonging to an

Arch-Deacon, *g.* a Church-Governour under the Bishop.

Archippus, *g.* Governor of Horses.

Architectonick, --*ical*, belonging to an

Architect, *g.* Master-builder.

Architecture, *g.* the Art of building.

Architrave, the Chapiter of a pillar, also the chief beam in building.

Archive, the place where old Records are kept.

Archontes, *g.* the chief *Athenian* Governours.

Archon, one of them, also the first authour of the

Archonticks, Hereticks denying the Resurrection and affirming the world to be the work of Princes.

Architas, *Archytas*, made a wooden Dove to fly.

Arcitenent *l.* bow-bearing.

Arctation, *l.* streightning.

Arctick, *Artick*, Northern.

Arcturus Boötes, [a star by the tail of] *Charle's wain*.

Arcuate, *l.* make or made like a Arch.

Ardelion, *l.* busie-body.

Ardently, earnestly.

Ardenna, (*ga.* a wood.) a Forest in *Warwickshire*, and another in *Germany* [500 miles long.]

Arders, fallowing or plowings.

Ardour, *l.* great heat.

Arduity, *l.* steepness.

Areatour, *l.* thresher or cleanser of

Area, *l.* floor.

Arefaction, *l.* a drying.

Arelatum, *l.* *Arles* in *France*.

Arenaceous, *Arenated*, Sandy.

Areopagites, *Athenian* Judges who sat in the

Areopagus, -*gos*, -*gy*, *g.* a street in *Athens*.

Areopagetical, belonging thereto.

Arescation, *l.* a drying or withering.

Aret, *o.* account.

Aretaloger, -*gon*, *g.* a talker [only] of vertue.

Aretaphila, *g.* a she-friend of virtue.

Arethusa, Daughter of *Nereus* a River of *Sicily*; also an *Armenian* fountain in which nothing sinks.

Aretine, belonging to

Aretium, *Arezzi* in *Italy*.

Argent, -*try*, *l.* Silver, also white.

Argentanginy, *l.* silver-squincy, when for mony one feigns himself sick and dumb

Argentifer, maker of Silver

Argentina, *l.* wild tansey, also *Strasburgh* in *Germany*.

Argentum Dei, Gods [*i. e.* earnest] Mony.

Argile, *Arguithil* (near the Irish) part of North *Scotland*.

Argiletas, *l.* a place near the palace in *Rome*.

Argillous, *l.* clayie, clammy.

Argives, *l.* Grecians.

Argoil, *o.* clay.

Argonauticks, Books treatin of Navigation.

Argonauts, *Jason* and the rest that went to *Colchos* for the golden fleece, in

Argo, the ship in which they sailed.

Argos, a Town in *Greece*.

Argument, *l.* reason, proof; also the matter of which you

Argue, dispute.

Argus, King of *Peloponnesus*, for his wisdom feigned to have 100 eyes,

Argute, -*tious*, *l.* subtile.

Argyra, *g.* an Indian Island full of Silver and Gold.

Argyritis, litharge of Silver.

Ariadne, Daughter of *Minos*.

Aridate, *l.* to make

Arid, *l.* dry, barren.

Aridity, *Aritude*, driness.

Arided, *ar.* the swans tail a star.

Arietine, *l.* belonging to

Aries, *l.* a ram; a Roman battering Engine; also the first sign of the *Zodiack*.

Arietation, *l.* butting, battering.

Ariminum, *Rimini* in *Italy*.

Ariobarzanes, one of *Darius*'s Captains.

Ariolation, *l.* South-saying.

Arion, a famous Musician of *Lesbos*.

Arist, *o.* he arose.

Aristæus, King of *Arcadia*, he found the use of Bees.

Aristarchus, *g.* best Governour.

Aristides, an Athenian Justice.

Aristippus, *g.* best horseman.

Aristocratical, belonging to

Aristocracy, *g.* Government

ment of a Common-wealth by Nobles.

Aristolochia, the herb Birthwort.

Arite, *o.* arrest, stay.

Arithmancy, *g.* Divination by numbers.

Arithmetical, belonging to

Arithmetick, *g.* the Art of Numbring.

Ark, *l.* *Noah's* Ship, also the chest that kept the Law-tables.

Arles, *Earles*, earnest [-penny.]

Armada, *Sp.* a great Navy.

Armadillio, a West-Indian-Beast with skin like Armor.

Armagh, an Arch-Bishops-seat in *Ireland*.

Arma moluta, cutting weapons.

Armature, *l.* Armour, also skill in Arms.

Arm a shot, bind *Ocum* in Canvas to the spike of a cross-bar-shot.

Armenia, part of *Asia*.

Armiferus, *l.* bearing arms.

Armiger, *l.* the same, also an Esquire.

Armil, *l.* one of the Coronation garments, also a bracelet.

Armillate, wearing a bracelet.

Armillet, a little Bracelet.

Arminians, Hereticks following

Arminius, a Divinity Professor at *Leyden* in *Holland*.

Armipotent, *l.* powerful in arms.

Armomancy, divining by the shoulders of Beasts.

Armoniack, a gum issuing from the plant Fennel-giant

Armoricans, people of

Armorick, *Britain* in *France*.

Armory, where arms are kept.

Armusia, a County of *Carmania*, full of Vineyards.

Arnabo, a kind of sweet-sented Tree.

Arobe, a *Portugal* measure of Sugar, 15 bushels.

Aromatical, *-tick*, *l.* Spicy.

Aromatize, to perfume, or Spice.

Aromatization, perfuming.

Aron, Wake-Robin, Cuckoe-pit.

Arphaxad, *Arpachshad*, *h.* the Son of *Shem*.

Arpent de France, contains 100 perches, square, 18 foot each.

Arquebusier, one that serves with

Arquebuse, *f.* large Musket.

Arquebusade, a shot thereof.

Arragon, part of *Spain*.

Arraign, bring to trial.

Arran, *Cluid* part of North *Scotland*.

Arras, rich tapestry of

Arras, a Town in *Artesia*.

Array, ranking of Soldiers, also setting forth a Jury.

Arrearage, *f.* debt due on some old account.

Arrayers, Officers ordering the Soldiers arms.

Arrendare, *Sp.* to let out lands yearly.

Arrentation, license (for yearly rent) to enclose lands.

Arreptitious, *l.* snatch'd away; also crept in privily.

Arrere, *o.* apart.

Arrest, *f.* stop, seisure, also a Court-decree.

Arrestandis bonis ne dissipentur, a Writ to secure goods taken away.

Arpetteth, *o.* laying blame.

Arretted, brought before a Judge.

Arrianism, Doctrine of the

Arrians, Hereticks following

Arrius, a *Lybian* who deny'd the Son to be of the same substance with the Father.

Arride, *l.* to consent [by smiling.

Arrision, smiling upon

Arrogate, *l.* take to much to ones self.

Arrogancy, taking too much &c.

Arrogant, he that takes, &c.

Arrow-head, a water-herb

Arsenal, *I.* *Arcenal*, *f* storehouse of armour and Ammunition.

Arsenick, Orpiment, Orpine, Rats bane.

Arseverse, *T.* a spell to keep the house from burning, also as

Arse-versie, preposterously, the wrong way.

Arsura, things relating to coynage.

Arsmart, the herb water-pepper.

Arsons *f.* the saddle-bow.

Artaxerxes, *Artahshash't*, *h.* light, malediction, or fervent to spoil.

Artemisia, Queen of *Halicarnassus*, also Mug-wort.

Artemisian, [month] *May*.

Arten, *o.* constrain.

Arteries, *l.* pulses, hollow vessels like to veins, wherein the thinnest and the hottest bloud (with the vital spirits) passeth.

Arterial, belonging thereto.

Arterious, *l.* full of Arteries.

Arteriatomy, *-otomy*, *g.* a cutting of Arteries.

Arthel *Arddelw*, *Br.* avouching, vouchee.

Arthritical, Gouty.

Arthropia, *g.* the ligament that joyns the bones together.

Arthur, *Br.* strong man.

Articular, belonging to an

Article, *l.* joint or member.

Articulate, *l.* distinct, joyned; also to joint and make Articles of Agreement.

Artifex, *Artificer*, *l.* Artisan, Artist, *f.* work-man, or Crafts-master.

Artificer, *l.* craft, device.

Artillery, *l.* War-instruments.

Arval [Brothers,] twelve Roman Priests, Judges of Land-marks.

Arvisian [wine,] from

Arvis or

Amista, in the Isle *Sio* or *Chios*.

Arundel, *Arundale*, a Town in *Sussex* upon the River *Arun*.

Arundiferous, *l.* reed-bearing.

Arundinetum, *l.* Reed-ground.

Aruspicy, l. altar-divination, by beholding the entrails.

Asa, h. healer.

Asabel, h. God hath wrought.

Asaph, h. gathering.

Asarabacca, a vomit herb

Asbatte, o. a buying.

Asbestes, a people of *Lybia*.

Asbestos, g. a precious-stone unquenchable when fired.

Ascalonite, *Herod*, born at

Ascalon, a Town in Jury.

Ascance, a looking on one side.

Ascanius, Son to *Æneas*, builder of *Alba* in *Italy*.

Ascarides, small worms in the fundament.

Ascaunces, o. as though.

Ascendant, l. *Horoscope*, g. that point of the Ecliptick which rises at ones birth.

Ascentive, l. climbing up.

Ascetick, g. Monastick, Monkish.

Ascertain, assure.

Asclepiad [verse.] a Spondee, Choriambus, and two Dactyls.

Ascribe, l. impute.

Ascriptitious, l. added to others [in writing.]

Aschenaz, h. fire as it were distilling.

Ashdown, *Assendown*, a Town in *Essex*.

Asher, h. happiness.

Ashtaroth, Goddess of the *Sydonians*.

Ashur, h. blessed or beholding.

Asiatick, belonging to

Asia, One of the Worlds four parts.

Asinine, l. belonging to an Ass.

Askaunce, o. if by chance.

Askaunt, o. side-wayes, asquint.

Asker, newt, Eft.

Askes, o. Ashes.

Asly, willingly.

Asmatographers, g. Composers of Songs.

Asmodeus, g. the name of an evil spirit [of Lechery.]

Asopus, a River of *Bœotia*.

Asotus, g a sot, intemperate.

Asparagus, l. *vulgô* Sparagrass.

Aspe, g. a venemous Creature with eyes in the Temples

Aspect, l. Sight, Countenance; also Position of the Stars.

Aspectable l. to be seen.

Asper, a Turkish coyn about five farthings.

Asperation, l. a making rough.

Asperity, l. roughness.

Aspernate, l. despise.

Aspersion, l. sprinkling, also slandering.

Asphaltick, Belonging to

Asphaltites, the dead sulphry lake where *Sodom* stood

Asphodil, the flower Kingsspear.

Aspike, a little venemous Serpent.

Aspirate, -*ation*, l. breathing, also the Greek mark for h.

Asportation, l. carrying away.

Assach, *Assath*, *Br.* purgation by the oaths of 300 men.

Assa-fœtida, Devils-dung, a strong-sented gum from the scarify'd root of Laserwort.

Assaier, a Mint-Officer for the trial of Silver.

Assail, *Assault*, f set upon.

Assart, f. to make glades in a Wood to lop Trees, grub up bushes; also an offence by rooting up woods in a Forest.

Assasines, a Sect of strict Mahometans, refusing no pain or peril to stab whom their Master appointed.

Assasine, -*nate*, l. to murther [for gain,] also he that so robs and murthers.

Assation, l. a roasting.

Assay, f. try, trial.

Assectation, l. a following.

Assentation, l. a flattering compliance.

Assert, maintain.

Assertion, l. affirmation.

Assess, f. to tax.

Assessor, l. one joyn'd in Authority to another.

Assestrix, a she-assistant, a Midwife.

Assets, f. goods enough for an Executor to discharge Debts or Legacies.

Asseveration, l. an earnest affirming.

Assidcans, h. Justiciaries, a strict Sect among the Jews.

Assiduous, l. daily.

Assiduity, l. diligence.

Assign, *Assignee*, f. one appointed by another to do any business.

Assignment, *Assignation*, l. an Appointment, also passing a thing over to another.

Assimilate, l. liken.

Assimulate, l. to counterfeit.

Assize, o. Order.

Assised, o. sure, firm.

Assist, l. to help.

Assize, f. the sitting of Justices upon their Commissions; also a writ; also the price of any Commodity set down.

Association, l. accompanying.

Assonate, l. to sound together or in answer.

Assoyl, o. acquit, also answer.

Assoylen, o. declare.

Assuefaction, l. an accustoming.

Assuete, l. accustomed.

Assuetude, l. custom.

Assume, l. take to ones self.

Assumpsit, l. a voluntary promise.

Assumption, l. a taking to, also the minor or second Proposition in a Syllogism.

Assumptive, l. taking to himself, or that is lifted up.

Astares a River in *Pontus* causing the sheep that feed near it to give black milk.

Asteria, g. *Gemma Solis*, a stone that sparkles like a star.

Astroit, the same.

Asterites, a stone having in the midst the likeness of an half-moon.

Asterisk, *g.* a little star.
Asterism, *g.* a Constellation.
Asterius, a King of *Creet.*
Asteriagour, *o.* Astrolabe.
Astert, *o.* passed.
Asthmatical, belonging to
Asthma, *g.* difficult breathing
Astipulation, *l.* an agreement.
Astite, *Astide*, *No.* as soon, anon.
Astism, *-mus*, *g.* a civil jest.
Astræa, [Goddess of] Justice.
Astræus, *Aurora*'s husband.
Astragal, a ring about the neck of a pillar or Canon.
Astragalize, *l.* to make Astragals; also to play at dice or Tables.
Astralish, natural gold ore.
Astriction, *l.* a binding.
Astrictive, *Astringent*, binding.
Astringe, *l.* bind fast.
Astriferous, *l.* star-bearing.
Astroarch, *g.* Queen of Planets, the Moon.
Astrobolism, *g.* a blasting or Planet-striking.
Astrihilthet, *Atra-*, *Atri-*, *Sa.* a forfeiture double the damage.
Astrolabe, *g.* a flat instrument to take the motions and distances of Stars.
Astrology *g.* foretelling things to come by the Motions of the Stars.
Astrological, belonging thereto.
Astrologer, one skil'd therein.
Astromela, a City of *Narbon* in *France.*
Astronomical, belonging to
Astronomy, *g.* knowledge of the stars and their courses.
Astronomer, one skil'd therein.
Asturia, part of *Spain.*
Astute, *l.* subtile.
Astyages, *Cyrus*'s Grandfather.
Asyle, *g.* Sanctuary, refuge for Offenders.
Asymbolick, *g.* Scot free.
Asymphony, *g.* disagreement [in musick.]
Asyndeton, *g.* putting comma's instead of Conjunctions.
Atabalipa, a King of *Peru.*
Atalanta, the swift Lady won by *Hippomane*'s three golden apples.
Atchievment, *f.* performance of some great exploit; also a Coat of Arms fully blazoned.
Atcheked, *o.* choaked.
Ateles, an Island famous for good Oyntments.
Aterst, *o.* indeed.
Athaliah, *h.* the hour or time of the Lord.
Athamas, Son of *Æolus*, and King of *Thebes.*
Atheistical, belonging to
Atheism, *g.* the Doctrine of an
Atheist, who believes there is no God.
Athelney, *Athelingy* (Isle of Nobles) in *Somersetshire.*
Athenian, belonging to
Athens, *g.* a City in *Greece.*
Athletick, *-cal*, *g.* belonging to wrestling.
Athol, part of South-*Scotland.*
Athos, a high hill between *Macedonia* and *Thrace.*
Athroted, *o.* cloyed.
Atlantick [Islands,]-*Hesperides*, the two fortunate Islands on the borders of *Lybia*
Atlantick [Sea,] the west part of the *Mediterranean.*
Atlas, *Anchisa*, *Monts claros*, a Mountain of *Mauritania*
Atmosphere, *g.* the sphere or Region of vapours, the 2d.
Atome, *g.* a mote in the Sun; the smallest part of any thing.
Atonement, reconcilement, making two to be at One.
Atramental, *-tous* *l.* Inky.
Atrate, *l.* made black, in mourning.
Atrick, *o.* an Usher of a Hall.
Atrocity, *l.* fierceness.
Atrabilary, *l.* troubled with Melancholy.
Atrophy, *g.* a Consumption [for want of nourishment.]
Atropos, *g.* (unchangeable) one of the three destinies, that cuts the thread of mans life.
Attachment, *f.* laying hands on [Body and Goods.]
Attacted, *l.* touched.
Attainder, *f.* the convicting any person of a new crime.
Attaint, *f.* try'd, found out.
Attainted, convicted.
Attamed, *o.* set on broch.
Attaminate, *l.* defile.
Attaque, *f.* Assault.
Attemperate, *l.* to temper, make fit.
Attendant, owing service or depending upon.
Attenes, *o.* at once.
Attentate, *l.* attempt.
Attentive, *l.* hearkning diligently.
Attenuation, *l.* a lessening.
Atterly, *o.* extremely.
Attermining, *f.* a longer time [to pay debts.]
Attercob, *Cu.* a spiders web.
Atter, [corrupt] matter.
Attestation, *l.* a witnessing.
Atthis, Daughter to *Cranaus*, King of *Athens.*
Atticism, *l.* the *Athenians* manner of speaking.
Attique, *ick*, *Athenian.*
Attiguous, *l.* near to
Attinge, *l.* touch [lightly.]
Attire, *f.* dress.
Attires, [of a stag,] large horns.
Attone, *l.* bring into tune consort or agreement.
Attornato faciendo, a writ commanding the Sheriffe to admit the Attorney.
Attoure, *o.* towards.
Attournment, *f.* Ones turning Tenant to a new Lord.
Attraction, *l.* a drawing.
Attraits, *f.* charming qualities [drawing the affections.]
Attrebatii, *Barkshire* people.
Attrectation, *l.* a handling, feeling.
Attribute, *l.* impute, also the thing Attributed or given
Attribution, Assignment, delivery, applying.
Attrition, *l.* rubbing, wearing, or dashing against; also imperfect contrition or sorrow for sin.
Attrite, *l.* worn, fretted, or imperfectly sorry, &c.

ap-

Atturney, Procurator, one appointed to act for another.

Avage, *Avisage*, a duty paid the Lord of *Writtel* in *Essex*, for pigs and hogs.

Avail, *o.* value.

Availed, *o.* assaulted.

Avale, *o.* descend.

Avaunce, *o.* advance.

Avauncers, *o.* the second branches of the Harts-horns.

Avaunt, *o.* before.

Avant, *f.* forward, away.

Avarice, *l.* Covetousness.

Avaricum, *l.* *Bourges*, *Chasteau-neuf* in *France*.

Aubades, *f.* morning lessons under ones window.

Aube, *o.* as *Albe*.

Auctive, *-ifical*, *l.* augmenting.

Auctor, *l.* an Increaser or Authour.

Aucupation, *l.* fowling; also hunting for gain.

Audacity, *l.* boldness.

Audible, *l.* that may be heard

Audience, *l.* a hearing, a being heard; also as

Auditors, *l.* hearers, also Officers that examine the accounts of under-Officers.

Auditory, *l.* hearing-place, also hearers.

Audiendo & terminando, a Commission for hearing and punishing misdemeanours.

Audita querela, a writ for the appearance of a Creditor

Audry, the foundress of *Ely-Church*.

Avelace, *o.* (for *Annelace*, from the Italian *Annela cio*, a great ring) the rings or gymews of a bag.

Avenaunt, *o.* pleasant, agreeable.

Avenage, *f.* Oats paid a Landlord, for some other duties.

Avenor, provider of Oats.

Avenio, *Avignon*, in *France* it hath seven Palaces, Parishes, Monasteries, Colledges, Innes and Gates.

Ave Marie, *l.* Her salutation by the Angel.

Avens, Herb bennet.

Aventure, *Adventure*, *f.* a mortal or deadly mischance.

Aventinus, one of the seven hills of *Rome*.

Avenue, *f.* access, passage to a place.

Aver, *o.* wealth, also bribery.

Averr, *f.* affirm, avouch.

Avera, a dayes-work of a plow-man, 8 pence.

Average, *l.* duty of Carriage [by horse or Cart,] also contribution for the loss of goods cast over-board; also pasturage.

Averia, Cattel.

Averdupois, *Avoirdupoix*, *f.* (to contain full weight) 16 ounces to the pound; also goods so weighed.

Avery, a place where Oats or Provender is kept.

Averment, *f.* the Justifying an exception pleaded in abatement of the Plantiffs act.

Avernal, *-nial*, belonging to *Avernus*, a deadly stinking lake in *Italy*; also Hell.

Averpenny, money gathered for the Kings Averages.

Averruncation, *l.* lopping off superfluous branches; also appeasing.

Averruncus, a Roman God who did

Avert or turn away evil.

Aversion, *l.* turning away; also Antipathy or secret hatred.

Aufidena, a City of *Italy*.

Augeus, King of *Elis*, had a stable of 3000 Oxen.

Augment, *l.* increase.

Augmentation, [Court,] for the revenues coming by the Monasteries supprest.

Auger, a boring tool.

Augrim, as Algorithm.

Augrim-stones, to cast account with.

Augurize, *l.* to use

Augury, *l.* Divination by Birds.

Augures-staff, a wand which the

Augures (in south-saying) held in their hands.

August, *l.* Royal, Majestical.

Augustals, Feasts in honour of

Augustus, the 2d. Roman Emperour.

Augustan [Confession,] made at *Auspurgh*, in *Germany*.

Augustin, *Austin*, Bishop of *Hippo* in *Africa*.

Austin-fryers, of his Order.

Augustinians, Sacramentaries, Hereticks following one.

Augustin a *Bohemian*, who who held that Heaven Gates were not open till the general Resurrection.

Aviary, *l.* a place to keep Birds.

Avice, *Hildeviz*, *Sa.* Lady defence.

Avid, *l.* Covetous, greedy.

Avidity, covetousness.

Avisee, *o.* look upon; advised.

Aviso, *Sp.* admonition.

Auk, *Aukward*, untoward.

Aulick, *l.* of the Court.

Aulis, a haven in *Bæotia*.

Aulnage, *f.* Ell-measure.

Aulnegeor, *f.* The Officer that looks to the assize of woollens.

Aume, [of Rhenish wine,] forty gallons.

Aumener, *o.* cupboard:

Aumer, *o.* amber.

Aumere, *o.* welt, skirt, or border.

Aumone, *f.* (Alms) tenure by divine service.

Auncetry, as Ancestry.

Auncient demesne, Demean, or Domain, Kings Lands in Dooms-day-book.

Aunder, *Oneder*, *Che.* the afternoon.

Auntreth, *o.* adventureth.

Aunters, peradventure, or if.

Avocation, *l.* a calling away.

Auntrous, *o.* adventurous.

Avocatory, calling away.

Avoidance, a Benefices becoming void.

Avoided, denied.

Avouch, *f.* maintain justifie.

Avowable, Justifiable.

Avowry, *Advowry*, *f.* the maintaining of an act formerly done, as of distress for rent, &c.

Avouter, an Adulterer.

Aurea Cherfonefus, an *Indian Peninfula*.
Aurelia, *Orleance* in *France*.
Aurenches, heretofore Barons of *Folk-ftone* in *Kent*.
Auricular, belonging to
Auricle, *l.* an ear.
Auriculum, *Calx*, a mineral with Gold in it, alfo Gold calcined to powder.
Auriferous, *l.* gold-bearing.
Auriflamb, *Oriflambe*, *f.* St. *Dennis*'s purple ftandard born againft infidels, loft in *Flanders*.
Auriga, *l.* Stars on the horns of *Taurus*.
Aurigation, *l.* the guiding of any Carriage.
Aurigia, *Arion* in *Spain*.
Aurigraphy, writing with Gold.
Auripigmentum, *l.* Orpine.
Aurift, that is skil'd in the ears.
Aurney, *Aurigney*, *Aurica*, a *Brittifh-Ifle*.
Aurora, *l.* morning.
Aurum Philofophorum, Lead in Chymiftry.
Aurum potabile, *l.* drinkable Gold.
Aurum Reginæ, Queen-gold
Aufcultation, *l.* hearkning, obeying.
Aufes, *African* Virgins ufed to combat in honour of *Minerva*.
Aufones, an old people of *Italy*.
Aufpical, belonging to the
Aufpices, *l.* Sooth-fayers that obferve the flight of Birds.
Aufpicious, *l.* lucky.
Auftere, *l.* four, ftern.
Aufterity, crabbednefs.
Auftral, *l.* Southern.
Auftralize, to turn to or from the South.
Auftrafia, *Brabant* and *Lorrain*, one of the four Kingdoms of *France*, the other three were *Soiffons*, *Orleans*, and *Paris*.
Autar, *o.* Altar.
Autem, (for Antem or Anthem) a Song.
Auftria, part of *Germany*.
Auftromancy, *g.* divination by the South-wind.
Aufturcus, a Gofhawk.
Autarchy, *g.* contentednefs, felf-fufficiency,
Authentick, *g.* allowed, of good authority.
Authorize, *l.* Impower.
Autochthones, *g.* Aborigines.
Autem, *c.* Church; alfo married.
Autocrafy, *g.* felf-fubfiftence
Autogeneal *g.* felf-begotten.
Autograph, *-phical*, *g.* of the Authors own writing
Autoleon, a Captain of the *Crotoniates*.
Autolicus, *Mercury*'s Son who could change all he ftole into what he would.
Autology, *g.* fpeaking of or to ones felf.
Automatous, *-tarian*, belonging to an
Autome, *-maton*, *g.* an inftrument moving of it felf.
Autonoe, *Actæon*'s Mother.
Autonomy, *g.* living after ones own law.
Autoptical, belonging to
Autopfy, *g.* felf-beholding.
Autotheifm, *g.* Gods being of himfelf.
Autremite, *o.* an [other] attire.
Autumnal, belonging to
Autumn, *l.* the Harveft-quarter.
Auturgie, *g.* felf-working.
Avulfion, *l.* a plucking from.
Aux, as *Abfis*
Auxiliary, coming to
Auxiliate, *l.* aid, help.
Auxilium ad filium militem faciendum, a writ to leavy aid of the Tenants toward the Knighting the landlords eldeft Son or marrying his Eldeft Daughter.
Avyfions, *o.* vifions.
Award, Judgment, arbitration.
Await, *-ayte*, *o.* waiting; alfo caution, heed.
Awaits, *o.* ambufhments.
Awdley, *Aldethelighe*, an ancient Family.
Awhaped, *o.* amazed, aftonifhed.
Awhere, *o.* a defire.
Awm, *Awame*, as Aume.
Awn, the beard of any Corn.
Awning, a canvafs fail fpread above the deck.
Awnfel. [weight] *quafi* handfale, poifing meat only by hand.
Awreaked, *o.* wreaked.
Awreaketh, *o.* revengeth.
Axefs, *o.* as accefs; ague.
Axillar, *-ary*, *l.* belonging to the Armpits.
Axinomancy, *g.* a divination by hatchets.
Axiom: *g.* a maxime or general ground in any Art.
Axicle, *l.* a lath; a pulley-pin.
Axis, *l.* an *Axel-tree*; the diameter of the World.
Axminfter, *Axanminfter*, a Town in *Cornwal*.
Ay, *Ea*, *Eye*, *Sa*, a watery place.
Ay, *o.* Egge.
Aye, *o.* for ever.
Ayen, *o.* again.
Ayenft, *o.* againft.
Ayenward, *o.* back again.
Ayl, *o.* alwayes.
Azamoglans, thofe intended to be enrolled *Janizaries*.
Azariah, *h.* the Lords help.
Azebone, *A.* head of the 16 manfion.
Azemech, *A.* the Virgins fpike, a ftar.
Azemen, [degrees] afcend at that birth which hath fome incurable defect.
Azimuthal, belonging to the
Azimiuths, or *Azimuths*, Circles that meet in the *Zenith* and pafs through all degrees of the Horizon.
Azure, *lazul*, *A.* skie-colour'd.
Azyme, *g.* without leaven or mixture.
Azymes, *g.* a feaft of feven daies (beginning the morrow after the Paffeover) wherein no leavened bread might be eaten.

B.

B*aal*, *h.* Lord, Jupiter, *Baalzebub*, *Belzebub*, *Beel-*, *h.* Lord of flies, or Devils,

Baasha, h. in making or pressing together.
Babel, *Babylon*, *Bagadeth*,
Bagda, h. confusion [of tongues.]
Babion, a large kind of Monkey.
Bablac, a Town in *Oxfordshire*.
Babewries, *Babeuries*, o. strange antick works.
Babys, Brother of *Marsyas*,
Bac, f. a ferry,
Bach, *Beak*, *Bec*, a River.
Bacchanalize, to imitate the
Bacchanals, mad feasts of *Bacchus*.
Baccharach, *Bachrag*, Rhenish [wines.] from
Baccharag, a *German* City.
Bacchation, l. rioting.
Bacchean, belonging to
Bacchus, God of Wine.
Bacciferous, l. berry-bearing.
Bachyllion, a song or dance of
Bachyllus, a Tragedian.
Backberond, Sa. a Thief taken with the goods about him.
Bactriana, part of *Scythia*.
Badbury, a Town in *Dorset*.
Badge, Arms, Cognizance.
Badger, f. a transporter and seller of Provision; also a Brock or Grey.
Badinage, f. foolery, buffoonry
Badelynge of Dokys, o. padling Company of Ducks.
Badonicus, *Bannesdown-hill* in *Sommersetshire*.
Bætica, part of *Spain*.
Bagates, f. toy, trifle.
Baggeth, o. disdaineth
Bagginly, *-ingly*, swellingly, proudly.
Bajazet, a Turkish Emperor.
Bail, f. surety for ones appearance.
Bailly, o. Government.
Baily-wick, Jurisdiction of a
Baily, *Bailiffe*, f. principal deputy to the King or other Lord.
Bain, f. a Bath; also willing, and limber, Sf.
Bainards Castle, Earl of *Pembrooks* house in *London*.
Baisemains, f. kiss-hands, Complements, humble service
Baiton Kaiton, A. the whales belly, a star.
Baize, fine freeze of
Bay, a City of *Naples*.
Balaam, *Bileam*, h. the ancient of the People.
Balade, f. ballet, poem; also a dance.
Balais of entail, f. rubies [or other jewels] cut.
Bales Turkes Turkish ruby.
Balak, h. covering or destroying.
Balasse, sa. Gravel (or any weight) in the bottom of a ship.
Balatron, l. babler.
Balaustium, the blossom of the Pomegranate-tree.
Balcone, I. a bay window.
Baldwin, ge. bold victour.
Baleyne, f. whale-[bone.]
Bale, f. pack [of merchandize.]
Balkful, o. Sorowful.
Balk, sa. a little peice left unplough'd, also a beam.
Balkes, forreign pieces of Timber.
Balk-staff, a quarter-staff.
Ball, f. a dancing-meeting.
Balladin, f Galliard-dancer.
Balliol [Colledge] in *Oxford*.
Ballist, l. a large cross-bow.
Ball-money, given by a new bride to her old Play-fellows.
Ballon, f. a large ball; also the round Globe or top of a pillar.
Ballotation, *Balloting*, Election, casting lots [by balls.]
Ballustrade, jutting out of a window or Portal.
Balm, juice of a Tree in *Judæa*.
Balmerinoch, a Scotch Abbey.
Balneary, l. a bathing place.
Balneation, bathing.
Balneator, bath-keeper.
Balneatory, belonging to bath.
Balneum arenæ, infusion of flowers, &c. in a close vessel (with water) set in hot sand.
Balneum Cinerum, the same set in hot ashes.
Balneum Mariæ, or *Maris*, the same put into a bigger vessel of water o're the fire.
Balthasar, h. (without treasure) *Melchior* and *Jasper*, the three wise men mentioned, *Mat*. 2.
Baltick, belonging to
Baltia, *Scandia*, *Scandinavia*, an Isle in the *German* Ocean.
Balsamon, a Patriarch of *Antioch*, *Anno*, 1185.
Bambalio, a faint hearted man.
Band, f. a foot Company.
Bandie, f. to toss up and down, also to follow a faction.
Banditi, Outlaws, condemned by
Bando, I. proclamation.
Banderol, *Bannerol*, f. a little flag or streamer.
Bandle, an Irish measure of two foot.
Bandog, Mastive.
Bandon, f. custody; license, also Sect, or Company.
Bandore, I. a Musick-Instrument.
Bane, Sa. poyson; destruction.
Banns, *Bans*, f. proclamations, and particularly of Marriages.
Bangle[*eard*] like a Spaniel.
Bangue, a pleasant drink in the Eastern Countries.
Banker, Exchanger of forreign money.
Bankers browded, o. embroider'd cushions.
Bankrout, *Bankrupt*, one that has consumed all.
Bannock, *La*. a cake of Oatmeal and water only.
Bannavenna, *-venna*, *Wedon* in *Northamptonshire*.
Banner, f. flag, ensign.
Bannians, crafty Merchants of *India*.
Banleucum, *Banleuga*, precinct.
Bantam, the chief City of *Java Major*, in the *East-Indies*
Baptismal, belonging to
Baptization, *Baptism*, g. washing or dipping in water.
Baptist, g. washer, dipper.
Baptistery, a vessel or place to wash in, a font.
Barabbas, Sy. Fathers Son.
Barak, h. lightning.
Baratta, rare *East-India* Balsom.
Baralipton, an imperfect Syllo-

Syllo.

Syllogism of two universal and a particular affirmative.

Barbara, a perfect syllogism of three universal affirmatives.

Barbarian, belonging to

Barbary, -*ria*, part of *Africa*.

Barbarism, g. rudeness of speech or behaviour.

Barbarous, cruel, inhumane.

Barbarity, cruelty.

Barbe, a mask or vizard.

Barbed, *l*. bearded.

Barbel, bearded fish.

Barbican, *f*. an Out-work.

Barbitist, *g*. Lutinist.

Barce, the cheif City of *Lybia*.

Bards, the British Scholars.

Bardes, *Barbes*, horse-trappings.

Bargh, *T*. a steep horse-way.

Bargaret, -*net*, *o*. a ballet; song or dance.

Bar-Iesus, *Ch*. Son of Jesus.

Bar-Ionah, *Ch*. Son of Jonah.

Barkary, bark- or tan-house

Bark-fat, Tanners-tub.

Barkman, boatman.

Barm, yest, also a lap.

Barm-cloth, *o*. apron.

Barn, *Bern*, *sa*. Child.

Bearn teams, broods of Children.

Barnabas, -*by*, *Ch*. Son of Comfort.

Barnacle, a fish that eats through the planks of Ships, also a Scotch or Soland-goose growing (they say) on trees, also a brake to put on the noses of unruly horses.

Baroco, a Syllogism of an universal affirmative and two particular negatives.

Barometer, *g*. an instrument to find the pressure of the air.

Baronage, tax laid upon

Baronies, Estates of

Barons, *f*. Lords.

Baroscope, *g*. an instrument shewing all the changes of the air.

Barre, a Defendants sufficient answer, also two lines overthwart an Eschutcheon.

Bar-fee, 20 d. to the Gaoler.

Barettor, *Barratour*, *f*. who sets men at variance.

Barratria, -*try*, Simony.

Barcaria, -*ium*, a Sheep-coat, also a Sheep-walk.

Barricado, *Sp*. a Defence of barrels fil'd with Earth.

Barriers, *f*. an exercise with short swords within barres.

Barresters, -*rasters*, who (after 7 years study) are admitted to the bar.

Barsalona, *Barcellona*, *Barcino* a City of *Spain*.

Barter, *Sp*. truck or change.

Bartle, warm pasture.

Bartholomew, *Ch*. the Son of him that makes the water ascend.

Barton, *Barken*, a place to keep Poultry in.

Baruch, *h*. blessed.

Barulet, the fourth part of a bar.

Barzillai, *h*. hard as Iron.

Bas. a Scotch Island.

Bascuence, *Sp*. the Biscay-tongue.

Base, *Basis*, *l*. the bottom or foundation of a thing.

Base-Court, not of Record.

Base-estate, at the Lords will.

Basels, an old abolished coyn.

Baselards, *o*. daggers, wood-knives.

Basiate, *l*. to kisse.

Basha Bassa, a Turkish Commander.

Basil, an herb, also as

Basilical, *g*. Royal, Magnificent.

Basilick vein, the Liver-vein.

Basilisk, *g*. a Cockatrice, also a large canon; also the Lions heart, a star.

Basilisks, *g*. stately buildings at *Rome*.

Basinet, *f*. a little basin.

Baskervile, an ancient Family.

Basse, *o*. A kisse, or the lower [lip.]

Bast, Lime-tree wood made into ropes and Mats, also to sew, *o*.

Bastardy, the being a

Bastard, born out of wedlock.

Bastardize, corrupt, make worse.

Bastile, -*ilde*, -*illion*, *f*. that is to *Paris*, as the Tower is to *London*.

Bastion, *f*. Cullion-head, a Fort.

Baston, *f*. a Cudgel, also an Officer to the Warden of the Fleet.

Bastonado, *Sp*. a cudgeling.

Batable *quasi* debatable [ground,] between *England* and *Scotland*.

Bataunly, *o*. boldly.

Batavians, people of

Batavia, *Holland*.

Batner, *c*. Oxe.

Bath, a City in *Sommerset*.

Bath, *o*. both.

Battail-field, by *Shrewsbury*.

Battalion, *f*. the main body of an Army.

Battery, *fa*. beating, assault.

Battology, *g*. vain repetition of words.

Batting, a Hawks fluttring, striving to fly away.

Battle, (size) take provision on the Colledge book.

Battle-bridge, *Stanford-bridge* in *York-shire*.

Battailed, *o*. having.

Battlements, turrets of houses built flat.

Battus, a perfidious fellow turn'd to a stone by *Mercury*

Batune, a note of bastardy in heraldry.

Batus, *Sa*. boot.

Bavaria, a *German* Dukedom

Baubels, *o*. Jewels.

Baubee, farthing.

Baucis *Philemons* wife.

Baud, *o*. bold.

Baude. a brave, a Gentleman, also a Ruffian.

Baudkin, a glistering stuff.

Baudons (for bandon) *o*. Custody.

Baudrick, *Bawd*, *o*. furniture, also a sword-girdle, also an old-fashion'd jewel.

Bavin, Brush-wood [fagots.]

Baulk, *o*. to crosse [a River]

Baudly, *o*. bravery, boldness.

Bawsin, *o*. big. gross.

Bawsyn, *o*. a badger.

Bay, a stop for water, a road for ships, a brown-red colour, also a stake, *o*.

Bayard, *f*. bay-coloured [horse.]

Bay [window] that boundeth out round.

Baxter, *sc.* baker.

Bazar, an Indian Market-place.

Baven, *o.* to bark.

Bdellium, an *Arabian*-Gum like wax, sweet in smell, but bitter in taste.

Beaconage, money to maintain.

Beacons, high lights for warning.

Beadroll, *Sa.* a list of those that use to be pray'd for.

Beak, the crooked upper part of a hawks bill.

Beak-head, is fastned with a knee upon the stem of a ship.

Beal, *Bel*, *f.* Fair.

Beam, whereon the starts of a stags head grow, also long [feathers of a hawks wing.]

Beam, *o.* *Bohemia.*

Beards, prickles on the ears of Corn.

Bearers, maintainers, abetters.

Bearn, *o.* a wood, also a Child.

Bears-breech, brank ursine, a lively-green herb.

Bears-foot, the herb Setterwort.

Bear in [with the harbour,] sail into it with a large wind.

Bear off [from the land,] go more room than your course lies.

Bear up, sail more before the wind.

Beasel, *Bezill* *Bezil*, the upper part of the collet of a ring, which contains the stone.

Beastail, *f.* all Cattel.

Beat, search for hare, &c.

Beating, *T.* with Child, breeding.

Beätifie *l.* to make happy.

Beätifick, *-cal*, *l.* that which makes happy.

Beätitude, *l.* blessedness.

Beatrice, *-trix*, *l.* she that makes happy or blessed,

Beavis, *Bellovesus*, proper name

Beau-champ, *f.* a title confer'd on the Family of *Seimours.*

Beaumont, *f.* one of the greatest Families of the Nation.

Beau-pleading, fair pleading.

Beau Sir, *o.* fair Sir.

Beazar Beazoar, [stone,] bread in the maw of a

Beazar, *Bazar*, an Indian Goat.

Bec, [*Phrygian*-]bread.

Becalmed, not able to sail for want of wind.

Beebic, *-cal*, belonging to a Cough, as Lozenges, &c.

Beclap, *o.* accuse, catch or arrest.

Bed, a plank on which the Canon lies in the carriage.

Bede, a Venerable English Monk near *Newcastle*, also to offer, also dwelled, *o.*

Beddeth [the Roe] lies down.

Bedes-man, *Beads-man*, *Almsman*, who prays for a Benefactor.

Bedrawled, bedrabled, drivel'd.

Bedrepe, *Bidrepe*, duty of some Tenants, to reap their Landlords Corn in Harvest.

Bedolven, *o.* dugg, delved.

Bedlam, *Bedlem*, *Bethlem*, *h.* [house of bread,] for Madmen.

Bede'an, the walk of a

Bedle, *Beadle*, *Bedel*, (D. Cryer) waits upon a Magistrate.

Beer-sheba, *h.* Well of the oath.

Beer, *birre* might, *Che.*

Bee-mol, *f.* the Musick flat key.

Beem, *o.* tree.

Beest[*ings*,] the first milk after birth.

Begon, *Bi-*, *o.* beset [with gold,] decked.

Beglerbeg, [*Tu.* Lord of Lords] of *Greece* and *Natolia.*

Beenship, *c.* worship, good ness.

Beguines, *f.* an order of old Nuns.

Beheft, a promise also a precept.

Behight, *-hete*, *o.* promised.

Behither, on this side, *Sf.*

Beiram, a Turkish feast.

Beight, bought, bending, *Che.*

Beknew, *o.* learnt out, knew.

Bekyth, *o.* wipeth her beke.

Bel, *Chald.* the Sun, or Lord.

Belage, fasten any [ship-] rope when haled.

Belamy, *f.* fair friend.

Belchier, *f.* good Countenance.

Bel-chose, *f.* fair thing.

Beleagre, *-guer*, *D.* besiege.

Belgick, *-ian*, belonging to

Belgia, *l.* the Low-Countries.

Belgrade, a City of *Hungary.*

Belial, *h.* wicked, unprofitable, without yoke, also the Devil.

Belides, *Danaus*'s 50 Daughters.

Belive, *qu.* by the *Eve*, anon.

Belisarius, a Roman General forced to beg his bread.

Bellacity, *l.* warlikeness.

Bellatrix, the left shoulder of *Orion*, a star.

Bellatrice, *l.* a she-warriour.

Bellerophon, Son of *Glaucus*, kil'd *Chimæra*, by the help of *Neptunes Pegasus.*

Belle I saude, I said or spoke very well.

Bellicose, *l.* warlike.

Bellyth, the Roebuck (probably) maketh such a noise.

Belligerate, *l.* make war.

Bellipotent, *l.* strong in arms.

Bellitude, *l.* beauty.

Bell-mettal, a mixture of Tyn and Copper-oar.

Bellona, Goddess of war.

Belluine, *l.* Beast-like.

Belly-cheat, *c.* an apron.

Belomancy, *g.* Divination by arrows.

Belperpis, (*q. pyropis*,) jewels.

Bel-videre, *I.* (fair to behold) the Popes palace, so

Belvoir [Castle,] in *Lincoln-shire.*

Belus, the first or second King of *Assyria*, also *Jupiter.*

Bement, *-eint*, a bemoaned.

Bemes, *o.* trumpets.

Benajah, *h.* the Lords building.

Benacus, a lake in *Lombardy* with gold-sands.

Bendlet, *f.* a little,

Bend, a line from the dexter chief to the finister base of a Scutcheon; also a muffler, caul or kercher, *o*.

Bend, [the Cable to the anchor,] fasten it to the ring.

Benediction, *l.* a blessing.

Bener, *-nar*, *c.* better.

Benet, contracted of

Benedict, *l.* blessed, happy, also a good saying.

Benedictins, *Benedictine-Monks*, in black.

Benerth, Plough and Cart-service to a Landlord.

Benefactor, *l.* he that doth a

Benefact, *l.* benefit, good deed.

Benefice, *l.* a spiritual living.

Beneficence, *l.* bounty.

Benegro, make black.

Beneplacity, *l.* wel pleasing.

Benemerent, *l.* a wel-deserving

Benes, *o.* bones.

Benevolence, *l.* good-will.

Benevolent [Planets] *Jupiter* and *Venus*.

Bengala, an *East-India* Kingdom.

Bengi, an *Indian* powder of hemp exciting luxury.

Benhadad, *h.* Son of noise.

Benjamin, *h.* Son of dayes or old age, called by his Mother,

Benoni, *h.* Son of sorrow.

Benjamin, *Benzoin*, *Assa dulcis*. a sweet gum from *Java*.

Bensel, beat, bang. *Y*.

Benign, *l.* favourable.

Beningly, *o.* benignly, kindly.

Benignity, *l.* kindness.

Bent, where rushes grow.

Benimmeth, *o.* bereaveth, taketh away.

Beorh, a heap.

Benison, *f.* a blessing.

Bercaria, as *Barcaria*.

Berecynthia, *Cybele*, the Mother of the Gods.

Berenice, *Ptolomy's* Daughter.

Bergh master, *Sa.* an Officer amongst the *Derbyshire* Miners.

Bergh-mote, a Court held there.

Beringarius, a great Scholar.

Beris, a high *Armenian* hill.

Berkhamsted, a Town in *Hertfordshire*.

Bern, cheif City of *Switzerland*.

Bernardines, *Cistertian* Monks of the order of St.

Bernard Sa. Bears heart or Bear-ward.

Bernard Colledge, St. *John Baptist Colledge*.

Bernet, a Town in *Hertfordshire*.

Berry, to threfh, also as *Bury*, *Sa.* a Mannor-house.

Berth convenient Sea-room

Berthing [the Ship-sides] is also the building or bringing them up.

Bertha, *ge.* bright.

Berthinsec, *Birdinsec*, a Scotch Law which only whips men for stealing so much meat as they can cary [in a Sack.]

Berton, a Farm house.

Bertram, proper name, also *Pellitory* of *Spain*.

Berubium, *Urehead* in *Scotland*.

Berwica, an appurtenant to some place.

Beryl, *g.* an *Indian* green-stone.

Beseech, *o.* beseech.

Bezant, *Besant*, *Besance*, *Bisantine*, *Biz-*, *Byz-*, an old gold coyn about a ducket, also (in Heraldry) a round plate of gold, by some worth 15, by other 3750 pounds, from

Byzantium, *Constantinople*.

Besca, a spade or shovel.

Besieged [Planet,] placed between two malevolents.

Beset, set packing, also employed.

Besestein, *Bisestano*, the exchange of *Constantinople*.

Besey, *o.* become.

Well Besey, of good aspect.

Beshet, *o.* shut up.

Besmottered, *o* besmutted.

Besprengyd, *o.* besprinkled.

Bestad *o.* lost.

Beswike, *o.* betray.

Besyen, *o.* trouble, grief.

Betake, *Beteach*, *Sa.* to deliver, to commend.

Bet, *o.* to pray, also better, also quickly.

Bete, *o.* boot, help, also to make or compel.

Beten, *o.* kindle, also abate.

Beth, *h.* a house.

Bethaven, *h.* house of vanity.

Bethel, house of God.

Bethesda, Alms house, &c.

Bethlemites, Fryars that wore a star on their backs.

Betle, *Betre*, Bastard-Pepper an Indian plant.

Betrassed, *o.* deceived.

Betreint, *-cut*, *o.* sprinkled.

Betty, *c.* an instrument to open doors.

Beverage, *f.* mingled drink.

Bevy, Company [of Roes, quails, Fairies, &c.]

Bevy-grease, fat of Roes.

Bewits, leathers to which the hawks bells are fastened.

Bewared, *o.* spent, expended.

Bewreck, *o.* revenged.

Bewryen, *o.* declare, also betray.

Bey, *o.* buy.

Beyaped, *o.* cheated.

Beyet, *o.* begotten.

No Beyete, not a bit, no whit, not at all.

Bezaliel, *h.* in Gods shadow.

Bezeil, as *Beasel*.

Bezoar, as *Beazar*.

Bialacovl, *o.* fair welcoming

Bibacious, *l.* given to

Bibacity, immoderate love of drink, tipling.

Bibliographer, *g.* Book-writer.

Bibliopolist, Book-seller.

Bibliothecary, keeper of a

Bibliotheque, *g.* Library.

Bice, a blew paint, also green.

Bickering, skirmishing.

Bicipital, *-tous*, *l.* with two heads.

Bicolor, *l.* of two colours.

Bicornous, *l.* with two horns.

Bicorporal, *l.* with two bodies.

Bid, *o.* both.

Bid a boon, *o.* desire a request.

Bidding of beads, *Sa.* calling to prayers.

Bid-ale, *Bidderale*, help-ale, bidding friends to a Feast to gain their Charitable help.

Bidental, *l.* with twoo teeth, also a place where sheep were sacrificed.

Bien

Bien & loyalment, f. well and faithfully.

Biennial, l. of two years.

Bifarious, l. of two meanings.

Biformed, l. of two shapes.

Biferous, l. twice-bearing.

Bifoyl, l. the herb tway-blade.

Bifront, l. with two foreheads.

Bifurcous, l. two-forked.

Biga, any carriage.

Bigamist, g. committer of

Bigamy, g. the having two wives [at one time.]

Bigat, a Roman peny.

Biggening, up-rising [of women.]

Biggins, *Lancashire* buildings.

Bigge, a pap or teat, *E.* build, o.

Bight, any part of a rope coiled up (see *Beight*) also the Neck.

Bigot, f. a scrupulous superstitious fellow; also hypocrite.

Bigottery, such practice.

Bighes, o. (for *Bagues*) jewels.

Bikenne, o. acknowledge.

Bilander. *By-lander*, a small kind of ship.

Bilanciis deferendis, a Writ for the weighing of Wool to be transported.

Bil-berries, *Whortle-*, Dewberries.

Bilbilis, a Spanish Town.

Bilboa, *Bilbo*, another, where the best Blades are made.

Bildge, *Buldge*, the breadth of the floor wherein the ship rests when she's aground.

Bilged, springs a leak, by striking against a rock or Anchor.

Bilinguis, l. double-tongued, also a Jury made up of English men and Aliens.

Bilious, l. Cholerick.

Bilk, A. nothing, also to deceive.

Billard, Sf. bastard Capon.

Billa vera, l. the indorsement of the Grand Inquest upon a presentment seeming probable.

Billows, great waves.

Billet, f. a litle note, also a wedge [of Gold.]

Bimatical, l. of two years.

Bimensal l. of two Months.

Binarious, *-ry*, l. belonging to two.

Binaria, l. the number of two.

Bineme, o. take away.

Binarchy, g. a Government which is under two.

Bindeweed, withwind

Bing awast, c. go away.

Binne, o. manger, also a place to keep bread in.

Binomical, *-ious*, l. of two Names.

Bint, o. bound.

Bipartite, l. divided in two.

Bipatent, l. open two ways.

Bipedal, *-aneous*, *-dical*, l. of two foot.

Biquintile, (Bq.) an aspect consisting of 141 degrees.

Bird, Sf. sight [of the eye.]

Birlet, *Birret*, o. coife or hood.

Birlings, sc. small sea-vessel.

Bismare, o. curiosity.

Bismutum, *Wismuth*, counterfein, Tinglass, whiter than black and blacker than white Lead.

Bison, f. Bugle, Buff, Wild Ox.

Bisque, a fault at Tennis, also a compound dish.

Bissected, l. cut in two equal parts.

Bissextile, leap-year, every fourth year, when *February* hath 29 dayes and St. *Matthias*, removes from the 24th. to the 25th. day.

Bistort, Snakeweed.

Bisumbres, as *Amphicii*.

Bite, c. to cheat, also to steal.

Biton and *Cleobis*, rewarded with death for their piety to their Mother *Argia*, in drawing her Charet to the Temple.

Birrent, o. compass, bind about.

Bits, two square peices of Timber to belage the Anchor Cable to.

Bittacle, the Compass-box on the steerage.

Bitter, vere out the Cable by little and little.

Bittersweet, Woody Night-shade with blewish flowers.

Bittourn, a kind of Heron having (they say) three stones

Bituminous, belonging to

Bitumen, l. a fat Clammy substance used for morter.

Bituminated, done therewith.

Bituriges, the people of *Berry* in *France*.

Biwopen, o. sprinkled with tears.

Bizend, *Beesend*, *Bison'd*, blinded.

Black-book, treats of all the Exchecquer-Orders.

Blake, o. naked

Blacklow, a hill in *Warwickshire*, on which *Pierce Gaveston* was beheaded.

Black-maile, contribution for protection against Thieves and Robbers in the North.

Black-more Forest, white-hart-forrest in *Dorsetshire*.

Black-munday, Easter, Munday 1359. when Hail-stones kil'd both Men and Horses in the Army of our *Edward* the 3d. in *France*.

Black-rod, the Usher belonging to the order of the garter

Black-buried, gone to Hell.

Blain, a push more painfull and red than the small pox.

Blanch, f. white.

Blakes, *Casings*, [Cow-]dung dried for fuel.

Blanching, peeling of Almonds, &c. in hot water.

Blandiloquence, l. fair speaking, also flattery.

Blandishment, f. flattring.

Blank, 8d. coyn'd by *Henry* the 5th. in *France*.

Black-bar, Common-bar, a plea compelling the Plantiff to assign the place of trespass

Blankers, o. white garments.

Blank-manger, f. a kind of delicious white-meat.

Blasco, the Isle *Languillade*, in the mouth of *Rhene*.

Blase, g. sprouting forth.

Blasours, c. Praisers.

Blasphemy, g. reproach.

Blatant, barking.

Blatteration, *l.* babling.

Blatta Bizantia, a ſweet Indian Sea-fiſh-ſhel.

Blaze, *D.* ſpread abroad, alſo a fire in memory of the blazing ſtar (*Jan.* 5.)

Blazon, *f.* the deſcription of a Coat of Arms.

Blay, *Bleak*, a [whitiſh] fiſh.

Blee, *o.* Corn, alſo as

Ble, *o.* ſight, aſpect.

Bleating-cheat, *c.* a ſheep.

Bleach, whiten [in the Sun.]

Bleit, *Blate*, *Sc.* ſhamefaſt.

Blemiſhes, Hunters marks where the Deer hath gone.

Blench, a tenure by payment of a peny, roſe, &c. on demand.

Blend, mingle together, alſo blind, *o.*

Blent, *-cint*, *o.* ſtopped.

Blepharon, *g.* he that hath great eye-brows.

Bleſiloquent, *l.* ſtammering.

Blue-mantle, an Office belonging to one of the Purſivants at Arms.

Bleve, *-ven*, *D.* tarry, abide.

Blight, a blaſting.

Blinks, boughs caſt in the Deers way.

Bliſſom, to tup [as the Ram doth the Ewe.]

Blite, *l.* a taſtleſs herb.

Blith, *Br.* yielding milk, profitable; alſo as

Blithſom, pleaſant, jovial.

Blive, as *Belive*, *o.* readily, preſently.

Blo, *o.* blue [colour.]

Blocks, the wooden things in which the ſhip ropes run.

Blois, a City of *France*.

Blomary, the firſt forge in an iron-mill.

Blonder, *o.* blunder.

Bloom, bloſſom, bloſme.

Blot the Skrip, *c.* enter into Bond.

Blote, to ſmoke, alſo ſmoked [herrings.]

Bloten, *Che.* fond (as a Nurſe.)

Bloud-ſtone, a reddiſh ſtone ſtopping bloud.

Bloud-wit, *Sa.* an amercement for ſhedding bloud.

Blower, *c.* a Quean.

Blubber, Whale-Oyl [imperfect.]

Bluffer, *c.* an Hoſt or Landlord.

Bluffe, *Bluff-headed*, when the Ships ſtern is as it were upright; alſo to blind-fold.

Blunderbuſs, a large gun carrying 20 piſtol bullets.

Blyn, *o.* Ceaſe.

Blyſs, *o.* joy.

Boa, Swine-pox.

Boanerges, *h.* Sons of thunder

Boas, a monſtrous Serpent, in who's belly *Pliny* ſayes a whole infant hath been found.

Boatſwain. the under-pilot.

Boccaſine, *f.* fine buckrum.

Bobtail, a kind of ſhort arrow-head, alſo a whore.

Bocardo, the name of a Priſon in *Oxford*; alſo a Syllogiſm who's firſt and laſt Propoſitions are particular Negatives and the other an univerſal Affirmative.

Boccone, *I.* a morſel or bit alſo poyſon.

Boc-hord, *Sa.* where Books or writings are kept.

Bockland, held by Book or Charter.

Bode, *D.* Meſſenger; alſo foretel; alſo to ask news.

Bodotria, *Bederia*, *Edenburgh Frith* in *Scotland*.

Bodykin, *o.* a little Body.

Bœotia, *Ogygia*, part of *Greece*.

Boer, *Boor*, *D.* a Countryman from

Bo, (*Gothick*) a village.

Boetherick that part of Phyſick which removes diſeaſes.

Bohemia, part of *Germany*.

Bois de Vicennes, a ſtately Palace near *Paris*.

Boiſtousneſs, *o.* rudeneſs.

Boiſtous, *o.* lame, halting.

Boke, point [at one,] *Che.* alſo belch and be ready to vomit, *Li.*

Bokeler, *o.* buckler.

Boken, *o.* ſtrike.

Boket, *o.* *Bucket*.

Bolas, *-les*, *o.* *Bullace*, *-lis*, wild plum.

Bole Armeniack, or *Armo-*, a ſoft crumbling ſtone found in *Armenia*.

Bold, *o.* Fenne.

Boling, the Cord that draws the ſail to gather wind.

Bollen, *o.* ſwelled.

Bollingbroke, a Caſtle in *Lincolnſhire*.

Bolmong, *Mong-Corn*, *Maſſelin*,

Bolt, [a Cony,] raiſe her.

Bolting, *Sa.* a [houſe-] exerciſe inferiour to Mooting.

Bolts, Iron pins belonging to ſhips rigging.

Bolt-rope, into which the Sail is made faſt.

Bolt-ſprit, a ſlope Maſt at the head of a ſhip.

Bolus, as *Bole Armoniack* alſo a Phyſical pellet.

Bombard, *l.* gun.

Bombardical, belonging thereto.

Bombaſine, ſtuff made of

Bombaſt, or *Cotton*, an *Aſia* plant a cubit high.

Bombilation, *l.* humming of Bees.

Bombycinous, *l.* made of ſilk.

Bonâ fide, *l.* Faithfully.

Bona Patria, Scotch Jury.

Bona Notabilia, Goods (above 5 *l.*) in another Dioceſs than that he dies in.

Bonaught, an Iriſh tax for the maintenance of Knights.

Bonair, *f.* courteous

Bonairite, Courteſie.

Bonaroba, *I.* a Whore.

Bonaſus, a wild horſe with a Bulls head.

Bonaventure, a famous *Franciſcan* Fryar.

Bone-breaker. an Eagle.

Bon Chretien, *f.* Good Chriſtian, a large French Pear.

Bondy, *T.* Simpleton.

Bonwell, a Well in *Hereford-ſhire*, full of little bones.

Bongrace, *f.* good Grace, alſo a kind of half-bonet to keep the Sun from the forehead.

Bon hommes, *f.* good men, an Order of Fryars.

Boniface, *f.* Well-doer.

Bonifate, having good luck.

Bon jour. *f.* good morrow.

Bonis non amovendis, a writ ſtopping the removal of Goods.

Fonito, a leaping fish.

Bonium, *Bangor*-Monastery.

Bonne mine, *f.* good aspect.

Bonnet, a short sail to be joyn'd to another sail.

Boodeth, *o.* Sheweth.

Boolie, *o.* beloved.

Boom, a pole to spread the clew of a sail further out.

Booming, with all sails out.

Boon, *o.* a request.

Boor, *Cu.* Parlour or Bed-chamber.

Boot, *Bote*, *Sa.* recompense also help, advantage.

Boot of bale, *o.* ease of sorrows.

Booting-Corn, certain Rent-corn.

Boot-baling, *No.* stealing.

Booting, *Sc.* a punishment by pegging-on an iron boot.

Bostock, with one stone.

Bostal Sf. a way up a Hill.

Boötes, as *Arctophylax*.

Boöz, *Boäz*, *h.* in strength.

Booz, *c.* drink.

Boracho, *Sp.* a pitched bottle made of a Pigs skin.

Borametsy, a Scythian Lamb-plant, eating the grass about it and then dying.

Borax, *Borace*, *Chrysocolla*, a green shining Mineral [to soder Gold or Silver,] or made of Childrens Urine.

Borbonia, a French Dukedom.

Bord, *c.* a shilling.

Bordarij, *Borduanni*, *Bores*, Husband-men, Cottagers.

Bordel, *I.* Brothel-house.

Bordagium, the same as

Bordland, kept in the hand of Lords for maintenance of their bord.

Bordue, a circumference drawn about the Arms.

Boreal, *-an*; belonging to

Boreas, *g.* North-wind.

Borith, an herb used by Fullers.

Born. *o.* burnish.

Borrel, *o.* head-geer; also rude, plain.

Borrow, *o.* pledge or surety.

Borysthenes, a Scythian River.

Boscage, a place full of Trees. also the Mast of Trees.

Boscaria, Wood-houses, or Ox-houses.

Boscus, *Bois*, *f.* Wood.

Bosinnus, a rude wind-instrument.

Boscobel, *f.* Fair Wood.

Bosenham, *Bosebam*, a Town in *Sussex*.

Bosphorus, the name of two Seas over which *Jupiter*, (like a Bull) carry'd *Europa*.

Botachide, a place in *Arcadia*.

Botachus, *Lycurgus*'s Nephew.

Botanical, *g.* belonging to Herbs.

Botanomancy, *g.* herb-divining.

Botargo, a kind of Saussage.

Bote, *o.* bitt.

Bothna, *Buthna*, *Sc.* a Park.

Botha, a Booth.

Botiler, *f.* Butler.

Botin, *f.* a buskin.

Botolph, *Sa.* helpful.

Bottle, *No.* house.

Bottomry, *Bottomary*, *Bottomage*, borrowing Money on the Ship.

Bottom, *o.* blossom, bud.

Boughrct, *-relet*, a Field-Faulcon.

Bovata terræ, 18 Acres.

Boveria, an Ox-stall.

Bovicide, *l.* a Butcher.

Bouched him, *o.* stopped his mouth.

Bouds, Weevils [in Malt] *Nf.*

Bouffe, *o.* an Elegant expression of the Noise of of belching.

Bougerons, *f.* buggering.

Bovillæ, a Town near *Rome*.

Bovillon, *f.* a boyled hotchporch of several ingredients.

Boulter, seive.

Boun, *o.* ready, bound.

Boun and unboun, dress and undress.

Bounsing cheat, *c.* a botle.

Bouchier, *Bower*, an ancient Family in *Essex*.

Boure, *o.* bed-chamber.

Bourd, *f.* Jest.

Bourgeon, *f.* bud.

Bourges, *f.* a free Denison.

Bourn, *l.* the head of a spring

Bourreau, *f.* Executioner.

Bourough, a Town incorporate, not a City.

Bourrough-English, or

Burgh-English, lands coming (by Custom) to the youngest Son or Brother.

Boursser, *-sier*, *Bouser*, *g.* the purse-bearer or Treasurer.

Bout, *Che.* without [doors, &c.]

Boutefeu, *f.* Incendiary, make-bate.

Bow, an instrument to take the height of any thing.

Bow, [of a Ship,] the fore-part.

Bow-bearer, an under-Officer in a Forrest.

Bowet, *Bowess*, a young hawk beginning to clamber on the boughs.

Bowge [*of Court*,] a Princes bounty above the ordinary allowance, also a rope on the outside middle of the Sail, keeping it close to the wind.

Bouche or Budge of Court, *id.*

Bowk, body, belly, stomach, *li.*

Bowl, a round thing at the head of a Mast to stand in.

Bown, swelled, *Nf.*

Bowr, the anchor commonly carried at the bow.

Bowse, pull [the tackle] all together.

Boxa, *Boza*, a kind of Turky-drink.

Boy, *Booy*, *Buoy*, *Sp.* a swimming thing tyed to the anchor to give notice where it is.

Boyar, a title of Nobility in *Russia*.

Brabant, *-tia*, is parted from *Flanders* by the River *Schelde*.

Braccata Gallia, *Provence* in *France*.

Brace, *f.* that which fastens beams in building, and joins words in Printing; a Cable of a Ship, also a couple [of hares, &c.]

Bracer, the thing laced on the Archers arm.

Brachial, *l.* belonging to the arm.

Brachygraphy, *g.* short-writing

Brachylogy, *g.* short speech.

Bradford, (*q. Broadford*,) in *Wilts*.

Brackets, *Braggets*, pieces sup-

 port-

porting the Ships Gallery.

Brackmans, Bramans, Indian Philosophers feeding on herbs.

Braggadocio, a bragging fellow.

Bragget, Welsh drink of honey, &c.

Braid Albin, the Highlands of *Scotland*.

Braied, *o.* blew [with a trumpet, &c.]

Brake, snafle for horses; handle of the Ships pump; Female fern, also a flax-dressing-instrument.

Brailes, small ropes belonging to the mizzen and main-top-sail, to put them into a fighting posture.

Brainford, Brentford, from

Brent, a River falling into the *Thames* there.

Brancher, as Bowet.

Brand-goose, a water fowl less than a Goose.

Brand-iron, Trevet [to set a pot on.]

Brandish, make to shine [with gentle moving.]

Brandrith, a rail about a wells mouth; also as Brand-iron.

Brandy, *d.* burnt [wine,] distilled from wine lees.

Brankursin, bears-foot.

Branonium, Wigornia, Worcester

Brant, Burgander, Barnacle, Soland-goose.

Brasiator, a Brewer.

Brasium, Malt.

Brasses, ropes for squaring and traversing the yards.

Brassets, *f.* armor for the Arms.

Brast, *o.* break.

Brat, *o.* a ragg, also a course apron, *Lin*.

Brava, an *American* Isl where the Sea is thought to be deepest.

Bravad, *Sp.* a daring.

Braughwham, *La.* Cheese, Eggs, clap-bread and Butter boild together.

Braunce, *o.* branch.

Bravy, Brave, *o.* a reward [the Conquerour.]

Brawdery, *o.* engraven work.

Brawl, *f.* a kind of dance.

Brayd, *o.* break out.

Brayed, awoke, arose, took.

Brade or *breid of*, *sc.* to be like [in conditions.]

Bread, *o.* appearance.

Bread of treet or trite, boulted or course Bread.

Break, *Nf.* Land plowed the first year after lying fallow.

Breaming, Brooming, washing a Ship burning her filth off [with reeds or broom.]

Breche, *o.* breeches.

Breck, *o.* a bruise, breach.

Breda, a City [of the Prince of *Orange*,] in the Low-countries.

Brede, Braide, *o.* breadth; abroad; also to make broad.

Bredgen, *o.* abridge.

Bree, frighten.

Breez, fresh gale of Wind.

Breetch, the aftermost part of a Gun.

Breetchings, ropes lashing Ordinance to the Ship-side.

Brehon, an Irish Judge.

Breme, *o.* furiously.

Bren, *o.* bran.

Brennus, a Gaulish Captain who took *Rome*.

Brent, *o.* burnt.

Brest-rope, keeps the yard close to the Mast.

Bretful, *o.* topful.

Bretoyse, [the Law] of the *Britains*, or Welsh-men

Bret, a wholsom Fish.

Brevan, strong German Ale.

Breve, a Writ.

Brevet, *o.* a brief, Popes-bull.

Brevibus & rotulis liberandis, a writ to the old Sheriff to deliver up all to the new.

Breviary, a short Collection, also a mass-book.

Breviloquence, a brief speaking.

Brevity, *l.* shortness.

Brian, *f.* thrill voice.

Briareus, Ægeon, a Gyant with an hundred hands.

Bricole, *f.* brickwall, a side stroke at Tennis.

Bricols, battering engines.

Brid, *o.* bird.

Bridgume, *o.* Bridegroom

Bridg-bote, Brig-bote, Bruck-, *Brug-, Brugh-bote*, [exemption from] contribution toward mending of Bridges.

Brichoe, *Che.* Brittle.

Bricken, bridle up the head.

Bridgenorth (for *Burgmorf*) a Town in *Shropshire*.

Brie, Brieze, horse-fly, gad-bee

Brief, as *Breve*, also two full times (in Musick.)

Briewr, as Bruyere.

Brigil, *f.* debate.

Brigade, *-do*, *f.* three squadrons of Soldiers, 1512 men.

Brigand, *f.* a robber, a foot-man serving with a

Brigandine, a Coat of male, also as

Brigantine a swift pinnace.

Brigantes, the Northern people of *England*.

Brigidians, Fryers and Nuns of the Order of

Brigidia, Brigit, Bride, a Princess of *Swedeland*, also an Irish Saint.

Brike, *o.* narrow, strait.

Brillant, *f.* glittering.

Brime, bring, *Sf.*

Bringer-up, the last man of a file.

Brinne, *o.* burn.

Brione, wild-vine.

Briseis, Achilles's Mistress.

Brite, [the hops] shatter.

Britannia, This Island of *England, Wales* and *Scotland*, from

Brith, *Br.* painted.

Bristol, *-ow*, a City partly in *Sommerset*, and partly in *Glocester-shire*.

Britomartis, a *Cretan* Lady Inventress of hunting-nets.

Brittonner, *o.* a bragger, boaster.

Brize, as Breez.

Broach, the next start above the beam-antler of a stag.

Brocado, *Sp.* cloth mixt with Gold or Silver

Brocerij, *sc.* Mediators in any business.

Brochity, crookedness [of Teeth.]

Brocket, pricket, spitter, a red Deer two years old

Broch, Brooch, *o.* a picked ornament [of Gold,]

Brock, Badger.

Brock-

Brocking, o. throbbing.
Brode-half-penny, *Bord-*, *Bort-h.* Custom for setting up boards in a market or fair.
Broke, o. keep safe.
Brokage, *Broc-*, the hire or trade of a
Broker, Breaker of prices between buyer and seller; also a seller of old broken wares.
Brocker, *Blocker*, *Brogger*, *sc* the same.
Broll, o. part, piece.
Bronchocele, g. a great round swelling in the throat.
Bronchiæ, g. branches of the wind-pipe dispersed through the lungs.
Bronde, o. a fury.
Brontes, one of the *Cyclops*.
Brooklime, a Physical herb.
Broom-rape, a plant at the root of broom, with a root like a Turnip.
Brotel, *brutel*, o. britle, brickle.
Brothel-house, Bawdy-house.
Brothelry, Whoredom.
Brouch, o. a jewel: see *Broch*.
Brow-antler, the start between the stags head and Beam-antler.
Browded, o. imbroidered.
Browk, *broke*, *bruke*, o. to use or injoy.
Brownists, rigid Independents.
Browster, *sc.* Brewer.
Browze, feed on shrubs, &c.
Brutte, *Sf.* the same.
Bruges, a City in *Flanders*.
Bruarts, *Che.* [hat] brims.
Bruit, *f.* a report.
Brunn, o. Fountain.
Bruyere, *Bruiere*, *f.* heath.
Brumal, *l.* Winter-like.
Bruma, *l.* the shortest day.
Brundusium, a Town in *Italy*.
Brusle, *c.* run away.
Brush, *Tenne*, a tawny-colour (in Heraldry.)
Brike, o streight, narrow.
Brymme, (to go to *br.*) when a swine desires copulation.
Buer, a Gnat.
Bubo, *c.* Pox.
Bubo, a large fiery pimple.
Bubulcitate, *l.* play the Neat-herd.

Buccinate, *l.* sound a trumpet.
Buccellation, *l.* dividing into gobbets.
Bucculent, *l.* wide-mouthed.
Bucentoro, the *Venetian* Gally wherein they espouse the Sea on holy Thursdays.
Bucephala, a Town built in honour of
Bucephalus, *g.* (bull's head) *Alexanders* horse.
Buck, *Sf.* breast, also body. See *Bowk*.
Buckaneers, the rude rabble in *Jamaica*.
Buckeldians, a kind of Anabaptist-hereticks.
Buckerels, an old play among *London*-boys (forgotten.)
Buck-hurst, a Baron-title of the *Sackvils*.
Buckingham, so called from
Bucken, *sa.* Beeches.
Bucks-horn, an herb with small jagged leaves.
Buck-stal, a large Deer-net.
Buck-wheat, Beech-corn, *French*-wheat, Brank, Crap.
Bucolicks, *g.* pastoral songs.
Bud, *Sf.* a calf of the first year weaned.
Buda, *Offen* in *Hungary*.
Bularis, *Heidelbergh* in *Germany*.
Budg, Lambs-fur, also *f.* to stir or move, also *c.* he that slips in to steal cloaks, &c.
Budg-barrel, a little tin powder-barrel.
Buffle, wild-ox.
Bughar, *c.* a dog.
Bugle, a wound-herb.
Buglosse, *g.* a Cordial herb.
Bulbous, belonging to
Bulbe, *l.* a round root.
Buffoon, *f.* Jester.
Bulgaria, a Country by *Thrace*.
Bulimy, *bou-*, dog-hunger.
Bulk-head, a partition of boards in a ship-room.
Bulk and file, *c.* one jostles you while the other picks your pocket.
Bull, a round hollow jewel; also the Popes mandate.
Bullen, hemp stalks pilled.
Bull-head, a kind of Fish.
Bullenger, a kind of boat,

Bullimong, *Ef.* Oats, pease and vetches mixt.
Bultel, refuse of bulted meal; also the bulting or boulting bag.
Bullion, Money in the mass or billet; also the place where 'tis try'd and changed.
Bully-Rock, Hector, Bravo.
Bumbeth, soundeth, *o.*
Bummed, o. tasted or desired.
Bundles, Records of Chancery,
Bung, *c.* purse.
Bunt, the hollowness allow'd in making sails.
Bunt[-lines] to trise up the bunt of the sails.
Buquan, part of South-*Scotland*.
Burbrech, *Borg-*, *Burgh-*, *sa.* [a being quit of] trespasses against the peace.
Burcheta, a kind of gun.
Burdegala, *Bourdeaux* in *France*.
Burden, *f.* a deep base; the humming of bees, also a pilgrims staff.
Burel, fine glass.
Burford, a Town in *Oxfordshire*.
Burghware (*q. Burgi vir*) a *Burgess*, or Citizen.
Burgage, a tenure [for a certain yearly rent] of
Burghers, Men of Cities and Burrowes.
Burganet, *f.* an helmet.
Burgeon, grow big about.
Burgh-Grave, a *German* Count of a Castle, &c.
Burglary, *f.* Fellonious stealing into a house.
Burgundia, *-die*, in *France*.
Burjon, *f.* a bud or sprought [of a vine.]
Burled, o. armed,
Burlesque, *f.* in a drolling way.
Burlet, *f.* a Coife.
Burly-brand, o. a great sword, also great fury.
Burnet, o. Woollen, also a hood.
Burned, o. for burnished.
Burnish, *l.* polish, also Harts spread-

spreading their horns.
Bur-pump, with a long staff only, and a bur at the end.
Burr, the roll of horn next the Harts head.
Burras-pipe, to keep corroding pouders in.
Bursholder, *Burrow-holder*, Headborough.
Busca, --*cus*, under-wood, brush-.
Busk, o. bush; also to shut up.
Buscumducis, *He togenbush* in *Brabant*.
Buscarles, *Buze-*, Seamen.
Bush, a Foxes tail.
Busiris, a Tyrant slain by *Hercules*.
Buskin, a kind of boot.
Busones, *Buzones* [*Comitatûs*] Justices.
Bustard, *Bistard*, a great sluggish bird.
But, *sc.* without.
But my list, o. Except I list.
Butchers broom, a shrub like Myrtle (but prickly.)
But-end, the fore-end of ships.
But-heads, the ends of planks.
Buthus, a wrestler that ate an ox every day.
Butlerage, impost on wines paid the Kings butler.
Buttens, *Burls*, the first puttings up of a stags head.
Butterburre, pestilent wort.
Butterwort, *Yorkshire*-Sanicle.
Buttington, a *Welch* Town.
Buttress, a prop supporting the but-end of a building.
Buttock, the ships breadth right-a-stern, from the tuck upwards.
Butyrum Saturni, the sweetest liquor of Lead.
Buxiferous, *l.* box-bearing.
Buxom, *Buxsom*, (*D. boogsaem*) pliant, obedient; also blithe, merry.
Buxioning, (for *Burjoning*) budding.
Buzzar, a Market-place among the *Persians*.
Buzzard, a large Kite.
By, o. habitation.
Bydding, o. abiding.
Byblus, a Town of *Phœnicia*.
Byg, *Bigg*, o. build.
Byker, o. a fray.
By-, *Byr-*, *Bur-laws*, determined by persons elected by common consent of Neighbours.
Byme, for By me.
Byndon, a Town in *Dorset*.
Byraft, bereft, o.
Byram, The Turks Carneval or Shrovetide.
Byramlick, a Turkish present like our New-years-gift.
By-spel, *sa.* Proverb.
Byssine, g. made of silk.
Bytrent, o. catcheth about.
Bywopen, *Bywoopen*, o. made senseless.
Byzantium, *Nova Roma*, *Constantinople* in *Thrace*.
Byzamine, see *Besant*.

C

C*As*, *f.* Chance.
Cab, *b.* three pints.
Caback, a *Russian* Inne or Victualling-house.
Cabades, King of *Persia*.
Cabal, *l.* a [jade] horse.
Cabalistick, belonging to
Cabala, -*la*, *b.* (receiving) Jewish tradition; their secret science of expounding divine mysteries; also a secret Council
Cabalist, one skil'd therein.
Caballine [fountain,] of the Muses.
Cabanne, *f.* a Tilt-boat.
Cabane, *Cabin*, a Cottage; also a little room in a ship.
Catern, the same.
Cabbage, that part of the Deers head where the horns are planted.
Cablish, Brush-wood.
Cabos'd *sp.* having the head cut off close to the Shoulder.
Cabura, a fountain of *Mesopotamia* where *Juno* used to wash.
Caburn, small yarn- line, to bind Cables withal.
Cacams, Jewish Doctors.
Cacafuego, -*fogo*. *sp.* shite-fire.
Cacao, an *Indian* tree, also the fruit, and kernel thereof.
Cachectick, g. having a
Cachexy, ill disposition of body.
Cachinnation, *l.* loud Laughter.
Cacique, *Casique*, an *Indian* King.
Cackling-cheat, *c.* a Chicken.
Cackling-farts, *c.* Egges.
Cackrel, a kind of fish.
Cacochymy, g. ill juice through bad digestion.
Cacodemon, g. evil spirit.
Cacography, g. ill-writing.
Cacology, g. ill language.
Cacophony, g. ill sound or pronunciation.
Cacosyntheton, g. a bad composition of words.
Cacozelous, g. ill affected.
Cacuminate, *l.* make sharp at the top.
Cacus, an *Italian* Shepherd slain by *Hercules* for stealing his Oxen, drawing them backward into his Cave.
Cadaverous, *l.* like or full of *Carcasses*.
Cadbait-fly, *Caddis*, *Cadworm*, a bait for trouts, &c.
Cadbury, a Town in *Somerset*.
Cade, *l.* a Pipe, two hogsheads; of Herrings, 500. of Sprats, 1000. also as
Caddee, *a.* Lord, Magistrate.
Caddow, *Nf.* a Jack-daw.
Cade-lamb, brought up by hand.
Cadence, -*cy*, *l.* a falling; also prose.
Cadent [*houses*] are the 3d 6th 8th and 12th houses [of a Scheme.]
Cadet *f.* a Younger Brother.
Cadge, on which they bring hawks to sell.
Cadier Arthur, King *Arthurs* Chair, the top of a Hill in *Brecknockshire*.
Cadis, *Cadiz*, *Cales*, *Calis-Malis*, in *Spain*.
Cadmine, belonging to
Cadmia, *lapis Calaminaris*, Brass-oar.
Cadmus, Son of *Agenor*, Brother of *Europa*, and founder of *Thebes*, whither he brought the *Greek* letters from *Phœnicia*.

Cadrou, *Cadzou*, a Barony in *Scotland*.

Caduccan, belonging to

Caduce, *l.* *Mercury*'s snaky staff, wherewith he kil'd or made alive; also the *Roman* Heralds staff, a sign of peace.

Caduciferous, carrying the same.

Cecity, *l.* blindness.

Celibat, *l.* a single life.

Ceneus, an invulnerable man, transformed from

Cenis, a *Thessalian* Virgin ravished by *Neptune*.

Caer, *br.* a City.

Caercaradoc, a hill in *Shropshire*, so called from

Caratacus, a *British* King.

Caerdiff, a Town in *Glamorganshire*.

Caerfuse, *Caersusc*, a Town in *Montgomeryshire*.

Caermarden, *Maridunum*, the birth-place of *Merlin*.

Caernarvon, the birth-place of King *Edward* 2. built by King *Edward*. 1. where the Princes of *Wales* kept their Chancery, Exchequer and Courts of Justice.

Cesar, *Keisar*, *Czar*, Emperour.

Cesura, making a short syllable (after a compleat foot) long.

Ceyx, as *Alcyon*, or *Halcyon*.

Cageole, *f.* to prate much to little purpose, also to inveigle one with fair words.

Cajole, the same.

Cainsham, *Canes-*, a Town in *Sommerset*.

Cainsham smoke, a mans weeping when beat by his Wife.

Cair, *Cairo*, *Grand Cairo Cairus*, *Alcairus*, *Babylon Ægyptia* a great City of *Ægypt*.

Caishoberry, a great house by *Watford* in *Hertfordshire*.

Caitive, *l.* wretched, wicked.

Caitifned, *o.* chained.

Calaber, a kind of Squirril.

Calabria, part of *Italy*.

Calaen, an East-Indian mineral.

Calamary, Cuttle-fish.

Calamina, as *Cadmia*.

Calamint, *l.* the herb Mountain mint; also a green Frog.

Calamist, a Player upon

Calamus, *l.* a reed.

Calamus Aromaticus, a Physical sweet cane.

Calamity. *l.* misery.

Calamize, to pipe.

Cala peregrinorum, Tartar.

Calangium, a challenge, or claim.

Calasticks, purging Oyntments.

Calatravo, in *Spain*.

Caloanthous, belonging to

Calcanth, Vitriol.

Calcar, *l.* a spur, also a calcining furnace.

Calcation, *l.* treading.

Calceate, *l.* to shooe.

Calcedon, *-ny*, a precious stone, also a vein in a Ruby, &c.

Calcetum, *-cata*, a causey or *Causway*, (Chalky or flinty.)

Calceya, *Casea*, *Calsetum*, and *Calceis*, *Caucies*, the same.

Calchas, seeing a Serpent devour 10 young Sparrows, prophesied that *Troy*, should be taken the tenth year.

Calcine, *-nate*, *-nize*, *l.* reduce metals to a calx or crumbling substance.

Calcitrate, *l.* kick.

Calcule, *l.* an accounting, also a Chesman or Counter.

Calculosity, *l.* fulness of stones or Counters.

Calcent, a great Mart Town of *India*.

Caleb, *h.* dog, or hearty.

Caledonian, belonging to

Caledonia, *Calyd-*, *Scotland*.

Calefactive, *l.* causing

Calefaction *l.* a warming.

Calefie, to heat.

Calendar, *l.* Almanack.

Calender, to set a glo's upon [Cloth.]

Calends, *l.* the first day of every month.

Calent, *l.* hot or warm.

Calenture, *sp.* heat; also a burning Fever.

Calewise, *o.* warmly.

Caletum, *Calis* in *France*.

Caliburn, Prince *Arthurs* sword.

Calico, stuff that comes from

Calicut, a Country in *India*.

Calid, *l.* hot, also fierce.

Calidity, *l.* heat.

Caliduct, *l.* a stove.

Califactory, *l.* the warming room [in a Monastery.]

Caligate, *l.* one wearing stockings.

Caligate Soldier, a common Soldier, also a faint hearted Coward.

Caliginous, dim.

Caligation, *l.* dimness.

Caligula, the 4th. Emperor of *Rome*.

Caliph, a Persian King or Emperour.

Calisto, one of *Diana's* Nymphs, corrupted by *Jupiter* and turn'd out of her train

Caliver, *Call-*, a small Seagun.

Calked, *o.* cast out, or (rather) up.

Calk, [the Ship,] beat in *Okum*, between every plank.

Calle, *c.* a Cloak.

Call, *o.* bravery.

Callent, *-lid*, *l.* Crafty.

Callidity, *l.* subtilty.

Calligraphy, *g.* fair writing.

Calliope, one of the nine Muses.

Callipolis, one of the *Ægean* Islands called *Cyclades*.

Callirrhoe, her 30 suiters having kil'd her Father *Phocus*, (King of *Bæotia*) were burnt to death.

Callosity, hardness or thickness of skin.

Callous, *l.* hard, brawny.

Calot, *f.* a cap and border, also as

Callot, *sa.* a wanton woman

Callow, downy, unfledg'd, not feathered.

Calour, *l.* heat.

Calpe, a Spanish hill, one of *Hercules* pillars.

Calsining, *o.* calcining.

Calsounds, a kind of Turkish linnen drawers.

Caltropes, *Calthrops*, *Sa.* four square Iron pricks to cast in the enemies way.

Calviniftical, belonging to
Calvinift, one that follows
Calvin, a *Geneva*-Reformer
Calvity, *l.* baldnefs.
Calumniatour, *l.* one alledging faults that were never committed.
Calumnious, full of cavils, or falfe accufations.
Calydonian, Scotifh.
Camail, *f.* a hood for wet weather, alfo a Bifhops purple ornament worn over the Rochet.
Camerina, a Lake in *Sicily*.
Cambel, a famous Caftle of *Argile* in *Scotland*.
Cambering, the deck of a Ship lies cambering, when 'tis higher in the middle than at either end.
Camlio, *fp.* an Exchange.
Cambfer, a Banker,
Cambles, a Lydian King who devoured his own Wife.
Cambren, *Br.* a crooked ftick. [to drefs a fheep on, &c.]
Cambrian, belonging to
Cambria, *Wales*.
Cambridge, built on the River
Cam, reported to be built by
Cantaber, a *Spaniard* 375 years before Chrift.
Cameletto, a ftuff partly filk and partly Camels hair.
Camelford, a Town in *Cornwall*.
Camelot, a Scotch Town.
Cameline, of Chamlet.
Camels-hay, a kind of fweet-fmelling rufh brought out of the Eaftern Countries.
Cambyfes, King of *Perfia* who added *Egypt* to his Dominions.
Cameracum, *Cambray*, a City of the Low-Countries.
Cambrick, fine Linnen-cloth coming from thence.
Camelionize, to play the
Camelion, a beaft like a Lizard, that lives by the air, and often changes colour.
Camelopardal, half-camel and half panther.
Cameral, *l.* belonging to a chamber or vault.
Camerade, *fp.* a Cabin- or Chamber-fellow.
Camerated, *l.* vaulted, arched.
Camefires, a fyllogifm who's firft propofition is an univerfal affirmative, the other univerfal negatives.
Camifado, *fp.* a fudden affault or furprize, alfo a fhirt put over their arms.
Camifed, *o.* Crooked.
Cammock, Reft-harrow.
Camœnæ, *l.* the Mufes.
Camois, *br.* Crooked.
Campaine, -*agne*, *f.* plain field, alfo an armies expedition or taking the field.
Campania, *Terra del Lavoro* in *Italy*.
Campden-broad, a Town in *Glocefterfhire*.
Campernulphs, *Champernouns* an antient family of *Cornwal*.
Campeftral, *l.* belonging to the Champain, or plain fields.
Camphire, *l.* a drug found on the *Indian* fhore, by fome a gum, by others a mineral.
Campions, a kind of *Lychnis* or Batchelors buttons.
Campfor, as *Cambfor*.
Campus lapideus, a field in *France*, where *Hercules* (with a fhowr of ftones fent from *Jupiter*) kil'd 2 Giants.
Campus Martius, *Mars*'s field by *Rome*, for exercife and popular affemblies.
Campus fceleratus, where the incontinent Veftal Nuns were buried alive.
Camolodunum, *Camul-*, *Colchefter* or *Maldon* in *Effex*.
Camulus, *Mars*.
Canaan, *h.* a Merchant
Canace, Daughter of *Æolus*, with child by her own Brother.
Canachus, a fountain near *Nauplia*, where *Juno* ufed to bath, to recover her Virginity.
Canaeus, a *Spanifh* hill with a bottomlefs well on the top.
Canakin, *c.* the plague.
Canary, belonging to
Canariæ, the *Canary* or fortunate Iflands in the Adriatick Sea.
Cancel, *l.* to rafe or blot out.
Canceline, *o.* Chamlet.
Cancer, *l.* a Crab, one of the 12 Zodiack-figns, alfo a hard and rough fwelling.
Candefy, *l.* whiten.
Candia, *Creet*, *Crete*, a Mediterranean Ifle where *Jupiter* was born.
Candid, *l.* white, fair, fincere.
Candida Cafa, *Witherd* in *Scotland*.
Candidate, *l.* one that ftands for any place or Office.
Candiope, being ravifht by her brother *Theodotion* brought forth *Hippolagus*.
Candlemafs, Purification of the Virgin *Mary*, Feb. 2.
Candour, *l.* whitenefs, alfo fincerity and ingenuity.
Canhooks, hooks at the end of ropes, for hoyfing things in or out of a fhip.
Cankdorte, *o.* woful cafe.
Canken, for Cauken, *f.* to tread [the hen.]
Canibals, *Indians* feeding on Mans flefh.
Canicular, belonging to
Canicula, the little dog-ftar.
Canine, *l.* dog-like.
Canitude, *l.* hoarinefs,
Cank, *c.* dumb.
Cannæ, a Town in *Italy*, where *Hannibal* beat the *Romans*.
Cannel-, or *Canel-bone*, the neck or throat-bone.
Cannifter, a Coopers inftrument in wracking of wine.
Canonical, according to
Canon, *g.* a Ruler, alfo a Rule or [Church-]law, alfo one that enjoyes a living in a Cathedral Church.
Canonift, a profeffour of the Canon-law.
Canonium, *Chelmerford*, *Chensford*, on the River *Chelmer* in *Effex*.
Canonize, to examine by rule, alfo to regifter for a Saint.

Canopus, a City of *Egypt*, alſo the bright ſtar in *Argo*.

Canorous, *l.* loud, ſhrill.

Canor, Melody, ſweet ſinging.

Canow, an Indian boat.

Cant, *Che.* [to grow] ſtrong and luſty.

Cantabrians, People of

Cantabria, *Biſcay*, *Guipuſcoa*, part of *Spain*

Cantabrize, to follow the faſhions of [*Cantabria*, or rather]

Cantabrigia, *Cambridge*.

Cantæ, an ancient people of *Roſs* in *Scotland*.

Cantation. *l.* a ſinging, alſo an enchanting.

Cantel, lump, or heap.

Canterbury, the old royal Seat of the *Kentiſh* Kings.

Cantharides, *g.* green venemous *Spaniſh* flies.

Canticle, *l.* Song.

Cantilene, *l.* a ſong or tale.

Canting-coines, ſhort pieces of wood with ſharp edges to lie between Casks.

Canting, the Language of Rogues and Beggars.

Cantium, *Kent*.

Cantlow, an ancient family in *Cornwall*.

Canto, *I.* a diviſion in an *Heroick poem*, alſo as *Canton*, a corner, alſo a diviſion of the Country of *Switzerland*.

Cantonize, to divide into *Cantons*.

Cantor, *l.* a ſinger or Charmer.

Cantreds, *br.* the hundreds into which their Countries are divided, or rather

Cantreſs, *br.* the ſame.

Cantus, *l.* the mean or Counter-tenour in Muſick.

Cantyre, (in *Iriſh*, Lands-head), part of South-*Scotland*.

Canvas, to ſift [a buſineſs.]

Cana, *-num*, *S.* a duty paid to Biſhops [or other Lords.]

Canute, firſt *Engliſh* Monarch of the *Daniſh* bloud, becauſe the water would not obey him ſitting by the Sea-ſide, he would never after wear his Crown.

Canzonet, *I.* Song, Sonnet.

Cap, a ſquare piece put over the head of a maſt, to receive into it a top-maſt or flag-ſtaff.

Cap of maintenance, ſent from Pope *Julius* to *Henry* 8. and is ſtill born before the King at great ſolemnities.

Capacitate, *l.* to put one into a

Capacity, *Capability*, a being

Capable, able or fit to do or ſuffer any thing.

Cap-a-pe, from head to foot.

Caparaſſon, *-riſon*, *f.* horſe-trappings or furniture.

Capcaſtles, among ſtreets and villages, are the ſame as Metropoles among Cities.

Cape, *Sp.* promontory, neck of Land running into the Sea.

Capel, Chapel, alſo a horſe.

Caperate, *l.* frown.

Capharnaits, thoſe of

Capharnaum, *Caper-*, in *Paleſtine*, who firſt doubted of the myſtery of the bleſſed Sacrament.

Capias [*ad reſpondendum*,] a writ before judgment requiring perſonal appearance.

Capias [*ad faciendum*, *pro fine*, *&c.*] Writs of execution.

Capillary, *l.* hairy.

Capillation, *l.* hairineſs, or cauſing hair to grow.

Capillature, *l.* a buſh of hair; alſo a frizling of the hair.

Cape, a writ touching plea of land or tenements.

Cape magnum or *Grand Cape*, lies before appearance.

Cape parvum or *petit Cape*, upon default afterwards.

Capirotade, a compound ſtewed minced meat.

Capiſtrate, *l.* to muzzel.

Capitation, *l.* poll-money.

Capite, a holding of lands immediately of the King.

Capital, *l.* belonging to the head; Chief: alſo deadly or deſerving death.

Capitolinus, belonging to the

Capitol, an ancient Citadel of *Rome*, in digging whoſe foundation they found a mans head.

Capitulate, *l.* to make Articles of agreement.

Capnitis, a kind of *Cadmia*

Capnomancy, *g.* divination by obſerving the Altar-ſmoak.

Capon-faſhion, as Bobtail in the firſt ſenſe.

Capo, one of the *Capi*, 3. chief *Venetian* Officers.

Capo, *Che.* a working horſe.

Capouchins, *Capucines*, Fryers inſtituted by *Mat. Baſci* of *Ancona*, without ſhirt or breeches; from

Capouche, *f.* the Cowl or hood they uſed to wear

Cappadine, ſilk whereof the ſhag of a rug is made.

Cappadocia part of *Aſia*.

Capriccio, *I.* *-icho*, *Sp.* the firſt draught or invention of a thing; alſo a fantaſtical humour.

Capricious, *-chious*, whimſical, giddy-brain'd.

Capricorn, *l.* a goat, one of the Zodiack-ſigns.

Caprification, *l.* the dreſſing of wild vines or figtrees.

Caprifoile, *l.* woodbine, honey-ſuckle.

Capriole, *f.* a Caper in dancing, alſo the Goat-leap on horſ-back.

Capſquares, 2 broad irons covering the trunnions of a great gun.

Capſtand, *--ſtern*, a wind-beam or draw-beam [in a ſhip.]

Capſulary, belonging to

Capſula, *l.* a ſmal cheſt.

Capſulated, lockt up therein.

Captation, *l.* a Catching-at.

Caption, a Certificate of a Commiſſion executed.

Captious, *l.* apt to take exceptions, quarrelſome.

Captivate, *l.* take priſoner.

Captivity, l. bondage.

Capture, l. the taking a prey; also an Arrest or Seisure.

Capuched, f. hooded.

Capuchin, as *Capouchin*.

Car, o. a pool.

Car-fick, T. a kennel.

Caracol, f. Soldiers casting themselves into a ring.

Caradoc, Br. Dearly beloved.

Caranna, a *West-Indy* Gum good for the tooth-ach.

Caratux, a wise (yet contemptible) Counsellour to *Saladine* the *Turk*.

Caravan, f. a Convoy of Soldiers, also a kind of wagon.

Caravel, Sp. a swift light round vessel.

Carawaies, an herb whose leaves resemble those of Carrets.

Carbantorigum, *Caerlaverok*, a very strong Town in *Scotland*.

Carbine, *Carab-*, a petronel or short gun, also an horsman that serves therewith.

Carbonado, I. a gash in the flesh; also a piece of flesh broild on the Coals.

Carbuncle, l. a precious stone, also a fiery botch or sore.

Carcanet, a rich chain to wear about the neck.

Carcedony, a precious stone.

Carcedon, *Carthage*.

Carcellage, prison-fees.

Carceral, belonging to a prison.

Cardamome, Grain of paradise, a spicy seed brought from the *Indies*.

Card, *Chart*, Sea-map.

Cardiaca, g. the Liver-vein.

Cardiacal, g. Cordial, belonging to the heart.

Cardiacle, *Cord-*, o. the passion of the heart.

Cardiac line, the heart-line or line of Life [on the hand.]

Cardigan, *Abertivy* (the river *Tivy*'s mouth) in *Wales*.

Cardinal, l. (belonging to a hinge) chief, principal; also the 70 chief Roman Church men, which Colledge chooses one for pope.

Cardinal Numbers, One, Two, &c.

Cardinals Flower, a kind of *American* Throatwort or Bellflower, very rare.

Cardiogmos, g. heart burning.

Cardiognostick, g. knower of the heart, *viz.* God.

Cardones, an *Indian* healing herb.

Cardoon, *Cha-*, f. a salad-plant like Artichoke.

Carduus benedictus, an herb called Blessed thistle.

Care cloth, a fine linen cloth laid over the new married couple kneeling, till Mass was ended.

Carecks, *Carectes*, o. Marks.

Carecta, *-ata*, a Cart or *Cart-load* (in law.)

Caretarius, a Carter.

Careening, trimming of the Ship [under water.]

Carefax, *Carefox*, *Carfax*, *Oxford* Market-place, where 4 wayes meet.

Carects, o. Marks.

Caresbroke, *Whitgaraburgh* (*Whitgars* town) in the Isle of *Wight*.

Caresse, f. a making much of.

Caret, l. (it wanteth,) *Clavis*, a mark directing where to insert any thing omitted, (^).

Carfe, o. cutt.

Cargaison, *-ason* f. the Ships freight.

Cargo, the same.

Caria, part of *Asia* the less.

Carine, l. the ships keel.

Carinthia, a Country joyning to the *Alpes* on the South.

Caristie, It. the same as

Carity, l. dearth, scarcity.

Cark, a bundle or load: the 30th part of a Sarplar of wool.

Carle, *Sa.* a clown.

Carl-cat, *No.* a bore-cat.

Carlile, a city in *Cumberland*.

Carline thistle, a plant by which *Charles* the great kept his army from the Plague.

Carlings, Timbers from one Ship-beam to another.

Carling-knees, timbers from the Ship-sides to the hatches.

Carlo Sancto, a *West-Indy* root of pleasant smel and bitter tast.

Carmania, part of Great *Asia*.

Carmasal, *-musol*, a kind of Turkish ship.

Carmelites, Fryers begun at

Carmelus, a Town in *Syria*.

Carmenta, *Nicostrata*, an *Arcadian* Prophetess who first gave the Oracle in verse.

Carminate, l. to card [wool.]

Carminative, [medicines] breaking wind.

Carmouth, a Town, in *Dorset*.

Carnage, f. eating of flesh; also the flesh (in hunting) given to the dogs: also slaughter.

Carnalist, one given to

Carnality, l. fleshliness.

Carnacion, a raw-flesh colour.

Carnaval, f. Shrovetide.

Carnel-work, building of ships with timbers and beams before they plank them.

Carnes, o. stones.

Carney, a horse-disease furring their mouthes.

Carnificine, l. the place of Execution, also the Office.

Carnify, l. cut in pieces, also to torment.

Carnivorous, l. flesh-devouring.

Carnogan, *br.* a kind of wooden dish or piggin.

Carnose, the bale ring in a great gun.

Carnosity, l. fleshiness.

Carnous, l. fleshy.

Carodunum, *Cracovia*, the chief City of *Poland*.

Carol, a Christmass-song.

Caros, dulness, heaviness of

of head [from bad concoction.]

Carotick [Artery,] issues from the Axillar (in two branches) toward the head.

Carove, a kind of fruit; also the root St. *Johns* bread.

Carouse, d. (all out) drink lustily.

Carpathus. the Mediterranean Isle *Scarpanto*.

Carpemeals, a course kind of our northern cloth.

Carpobalsamum, g. the fruit of Balsamum.

Carpocratians, Gnosticks, Hereticks that deny'd the Creation and Christs Divinity.

Carp-stone, found in the chap of a Carp, triangular.

Carrack, *-rick*, a great Ship.

Carrat, the 3d. part of an ounce (of Gold or Silver,) and in jewels the 192d. part.

Carre, o. a wood in a boggy place.

Careta, as Carecta.

Carriage, that whereon the Ordnance is mounted.

Carrict, *-ta*, part of South *Scotland*.

Carriere f. running of horses full speed; also the place of running.

Cartage, as Cartouche.

Cartel, f. a Challenge.

Cartesian, belonging to *Des-Cartes*, the modern fam'd Philosopher opposing *Aristotle*.

Carthage, the chief City of *Africa*, built by *Dido*.

Carthamus, Bastard-Saffron.

Catharist, g. Puritan.

Carthismandua, a Britith Queen who casting off her husband *Venusius*, married and Crowned his Armour-bearer *Vellocatus*.

Carthusians, Fryers instituted by *Bruno* of *Cullen*, 1101.

Cartilagineous, belonging to *Cartilage*, l. a gristle.

Carucata or *Hilda terræ*, a Carve, or hide of land, as much as may be plough'd in a year by one plough.

Carucage, such a taxation.

Carve, *kerve*, Che. to grow soure (of Cream.)

Caruncle, l. a bit of Flesh [growing out any where.]

Cartouch, f. a roll adorning the *Cornish* of a pillar; also as

Carthrage, a charge of powder and shot made ready in a Paper.

Carvage, a being quit, when land is tax'd by Carves.

Carvel, a kind of ship.

Casan, the cheif City in *Parthia*.

Casani, Indian bread.

Casbine, the chief City in *Media*.

Casemate, I. loop hole in a wall, [to shoot through.]

Cases, changes in the endings of words.

Case-shot, small shot in a case to shoot from Ordnance.

Cash, ready mony.

Cashire, f. disband.

Casings, dry'd Cows-dung (for fewel,)

Caskets, small strings in farthelling the Sails.

Caspian Sea, or lake, between the *Caspian* and *Hircanian* Mountain, it neither ebbs nor flows.

Cassandra, a Prophetess the Daughter of *Priam* and *Hecuba*.

Cassan, c. Cheese.

Cassation, l. making void.

Cassia, *Cassia fistula*, a sweet *Ægyptian* reed or shrub.

Cassia lignea, a sweet wood like to Cinnamon.

Cassidony, o. as calcedony.

Cassiope, *-pea*, *Cepheus's* Daughter placed among the stars.

Cassivellaunus, *-ibellinus*, the British King conquered by *Julius Cæsar*.

Cast the Hawk to the pearch that is, put him upon it.

Casting, feathers, &c given the Hawk to cleanse her gorge.

Castaldie, l. stewardship.

Castalian, belonging to

Castalia, a Nymph, who flying from *Apollo*, was turned into a Fountain by *Parnassus*.

Castanets, snappers [for dancing] like Chesnuts.

Castellain, l. the Constable of a Castle.

Caster, *Chaster*, *Cester*, *Chester*, o. a walled Town.

Castifical, l. making chaste.

Castigate, l. chastise, punish.

Castilian, belonging to

Castile, part of *Spain*.

Castlecomb, a Town in *Wiltshire*.

Castlesteed, o. a fortress or Bulwark.

Castleward, the Compass of Land subject to a Castle, also an imposition on such as dwell there.

Castor and *Pollux*, Sons of *Jupiter* (in the shape of a Swan) by *Leda*.

Castoreum, the Cod of a

Castor, l. Beaver.

Castrametation l. encamping.

Castrensian, l. of a camp.

Castrated, l. gelt.

Casual, accidental, happening by

Casualty, chance.

Casu consimili, a writ of entry granted, where the Tenant doth alienate.

Casu proviso, where a Tenant in dower doth alien.

Casuist, one that writes cases of Conscience.

Casule, a Mass-priests vestment, resembling Christs purple robe of mocquery.

Cat, a piece of Timber, to trise up the Anchor from the hause to the fore-Castle.

Catabaptists, g. Enemies or abusers of Baptism.

Catachrestical, *-ick*, belonging to

Catachresis, g. (abuse) putting an improper word for a proper one.

Cataclysm, g. Flood.

Catadoup, *-dupa*, as *Cataract*.

Catadrome, g. a kind of Crane for building, also a Tilt-yard or horse-race.

Cataglottism, g. a thrusting out the Tongue [in kissing.]

Catagmatical, belonging to

Catagmaticks, g. Medicines for broken bones.

Catagraph, g. the first draught [of

[of a Picture.]

Catallis reddendis, a writ of delivery.

Catals, as Chattels.

Catalepſy, *g.* apprehenſion, alſo a brain diſtemper.

Cataline, *-eline*, as *Catiline*.

Cataloguize, to put into a

Catalogue, *g.* a roll or liſt.

Catalonia, part of *Spain*.

Catamidiate, to put one to open ſhame and puniſhment, for ſome notorious offence.

Catamite, *Catem-*, *g.* Ingle, a boy kept for Sodomy.

Catapaſms, *g.* ſweet powders.

Cataphor, *-ra*, *g.* a ſleepy diſtemper in the head.

Cataphyſick, *g.* againſt nature.

Cataplaſm, a kind of thick pultis of meal and herbs.

Cataphrygians, Hereticks baptizing the dead, forbidding ſecond marriage, &c.

Catapuce, the herb ſpurge.

Catapult, *l.* as *Baliſta*.

Cataract, *Catarr-*, *g.* a great fall of waters; a Portcullis; alſo a diſtemper in the eyeſight.

Caractonium, *Catarac*

Catarrick-bridge, by *Richmond*.

Catarh, *g.* a Rheume or diſtillation of humours from the head,

Cataſtaſis, *g.* the third act of a play.

Cataſtrophe, *g.* the concluſion [of a play.]

Catch-fly, a flower with clammy ſtalks.

Catchpoll, *Chachepollus*, *Cacep-*, a Serjeant, Bailiff, or any that arreſts upon an action.

Catch-land, *Nf.* uncertain to what pariſh it belongs, and tithed by the firſt comer.

Catechetical, *-chitical*, belonging to inſtruction.

Catechumen, *g.* one that is

Catechized, inſtructed [for the Communion.]

Categorematical, belonging to

Categorem, *g.* the predicated, or latter part of a propoſition.

Categorical, belonging to

Category, *g.* Accuſation, alſo as Predicament.

Catenate, *l.* to chain.

Caterlogh, *Carlogh*, part of *Ireland*.

Cathaneſs, *Cathneß*, part of South *Scotland*.

Cathæa, part of *India*, where they chooſe the handſomeſt man for King.

Catharine, *g.* pure.

Catharians, Hereticks, rejecting baptiſm and original ſin.

Cathariſts, a ſort of Manichees.

Catharpings, ſmall ropes to keep the ſhrouds tight and the maſt from rowling.

Cathartical, *g.* purgative.

Catharticks, *g.* all purging medicines.

Cathay, *Scythia*, *Sinarum Regio* under the great *Cham*.

Cathedral, *g.* belonging to a chair; alſo the chief [church] in a Biſhops See.

Cathedratick, 2 *s.* paid by the Clergy to the Biſhop.

Cathedrarious, belonging to a chair or ſeat.

Cathelaunum, *Catal-*, *Chaalons* in *France*.

Catherplugs, ſmall ropes forcing the ſhrouds, to eaſe and ſecure the Maſt.

Catheter, *g.* an inſtrument to cleanſe the yard of gravel.

Cathetus, the perpendicular ſide of a right-angled triangle.

Catholiciſm, univerſality, or the Orthodox faith of the whole Church ſo called

Catholick, *g.* univerſal, alſo Orthodox, and ſometimes (corruptly) Roman Catholick or Papiſt.

Catholick Majeſty, the King of *Spain*.

Catholicon, a general purging Medicine.

Catholiſation, the being or becoming a Catholick.

Cathore, *-rius*, the value of nine kine.

Catilinariſme, the practice of *Catiline*, a famous conſpiratour againſt his own Countrey [*Rome*.]

Catini, people of *Cathneſs*.

Catkins, winter excreſcences in Nut- and Birch-trees.

Catling, a knife uſed in cutting off any joint.

Catmint, an herb.

If you ſet it, Cats will eat it;
If you ſow it, Cats can't know it.

Catoblepa, a beaſt that kills, only with the ſight.

Cato, the name of ſeveral famous men of *Rome*.

Catonian, *-ien*, grave, ſevere.

Catopticks, Profeſſours of the Opticks or ſpeculative Art.

Catoptographicks, books treating of Glaſſes.

Catoptrick, belonging to

Catopiron, *g.* a kind of Optick glaſs.

Catoptromancy, divination by viſion in a glaſſe.

Catry, a place to keep

Cates, or [dainty] victuals.

Cats-tail, reed-mace, who's top reſembles it.

Catieuchlani, *Caſſij*, certain *Britans* under *Caſſivellaunus*.

Cavalcade, *f.* a riding or ſhow on horſ-back.

Cavalier, *f.* *-lero*, *Sp.* a brave man [on horſeback.]

Cavalry, *f.* the horſ [men] in an army.

Cavation, *l.* hollowing [the ground for Cellerage.]

Caucaſus, part of the mountain *Taurus*, parting *India* from *Scythia*.

Cavea, the triangle in the hollow of the hand.

Caveare, *-ri*, *Ickary*, a Ruſſian meat made of ſeveral fiſh roes.

Caveat, *l.* a Caution or warning.

Cavechin, *-eſan*, *f.* a falſe rein [to lead a horſe in.]

Cavern, *l.* a Cave.

Cauf, a cheſt with holes to keep fiſh alive in the water.

Cavillation, *l.* a mocking, alſo wrangling.

Cavity, *l.* hollowneſs.

Caulk, as *Calk*.

Cavon, part of *Ireland*.

Caupes, *Calpes*, *ſc.* a gift given the Maſter for maintenance

tenance and protection.

Cauphe, Coffa, a *Turkish* drink made of brown berries.

Cauponate, *l.* sell [wine or victuals.]

Caurymaury, *D.* Mock-garments.

Caurus, North-east-wind.

Caursines, *Lumbards*, *Italian* Bankers coming hither 1235. and terming themselves the Popes Merchants.

Causam nobis significes, a writ for the Major to shew why he delayes, *&c.*

Causal, *l.* causing.

Causality, a being the cause; also as

Causation, *l*, an excusing, or alledging of a cause.

Causidick, pleader of

Causes, Tryals, actions.

Caustick, *g.* searing, burning.

Cautele, *l.* a taking heed.

Cauterism, *g.* a searing.

Cautery, *g.* a searing iron.

Cauterize, to sear.

Cautione admittenda a writ against the Bishop, holding an excommunicate person in prison who promises obedience [under Caution.]

Cautionary, *l.* given in pawn. also as

Cautional, pertaining to

Caution, pledg, instruction, wariness.

Cawston, a Town in *Norfolk*.

Cautor, *l.* he that foresees or bewareth.

Caya, *Sa.* a Kay, Key, or Water-lock.

Cayer, a quire of [written] paper, or part of a written book.

Cazemate, as *Casemate*.

Cazimi, *Ar.* in the heart of the Sun, when the planet is not 17 minutes distant.

Cebratane, *f.* a trunk to shoot clay pellets.

Ceca, a Monastery of *Corduba* in *Spain*.

Cecity. *l.* blindness.

Cecrops, an Egyptian King of *Athens*, he first civilized them and instituted marriage.

Cecutiency, *l.* purblindness.

Cedar, a tall upright *African* Tree.

Cedrosij, barbarous people cloath'd in wild beasts skins.

Cefala, an African Isle, three miles in length and one in breadth, a *Portugal* Kingdom.

Celænæ, the Hill in *Asia*, where *Marsyas*, contended with *Apollo*.

Celarent, a Syllogism who's second Proposition is an universal affirmative, the other universal Negatives.

Celature, *Cæl-*, *l.* carving or engraving.

Celebate, as Celibate.

Celebration, *l.* a solemnizing or making famous.

Celebrity, *l.* famousness.

Celerer, *o.* a Butler.

Celeripedean, *l.* swift-footed.

Celerity, *l.* swiftness.

Celestifie, to make

Celestial, *l.* heavenly.

Celestines, an Order of Fryars instituted by *Pope*

Celestine the fifth, 1215.

Cellarist, the Butler in a Religious house.

Celostomy, *g.* a speaking hollow in the mouth.

Celsitude, *-ty*, *l.* Highness.

Celtique, belonging to the

Celtæ, *Gauls*, inhabiting between the Rivers *Garonne* and *Sein*.

Celtiberia, *Arragon* in *Spain*.

Celurca, *Montros* in *Scotland*.

Cementation, a joyning with

Cement, *Cim-*, *l.* strong mortar

Cemetery, *Cœm-* *g.* a Church-yard.

Cenatical, *-tory* *l.* belonging to

Cene, *l.* a Supper.

Cenchris, a green venemous biting Serpent.

Cenosity, *l.* filthiness.

Cenotaph, *g.* an empty Tomb in honour of some great person.

Cense, a mustering of an Army, also cessing of the people.

Censer, wherein the Priest burns incense.

Cension, *l.* a punishment inflicted by the

Censor, *l.* a Roman Officer to cesse Estates, reform manners, *&c.*

Censorious, *-ian*, belonging thereto.

Censure, to judg, give sentence

Centaurs, half men and half horses (of *Thessaly*.)

Centaury, an herb of *Mars*.

Centenary, *l.* belonging to

Cent, *f.* an hundred.

Center, *-tre*, *l.* the middle of a circle, also wooden things to turn arches upon.

Centiloquy, a hundred-fold-discourse.

Centinodie, *l.* knot-grass.

Centoculated [*Argus*] having 100 eyes.

Centon, *l.* a patched coat.

Central, in the Center.

Centrie, Sanctuary, place of Refuge for Malefactors.

Centum-viri, *l.* (a hundred men) Roman Judges.

Centuplicated, made

Centuple, a hundred fold.

Century, *l.* the number of an hundred [years, *&c.*]

Centuriate, *l.* divided by hundreds.

Centurion, *l.* Captain over an hundred men.

Centurists, four *German* Ecclesiastical Historians, dividing their work into Centuries

Cephaleonomancy, *g.* Divination by a broil'd Asses head.

Cephalick, [line, plaister, vein, &c.] *g.* belonging to the head.

Cephalus, shot his jealous wife in a bush (instead of a wild Beast) and was turned into a stone.

Cephas, *Sy.* (a stone) *Peter*.

Cepi Corpus, a Sheriffs Return that he hath taken the body of such a man.

Ceramite, a precious stone.

Cerast, *g.* a horned serpent.

Ceratine, *l.* made of wax.

Ceratine, *g.* horned, subtile [arguments.]

Cerberus, a three-headed dog Porter of Hell.

Cercel, a Teal.

Cerebrosity. *l.* a being cock-braind, or brainsick.

Cerebrum Jovis, burnt Tartar (in Chymistry.) *Cer-*

Cerdonists, Hereticks holding two contrary principles (a good and bad God) in all causes.

Ceremonious, -*ial*, belonging to or full of

Ceremonies, *l.* Customs and Rites [of the Church,] also complements.

Cereal, pertaining to

Ceres, Goddess of Agriculture, daughter of *Saturn* and *Ops*, also Corn.

Cerinthians, a sort of Hereticks that followed one

Cerinthus, who held, that Christ at his second coming would give all carnal pleasures.

Cerna, an Ethiopick Isle.

Ceromancy, divination by wax in water.

Ceromatick, *g.* anointed.

Ceroferarie, Candlestick or Candlemaker, also he that has the care of the [wax-] Candles.

Cerones, ancient inhabitants of *Assin-shire* in *Scotland*.

Cerote, *g.* a kind of searcloth or plaister.

Certaminate, *l.* contend.

Certes, *f.* certainly, surely.

Certificate, a writing to give notice of any thing done.

Certification of Assize of novel disseisin, a writ for the examining of a matter passed by Assize before the Justices.

Certificando de recognitione stapulæ, a writ for the Major to certifie to the Chancellor the staple taken before him, when the party refuses to bring it in.

Certiorari, a writ from the Chancery to an inferiour Court, to call up the records of a cause there depending.

Cert mony, (certain money)

Certum litæ, head mony or common fine, paid the Lords of Leets.

Cervical [Artery] passes from the Neck-bone to the brain.

Cervine, *l.* belonging to an Hart, also tauny.

Ceruleated, sky-coloured.

Ceruse, -*ussi*, *l.* white lead.

Cesare, as *Celarent*.

Cesariated, *l.* wearing long hair.

Cesata, -*ada*, a City of *Spain*.

Cespitate, *l.* stumble.

Cessant, *l.* lingring, doing nothing.

Cessation, *l.* a leaving off

Cessavit, a Writ, when Rent or service (according to tenure) is neglected.

Cessure, -*ser*, a ceasing, giving over or departing from.

Cesse, *l.* leave off, or be idle; also to rate or tax.

Cessibility, aptness to cease.

Cession, *l.* yielding or giving place to another.

Cessor, *l.* a loiterer.

Cest, *l.* the Brides wedding-girdle untied (the first night) by the Bridegroom.

C'est sans dire, *f.* to say no more.

Cestui qui vie, (*Cestui à vie de qui*) he for who's life any Land or Tenement is granted.

Cestui que use (*Cestui à l' use de qui*) he to who's use another is Enfeoffed.

Cestui qui trust, he that is entrusted for the benefit of another.

Cesurate, *l.* cut, notched.

Cetacious, -*reous*, *l.* belonging to a Whale.

Cete, *l.* a Company.

Ceterach, *Ar.* Finger-ferne, spleen-herb resembling fern.

Ceus, *Ceos*, an Isle, where all above sixty years old, were bound to poison themselves.

Cha, a China-leaf, who's infusion makes their ordinary drink.

Chabane, *o.* a Cabbin.

Chable, as Cable.

Chace, *f.* a Warren.

Chachshirs, Turkish breeches reaching down to the heels.

Chafe, gaul, or fret [a rope.]

Chaffers, wares, Merchandize.

Chaffewax, a Chancery Officer preparing the wax for writs, &c.

Chaft, *c.* beaten, bang'd.

Chagrin, *f.* care, Melancholy.

Chain-shot, two bullets with a chain between them.

Chalcedon, a City of *Asia* built by the *Megarenses*.

Chalcographer, *g.* an ingraver in Brass.

Chalcography, *g.* the Art of engraving.

Chaldæan, belonging to

Chaldæa, part of greater *Asia*, famous for Astrology and Magick.

Chaldese, to tell fortunes.

Chaldron, -*der*, six and thirty bushels [of Coals.]

Chalice, *l.* the Communion-cup.

Challenge, exception against Jurors, &c.

Chalmer, *sc.* Chamber.

Chalmerlan, Chamberlain.

Chaloner, the Name of an ancient Family.

Chalons, *f.* blankets, Coverings.

Chalybeat, -*bete*, *l.* like steel. [water] wherein steel hath been quenched.

Chalybes, people of *Asia* the less having great store of steel-Mines.

Chamber [of a great gun] so far as the charge reaches.

Chamberdekins, *Chaumberdakyns*, Irish begging Priests.

Chamberer, Chamber-maid.

Chamberlain [of a City] the cheif keeper of the publick Treasury.

Chamfered, [stalks] having impressions like a gutter or crevice.

Chamelæa, spurge Olive, a shrubby surculous plant.

Chamelet, *Chamolet*, *Chamblat*, a watered stuff mixt with Camel-hair.

Chamfer, an artificial gutter or crevice in a pillar.

Chamfred, *o.* chapt, wrinkled.

Chamois, [leather] made of the skins of a

Chamois, -*moy*, Wild Goat.

Champain, open Fields.

Champernouns, as Campernulphs.

Champertors, they that use

Champarty, *f.* the maintaining of a man in his suit, on condition to have part of the Land

land or goods when recovered.

Champion, f. one that fights (or is ready to fight) in anothers behalf.

Chananæa, Canaan, the holy-land.

Chancellour [of either Univerſity,] the Chief Governour.

Chancellour [of the Dioceſs] the Biſhops official.

Chancellour [of the Dutchy of *Lancaſter.*] Judge in that Court.

Chancellour [of the Exchequer] appointed to moderate extremities there.

Lord Chancellour, Chief Judge in the

Chancery, Court of Equity and Conſcience, moderating the ſeverity of Common law.

Chanfron, an Italian Coin about 20 pence.

Chantepleur, f. he that ſings and weeps both together.

Chanter, a [Church] ſinger.

Chanticleer, f. the Cock,

Chaomancy, divination by the air.

Chaonia, the hilly part of *Epirus,* from

Chaon, Priam's ſon, ſlain by chance by his brother *Helenus* in hunting.

Chaos, g. a confuſed heap.

Chaperon, f. a hood; alſo the little Scutcheon on the horſes forehead.

Chapin, ſp. a high Cork-heel'd ſhooe.

Chapelry, is to a Chapel, as a Pariſh to a Church.

Chaplet, Garland [for the head.]

Chapt, c. dry, thirſty.

Chapter, -piter, the top or head of a pillar; alſo a Company of Cathedral [or Collegiate] Clergy men who chooſe the Biſhop.

Char, a particular buſineſs; alſo a kind of trout,

Character, g. the print of any thing, or mark in ſhort-hand, or any letter; alſo as

Characteriſm, a lively deſcription of a perſon.

Characters in printing are 1. Pearl, 2. Non-pareil, 3. Breviar, 4. Minion, 5. Long primer, 6. Smal pica, 7. Pica, 8. Engliſh Roman, 9. Great primer, 10. Double pica, 11 Smal Canon, 12. Fat Canon 13. Capitals. And moſt of theſe have a black Engliſh letter anſwering them.

Characteriſtick-cal, belonging thereto; alſo diſtinguiſhing, alſo that letter which immediately precedes the varying termination of any word.

Characterize, to deſcribe, alſo to take in Characters or ſhort-hand.

Charactery, a writing by Characters.

Caratux, as *Caratux.*

Chardford, Cerdeford, a Town in *Hantſhire.*

Charde, a Town in *Somerſet.*

Chare, a fiſh proper to *Winandermer* in *Lancaſhire.*

Chare [the Cow,] ſtop or turn her.

Charge, that which fills the field of an Eſcutcheon: in a ſhip, the water ſhe draws.

Charientiſm, g. gracefulneſs alſo a pleaſant piece of raillery ſoftening a taunting expreſſion.

Charing-Croſs, erected by King *Edward* 1. in memory of Queen *Eleanor* who ſuckt the poiſon out of his wounds made by a Moors envenom'd ſword at the holy war.

Charites, g. the Graces, *Thalia Aglaia, Euphroſyne.*

Charivary, f. a publick defaming or traducing of another.

Charlatanerie, f. a Cheating or cogging, from

Charlatan, a Mountebank

Charles, Sa. all Noble.

Charles-wain, ſtars near the North pole, like 4 wheels and horſes drawing them.

Charlock, wild muſtard among corn, with a yellow flower.

Charmer, one that uſeth

Charms, bewitching or unbewitching expreſſions.

Charnel-houſe, where dead bones are laid,

Charon, the ſouls ferry-man over the Stygian-lake.

Chart, l. paper, parchment or written deed.

Charter-houſe, Chartreuſe, a Monaſtery of the *Chartreux* (*Carthuſian* Fryers) *Suttons* Hoſpital, founded by Sir *Walter Marny* of *Hewault,* who ſerved under *Edward* 3. in the *French* wars: alſo a town in *Somerſet.*

Charter-land, holden by

Charter, Letters patents of priviledges granted by the King.

Charter-party, an Agreement between a Merchant and the Maſter of a ſhip.

Chartis reddendis, a writ againſt him that refuſes to deliver Charters of feofment entruſted with him.

Chartulary, keeper of a Regiſter, or reckoning book.

Charvil, Chervil, an herb.

Charybdis, Gorophare, a Gulph in the bay of *Sicily.*

Chaſmatical, belonging to a

Chaſm, -ma, g. a wide gap or opening of the earth or air.

Chaſteleyn, o. a Gentleman or Woman of a great houſe.

Chaſtilleine, as *Caſtellaine.*

Chaſuble, f. a kind of Cope worn at Maſs.

Chats, c. the gallows.

Chattels, all kind of goods, except free-hold.

Chattesworth, a ſtatelie houſe in *Darbyſhire.*

Chauſynges, o. heatings.

Chaumound, an ancient and Noble Family in *Cornwall.*

Chaud-mille, ſc. a fault committed in a ſudden tumult.

Chaviſh, Sſ. a prating noiſe.

Chauncel, the moſt ſacred ſeparated part of a church or temple.

Chaunce-medley, killing of a man by chance.

Chauncery, as *Chancery,*

Chaundler, a candleſtick.

Chauntry, *f.* a church, chappel or quire endowed with maintenance for ſingers of Divine ſervice.

Chaworth, a noble family of *Alesbury*.

Cheapgild, a reſtitution made by the county or hundred for wrong done by one *in plegio*.

Chechiface, *Chechivache*, *f.* a ſtarved, hungry cow : ſee *Chittyface*.

Check, when a hawk forſakes her natural flight to follow other Birds that come in view.

Check-roll, *Chequer-roll*, containing the names of the Kings [or other great perſons] menial ſervants.

Checks, thick ſpliced clamps of wood at the top of a maſt.

Cheerte, charity, *o.*

Checkie, (in heraldry) conſiſting of three panes of checquer-work.

Cheffes, *o.* chevins or elſe calves.

Chegford, a Town in *Devon*.

Cheigo, a ſmall *Barbados* animal getting into ones feet and tormenting them.

Chief, as *Capite* ; alſo a line in the chief or upper part of the Eſcutcheon containing one third of it.

Chiefage. *Chevage*, *Chivage*, *-gium*, head-ſervice, money paid by Villains to their Lords.

Chief-pledge, Headborough.

Chekelaton, *o.* a ſtuff like Motly.

Chelaundri, *-aundre*, *o.* a goldfinch, or a lark

Chelidonius, a precious ſtone in a ſwallows belly.

Chelidonie, *Celandine*.

Chelmerford, *Chelmesford*, *Chensford*, a Town in *Eſſex*.

Chelonophagi, people feeding only upon Tortoiſes, covering their houſes and building ſhips with the ſhels.

Chelſey, *g.* *Shelfsey*, in *Middleſex*.

Cheltenham, a Town in *Gloceſterſhire*.

Chemnis a floting Iſland.

Chent, corruptly for *Kent*.

Chentſers, quit-rent, or chief Rent.

Cheape, *o.* buy.

Cherſet, as Churcheſſet.

Cheriſaunce, *o.* comforts.

Cherſoneſus, *Cherro-*, *g.* *Peninſula*, *l.* a tract of land almoſt environ'd with the Sea.

Cherketh, *o.* Chirpeth.

Cherme, *o.* a company [of birds.]

Chert, *Cheort*, *Cherte*, *o.* love, alſo jealouſie.

Chertes, *o.* merry people.

Cherubim, *h.* *-bin*, *ch.* the plural number of

Cherub, *h.* fulneſs of knowledge, the ſecond of the nine orders of Angels.

Chervel, *Charwel*, a River on the Eaſt ſide of *Oxford*, famous for dreſſing of Leather.

Cheſlip, hog [louſe,] a little vermin, turning it ſelf round like a pea.

Cheſe, *o.* choſe.

Cheſs-bowls, Cheeſe-bowls.

Cheſten, *-tin*, *f.* Cheſnut.

Cheſter, as *Weſt-cheſter*.

Cheſterfield, a Town in *Darbyſhire*.

Cheſtoul, Poppy.

Chetrones, two ſmall pieces with holes, to which the tack is haled down.

Cheve, *o.* to thrive.

Cheveril, *f.* a wild goat.

Cheverel [leather,] ſee Chervel.

Cheveſal, *-ſayl*, *o.* a gorget.

Chevice, *o.* redeem.

Chevin, a fiſh with a great head.

Cheviſaunce, *-ſſance*, *f.* Compoſition between Creditor and Debtour.

Chevitiæ, *-iſcæ*, head-lands.

Chevrons, *f.* the ſtrong rafters meeting at the houſe-top, alſo one of the Ordinaries of a Eſcutcheon made in faſhion of a triangle.

Chevronel, half a *Cheveron* (in Blazon.)

Chibbol, a little Onion.

Chiche, chicket, niggardly, *f.*

Chicanerie, *f.* wrangling, Impertinent perplexing of a cauſe.

Chicheſter, *Ciſſanceſter*, in *Suſſex*, built by

Ciſſa, King of the South-*Saxons*.

Chidleigh, a Town in *Devonſhire*.

Chieve, ſucceed, befall.

Childermas, Innocents day.

Childing [plants,] who's offſpring exceeds the number of the ordinary kind.

Childwit, power to take a fine of your bondwoman gotten with child without your conſent, alſo of the reputed Father of a Baſtard.

Chiliad, *g.* a thouſand.

Chiliarch, *g.* a Colonel.

Chiliaſm, Opinion of the

Chiliaſts, Millenaries, holding that Chriſt ſhall reign perſonally upon earth a thouſand years.

Chilonick, *-ian*, belonging to

Chilo, one of the ſeven wiſe men of *Greece*, who's ſentences were very brief.

Chilperick, a worthleſs King of *France*.

Chiltern, *ſa.* the hilly, cold and chalky part of *Buckinghamſhire*.

Chily, an *American* Kingdom.

Chimæra, a hill in *Lycia*, who's top, middle and bottom, had Lions, Goats and Serpents ; alſo an idle conceit, or a feigned monſter with a Lyons head, Goats belly and Dragons tail.

Chimerical, imaginary, phantaſtical.

Chimbe, the uttermoſt part of a barrel.

Chimin, *f.* the Kings highway.

Chiminage, toll for paſſage through the Forreſt.

Chimmar, a Biſhops black ſleev-leſs veſtment worn between the Gown and Rochet

Chimney-money, hearth-money, 2 s. *per annũ* paiable at *Michaelmas* and *Lady day*.

China, a Kingdom in *Asia* containing 600 Cities, 2000 walled Towns, and 4000 unwalled.

Chincery, o. (for *Chicherie*, f. niggardliness.

Chinquita, a Colony of Spaniards in *America*.

Chione, Daughter to *Deucalion*, with child by *Mercury* and *Phœbus*, brought them at once *Antolycus* and *Philemon*.

Chios, an Island in the *Ægean* Sea between *Lesbos* and *Samos*.

Chipnam, a Town in *Wilts*.

Chipping-Norton, a Town in *Oxfordshire*.

Chipping-Sodbury, a Town in *Glocestershire*.

Chiragrical, having the

Chiragra, g. hand-gout.

Chirchsed, as *Churches sed*.

Chirking, o. chattering noise,

Chirograph, g, ones own hand writing.

Chirographer, he that gives a bill of his hand; also he that records the fines acknowledged in the Common pleas Office.

Chirologie, g. a discoursing by signs.

Chiromancer, one that professeth.

Chiromancy, Palmestry, divination by the hand-lines.

Chiromantick, -*cal*, belonging thereto.

Chiron, *Sagitarius*, half man, half horse, begotten by *Saturn* in the shape of a horse.

Chironomer, g. a teacher or user of hand-gestures in dancing, pleading, &c.

Chirrichote, a word of derision from the Spanish to the French pronouncing

Chirrie, for *Kyrie*.

Chirurgery, Surgery, the Art of curing wounds.

Chitty-face, *Chiche-face*, f. a pitiful, wretched, sneaking fellow.

Chivalrie, f. horsmanship, also a tenure by Knights service.

Chivauchie, -*ancy*, the same.

Chit, the seed chits when it shoots the small root out of the Earth.

Chiven, as *Chieve*.

Chiver, o. to shiver.

Chives, the small parts of roots (as of garlick, &c.) by which they are propagated.

Chizzel, *Sf*. k. bran.

Chevasme, as *Epicertomesis*.

Chloris, *Flora*, the Wife of *Zephyrus*.

Chlorosis, white Jaundies, or green sickness.

Chocolate, an Indian drink made of *Cocao*.

Chœnix, g. a measure somewhat more than a wine quart

Choldmonley, *Cholm*-, and

Cholmley, a Town and Family in *Cheshire*.

Cholog gon, g. purging of Choler

Chondril, a herb like savoury.

Chop-Church, changing of one Church for another.

Choral, one of the quire.

Chord, subtense, Hypotenuse, a right line subtending an arch of a circle.

Choriambick, g. a foot of four syllables, the two middlemost short, the other two long.

Chorion, the outermost tunicle that enwraps the birth.

Chorister, g. Quirister, singing man or boy.

Chorographer, g, describer of places.

Chorography, the description of a Country, Kingdom, &c.

Chorus, a Company of Singers [in a Quire.]

Chose, f. a thing.

Chowse, to cozen or deceive.

Chiaux, a Turkish messenger hath the very same sound.

Chrismatory, a vessel receiving the liquor from the two Olive branches by golden pipes in the Temple, also a vessel containing the

Chrism, g. ointment used in Popish baptism, and at Kings Coronations.

Chrisme, a white cloth put on the child after baptism, also a child dying before baptism or within the moneth of wearing the Chrisom-cloth.

Chrisom-calf, kil'd before 'tis a month old.

Christianism, -*ity*, the profession of the Christian Religion.

Christ, g. anointed.

Christopher, g. Christ-carrier.

Chromatick, g. keeping its colour, delightfull, also as *Acroamatick*.

Chronical [*diseases*] not acute but lingring.

Chronical or *Acbr-rising*, is when a star rises at Sun setting.

Chronicle, g. History of the Times.

Chronodix, g. a Dial.

Chronogram, g. a collection of the numeral letters out of a sentence.

Chronography, g. a writing of *Chronicles* or Annals.

Chronographer, such a writer.

Chronology, g. computation of years and comparing of Histories.

Chronologer, a computer of times.

Chronologicks, books treating of Chronology.

Chrysites, a kind of Litharge, from its golden colour.

Chrysocol, as *Borax*, Goldsmiths soder.

Chrysolite, an *Æthiopian* gold-coloured stone.

Chrysopæa, g. the Art of making gold.

Chrysopolis, Scutary a promontory of *Asia*.

Chrysoprase, an Asian greenish precious stone.

Chrysostom, -*mus*, g. golden mouth, Bishop of *Bizantium*.

Christalline [*heaven*], the ninth.

Chrystal, a precious stone engendred by cold.

Chrystallization, a Chymical purifying of Salts.

Chuck, *Sf*. chunk, a great chip.

Churlich, o. plainly, homely.

Churle, *Sa*. carle, clown.

Church-litten, *W*. Church-yard.

Church-choppers, they that change away one Church for another.

Church-reve, a Church-warden

Church-set, *Churchesset*, *Churchesed*, *Church-seed*, Wheat formerly paid the Church on St. *Martins* day.

Chylifactory, causing

Chylification, the turning of nourishment into

Chyle, g. a milky substance ready to be turned to bloud.

Chymistry, the art of dissolving metals, and extracting quintessence.

Chymere, as *Tabard*.

Cibarious, l. belonging to meat.

Ciboire, f. a pix, cup, or box, wherin the *Roman* host is kept

Cibosity, l. store of food.

Cicatrice, l. a scar.

Cicely, l. Grey-eyed.

Ciceronian, *-ical*, belong to

Cicero, a famous Roman orator and Philosopher.

Cicers, l. Italian pease.

Cicurate, l. to tame.

Cid, *Sp.* valiant [Captain.]

Caide, *Ar.* Lord, great man.

Cidaris, the Persian attire for the head.

Cierges, o. wax-candles.

Cileric, *Sp.* the drapery or leavage wrought upon the heads of pillars.

Cilicia, *Caramania*, or *Turcomania*, in lesser *Asia*.

Cilicious, belonging to

Cilice, l. hair-cloth.

Cilinder, as *Cylinder*.

Cimbal, as *Cymbal*.

Cimbick, g. a niggard.

Cimbrians, ancient people of *Denmark*.

Cimeliark, l. a place for vestments or jewels.

Cimice, *-isse*, l. a wood-louse, a small red insect.

Cimiter, as *Scymiter*.

Cimmerian, belonging to the *Cimmerians*, Northern people, also Italians (in deep vales) who seldom or never the Sun.

Cincantenier, f. a Commander of 50, also an Officer in *Paris*.

Cincture, l. encompassing with see a girdle.

Cindalism, dust-point, a boyish play.

Cinefaction, a burning to ashes.

Cinefy, l. bring to ashes.

Cinerulent, l. full of ashes.

Cingulum Veneris, l. (the girdle of *Venus*) the semicircle from the space between the fore-finger and middle finger to the space between the ring-finger and little finger.

Ciniph, l. a gnat.

Cinque-foil f. five-leaved grass.

Cinnaber, f. a red mineral stone used for a vermilion colour.

Cinople, *Sinople*, rudle.

Cinque-Ports, f. (five havens) *Hastings*, *Hith*, *Dover*, *Rumney* and *Sandwich*.

Cion, *Sion*, *Scion*, f. a young shoot from the root or stock of a tree.

Ciperus, a three square rush who's root is odoriferous.

Cipher, any figure or number, especially the nought (o), also as character.

Cippus, l. a pair of stocks.

Cipress, fine curled linnen.

Circe, a witch who turn'd *Ulysses* companions into Swine.

Circester, *Cirencester*, an ancient City of *Glocester-shire*.

Circinate, l. make a circle with a pair of compasses.

Circination, a circling or turning round.

Ciric seat Circesed, as *Churchsed*

Cirk, *Cirque*, l. a round Roman show-place.

Circensial, belonging thereto, or the plaies there exhibited.

Circuit of action, a longer course of proceeding (in law) than is needful.

Circuition, *-citure*, l. a going about.

Circular, l. round, in a circle.

Circulation, l. a fetching of a [round] compass to the same place again, also extraction of waters by limbeck.

Circumaggeration, l. a heaping round about.

Circumambient, l. incircling, flowing all about.

Circumambulation, l. a walking about.

Circumbilivagination, circular motion, or going round.

Circumcellions, *-celians*, Hereticks who (to get them a name) laid violent hands upon themselves.

Circumcession, a general yielding.

Circumcinct, girt about.

Circumcision, l. a cutting off the fore-skin.

Circumduction, *Circund-*, l. a leading about, also deceiving.

Circumference, l. a line drawn round a centre.

Circumferenter, a Mathematical instrument to find the hour of the Sun.

Circumflex, l. bowed about, an accent shewing a long or contracted syllable, thus (^) or thus (~).

Circumflexion, a bending about.

Circumfluent, *-uous*, flowing about.

Circumfodient, digging about.

Circumforaneous, l. pitiful, pedling, loitering [about the market.]

Circumfulgent, shining about.

Circumfusion, l. a powring about.

Circumgyration, l. a wheeling round about.

Circumjacent, l. lying about.

Circumincession, l. a going round, the reciprocal Being of the Persons of the Trinity in each other.

Circumligation, *Circunli-*, l. a binding about.

Circumlition, l. a daubing or plaistering about.

Circumlocution, l. many words to express one thing, a going about the bush.

Circumplication, l. a folding about.

Circumposition, l. laying [the mould] about [a bough, which is to be taken off.]

Circumrotation, l. a wheeling about.

Circumscribed, enclosed.

Circumscription, l. a writing about.

Circumscript, drawn about with a line, also deceived or disanulled.

Circumspection, *l.* looking about, wariness.

Circumstantial, belonging to

Circumstance, *l.* a quality that accompanies any thing, as time, place, &c.

Circumstantiate, to do or describe a thing with its circumstances.

Circumstantibus, [make up the number of the Jurours] of those that stand about.

Circumstation, a standing round about.

Circumvallation, *l.* an enclosing or trenching about.

Circumvection, *Circumv-*, *l.* a carrying about.

Circumvest, cloath or garnish round about.

Circumvent, *l.* deceive, overreach.

Circumvolate, *l.* fly about.

Circumvolve *l.* roll about.

Circumvolution, *l.* a rowling about, or wheeling about.

Circumdate, *-undate*, *l.* to compass about.

Circumsonate, *-unsonate*, *l.* to sound round about.

Circundolate, chip, or cut about

Circunspicuous, to be seen on all sides.

Circunvagant, wandring about.

Cirrous, belonging to curled hair.

Cisalpine, *l.* on this side the *Alpes*.

Cisbury, a Town in *Sussex*, from

Cissa, 2d. King of the South-*Saxons*.

Cista gratiæ, a Church-coffer where peoples charity was kept

Cistercian, as *Bernardine*.

Cistus, the holy rose, a bramble.

Citation, *l.* quoting, also summoning to appear.

Citharist, *l.* a Harper.

Citharize, to Harp.

Citherides, the Muses.

Citrial, *o.* a Cittern, Ghittern, or a dulcimer.

Citrine, *-rean*, [colour] of a Pom-citron, golden.

Citrination, perfect digestion, or the colour proving the Philosophers stone.

Citrull, a kind of cucumber.

Citadel fort, fortress.

Cives, leeks.

Civet, *Ar.* a sweet unctious excrement of some beast.

Civick, [Crown] given to deserving Roman Citizens.

Civilize, make civil.

Clack [*wool*,] cut off the Sheeps mark, to make it lighter.

Claick-geese, as *Barnacles*.

Claim, challenge.

Clamorous, full of

Clamour, *l.* noise.

Clamps, thick Timbers under the beams of the first *Orlop*.

Clan, *sc.* tribe, family.

Clancular, *-rious*, *l.* private, secret.

Clandestine, *l.* the same.

Clangour, *l.* a great sound, or cry.

Clap, the neather part of a Hawks beak.

Clap-bord, board ready cut to make cask or vessels.

Clap bread, *La.* thin hard oat-cakes.

Clapperdogeon, *c.* a begger born.

Clapers, *f.* Warren pales or walls.

Clara, *l.* clear.

Clare, a Tower in *Suffolk*.

Clarentieux, *-tiaux*, *-tius*, one of the Kings at Arms.

Claricord, *Cler-*, an instrument somewhat like a cymbal.

Clarifie *l.* make clear.

Clarigation, *l.* as reprisal.

Clarion, a kind of shrill Trumpet.

Clarissonant, *-isonent*, *l.* shrill-sounding.

Clarity, clearness.

Clark, a Clergy-man, Scholar, Secretary, &c.

Clarmarthan, *sc.* the warranting of stolen goods.

Classe, *l.* a rank, order or degree, also a Navy.

Classick, *-ical*, belonging thereto, approved, of good authority.

Claudicate, *l.* halt.

Claudity, lameness.

Clavecymbal, *Claricy-* an instrument with wire strings, by some an Harpsical or Virginal.

Claver, Trefoyl, an herb.

Clavicular, *-rious*, belonging to

Clavis, *l.* a key.

Claves Insulæ, twelve men in the Isle of man to whom all doubtful and weighty cases are referred.

Clavigerous, bearing or keeping keyes.

Clause, an Article or conclusion.

Claustral, *l.* belonging to a *Cloyster*, or close place.

Cleam, *Li.* glue together.

Cleat, a little wooden wedge on the yards, to keep the ropes from slipping.

Cleavers, as *Goose-grass*.

Cledgy, *k.* stiff.

Clemd, *Clamd*, starved, also thirsty.

Clement, *l.* mild.

Clemency, gentleness.

Clementines, certain decretals collected by Pope *Clement*.

Clenge, *o.* cleanse, also factious, disorderly.

Cleopatra, Queen of *Ægypt* loved by *Julius Cæsar*.

Clep, *sc.* certain solemn words used especially in criminal causes.

Cleped, *Cleeped*, *sa.* named.

Clepen, *o.* they call.

Clepsydry, *g.* a water hourglass.

Clergion, *o.* a Clark.

Clergial, learned, belonging to the

Clergy, the who company of Ministers, also allowance of the book to a Prisoner.

Clerico admittendo, for the Bishop to admit a clark to a Benefice.

Clerk, as *Clark*.

Clerk of the Axe, marks timber for the use of the Kings Navy.

Clerk of the Check, Orders the Yeomen of the guard, sets the watch every night, &c, another of this name in the Navy.

Clerk of the Chest, Where is kept the mony collected for

sick and wounded Seamen.

Clerk Comptroler of the Kings house, Two *Court*-Officers that allow or disallow the charges of Pursuivants, &c.

Clerk of the Crown [*Office*,]

Clerk of the *Crown* of the Kings Bench.

Clerk of the Crown in Chancery, Attends on the Lord *Chancellour* or *Keeper*.

Clerk of the Errours, in the *Common Pleas*, transcribes the tenour of the Records of the cause into the Kings Bench.

Clerk of the Errours, in the *Kings Bench*, transcribes the Records of such causes into the Exchequer.

Clerk of the Errours, in the *Exchequer*, prepares the Records certified thither for Judgment.

Clerk of Essoyns, keeps the Essoyn-rolls (in *Common-Pleas*.)

Clerk of the Estreats, Writes out the Estreats to be levy'd for the King.

Clerk or Warden of the hamper or *hanaper*, (in the *Chancery*) receives all mony due to the King for the Seals of Charters, Patents, Commissions and Writs.

Clerk of the Juries or Jurata-Writs, makes out writs in the Court of Common Pleas.

Clerk of the Kings Silver, receives the fines in the Court of Common Pleas.

Clerk of the Market, keeps the standards (examples) of all measures.

Clerk Marshal of the Kings House, Attends the Marshal in his Court, and Records his proceedings.

Clerk of the Nichils or Nihils, (in the *Exchequer*.) Makes a roll of all such sums as are nihilled by the Sheriffs, upon their Estreats of Green wax, &c.

Clerk of the Outlawries. Servant or deputy to the Kings Attorny General.

Clerk of the Peace. Reads Enditements, &c. at the Sessions.

Clerk of the Pell, or Parchment roll (in the Exchequer) wherein he enters every Tellers bill.

Clerk of the petty Bag, Three Officers in Chancery, whereof the Master of the Rolls is chief.

Clerk of the Pipe, (or great Roll) in the Exchequer, looks to all Accompts and Debts due to the King.

Clerk of the Pleas, in the Exchequer, in his Office all Court-Officers must sue and be sued.

Clerk of the Privy Seal, Four that attend the Lord Privy Seal.

Clerk of the Signet, Four that attend (by turns) on his Majesties Principal Secretary.

Clerk of the Treasury, keeps the Records of the Court [of Common Pleas.]

Clerk of the Warrants, belongs to the Court of Common Pleas.

Clermatine[*bread*] fine, white

Cleromancy, *g*. Divination by lots or dice.

Clever, neat, smooth, dextrous.

Clevis, *o*. clifts, Rocks.

Clew [*of a Sail*.] the lower corner.

Clewgarnet, a rope made fast to the clew of the main-sail, and fore-sail.

Clew-line, is the same to top sails.

Clicket, the clapper of a door; also a key, *o*.

Cliquets, *f*. flat ratling bones for boys to play with.

Clicketing, when a Fox desires copulation, he goes a *Clicketing*.

Cliental, belonging to a *Client*, one that goes for counsel to a Lawyer.

Clientele, *l*. a taking of Clients into protection.

Cliff, a Cleft or side of a hill, a broken rock by the Seaside.

Cliff, *f*. (key) the whole scale of Musick is divided into 3 Cliffs, Basse, Mean and Treble.

Climacter, an account or reckoning made by degrees.

Climacterical, *Climat*-, [year] every 7th. and 9th. year of ones age, to the 63d, which is accounted the great Climacterical and most dangerous of all.

Climate, *Clime*, *g*. such a space of Earth (between two parallel lines) as makes half an houres difference in the Sun-dials and length of the daies.

Climax, *g*. (ladder) a gradual proceeding from one thing to another.

Clinch [of the Cable] that part which is seased about the ring of the anchor.

Clinch the Ports, drive a little *Okam* into their seams.

Clink, *o*. key.

Clinker, *c*. a crafty fellow.

Clinick, *g*. bed-rid.

Clinopaly, *g*. bed-wrestling.

Clio, one of the 9 Muses, Inventress of History.

Clito, as *Clyto*

Clitoris, *g*. the sinewy part of the womb.

Clitumnus, a River in *Italy* turning the Oxen (that drink it) white.

Cloacal, filthy, from

Cloaca, *l*. a sink or house of Office.

Clochier, *f*. a steeple.

Clodius, a notable Adulterer of *Rome*.

Cloath, a sail cloathes the mast, when it is so long that it touches the hatches.

Clælia, a noble *Roman* Virgin who swam over *Tybris* from *Porsenna* with whom she was left an hostage.

Cloffe, *Tare*, the bag, barrel, &c. in which the Commodity is.

Clomben, *o*. climbed.

Closet, half a barre (in heraldry.)

Clotlese, *o*. Clotburre.

Clottend *o*. Clotted.

Closh, the forbidden game at

Closh-cayles, Nine-pins.

Clotho, one of the 3 destinies carrying the thrid of mans life.

Cloy,

Cloy, *c*. steal.

Cloy'd, a peece is cloy'd, when any thing hinders the priming-powder from giving fire to the rest.

Cloudsberry, a plant proper to *Pendlehill* in *Lancashire*

Clove, 8 pound, the two and thirtieth part of a weigh of cheese.

Clough, *Sa*. a deep descent between hills.

Clowys of Gelofre flores, *o*. Clove gillyflowers.

Clum, *o*. a note of silence.

Clumperton, a clown,

Clumps, *Li*. Lazy, unhandy.

Clussum'd[*hand*,]*Che*. benummed with cold.

Clun-Castle in *Shropshire*,

Cluniack[*monks*] Benedictines reformed by *Odo* Abbot of

Cluni in *Burgundy*.

Clusive, shut up.

Cly the jerk, *c*. to be whipt.

Clymbe, *o*. a noise.

Clyptica, *g*. Medicines to beautifie the skin.

Clysterize, to give a

Clyster, *g*. an instrument to convey a purge through the Fundament to the guts; also the purge it self.

Clytemnestra, lived in Adultery with *Ægisthus*, and with his help kild her Husband *Agamemnon*.

Clytia, slighted by *Apollo*, pined away to an *Heliotrope*.

Clyto, *g*. (Excellent,) a title of honour anciently appropriated to our Kings Sons.

Cnidus, *Cab crio*, in *Caria*, where *Venus* was worshipped.

Cnossus, *Gnossus*, *Ceratus* in *Crete*, where *Minos* kept his Court.

Cnouts delf, *Swerds delf*, *Steeds dike*, made by *Canute* the *Dane* between *Ramsey* and *Whitlesey*.

Coacervate, *l*. heap toge-

Coacervation, a heaping or gathering together.

Coaction, *l*. the same, also a compelling.

Coadjutor, *l*. fellow-helper.

Coadjuvate, *l*. to help or assist together.

Coadunation, *l*. an assembling, or bringing together.

Coætaneous, *l*. of the same age.

Coæternal, *l*. Equal in Eternity,

Coagitate, to move or stir together.

Coagmentation, *l*. a joyning together, also (in chymistry) dissolving things and hardening them again.

Coagulation, *l*. a curdling; in chymistry the reducing any liquid thing to a thicker substance,

Coalesce, *l*. to grow together, to close together again.

Coalition, *l*. a growing together, an increasing.

Coamings, see *Comings*.

Coangustation, a making one thing straight (or narrow) with another.

Coaptation, *l*. a fitting together.

Coarctation, *l*. a straightning, or pressing together.

Coart, *o*. Enforce.

Coassation, *l*. a joyning together with boards.

Coates, peeces of tarr'd Canvas put about the masts at the deck, to keep the water out.

Coaxation, the croaking of Frogs.

Cob, a forced harbor for ships.

Cobby, stout, or brisk.

Cob-iron, *Es*. Andiron.

Coble-colter, *c*. a Turky.

Cobus, a River of *Colchis*, having golden sands.

Cobweb-morning, *Nf*. a misty morning.

Coccinean, of a crimson or scarlet colour.

Coccium, *Cockley* in *Lancashire*,

Cochineale, *Cuchanel*, a costly grain made of little worms proceeding from the fruit of the Holm-Oak, much used in dying Scarlet.

Cock-on-hoop, at the height of mirth and jollity; the Cock (or Spigot) being laid on the hoop, and the Baril of Ale stunn'd (as they say in *Staffordshire*) that is drunk out without intermission: or else

Cock-a-hoop, *Coq-à-hupe*, *f*. a Cock with a cop, crest or comb; also proud, stately, &c. and in this sence I have seen it joyn'd with *Top and top gallant*, which signifies Lofty, standing upon high terms.

Cockatrice, as *Basilisk*.

Cocket, brisk, malapert.

Cocket, the Custom-house-seal; also their Warrant to the Merchant that his goods are Customed.

Cocket-bread, Wheaten, next to wastel or white bread.

Cock-feather, that which stands upward in the right nocking of a shaft.

Cockle, a shel-fish; also a Cornweed.

Cockleary, pertaining to

Cockle-stairs, winding stairs.

Cockney, a child that sucks long, wantonly brought up, one born and bred in *London*, or (as they say) within the sound of Bow-bell; also an ancient name of the River *Thames*, or (as others say) the little brook by *Turn-mill street*: or else

Cockneigh, as if they could not distinguish the Crowing of a Cock, and the Neighing of a horse. See *Cokeney*.

Cocles, one born with one eye; also a *Roman* who alone withstood all the force of King *Porsena*, till the bridge was cut down from under him.

Coctile, *l*. easie to be boyled.

Coction, *l*. a seething, also digestion of meat.

Coctive, *l*. soon boil'd, soon ripe.

Cocks, square brasses (with holes) put into wooden sheaves, to keep them from splitting by the block-pin whereon they turn.

Coculus Indiæ, *Oculus In-*, a venemous drug used in the killing of lice, foxing of fish, Crows, &c.

Cocytus

Cocytus. a River of hell.

Cod, a pillow.

Code, *l.* book or volume of the Civil law.

Codebec, a kind of *French* hat so called, from

Codebec, a town upon the *Seine* in *Normandy*.

Codeta, Orchards about *Tiber*, wherein grow shrubs like horse-tails.

Codicil, a supplement to a will.

Codiniack, *f.* Marmalade of Quinces.

Codrus, an *Athenian* King who (in a disguise) exposed himself to death for his Country; because the Oracle said the *Peloponnesians* should overcome if they did not kill him.

Codware, Grain contained in Cods, as pease, &c.

Cœliaque artery, a main branch of the great artery, descending to the midriff and entrails.

Cœliacal vein, a second branch of the Mesenterique running to the blind gut.

Cœmitarie, *g.* Church-yard.

Coemptional, belonging to

Coemption, *l.* a *Roman* Ceremony. whereby the husband and wife seemed to buy one another.

Cœnotes, *g.* Community; also a figure whereby several clauses end alike.

Coëqual, *l.* equal to one another.

Coercible, which may be restrained.

Coercive, restraining, compelling.

Coertion, *l.* a restraining.

Cœrulean, *l.* sky-coloured.

Coessential, *l.* of the same essence.

Coetaneous. as *Coeta-*.

Coeternal, as *Coeter-*.

Coeval, of the same age or time.

Coexistent, having a being at the same time.

Coffa, and Coffee, as Caupbe.

Cofferer of the Kings h...hold, he is under the Controller, overlooks and paies the other Officers, &c.

Cog. *Cogle*, *o.* a Cockboat.

Coggeshall, a town in *Essex*.

Cogitation, *l.* a thinking.

Cogitative, thoughtfull, pensive, Musing.

Cognation, *l.* kindred [by bloud.]

Cogmen, dealers in

Cogware, Course Northern *English* cloth.

Cognisance, *-zance*, *f.* knowledge, a badge in armes, a Judicial hearing of a thing; also an acknowledging of a fine.

Cognisee, he to whom the fine is acknowledged.

Cognisour, he that acknowledges a fine.

Cognition, *l.* a knowing or Judging of a thing.

Cognitionibus mittendis, a writ, for him that takes a fine to certify it in the Common Pleas.

Cognominal, having one and the same name or Surname.

Cognominate, *l.* to give a Surname to any.

Cognoscible, *l.* knowable.

Cognoscitive, that knows or may be known or enquired.

Cogs, the outmost knots in a Mill-wheel, also a kind of boat.

Cohabite, *l.* dwell together.

Cohabitation, a dwelling together.

Cohere, *l.* hang together.

Coherence, *Cohesion*, *l.* a sticking or hanging together.

Cohibition, *-bency*, *l.* a restraining or keeping back.

Cohobation, pouring the distilled liquor on the dregs and distilling it again.

Cohort, *l.* the tenth part of a *Roman* Legion, 500 men.

Cohortation, exhortation, perswasion.

Coilons, *f.* the stones.

Coincidency, a happening at the same time, a being

Coïncident, *l.* falling out together, or one upon another.

Coins, *quines*, corners of walls, pieces of wood in mounting Ordinance, also Printers pins to fasten letters into the frames.

Coin the house, lay the corners or foundation with brick or stone.

Coinquinate, *l.* defile.

Coint, *o.* strange.

Coition, *l.* [carnal] coming together, also when the Sun and Moon are in the same sign and degree.

Cokermouth, a Town in *Cumberland*.

Coke, (*q. Coct.*) pit-coal (or Sea-coal) charred, also *Cook*, *o.*

Coker, *c.* a lye.

Cokeny, *o.* Cocket-bread.

Cokewold, *o.* Cuckold.

Cokoar, *Cocoar*, an Indian Nut-tree that bears both meat, drink and apparel.

Colaphize, *l.* buffet with the fist.

Colation, *-ture*, *l.* a straining.

Colatory, *l.* a strainer.

Colbrand, the Danish Giant overcom'n by *Guy* Earl of *Warwick*.

Colbrook, a Town upon

Cole, a River in *Bucks*.

Colechester, a Town upon.

Colne, a River in *Essex*.

Colchis, a Country in *Asia*, where *Æetes* reigned, with whom the *Argonauts* made war for the golden fleece.

Colfox, *o.* blackfox.

Colcothar, a caustick medicine.

Cole, keal, pottage.

Colefire, so much fire-wood as (when it is burnt) contains a load of Coals.

Coliberts, such as of Villains were made free men.

Colisæus, the Amphitheater of *Titus* at *Rome*.

Colick, a greivous pain of the bowels with difficulty of stool and wind.

Collabefaction, *l.* a destroying, wasting or decaying.

Collachrymate, *l.* weep or lament with others.

Collactaneous, nursed together, sucking at the same time.

Collapsed, *l.* fallen to decay.

Collaqueate, *l.* to entangle together.

Collaterally, ſide by ſide.

Collateral kindred, Uncles, Coſins, &c.

Colateral ſecurity, over and above the deed it ſelf, as a bond to a Covenant.

Collaterate, *l.* joyn ſide by ſide.

Collar, a great rope about the beakhead, to which the main-ſtay is faſten'd, alſo another about the main-maſt-head.

Collation, *l.* a little banquet, a comparing, a beſtowing [of a Benefice,] alſo folding of printed ſheets by the letters of direction.

Collatitious, done by conference or contribution of many.

Collative, *l.* Subſtant. an unanimous contribution of the people to any publick work, Adject. conferred together, made large, mutual.

Collaud, *l.* to praiſe with others.

Colleague, *l.* a partner in Office.

Collegate, *l.* to ſend together.

Collection, *l.* a gathering or Levy.

Collectitious, *-ctaneous*. *l.* gathered out of ſeveral things or places.

Collective Noun, though ſingular, comprehends many particulars, as a Company, &c.

Collect, *l.* gather together.

Collects, things gathered from others works, alſo ſelect prayers for certain times

Collegiate, one of the ſame

Colledge, *l.* ſociety [of ſtudents.]

Collens earth, a ſort of paint.

Colignia, a Town in *Braſile*, peopled by the French, and taken from them by the *Portugeſe*.

Colles Paſſion, *o.* the Cholick.

Collerage, a French fine upon the collars of Wine drawing Horſes or men.

Coller-dayes, Feſtivals, on which the Knights of the Garter wear their collars.

Collet, as *Beazel*, of a ring, alſo the throat.

Colly, the hawk collies, that is, beaks.

Collide, *l.* to knock or bruiſe together.

Colligate, *l.* tye together.

Colligence, a knitting, bringing or gathering together.

Collimation, *l.* an aiming.

Collineate, to level at, or hit the mark.

Colliquation, *l.* a melting.

Colliſion, *l.* a cruſhing together.

Colliſtrigiated, having ſtood in a

Colliſtrigium, *-idium*, Pillory.

Colligant, wrangling together.

Collocation, a placing in order, alſo a letting out to hire.

Collock, *Sa.* a one-handed pail, or great piggin.

Collogue, flatter.

Collonel, as *Colonel*.

Colloquy, *l.* diſcourſe between two.

Colluctation, *l.* a ſtrugling together.

Colluſion, *l.* fraud, deceitfull dealing.

Collybiſt, *g.* Mony-changer.

Collyrie, *-yre*, *g.* a medicine for the eyes.

Colne, a Town in *Lancaſhire*.

Colobe, an old kind of ſhort coat reaching to the knees.

Coloferos, a Religious order of *Grecians*.

Colon, *g.* half a period (:) alſo one of the three great guts.

Colony, *l.* a company ſent out of one Country to dwell in another.

Colophonia, the *Caput mortuum* of Turpentine, uſeful in ſalves, the liquid part being diſtilled into Oyl.

Coloquintida, *Collo-*, a purging wild gourd.

Coloration, *l.* the brightning of [obſcured] gold or Silver.

Coloſs, a ſtatue of a vaſt bigneſs, as that of the Sun at *Rhodes*, between whoſe feet the ſhips ſailed, alſo a Town in *Phrygia*.

Coloſtration, a diſtemper in Childrens Stomachs by ſucking the beeſtings or firſt milk.

Colp, *o.* a blow, alſo a bit of any thing.

Colpindach, *Cowdach*, *Sc.* a young cow or heifer.

Colquarron, *c.* a [mans] neck.

Colran, *Krien*, a County in *Ireland*.

Colubraria, an *Iberian* Iſland full of Snakes.

Colubriferous, *l.* that bears Snakes or Serpents.

Coludum, *Coldana*, *Coldingham*, in *Scotland*, where the Nuns (and Prioreſs *Ebba*) cut off their lips and noſes, to ſhun the luſt of the *Danes*.

Columb-Great, A Town in *Cornwall*.

Columbary, *l.* Dove-houſe.

Columbine, *l.* Dove-like.

Columity, *l.* health, ſafety, ſoundneſs.

Column, *l.* Pillar; alſo one diviſion of a page at length.

Columnary tribute, was exacted for every pillar in a houſe.

Columnæ Herculis, *Hercules*'s Pillars; by ſome, two brazen pillars in *Cadez*; by others, two weſtern Mountains ſeparated by *Hercules*, *Calpe* in *Europe* and *Abyla* in *Africa*.

Columpton, A Town in *Devon*.

Colures, Two Circles which paſs through the Poles, and divide the Globe (like an apple) into four equal parts.

Colus, A whitiſh beaſt with a hogs head, that drinks through the noſtrils.

Colutea, a kind of baſtard Sena, in gardens of rarities.

Coma Berenices, a triangle in the tail of *Leo*.

Comald, *-da*, an Order of *Italian* white Fryars inſtituted, *Anno* 1012.

Comarch, *-ark*, *g.* a Governour

nour of town or city, an Earl.

Comaunce, o. community.

Combat, (in law) the tryal of a doubtfull cause by two Champions.

Combe, f. a valleybe tween two high Hills.

Combe, 4 bushels; also a small piece of Timber under the beak-head, used in bringing the tack aboard.

Combinational, belonging to

Combination, l. a joyning together; also a conspiracy.

Combustible, l. apt to take fire, as brush-wood, &c.

Combustion, a burning together, also a tumult.

Combustion of a Planet, when he is not 8 Degrees and 3 minutes distant from the Sun.

Comeling, Sa. a New-comer, a stranger.

Commessation, l. Revelling, intemperate eating and drinking.

Comestible. eatable.

Comestion, l. eating up.

Comet, g. a [hairy] Blazing star.

Comical, pertaining to

Comedies, Merry Playes: and

Comedians, the Actors, or as

Comediographers, Writers of Comedies.

Comfry, *Bone-set*, an herb usefull both in meat and medicine.

Comings [*of the hatches*,] the planks that bear them up above the deck.

Comminus pugnator, l. he that fights hand to hand.

Comitatu Commisso, a writ authorizing the Sheriff to take the county upon him.

Comitatu & Castro Commisso, the committing of a county (together with a castle) to the Sheriff.

Comity, l. courteous and civil behaviour.

Comitial, belonging to

Comices, l. Solemn assemblies of the people of *Rome*.

Comitial [*disease*,] the falling sickness.

Comma g. (Section, cutting,) the smallest of our stops (,).

Commaculate, l. defile.

Commasculate, to take heart or hardiness.

Commaterial, l. made of the same substance or matter.

Commaundry, -*andry*, Lands formerly belonging to the priory of St. *John* of *Jerusalem*.

Commeator, l. a Messenger that goes to and fro.

Commemoration, l. remembrance or calling to mind.

Commence, f. begin, also proceed in a suit; also take a degree in the University.

Commencement (at *Cambridge*) the same as the Act at *Oxford*, when they become graduates.

Commendaces, prayers for the dead, also Verses or Orations in their praise.

Commendatary, he that hath or sues for a

Commendam, He hath a Benefice in *Com.* to who's care it is commended, till it can be conveniently supply'd.

Commendatory [*letters*] recommending one.

Commendation, l. praise.

Commendator, a *Dutch* President or Consul in the *Indies*.

Commensal, l. Fellow commoner, companion at Table.

Commensuration, l. a measuring one thing with another.

Commensurability, an equal proportion or measure of one thing with another.

Comment, -*tary*, f. an exposition of any text.

Commentatour, he that doth

Comment, write Comments.

Commentitious, l. feigned, counterfeit.

Commerce, f. Trade

Commessation, as *Comess*-.

Commigration, l. a removing from one place to another.

Commilitone, l. a comrade, fellow-souldier.

Commination, l. a vehement threatning.

Comminuible, that may be bruised, or broken in pieces.

Comminution, a breaking to pieces.

Commiseration, compassion.

Commissary, he exercises Ecclesiastical jurisdiction in the remoter parts of the Diocess, also (in war) one that looks to the distribution of Victuals in the Army and Garrisons.

Commissioner, he that hath a

Commission, l. a delegation, Mandate or Warrant given for the exercising of a jurisdiction.

Commission of Association, is to associate others to the Justices in their circuits.

Commission of Anticipation, was for the collecting a subsidy before the day.

Commission or Writ of rebellion is for the apprehending of such a one as a rebel, who doth not appear upon proclamation.

Commissure, l. a putting together, the joyning of the skul on the mould of the head; also of planks, stones, or any materials.

Committee, he or they to whom the ordering of any matter is referred.

Commixtion, l. a mingling together.

Commodious, profitable, or convenient.

Commodity, convenience, also Merchandize.

Commoigne, f. A fellow-Monk of the same Convent.

Common, Soil or water, whose use is common.

Commoning, Partaking.

Common Hunt, The Lord Major of *London's* Cheif huntsman Esq; by his place.

Commonalty, *Commin-* the common people.

Common Bench, as

Common-pleas, A Court in *Westminster* erected by *Hen.* 3. for all civil causes real and personal.

Common fine, Cert-money.

Common Law, is sometimes oppos'd to Spiritual, Admiralty, &c. Sometime to Customary & all other base courts, but most usually it is such laws as were before any statute altered them.

Commoration, *-rance*, *l.* a tarrying.

Commotion, *l.* a stir or tumult.

Commote, *Commoithe*, *Br.* 50 Villages, half a Cantred or a Hundred of a shire, or a Collection made there.

Commune, common; also to discourse.

Communication, Conversation, also as

Communicating, imparting to one another.

Community, mutual participation, injoying in Common.

Communion, the same; also the Sacrament of the Lords supper.

Communition. *l.* a fortifying.

Commutation, *l.* a changing one thing for another.

Commutative justice, in buying and selling, borrowing and lending, performing Covenants, &c.

Comædy, as Comedy, a pleasant personal representation of the common actions of humane life.

Compact, *l.* agreement.

Compaction, *-page*, *l.* a joyning close together, Contraction.

Compaginate, *l.* to couple or knit together.

Compagnia [*de morti*,] a Religious Order in *Italy*, who are to bury the dead and visit condemned persons.

Companion of the Garter, one of those Knights.

Companage, *l.* all kind of victuals eaten with bread.

Compar, as Isocolon, of equal members or parts.

Comparats, *l.* things compared together.

Comparition, *l.* an appearing in open view.

Comparative, belonging to

Comparation, Comparison, comparing together.

Comparative degree, hath the sign *More* or termination *er*, as harder or more hard.

Compart, *Compartment*, *f.* a square [stone] piece in building; a Garden-bed or border; a partition or equal division.

Compartition, the same; also a graceful and usefull distribution of the whole plot of ground, for all kind of rooms.

Compass, a pair of Compasses wherewith Circles are made, also (at sea) a round pastboard with all the 32 winds described, and (under the North) a needle pointing Northward.

Compass Callipers, (with blunt ends) are used in disperting a piece of Ordnance.

Compassionate, tender-hearted, full of

Compassion, a fellow-feeling, suffering together.

Compatible, *f.* which can abide, agree or be together.

Compatient, *l.* suffering together.

Compatriot, *l.* one of the same City or Country.

Compeer, *l.* Consort, fellow, also Gossip, and (in some places) all the young men invited to the same wedding.

Compel, *l.* to force.

Compellation, *l.* a calling one by their name; also an opprobrious mentioning.

Compendiousness, a being

Compendious, *l.* short or brief.

Compendium, *l.* abridgment also a gaining by Thrift.

Compensable, *f.* able to recompense, or make amends.

Compensation, *l.* requiting, making up, repaying [a good or bad turn.]

Comperage, *f.* gossiping, also the affinity or friendship gotten by being Gossips.

Comperendination, *l.* a deferring or putting off [from day to day.]

Competency, *l.* a sufficiency, enough.

Competize, to stand in

Competition, *l.* a rivalship, the being

Competitour, *l.* a rival, one that seeks after the same thing as you do.

Competible, that may be sued for with another; also that may be convenient or agreeable.

Compile, *f.* heap together.

Compinable, *o.* fit for company.

Compitalitious, belonging to

Compitals, feasts celebrated in the

Compita, *l.* Cross-waies.

Compital. belonging thereto.

Complaisant, *Complacential*, *-tious*, *l.* of a courteous pleasing behaviour.

Complainant, complaining to a Magistrate [for relief.]

Complaisance, *f.* an obliging carriage, aptness to comply.

Complacence, the same, also as

Complacency, a taking delight or being well pleased with.

Complemental. belonging to

Complement, *l.* a filling up; also a choice of the best words to express our minds by; and (corruptly) too much ceremony in speech and behaviour.

Complement [*of an Angle*,] so much as it wants of 90 degrees.

Completes, *Sp.* the last or closing prayers of the Evening: See *Compline*.

Completion, *l.* a fulfilling performing.

Complex, *l.* compounded of several [things, notions, &c.]

Complexion, *l.* the state and constitution of the body; also (the index thereof) the colour; countenance.

Complicate, *l.* wrap or fold up.

Complicated disease, of many distempers meeting together.

Complices, Partners [in evil.]

Complicity, such partnership.

Compline, *f.* *Complitory*, *l.* the last of the Canonical hours, beginning at nine a clock at night.

Complore, *l.* bewail or weep together.

Comportment, *f.* carriage or behaviour.

Composition, *l.* a putting together, also a [written] work also a compounding or agreement.

Compositor, he that doth

Compose, *l.* put [the printing letters] together.

Compost, *f.* a composition, also soil or dung for trees, Land, &c.

Compotation, *l.* a drinking-bout, a merry meeting.

Compotist, *Computist*, *l.* a computer, reckoner, calculator, caster of accounts.

Comprecation, *l.* a praying,

Comprehension, *l.* a taking in or together, also understanding or finding the depth of a mystery.

Comprehensible, that may be

Comprehended, contained and laid hold of.

Comprehensive, large, taking in, or containing much.

Compression, *-sure*, *l.* a pressing together.

Comprint, to print anothers copy or to print one upon another.

Comprise, comprehend, contain, take in.

Comprobation, *l.* a mutual approving or allowing.

Compromise, *f.* a mutual promise of Parties at difference, to refer the business to Arbitratours also that power of the Arbitratours to decide the matter.

Compromissorial, belonging thereto.

Compton in the hole, a Town in *Warwik shire*.

Comptroller, as *Controller*.

Compulsion, *l.* a constraining.

Compunction, *l.* pricking, remorse, trouble of mind for a fault committed.

Compurgation, *l.* a justifying (by oath) the report or oath of another.

Compurgator, *l.* a cleanser, clearer, purger.

Computable, capable of

Computation, *l.* a reckoning, or casting of accounts.

Computo, the same as

De Computo reddendo, a writ compelling a Bailiff, &c. to give up his accounts.

Comrade, or *Camerade*.

Comsed, *o.* (for commenced) began.

Comus, a Heathen God, the cheif patron of revellings and debaucheries.

Con, *o.* ken.

Conabel, *-byl*, convenient.

Concani, *Gargani*, people of

Conaught, *Connaught*, a Province in *Ireland*.

Conoamerate, *l.* to arch or make a vaulted roof.

Concatinate, *l.* to chain together.

Concatination, a linking together.

Concave, hollow, also hollowness, the bore of a piece.

Concavity, *l.* hollowness.

Concavous, hollow.

Concealers, they that find out Lands privily concealed from the King or state.

Concede, *l.* yield, grant.

Concent, *-tion*, *l.* an agreement or harmony [in musick.]

Concentrick, having one common center.

Concepticle, *l.* a large hollowness able to receive [any thing.]

Conception, a conceiving with Child, also a thought, fancy or conceit.

Concern, to busie, regard or belong to.

Concern, *-nment*, business, affair, also moment or weight.

Concert, *f.* as *Concent*, also to set [a business] in order.

Concertation, *l.* a striving or disputing together.

Concessi, *l.* (I have granted) this word (in Law) creates a Covenant.

Concession, *l.* a grant or yielding.

Concidence, a falling or making a Cadence together.

Conciliate, to procure, also to make to agree.

Concinnate, *l.* apt, fit, proper, also neat.

Concinnity, *l.* handsomeness, aptness, decency.

Concional, belonging to

Concion, *l.* a publick speech.

Concionator, he that preaches or makes an Oration to the people.

Concise, *l.* cut short, of few words.

Concision, *-sure*, *l.* a cutting dividing, rent or schism.

Concitation, *l.* a stirring up or provoking.

Conclamation, *l.* a great noise or shouting of many.

Conclave, a closet or inner room, also the chamber or Assembly of the Roman Cardinals.

Conclavist, one that meets there, or has the keeping of it.

Conclusion, *l.* a shutting up, the ending of a business.

Conclusive, concluding, shutting up, ending.

Concoction, a boyling, also digesting of the meat in the Stomach.

Concomitant, *l.* bearing company or going along with.

Concord, *l.* agreement, also (in musick) an agreeing Note as an eight, fifth, &c.

Concordance, the same, also a Catalogue of all (or the cheifest) Bible-words, and their places.

Concordate, *l.* to agree.

Concorporation, *l.* a mixing of bodies together.

Concourse, l. a meeting together.

Concratitious, l. watled with rods made like hurdles, &c.

Concredited, delivered, lent or trusted together.

Concrete, l. joyned or grown together. also an accident or quality joyned with the subject.

Concreted, -*tive*, congealed or grown together.

Concretion, -*ment*, l. a growing or joining together.

Concrimination, a joint accusing.

Concubinage, f. fornication, also an exception against her that sues for dowry alledging that she is not wife but concubine.

Concubinal, -*nary*, belonging to a

Concubine halfwife.

Conculcate, l. to trample upon, or tread under foot. (ther.

Concumbence, l. a lying toge-

Concupiscence, l. lust or vehement desire.

Concupiscible, desiring earnestly or naturally, also desireable

Concupiscible faculty, the sensual power of the soul, seeking only pleasures.

Concurrence, l. a meeting together, an agreeing.

Concussion, l. a shaking together, also a publick extortion by threatning.

Concussionary, an Officer extorting gifts and bribes, under pretence of authority.

Cond, *or Cun the ship*, give directions to him at helm, which way he should steer.

Condense, l. thicken.

Condensity, l. thickness.

Condensation, l. a making thick.

Condercum, *Chester* on the Street, a Town in the Bishoprick of *Durham*.

Conders, *Huers*, *Balcers Balkers*, they stand on hills (by the sea) with boughs in their hands, to direct the Fishers which way the Herrings pass. (down

Condescend, l. step or stoop

Condescension, a compliance, or yielding to

Condict, l. an appointment or composition.

Condign [punishment] worthy, deserved.

Condiment, l. sauce, seasoning.

Condisciple, l. school-fellow, fellow-student.

Condise, o. Conduits.

Conditaneous, l. that which may be

Condited, l. seasoned, sawced, preserved.

Condite, o. conduct.

Condition, nature or disposition, estate or fortune, also a supposition (if, &c.)

Conditional, having a condition or supposition.

Conditor, l. a builder, maker.

Conditor, l. a seasoner, temperer.

Condolence, l. a grieving with another.

Condone, -*nate*, l. forgive.

Condonation, l. a pardoning or forgiving.

Conducible, l. profitable, also to be hired.

Conductor, he that doth

Conduct, f. guide or lead.

Conduct, guidance, also management of business.

Conductitious, that may be led, hired, or gathered together.

Condylome, g. excrescent flesh or swelling (like a knuckle) about the fundament.

Cone, l. a Geometrical figure like a pyramid, nine-pin or sugar-loaf.

Cone & Colne, sa. an account. A Woman was reckon'd to be of competent years, when she was able to keep

Conc and key, the account and keyes [of the house.]

Confabulation, a discoursing together.

Confarreated, married with

Confarreation, l a wedding ceremony, like the breaking of our Bride-cake.

Confeck, c. counterfeit.

Confection, l. a finishing or mingling, also the making of

Confits, *Comfits*, sweet-meats.

Confectioner, a maker of sweet-meats.

Confectionary, the same, also the place where they are kept.

Confeder, to joyn together in a league.

Confederate, as *Confœderate*.

Confertion, a stuffing.

Confessionary, f. belonging to [auricular] Confession; also the confession seat.

Confessour, he to whom you confess your self.

Conficient, finishing, procuring, working.

Confide, l. to trust, rely upon

Confidence, boldness, assurance.

Confident, bold, sure, assured, [sometimes] impudent, also he to whom trust and secresie is committed.

Configulate, l. play the potter.

Configulation, l. making of earthen ware.

Configuration, l. likeness of figures, the mutual aspects of Planets.

Confines, f. borders of a Country.

Confer, l. compare, also to talk or reason together.

Conference, a meeting together [for discourse.]

Confine, to limit, to imprison.

Confinement, imprisonment, or being ty'd to a certain place.

Confirmation, l. a strengthening or making sure.

Confiscation, l. taking away goods (as forfeited) to the *Fiscus* or publick treasury.

Confitent, penitent, confessor.

Conflagitate, l. to desire a thing importunately.

Conflagration, a great burning.

Conflagrant, burning; also earnestly desiring.

Conflature, l. the melting or casting of metal

Confluctuate, l. to flow together, to be uncertain what to do.

Confluence, *-flux*, *l.* a flowing or meeting together.

Confluxibility, an aptness to flow or be mingled together.

Confederate, joyned together [by Covenant.]

Conforaneous, *l.* of the same court or Market place.

Conformable, agreeable, suitable.

Conformist, one that doth

Conform, suit himself to [the Church of *England*.]

Confrairie, *f.* fraternity, society, brotherhood.

Confrication, *l.* a rubbing.

Confreres, *-freres*, *f.* Brethen or fellows of the same house.

Confront, *f.* come face to face, oppose; also compare.

Confusion, *l.* pouring, mixing, or jumbling together, disorder, disturbance, also blushing or being out of countenance.

Congayne, *o.* convince.

Congaye, *o.* send away.

Congé, *f.* leave, also a ceremony (bowing, &c.) in taking ones leave.

Congéd' accorder, *f.* (leave to agree) desiring the Justice to give them leave to agree.

Congé d' elire, or *eslire*, *f.* (leave to choose) the Kings permission to a Dean and Chapter to choose a Bishop.

Congeable, lawful, or lawfully done.

Congenerous, *-nious*, *l.* of the same sort or kinred.

Congeniality, a being

Congenial, *l.* alike in Genius, fancy or disposition.

Congelation, *l.* a congealing, freezing, or growing like to Ice.

Congelative, having the power to Congeal or dry up.

Congeon, *o.* a Dwarffe.

Conger, *l.* a large Sea-Eel.

Congeriate, pile up, heap together.

Congersbury, a Town in *Somersetshire*, from

Congar, an Eremite there, affirmed (by *Capgrave*) to be the Emperors Son of *Constantinople*.

Congius, *l.* a Gallon [and a little more.]

Congiary, *l.* a Great persons gift to the people.

Conglaciate, *l.* to freeze, also to be idle.

Congleton, a town in *Chesh.*

Conglobation, *l.* a gathering round, into a Globe.

Conglomeration, *l.* a rolling or winding up into a bottom or heap.

Conglutinative, that which hath strength to

Conglutinate, *l.* glue or joyn together.

Conglutination, *l.* a gluing together.

Congratulation, *l.* a rejoycing with another.

Congregational, belonging to

Congregation, *l.* an Assembly assembling or gathering together.

Congregationalists Independants, Dissenting Brethren, who gathered particular Congregations in a middle way between *Presbytery* and *Brownism.*

Congress, *l.* a meeting, encounter.

Congruence, *-ity*, *l.* agreeableness, a being

Congruous, convenient, fit.

Conical, belonging to a *Cone.*

Conical sections make the *Ellipsis*, *hyperbole* and *parabola.*

Conjectural, belonging to

Conjecture, *l.* guess.

Coninesborough, a Castle in *Yorkshire*, where *Hengist* was beheaded.

Coniferous trees, bearing

Cones or *Clogs*, as the fir, pine, &c.

Conjugal, belonging to marriage.

Conjugates, *l.* things of the same rank, order or original.

Conjugation, deriving of things under the same order, particularly of verbs in their moods, tenses, &c.

Conjunction, *l.* a joyning or meeting together, also the particle that joyns or disjoyns words and sentences.

Conjunctive, belonging thereto.

Conjunctive mood, Subjunctive.

Conjunctiva, a Coat of the eye [sticking fast.]

Conjuncture, a joyning together.

Conjuration, *l.* a conspiracy or plot, also a Charm.

Conjurer, he that doth

Conjure, *l.* raise or deal with the devil.

Conjúre, swear together, also to swear one in the name and power of another.

Conizee, as *Cognisee.*

Conizour, as *Cognisour.*

Connascency, *l.* a being born or springing together.

Conne, *ken*, learn [without book.]

Connen, *o.* Can.

Connexive, having the power of, or belonging to

Connexion, *l.* a knitting or joyning together.

Connex (in Logick) things joyn'd without any dependence or Consecution.

Connictation, a twinkling of the eye.

Connivence, *l.* a winking [at a fault.]

Connubial, belonging to wedlock.

Connutritious, nourished or brought up together.

Connovium, *Conwey* in *Wales.*

Conquassation, *l.* a shaking or dashing together.

Conquest, *f.* Victory; also Lands held by some private Title, not by Inheritance.

Conquestion, *l.* a Complaining together.

Conradus, *Ge.* able Counsel.

Consanguinity, Kindred by Bloud.

Consarcination, *l.* a patching together.

Conscension, *l.* a Climbing.

Conscientious, according to

Conscience, the witness of ones own heart.

Conscious, *l.* [knowing ones self] guilty.

Conscission, a cutting.

Conscissure, a gash, cut or rent.

Conscription, *l.* a registering,

Consecration, l. Hallowing, setting apart for divine service.

Consectaneous, *-cutif*, *-tive*, following, or succeeding.

Consectary, l. That which follows upon the demonstration of an argument.

Consectatour, He that follows or pursues.

Consecution, A following.

Consecution-month, the space between each Conjunction of the Moon with the Sun.

Conseminate, l. Sow divers seeds together.

Consentient, l. Agreeing.

Consequence, l. a following or conclusion, Also weight and moment.

Consequent, Following, or a following Conclusion.

Consequentious, important, necessarily following.

Conservation, A preserving.

Conservator, l. Keeper, overseer.

Conservatory, [A place for] preserving or keeping.

Conserves, f. Fruits being

Conserved, Condited.

Consession, A sitting together.

Consideration, An advising or taking heed; also a condition upon which a thing is done, an allowance.

Consignificative, Of the same signification with another.

Consignation, Ones own signing of a Bil.

Consign, Present, deliver, assign over.

Consimilarity, Likeness.

Consistence, a being, also setling and growing stiff or hard

Consistent, Agreeable, also standing, not fluid

Consistory, l. An Assembly of Church-men, also the place.

Consition, l. A planting together.

Consolatory, Comforting, belonging to

Consolation, l. A Comforting.

Consolidation. A strengthening or making sold; also the uniting a Benefices, also the joyning of possession or profit with the property.

Consomniation, A sleeping or dreaming together.

Consonant, agreeing [in sound;] also a letter which is not a vowel.

Consort, A Companion; also a company [of Musicians.]

Consound, Cumfry, backwort, knit-back.

Conspersion, a sprinkling.

Conspicuous, l. easie to be seen.

Conspiratione, a writ against

Conspiratours, guilty of

Conspiracy, evil and malicious plotting together.

Conspurcation, a defiling.

Consputation, a spitting upon.

Consputator, he that spits upon others.

Constablerie, o. the office, jurisdiction and dignity of a

Constable, f. (q. *Comes stabuli*) master of the horse.

High Constables, are over hundreds,

Petty Constables in Parishes, for conservation of the peace.

Constable of the Tower, *Dover-Castle*, &c. cheif Governour.

Constant, l. standing firm.

Constantinople, *Byzantium* the Port, the seat of the Great Turk, repaired, beautify'd and named from

Constantine the great, the first Christian Emperour of *Rome*

Constat, l. (it is evident) a certificate given out of the Court of all that is on record touching such or such a matter.

Constellation, a Company of stars in some figure.

Consternation, amazement.

Constipation, a standing close together, a guarding.

Constitution, an appointment, also the state and condition [of any thing.]

Constrain, to compel.

Constraint, force.

Constriction, the same, also a binding together.

Constrictive, binding.

Construction, a placing or joyning together, also interpretation or meaning.

Construe, expound, unfold.

Constupration, a ravishing of a virgin.

Consubstantiality, a being

Consubstantial, of the same substance.

Consuet, *-tudinal*, usual, accustomed.

Consuetude, l. a custom.

Consuetudinibus & servitiis, a writ for rent or service failing.

Consular, belonging to the

Consulship, the office of a

Consul, chief Governour.

Two *Consuls* were chosen yearly at *Rome*, instead of the Kings.

Five yearly *Consuls* (at *Paris*) determine all cases of debt not exceeding 4000 livres.

Consultation, a taking Counsel; also a writ returning a cause from the Kings to the Ecclesiastical Court.

Consummate, summe up, make perfect, also as

Consummated, perfected, accomplished.

Consummation, l. a fulfilling, perfecting.

Consumption, a wasting.

Contabulation, planking, fastening of planks together.

Contaction, a touching together.

Contagion, infection.

Contagious, l. infectious.

Contamination, a polluting.

Conteke, *-teck*, o. strife, contention,

Contemeration, a violating, deflowring.

Contemplation, a deep considering, meditating.

Contemplative, thereto belonging.

Contemplatives, Fryers of the Order of St *Mary Magdalene*.

Contemporianism, Coexistency, a being

Contemporal, *-ary*, *-aneous*, of the same time.

Contemptible, l. base, to be

Contemned, slighted, scorned.

Con-

Contemptuous, reproachful, scornful, slighting.

Con-tenement, the freehold which lies to a tenement.

Contention, *l.* strife.

Contermination, a bordering upon.

Conterpleted, *o.* controlled.

Conterraneous, of the same Land or Countrey.

Contesseration, entring into league or friendship.

Contest, *l.* a fellow witness.

Contestate, to bear or prove by witness.

Contestation, Calling to witness.

Context, *-ture*, *l.* (weaving together) the form or style of a process or discourse, also the adjoyning matter of it.

Contignation, raftering, the floor-work.

Contiguity, a being

Contiguous, near or touching one another.

Continence, *-cy*, *l.* a being

Continent, temperate, also the main Land.

Contingent, casual, hapning.

Contingence, *-cy*, a falling out by chance.

Contingent propositions, may (as it fals out) be true or false.

Continual, without intermission.

Continual claim, (to Land, &c.) made from time to time, within every year and day.

Continuance untill next Assizes, Prorogation, putting off till then.

Continuand, when the Plaintiff would recover dammages for several trespasses in the same action.

Continuation, *-nity*, a lengthning or going on with a business.

Contorsion, a wresting, pulling awry.

Contrabanded, [goods] forbidden importation.

Contraction, *l.* *Contratation*, *Sp.* making of a

Contract, or bargain.

Contract, *l.* shorten, draw together.

Contraction, a drawing together.

Contradictory, contrary by Affirmation and Negation, full of

Contradiction, 'gainsaying.

Contrafaction, a counterfeiting.

Contra formam collationis, a Writ against an Abbot for making a Feoffement of Land given to the Abby.

Contra formam Feoffamenti, when a Tenant enfeoffed by the Lords Charter to make certain suit and service to his Court, is distrained for more than is there contained.

Contramure, *Counterscarf*, an out-wall built about another wall.

Contrariety, a being

Contrary, against one another

Contraries, opposites wherein one is oppos'd to the other.

Contrasto, *Sp.* Contention.

Contragerva, a West-Indian-plant much used in Counterpoysons.

Contratation, *Sp.* a contract or bargain.

Contravention, a coming or speaking against.

Contrectation, [a wanton] handling.

Contribution, mony or supplies (given or forced) from many.

Contribution facienda, a writ, when the whole burden lies upon one, though more be bound thereto.

Contristation, *l.* a grieving or making sad.

Contrite, bruised, also penitent.

Contrition, *l.* a bruising or breaking, also remorse or trouble of mind.

Controller, an Officer who keeps a roll of other Officers accounts.

Controller of the hamper, he takes all things sealed in leather-bags from the Clark of the hamper.

Controller of the Pipe, he writes summons to the Sheriffs, to levy the debts of the Pipe.

Controller of the Pell, keeps a Controlment of the Pell, of Receipts and goings-out.

Controve, *o.* devise, contrive.

Controver, he that invents false news.

Controversie, a dispute.

Controverted [points] argued pro and con.

Contrucidate, *l.* kill.

Contumacy, *l.* stubbornness.

Contumelious, full of

Contumely reproach.

Contumulation, an intombing or burying together.

Contune, *o.* for continue.

Contund, knock down, beat in pieces, subdue.

Contusion, a bruising, beating, pounding to powder.

Convail, *o.* to recover.

Convalesce, *l.* to wax strong.

Convalescency, a recovering of health.

Convalidate, strengthen, confirm.

Convene, *l.* come together, also to summon one to appear.

Convenience, *-cy*, fitness.

Convent, *Covent*, Monastery, a Religious House.

Conventicle, *l.* a private assembly.

Conventional, belonging to

Convention, an assembly, also a summoning.

Conventione, a writ for the breach of a written Covenant.

Conventual, belonging to a company of religious persons.

Conventual Church, belonging to a Convent.

Conversation, a being

Conversant, keeping company.

Conversion, a change.

Convert, *l.* turn.

Convert, one turned [to the Faith.]

Convertite, the same.

Convex, of a round outside.

Convexity, the outside of a Globe.

Convict, *-ed*, proved guilty.

Conviction, proving a man guilty (by witnesses or confession.)

Convictor, *l.* a boarder.

Convi-

Convivial, belonging to a feaſt.

Convocation-houſe, for the *Convocation*, Aſſembly of the Clergy.

Convoke, *l.* call together.

Convoy, *f.* Conduct, guide.

Conuſant, *f.* knowing, underſtanding.

Convulſion, a violent pulling together [of Sinews, &c.]

Cooliß, *Coulis*, as *Cullis*.

Coom, the ſoot that gathers over the ovens mouth.

Cook-room, a ſhips Kitchin, in a Merchant mans forecaſtle, and (generally) in a Frigates hold.

Coomb, *So.* half a quarter of Corn.

Co-operate, *l.* to work together.

Coöptate, *l.* to Elect or chuſe together.

Coöpertura, a thicket or covert of wood.

Coot, a Moor-hen.

Copal, a perfume, of white Roſin from the Weſt-Indies.

Cope, Cloak, alſo a veſtment Biſhops were wont to wear, alſo a cuſtom (6d a load) paid out of the lead-mines in *Derbyſhire*, alſo the top of an high hill.

Cope the Wall, cover it.

Cope, *Nf. Sf.* Chop or exchange.

Coparceners, *Parceners*, ſuch as have Equal ſhare in the inheritance of their Anceſtors.

Copes-mate, a partner in Merchandize.

Cophoſis, *g.* a growing deaf.

Copia libelli deliberanda, a writ for the Copy of a Libel from an Eccleſiaſtical Judge.

Coping, the top or roof of a wall.

Copy-hold, a tenure by a Copy of the Rolls made by the Lords Steward.

Copioſity, a being

Copious, *l.* plentifull

Copiſe, *Copſe*, a little wood of underwoods to be cut down before they be great trees.

Copland, *Sa.* a headland or hadland into which the reſt of the lands in a furlong do ſhoot.

Coporas, Vitriol.

Coppenhagen, the Chief City in *Denmark*.

Copulation, a joyning together.

Copulative, joyning, coupling.

Copie, *-py*, *l.* plenty.

Coquettery, *f.* a prating like a Goſſip.

Coquinate, to play the Cook.

Coquination, a Cooking of meat.

Coraage, an impoſition upon certain Meaſures of corn.

Cor Scorpij, the heart of the Scorpion, a Conſtellation.

Coral, *Corral*, *l.* a Sea-plant growing hard as ſtone and red, when taken out of the water.

Coralline, Sea-moſs, Coral-moſs, a plant.

Coralwort, *Toothwort*, an herb near *Mayfield* in *Suſſex*.

Coram non judice, in a cauſe whereof the Judges have no juriſdiction.

Coram nobis, *l.* before us.

Coranto, a *French* running dance, alſo a News-book.

Corare, *o.* overcome.

Coraſines, Northern people of *Aſia*, who (by the Conſent of the Sultan of *Babylon*) ſubdued all the *Elpians* in *Paleſtine*, and were themſelves utterly rooted out by the Sultan.

Corban, *Kor-*, *h.* a gift dedicated to God, alſo the cheſt (in the Temple) receiving it.

Corbel, *-bet*, *-bil*, a ſhouldering piece in timberwork, jutting out like a bragget.

Corbets an Ancient Family in *Shropſhire*, alſo, *o.* ſtones wherein images ſtand.

Corciouſneß, *o.* corpulency.

Corck, *Orchal*, a kind of blue paint.

Cord [*of firewood*] 4 foot in breadth, 4 in height, and 8 in length.

Cordage, the tackle of a ſhip, alſo ſtuff to make ropes of.

Cordelier, *f.* a Gray Franciſcan Fryer.

Cordial, *l.* hearty.

Cordon, *o.* reward, alſo the end of the parapet towards the muraille.

Corduvan, belonging to *Corduba*, a City in *Spain*.

Cordwane, *o.* a dry hide.

Cordwainer, *Cordinar*, *f.* a Shoe-maker.

Coriander, an herb like parſley.

Coriged, *o.* corrected.

Corinæus, *Brutus's* Companion who ſlew the giant *Gogmagog*.

Corinthian, belonging to *Corinth*, a City of *Achaia*.

Coritani, the ancient inhabitants of *Northampton*, *Leiceſter*, *Rutland*, *Lincolnſhire*, *Nottingamſhire*, and *Darbyſhire*.

Cork, part of *Ireland*.

Cormandel, in the Eaſt-Indies, where ſtands Fort St. *George*.

Cormorant, a Sea-Raven.

Cornage, an impoſition upon Corn; alſo a Northern tenure by blowing of a horn on the approach of an enemy.

Cornalin, a kind of precious ſtone.

Cornavij, ancient inhabiters of *Warwickſhire*, *Worceſter*, *Staffordſhire*, *Shropſhire*, and *Cheſhire*.

Corn-flower, blue-bottle.

Cornea, the horny Coat of the eye.

Cornelian, *Corneol*, a red precious ſtone.

Corneltan law, made by *Cornelius Sylla*, Dictatour of *Rome*, that all that followed him to the war, ſhould be capable of bearing office before their time.

Cornel, *o.* Corner; alſo the forepart of a houſe.

Corneol, *Sardis*, *Onyx*, a ſtone uſed much for ſeals.

Corneous, horny.

Cornet, *f.* a black taffaty the badg of Doctors of Phyſick or Law, alſo the Enſign of a Troop.

Cornice, *frize*, *f.* the Creſts or flouriſhing work at the upper end of a pillar.

Cornicle, *l.* a little horn.

Cornigerous, horn-wearing [*Bacchus*.]

Cornil tree, horn-tree.

Cornimuſe, *f.* bag-pipe.

Cornix, as *Cornelix*, *Corneol*.

Cornu Cervi, the mouth of an *Alembick*.

Cornucopia, *-pie*, a horn (with plenty of all things) given by *Jupiter* to his nurſe *Amalthea*.

Cornuted, horned.

Corny ale, *o.* ſtrong.

Corody, *Corr-*, an allowance to any of the Kings ſervants from an Abby, &c. whereof he is Founder.

Corodio habendo, a writ for the exacting thereof.

Corollary, advantage above the ordinary meaſure, alſo a gift to the people at publick feaſts.

Coromandel, part of *Eaſt-India*.

Corona, *l.* Halo, a clear circle about the Moon, &c. alſo a Conſtellation on the Shoulder of *Boötes*.

Coronal arterys, two little branches of the great artery, to the left ventricle and broad end of the heart.

Coronal vein, a branch of the Spleen-vein, about the heart like a Crown.

Coronal ſuture, the foremoſt ſeam of the skull, from temple to temple.

Coronary, belonging to a Crown.

Coronation, *l.* a Crowning.

Coronatore eligendo, a writ for the Freeholders to chooſe a

Coroner, an Officer who is to enquire into all untimely deaths, (uſually 4, ſometimes but 1 in a County.)

Soveraign or Chief Crowner, The Lord Chief Juſtice of the Kings bench, wherever he be.

Coronet, *f.* a little Crown.

Corporal, belonging to the Body; the leaſt Commander in a foot company, alſo the fine linen wherein the Sacrament is put.

Corporation, *l.* a body politick, form'd by the Kings Charter.

Corporature, *l.* the frame or conſtitution of the Body.

Corporeal, bodily.

Corporeity, *-eature*, the being a bodily ſubſtance.

Corporification, a making into a body, a Spirits reaſſuming its body and appearing.

Corps, *f.* a [dead] body.

Corps-du-Gard, *f.* the body of the Guard.

Corpulent, groſs, having

Corpulency, fulneſs of Body.

Corpus Chriſti, *l.* Chriſts body, a Colledge in *Oxford*.

Corpus cum cauſa, a writ of Chancery to remove into the Kings bench.

Corpuſcule, *l.* a little body.

Corr, two quarts.

Corrade, *l.* ſcrape together, extort.

Corraſive, ſcraping together

Correction, amendment, chaſtiſement.

Correctour of the Staple, a Clark recording all bargains made there.

Correlative, having mutual relation.

Correptory, belonging to

Correption, a ſudden ſnatching away; alſo reproof.

Correſpond, *l.* anſwer, agree.

Correſpondent, [one] holding.

Correſpondency, mutual commerce and familiarity, alſo the anſwerableneſs or proportion of one thing to another.

Corridor, as *Cortine*, *-na*.

Corrigible, which may be corrected or amended.

Corrigidor, *Sp.* the Chief Governor of a Town or City.

Corrival, as Competitour.

Corrivality, Corrivalſhip.

Corroboration, a ſtrengthning.

Corrode, gnaw, fret.

Corrodible, that may be gnawn or eaten away.

Corroſives, Medicines that are

Corroſive, belonging to

Corroſion, gnawing, fretting.

Corrugation, a wrinkling, frowning.

Corruption, infection, a ſpoiling, tainting.

Corruption of bloud, of the whole iſſue, honour and Eſtate (by Felony or Treaſon.)

Corſary, *-ſaire*, *f.* a Courſer, a Rover, a Pirates ſhip.

Corſe-preſent, Mortuary, a beaſt or other offering to the Prieſt from a dead mans Eſtate.

Corſeint, *o.f.* holy or bleſſed heart.

Corſlet, *I. Cuiraſſe*, *f.* [armour for] back and breaſt.

Corſure, *Courſer*, *o.* Broaker.

Corſtopitum, *Corbridge* in *Northumberland*.

Cortex Winteranus, a kind of Cinamon brought firſt from *India*, by Captain *Winter*.

Corticated, covered with a bark.

Cortin, *f.* that ſpace of the Terraſſe or Muraille that is between the Baſtions,

Corven, *o.* carved.

Corvet, praunce.

Corvetta, *I.* prauncing.

Corvine, *l.* of a Crow or Raven.

Corviſer, as Cordwainer.

Coruſcant, ſhining, glittering.

Coruſcation, *l.* Lightning, a flaſhing of Light.

Corybantes, the Prieſts of *Cybele*.

'*Coſſet* [*lamb*] brought up without the dam.

Coscinomancy, *Coski-*, *g.* divination with a sieve.

Costnage, a writ for the heir against an intruder.

Coshacks, *Turkish*-womens girdles.

Cosier, *o.* Sowter, Botcher.

Cosignificative, of the same signification.

Co-sine, the Complement of the Radius or whole sign to a quadrant or 90 degrees.

Cosmeticks, things to clear and purify the skin.

Cosmical, of the world.

Cosmical rising [*of a star*,] is together with the Sun.

Cosmographical, belonging to

Cosmography, *g.* a description of the world.

Cosmographer, a describer, &c.

Cosmodelyte, one fearing or serving the world.

Cosmology, a speaking of the world.

Cosmarchy, the government of

Cosmos, *g.* the world.

Cosmopolite, *-tan*, a Citizen of the world.

Cosmometry, *g* a measuring of the world by degrees and minutes.

Cossacks, Polish Outlaws form'd in a Militia, partly under the Rebel *Dorosensko*, partly under the Crown.

Cosset [*Lamb*, *Colt*, *&c.*] brought up by hand.

Cossick [*numbers*] used in *Algebra*.

Cost, (in blazon) the fourth part of the bend or half the Sarier.

Costay, *o.* to Coast up and down.

Costive, having the belly bound.

Costmary, Alecoast, Maudlin herb.

Cost el. *Cas-*, *o.* a wine-pot.

Costus, an *Indian* drug, (the sweet and the bitter.)

Cot, *Cote*, refuse or clotted wool, also a Cottage or Sheepfold.

Coteswold, *o.* a company of Sheepcoats, and sheep feeding on hills: also hills in *Glocestershire* whose Sheep are famous for fine wool.

Cottager, *-arius*, he who's cottage hath not above four acres of Land to it.

Cotterel, *Cottarel*, *o.* a poor Cottager.

Cottre, *De.* a trammel to hang the pot on over the fire.

Coton, frize, bombasin.

Cotula, *l.* May-weed.

Cottis, as *Cost*.

Cotyledones, *g.* *Acetabula*, *l.* the mouths of the veins in the womb, through which the monthly bloud is derived.

Couch a Hogshead c. go to sleep.

Couchant, *f.* lying close to the ground.

Coucher, a Factour, also a General Register-book of a Corporation, &c.

Cove, *Cuffin*, *c.* a man.

Cove, *We.* a little harbour for boats.

Covenable, *Conv-*, *f.* Convenient, suitable.

Covenant, *f.* bargain, also a writ that lies for the breach thereof.

Coventry, *-tree*, a City in *Warwickshire*, from a Covent of Monks there.

Coverchief, *o.* Kerchief.

Covercle, *Coverkil*, *o.* a Cover.

Covert, *f.* a shady place for Deer, &c.

Coverture, *Covert-barn* or *-Baron*, *f.* the Condition of an *English* wife, who can make no bargain without her husbands consent.

Coughton, the Mansion of the *Throgmortons* in *Warwickshire*.

Covie, *f.* a nest or brood [of Partridges.]

Covin, fraud, deceit [by conspiracy.]

Coulant, *f.* flowing, gliding along.

Couldray, *f.* a hazel grove.

Coule, a water-tub, a fryers hood, and (in Archery) to cut the feather of a shaft high or low.

Coulpe, *f.* a fault.

Coulter, *l.* a Plow-share.

Counsellour, he that give h

Counsel, *f.* advice, also as

Council, *-cil*, *l.* an Assembly of Counsellours.

Count, *f.* Earl, also the Original declaration in a process.

Countenance, *f.* visage, also credit, estimation, also to favour or favour [shown.]

Counter, *f.* a counting thing or place; a Shop Chest, also the name of 2 Prisons for debt in *London*.

Counters, *Con-*, *f.* Advocates which speak in Court for one [absent.]

Countercharge, Charge again or against.

Counter-check, blame him that blames you.

Counter-componed, Compounded of two colours (or more.)

Counterfeit, *f.* feign or feigned.

Counterfeits and trinkets, *Chet* Porringers and Saucers.

Countermarch, When fileleaders turn to the hand directed, and pass through the Company, their followers make good their ground, then turn and follow them.

Countermand, *-maund*, *f.* recalling a former command.

Countermine, Mine against mine.

Countermure, wall against wall.

Counterpane, *-pain*, one part of a pair of deeds or Indentures.

Counter-plea, *-plee*, a reply to *Ayde-prier*, (a petition in Court for the calling-in of help from another.)

Counterpoint, opposition, composing parts (in Musick) by setting point or note against note, also back-stitch, or quilt-stitch, also the quilt, Carpet, &c.

Counterpoise, *f.* to weigh one against the other, also the weight, &c.

Counterpoison, an antidote, or a contrary poison.

Counter-balance, as *Counterpoise*.

Counterbarred, on both sides.

Counter bond given to your surety to save him harmless.

Counter-rail, rail against tail.

Counter-rolls, of the same contents.

Counter-round, Officers visiting the common round or Sentinels.

Counterscarf, *-scarp*, *f.* a rampire or bank [of a moat] opposite to a Fortress, Town-wall, &c.

Counter-security, mutual.

Counter-Sophister, who holds the adverse part of Sophistry.

Counter-tail, *-tally*, one of the tallies or wooden scores, also as

Counter-tenour, against the tenour, a middle part in Musick.

Countervale, be of equal value, make amends for.

Countess, *f.* an Earls wife.

Counter, *f.* an accomptant, a reckoner.

Counting-house of the Kings Houshold, the Green Cloth, where sit the Lord Steward, Treasurer of the Kings-house &c.

County, *f.* shire.

County-Court, held monthly by the Sheriff or under Sheriff.

Coup, *o.* a piece cut off (or out.)

Coupant, *f.* cutting.

Coupé, *f.* cut off.

Couped, [trees] cut from the trunk (in heraldry.)

Coupe-gorge, *f.* a cut-throat

Couple-close, the 4th. part of a Cheveron.

Courant, *f.* a news-book.

Coure, as *Cowre*.

Courfine, *o* fine heart.

Courier, a [riding] post, *f.*

Courratier, a horse-courser.

Course, that point of the compass the ship is to sail on.

Courser, *f.* a [race] horse.

Court Baron, which every Lord of a Mannor keeps.

Court of Requests, a Court of Equity, like the Chancery.

Court of the Legate, obtained of Pope *Leo.* 10. by Cardinal *Woolsey*, to dispense with offences against the Spiritual Law.

Court Christian, Spiritual Court.

Court of Chivalry, the Marshals Court where the Earl Marshal (one of the Judges) is to see Execution done.

Courtesie of England, *Lex Angliæ*, a mans tenure (during life) of Land which his wife died possest of, if he had a Child by her.

Courtilage, *Curt-* a garden or piece of void ground belonging to a Messuage.

Courtisane, *f.* a Court Lady, also a Strumpet.

Courtlass, *Coutlass*, a short sword.

Courtmantle, *-til*, *f.* a short Cloak.

Courtpy, *-pies*, *o.* a kind of short coat.

Couth, *o.* (*q. Kennouth*) knew

Couthoutlaug, *Couthut- Sa.* he that harbours an Outlaw.

Cowde, *o.* gobbet.

Conde, *f.* elbow, cubit.

Cowl, *E.* tub, as *Coule*.

Cowre, kneel, fall down for fear, also ruck down (*ut mulier ad mingendum*) *so.*

Cowneer, the hollow arching part in the ship-stern.

Coy, *Coyen*, *o.* nice, dainty, also to quiet [by flattering.]

Coyse, *o.* jollines, joyes.

Crab, a wooden engine with three claws on the ground for the lanching of Ships, &c.

Crablat, *f.* comely, also a womans gorget, also a

Cravate, worn first (they say) by the *Croats* in *Germany*.

Cracker, *c.* the breech.

Crackmans, *c.* hedges.

Cracovia, *Cracow*, a City of *Poland*.

Cradle, a frame on the Ship sides for easie lanching, also a frame fasten'd to sythes, also the place where the bullet lies in a Crosse-bow.

Craddanly, *La*, as *Crassantly*.

Crabs-eye, a stone (like an eye) found in a Crab.

Craft, all kind of fishing tools; also small vessels as ketches, &c.

Crakel, *o.* make a chattering noise.

Crakers, *Creekers*, *Kr.* choise English soldiers in *France*, in the time of *Henry the* 8th.

Crallit, *o.* engraven.

Crambe, *g.* Colewort.

Cramborne, a Town in *Dorcetshire*.

Cramp, a disease in the hawks wing (by taking cold.)

Crampesh, *-eth*, gnaws, cratcheth.

Cramp-rings, *c.* bolts or shakles.

Cramp-fish, causing the Cramp by touching it.

Cranage, money paid for the use of a

Crane, an engine to draw up wares.

Cranbroke, a Town in *Kent*.

Crank, *E.* lusty, jovial, brisk.

Crank-sided, when a ship will bear but small sail.

Crany, *g.* the skull or brainpan, also as

Cranny, a cleft, chink.

Cranny lad, *che.* jovial, lusty lad

Crap, *Sf.* darnel, also (in other places) Buck-wheat.

Crapulent, *l.* glutted, having taken a surfeit.

Crased, *o.* cracked.

Crashing-cheats, teeth. *c.*

Crasie, sick, distempered, weak.

Crassantly lad, *che.* a Cowardly lad.

Crassulent, full of

Crassitude, *-ty*, thickness, grossenes.

Crasse, *l.* thick, also heavy or dull.

Crastinate, *l.* put off from day to day.

Cratched, *o.* scratched (with the Fullers Teasel.)

Cratch, *Critch*, a rack, *So.*

Crater, the bottom of the pitcher in *Virgo*, also the line to which Hawks are fasten'd when reclaimed.

Craven, *Cravent*, *-vant*, (*q.* craving mercy) a horrid word, to be pronounced by the vanquished,

quished in a trial by battel, a Coward.

Crawly-mawly, *Nf.* pretty well.

Crayer, a kind of small ship.

Cray, a disease hindring the Hawks muting.

Creamer, *D.* he that hath a stall in the Fair or Market.

Cream, *No.* to mantle as drink doth.

Creance, *-aunce*, *f.* trust, confidence, also a long small line fasten'd to the Hawks leash when first lured.

Creansour, a Creditor.

Creast, as *Crest*.

Crest-tile, roof-tile.

Create, *l.* make [of nothing.]

Creation, *l.* the making [of the World.]

Crebrous, *l.* often, usual.

Crebrity, frequency, multitude.

Credibility, a being

Credible, *l.* that may be believed.

Creditable, bringing

Credit, esteem, belief, trust.

Crediton, a Town in *Devonshire*.

Creditor, *-tour*, *l.* a lender.

Credulity, a being

Credulous, *l.* apt to believe.

Creed, belief.

Creek, *Sa.* a landing place in a haven.

Creem it into his hand, *Che.* put it in slily and secretly.

Creeze, a broad, sharp waved and envenomed Indian weapon about two foot long.

Crekelade, a Town in *Wilts*.

Cremaster, *g.* the muscle that holds up the Stones.

Cremation, *l.* a burning.

Crenated, *l.* notched.

Crenelle (in heraldry) a line dented like the battlement of a wall.

Creon, he resigned his Kingdom of *Thebes* to *Oedipus* for expounding *Sphinxes* riddle.

Crepitation, *l.* a crackling noise.

Crepusculous, belonging to

Crepuscule, *l.* twilight.

Crescent, *l.* encreasing.

Cressant, *f.* the figure of a half-moon.

Cressee, nose-smart.

Cresset, *o.* lanthorn, beakon.

Crest, *f.* the upper part of an helmet and Escutcheon.

Crestmarine, Rock-samphire

Cretians, *-ian*, belonging to

Crete, *Creet*, *Hecatompolis* the Isle *Candy* in the *Mediterranean*.

Cretism, *Creticism*, lying, perfidiousness.

Crevequers, an ancient Family in *Kent*.

Creuet, *Cruset*, a Goldsmiths melting-pot.

Creusa, wife to *Æneas*, lost by him coming out of *Troy*.

Crible, a sieve.

Cribration *l.* a sifting.

Crick, *Crock*, *Cruche*, *f.* an Earthen pot or pitcher.

Criminal, *-nous*, guilty, an offender, belonging to a

Crime, great fault.

Crined, hairy.

Crinel, belonging to the hair.

Cringles, *Creengles*, little ropes spliced into the bolt-ropes of sailes.

Crinigerous, having or wearing hair.

Crinisus, a river of *Sicily*, which (in the form of a Bear) ravishing *Hegesta*, begat *Acastes* King of *Sicily*.

Crinites, the small black feathers (like hairs) about the sere of a Hawk.

Crenosity, hairiness.

Criplings, short spars on the side of a house.

St. *Crispin*, *Cre-*, the Patron of the Shooemakers.

St. *Crispins lance*, an Awl.

Crispitude, a being

Crispid, *l.* curled.

Crist, a *Crest*, tuft, plume.

Cristal, as *Crystal*.

Criticism, a playing the

Critick, one of a nice judgment, apt to censure.

Critical, belonging thereto.

Critical dayes, wherein the disease comes to its

Crisis, *g.* Judgment, sudden change (for better or worse) *viz.* the odde dayes, and fourteenth (especially.)

Critilogy, *g.* a gathering in the first fruits [of Corn.]

Cro, *Croy*, *Sc.* which the Judge (if he minister not justice) is to pay the nearest of kin to a slain man.

Crocard, an old forbidden Coin.

Crocation, *Crocita-*, *l.* the kawing of Crows, &c.

Croc, *sc.* pot.

Crock, *e.* to black with a pot or soot.

Croce, *o.* Shepherds staff.

Croches, the little tips of the Harts horns.

Crocolana, *Ancaster* in *Lincolnshire*.

Crockets, *o.* locks of hair.

Crocodile, an *Ægyptian*, *Amphibious* Creature shaped much like an Eft, but (sometimes) twenty or thirty foot long.

Crocodiles tears, false, treacherous, because (they say) he weeps when he devours a man.

Crocus, *g.* Saffron, also flowers resembling it; also a Chymical preparation, as

Crocus Martis, a preparation of iron.

Crocus Veneris, of Copper, &c.

Crocute, a certain beast imitating mans voice.

Crœsus, a very rich King of *Lydia*, taken by *Cyrus* and made one of his Counsel.

Croft, a small close adjoyning to a house.

Crogen, *Crogy*, *Br.* hang.

Crois, *f.* a Cross.

Croisada, the Popes Bull granting the sign of the cross to Christians warring against Infidels.

Croiseri, *o.* those for whom Christ suffered.

Croises, Pilgrims, also Knights of St. *John* in *Jerusalem*, created for the defence of Pilgrims.

Crokethorn, a Town in *Somersetshire*.

Crokes, *o.* hooks.

Crome, Corm, o. an iron crow
Crompe, o, a crop.
Cromer, a Town in *Norfolk*.
Cronical, as *Chronical*.
Crones, old Ews, *So*.
Cronie, a contemporary disciple, or intimate companion.
Cronus, *Diodorus* the Philosopher, from his Master *Apollonius Cronus*.
Crool, o. mutter. growl.
Crop, o. top.
Croppin-ken, c. a privy.
Crosier, a Bishops staff.
Cross avellane, whose ends shoot forth like a filberds husk.
Cross-fitched, fixed (in the coat of arms) with a sharp end.
Cross fourche, forked.
Cross flurry, with a flower-de-luce at each end.
Cross milrine, whose ends are clamp'd and turn'd again like the milrine which carries the milstone.
Cross voided, when the field is seen through the cross.
Cross-wort, whose leaves and flowers both grow like crosses
Cross-bar-shot, a round shot with a long spike of iron (as it were put thorow it.
Crosslet, f. a little cross, also as *Crucible*.
Cross-jack a yard flung under the top of the mizzen-mast.
Cross-staff, an instrument to take the height of any thing.
Crosstrees, cross pieces on the head of a mast.
Crotaphique artery, a great sinew near the Temples.
Crotaphites, g. the two Temple-muscles.
Crotch, the forked part of a Tree.
Crochet half a minim, also a whimsey; also (in printing) the mark of a parathesis, [ ].
Crochets, a Foxes chief master teeth.
Crotels, *Croteying*, the ordure of a hare.
Crotyith, -*eth*, o. dungeth.
Crouch, o. cross, whence
Crouch, o. bless [with a cross]

Croupe, f. a buttock.
Crow, a southern Constellation, upon *Hydra's* tail.
Crowfoot, yellow crey, a very biting plant.
Crowland, a Town in *Lincolnshire*, haunted with spirits till *Guthlac* (the Hermite) lived there.
Crownet, as *Coronet*.
Crows-bill, an instrument to draw forth bullets, bones, &c.
Crowse, *No.* brisk.
Crows-feet, small ship lines reev'd through the dead-mens eyes (here and there for ornament.
Croydon, a Town in *Surrey*.
Cruciate, l. afflict, torment.
Crucible, a chymick-glass wherein things are burnt and prepared for powdering.
Crucicola, l. (cross-worshipper,) an old Pagan name for a Christian.
Cruciferi, *Crouched*, *Crutched*, *Cruchet* or *Crossed Fryers*, who came into *England*, 1244.
Crucif rous, cross-bearing.
Crucifie, l. nail to a crosse.
Crucifix, the image of Christ upon the crosse.
Crucifixion, a being Crucifyed.
Crude, l. raw undigested.
Crudity, rawness [of Stomach.]
Cruental, cruel, bloody.
Cruet, *Crewet*, *Cruse*, a vial or narrow-mouth'd glass.
Cruise, *Creffera*, *Sc.* hogsty.
Cruis, o. Prayers.
Cruise, *Crose*, *Crosse* or *Coast*, up and down at Sea [for prize, &c.]
Crul, o. smooth, or [rather] curled.
Cruor, l. gore-blood.
Crural, l. belonging to the Thighs.
Crush, *Crussel*, o. grisle.
Crusible, as *Crucible*.
Crustaceous, l. crusted, or cover'd with a hard shell.
Cruzada, as *Croisada*.
Cruzado, a *Portugal* peice of Gold worth 10 s.
Cruzet, as *Crucible*.
Cryptick, -*cal*, g. hidden, secret,

Cryptography, [the art of] secret writing.
Cryptology, g. secret speaking, whispering.
Crystal, a bright transparent Mineral, like ice or the clearest glass.
Crystalline, belonging thereto.
Crystalline humour, the first instrument of sight, not flat nor round, seated in the center of the eye.
Cubbridg-head, as *Bulk-head*.
Cubbridg-head afore the Bulkhead of the fore-castle.
Cubbridg-head abaft, the Bulkhead of the half-deck.
Cubic, belonging to a
Cube, a solid square body of six equal sides, also the product of a square number multiplied by its root.
Cubebs, an Indian fruit like ivy-berries.
Cubical artery, a branch of the Axillar.
Cubicular, l. belonging to a Bed-chamber.
Cubit, a measure from the elbow to the fingers end.
Cubiture, a lying down.
Cuchaneal, as *Cochineal*.
Cucking-stool, *Ducking-stool*, *Cokestool*, or Tumbrel.
Cuckopint, *Aram*. a biting herb.
Cucullated, l. having a Monks coule (or hood) on
Cucubite, howl or whoop like an Owl.
Cucupha, caps quilted with things good for the head.
Cucurbate, l. a gourd, also a *Cupping-glass*, apply'd to the body (with towe on fire) to raise a blister or draw blood.
Cucuye, a bird in *Hispaniola*, with eyes under the wings shining in the night.
Cudweed, Cottonweed.
Cue, an Item given stage-players, what or when to speak.
Cuerpo, *sp.* a body, also a corporation.
In Cuerpo, without a cloak.
Cuffin quire, c. a Justice of Peace.
Cui ante Devortium, a writ em-

empowering a divorced woman to recover her lands from him to whom her husband did (before the divorce) alienate them.

Cui in vita, a writ of entry (for a widow) upon her lands alienated by her husband.

Cuinage, the making up of Tin fit for carriage.

Cuirassier, f. one armed with a

Cuirasse, -rets, -rats, corslet, armour for the back and breast.

Culagium, when a ship is a repairing in the Dock.

Culdeis, (q. *cultores Dei*) a sort of Religious people formerly in *Scotland* and *Ireland*.

Culrage, f. lechery, also the herb Arse-smart or Water-Pepper.

Culinary, belonging to the kitchin.

Cullers, bad Sheep separated from the rest.

Culleth, o. pulleth, enforceth;

Cullion-head, Schonce, Bastion, Block-house.

Cullion, a fleshy stone.

Cullis, the strained juice of boild meat.

Culleton, a Town in *Devonshire*.

Cullot, f. a cushion to ride post upon.

Cully, I. a fool.

Culm, smoak or soot.

Culminate, l. to get up to the top, also to appear (as a Planet) in the Meridian, or Mid-heaven.

Culpons, o. heaps, also little bits.

Culrach Col-, sc. a pledge or cautioner left for the repledging of a man from one Court to another.

Culpable, l. guilty, blameable.

Cultivation, l. a manuring.

Culture, l. the same.

Culver, So. Pigeon.

Culvertage, faint heartedness, or turning the tail [to run away.]

Culverine, a piece of Ordnance.

C V

Culvertaile, a fastening of boards (or any Timber) by letting one into another.

Cumble, f. full heaped measure.

Cumæ, an Italian City by the Sea-side.

Cumatical, blew [colour.]

Cumini sector, l. a niggardly divider of the small seed of

Cummin, l. a plant like (but less than) Fennel.

Cumulation, l. a heaping up together.

Cunctation, l. a delaying.

Cuneglassus, a cruel Welsh Tyrant.

Cuneus, a Mint.

Cuniculous, full of

Cunicles, l. Mines or Cony-burroughs.

Cunobelinus, King of the *Trinobantes*, when *Cæsar* entred *Brittain*.

Cuntey Cunty, a Jury, or trial by ones Country.

Cupidous, -*dinous*, full of

Cupidity, l. lust, Covetousness.

Cup-glass, *Cupping-glass*, see *Cucurbite*.

Cupulo, -*polo*, I. a high arch in a building, a round loover.

Cupreous, l. of Copper.

Curator, overseer, provider of necessaries.

Cure bulli, *Cuir bouillie*, f. tanned Leather.

Curfew, f. covering the fire (in the time of *William* the Conqueror) at the ringing of the

Curfeu-bell, eight a clock bell.

Curia advisare vult, a deliberation in Court before Judgment.

Curia claudenda, against him that refuses to fence or enclose his ground.

Curia Penticiarum, the Sheriffs Court in *Chester*, under a pentice or shed of boards.

Curia Ottadinorum, supposed the same as *Corstopitum*.

Curialitas Scotiæ, the courtesie of *Scotland*, equivalent to the Courtesie of *England*.

Curlew, a bird about the bigness of a Pigeon.

C V

Curnock, 4 bushels.

Curranto, f. a running French dance.

Curricurre, -*ro*, an East-Indian barge.

Curriedew, *Curriedow*, o. a curry-favour or flatterer.

Current, l. a stream.

Cursiters, *Cursitory*, the office of 20 Clerks in Chancery who make out Original writs.

Curtezan, as *Courtisan*.

Curtesie, as *Courtesie*.

Cursorily, in a flight or running manner.

Curteyn, the sword of King *Edward* the Confessour, carried before the King at Coronations.

Curteis, o courteous.

Curtilage, as *Courtelage*.

Curvature, a bending, crookedness, a roundle.

Curvetta, *Corv-*, I. the prauncing of a Horse.

Curvilineal, who's lines are crooked.

Curvity, l. crookedness.

Curules, Roman Senatours caried to Court in a

Curule Chair, an ivory seat in a chariot.

Curule [wit,] Senatorian.

Curvous, l. crooked.

Cusco, a great City in *Armenia*.

Cuspidate, l. sharpen the point.

Cuspe, the first beginning or entrance of any house (in Astronomy.)

Custance, o. for *Constance* or *Constantine*.

Custode admittendo, a writ for the admitting of a Guardian.

Custode amovendo, a writ for the removing a Guardian.

Custody, l. safehold.

Customary, usual, see *Custu-*.

Customary tenants, hold by the custom of the mannor.

Custos brevium, keeper of the writs, in the Court of Common pleas.

Custos rotulorum, keeper of the rolls and records of the Sessions.

Custos placitorum coronæ,

seems

seems to be the same.

Custos Spiritualium, Guardian or keeper of the Spiritualties during the vacancy of the See, *viz.* the Dean and Chapter.

Custrel, *f.* the servant of a man at arms or of a Lifeguard-man, as in *Henry* 8.

Customary, belonging to *custom*, also the book wherein

Customs are recorded and described.

Cuth, *o.* known, knowing, knowledge.

Cuthbert, *Sa.* famous knowledge.

Cuthwin, skilfull Victor.

Cuticle, *l.* the thin skin which covers the other all over the Body.

Cuticular, full of pores or little holes.

Cutter of tallies, an Officer in the Exchequer.

Cut, *c.* speak.

Cut the sail, let it fall.

Cuttle fish, he escapes the fisher by obscuring the place about him with an inky juice.

Cutilia, an *Italian* Lake wherein is a moveable Island.

Cutlu-Muses, the second King of the *Turks* who took *Jerusalem.*

Cutwater, the sharpness of the ship before; also a false stem put on a ship that is too bluffe.

Cyamba, a City of *Asia*, which uses Coral instead of money.

Cybele, *Cib-*, *-elle*, *Berecynthia*, *Dindymene*, *Ops*, *Rhea*, *Vesta*, *Magna mater*, or the Mother of the Gods.

Cyclades, *g.* *Isole del Archipelago*, *I.* 50 Islands in the *Ægean* Sea.

Cycle, *g.* Circle.

Cycle of the moon, the space of 19 years.

Cycle of the Sun, 28 years, wherein their motions return to the same point.

Cyclometry, *g.* a measuring of Circles.

Cyclopædie, *g.* the whole Circle of Arts and Sciences.

Cyclopes, *Bronte*, *Sterope*, and *Pyracmon* (or *Harpe*,) *Vulcans* servants (with one eye in their forehead) who made thunderbolts for *Jupiter.*

Cyclopick, *-pean*, belonging to the foresaid giants, or the old inhabitants of *Sicily.*

Cycnus, the son of *Mars* killed by *Hercules*; also the son of *Neptune* (invulnerable) stifled by *Achilles* kneeling on his neck.

Cydoniarum, Marmalate of Quinces.

Cygnus, *l.* Swan.

Cylindrical, pertaining to or like a

Cylinder, *g.* a Garden-roller, or any thing of that form; also the empty part of a laden piece.

Cymace, *g.* Carved work resembling waves.

Cymbalist, he that playes on a

Cymbal, a Musical instrument of brass plates, resembling a small boat.

Cymraecan, *-acean*, *-aeg*, *Br.* *Welsh.*

Cynanthropy, *g.* a mans conceiting that he is a dog.

Cynarctomachy, *g.* a fight betwixt dogs and bears, bearbaiting.

Cynegeticks, *g.* Treatises of Hunting.

Cynegirus, *-ris*, an *Athenian* who (after his hands were cut off) held his Enemies ship fast with his teeth.

Cynical, *g.* belonging to the *Cynick* (dogged) crabbed, severe Philosophers.

Cynocephalist, a baboon.

Cynosure, *g.* (dogs tail) *Ursa minor*, near the Northpole, directing sailers.

Cynorexie, *-ia*, *g.* Dog-hunger.

Cynthia, *Diana*, twin-sister to

Cynthius, *Apollo*, born near *Cynthus*, a hill in *Delos.*

Cyon, a young sprout from an old tree.

Cypher, as *Cipher*, to cast account, a thing of nought, &c.

Cyprian, belonging to

Cyprus, an Isle in the *Carpathian* Sea dedicated to

Cypria, *Venus.*

Cyprine, belonging to a

Cypress-tree, once cut it never reflourisheth.

Cyrenaica, *Pentapolitana*, part of *Africa.*

Cyricsceat, as *Churchesset.*

Cyrus, King of *Persia*, he overthrew the *Assyrian* Monarchy.

Cystick, belonging to

Cystis, *g.* the bag of gall.

Cystepatique artery, a branch of the *Cœliaque*, to the liver and gall.

Cystick vein, a branch of the *Port-vein*, to the neck of the gall.

Cyzicus, an Island in the *Propontis*, joyn'd to the Continent with two bridges.

Czar, (*q.* *Cesar*) the great Duke or Emperour of *Muscovy.*

D.

Dae, People inhabiting part of *Scythia Europæa.*

Dabuze, a weapon (or mace) carried before the Grand Signior.

Dacker, *Li.* Waver, stagger.

Dacia, part of *European Scythia.*

Dactyle, *g.* a finger, a date; also a foot of one long syllable and two short.

Dactylogie, discoursing by signs.

Daddock (*q.* dead oak) the rotten heart or Body of a tree.

Dædalean, belonging to

Dædalus, a famous artist, *Icarus* father, authour of the *Cretian* Labyrinth.

Dæmoniack, *-cal*, belonging to, also possessed of a

Dæmon, *g.* Devil.

Dæmonologie, a treatise of angels, spirits or Devils.

Daff, *o.* Dastard, Coward; also to daunt, *No.*

Daffock, *Dawgos*, *Dawkin*, *No.*

Vo. a dirty flut.

Daffadil, Narcissus, a flower.

Daft, No. stupid, blockish.

Dagged, o. digged, slitted.

Dagges, o. Leather-latchets.

Dagge, D. a Dagger.

Dagon, an idol having the upper part like a man, the rest like a fish; also a piece or remnant, *o.*

Dag-swain, a rough or course mantle.

Dakir, as *Dicker*.

D'alanson, Dallison, a Noble family in *Lincolnshire*.

Dalilah, Del-, h. he drew, or was drawn [out or dry.]

Dalmatia, part of *Illyricum* in *Greece*.

Dalmatian Cap, a Tulip, brought from *Tulippa* a Promontory of *Dalmatia*.

Dalmatick, a kind of vestment (white with purple studs) for Deacons or Sub-Deacons; and another used by Archbishops.

Dalrendini, Certain Scotch, conquered by the *Irish Renda*.

Damask prunes, Damasines, plums of

Damascus, the chief City of *Syria*.

Damber, c. a rascal.

Damiata, pelusium, a chief haven of *Egypt*.

Dammage, f. hurt; also allowance (in Court) for damage done.

Damage Cleer, a Gratuity given Protonotaries and their clerks for drawing special writs and pleadings (2 *s. per* pound.)

Dammage fesant, when beasts feed and spoil in other mens grounds without leave.

Dammask, fine stuff, first made in *Damascus*.

Damnation, l. a condemning.

Damocrita, a *Roman* Matron who kil'd her Daughters and her self, being forbidden to follow her banisht husband *Alcippus*.

Dan, h. Judgement, also as Don, Monsieur, Sir, *o.*

Danaë, Daughter of *Acrisius* King of *Argos*.

Danai, *Grecians*, from

Danaus, Son of *Belus* and King of *Argus*.

Dancers, c. stairs.

Dancet, like Indented, only the lines are deeper and wider.

Dandelion (Dent de lion, f.) piss-a-bed, a plant.

Dandy-prats, a small coyn made by *Henry* 7. also little folks.

Dandruff, -raff, head-scurfe.

Dane-gilt, -gelt, -geld, -gold, 12 d. paid the *Danes* for every hide of land.

Danewort, Wallwort or dwarf-elder.

Dagwallet (q. Danglewallet) o. excessive.

Dania, Denmark.

Daniel, h. Judgment of God.

Danistick, belonging to a

Danist, he that takes

Danisme, g. Usury.

Dank, o. damp, moist.

Danmonij, the people of *Devonshir* and *Cornwal*.

Dantiscum, Dantzick, -zig, a town in *Poland*.

Dantoned, o. tamed.

Danubius, Ister, Danow, the greatest river in *Europe*.

Danwort, as *Danewort*.

Dapatical, sumptuous.

Daphne, flying from *Apollo's* lust was turn'd into a Laurel or Bay-tree.

Daphnælion g. Oil of Bay.

Daphnomancy, g. Divination by Laurels.

Dapifer, Sewer, that orders and serves up a Banquet.

Dapper, neat, spruce.

Daping, angling near the top of the water.

Dapocaginous, I. low-spirited, narrow-hearted, of litle worth.

Darapti, a syllogism of the two first Universal and the last a particular Affirmative.

Darby (q. Derwentby) built on the river *Derwent*.

Darcy, D'Adrecy, an ancient family in *Lincolnshire*.

Dardanum, Troy, built by

Dardanus, Son of *Jupiter* and *Electra*, also a Magician.

Dardanian art, Witchcraft.

Dare, o. stare upon, also hurt, *No.*

Darick, 2 s. a coyn of

Darius, King of *Persia*.

Darking, a town in *Surrey*.

Darkmans, c. night, evening.

Darling, (q. Dearling) fondling.

Darlington, a Town in the Bishoprick of *Durham*.

Darnel, a rushy corn-weed very seedy.

Darrein [presentment,] f. the last.

Darreign, Daren, o. attempt.

Dartos, one of the skins that enwraps the stones.

Dartford, Darf-, Darens-, a town in Kent, upon

Daren, a River there.

Dartmouth, a town in *Devon*.

Darij, a syllogism of the first universal and the two last particular affirmatives.

Dart, jaculus, an ash-colour'd serpent darting it self from trees, &c.

Datary, a *Roman* Office, for the collation of Benefices.

Date, the palm-tree-fruit, also the time of writing a letter, &c.

Dates, o. accounts.

Datise, that may be given or disposed of.

Dation, l. a gift.

Dathan, h. an Edict of law.

Datisi, as *Darij* (in another mood.)

Datism, a heaping together *Synonyma's* or words of the the same signification, from

Datis a Noble-man of *Greece*.

Dative, l. belonging to giving.

Dative Case, that which ispue acquisitively, to or for ones use, benefit or dammage.

Daudery, a town in *Lincolnshire*.

Davitt, a piece of timber with a notch at one end, whereon they hang the fish-block.

Davenport, Damport, a town in

in *Cheshire*, also an ancient family.

Daventree, *Daintry*, a town in *Northamptonshire*.

David, *h*. beloved.

Davids-staff, contains an entire quadrant between the circle of the arched bases of two united triangles.

Daulphin, or *Dolphin* [of *Viennes*] the title of the King of *France*'s eldest son.

St. *Davids day*, *March*, 1. in Honour of *St. David* Arch-Bishop of *Menevy* above 60 years. The Leek denotes a great victory obtained against the *Saxons* by the *Britains* wearing Leeks by *St. Davids* direction.

Daungere, *o*. a Trap.

Daungerous, *o*. coy or sparing.

Daunsette, as *Dancet*.

Dauntry, an ancient Family in *Suffex*.

Day-lights-gate, the going down of day-light.

Dawe, *o*. dawn, also thrive, *no*.

Dawes, *o*. days.

Dawkin, as *Daffock*.

Days in bank, when the writ is to be returned, or the party to appear.

Days-man, Arbitrator. *no*.

Dazed [*bread*,] Dough-baked, *Li*.

I's *Dazed*, I'm very cold, *no*.

Dea bona, the Goddess *Fortuna*, and sometimes the Earth, cal'd also *Ops*, *Fatua*, and *Fauna*, whipt to death with myrtle by her husband *Faunus*, for being drunk with wine of Myrtle-berries.

Dea viri-placa, a Goddess in who's chappel man and wife were reconciled.

Deaction, *l*. a finishing or perfecting.

Deacon, *g*. (Minister, Servant) a Church Officer [looking anciently to the poor, now also] reading in the Church.

Deadmans-eyes, Ship blocks full of small ropes.

Dead-pledge, Mort-gage, pawning of things for ever, if the money be not paid at the time agreed on.

Deafly, dearn, solitary, far from neighbours, *no*.

Deadwater, the eddy water at the stern of a Ship.

Deafforested, discharged from being a Forest, or freed from Forest Laws.

Dealbate, *l*. whiten.

Deambulatory, *l*. walking up and down, also a walking place.

Deanric, the Office and place of a

Dean, set over [ten] Canons.

Deans rural, who have a Jurisdiction assign'd by the Bishop over other Ministers and Parishes adjoyning.

Dean-great, a Town in *Glocestershire*.

Deark, as *Decark*.

Deauration, *l*. gilding over.

Debauch, to corrupt in manners, also as

Debaucherie, *Desboshrie*, *f*. riot, disorderly revelling.

Debellation, an overcoming [in war.].

Debenham, a Town in *Suffolk*.

De bene esse, when a Defendants deposition is only allow'd of, for the present.

Debentur, (*l*. they are owing) a bill charging the Commonwealth to pay the Soldier creditour his arrears.

Debet & solet, a writ of right, a suit to a mill, common of Pasture, &c.

Debilitation, *l*. a weakening.

Debility, *l*. weakness.

Debito de debito, a writ for mony due by obligation or bargain.

Debonairity, a being

Debonair, *f*. courteous, sprightly, complaisant.

Deborah, *h*. a word or bee.

Deboistness, a being

Deboist debauched.

Deboshrie, debauchery.

Debulliate, *l*. seethe over.

Decachord, *g*. an instrument of ten strings,

Decacuminate, *l*. take off the top of any thing.

Decade, *g*. a number of ten.

Decadency, *l*. a falling down

Decadist, a writer of Decads, as *Livy*, &c.

Decagon, *g*. a figure of ten angles or corners.

Decalogue, *g*. the ten Commandments.

Decameron, *g*. *Boccaces* book of Fables in 10 parts.

Decant, *l*. report, sing enchant

Decantation, *l*. a praising, also the pouring off of liquor setling by inclination.

Decapitation, *l*. a beheading.

Decapolis, *g*. part of *Syria*.

Decark, *g*. a Governor of ten.

Decede, *l*. depart.

December, *l*. the 10th. month from *March*.

Decempedal, of ten foot.

Decem tales, the Judges granting a supply of ten such Jurors as do appear, or as are not excepted against.

Decemvirate, the office and authority of the

Decemviri, ten *Romans* chosen to govern instead of the two Consuls.

Decenna, see *Deciners*.

Decennial, *l*. of ten years.

Deception, *l*. a deceiving.

Deceptione, a writ against him that doth any thing deceitfully in the name of another.

Deceptive, *l*. apt to deceive.

Decerp, *l*. pluck off or away, gather.

Decerption, *l*. a cropping off.

Decertation, *l*. a striving.

Decession, a departing.

Deciduous, hanging or falling down.

Decies tantum, ten times as much, recoverable from the Juror bribed to give his verdict.

Decimal, belonging to the number of ten.

Decimate, *l*. to tythe or take the Tenth.

Decimate, *l*. a tithing, also punishing every tenth man.

De decimis solvendis, a writ for recovery of Tythes of them that had farm'd the Priors aliens Lands of the King.

De-

Decenna, *-ary*, the jurisdicti-on of the

Deciners, *Decenniers*, *Deziners*, who were to keep the Peace within ten *Friburghs*.

Decide, *l.* determine controversies.

Decircinate, *l.* bring out of compass, unbind.

Decision, a determining or ending of a controversie.

Decisive, *-sory*, apt to determine.

Decius, a Roman Emperor who persecuted Christians.

Deck, floor [of a ship.]

Declaim, *l.* to make a

Declamation, crying out, also an Oration.

Declarative, which doth

Declare, *l.* make a

Declaration, manifestation, shewing forth, also a shewing the Plantiffes grief in writing.

Declension, *Declination*, a declining, bending or bowing [down,] also the variation of Cases in Nouns, &c.

Declinator, an instrument to take the

Declination of Planets, their distance from the *Æquator*.

Declivity, *l.* steepness.

Decoctible, easie to be sodden.

Decoction, *l.* a boiling away.

Decollation, *l.* a beheading.

Decomposite, *-pound*, *l.* compounded of more than two.

Deconate, as *Decury*.

Decoped, *o.* copped, peaked.

Decor, *l.* comliness.

Decorate, beautifie.

Decorticate, pill off the rinde.

Decoration, *l.* an adorning.

Decortication, a pulling off the bark.

Decorum, *l.* decency, comeliness, order.

Decretist, one that studies the

Decrees, *Decretals*, a volume of the Canon-law compiled by Gratian a monk.

Decrement, *l.* a decreasing.

Decrements, are paid by Schoars for the use (or wasting) of things at *Colledge*.

Decrepit, *l.* weak [with age.]

Decressant, *l.* waining.

Decretaliark, an absolute Commander.

Decrustation, a taking away the rinde or crust.

Deculcate, *l.* trample on.

Decumbence, *l.* a lying down.

Decumbiture, *l.* the taking ones bed, or first lying down in a sickness.

Decuple, *l.* ten fold.

Decurion, *l.* the chief of a

Decuria, a company of ten.

Decursion, a running down.

Decussate, *l.* to make a

Decussation, *l.* a cutting in the form of an X.

Decussion, *l.* a shaking off.

Decutient, shaking or beating down.

Dedalus, as *Dædalus*.

Dede, *o.* death.

Dedecoration, *l.* a disgracing.

Dedentition, *l.* a shedding of Teeth.

Dedi, (*l.* I have given) a warranty to the Feoffee and his Heirs.

Dedignation, *l.* a disdaigning.

Dedimus potestatem, a delegation or commission to a private man for the speeding some Judicial act.

Deeping-market, a Town in *Lincolnshire*.

Neither Dees nor Daws, No. neither dies nor mends.

Dedition, *l.* a surrendring.

Deed, *o.* dead.

Deeds, writings of contract.

Deemsters, *Demsters*, Judges (in the Isle of man) deciding all controversies, without process, charges, &c.

Deep-sea-lead, about fourteen pound hung at the

Deep-sea-line, to sound in deep waters.

Dees, *o.* a Canopy.

De essendo quietum de Tolonio, priviledge from payment of Toll.

Deësis, *g.* beseeching, earnest entreaty or calling to witness.

De expensis militum, a writ to levy 4 s. per day, a Knight of the Shires expenses.

Defailance, *f.* a failing.

Defaited, *o.* decay'd.

Defatigable, easily wearied.

Defatigation, *l.* a wearying.

Defamation, *l.* a slandering.

Defaulking, *f* the same as

Defalcation, *l.* an abating or cutting off

De facto, actually done.

Default, omission of what we ought to do.

Defeasance, *Defeisance*, *f.* the making void an act, obligation, &c. by performing a condition thereto annexed.

Defecated, refined.

Defecation, *l.* a refining or cleansing [from dregs.]

Defection, *l.* a failing, also revolting or falling away.

Defend, *f.* forbid.

Defendant, *f.* he that is sued in an action personal, as Tenant in an action real.

Defendemus, a binding the Donour to defend the Donee.

Defender of the Faith, a Title of the Kings of *England*, given *Henry* the 8th. by *Leo*. 10. 1521.

Defenestration, a throwing out at window.

Defeneration, a taking of money upon usury.

Defensatives, medicines diverting the humour.

Deficiency, *l.* a want or failing.

De fide, *l.* of Faith, necessary to be lieved.

Define, *l.* make a

Definition, explication, an unfolding the essence of a thing [by the genus and difference.]

Definite, certain, limited.

Definitive, limiting or determining.

Deflagration, a burning.

Deflection, *-exure*, a turning down or away.

Defletion, a bewailing.

Defloration, *l.* the same as

Deflowring, ravishing.

Defluxion, *l.* a flowing down [of humours.]

Deft, *o.* little and pretty.

Deforcement, a forcible withholding lands, &c.

Deformatio, as *Prosopopæa*.

Deformity, *l.* a being

Deformed, ugly, mis-shapen.

Deforsour, *-ceor*, *-ciant*, he that dispossesses one by force, as

Desseisour, without force.

Defouled, *o.* shamed.

Defray, make free, also to pay [anothers] charges.

Defunct, *l.* dead.

Defie, to chalenge.

Degenerous, he that doth

Degenerate, *l.* fall from the [better] kind, from vertue, to vice, &c.

Deglutination, *l.* an unglueing.

Deglutition, *l.* quick devouring, also the appetite of swallowing.

Degowtdy, *o.* moulting.

Degrade, *l.* cast down [from Office or Honour.]

Degradation, a degrading.

Degrandinate, *l.* to hail much.

Degree, *f.* a step or stair, a state or condition, also (in Astronomy) the 30th. part of a Sign.

Dehort, *l.* disswade.

Dehortation, a disswading.

Dejanira, *Hercule's* wife, who slew her self, because he burnt himself to avoid the torment caused by the shirt she gave him (to gain his love) presented her by the Centaure *Nessus* wounded by *Hercules's* arrow, for attempting to ravish her when carried by him over the River *Evenus*.

Deiden, *o.* dy'd.

Deicide, *l.* a killer of God.

Dejeration, *l.* a solemn swearing.

Deiformity, the form of God.

Deifie, *l.* make a God of one.

Deiphobus, *Priam's* Son, who causing *Paris* to be murdered, married his wife *Helena*.

Deignous, *o.* disdainful.

Deintie, *o.* desire or dainty.

Deipnosophists, *g.* wise men discoursing at supper.

Deirie, *o.* dairy.

Deis, *o.* a seat.

Deists, Anti-Trinitarians.

Deity, *l.* Godhead.

Delamere, a Forrest in *Cheshire*.

Delatour, *l.* an accuser, informer.

Delayed [*wine*] mingled with water.

Delegate, *l.* appoint another in ones stead, also he that is so appointed.

Delenifical, mitigating, pacifying.

Deleted, defaced, destroyed.

Deletry, [*medicines*] deadly, venemous.

Deletorious, apt to blot or rase out.

Deletion, *l.* a bloting out.

Delgovitia, supposed to be *Wighton* in *Yorkshire*.

Delibation, *l.* tasting, also a sacrificing.

Deliberate, *l.* with advice, leisure and consideration.

Deliberation, a debating or consulting.

Delibrate, *l.* peel off the bark.

Delict, *l.* offence.

Delignate, destroy wood.

Delimate, *l.* file off.

Delineate, *l.* draw the first draught of a picture, also to describe.

Delinquent, *l.* offender.

Deliquium, a fainting away, also the dissolving of a hard body (as salt, &c.) into liquor, in a moist place.

Delirous, belonging to or full of

Deliration, *-rium*, a doating.

Deliver, *o.* active, nimble.

Delian-twins, *Apollo* and *Diana* born in

Delos, cheif of the *Ægean Cyclade-Isles*.

Delle, *o.* Dike.

Dell, *Doxy*, *c.* a wench.

Delph, an abatement in the midst of an Escucheon, proper to him that revokes his challenge and eats his own words.

Delphick, belonging to

Delphos, a Town of *Phocis* in *Greece*, famous for *Apollo's* Oracle and Temple.

Deltoton, *g.* a Constellation resembling the greek delta

Delusion, *l.* a deceiving or being

Deluded, deceived.

Deluge, *f.* flood, inundation.

Dely, *o.* little.

Demagogue, *g.* leader of the people, head of a party.

Demain, *-mene*, *f.* manage.

Demandant, in real actions is the same as Plaintiff in personal ones.

Demean, behave, also bemoan, *o.*

Demene, *o.* dwell.

Demeanour, behaviour.

Dementation, a making or being besides ones self.

Demesne, *Demean*, *f.* land holden originally of ones self.

Demerit, an ill deserving.

Demas and Gesmas, (in the Gospel of *Nicodemus*) the two thieves crucified with Christ.

Demetrius, belonging to

Demeter, *g.* *Ceres*.

Demi- *l.* half-.

Demi-chase, *f.* half-hunting, Summer-riding-boots.

Demigrate, *l.* flit, remove.

Demin, *o.* a Judge.

Demipho, *g.* light of the people.

Demise, *l.* farm or let out.

Demission, a casting down or abasement.

Demit, *l.* lay down, to humble.

Democratical, belonging to

Democracy, *g.* a Government whose Magistrates are chosen from among and by the people.

Democritick, belonging to

Democritus, a Philosopher who laughed at all the world, and (for contemplation sake) put out his own eyes.

Demolition, a demolishing casting down and ruinating.

Demonachation, an expelling from, or forsaking the Monkish order.

Demoniack, as *Dæmoniack*.

Demonicracy, the Government of Devils.

Demonstrative, belonging to

Demon

Demonstration, l. a shewing or making plain.

Demonologie, a discourse of or with Devils.

Demophoon, succeeding his Father *Theseus* (in the Government of *Athens*) forgat *Phillis* whom he had married in *Thrace*, driven thither by storm, whereupon she hang'd her self on an Almond-tree.

Demosthenes, a famous Oratour, that was banished by *Philip* of *Macedon* and poisoned himself.

Demur, -*rrer*, f. stop at any case of difficulty.

Demy, an half-fellow [at *Magdalen Colledge* in *Oxon*.]

Denariata terræ, a farding-deal, or farundel of Land, the 4th. part of an acre.

Denary, the number of 10, also as

Deneer, -*ier*, f. the tenth (now the 12th.) part of a peny.

Denbigh, a Town in *Wales*.

Denwere, o. double.

Dene, o. a small valley, contrary to doun.

Dendrologie, the or a discourse of Trees.

Dene-lage, the law of the *Danes* before the Conquest.

Denis, *Dionysius*, a mans name.

Denis, *Diana*, a womans name.

Deneck, a. the swans tail.

Deneck eleced, a. the Lions tail.

D.neck alihedi, a. the bowing of the back, or doubling of the tail of the Goat.

Denigrate, l. make black.

Denizon, *Dennizen*, (q. *Danes* Son, or *Dinesidd*, *Br.* Citizen) an alien infranchised and made capable of Office or purchasing, but not of inheriting by descent (as one that is naturalized.)

Dennington, a Castle in *Berks*, once the residence of Chaucer.

Denomination, l. the giving of a name.

Denshire, *Devonshire*.

Denotation, a marking.

Dense, l. thick.

Densitie, l. thickness.

Dent, indented like the teeth of a saw, also dint, blow, impression, o.

Dental, belonging to the Teeth, also a small shell-fish like a dogs tooth.

Dentati, l. such as are born with teeth.

Dentelli, *Asseri*, the teeth above the *Cymatium* (in Architecture.)

Denticle, l. a little tooth.

Dentifrice, l. any thing to rub the teeth with.

Dentiloquent, l. lisping [through the teeth.]

Dentiscalp, l. a tooth-picker.

Dentition, l. a breeding teeth.

Denudation, l. a making bare or naked.

Denumerate, pay down.

Denuntiation, l. a denouncing or proclaiming.

Denwere, o. doubt.

Deobturated, l. shut or stopped from.

Deodand, a thing devoted (sold for the poors use) to expiate the mischief it hath done, as a Cart running over and killing a man, &c.

De Deoneranda pro rata portionis, when one is distrained for rent payable by others in proportion with himself.

Deosculation, l. an eager kissing.

Deperdeux, (*De par dieu*) f. from God.

Departer, -*ture*, waving the first thing pleaded (being replied to) and producing another.

Departers, parters, finers, refiners of Gold or Silver from the courser sort.

Departure in despight of the Court, when a Defendant appears to an action, but makes default in not appearing afterward.

Departed even, o. equally mixt, or divided.

Depauperate, l. make poor.

Depeculation, l. a stealing from the publick.

Depeloupe, o. (for *Deve-*) transparent.

Depend, l. hang or rely upon.

Dependance, -*cy*, a relying or staying upon.

Depension, l. a weighing or paying.

Deptford, *West-Greenwich* in *Kent*.

Depilatory, that which is apt to

Depilate, take away hair.

Depilation, a making bald.

Depilous, bald without wool, fur, or hair.

Deploration, l. a bewailing.

Deplantation, a taking up of Plants.

Deplume, l. strip off Feathers.

Depolition, a polishing.

Deponent, l. laying down, he that doth

Depose, -*site*, l. lay down upon oath.]

Deponent verbs, which have laid aside their passive signification.

Depopulatores agrorum, those that are guilty of

Depopulation, l. a spoiling, wasting or unpeopling [of a Country.]

Deportation, l. a carrying away.

Deportment, f. carriage, behaviour.

Depositary, he that keepeth a

Depositum, l. a pledge in Feoffee or trust.

Deposition, a laying down, an oath, also death.

Depravation, l. a spoiling, or making naught.

Deprædation, l. a preying upon, robbery.

Depredable, that may be rob'd or spoild.

Deprecation, l. a praying against [judgments, &c.]

Deprecate, divert by Prayer.

Deprehension, l. a taking unawares.

Depression, l. a pressing down

Depretiate, beat down the price.

Deprivation, *l.* a bereaving.

Deprome, *l.* draw forth.

Deprompsion, *l.* a bringing out.

Depudication, *l.* a deflouring.

Depulsion, *l.* a driving from.

Depuration, a cleansing [of a wound.]

Deputy, one appointed in the stead of another.

Dequace, *o.* dash, (*q. Dequash.*)

Dequantitate, to lessen the quantity.

Deradiation, *l.* a casting forth of raies or beams.

Derbent, a famous Port in *Persia.*

Derbices, people of *Asia* who eat their kindred at 70 year old.

Derceto, half woman, half fish, an Idol Goddess at *Askalon.*

Dercyllidas, a famous *Lacedemonian* Commander against the *Persians.*

Dere, *o.* to hurt, grieve.

Dereham East, a Town in *Norfolk.*

Dereliction, *l.* an utter forsaking.

Derelinquish, *l.* utterly to forsake.

Derein, *Deraign*, prove an action.

Dereinment, proof, also turning aside, departure.

Derham, a Town in *Glocestershire.*

Derick, *Theodorick.*

Derision, *l.* a laughing to scorn.

Derivation, a drawing from the Fountain or Original.

Dertmouth, a port-Town in *Devonshire.*

Derogatory, apt to

Derogate, disparage, diminish.

Derogation, a detracting from the worth of any thing.

Deruncination, *l.* a weeding out.

Dervises, *-vceshes*, a strict and severe sort of Religious Turks.

Desarcinate, unload.

Descalsas, Spanish bare-leg'd Fryers.

Descant, the answering of quick notes in one part to a slower measure in the other, also as Comment.

Descent, *l.* a going down, also a pedigree.

Descention, a going or faling down.

Deschevel, as *Dishevel.*

Describe, *l.* to make a

Description, imperfect definition, shewing the nature or property of a thing.

Descry, discover a far off.

Desecate, *l.* cut off.

Desection, *l.* a cutting down

Desecrate, degrade, discharge from holy Orders.

Désart, *-sert*, *l.* wilderness.

Desért, *f.* merit.

Desertion, *l.* a forsaking.

Deserter, *-tor*, *l.* renegado, that leaves one Religion, Prince or Captain for another

Desiccative, apt or able to dry up.

Desiccation, *l.* a drying up.

Desiderate, *l.* to desire.

Desiderative, desiring [to do what the primitive verb signifies.]

Desidery, *o.* desire, lust.

Designation, *l.* design, *f.* a purposing or contriving.

Desidious, *l.* negligent.

Desipience, *l.* foolishness, dotage.

Desist, *l.* leave off.

Deslavy, *o.* (*q.* deslawy) lawless, leacherous, beastly.

Desmonia, *Desmond* in *Ireland.*

Desolation, *l.* a laying or a lying waste.

Desolate, *l.* forsaken, left alone.

De son tort Demesne, *f.* the trepass was done of his own head, without command of Master, &c.

Despection, *l.* a looking downwards.

Desperation, *l.* a despairing or giving over.

Despicable, *l.* base, to be slighted.

Despoliation, *l.* a robbing or spoiling.

Despond, *l.* to despair.

Despondence, *-cy*, *l.* a being cast down, quite disheartened.

Despondingly, despairingly.

Desponsation, *l.* a betrothing.

Despotical, belonging to a

Despote, *g.* Lord, Governour.

Despumation, *l.* a taking off the scum or froth.

Dessert, *f.* the last course at a Feast.

Destination, *l.* an appointing.

Destiny, fate.

Destitute, *l.* forsaken, wanting.

Destitution, *l.* a forsaking.

Destrer, *o.* a war-horse.

Destruction, *l.* a destroying.

Desuetude, *l.* a disuse, desisting from any custom.

Desultorious, *-ry*, *l.* belonging or given to leaping or vaulting; also unconstant, mutable.

Desumption, *l.* a Chusing or taking out.

Detection, *l.* a discovering or laying open.

Detenebrate, *l.* dispel or drive away darkness.

Detention, *l.* a with-holding.

Deterioration, a making worse.

Determination, a purposing, appointing.

Deterred, *l.* affrighted, discouraged.

Detersion, *l.* a wiping or cleansing.

Detestation, an abhorring.

Dethrone, *l.* to depose or put from the Throne.

Detinue, *f.* a writ against him that refuses to deliver goods delivered him to keep.

Detonation, a thundring down, also driving away all impure Sulpherous and Mercurial parts of a body.

Detorsion, a wresting away.

Detraction, *l.* a drawing away, also a slandering.

Detrectation, a drawing back a refusing.

Detri-

Detrimental, having or bringing

Detriment, *l.* dammage.

Detrition, *l.* a wearing away.

Detrite, worn out, bruised, consumed.

Detrusion, a thrusting away.

Detruncation, a cutting off [limb or branch.]

Deturpation, *l.* a defiling.

Devastation, a laying waste.

Devastaverunt bona Testatoris, a writ against Executors for paying Legacies and debts without specialties, to the prejudice of Creditors having specialties.

Deucalidonians, the *Picts* in the West of *Scotland*.

Deucalion & Pyrrha, all that were saved in the General floud, restored mankind by throwing stones over their heads.

Devection, *l.* a carrying away or down.

Devest, uncloath, deprive.

Devexity, *l.* the hollowness of a vally, a bending down.

Devils-drop, [the reliques of a beacon on] a high hill at *Dover*.

Devils-bit, a plant who's root seems bitten [by the Devil, out of envy to mankind, for its rare virtues.]

Devenerunt, a writ commanding the Escheatour to enquire what lands came to the King, by the death of the Kings tenant.

Developed, *f.* unfolded.

Deviation, *l.* a going astray.

Devious, *l.* -*iant*, *f.* wandring, out of the way.

Devirgination, a taking away Virginity.

Devinals, *f.* wizards, or their predictions.

Devise, *Div-*, bequeath by Will, also to declare or tell, *o.*

Devisee, to whom goods are

Devised or bequeathed.

Devise, Motto, conceit, impress in a Coat of arms, *&c.*

Devises, -*izes*, a Town in *Wilts*.

Devonshiring, *Den-*, of land, is improving it by spreading on it the Ashes of burnt Turfs.

Deumo, an *East-Indian* Idol.

Devoir, *f.* duty.

Devolve, *l.* roll down.

Devolution, *l.* a rolling or falling from one to another.

Devote, *l.* vow, consecrate.

Devotion, *l.* a consecrating, also piety, a being

Devout, Religious.

Deuseaville, *c.* the Country.

Deuswins, a twopence.

Deusan, any hard lasting fruit.

Deuterogamy, *g.* second marriage.

Deuteronomy, *g.* the second law, a repetition of it.

Deuteral, pertaining to a second or weaker [wine, *&c.*]

Deutroscopy, *g.* a second aim, intention or thought.

Dewclaw, the little nail behind the foot of a Deer, *&c.*

Dewlap, the skin hanging under the Oxes throat.

Dex, *o.* for Desk.

Dexterity, *l.* a being

Dexterous, handy, active.

Dexter aspect, contrary to the succession of the signs.

Dexter point (in heraldry) begins in the Chief of the right corner.

Dexter-Epiploik vein, the 2d branch of the spleen-vein, passing to the *Epiploön* and *Colon*.

Dextral, a bracelet for the right arm.

Dey, *o.* Dairy-woman.

Diabetical, troubled with

Diabetes, *g.* the running of ones water without any stay.

Diabolical, *g.* Devilish.

Diacalaminthe, a powder of mountain *Calamint*.

Diacatholicon, a Composition of universal use.

Diachylon, a softening and concocting plaister of juices or mucilages.

Diacodium, a syrup of poppy-tops and water.

Diaconal, belonging to a Deacon.

Diacope, as *Diastole*

Diacydonium, Marmalade of Quinces.

Diacyminon, *g.* *Diacuminum*, *l.* a Composition of Cummin, *&c.*

Diadem, *g.* a linnen wreath for the head [of Kings;] also a Crown.

Diæresis, *g.* Division, also the mark thereof on the head of a vowel (¨).

Diagalanga, a Confection of *Galingale*, and hot spices, for the wind-cholick, *&c.*

Diagnostick, discerning, also apparent at present, also a sign or mark of distinction [in herbs, *&c.*]

Diagonal, *g.* passing from corner to corner.

Diagram, *g.* a decree, title of a book, Geometrical figure, also a proportion of measures in musick.

Diagraphical, belonging to the art of painting or graving.

Diagrydium, the prepared juice of Scammony-roots.

Dialacca, a confection of the gum Lacca, &c.

Dialectick, belonging to

Dialect, Logick, speech; also a particular propriety or Idiom of the same speech.

Dial, belonging to the day.

Diallel [*lines*] running cross and cutting one another.

Dialogism, a mans reasoning with himself.

Dialogical, belonging to

Dialogue, a discourse between two.

Dialyto, as *Asyndeton*.

Diamargariton, a restorative pearl powder.

Diamber, a Confection of Amber and hot spices.

Diamerdis, a Confection of Pilgrims salve, also a shitten fellow.

Diametrical, belonging to

Diameter, a streight line drawn

drawn through the center.

Diamond, *Adamant*, *g.* untamable (by reaſon of the hardneſs.) alſo the Rhomb or picke at cards.

Diamoſcʋu, a medicinal musk-powder.

Diana, the maiden Goddeſs of woods and hunting, twin-ſiſter to *Apollo*, by *Jupiter* and *Latona*: the Moon.

Dianoëtick, belonging to

Dianæa, Conſideration, alſo argumentation.

Diapaſm, Pomander or perfume of dry powders.

Diapaſe, *-ſon*, *g.* an Eight, the moſt perfect concord.

Diapente, a fifth, alſo a Farriers compoſition of *Myrh*, *Gentian*, *Birthwort*, *Ivory*, and *Bay-berries*.

Diahexapla, the ſame with an addition of Honey.

Diaper, linnen wrought with flouriſhes and figures.

Diaper'd, *-pred*, [bordure] in heraldry, where it is fretted all over, and ſomething appearing within the frets.

Diaper. (in painting) over-run the finiſht work with branches, &c.

Diaphanous, *g.* that may be ſeen or ſhon thorow.

Diaphanity, tranſparency.

Diaphonicon, an electuary of dates, &c.

Diapnoetica, medicines to ripen a ſwelling.

Diapranum, an electuary of *Damask-prunes*, *&c.*

Diaphoniſt, he that makes a

Diaphony, a diſcord or harſh ſound.

Diaphora, *g.* difference.

Diaphoretick, piercing through, diſcuſſing [humours.]

Diaphragmatick, belonging to the

Diaphragm, a fence, a partition; the skin, muſcle, midriff or apron parting the breaſt and ſtomach.

Diapedeſis, the ſweating of bloud.

Diaporeſis, a doubting, (either real or feigned.)

Diarrhoetick, belonging to a

Diarrhæa, a gentle flux of of the belly, without inflammation.

Diary, *l.* a day-book.

Dias, *drive away death with*

Dias and *Dragges*, *i. e.* dulneſs and dregs, or (perhaps) Diets and Drugs.

Diaſantalon, a confection of the wood Sahders.

Diaſatyrion, an Electuary of *Satyrion*, *&c.*

Diaſcordium, an Electuary of *Scordium*, &c.

Diaſena, *-ſenna*, *-ſonna*, an Electuary of *Sena*, *&c.*

Diaſtole, Extenſion, prolonging a ſhort ſyllable; alſo that motion of the pulſes which dilates the heart and arteries, as Syſtole contracts them.

Diaſyrmus, *g.* an extolling of a perſon(or thing) by way of deriſion.

Diateſſaron, a fourth (in muſick,) alſo a plaiſter of four ingredients,

Diatonick muſick, plain-ſong

Diatragantb, a confection of the gum *Tragantb* &c.

Diatribe, a place where Orations and diſputations are held.

Diatrionpipereōn, a medicine of 3 ſorts of pepper.

Diatypoſis a very exact and lively deſcription of a thing.

Diaturbith, an Electuary of *Turbith*, &c.

Dibble, a forked ſetting-ſtick.

Dicacity, *l.* taunting or mocking.

Dicæarchy, *g.* Government by a

Dicæarch, *g.* a juſt Prince or Governour.

Dicæologia, a brief expreſſing the juſtice of a cauſe.

Dication, *Dedication*, *l.* a devoting or conſecrating.

Dichling, a town in *Suſſex*.

Dichotomy, *g.* a cutting in two, dividing a diſcourſe.

Dicker [of Leather] ten hides

Dictamen, *l.* a thing written by the inſtruction of another.

Dictate, *l.* tell one what he ſhould write, alſo an Engliſh dictated for tranſlation, &c.

Dictitate, *l.* ſpeak often, plead.

Dickins, *Devilkins*, little devils.

Dictature, *l.* the ſame as

Dictatorſhip, the Office of a

Dictator, who's word was a law, choſen upon great and urgent Occaſions.

Dictionary, *l.* Lexicon, *ga.* ſtore houſe of words orderly digeſted and explained.

Dictum, *Diganway* in *Caernarvanſhire*.

Dictum de Kenelworth (Caſtle in *Warwickſhire*.) a compoſition between King *Henry* 3d. and the Barons, &c. for their Eſtates forfeited in that Rebellion.

Dictynna, *Diana*.

Dido, Queen of *Carthage* in *Africa*, ſhe kil'd herſelf, becauſe *Æneas* would not marry her, or (rather) becauſe ſhe would not be forced to marry *Jarbas* King of *Getulia*.

Didapper, diver, a bird.

Didram, *g.* a Roman coyn of fifteen pence.

Didactick, *-ical*, *g.* doctrinal, inſtructive.

Didaſcalick, pertaining to a Maſter or Teacher.

Didder, *No.* quiver [with cold.]

Didymus, *g.* *Thomas*, *h.* a twin.

Diem clauſit extremum, a writ for the Eſcheator to enquire into the Eſtate and next Heir of a Kings Tenant.

Diennial, *l.* of two years.

Dies datus, a reſpite given (by the Court) to the Tenant or Defendant.

Dieretick, belonging to

Diereſis, as *Diæreſis*.

Dieſpiter, *Lucetius*, Jupiter.

Diet, a German Parliment.

Dieta,

Dieta rationabilis, a reasonable dayes journey.

Dietary, treating of or belonging to a Diet

Dietical, daily, regular.

Dietetical, belonging to a prescribed Diet.

Dieu et mon droit, *f*. God and my right. First used (they say) by *H. n.* 8.

Diezeugmenon, *Epiz-*, *g*. the reference of several clauses to one verb.

Diffamation, *Def-*, *l*. a taking away ones good name.

Diffarreation, *l*. a *Roman* ceremony at divorcement.

Diffibulate, *l*. unbutton.

Difficulty, *-cacity*, *l*. hardness uneasiness.

Difficilitate, make difficult.

Diffidence, *l*. a doubting mistrusting,

Diffident, *l*. distrustful.

Diffoded, *l*. digged.

Difflation (in Chymistry) when Spirits (through heat) are blown and coagulated in the adverse Camera, a blowing down or about.

Diffluence, *l*. a flowing asunder or several wayes.

Diffusion, *l*. shedding abroad, dilating of a substance into more parts.

Digamist, *-ite*, as *Bigamist*.

Digamma, *g*. an *Æolick* letter, in force and figure like the Latin F.

Digestive, (in Chirurgery) that which prepares for cleansing.

Digestion, *l*. a disposing, concocting.

Digests, *l*. *Pandectes*, *g*. a Volume of the Civil law.

Dight, *No*. decked, made ready; also to foul or dirty one, *Che*.

Digit, any single figure in Arithmetick.

Digital, *l*. of a finger.

Digitation, a shewing or pointing with the fingers, also an expressing the form of them.

Digladiation, *l*. a combating [with swords.]

Digne, *f*. Worthy, neat, gentle, also disdainful.

Dignitary, a Church Officer without cure of Souls, as Dean, &c.

Dignity, *l*. honour, advancement.

Dignities of Planets, their being in their own houses, exaltations, triplicities and faces.

Dignorate, to set a mark on

Dignosce, *l*. discern, distinguish.

Digression, *l*. a going aside.

Dijudication, *l*. deciding a difference.

Dike-Grave, *D*. Overseer of the Low-Country Dikes and Banks.

Dilaceration, *l*. a rending or tearing asunder.

Dilaniation, *l*. tearing in pieces [like a Butcher.]

Dilapidation, *l*. a taking away of stones, also a wasting.

Dilatable, *l*. capable of

Dilatation, *l*. a widening.

Dilatory, *-ter*, a Chirurgeons widening instrument.

Dilatory, *l*. making delayes.

Dildo, *passa-tempo*, *l*. *penis succedaneus*.

Dilection, affection, love.

Dilemma, *g*. a forked or horned syllogism, where two propositions are so framed, that neither can well be denied.

Dill, an herb resembling fennel.

Dilling, *Darling*, a Child born when the parents are old, the youngest.

Diloricate, rip a sewed coat.

Dilstone, *Divelstone*, a town on

Divelsburn, a River in *Northumberland*.

Dilucid, *l*. clear, manifest.

Dilucidation, *l*. a making clear.

Dilute, *-ed* [wine] mingled with water.

Diluvial, belonging to a flood.

Dimber, *c*. pretty.

Dimension, *l*. the just measure or proportion, length, breadth, depth.

Dimetient, *l*. measuring.

Dimetæ, the ancient inhabitants of *Caermarthen*, *Cardigan* and *Pembrokeshire*.

Dimication, *l*. a skirmishing.

Dimidiation, *l*. a dividing in the midst.

Dimidietas, the one half.

Dimocks, an ancient family in *Cheshire*.

Diminutive, *l*. little, diminishing the signification of the primitive, blemishing or staining a part of the Escucheon, also lessening a pillar all along by degrees.

Dimissory, dismissing, discharging.

Dimissory [letters] of appeal.

Dinah, *h*. Judgment.

Dinarchy, *g*. a government by two.

Dingle, a small valley between two steep hills.

Ding, *No*. beat, also a blow, also to fling.

Diocese, *g*. the jurisdiction of a

Diocesan, a Bishop.

Dioclesian, a *Roman* persecuting Emperour, who (after two years) resign'd his Crown for a private life.

Diogenes, a Cynic, churlish Philosopher, who dwelt in a kind of tub.

Diomedes, King of *Ætolia*, one of the chiefest Hero's at the *Trojan* wars: also a King of *Thrace* who fed his horses with mans flesh, till *Hercules* gave them him for their meat.

Dionymal, *g*. of two names.

Dyonisia, a gemm which being bruised and drunk, tastes like wine and resists drunkenness.

Dionysius (of *Bacchus*) *Denis*.

Dioptick art, searching by perspectives the distances of planets.

Dioptrical, belonging to a

Dioptra, a Geometrical quadrat.

Diphryges, the dross of brass, sticking (like ashes) to the bottom

bottom of the furnace.

Dipthong, g. a double or compound sound, as *ei*, *ai*, *oy*, *ou*.

Diple, a marginal mark for the correcting of a fault.

Diploma, letters patent, a writ or Bull.

Dipondiary, l. of a pound weight.

Dipsas, a serpent who's biting brings a deadly thirst.

Dipseiline, as *Deep-sea-line*.

Diptote, g. a noun of two cases only.

Diptychs, g. tables with the names of famous men recited at the Altar, the living on one side, dead on the other.

Dire, l. cruel, dreadful.

Direction, l. instruction, putting in the right way.

Direct, straight.

Direct Planet, moving on in its natural course.

Number of direction, the 35 years between the highest and lowest falling of the moveable Feasts.

Directory, apt to direct or put in the right way, also a book of rules for Divine service, instead of the Common-prayer-book.

Diremption, l. a separation or setting apart.

Direption, l. a taking or snatching away, a robbing or plundering.

Dirge, (for *Dirige*, l.) Prayers for the dead.

Diribitory, the place of mustering and paying Soldiers.

Dirity, l. terribleness.

Diruption, l. a bursting in sunder.

Dirutor, l. he that destroys or pulls down.

Disability, a being [made] uncapable.

Disalt, to disable.

Disamis, a Syllogism whose midle proposition is an universal affirmative, the other two particular.

Disard, a block-head.

Disarmed [*Deer*] when the horns are fallen.

Disboscatio, assarting, turning wood-ground to arable or pasture.

Discalceate, l. unshooe.

Discarcatio, an unloading.

Disaster, f. misfortune.

Disastrous, unlucky.

Disceit, deceit, deception.

Discent, an order or means whereby land is derived to a man from his Ancestors.

Disceptation, l. contentious disputing.

Disceptator, a Judge or Arbitrator.

Discern, perceive, distinguish.

Discerption, l. a tearing in pieces.

Discession, l. a departing.

Discever, o. spend, consume.

Discheveled [*hair*,] f. hanging loose, out of order.

Discinct, l. ungirded, careless.

Disciple, l. Scholar, learner.

Disciplinable, capable of

Discipline, l. order, instruction, correction.

Disciplinants, Fryers that scourge themselves.

Disclaimer, an express denial or refusal (in law.)

Disclaim, f. renounce.

Disclose, reveal, discover.

Disclosed [*hawks*,] newly hatcht.

Disclusion, a shutting out.

Discolor, l. of divers colours.

Discolour, l. to change into another colour.

Discomfiture, f. a routing or vanquishing an enemy.

Disconsolate, f. comfortless.

Discontinue, f. leave or break off.

Discontinuance, -*uity*, interruption or breaking off.

Discontinuance of possession, a mans incapacity of entering on his own alienated lands, except in a legal way.

Discontinuance of Plea or Process, when (the opportunity of prosecution being lost) the suit must be begun afresh.

Discontinued, put without day, finally dismist the Court for that time.

Discordance, l. disagreement.

Discords [*in Musick*,] harsh, disagreeing notes.

Discrasy, as *Dyscrasy*.

Discount, set off, count how much less you have to pay.

Discrepance, l. a differing.

Discrepant, l. disagreeing.

Discretion, l. a distinguishing, also prudence.

Discriminating, distinguishing.

Discrimination, l. a putting of a difference between things.

Discubation, the same as

Discumbence, l. a lying (or sitting) down [to meat, &c.]

Discure, o. discover, show.

Discurrent, l. wandring about.

Discursion, l. a running up and down.

Discursive, l. belonging to discourse.

Discuss, l. shake up and down, handle, search narrowly into.

Discussion, a shaking, handling, searching, &c.

Disembarque, *Disimbark*, f. to land [goods] out of a ship.

Disembogue, Sp, Vomit up, also to sail out of the straight mouth of a gulph.

Disertitude, l. Eloquence.

Desesperance, f. dispair.

Disfranchize, f. take away ones freedom.

Disgrade, as *Degrade*.

Disgregation, a scattering or separating [from the flock.]

Disguise, f. put into another guise or form.

Disgust, f. distaste.

Dish-meat, *Kspoon-meat*.

Disherison, a disinheriting, dammage.

Disheritour, *Disheriter*, endammager.

Disherit, *Disinherit*, f. put out of Possession or right thereto.

Disimbellish, f. disfigure.

Disjugate, disjoyn.

Disjoynt, o. a hard case, danger.

Disjunctive, belonging to

Disjunction, l. a separating or disjoyning.

Dis-

Disjunctum, as *Diezeugmenon*.

Dislocation, a putting out of joint, out of the right place.

Dislodge, *f.* rowse, raise [a Buck.]

Disloyalty, *f.* unfaithfulness.

Dismal, dreadful.

Dismantle, *f.* take off a cloak, also beat down the walls of a Town, Fort, &c.

Dismay, astonish.

Dismember, *f.* cut off a member or joynt.

Dismembering-knife, as *Cutling*.

Dismes, *f.* tithes.

Dismiss, *l.* send away.

Dismount, *f.* take down, unhorse.

Dismount a piece, take her off the carriage.

Dispand, *l.* stretch out.

Dispansion, *l.* a spreading abroad.

Disparage, *f.* disgrace.

Disparagement, an undervaluing, also the marrying of an Heir or heiress under their degree.

Disparates, *l.* opposites wherein one thing is opposed to many.

Disparility, the same as

Disparity, *l.* inequality, unevenness.

Disparition, *l.* a disappearing.

Disparpled, *-perpled*, *-perpelled*, loosly scattered, shooting it self into divers parts (in heraldry.)

Dispaupered deprived of the Priviledge of *forma pauperis*.

Dispend, *f.* spend [money.]

Dispensation, *l.* a distributing or dealing, performing the office of a

Dispenser, *-sator*, *l.* Steward.

Dispensatory, *f.* *Pharmacopœa*, *g.* directions (from the Colledge of Physicians) for making all Physical compositions, &c.

Dispertion, *l.* a scattering.

Dispert a peice of Ordnance, find the different diameters between the mouth and breech.

Dispicience, *l.* looking diligently, considering.

Dispitous, *o.* angry, full of spite.

Display, *f.* unfold, spread abroad.

Displant, *f.* pluck up.

Displicence, *l.* a displeasing.

Displosion, *l.* a bursting in two, also the shooting a gun off.

Dispoliation, *l.* a spoiling, rifling, robbing.

Dispone, *o.* dispose, set in order.

Disport, *o.* sport.

Disposition, *l.* a disposing, also the Constitution [of body or mind.]

Dispositor, *l.* a disposer.

Dispossesse, *f.* put out of possession.

Disproportion, inequality.

Dispurveyed, *f.* bare, indigent, unprovided.

Dispute, *l.* strive, contend (either by words or blows.)

Disquammation, *l.* a scaling [of fish, &c.]

Disquisition, *l.* a narrow search.

Disrationare, *o.* *Traversare*, to traverse.

Dissasina, *f.* Dispossession.

Dissection, *l.* a cutting in two or in pieces.

Desseisin, *f.* unlawful dispossessing one of Lands or goods.

Disseisin upon Disseisin, when the

Disseisour, (or Dispossesser) is

Disseised, (dispossest) by another.

Dissemination, *l.* a sowing or scattering up and down.

Dissentaneous, *l.* disagreeing.

Dissentery, as *Dyssentery*.

Dissentiment, *f.* disagreement [in opinion.]

Dissentory, *o.* a kind of still.

Disserve, *f.* do a

Disservice, *f.* an ill office, a bad turn; disclaiming ones service.

Dissidence, *l.* a disagreeing, a falling out.

Dissilience, *l.* a leaping up and down, a falling asunder.

Dissimilar, *-ry*, *l.* unlike, compounded of several similar parts.

Dissimilitude, *l.* unlikeness.

Dissimulation, *l.* a dissembling.

Disheveled, as *Desch-*, *Dish-*.

Dissipable, capable of

Dissipation, *l.* a scattering, dispersing.

Dissite, *l.* remote.

Dissociation, *l.* a separating.

Dissology, Dialogue.

Dissolve, *l.* Melt, destroy, undo, put an end to.

Dissolute, loose, debauched, lawless.

Dissoluble, capable of

Dissolution, *l.* a dissolving, also death.

Dissonance, *l.* disagreement [in sound.]

Disswade, *l.* perswade against.

Disswasion, a perswading against.

Dissyllable, *g.* a word of two syllables.

Distantial, belonging to

Distance, *l.* space, a being

Distant, asunder, far off.

Distaunce, *o* Discord.

Distemper, sickness, also size for [ancient] painting.

Distend, *l.* stretch out, enlarge.

Distention, an enlarging.

Distermminate, *l.* divide place from place.

Distick, *g.* a couple or pair [of verses.]

Distillation, *l.* a dropping down, a

Distilling, extracting the moisture of things by heat, and condensing the vapour again by cold.

Distillatio per descensum, when the liquor falls into a vessel below the distilled matter.

Distinction, *l.* Distinguishing, putting a difference between; shewing the several meanings of a thing.

Distinguement, the same as

Distorsion, *-tion*, *l.* a wresting, writhing, pulling awry.

Distrain, take away goods for the payment of a debt; also to grieve, vex, *o.*

Distress, a distraining, also great affliction.

Distract, *l.* draw asunder, perplex, also to cause

Distraction, Madness.

Distreine, *o.* Constrain.

Distreineth, *o.* Effecteth.

Distributive, *l.* belonging to

Distribution, *l.* a dividing among many, resolving the whole into parts, also as *Dieresis*.

Districation, Disentangling, ridding out of trouble.

Disturn, *o.* turn away.

District, *-tus*, *l.* jurisdiction, the compass within which a man may be compel'd to appear, or be distrained.

Distrigilation, *l.* a currying.

Distringas, a writ for the Sheriff to distrain.

Distringent, wiping off, also troubling.

Disturbance, *-ation*, *l.* a causing of trouble.

Disveloped, as *Developed*.

Disvirgin, Deflour.

Disunited, *l.* severed.

Dite, *o.* (for indite) a treatise.

Dithyramb, *f.* a jovial song [to *Bacchus*.]

Dition, *l.* Dominion, jurisdiction, territory.

Dittander, *Dittany*, *Dictamnum*, *Lepidium*, *Piperites*, *Pepperwort*, a cleansing herb, from

Dicte, a Promontory of *Creet*.

Ditto, *I.* the same, the said.

Dittology, *g.* a double reading or meaning.

Ditty, Song.

Divagation, *l.* a going astray.

Dival, Divine.

Divan, *-no*, the *Turkish* and *Persian* great solemn Council or Court of Justice.

Divaporation, exhalation of vapour by fire.

Divarication, *l.* a being

Divaricated, spread as a fork.

Divelled, pulled away, ravished.

Diventilate, winnow.

Diverberation, *l.* a beating.

Diversify, *l.* vary, alter.

Diversity, *l.* a being

Diverse, *l.* different [in circumstance.

Divers, many, several.

Diversiloquent, speaking diversly.

Diverticle, *l.* a turning, a by-way, also a shifting device.

Divertisement, *f.* recreation.

Dividend, *l.* the thing to be divided, the dividing, also the division or share.

Dividual, *l.* apt to be divided.

Dividuity, division, aptness to divide.

Divinale, *-ail*, *o.* a ridle.

Divination, *l.* foretelling of things to come.

Divine, *l.* guess; also heavenly, also a professour of

Divinity, *l.* the mystery of heavenly things, also as Deity.

Divinistre, *o.* a smatterer in Divinity.

Divinize, to [make] Divine.

Divisibility, *l.* a being

Divisible, capable of

Division, Dividing or being divided.

Divitiate, enrich.

Divitiosity, a being very rich.

Divitiacus, King of the *Gauls*.

Divorce, to separate (also the separation) from the bond of Wedlock.

Diuretical, *g.* provoking urine.

Diurnal, *l.* belonging to the day, also a day-book or News-book.

Diuturnity, *l.* lastingness.

Divulgation, *l.* a publishing abroad.

Divulsion, *l.* a pulling asunder

Dizain, *f.* half a score.

Dize, *No.* put tow on a distaffe.

Dizen'd, *No.* drest.

D. La sol re, the fifth note in the common Gamut or Scale of Musick.

Dobeler, a great dish or platter.

Dobuni, antient inhabitants of *Oxford* and *Glocestershire*.

Doced, *Douced*, a Dulcimer.

Docility, *Docibility*, *l.* a being

Docile, teachable apt to learn.

Docilize, make tractable.

Dock, a place where ships are built or laid up, also the fleshy part of a Boars chine between the middle and the buttock.

Docket, a brief in writing, or a subscription (under the Letters Patents) by the clerk of the Dockets.

Doctiloquent, *l.* speaking learnedly.

Doctoral, belonging to a

Doctor, *l.* teacher, he that hath taken the highest degree in Divinity, Physick, Civil-law or Musick.

Doctorate, *f.* Doctorship.

Document, *l.* instruction.

Dodded, *o.* having the branches or horns cut off.

Dodder, a weed winding about herbs.

Dodecaedrie, *-dron*, *g.* a figure of twelve sides.

Dodecagon, *g.* a figure of 12 Angles.

Dodecatemorie, *g.* one of the twelve parts of the Zodiack.

Dodkin, by some a farthing, by others the 8th. part thereof.

Dodman, *So.* *Hodmandod*, *Nf.* a shel-snail.

Dodona, a City in *Greece*, near which *Jupiter* had an Oracle in a wood whose trees were supposed to be vocal and to return the answers of the Oracle.

Dodo, (*Dors*, *Dors*, *f.*) sleep, sleep; lullaby.

Dodonæus, a Physician of *Mechlin* in *Germany* author of a famous herbal.

Dodrantal, of nine ounces.

Dodu, a chuffe or fat-chaps.

Dogana, a custom-house in the *East-Indies*.

Doeg, *h.* careful.

Dog-

Dog-days, in *July* and *August*, when the Dog-star, rising with the Sun, encreases his heat.

Dog-draw, when a man is found drawing after a Deer by the sent of a dog in his hand.

Doge, Duke [of *Venice*.]

Dogger, a kind of ship.

Dogget, as *Docket*.

Dogmatical, imposing his own opinions, also prudent.

Dogmatist, introducer of new opinions.

Dogmatize, to impose a Doctrine, also to instruct.

Dogs-bane, a dog-killing herb.

Dogs-grass, common in Gardens and ploughed fields.

Doke, *E. Sf.* deep dint or furrow.

Dolation, *l.* a smoothing, plaining.

Dole or *Dool*, *No.* (*q. dale.*) a long unplowed green in a plowed field.

Dole, *l.* deceit, grief, also a distributing of Alms.

Doleans, *f.* a lamentation.

Dole-fish, which the north-sea Fishers do by custom receive for their allowance.

Dolg-bote, *Dolgbot*, satisfaction for a wound.

Dollar, a dutch crown less than ours.

Dolgelle, a Town in *Merioneth-shire*.

Dolling, *o.* warming.

Dolorous, *l.* painful.

Dolphin, a fish that loves men, the eldest Son of *France*, also a Constellation of nine bright stars.

Dolt, for block-head.

Dolven, *o.* buried.

Doly. *Dooly*, *o.* mourning, sad.

Dolyman, a Turkish garment

Domable, *l.* tameable.

Dome, *I.* a Town-house.

Domestick, *-cal*, *l.* belonging to the house or Family.

Domes-man, *o.* confessor, or Judge.

Domicil, *l.* a dwelling-place.

Dominative, belonging to

Domination, *l.* a ruling or Lording.

Dominical, of the Lord.

Dominica in ramis palmrum, Palm-sunday.

Dominica in albis, Whitsunday.

Dominical Letter, shewing the Lords-daies in an Almanack.

Dominicide, *l.* killer of his Master.

Dominicans, an order of Fryers instituted, 1206. by

Dominick, a *Spaniard*, the author (as they say) of the Inquisition.

Domicellus, *-la*, titles given *John* of *Gaunts* Son and Daughter in their naturalization.

Domino, a hood worn by Canons, also a womans mourning veil.

Domitian, a persecuting Emperour of *Rome*, who was wont (when alone) to kill flies.

Dompte-vilain, *f.* tame-knave a good cudgel.

Domition, *-ture*, *l.* a taming.

Domnerar, *c.* a madman.

Domo reparanda, a writ against him that lets his house go to decay, and endanger his neighbours.

Domus Conversorum, a house appointed by King *Henry* the third, for Jews converted to the Christian Faith, now the rolls.

Don, *Doun*, *sa.* a hill.

Donary, *l.* a gift or present.

Donatists, hereticks detracting from the Son and Holy Ghost, and holding the true Church to be only in *Africa*, from

Donatus, Bishop of *Carthage*.

Donnat, *Donnaught*, (*q.* do nought, or naught) idle, good for nothing, naughty, *T.*

Donation, *l.* bestowing, a gift.

Donative, apt to give, also a gift, a Benefice.

Done houres, *o.* [to observe] Canonical, given or consecrated houres.

Doncaster, a Town in *York-shire*.

Dondon, *o.* a short fat woman.

Donegal, as *Tyrconel*.

Donee, to whom lands are given.

Donour, he that gives [lands, &c.]

Doniferous, gift-bearing.

Donwich, a Town in *Suffolk*.

Doom, *Sa.* judgment, sentence, also sence or signification.

Dooms-day-book, made in the time of *Edward the Confessor* (or *William the Conquerour*) wherein all the demeans of *England*, (and the possessours) were registred.

Dont vient la destenie (or *le destin*) *f.* whence the fate or destiny comes.

Dooms-man, *sa.* a Judge.

Dorado, *Sp.* guilded over.

Dorcas, *g.* a Deer or Roebuck.

Dorchester, the cheif Town in *Dorcetshire*, and another in *Oxfordshire*.

Dordrectum, *Dort* in *Holland*

Dorias's woundwort, an herb with broad leaves, wherewith he used to cure himself and his Soldiers.

Dorick, one of the five greek Dialects, also a kind of work in Architecture.

Dorick-mood, *Dorian-musick*, of a slow solemn time, from *C sol fa ut* to *A la mi re*.

Doris, wife to *Nereus*, and Mother of the Sea-nymphs *Nereides*.

Dormant, *f.* in a sleeping posture, having a blank to put in a name.

Dormant-tree, the summer or beam lying cross the house.

Dormant, (*q. demeurant*, *f.*) unremoved.

Dormers, windows in the roof of a house.

Dornix, a kind of stuff for curtains, &c. from

Dornick, a City in *Flanders*.

Dorothy, *g.* the gift of God.

Dorp, *Thorp*, a village.

Doronicum, a Cordial herb resisting poyson.

Dorrie, a fish that shines like gold.

Dortor, -*ture*, *Dortoire*, *f.* *Dormitory*, *l.* a place where many sleep together, a burying place.

Dose, *g.* so much of a Medicine as is given or taken at a time.

Dosology, *g.* a discourse concerning the several Doses.

Dosome [*beast*] *Che.* content with nothing; also thriving.

Dosel, *Dorsel*, a Princes Canopy, also the Curtain of a Chair of state.

Dosser, *Dorser*, a panier.

Dotal, belonging to a Dowry.

Dote assignanda, a writ for the Escheator to assign a Dowry to the widow of a Kings tenant, swearing in Chancery not to marry without the Kings leave. These are the Kings widows.

Dote unde nihil habet, a writ of Dower for a widow, of the land sold by her husband, whereof he was so seised as the issue of them both might have inherited.

Doted, *l.* endowed, having a joynture.

Dotkin, as *Dodkin*, or (by some) the 8 part of a Sol or *French* peny.

Dottrel, a foolish bird (in *Lincolnshire*) imitating the Fowlers, till it be caught.

Douane, *f.* Custom, the Custom-house at *Lyons*.

Double quarrel, a Complaint to the Archbishop against an inferiour Ordinary for delay of justice.

Doubles, Letters patents.

Doubleth, when a hair winds up and down, to deceive the dogs.

Doublet, a precious stone, of two pieces joyned.

Doublets, a low game at Tables.

Doublings, linings of Robes (in Heraldry.)

Dover a Sea-town in *Kent*.

Doves-foot, a kind of Cranes-bil, an herb.

Dove-tail, a kind of Joyning by laying one piece into another.

Doughty, *o.* stout, valiant.

Douglas-town, in Man Island.

Doulcets, *Dowsets*, the stones of a hart or stag.

Doundrins, *Der.* afternoons drinkins.

Dousabel, *f.* *Dulcibella*, *l.* sweet and fair.

Douset, *Doulcet*, a Custard.

Doutaunces, *f.* doubtings, suspicions.

Doutremere, (*d' outre mere*, *f.*) from beyond sea, sea-faring.

Dow, *o.* (*q. Da*, *l.*) Give, also thrive, mend, *No.*

Dowager, applyed to widows of Princes, &c.

Doway, an *English* Seminary in the *Netherlands* instituted 1568. by the procurement of one *W. Allen* of *Oxford*.

Dowl, *o.* Deal.

Downs, *Sa.* hilly plains, also a harbour between *Deal* and the *Goodwin sands*.

Downeham, a town in *Norfolk*.

Dow-gate, (*q. down-gate*, or *Dour-gate*, *Br.* Watergate) where the water runs faster into the *Thames* than in any other street in *London*.

Dower, Dowry, a wives portion.

Dowsets, as *Doulcets* or *Douset*.

Dowtremere, as *Doutremer*.

Doxie, *o.* a she-beggar, trull.

Doxology, *g.* *Gloria Patri &c.* repeated (in the Liturgy) at the end of Psalms, &c.

Dozens, *Devonshire* Kersies.

Dozein, as *Deime*.

Drabler, a piece added to the bonnet, when there is need

Draco's laws, very severe, from

Draco, an *Athenian* Governour.

Drafty, *o.* Irksom, troublesome.

Dragant, *Tragacant*. Goats horn, a gum Distil'd from an herb so called.

Dragges, *o.* Dregs or Drugs.

Draggts, whatever hangs over the ship in sea, as shirts, &c. also the boat, and all hind'rances of sailing.

Dragons-head, a node or place in the Eclipticka which the Moon cuts ascending *Northward*.

Dragons-tail, the node (opposite to the *Dragons head*) which the Moon cuts descending *Southward*.

Dragons, Serpentary, Vipers Bugloss.

Dragonstone, a kind of precious stone in a Dragons head.

Drags, pieces of wood joyn'd to carry wood &c. down a river.

Draiton, *Drayton*, a town in *Shropshire*.

Draitwitch, a town in *Worcestershire*.

Drake, a field piece of Ordnance.

Sir *Francis Drake*, in two years space sail'd round the world.

Dram, *Drachm*, *g.* the 8 part of an ounce.

Dramatick poetry, Comedies and Tragedies.

Dran, *o.* bran.

Drap de Berry, thick *French* cloth of *Berry*.

Drape, *No.* a farrow-Cow, whose milk is dry'd up.

Drape-sheep, *No.* Culled, Bad.

Drapery, Cloth-wares, cloth-market, also a representing of Cloaths in painting.

Draught, a Drawing.

The ship Draws much water, i.e. goes Deep in water.

Draule, *o.* speak dreamingly.

Drawers, *c.* stockings.

Draw-latches, Roberts-men, Night-thieves.

Drede, *o.* dread.

Dregge, Draw a little Crapnel on the ground, to find a cable, &c.

Dredgers, Oister-fishers.

Dreint, *o.* drowned, drench'd.

Dreit-dreit, a double right (of possession and Dominion.)

Drenched, *o.* over-com'n.

Drenie,

Drenie, *o.* sorrowful.
Drengage, the tenure of a
Dreynghe, *Drenge*, *Drench*, a tenant in *Capite*.
Dretch, *o.* dream, tarry.
Dry exchange. Usury.
Dribblets, *o.* little bits.
Dree, *No.* long, tedious [way] also a hard [bargaine.] *q.* dry.
Driffield, a Town in *Yorkshire*.
Drift, a driving, a scope or intent, Counsel or Policy.
Drift of the Forest, an exact view of the Cattel.
A Drift, a-float, swimming down stream.
Drift-sail, to keep the ships head right upon the Sea (in a storm, &c.)
Drill, a baboon, also a tool to bore holes in Marble, Iron, &c.
Drink-lean, Scot-ale, provided by the Tenants to entertain their Lord or his Steward.
Drivebolt, a long piece to drive out a nail, &c. (in a ship.)
The ship drives, when the anchor will not hold her.
Drogeday, *Tredah in Ireland*.
Drofdenn, *Sa.* a grove.
Drofland, *Dryfland*, rent paid the Landlord for driving Cattel through the Mannor, to fairs or Markets.
Drogoman, *Truchman*, *Tu.* an interpreter.
Droit, *f.* right.
Drol, *f.* a little stage-play, also he that uses
Drollerie, *f.* jesting, joquing.
Dromedary, a kind of Camel with two bunches on his back.
Dronklew, *o.* given to drink.
Drovy, *o.* (*Droevigh*, *d.*) troubled.
Drozen, *No.* fond.
Dropacist, one that applies a
Dropax, *g.* a depilatory, or medicine to take away hair.
Dropsy, (for *hydropsie*,) *g.* a waterish distemper.
Dropping, a hawks muting (in drops) directly downward.

Dropwort, *filipendula*, an herb.
Drouk,
Drough, *o.* drawn.
Dru, *Drugo*, *Drogo*, *sa.* subtile.
Dradging, Oyster-fishing.
Drugge, *d.* any dry simple used in medicine, also drudge, *o.*
Drunk wort, Tabacco.
Druides, old Gaulish Priests.
Drungar, a Grecian Commander [of a squadron.]
Drury, *o.* modesty, sobriety.
Drusilla, *Dioclesians* wife.
Dry, *Drien*, *o.* suffer.
Dryads, *g.* Oak or Wood-Nymphs.
Duacum, *Doway*.
Dual, *l.* belonging to two.
Duality, *l.* a being two.
Duana, as *Divano*.
Duarchy, *g.* government by two.
Dub, *No.* a pool of water.
Dub, make [a Knight.]
Dubiosity, a being
Dubious, *l.* doubtful.
Dublin, the Chief City of *Ireland*.
Dubris, *l. Dover*.
Ducal, belonging to a Duke.
Ducape, a kind of silk.
Ducenarious, belonging to two hundred.
Duces tecum, a writ to appear in Chancery, and bring some evidence to be viewed.
Duck up the clew-lines, when a sail hinders the sight in steering, shooting, &c.
Ducks-meat, an herb swimming on the top of standing waters.
Ducket, *Ducate*, a Roman Gold coyn, about 6 s.
Ductarious, drawing, or leading.
Ductile, (mettals) to be drawn out and beaten into plates.
Ductible, capable of
Duction, *l.* a leading.
Dudman, (*q. Deadman*) a Maulkin or scare-crow.
Duel, *l.* a Combat between two.
Duls, *c.* Goods.

Duilus, a *Roman* that beat the *Carthaginians* by Sea, the first that triumphed after a naval victory.
Dulcacid, sweet and soure.
Dulcarnon, (by some) a proportion found out by *Pythagoras*, after a years study, also the Oxe which he sacrificed in thankfulness.
At Dulcarnon, in a maze, at my wits end, *Chaucer*, *l.* 3. *fol.* 161.
Dulciaries, *l.* sweetning things.
Dull, *D.* mad.
Dulcifie, *l.* sweeten.
Dulciloquent, sweet-spoken.
Dulcimer, a wire-string'd instrument.
Dulcisonant, *l.* sweet-sounding.
Dulcitude, *l.* sweetness.
Dulcoration, *l.* a sweetning.
Dulocratical, belonging to
Dulocracy, *g.* a Government where servants domineer.
Dulverton, a Town in *Somersetshire*.
Dumal, belonging to bryers.
Dumosity, *l.* fulness of bushes.
Dum fuit infra ætatem, a writ to recover land sold by one under age.
Dum non fuit compos mentis, a writ to recover land alien'd by one not of sound memory.
Dun, importune.
Dunbar, a Town in *Scotland*.
Dunch, *o.* deaf.
Dundee, a Town in *Scotland*.
Dunsets, *sa.* Mountainers.
Duni pacis, as knolls of peace.
Dunholm, a Town in *Lincoln-shire*.
Dunmow, a Town in *Essex*, where the Prior gave a flitch or gammon of Bacon to all that swore they repented not of marrying within a year and a day, or never made any nuptial transgression.
Dunnington, a Town in *Lincolnshire*.
Donington-Castle, a Town in *Leicestershire*.
Dunstable, a Town in *Bedfordshire*.

Dunster, a Town in *Somerset*.

Dunstan, *Sa.* most high, or as *Aaron*.

Duodecennial, of 12 years.

Duodecimo, of twelve [leaves in a sheet.]

Dup, *c.* enter [the house.]

Duplicity, *l.* a being

Duple, double, twofold.

Duplicate, *l.* Double, also a second letter of the same contents with the former.

Duplication, *l.* a doubling, also an allegation brought to weaken the reply of the pleader.

Dura mater, the outward skin that infolds the brain.

Duration, *l.* continuance, lasting.

Durense, *o.* (*Duracines*, *f.*) some kind of solid and lasting fruit.

Dures, *-ress*, a plea of exception by one constrained (by imprisonment, &c.) to seal a bond.

Durham, *Duresme*, *Dunholm*, *Dunelmum*, the Chief City of the Bishoprick of *Durham*,

Durham Colledge, Trinity Colledg in *Oxford*.

Durity, *l.* hardness.

Durnovaria, *Dorchester*,

Durotriges, *Dorcet-shire-Britains*.

Dursley, a Town in *Glocestershire*.

Duskie, Dark.

Dutchie-Court, where all matters relating to the Dutchy of *Lancaster* are Decided.

Duumvirate, the Office of the

Duumviri, *l.* two Magistrates of Equal authority in *Rome*.

Dwale, sleeping or deadly night-shade.

Dwas-light, *Sa.* Jack with a Lanthorn, *Will-a-wisp*.

Dwindle, shrink or consume away.

Dwyned, *o.* consumed.

Dyers-weed, used for yellow-colour.

Dyke-reeve, Overseer of the *Dykes and Draines* in Deeping-fens, &c.

Dyna, an *East-India* Coyn, about 30 *s.*

Dynamologie, *g.* a Discourse of power.

Dynaste, *-stick*, *g.* [a powerfull] Prince.

Dynastie, *g.* supream authority.

Dypticks, as *Diptieks*.

Dyrrachium, *Durazzo* in *Macedonia*.

Dyscrasy, *g.* a Distemper, an unequal mixture of the first qualities.

Dysentery, *g.* the bloudy-flux.

Dysnomy, *g.* evil constitution or ordering of the law.

Dysopsy, *g.* dimness, bad sight.

Dyspathy, *g.* evil passion or affection.

Dyspepsie, *g.* an ill digestion.

Dyspnœa, *g.* a difficult breathing.

Dyss, a Town in *Nf.*

Dysury, *g.* a scalding or stopping of the urine.

E.

EAd, *Eadith*, *Sa.* *Auda*, happiness.

Eadelman, *Adelman*, *Sa.* Nobleman, Earl.

Eadgar, *Sa.* happy power.

Eadulph, *Sa.* happy help.

Eadwin, *Sa.* happy victor.

Eaglestone, found in the nest of Eagles.

Eaglet, a little Eagle.

Ealderman, *Ealdorman*, Alderman, as *Eadelman*, or Earl.

Ealred, *Sa.* all-counsel.

Ealdred, *Sa.* all-reverent.

Eame, *Sa.* the Mothers brother; also Gossip, Friend, *No.*

Ean, bring forth [young.]

Ear, *ar*, *Sa.* honour.

Ear, *l.* till [the ground.]

Eardorburgh, *Sa.* Metropolis or Chief City.

Earing, that part of the bolt rope, which (at the Corners of the sail) is left open like a ring.

Earl, *Sa.* a Nobleman.

Earn, *No.* to run (like Cheese.)

Earning, *No.* Cheese-rennet.

Earnest, *c.* a part or share.

Ease the ship, slacken the shrouds when too stiffe.

Ease the helm, let her fall to the lee-ward.

Easel, a Painters frame for his Cloth.

Earthnut, pignut, a root in shape and taste like a nut.

Easement, a service from Neighbour to Neighbour (by Charter or prescription) as passage through his ground, &c.

Easie of dispence, *o.* of little expence.

Easter, *No.* the back or stock of the Chimney,

Easter, *Eoster*, *Aoster*, *Oster*, a *Saxon* Goddess, whose feast they observed in

Easter-month, April.

Easter, the Christian-Passover, in remembrance of Christs [Death and] Resurrection. On this depend all the other moveable feasts, and the most certain Rule to find it (according to the Church of *Englands* use) is this: Shrove-tuesday is alway the first tuesday after the first new moon that happens after *January* (whether that be in *February* or *March*) and the Sunday following is *Quadragesima* (or the first Sunday in Lent) and the sixth Sunday after is *Easter-day*.

Easterling [Mony] 'Sterling, current, pure, coyn'd by the

Easterlings, Inhabiting the *Eastern* parts of *Germany*.

Eastmeath, a County in *Ireland* containing 18 Baronies.

Eath, *Eth*, *Eith*, *o.* Easie.

Eath, *sc.* an Oath.

Eaton, above 20 towns in several Counties.

Eaves-dropper, one that Listens under the windows or house-Eaves.

Ebere-murder, *Sa.* open and inex-

inexplable murder.

Ebene, see *Ebony*.

Ebionites, Hereticks deny-ing Christs Divinity, and all Gospels but St. *Matthews*, Anno 71.

Ebissa, a Saxon-Captain assisting *Hengist* against the *Britains*.

Ebony, black, hard wood of the

Eben-tree, an *Indian* and *Ethiopian* tree, without leaves or fruit.

Eboracum, *Eburacum*, *Brigantium*, *York*.

Ebourn, a town in *Suffex*.

Ebrank, a British King.

Ebrack, *o*. *Hebrew* [tongue.]

Ebriety, *Ebriosity*, *l*. Drunkennefs.

Ebrious, *l*. [making] drunken.

Ebulo, as *Ybel*.

Ebullate, *l*. to bubble or burst out.

Ebullition, -*iency*, *l*. a boiling up

Eburnean, *l*. of Ivory.

Eccentricity, a being

Eccentrick, *l*. moving at unequal distance from the Center, out of order.

Ecclesiastick-cal, *g*. belonging to the Church.

Ecclesiastes *g*. The Preacher.

Eccleshall, a Town in *Staffordshire*.

Echen, *o*. Increafe or help.

Echidne, a *Scythian* Queen, who had three children at a birth by *Hercules*.

Echo, *Eccho*, a Nymph dying for the love of *Narcissus*, and turned into that voice.

Ekle, *Ettle*, *No*. To aim or intend.

Eclipse. *g*. want or defect [of light;] also to darken or obscure.

Eclipse of the Sun, by the interposition of the Moons body.

Eclipse of the Moon, by the interposion of the Earth.

Ecliptick [*line*] running through the *Zodiack*, in which the Eclipses happen, when the Moon is in Conjunction or opposition under it.

Eclegma, *Lohock*, a confection (thicker than a Syrup and thinner than an Electuary) to be lickt and softly melted down.

Eclogue, *Eglogue*, a Pastoral or Shepherds Dialogue.

Eclympastery, Son to *Morpheus* the God of sleep.

Ecphonesis, *g*. exclamation, crying out.

Ecstasie, *g*. making a short syllable long, also a trance or sudden rapture of Spirit.

Ecstatick, -*eal*, belonging thereto.

Ecthlipsis, *g*. a thrusting out [the letter m (and the vowel before it) when the following word begins with a vowel or h.]

Ectype, *g*. a draught from another copy.

Ed, *sa*. again.

Edacity, *l*. a greedy eating or devouring.

Edder, a fish resembling a Mackrel.

Eddish, *sa*. *no*. *Roughings*, new latter grafs, aftermathes.

Eddie, the turning round in a stream.

Eddy-tide, where the water runs back, contrary to the tide.

Eddy-wind, that which recoiles from a fail, &c.

Edelfleda, *Elfleda*, govern'd the Kingdom prudently eight years after the death of her husband *Ethelred*, King of the *Mercians*.

Eden, *h*. pleafure, paradife.

Edenburgh, -*borrow*, the chief Town in *Scotland*.

Edentate, *l*. make toothlefs.

Edge-hill, in *Warwick-shire*, here was fought the first pitcht battel between the King and Parliament.

Edgware, a Town in *Middlesex*.

Edict, *l*. Proclamation, Ordinance.

Edification, *l*. building, also instruction.

Edifice, *l*. a houfe, a building.

Edile, *Eadile*, *l*. the Surveyor of the buildings in *Rome*.

Edinton; *Eathandune*, a Town in *Wilt-shire*.

Edish, *Edise*, *sa*. later-math.

Edition, *l*. setting forth, impreffion.

Edifferator, *l*. a shewer or declarer.

Edituate, *l*. to defend or govern the houfe or Temple.

Edmund, *Sa*. happy peace.

St. Edmunds-bury, *Bedericksgueord*, a Town in *Suffolk*.

Edomites, posterity of *Edom*, (*h*. red,) *Esau*.

Education, *l*. a bringing up.

Edward, *sa*. happy keeper.

Eever, *che*. corner or quarter.

Eel-fares, *Eel-vares*, the fry or brood of *Eeles*.

Eem, *Che*. to have leifure, to spare time.

Effable, *l*. which may be exprest or utered.

Effascinate, *l*. to bewitch.

Effated, *l*. *o*. for *Ef*-, or defaced,

Effect, *l*. end, finishing, that which is caufed.

Effects, Merchants concerns.

Effection, *l*. a forming, expreffing.

Effete, *l*. having lately brought forth, also barren.

Efferous, *l*. fierce, cruel, violent.

Efficacious, full of

Efficacy, *l*. virtue, power, force.

Efficient, *l*. making, working.

Effiction, *l*. an expreffing or reprefenting.

Effigies, *l*. shape, reprefentation of any thing.

Effiguration, as *Prosopopæa*.

Efflagitate, *l*. importune, earnestly to requeft.

Efflated, *l*. blown away, yeilded or given up.

Efflorescence, a budding forth, or flourishing.

Effluence, *Efflux*, *Effluvium*, *l*. a flowing forth.

Effluent, -*uous*, *l*. running or flowing out.

Effocate, *l*. choak, strangle.

Effemination, a making

Effeminate, *l*, womanish.

Effe-

Efforts, *l.* strong assaies, endeavours, or impressions.

Effraction, *-ture*, *l.* a breaking open.

Effringed, *l.* broken, ground to pouder.

Effractores, Burglars, breakers-open of houses.

Effrænation, *l.* rashness, unbridledness.

Effronterie, as affrontedness.

Effund, *l.* pour out, consume riotously.

Effusion, *l.* a pouring out, prodigality.

Eft, *o.* again, also *Evet.*

Efters, *o.* waies, walls, walks, galleries, entries, hedges.

Eft soones, *o.* quickly.

Egal, *f.* equal.

Egbert, *Ecb-*, *sa.* ever bright, the first English Monarch.

Egean, as *Ægæan.*

Egestion, *l.* a voiding or throwing forth.

Egestuosity, *l.* extream poverty, a being

Egestuous, *l.* very poor or needy.

Eggement, *o.* procurement.

Eglantine, *f.* sweet-bryer.

Egilopical, *Ægi-*, belonging to the

Egilopa, *Ægi-*, a canker in the corner of the eye, the *lachrymale fistula.*

Eglogue, as *Eclogue.*

Eglomerate, *l.* unwind.

Egre, *o.* sore.

Egregious, *l.* excellent.

Egremont, *-mond*, a Castle and Town in *Cumberland.*

Egress, *-sion*, *l.* a going out.

Egrets, *o.* a kind of ravenous bird.

Egrimony, as *Ægrimony.*

Egritude, *l.* sickness, as *ægrotting*, as *Ægrotting.*

Egurgitate, *l.* draw out, empty, disgorge.

Egyptians, *'Gypsies*, (*Cingari*, *I.*) counterfeit vagabonds.

Eiud, *h.* praising.

Ejaculation, *l.* a casting forth; also a sudden and short meditation or prayer.

Ejaculatory, *l.* having the power or property of darting or sprouting forth.

Ejection, *l.* a casting out.

Ejectione Custodiæ, *l.* and

Ejectment de gard, *f.* a writ against him that casts out the heirs Guardian.

Ejectione firmæ, a writ for the Lessee ejected before the expiration of his term.

Eigh, *o.* Eyes.

Eign, eldest.

Eight, *Alney*, an Isle in *Glocestershire*, where *Edmund* King of *English* and *Canutus* King of *Danes* (in a single combat) try'd their right to the Kingdom.

Eighteth mow, *o.* might grant.

Einecia, Eldership.

Eirenarch, *g.* Justice of peace.

Eirenarchie, *g.* a keeping of the peace, the Office of Constable, Justice, &c.

Eisil, *Sa.* Vinegar.

Eitching, as *Etching.*

Ejulation, *l.* a yelling or howling.

Ejuration, *l.* a renouncing.

Eke, also; also to piece, lengthen or enlarge, also to kill, hurt or make to ake.

Ela, the highest note in the Common scale of Musick.

Elaborate, *l.* Done with exactness and great pains.

Elaboratory, *Labra-*, a [chymists] work-house or shop.

Elacerate, *l.* rend or tear in pieces.

Elamites, the posterity of

Elam, *h.* young man.

Elami, the sixt note in Musick.

Elapidation, *l.* a taking away of stones.

Elapsion, *l.* a slipping away.

Elapsed, *l.* slipt, gone, past.

Elaqueate, *l.* disintangle.

Elate, *Elated*, *l.* lifted up, proud.

Elation, *l.* a lifting up.

Elaterium, *g.* Concrete juice of wild Cucumbers.

Elaxate, *l.* unloose, widen.

Eld, *o.* age, Eldership.

Elder, *D.* and *No.* the udder.

Eleack, Philosophers instituted by *Phædo* an

Elean, of *Elis* in *Greece.*

Ele, *o.* help, assistance.

Elden, *No.* fewel for fire.

Eleanor, *Helena.*

Eleazar, *h.* the help of God.

El.campane, *Enula campana*, horse-heal.

Elect, *l.* choose, also as

Elected, chosen.

Elective, belonging or subject to.

Election, *l.* a choosing, choice.

Election de Clerk, a writ for the Choice of a Clerk assigned to take and make the bonds called Statute Merchant.

Elections, (in Astronomy) fit times elected for the doing any manner of work.

Electorat, the Office, power or territory of the

Electors, Electoral-Princes, who choose the Emperour of *Germany.*

Electriferous, *l.* yielding

Electrum, Amber, distilling from Poplar-trees.

Electricity, *l.* power to draw straws &c. like amber.

Electrine, belonging to, or made of Amber.

Electuary, a Confection of the choicest Drugs.

Eleëmosynary, *g.* of free gift also an Almoner.

Eleëmosynate, to give alms.

Elegance, *-cy*, *l.* a being

Elegant, *l.* Neat.

Elegiac [*verse*,] pentameter, of five feet (most commonly subjoyn'd to the Hexameter) belonging to an

Elegie, *g.* a kind of mournfull verse, or funeral song.

Elegiographer, a writer of Elegies.

Elegit, a writ for part of the land and goods, till the debt or damage given be satisfied.

Elementary, belonging to

Elements, *l.* unmixt bodies, the principles of all things.

things, fire, air, water, Earth; also the first Principles or Rudiments of any art, and the single letters of an Alphabet.

Elemi, a *West-India* gum.

Elenchical, *-ctick*, *-cal*, *g.* belonging to

Elench, *g.* a subtile argument, by way of reproof.

Elenge, *o.* strange, forreign.

Elengelich, *o.* strangely or miserably.

Elephansy, *Elephantiasy*, the Leprosie.

Elephantine, belonging to an Elephant.

Eles, *o.* Beles.

Elevation, Exaltation, lifting up; (in Chymistry) the rising of any matter in manner of fume or vapour.

Elevatory, an instrument to lift up broken pieces of the skull, draw out bullets, &c.

Elf, *Elve*. a fairy.

Elguze, the left shoulder of *Orion*.

Eliah, *Elijah*, *Elias*, *h.* [My] God the Lord

Eliakim, *h.* God ariseth.

Eli, *h.* My God, or the Offering, lifting up.

Elibation, as *Delibation*.

Elicitation, *l.* a drawing out, an enticing.

Elide, *l.* to dash, break, squeeze or strangle.

Eligible, *l.* to be chosen.

Elihu, *h.* he is my God.

Elimation, *l.* a filing off.

Elimination, *l.* a casting over the threshold, out of doors.

Elingued, *l.* tongue-tied, dumb.

Eliphaz, *h.* the endeavour of God.

Eliquament, *l.* fat juice of flesh or fish.

Elisa, *Dido* Queen of *Carthage*.

Elisha, *h.* my God saveth, or the salvation of God.

Elisæus, *-zeus*, as *Elisha*.

Elishaphat, *h.* my God judgeth.

Elision, *l.* a dashing or striking off or out.

Elixation, *l.* a seething.

Elixir, *-er*, *A.* strength, quintessence, also the Philosophers stone.

Elizabeth, *h.* the fullness or oath of God.

Elk, a strong swift beast like a stag, also a kind of Ewe for bows.

Ellinge, *Sf.* solitary, lonely.

Ellipsis, *g.* wanting, leaving out, also a crooked line in the bias-section of a Cone or Cylinder.

Elliptick, Defective.

Ellis, *Elias*, *h.* Lord God.

Elmer, *Ethelmer*, *Sa.* Noble, renowned.

Elmet, a certain Territory about *Leeds* in *Yorkshire*.

El-mother, *Cu.* a Step-mother.

Elocution, *l.* proper speech, handsom utterance.

Eloah, *Elohim*, *h.* God [the Judge.]

Elogie, *l.* commendation.

Eloinment, *f.* *Elongation*, *l* a removing far off.

Elopement, a womans leaving her husband, dwelling with an Adulterer, and losing her Dower,

Eloquence, as *Elocution*, a being

Eloquent, *l.* neat, and powerful in speech.

Eltham, a town in *Kent*.

Elth, *o.* old. See *Eld*.

Elucidaries, Expositions of obscure things.

Elucidation, *l.* a making bright, clear, plain.

Elucubration, *l.* a watching and studying by candle-light.

Elves, Fairies, hobgoblins.

Elvish, *o.* froward.

Elutheria, feasts to the *Elutherian God*, *Jupiter*.

Ely, a City in the midst of the fens in *Cambridgshire*.

Elychnious, without match, weik, or light.

Elysian fields, pleasant places whither the heathens supposed the Souls to pass.

Elysium, the same, paradise.

Elytroides, Vaginal tunicle, the inmost of the 3 tunicles covering the testicles.

Emaceration, a soaking, also as

Emaciation, *l.* a making lean.

Emacity, *l.* a desire of being alway buying.

Emaculation, *l.* a taking away of spots.

Emanation, *l.* a flowing from.

Emancipation, *l.* a legal setting of Children free from the power of their parents.

Emanuel, *Emm-*, *h.* God with us.

Emanuensis (for *Ama-*,) One that writes for another, a Secretary.

Emargination, *l.* a cleansing of sores from the scurfe about the brims.

Emasculation, *l.* a taking away of Manhood, Effeminating.

Embalming, the seasoning a dead body with gums and spices, to keep it from putrifaction, also wrapping it in Searcloth of wax, gum, &c.

Embarasment, *f.* a perplexing, intangling, hind'ring.

Embargo, *Sp.* a stop or arrest laid upon ships.

Embassade, *f.* Embassy, Message.

Embattel'd, set in battel aray, also as *Crenelle* (in Heraldry.)

Embelf [*circle*] *o.* oblique, or else Embolick, belonging to leap-year.

Ember-weeks, (when the Bishop sprinkled ashes on the Peoples heads in token of mortality) four Seasons in the year, set apart for fasting and prayer, immediately preceding the Ordination of Ministers.

Embellish, *f.* beautify.

Embezel, *l.* theevishly to consume or make away.

Emblematical, belonging to an

Embleme, *g.* a curious inlaying in wood, &c. also a device or picture Expressing something moral or divine.

Emblematist, a maker of Emblems.

Emblements, the profits of land [which hath been sowed.]

Embolism, g. the casting in of the day added to Leap-year.

Embolned, o. swelled.

Embossement, *Embouchement*, f. a putting into the mouth.

Embost, foaming at the mouth, (spoken of a hunted Dear.

Embracery, the act or offence of an

Embraceor, *-cor*, he that, (being no lawyer, but for reward) comes to the bar and speaks for either party, labours with the Jury, &c. the penalty is 20 *l.* and imprisonment.

Embring-daies, the Wednesday, Friday and Saturday, before every ordination Sunday.

Embrocation, *l.* by some, a bathing any part in liquor falling from aloft; by others, a rubbing the part affected or applying of clothes dipt in oyl, &c.

Embryous, belonging to an

Embryo, *-on*, g. the Child in the Mothers Womb not yet shaped, also any thing else before it come to perfection.

Embushment, as *Embossement*.

Embushment, f. the falling [of a river] into the Sea.

Embuscade, f. an Ambushment.

Embden, a City built upon *Ems*, a River in *Friezland*.

Eme, o. an Aunt.

Emendals, (at the foot of an account in the Temple) bank or stock for the house.

Emendation, *l.* a mending.

Emmition, *l.* a lying or forging.

Emerald, *Sp.* a precious stone of a green colour.

Emergency, a being

Emergent, *l.* rising up above water, appearing on a sudden, also of great importance.

Emeril, a *Garnsey*-stone, wherewith they cut and burnish other precious stones.

Emetical, *-ique*, g. purging the body by vomit.

Emersion, *l.* a rising, appearing or coming out.

Emication, *l.* a shining out.

Emigration, *l.* a passing out.

Emerlin, o. a Marlin, Hawk.

Emildon, a Town in *Northumberland*, birth-place of the subtile Dr. J. *Duns*, called *Scotus*.

Emforth, o. according.

Eminence, *-cy*, a being

Eminent, *l.* excellent, appearing above others.

Emissary, *l.* one sent abroad [to spy or give intelligence.]

Emission, *l.* a sending forth.

Emit, *l.* send or cast out.

Emme, a womans name, either as *Amie* or *Elgiva*, help-giver.

Emmoised, o. comforted.

Emmot, ant, pismire.

Emollid, *l.* soft.

Emollient, *l.* softning.

Emolument, *l.* mill-toll, profit.

Emotion, *l.* a moving out, a stirring up, also trouble of mind.

Empair, f. diminish, make worse.

Empale, as *Impale*:

Empanel, *-nnel*, enter the names of the Jury in a Schedule.

Emparlance, f. a petition (in court) for a day of respite.

Empasmus, g. powders to allay inflammations and scarifie the extremity of the Skin.

Empeor, o, grow worse.

Emphatical, having or done with an

Emphasis, *-sy*, g earnestness, an intent expression of ones mind.

Emplastica, g. clammy medicines stopping the pores of the skin.

Emphyteutick, g. set out to be improved, let out to farm.

Emphyteuticary, an improver making a thing better than he received it.

Empirick, g. a Physitian that cures by receipts taken upon trust.

Empirically, done like an Empirick, by practice without Theory.

Emplaister, *l.* plaister.

Emplasteration, *-tration*, *l.* an applying of a plaister, a dawbing, also a graffing.

Emporetical, belonging to an

Emporium, *-ry*, *l.* a Mart-Town, or an Exchange.

Emprimed, spoken of a Hart at first forsaking the Herd.

Emprize, o. enterprize.

Emprosthotonos, g. a kind of Cramp.

Emptional, to be bought.

Emption, *l.* a buying.

Emptory, as *Empory*.

Empturition, *l.* a longing to buy.

Empyema, g. corruption between the breast and lungs, after a Pleurisie.

Empyreal, g. fiery.

Empyreal Heaven, the highest.

Emrods, as *Hemorrhoides*.

Emucid, *l.* mouldy.

Emulation, *l.* a striving to excel others.

Emulgent, *l.* milking out.

Emulgent vein, pumping vein, one of the two main branches of the hollow vein passing to the Reins.

Emulsion, *l.* a stroking, any kind of cream or milky substance, seeds, &c. brayed in water and strained to the consistence of an Almond milk.

Emunctories, *l.* the kernels by which the principal parts void their superfluities, also a pair of snuffers.

Emuscation, *l.* a rubbing the moss off.

Enach, *Sc.* a satisfaction for any crime or fault.

Enacted, decreed, ordained.

Enaluron, when a bordure (in heraldry) is charged with any kind of Birds.

Enamel, f. to vary with little spots.

Enantiosis, g. contrariety.
Enargie, Evidence, clearness.
Enblaunched, o. adorned, whited.
Enbolned, o. swelled.
Encaustick, g. enameled, varnished, wrought with fire.
Enchase, f. to set in gold.
Enchant, f. conjure, bewitch.
Encheafed, o. heated.
Encheson, f. occasion, cause or reason why any thing is done.
Enchiridion, g. a hand- or pocket-book.
Enclitick, -cal, g. enclining, a particle joyn'd to the end of words and causing the accent to encline that way.
Encumbrance, f. an hindrance.
Encomiast, g. a Praiser of vertues.
Encomiastick, belonging to
Encomium, -ion, g. a speech in the Praise or Commendation of any.
Encontrewayl, o. prevent.
Encrees, o. Increase.
Encroachment, a pressing too far upon a neighbours ground.
Encyclical, round, belonging to
Encyclopædie, as *Cyclopædie*.
End for end, when a rope is all run out of the Block, &c.
Endammage, f. to hurt or damnify.
Endeynous, o. Disdainfull,
Endictment, *Enditement*, an accusation exhibited or presented to the Court.
En Dieu est, f. it is in Gods hand or power.
Endive, a cooling herb.
Endorse, f. write on the back-side.
Endorse, the fourth part of a pallet.
Endoubted, o. feared,
Endowment, f. the bestowing or assuring of a Dower.
Endowment de la plus belle part, a widows Dower of Lands holden in soccage, as the fairer or better part.
Endowment of a vicaridge, the setling of maintenance on a vicar (by some great tithes, &c.) when the rest of the Benefice is appropriated.
Endromick, -me, g. a long *Irish* robe, used before and after running, &c.
Endry, o. Endure.
Endymion, a Shepherd in love with the Moon, who stoops every night to kiss him, being cast into a perpetual sleep on the top of *Latmus* hill.
Endyd in untime, o. Yeaned before the time.
Enecated, l. killed.
Eneorema, g. a cloud in distilled waters, or in urines when the Disease is breaking.
Enewed, o. made new.
Encrees (of. *Denrées*) o. wares, or peny-worths.
Enervity, weakness.
Enewed, o. renewed.
Eneya, Sa. the principal part of the heritage, passing to the eldest son.
Energetical, belonging to
Energy, g. force, efficacy, powerfull working.
Enervation, l. a weakening.
Enfield-Chase, in *Middlesex*, belonging to the Earls of *Essex*.
Enfamined, o. famished.
Enfecteth, o. infecteth.
Enfranchisement, f. incorporating into a society or body politick.
Engastrimuth, g. one that speaks out of his belly.
Engel-bert, Ge. bright Angel.
Engine, l. devise, wit, o.
Engined, o. racked.
Englecerie, *Englecherie*, *Englescheyre*, f. a being an *Englishman*.
Englaymyd, -lemed, o. Nauseated.
Englutting, o. gluing, or glued, stopped.
Engonasi, -sin, g. *Hercules* on his knee, a Constellation.
Engrailed, as ingrailed
Engyscope, g. an instrument to discern the proportion of the smallest things.
Enharmonick, -iack, Musick] of many parts, differing from the other 2 kinds, *Chromatick*, and *Diatonick*.
Enhaunsement, f. a raising the price of a thing.
Enigma, as *Ænigma*.
Enion, Br. just, upright.
Enitia pars, as *Esnecy*.
Enlased, o. intangled.
Enlangored, o. Languishing.
Enneade, Nine. g.
Enneagon, g. a figure of 9 angles.
Ennealogue, g. a discourse of 9 points, or parts.
Ennoy, Sc. annoy.
Enochs pillars, (supposed) one of brick, the other of stone containing the whole art of Astronomy.
Enoch, *Henoch*, h. Dedicated to God.
Enodation, l. a taking away of knots.
Enormity, l. errour, unevenness, a being
Enormous, irregular, unmeasurable, out of rule.
Enosch, h. mortal, miserable.
Enpited, o. delighted.
Enprice, o. the fashion.
Enquest, f. the trial of causes by a Jury.
Enquitance, -aunce, o. Enquiry.
Enseame, purge a hawk of her glut and grease.
Enseeled, [a hawk] having a thread drawn through her upper ey-lids, and made fast under her beak.
Ensconse, D. Entrench.
Ensiferous, l. sword-bearing.
Ensign, f. an Escutcheon; also a banner, or he that bears it.
Ensise, o. quality, stamp.
To Ensile hawks, See *Enseeled*.
Enstall, set upon a throne, endow with a robe of honour.
Enstallment, a making

Knights of the Garter, &c.

Entail, f. (cut off) fee-tail, fee-entailed, limited, tied to certain conditions.

Entailed, o. engraven.

Entalenten, o. stir up.

Entangle, ensnare, perplex.

Entetched, o. defiled.

Entelechie, g. an understanding, soul, or power to move or act of it self.

Entendaunce, o. service.

Entendment, f. the true sense and meaning.

Entermelled, o. intermingled.

Enterfeire, -fere, -frir, f. to hit one against another, as a Horses heels, &c.

Entermined, o. robbed, emptied.

Enterlaced, as *Enlased*, contrary to unlased.

Enterplead, -plede, discuss or try a point accidentally happening, before the principal can be determined.

Entetched, *Entecched*, o. qualified.

Enthalamize, bring the bride and Bridegroom to bed.

Enthean, -ated, inspired with God.

Enthymematical, belonging to an

Enthymem, g. an imperfect Syllogism, part being retained in the mind.

Enthysiasmical, -astick, -cal, belonging to

Enthysiasm, *Enthusiasm*, the doctrine or principles of an

Enthysian, *Enthusiast*, g. one pretending to Divine revelation and inspiration, fanatick.

Entiertie, *Int*-, the whole.

Entierement vostre, f. entirely yours.

Entire Tenancy, a sole possession in one man.

Entire pertransient, a line crossing the midle of a shield and running diametrically the longest way of her position.

Entire pertingents, lines running the longest, way of the shields position, without touching the center.

Entitatively, according to the

Entity, an essence, being or subsistence.

Entoire, when a bordure is charged with all sorts of inanimate things, except leaves Fruits and Flowers.

Entoxicate, l. to poyson.

Entrails, f. bowels.

Entreague, Sp. a making good again, also a story (after manyentangled passages) brought to a calm end.

Entreat, o. to handle.

Entrecomune, o. f. converse together.

Entremees; -mes, f. intermingled.

Entremesse, entertainment between the messes, or courses.

Entremete, o. to deal or medle.

Entresse, o. entrance.

Entreteden, o. to handle.

Entry, a taking possession.

Entriked, o. deceived.

Entrusion, a violent entrance.

Entrusion de gard, a writ against an Infant within age, entring upon his lands and holding his Lord out.

Entunes, o. tunes.

Entwyssel, an ancient house and Family in *Lancashire*.

Enucleate. l. take out the kernel, also unfold, expound.

Envelope, f. infold, wrap up.

Environ, f. to compass about.

Enumerate, l. to reckon up, to number.

Enunciation, l. an uttering or pronouncing, also (in Logick) a proposition.

Enunciative, simply affirming or denying.

Envoy, f. (*Envoié*) a messenger sent [to an Ambassadour.]

Envoice, as *Invoice*.

Enure, to take place or effect or be available.

Envyron, o. as *Environ*.

Enurny, all borders of Coats charged with beasts (in heraldry.)

Eolian, belonging to *Æolus*, God of the Winds.

Epact, g. the addition of eleven dayes, to equal the Lunar year of 354, to the solar of 365 daies.

Epagoge, g. the comparing of things that are alike.

Epaminondas, a great Captain of the *Thebans* against the *Lacedemonians*.

Epanadiplosis, g. a beginning and ending with the same word in a sentence.

Epanalepsis, g. a repetition of the same word for enforcement sake.

Epanaphora, g. when the same word begins several sentences.

Epanodos, g. a repitition of things in an order inverted.

Epanorthosis, g. a recalling and correcting somthing before spoken.

Epatrides, g. certain Noblemen amongst the *Athenians*.

Eparch, g. the cheif Governour of a Province.

Epenthesis, g. the putting of a letter or syllable into the midle of a word.

Epha, an hebrew measure of nine gallons.

Epheby, g. a stripling.

Ephemera febris, a Fever that lasts but one day.

Ephemeron, daily, also as

Ephemeridian, belonging to

Ephemerides, g. Journals, also Almanacks.

Ephemerist, he that writes Almanacks, Calculations, &c.

Ephesian, belonging to

Ephesus, the chief City of *Jonia* in *Asia minor*, famous for the Temple of *Diana*.

Ephesian moan, like that of *Heraclitus* their weeping Philosopher.

Ephi, as *Epha*.

Ephialtes, g. the night-mare

Ephippiated, g. sadled.

Ephippiarchy, a body of 16 Troops of horse, 1024.

Ephod, a Linnen Garment worn by the Jewish Priests.

Ephori,

Ephori; *g.* certain Magistrates among the *Lacedæmonians.*

Ephraimites, the Off spring of

Ephraim, *h.* fruitfull.

Epibole, *g.* as *Epanalepsis*, only with respect to the matter, as that is to the style, a repetition of the same word at the beginning of several sentences.

Epick poetry, written in Heroick verse, not *Lyrick.*

Epicrasis, *g.* a slow and moderate evacuation of bad humours.

Epicedie, *g.* -*ium*, a funeral song.

Epicæne, *g.* comprehending both sexes under one gender.

Epichrists, *g.* ointments.

Epicure, -*ean*, belonging to

Epicurus, an *Athenian* Phylosopher holding Pleasure to be the chiefest good.

Epicurism, the manner or custom of an

Epicure, or voluptuous person.

Epicycle, a lesser orb, whose centre is in the Circumference of a greater, whereby they solve the irregular motions of Planets, &c.

Epidemick, -*cal*, belonging to an

Epidemy, *g.* a disease or contagion univerally catching.

Epidermis, *g.* the outward skin covering the main skin of the body.

Epididymis, *g.* one of the tunicles involving the testicles

Epigamy, *g.* affinity by marriage.

Epigastrick, *g.* belonging to the

Epigastrium, the outward part of the belly, from the stomach to the navel.

Epiglot, -*ttis*, *g.* the weasel of the throat, the little tongue closing the Larynx.

Epigram, *g.* a short and witty sort of poem, playing on the subject.

Epigrammatist, -*igrapher*, a maker or writer of Epigrams.

Epigraph, *g.* an inscription.

Epileptick, belonging to, or troubled with an

Epilepsy, *g.* a Convulsion of the whole body, the falling sickness.

Epilogism, a computation or numbring by way of repetition.

Epilogize, to make an

Epilogue, *g.* a conclusion, also a speech at the end of a play.

Epiloimick, *g.* good against the plague or any infection.

Epimenides, a *Cretian* poet. who slept (they say) 75 years in a Cave, as he kept his Fathers sheep.

Epimone, *g.* a tarrying long upon one subject or matter.

Epiod, *g.* a song before the burying of the corps.

Epephonema, *g.* Acclamation, a sententious clause of a discourse.

Epiphany, *g.* appearance [of the star to the wisemen,] Manifestation [of Christ to the Gentiles] *January 6.*

Epiphora, *g.* force, impression, repeating the same word (with respect chiefly to the matter) at the end of several sentences.

Epiplexis, *g.* an elegant upbraiding in order to conviction.

Epiploce, *g.* a gradual rising of one clause of a sentence out of another, much like to *Climax.*

Episcopal, *g.* belonging to a Bishop or Overseer.

Episcopate, to play the Bishop, overlook diligently.

Episcopicide, the killing of a Bishop.

Epispastick, *g.* drawing or blistering.

Epistolary, belonging to an

Epistle, *g.* a Letter sent.

Epistrophe, *g.* when divers sentences end alike.

Epistyle, *g.* the Chapiter of a Pillar, or architrave.

Epitaph, *g.* an inscription on a tomb or grave.

Epitasis, *g.* the second or busie part of a Comedy, before things are at full vigour.

Epithalamize, to make an

Epithalamy, -*mium*, *g.* a nuptial or wedding song.

Epithemetical, belonging to an

Epitheme, *g.* a liquid medicine appli'd by Cotton, Scarlet, &c.

Epithet, *g.* an Adjective, or concrete quality, expressing the nature of the thing to which it is added.

Epitimesis, *g.* as *Epiplexis* a rebuking.

Epitoge, a loose upper garment.

Epitomater, he that doth

Epitomize, make an

Epitome, -*my*, *g.* an abridgment.

Epitritos. *g.* a foot of four syllables the first short and the other three long.

Epitrochasmus, *g.* a slight running over several things for brevity sake.

Epitrope, *g.* permission (serious or ironical.)

Epizeuxis, *g.* an immediate repetition of the same word.

Epoch, -*che*, -*cha*, *g.* as *Æra.*

Epode, *g.* a kind of Lyrick Poesie, wherein the first verse is longer than the second.

Epostracism, *g.* Duck and a Drake and a white peny cake (with an oister-shell on the Water.)

Epping-street, a Town in *Essex.*

Epulary, *l.* belonging to a banquet.

Epulosity, a being

Epulous, *l.* full of banqueting.

Epuloticks, *g.* powders, &c. to dry up ulcers, &c.

Equanimity, *l.* evenness, quietness of mind.

Equation, *l.* a making equal even or plain.

Equator, as *Æquator.*

Eque-

Equestrian, *l.* belonging to an Horseman or Knight.
Eques auratus, *l.* a Knight [with gilt arms,&c.]
Equilateral, as *Æquilateral.*
Equinoctial-line, as *Æquator.*
Equiparates, *Æq-*, *l.* things compared or made equal.
Equippage, *f.* a furnishing, setting forth, also furniture.
Equiparable, comparable.
Equiangle, where the angles are equal.
Equipped, *f.* set forth, furnished, accoutred.
Equicrural, even-legged.
Equidial, having the daies and nights equal.
Equipensate, weigh or esteem alike.
Equipollence, *Æq-*, *l.* a being
Equipollent, *l.* of equal force or value.
Equidistants, Parallels.
Equiformity, *l.* likeness in form.
Equiponderous, of equal weight.
Equivalent, *Æq-*, *l.* of equal worth, or signification.
Equivocal, *Æq-*, *l.* having a double meaning.
Equivocate, to use
Equivocation, double or doubtfull speech.
Equorean, *l.* belonging to the Sea.
Equus, the Horse, *l.* a Constellation.
Er, *h.* a Watchman.
Eradicate, *l.* pull up by the roots.
Erarij, *Ær-*, Romans deprived of giving their vote, paid all tribute, and served in the war at their own charges.
Erased, *l.* scraped out, torn away.
Erasmus, *g.* amiable.
Erastianism, the doctrine of the
Erastians, followers of
Erastus, a *Swisse* Doctor (about 1580) who held that excommunication belong'd to the secular Magistrate, &c.
Erato, one of the nine Muses.
Erber, *o.* arbour.
Erchenbald, a Bishop of *London*, Son to King *Offa*.
Erean, *Ær-*, *l.* brasen.
Erebus, an infernal deity, Father of Night, Hell.
Erection, *l.* a raising upright.
Erector, *l.* a lifter up, one of the Muscles.
Eremitical, belonging to an *Eremite*, or *Hermite*, *g.*
Ereption, *l.* a snatching away.
Eretriack, as *Eleack*, from *Menedemus* born at
Eretria, a City of *Eubæa.*
Ergotique, belonging to
Ergotism, arguing, quarrelling, sophistry, from
Ergo, *l.* therefore.
Eriferous, *l.* bearing brass.
Erichthonius, King of *Athens*, Son of the Earth and *Vulcan* (striving with *Minerva*) he invented the Chariot, to hide his Dragons feet.
Eridanus, *Padus*, the *Po*, a River in *Italy*, a Constellation.
Erigone, Daughter of *Icarus*, who hang'd her self for her Fathers death, the Constellation *Virgo.*
Erimanthian, belonging to
Erimanthus, a Mountain in *Arcadia.*
Eriphile, for a bracelet betrayed her Husband *Amphiaraus* to the *Theban* wars, to his destruction.
Erke, *o.* weary, loathing.
Eristical, *g.* contentious.
Eristicks, books or Treatises of controversie or disputes.
Erivate, *l.* to dry up, or drain away by a stream.
Ermine, a little Beast whose fur is very costly.
Ermin-street, *Erminage-street*, the Roman high-way from *St. Davids* to *Southampton.*
Ernes, *o.* a promise in [earnest.]
Ern, *o.* greatly.
Ernest, *ge.* severe.
Earnfull, *so.* sorrowful, lamentable.
Erogation, *l.* a liberal bestowing.
Eros, *g.* Love, Cupid.
Erosion, *l.* a gnawing or eating away.
Erostratus, to get him a name set fire to *Diana*'s Temple.
Erotesis, *-tema*, *g.* asking of a question.
Ersh, *Sf.* *Edish*, the stubble after corn is cut.
Errant [Justices] riding the Circuits.
Errant [Knights] wandring all over the world, doing wonders.
Erre, *f.* a way.
Errata, *l.* faults [in print, &c.]
Erratique, *l.* wandring or creeping up and down.
Errhines, *g.* Medicines purging through the nose.
Erroneous, subject to or full of
Errours, *l.* mistakes.
Erst, *o.* earnest.
Erst my shirt, *o.* before my shirt [was made.]
Erugate, *l.* take away wrinkles.
Eruginous, *l.* rusty, cankered, corrupted, blasted.
Erubescency, *l.* a blushing.
Eructation, *l.* a belching out.
Erudition, *l.* an instructing.
Erumnate, *l.* impoverish, make miserable.
Eruncation, *l.* a weeding.
Eruption, *l.* a violent breaking forth.
Erewhile, *o.* a while ago.
Eryngus, Sea-holly.
Erysipelatous, troubled with an
Erysipely, *g.* St. *Anthonies* fire.
Ery, *D.* to honour or reverence.
Erythræan sea, the Red sea, the Gulph of *Arabia* or *Mecha.*
Eryx, a valiant man kil'd by *Hercules* at Whirl-bats.
Esaias, as *Isaiah.*
Esarhaddon, *h.* binding chearfulness.
Esau, *h.* working or doing.
Escal, *l.* fit for food.
Escambio, a licence to make

make over a bill of Exchange to another beyond-ſea.

Eſchaufeth, *o.* heateth.

Eſchange, as *Exchange*.

Eſchew, *f.* avoid or ſhun.

Eſcheat, Lands &c. fallen or forfeited to the Lord of the Mannor, alſo a writ to reco ver ſuch lands, alſo the Circuit within which they fall.

Eſcheator, the Officer appointed to obſerve the Eſcheats due to the King.

Eſclat, *f.* a ſplinter of wood.

Eſchequer, as *Exchequer*.

Eſcotcheon a ſhield or buckler, a Coat of arms.

Eſcrite, *f.* a writing.

Eſcuage, *f.* a tenure whereby the tenant is bound (at his own charges) to follow the Lord to the wars.

Eſculent, as *Eſcal*.

Eſcurial, a ſtately Edifice built by *Philip* 2. King of *Spain*, in 24 years, it contains the Kings palace, St. *Laurence* Church, the Monaſtery of *Jeronomites* and Free-Schools.

Eſkin, *No.* a pail or kit.

Eskippeſon, *Eskypeſoun*, ſhipping, paſſage.

Eſnecy, *f.* a prerogative allow'd the eldeſt copartner, of chooſing firſt.

Eſon, *Æſon*, King of *Theſſaly*, had his youth reſtored by *Medea* at the requeſt of his ſon *Jaſon*.

Eſons bath, the Bath or Medicines which reſtored his age.

Eſopical, fabulous, belonging to

Eſop, *Æſop*, authour of the Fables.

Eſpalier, *f.* a cloſe hedg-row of ſundry fruit-trees, alſo a ſhouldering piece in architecture.

Eſples, *Expleta*, *l.* the full profit of land.

Eſpervarius, *Sparverius*, a Spar-hawk.

Eſpelers, the 3d branch of the harts-horns.

Eſpeces, *f.* kinds.

Eſperance, *f.* hope.

Eſpire, *o.* as expire.

Eſploit, (for *Exploit*) perfection.

Eſpringold, *Eſpringalle*, *f.* a warlike Engine (diſuſed) for the caſting great ſtones.

Eſquiline, *-nus*, *l.* one of the ſeaven hills on which *Rome* was built.

Eſquiry, *f.* a querry or Princes ſtable, alſo a querryſhip, or the Office and dignity of an

Eſquire, *f.* he that bore the arms of a Knight, [now] that degree of Gentry next below a Knight.

Eſſay, *f.* to try, alſo a tryal or preamble.

Eſſay [of a Deer,] the breaſt or brisket.

Eſſedary, one that guides or fights in an

Eſſede, *l.* a warlike Chariot.

Eſſendi quietum de Tolonio, a writ for any Townſmen (when toll is exacted) having Charter or preſcription to exempt them.

Skeer the Eſſe, *Che.* ſeparate the dead aſhes from the embers.

Eſſenes, a kind of Monaſtick Philoſophers among the Jews, kept neither wife nor ſervant, referred all to deſtiny, thought the ſoul mortal, &c.

Eſſential, having or belonging to

Eſſence. *l.* ſubſtance, being.

Eſſential debilities, when planets are in their detriment, fall, or peregrines.

Eſſentifical, cauſing the Eſſence or being.

Eſſoine, an excuſe for one ſummoned to appear.

Eſtabliſhment of Dowre, aſſurance thereof to the wife, about the time of marriage.

Eſtandard, *'Standard*, the ſtanding meaſure to regulate all others in the land, alſo an Enſign in war.

Eſter, (*f. Eſtre*) *o.* ſubſtance, ſtate or being.

Eſther, *h.* ſecret.

Eſtiferous, *l.* bringing or bearing heat.

Eſtimate, *Æſt-*, *l.* to make

Eſtimation, account, valuing.

Eſtival, *l.* of Summer.

Eſtivate, *l.* to Summer.

Eſtopel, an impediment or bar of an action, from his own fact who otherwiſe might have had his action.

Eſtotiland, the moſt Northern Region on the Eaſtſide of *America*.

Eſtovers, ſuſtenance allowed an accuſed felon (and his family) out of his Eſtate during impriſonment.

Eſtreat, *Eſtreict*, *f.* *extractum*, *l.* the copy of an original writing.

Eſtraie, *'Stray*, *Extrahura*, *l.* a beaſt (not wild) found (and not owned) in any Lordſhip.

Eſtreignes moy de cœur joyeus, *f.* embrace me with a merry heart.

Eſtrepement, *-pament*, *Eſtropement*, *f.* Spoil made by a Tenant, to the prejudice of him in reverſion.

Eſtuate, as *Æſtuate*.

Eſurial, *l.* faſting, hungry.

Eſurion, *l.* a hungry fellow.

Eſurition, *l.* a being hungry.

Et je ſay bien que ce n'eſt pas mon tort, *f.* And I am ſure I have done no wrong.

Etching, graving with *aqua-fortis* eating into the Copper, &c.

Et cætera, *&c.* *l.* and the reſt, and ſo forth.

Eternize, *g.* to make eternal.

Etesiæ, Eteſian-winds, certain Eaſterly winds blowing yearly about the dog-dayes.

Ethe, *o.* Eaſie, gentle.

Etheling, as *Adeling*.

Ethelard, *Adelard*, *Sa.* Noble diſpoſition.

Ethelbert, *Edelbert*, *ſa*, nobly bright.

Ethelſtaine, *-an*, *ſa.* Noble Jewel.

Ethelward, *ſa.* Noble keeper

Ethelwold, *ſa.* Noble Governour.

Ethel-

Ethelwolph, *sa.* Noble helper
Etherial, as *Æthereal*.
Ethicks, *g.* [books treating of] moral Philosophy.
Ethiopia, as *AEthiopia*.
Ethnarchy, *g.* Principality.
Ethnick, *g.* heathenish.
Ethnicks, Heathens, Gentiles.
Ethologie, *g.* a discourse concerning manners.
Ethopœia, *g.* a representation of [some certain particular mens] manners.
Etiologie, as *AEtiology*.
Etna, as *AEtna*.
Etocetum, a Town in *Warwick-shire*, the second Roman station from *Manchester*.
Etymological, belonging to
Etymology, *g.* derivation of words from their Originals.
Etymologize, to interpret by deriving words, &c.
Evacuate, *l.* to empty.
Evade, *l.* to make an
Evasion, an escape, shift.
Evagation, *l.* a wandring abroad.
Evagination, *l.* a drawing out of the sheath.
Evan, *Ivon*, *John*.
Evander, an *Arcadian*, having slain his Father, he fled into *Latium*, where he made himself King.
Evangeliques, a sort of reformers not much differing from *Lutherans*.
Evangelism, *g.*, a bringing of glad tidings.
Evangelistary, a pulpit, also the office of an
Evangelist, *g.* one that doth
Evangelize, write or bring
Evangelium, the Gospel, good news.
Evanid, *l.* soon decaying.
Evaporation, *l.* a sending forth of vapours.
Evate, precious *Ethiopian* Wood for cups, that will endure no poison.
Eucharistical, belonging to the
Eucharist, *g.* thanks-giving, also the Sacrament of the Lords-Supper.
Eucrasie, *g.* a good temperature of body.
Euchamie, *g.* [a being supplied with] good juice.
Eudora, *g.* a good gift.
Eudoxie, *g.* excellency of name, good report or estimation.
Eve, *h.* living.
Eve and Treve, *sc.* Servants whose predecessors have been Servants to any man and his predecessors.
Eveck, *-ick*, *ibex*, *l.* a kind of Wild Goat.
Evection, *l.* a lifting up, or a carrying out.
Event, *l.* issue, success.
Eventeration, *l.* a taking out the belly of a thing.
Eventilate, *l.* sift or winnow [Corn,] strictly to examine.
Evershot, a Town in *Dorsetshire*.
Everych, *o.* every.
Everard, *g.* well reported.
Everwicscire, *Yorkshire*.
Eversion, *l.* an overthrowing.
Evertuate, take away the vertue or strength.
Evestigation, *l.* an earnest seeking or hunting after.
Evesholme, a Town in *Worcestershire*.
Euganian, belonging to a Country of the *Venetians* by the inner gulph of the *Adriatick-Sea*.
Eugeny, *g.* nobleness of blood.
Eviction, *l.* a convincing or vanquishing.
Evibration, *l.* a brandishing or darting forth.
Evidence, *l.* a testimony, or proof.
Evince, *l.* overcome, declare.
Evil, a Town in *Somersetshire*.
Evintegrous, *l.* bearing age well, without decay.
Eviration, *l.* an unmanning, a gelding.
Evisceration, *l.* a taking out the bowels.
Evitable, *l.* capable of
Evitation, *l.* an avoiding, or shunning.
Eviternity, *l.* everlastingness.
Eulogy, *-ge*, *g.* a praising.
Eum, *o.* equal.
Eulogical, *g.* well spoken.
Eumenides, the three Furies.
Eunuchate, *-chize*, to geld.
Eunuchism, the state or condition of an
Eunuch, *g.* (whose mind is right) a gelded man.
Eunomians, Hereticks holding, that Faith only was acceptable without works, or that no sin could hurt the faithful.
Evocation, *l.* a calling out.
Evolatical, *l.* flying abroad.
Evolution, *l.* a rolling or reading over.
Eupatory, liver-wort.
Euphemism, *g.* a speaking well of, putting a favourable interpretation on a bad word or thing.
Euphonie, *g.* a graceful sound.
Euphorbium, the gum of the *Lybian* gum-thistle.
Euphrosyne, *g.* burrage, also one of the 3 Graces.
Euridice, being fetch'd from hell by her husband *Orpheus*, was snatched back again, because he lookt back on her before she arrived upon earth.
Euripize, to imitate
Euripe, *-pus*, *Golpho de Negroponte*, which ebbes and flows seaven times a day.
Euroclydon, *g.* the Seamans plague, a furious North-east-wind.
Europæans, Inhabitants of
Europe, one of the Worlds four parts, separated from *Asia* by the River *Tanais*.
Eurythmy, *g.* the exact proportion of rooms in a building.
Eusebius, *g.* pious, godly.
Eustace, *Eustathius*, or
Eustachius, *g.* standing firm.
Eutaxie, *g.* good order or disposing of things.
Euterpe, one of the Muses.
Euthansie, *g.* an happy dying.

Euthymy, g. tranquillity, quietness of mind.
Eutrapelize, to use or exercise
Eutrapely, g. Courtesie.
Eutropius, g. Well-manner'd.
Eutychians, followers of
Eutyches (*An.* 443.) he held that there was but one nature in Christ, that he was not born of the Virgin *Mary*, &c.
Evulsion, l. a violent pulling up.
Ewage, o. colour.
Evyn, o. Even.
Exacerration, l. a purging or cleansing from chaffe.
Exacerbation, l. a making soure, also as *Sarcasmus*.
Exacination, l. a taking out the stone or kernel.
Exaction, l. a taking of unlawfull fees.
Exacuation, l. the making a thing sharp-pointed.
Exactor Regis, the Kings
Exactor, Customer or Exciseman, also the Sheriffe.
Exaggeration, l. a heaping up, also as *Aggravation*.
Exagitation, l. a stirring up.
Exaltation, l. a lifting up, also (in Chymistry) a bringing to greater purity.
Exalted, lifted up, sublime, excellent,
Example, l. pattern, copy.
Examussim, l. exactly.
Exanguious, l. bloudless.
Exanimate, l. to deprive of life, also to dismay.
Exanthems, g. the small pox, measles, or any wheales.
Exantlate, l. to empty, pump or draw out; also to overcome by great labour.
Exaration, l. a plowing up, also writing, engraving.
Exarchy, -*chate*, the office or dignity of an
Exarch, g. a Lieutenant or Vice Emperour.
Exarch of Ravenna, Governour of *Italy* under the *Constantinople* Emperours.
Exarticulation, l. a putting out of joynt.
Exartuate, l. disjoynt, carve or quarter.
Exasperation, l. a making sharp, a provoking.
Exaturation, l. a satiating.
Exauctoration, *Exaut*-, l. a depriving one of an office, a disbanding.
Exaugurate, l. to unhallow or prophane.
Exauspicate, l. to have ill luck, or do a thing unfortunately.
Excalfaction, l. a heating.
Excambio, an Exchange.
Excambiator, an Exchanger of land.
Excandescency, l. a being inflamed [with anger, &c.]
Excavation, a making hollow.
Excecation, l. a blinding.
Excelsity, l. highness, loftiness.
Excentrick, as *Eccentrick*.
Exception, l. (taking out) a bar or stop to an action.
Exceptions, irregularities, deviations from general Rules.
Take Exception at, be displeased or unsatisfied with.
Exceptor, l. a gatherer [of the speakers words.]
Excern, l. to seirce or sift.
Excerption, l. picking or choosing.
Excess, l. an exceeding, a going or doing out of measure.
Excester, *Exonia*, *Isca Danmoniorum*, the Chief City of *Devonshire*, upon
Ex, the name of the River.
Exchangeors, men licensed to return money beyond-sea by bills of Exchange.
Exchequer, the Court whither all the Crown-Revenues are brought.
Excision, l. a breaking down, wasting or destroying.
Excise, an imposition on Beer, Ale, Sider and other liquors.
Excitation, l. a stirring up.
Exclude, l. to shut out.
Exclusory, l. having power of
Exclusion, l. a barring or shutting out.
Exclusively, in a manner
Exclusive of, not taking in [the extreams, &c.]
Excogitate, l. to invent.
Excommengement, the same as
Excommunication, l. a separating from the Church or Communion of Saints.
Excommunicato capiendo, a writ for the apprehending and imprisoning him that obstinately stands excommunicated 40 dayes.
Excommunicato deliberando, a writ to deliver the excommunicate out of prison upon a Certificate of his conformity.
Excommunicato recipiendo, for the retaking an Excommunicate person unlawfully delivered from prison.
Excoriate, l. flea off the skin.
Excorticate, l. pull off the rind or bark.
Excreable, l. which one may
Excreate, l. Spit out.
Excrementous, -*titious*, belonging to
Excrements, l. dregs, ordure.
Excrescence, -*cy*, l. a growing out, or swelling.
Excretion, l. a voiding or purging of
Excrements or bodily superfluities.
Excruciate, l. to torment.
Excude, l. to beat or hammer out.
Exculcate, to tread, or kick up or out.
Exculpate, l. to clear ones self of a fault.
Excuriate, l. throw out of the Court.
Excursion, l. a roving or running out.
Excusatory, belonging to
Excusation, l. an excusing.
Excussion, l. a shaking off.
Exsection, l. a cutting out
Execration, l. a cursing.
Execrable, l. accursed, hor-

horrible, detestable.

Execution, *l.* the last performance of an act, inflicting of punishment.

Executione facienda, a Writ for the Execution of a Judgement.

Executione facienda in Withernamium, a Writ for the taking his Cattle who had conveyed another mans Cattle out of the County, so that they could not be replevyed.

Executor, *l.* he that performs any action, also he that is left by Will to dispose of the deceased mans estate.

Executor de son tort, who takes upon him the office without appointment.

Exegetical, belonging to

Exegesis *g.* explication.

Exemplary, belonging to

Exemplar, *l.* a person or thing containing an example

Exemplific, *l.* to give, make take out of an example or copy.

Exemplificatione, a writ granted for the exemplification of an Original.

Exemption, *l.* a taking out or a freeing [from duty, &c.]

Exenteration, *l.* a taking out the guts or bowels.

Exequial, belonging to

Exequies, *l.* funeral rites.

Exercitation, *l.* a frequent exercising, also a critical Comment.

Exergasia, *g.* an adorning, polishing.

Exert, *l.* to put forth.

Exesion, *l.* an eating up or out, consuming.

Exflorous, *l.* having flowers growing out of it.

Ex gravi querela, a writ for him to whom Lands are devised by Will, and the heir of the devisor enters and detains them.

Ex mero motu, (in the Kings Charters and Letters Patent) of his own will and motion, without the Petition or [false] suggestion of others.

Ex officio, an Oath *ex officio* might have been administred by any person authorized by Letters Patent, to force the supposed delinquent to accuse or clear himself; repealed.

Exoneratione Sectæ, a writ to disburden the Kings ward of all sute to the County, &c.

Exhalation, *l.* a vapour drawn up by the Suns heat, also a blowing or breathing out.

Exharmonia, discords in Musick.

Exhausted, *l.* drawn dry, wasted.

Exhibit, *l.* to shew, or present.

Exhibition, a shewing, also an allowance towards ones maintenance.

Exhilarate, *l.* to refresh, to make one merry or chearful.

Exsiccation, *l.* a drying up.

Exigendary, *-genter*, four Officers in the Common-pleas who make

Exigents, Writs where the Defendant cannot be found, nor any thing to be distreined

Exigent, *l.* a great streight or necessity.

Exiguity, *l.* slenderness.

Exiguous, *l*, slender, small.

Exilition, *l.* a leaping out.

Exile, *l.* banishment.

Exility, *l*, as *Exiguity*.

Eximiety, a being.

Eximious, *l.* excellent, famous.

Exinanition, *l.* an emptying. or making void, a being

Exinanited, *l.* robbed, pilled, reduced to nothing.

Existence, *l.* a being.

Existimation, *l.* a thinking or judging.

Exit, *l.* he or she goes out, also a going out or ending.

Exitial, *-itious*, *l.* dangerous, destructive, deadly.

Exodus, *g.* the going out [of the Isralites from *Egypt*.]

Exoine, as *Essoyn*.

Exolete, *l.* stale, out of use.

Exolution, *l.* full payment, also faintness and loosness all over the body.

Exonerate, *l.* unload.

Exoptable, *l.* desireable.

Exoptate, *l.* to desire earnestly.

Exorable, *l.* that may be entreated.

Exorbitancy, *l.* a being

Exorbitant, *l.* out of rule or measure.

Exorbitate, *l.* to go out of the right way.

Exorcism. the practise of an

Exorcist, *g.* he that doth

Exorcise, restrain the Devils Power (by prayer or Conjuration.)

Exordium, *l.* a preamble or beginning [of a discourse.]

Exornation, *l.* an adorning, or dressing up.

Exortive, *l.* belonging to rising or the East.

Exosseous, *l.* having no bones.

Exoster, *l.* a petard or engine to blow a gate open.

Exoterick [doctrine] of nice disputes.

Exotick, *g.* strange, forreign outlandish.

Expand, declare, display.

Expansed, *l.* displayed.

Expansion, *l.* an opening or spreading abroad.

Ex parte, *l.* partly, also done by one party onely.

Ex parte talis, a writ for a Bailiff or Receiver who cannot obtain reasonable allowance but is cast into prison by the Auditors assign'd to take his account.

Expatiate. *l.* walk at large or full liberty.

Expectant [*fee-*] *taile*, the having Lands given to a man and the heirs of his body, &c.

Expectable, to be expected.

Expectation, *l.* a tarrying or looking for.

Expectorate, *l.* to raise phlegme from the breast.

Expedient, *l.* fit, convenient

An Expedient, a convenient way, means, or device.

Expeditate, *l.* cut out the balls of the Dogs feet, (for preservation of the Kings game)

Expedite, *l.* prepare, dispatch finish.

Expedi-

Expedition, *l.* quick dispatch, also a setting forth upon a journey, war, &c.
Expel, *l.* drive out.
Expenditors, paymasters.
Expence, *l.* cost or charges.
Expensis militum levandis, a writ to levy allowance for the Knights of Parliament.
Experience, l. proof or trial upon sight or observation.
Experiment, *l.* a putting to trial or into practice.
Expetible, *l.* desireable.
Expiable, capable of
Expiation, *l.* a pacifying, satisfying or making amends for an offence.
Expiration, *l.* a giving up the Ghost.
Expire, *l.* to come to an end.
Explain, *l.* unfold, declare.
Explanation, a making plain clear or manifest.
Expleiten, *o.* make show.
Explement, the same as
Expletion, *l.* a filling up.
Expletive, *l.* filling, fulfilling, perfecting.
Explication, *l.* explaining or unfolding.
Explicite, *l.* unfolded, open.
Exploit, *f.* a notable act.
Exploration, *-orement*, *l.* a spying or searching out.
Explorator, *l.* a scout [Master]
Explode, *l.* to hiss off the stage
Explosion, *l.* an exploding, slighting, decrying, hissing, off, &c.
Ex post facto, *l.* the doing a thing after the time when it should have been done.
Expolition, *l.* a polishing.
Eposition, *l.* an expounding or interpreting.
Expostulate, *l.* reason the case, complain.
Express, pronounce, utter, declare, also a letter or packet of Letters.
Expressed, (in Physick) squeezed out.
Expression, *l.* an expressing, squeezing, also the thing expressed, &c. also as *Ethopœia*.
Exprobation, *l.* a reproaching or upbraiding.
Expugnable, capable of
Expugnation, *l.* a taking or winning by force.
Expuition, *l.* a spitting out.
Expulsion, *l.* a driving out.
Expumication, *l.* a sleeking or smoothing with pumice-stone.
Expunge, *l.* blot out.
Exquisite, *l.* exact, in the highest degree.
Exsufflation, *l.* a breathing out.
Extancy, being
Extant, *l.* appearing in sight [above others] also in being.
Extacy, as *Ecstasie*.
Extemporary, *-raneous*, *l.* that which is done
Ex tempore, presently, without any prævious study.
Extemporality, a promptness without præmeditation.
Extend, *l.* enlarge, stretch out.
Extensible, *-sive*, capable of
Extension, a stretching out.
Extent, whole breadth or compass, also a commission to seize and value lands, &c. also the act of seizing, &c. upon this writ.
Extendi facias, writ of extent, commanding Lands to be extended or valued.
Extenuate, *l.* make little, undervalue.
Extercorate, *l.* cleanse, or carry forth dung.
Exterminate, *l.* throw out or banish.
External, *-riour*, *l.* outward.
Exterraneous, *Extra-*, *l.* strange, forreign.
Extersion, *l.* a wiping off or out.
Extimate, *l.* outmost, contrary to intimate.
Extimulate, *l.* to spur on or provoke.
Extinct, *l.* put out, quenched.
Extinction, *l.* a quenching.
Extinguisher, an instrument to
Extinguish, *l.* put out [a candle, &c.]
Extinguishment of Rent, when the Rent and property are both consolidated into one possession.
Extirpate, *l.* utterly to destroy or root out.
Extispitious, belonging to southsaying by the entrails of Beasts.
Extorsion, *l.* a wresting or violent taking [of more than is due,] excessive usury.
Extort, *l.* to wrest or wring out of.
Extract, *l.* to draw out, also as
Extraction, *l.* a drawing out, also as Estreat, also a pedigree, or descending from such or such a Family.
Extracts, as *Estreats*.
Extrajudicial, done out of Court.
Extramission, *l.* a sending out or beyond.
Extramundane, [spaces] between one world and another.
Extraneous, *-terra-*, *l.* of a Forreign or strange Land.
Extraparochial, beyond or out of the Parish.
Extravagant, *l.* wandring beyond the due bounds.
Extravasal, beside or out of the vessel.
Extreat, as *Estreat*.
Extricable, capable of
Extrication, as *Distri-*, ridding one self of.
Extrinsick, *-cal*, *l.* outward, from without.
Extroversion, a turning [ones thoughts upon] outward [objects.]
Extrude, *l.* to thrust out.
Extrusion, a thrusting out.
Extuberate, *l.* [to cause] to swel or bunch up.
Extumescence, *l.* a swelling or bunching up.
Exuberance, *-cy*, *l.* an overflowing or abounding.
Exuberate, *l.* to abound, or be plentifull.
Exuccous, *Exsu-*, *l.* juiceless.
Exudate, *Exsu-*, *l.* to drop or send forth moisture, to sweat out.
Exuge, *l.* to suck up.
Exulate, to be banished or to

to live in exile.

Exulcerate, *l.* to blister or turn to an ulcer, also fret or vex.

Exult, *l.* leap for joy, triumph.

Exultation, *l.* a great rejoycing.

Exundation, *l.* an overflowing.

Exuperable, *l.* that may be exceeded, got over or overcom'n.

Exuperation, *Exsu-*, *l.* an excelling or surpassing.

Exustion, *l.* a burning or parching.

Exuthenismus, *g.* an extenuation or speaking contemptibly of any person or thing.

Ey, *o.* an egge, also a watery place.

Eye [of a plant,] where the bud puts forth, also the bud it self.

Eye-bite, to bewitch with the eyes.

Ey-bright, *Euphrasia*, an herb good for eyes, brain and memory.

Ey- [*of Pheasants*] the whole brood of young ones, the same as Covey in Partridges.

Eyess, a [watery-eyed] hawk brought up under a Kite.

Eyet, *Eyght*, a little Island.

Eyleth, *o.* aileth.

Eyre, the Court of Justices Iterant.

Eyre of the forest, the Court which was wont to be kept (every three years) by the Justices of the Forest.

Eyth, *Eth*, *o.* easie.

Eywood, a Town in *Surrey*.

Ezechias, *Hezekiah*, or *Hizkiah*, *h.* strength of the Lord.

Ezechiel, *h.* seeing or strength of God.

Ezenden, a town in *Rutland*.

Ezra, *h.* an helper.

Ezzab, a Province of *Africa*.

F.

F*Abal*, *h.* belonging to a bean.

Fabellator, *l.* an inventer of little tales.

Fabianus, Bishop of *Rome*, martyred under *Decius*.

Fabius Maximus, a *Roman* General famous for tiring and overthrowing *Annibal*.

Fabrication, *l.* the making a

Fabrick, *l.* a building; also a work-house.

Fabrick-lands, given for the building or repairing of a Church, Colledge, &c.

Fabulator, *-list*, an inventer or teller of Tales.

Fabulinus, the God suppos'd to look to Children when they begin to speak.

Fabulosity, a being

Fabulous, full of

Fables, *l.* invented tales.

Fac-totum, (*l.* do-all) a border, in whose midle any letter may be put for use, and taken out again.

Façade, *f.* the front or outside of a house.

Facetious, *l.* wittily-merry.

Facile, *l.* easie.

Facility, easiness.

Facinorous, *l.* belonging to notable exploits.

Fack, one circle of any queiled rope.

Facrere, *o.* dissimulation.

Fact, *l.* an act or deed.

Factious, given to

Faction, a withdrawing any number from the main body (of Church or state) governing themselves by their own Councels, and [openly] opposing the established Government.

Factist, a poet or play-maker.

Factitious, *l.* counterfeited, made like another.

Factor, *l.* a Merchants Agent beyond-sea.

Facture, *l.* the making or doing of a thing.

Faculty, *l.* power or ability, also a licence or dispensation, also a trade, mystery or profession.

Faculent, *l.* bright, clear.

Facundate, *l.* to make

Facundous, full of

Facundity, *l.* Eloquence.

Fader, *o.* Father.

Fadom, *Fathom*, Six foot.

Fage, *o.* a merry tale.

Faint, *Feint*, or *Fained Action*, whereby nothing can be recovered, though the words of the writ be true.

Fain, *o.* glad.

Faint pleader, a false and deceitful pleading.

Fair-pleading (*beau-pleader*) a writ on the statute of *Marl-bridg*, providing that no fines shall be taken for not pleading to the purpose.

Fairie, Goblin, Phantasm, also, *o.* a goodly sight.

Fairy-sparks, *Shel-fire*, *K.* often seen on clothes in the night.

Faisible, *f.* possible to be done.

Faitours, idle vagabonds.

Fakenham, a town in *Norfolk*.

Falang, *f.* a jacket or close coat.

Fall of a Planet, an essential debility, opposite to his exaltation.

Falarick, *l.* belonging to a dart thrown from towers besieged.

Falcator, *l.* a cutter with a bill or hook.

Falcation, *l.* a mowing.

Falchon, a short hooked sword.

Falcidius, a *Roman* Consul, author of the

Falcidian-law, treating of the Citizens right to dispose of his own goods.

Falciferous, *l.* bearing a hook or bill.

Falcon, a great Gun, next to the minion.

Falda, a sheepfold.

Faldage, the Lords liberty of folding his Tenants sheep.

Falding, a kind of course cloth.

Faldisdory, *-dorium*, *-tory*, the Bishops seat within the Chancel.

Fald-stool, placed on the Southside of the Altar at which the Kings of *England* kneel, at their Coronation.

Falern, *Fall-*, a diseafe in hawks, known by their white talons.

Falernian [wine] growing in

Falernus, a Field of *Campania* in *Italy*.

Falesia, a hill or Down by the Sea-side.

Fallacy, *l.* *Sophism*, *g.* [a proposition framed for] deceit.

Fallaciloquence, deceitfull speech.

Fallacious, deceitfull.

Fallax, *l.* the same; also deceit.

Fall-off, when the ship keeps not near enough to the wind.

Falls, the different lyings of the deck higher or lower.

Falls of the tackle, the small ropes which they hale by.

Falouque. *f.* a kind of Barge or Brigantine.

Falso returno brevium, a writ against the Sheriff, for false returning of writs.

False-keel, another keel put under the first, when the ship is too floaty.

Falstre, an Island in the *Baltick* Sea.

False-stem, another stem put on the first being too flat.

Falsed, *o.* falsifyed.

Falsification, *l.* the same as

Falsifying, counterfeiting, working or speaking of

Falsity, Falshood, untruth.

Famagosta, the chief City in the Isle of *Cyprus*.

Fambles, *c.* hands.

Famble-cheats, *c.* rings or Gloves.

Fam-grasp, *c.* agree with.

Famicide, *l.* a slanderer, destroyer of ones good name.

Famigeration, a divulging, reporting abroad.

Familiar, belonging to a

Family, or houshold, also an hide, Manse, Carucata or a Plough-land.

Familiar, [spirit] with whom there is a league or contract made.

Familist, one of the

Family of Love, Hereticks following one *H. Nicholas*, (1550) whose chief Tenet was, That Christ is already com'n to judgment.

Famulers, *o.* helpers.

Fanatical, belonging to

Fanatick, *Pha-*, *l.* frantick, mad; also a dissenter from the Church of *England*.

Fane, a Weathercock, also a Temple.

Fannian Law, repressing excessive banquets.

Fannel, *f.* an ancient ornament of Priests left arm in sacrificing.

Fantastick, *-cal*, whimsical.

Fantome, as *Phantome*, also lank or light, *No.*

Fanus, a Heathen Deity representing the year.

Faonatio, *Feo-*, the fawning of Does.

Fapesmo, a Syllogism whose first Proposition is an universal affirmative, the 2d. an universal negative, and the last a particular negative.

Farantly, *No.* handsome.

Farandman, *sc.* pilgrim or stranger.

Farce, *f.* any stuffing in meat, a knavish jig at the end of an interlude, a fond and dissolute play.

Farced, *l.* *Fassed*, *o.* stuffed.

Farcie, *-cines*, fashions, scurffe leprosie, a knotty creeping ulcer.

Farcinate, *l.* to stuffe.

Fardingdeal, Farundel of Land, the fourth part of an Acre.

Farding or *Farthing* of Gold, a Gold-coin worth 10 pence.

Fardel of Land, the 4th. part of a yard-land, or rather (as *Noy* saies) two Fardels make a nook, and four nooks make a yard-land.

Fare, *sa.* [the price of] a passage, also for Face.

Farinaceous, *-nous*, *l.* made or full of Corn or meal.

Farley, *-leu* something paid (at the death of a Tenant) in stead of a herriot.

Of Farlie or *Ferlie*, things, for Of Yearly, early or ancient things.

Farnham, a Town in *Surrey*.

Farriginous, belonging to a

Farrago, *l.* maslin, a mixture of several grains together.

Farreation, *l.* a Ceremony whereby the Priests confirmed marriage.

Farringdon, a Town in *Barkshire*.

Farrow, to bring forth [as a Sow.]

Farsang, *Parasang*, a *Persian* league, three miles.

Farthling, as *Farling*.

Farthing of Land, a yard-land.

Fascicular, made into a

Fascicle, *l.* a fardel, bundle.

Fasciculate, to tye up into a bundle.

Fascination, *l.* a bewitching by the eye.

Fasciate, to bind with

Fascia, *l.* a swathe.

Fasguntide, *Fasting-tide*, *N.S.* Shrove-tide, the beginning of Lent.

Fashion-pieces, Timbers in fashion of a great pair of horns, to which all the planks reaching to the Ships after-end are fastened.

Fast, *o.* wedded.

Fast-freits, *o.* full fraughted.

Fastidious, *l.* disdainful.

Fastigate, *-giate*, *l.* to raise or grow up to a sharp top.

Fastness, a strong hold, a place inaccessible, for bogs, bushes, &c.

Fastuosity, *l.* pride, disdainfulness.

Fat, *o.* eight bushels.

Fatality, *l.* fatalness, the being

Fatal, deadly, belonging to or appointed by

Fate, destiny, necessity.

Fathom, six feet in length.

Fatidical, prophesying, foretelling.

Fatiferous, *l.* bringing fate.

Fatigable, capable of

Fatigati-

Fatigation, *l.* a wearying.

Fatigue, *f.* wearisomness, toil, tediousness.

Fatiloquent, *l.* soothsaying, prophesying.

Fatome, as *Fantome*.

Fatuity, *l.* sottishness, stupidity.

Fatuate, *l.* to play the fool.

Favaginous, full of or like honey or honey-combs.

Faunus, the Son of *Saturn*, one of the oldest Italian Kings.

Faunes, Field and Wood-Gods.

Faunick, *l.* wild, rude.

Favonian, belonging to

Favonius, *l.* the West-wind.

Faukon heronere, a Falcon taking herons.

Faust, *l.* lucky, happy.

Faustity, good luck, happiness.

Fauntekyns, *o.* little infants.

Fautor, *l.* a favourer, cherisher or maintainer.

Fautress, *l.* she that favoureth or maintaineth.

Faw, fain, glad, *o.*

Fay, *f.* Faith.

Faytours, as *Faitours*, deceivers.

Faxed, see *fixed*.

Feabes, *Feaberries*, *Sf.* Gooseberries.

Feal, *No.* to hide.

Fealty, *f.* (fidelity) the Tenantsoath (at his admittance) of being true to his Lord.

Feasible, *Feac-*, *Feis-*, (*f. Faisible*) easie to be done.

Febricitation, *l.* a falling sick of an ague or Fever.

Febriculous, having or subject to a Fever.

Febris Catarrhalis, a Fever caused by distilling of Rheum from the head.

Feg.no. fair, also to flag or tire.

February, the moneth of

Februation, *l.* sacrificing and praying for the Souls of the dead.

Fecial, *Fæcial*, *l.* an herald.

Fecible, as *Faisible*.

Feculent, *Fæc-*, full of dregs.

Feculency, filthiness.

Fecundity, *l.* fruitfulness.

Fedity, *l.* foulness.

Federasy, *o.* confederacy.

Fee, *Fædum*, Lands held by perpetual right.

Fee-farm, Land held of another to himself and his heirs for ever, for a certain Yearly Rent.

Fee-simple, or absolute, to us and our heirs for ever.

Fee-taile, or conditional, To us and the heirs of our Body.

Fee of Greece (for *Free*, *Fre*, *Fretum*) the *Archipelago*

Feers, *o.* chess-men, fellows.

Feest, *o.* joy (for Feast.)

Feet, (for feat) *o.* fine.

Feffe, *o.* indue.

Felthe, *o.* feud, enmity.

Feige, *o.* to carp at.

Feintise, *f.* a dissembling.

Felapton, a Syllogism whose first proposition is an universal negative, the 2d. an universal affirmative, and the last a particular Negative.

Felaw, *o.* for fellow.

Felicitate, *-cifie*, to make

Felicitous, full of

Felicity, *l.* happiness.

Fellifluous, *l.* flowing with gall.

Fele, *o.* Sense, knowledge.

Fell, *o.* for field, a stony hill, *sa.* also cruel, raging.

Fellon, *-oun*, *o.* cruel also an angry blister at the fingers end, &c.

Felmonger, a dealer in [sheep] skins parting the wool from the pelts.

Felo de se, *l.* a self-murderer.

Felonious, belonging to

Felony, any offense next to petty treason, as murder, Theft, Rape, &c.

Feloque, and *Felacca*, the same as *Falouque*.

Feltred, *o.* entangled.

Feltron, *o.* strong rock.

Feme Covert, *f.* a married woman.

Feminie, *o.* the Womens (*Amazons*) Country.

Fence, *c.* to spend.

Fence-moneth, from *June*, the 9th. to *July*, 9th. when Deer begin to fawn, and it is unlawful to hunt in the Forest

Fencing Cully, *c.* a receiver of stoln goods.

Fend, *no.* defend, shift off.

Fendly, (*q. Fiendly*) ugly.

Fends, *Fend-bolts*, things hung over the ship-side, to keep it from rubbing against another, &c.

Fenestral, *l.* belonging to a window.

Fenerations, taken or given to

Feneration, usury.

Fenestere, a promontory of *Gallicia*.

Fenne, *A.* the division of a Book.

Fenny, *k.* mouldy.

Fenugreec, an herb growing plentifully in *Greece*.

Feodary, *Feud-*, *Feudatory*, an Officer belonging to the Court of wards and liveries, to survey and value the land, &c.

Feoffment, the gift or grant of Lands, &c. in fee-simple by delivery of seisin, by word or writing.

Fæminine, *l.* belonging to the Female sex.

Fæneration, *l.* a putting out to use.

Fer, and *Ferthest*, for Far and Farthest.

Feracity, *l.* fruitfulness.

Feral, *l.* dangerous, deadly.

Feral signs, *Leo* and the last part of *Scorpio*.

Ferde, *o.* Fear.

Ferd, *o.* Went.

Fercost, *J.* a small kind of ship.

Ferdella terræ, ten Acres.

Ferdendel, as *Fardingdeal*.

Fere, *Peere*, *o.* a companion [on the way.]

Ferdfare, an acquitment of a man to go into the wars.

Ferdinando, either from *Fredrand*, *sa.* pure peace, or as *Bertrand*, *sa.* fair and pure.

Ferdwit, an acquitment of murder in an Army.

Feretory, a place in the Church where are set the bier, Coffins, &c.

Feretrius, a name of *Jupiter*.

Ferial, belonging to

Feriation, *l.* a keeping holiday.

Ferient, *l.* striking.

Ferine, *l.* brutish, wild.

Ferio, a Syllogism whose first proposition is an universal, the last a particular Negative, and the second a particular affirmative.

Ferison, the same in the 3d figure, as *Ferio* in the first.

Ferit, *l.* a blow.

Ferity, *l.* fierceness, brutishness, salvageness,

Ferly, *o.* Strange. See *Farly*.

Ferling a farthi ng, also the fourth part of a Ward.

Ferlingata terræ, *Ferlingus*, *Ferdl-*, the fourth part of a yard-land.

Ferm, *c.* a hole.

Ferm, *Farm*, an house [and land] taken by lease in writing or parol.

Fermaces, *g.* Medicines.

Fermanagh, *Erdino*, a County in *Ireland*.

Fermisona, the winter season of Deer, as *Tempus pinguedinis* is the Summer season.

Fermary, *o.* (*q. Infirm-*,) an Hospital.

Fermerere, *o.* an Overseer of Cattel and Husbandry.

Fermentarious, belonging to

Ferment, *l.* leaven.

Fermented, *-tated*, leavened.

Fermentation, a puffing up [with leaven,] the working of beer, &c. and (in Chymistry) the ripening or resolving of any thing into it self.

Ferne year, *o.* February (*Fevrier*, *f.*)

Ferocious, *l.* Fierce, haughty.

Ferocity, *l.* Fierceness.

Feronia, a Goddess of the woods.

Ferrean, *l.* of or like iron.

Ferret, a little beast sent into the Coney-burroughs to drive them out.

Ferried, carried by

Ferry, a passage over the water.

Ferry, a town in *Kent*,

Ferruginous, full of or like

Ferrugo, *l.* the rust of

Ferrum, *l.* Iron.

Ferrumination, a Chymical soldering of metals together.

Ferrure, *f.* the shooing of horses.

Fers, *Feers*, *Feerses*, *o.* Chessmen,

Ferth, *o.* Fourth.

Ferthing, *o.* a thin scale.

Fertility, *l.* a being

Fertile, *l.* fruitfull.

Fertilize, to make or grow fruitfull.

Fervent, the same as

Fervid, *l.* hot, eager.

Ferulaceous, like unto or full of

Ferula, *Fennel-giant*, an *African* herb, from whose root comes Gum Arabic; also as

Ferular, a palmer or hand-clapper.

Fervor, *l.* a burning heat, vehemency.

Fesse, a Considerable Kingdom of *Africa*.

Fesaunce, *o.* a Pheasant.

Fesse-point, (*l. fascia*) the girdle of honour, a line going thorow the midst of the Escutcheon.

Fessitude, *l.* weariness.

Festination, *l.* a making haste.

Festingmen, *Sa.* Frank-pledge.

Festino, a Syllogism whose first proposition is an universal, and last a particular Neg. the midlemost a Partic. Affirmative.

Festivous, *l.* full of

Festivity, *l.* merriment.

Festoon, *-ton*, *f. Encarpo*, *g.* a garland of fruits or flower-works [in graven or imbossed work.]

Festucous, belonging to or having tender sprigs or branches.

Fetid, *l.* stinking.

Fetiferous, *l.* bringing forth fruit or young.

Fetise, *o.* handsome.

Fetor, *l.* a stink, ill-smell.

Fetously, *o.* featly.

Fette, *o.* fetched.

Fettle, *No.* to go about any business,

Feu, a very high Mountain in *China*.

Feud, *feed*, *feid*, *Ge.* a deadly and implacable hatred.

Feudal, belonging to or held in fief or fee.

Feud-boot, *Sa.* a recompence for engaging in a feud or faction.

Feudist, one that bears a feud or writes of Fee, &c.

Feverfew, *Febrifuga*, *Parthenia*, *Matricaria*, *Mother-wort*, a cleansing and opening herb.

Feveriere, *-rere*, *o.* February.

Feversham, a town in *Kent* where K. *Stephen*, his Wife and Son lie buried.

Fewterer, a dog-keeper, or leader of a Lime-hound, &c.

Few, *No.* to change

Fewmets, *-mishing*, the dung of a Deer.

Fey, *Sc.* Foolish.

Fey, or *Feigh it*, *No.* to do any thing notably.

Fey meadows, *ponds*, &c. Cleanse them.

F fa ut, the seventh musick note, the Cliff-note of the basse-part.

Fiants, *f.* the dung of a Badger, Fox, and all vermine.

Fib, *c.* to beat.

Fibrous, belonging to

Fibres, *l.* small strings about roots, veins, &c.

Fibulation, *l.* a buttoning, or joyning together.

Fictile, *l.* made of Earth.

Fictitious, *l.* feigned, invented.

Fiction, *l.* a feigning, also the thing feigned.

Ficus, *l.* *Alanisca*, *Sycon*, *Sycosis*,

Sycosis, *Hæmorrhoides*, the piles in the fundament.

Fid, Okum put into the touch-hole and covered with lead to keep the powder dry, also an iron pin to open the strands in splising of ropes.

Fideicide, a faith-destroyer, breaker of his word or trust.

Fideicommissor, *l.* he that commits a thing to anothers trust or dispose.

Fidelity, *l.* Faithfulness.

Fide-jussor, *l.* a pledge or surety.

Fidius, the God of faithfulness, (for *Filius*) the Son [of *Jupiter*.]

Fiduciary, *l.* trusty, also a Feoffee in trust.

Fiduciate, *l.* to commite a trust, or make condition of trust.

Fiera'rms, *f.* fierce at arms, a Braggadocia.

Fieri facias, a writ for the Sheriff to levy (within the year and day) the debt or damages recovered.

Fife, an Eastern County of *Scotland*.

Fifteenth, a Parliament-tribute on every City or Borough in the Realm.

Fightwite, *Sa.* a forfeiture for fighting and breaking the peace.

Fights, *Coverts*, any places where men may stand unseen and use their arms (in a ship.)

Figment, *l.* a feigned story.

Figulated, *l.* made of earth

Figuration, as *Ethopeia*.

Figurative, belonging to or spoken by a

Figure, a word or speech not strictly proper or literal; (in Grammar) a distinguishing of words into simple and compound, (in Logick) a threefold disposition of the Argument or middle term with the two extreams, *viz.* *Sub præ primis*, *Bis præ secunda*, *Tertia bis sub*.

Figuretto, a kind of stuff

Figured or flowered.

Filaceous, *l.* made of thread or flax, also full of

Filaments, *l.* as *Fibres*.

Filanders, little worms in hawks, also Nets for wild beasts.

Filazers, Fourteen Officers in the Common pleas, filing original writs that issue from the Chancery, and making out process thereupon.

Filch, *c.* a staff with a hole for a hook upon occasion.

Filctale, *Filgale*, *Fictale*, *Sothale*, an extortion (under pretense of Compotation) by Bailiffs in their hundreds.

File, *f.* a thread or wire, a difference in Cout-Armours, also the order of Soldiers in depth usually six.

File-leaders, all in the first rank.

Filial, *l.* belonging to a son.

Filiaster, *f.* a Son in law.

Filiation, Son-ship.

Filjan-tages, a Cap that the *Turkish* Sultanas wear.

Filiolus, *l.* a little son, also a Godson, Nephew, &c.

Filimot, (*fueille mort*) *f.* [the colour of] a dead leaf.

Filipendula, Dropwort.

Fillet, a line added under the Chief (in Heraldry.)

Fill, *o.* pleased or thought convenient.

Filly-foal, a Mare-colt.

Film, a thin skin.

Filipinas, *Indian* Islands found and reduced by *Philip* the 2d King of *Spain*.

Filozella, a kind of stuff.

Filtration, *l.* a straining or distilling through a felt, woollen-cloth, &c. hung over the brim of a pot.

Fimashing, as *Fewmets*.

Fimble [*hemp*] *So.* Early ripe.

Fimbriated, *l.* edged or bordured with another colour (in heraldry.)

Final, *l.* belonging to, brought to, or having an end.

Financer, a receiver or teller in the Exchequer.

Finance, *-cy*, *f.* Wealth, Revenue, treasure.

Finders, searchers [for goods not customed.]

Find the Ships trim, find how she will sail best.

Findible, *l.* which may be cleft.

Fine, a mulct or penalty, also a formal conveyance of Land, &c. before a Judge, by acknowledging a final agreement.

Fine adnullando levato, &c. a writ to Justices, for disannulling a fine levied of Lands holden in ancient Demesn, to the prejudice of the Lord.

Fine capiendo pro terris, a writ for one (committed to Prison and his goods in the Kings hand) to be released for his fine.

Fine levando de tenementis, &c. a writ licensing the Justices of Common-pleas to admit a fine for the sale of Lands holden in *Capite*.

Fine non capiendo, &c. a writ forbidding Officers of Courts to take fines for fair pleading.

Fine pro redisseisina, &c. a writ for the release of one laid in prison for a *Redisseisin* upon a reasonable fine.

Fine force, *f.* an absolute necessity or constraint.

Finesse, *f.* craft, subtilty.

Finite, *l.* limited, bounded.

Finland, part of *Swedeland*.

Finors of Gold, &c. as Parters and Departers.

Fint skiles, *o.* it finds or feigns skills.

Firdstole, as *Fridstole*.

Firebares, *o.* Beacons.

Fire-boot, allowance of competent fire-wood to the Tenant.

Fire-drake, a fiery Meteor, a great unequal exhalation inflamed between a hot and a cold cloud.

Fire-cross, a Scotch Proclamation (by fire brands on a spear) for all between 16 and 60 to repair to a place of Rendezvous.

Firkin, a vessel of nine gallons.

Firma, *sc.* the duty which the Tenant paies to his Landlord.

Firmament, *l.* the starry heaven, finishing its course in 250 thousand years.

Firmity, *l.* firmness, stableness, constancy.

Firmus, a *Roman* Emperour of a vast strength.

First-fruits, Annates, one years profits of every benefice.

Firth, for *Frith*.

Firthe, Fyrte, Fyrt, *o.* a bugbear, a Ghost, or apparition.

Fiscal, belonging to a

Fisque, *l.* a treasury or Exchequer.

Fish-garth, a dam or wear for the taking of fish.

Fishing, piecing of masts or yards to strengthen them.

Fissility, *l.* aptness to be cleft.

Fissiped, *l.* cloven-footed.

Fissure, *l.* a cleft or division.

Fistic-nuts, brought out of hot countries and useful in Physick.

Fistulary, belonging to a

Fistula, *l.* a pipe, also an ulcer eating in and running like a pipe.

Fitch, the [fur of the] polecate.

Fitc'tel, a town of *Mecklenburgh* in *Germany*.

Fitched, sharp at the end. See *Cross*.

Fithwite, as *Fightewite*,

Fitz, (*f. fils*) a son.

Five-finger, a fish like a spurrowel, to be destroyed by the Admiralty law, because destructive to Oysters.

Fixation, *l.* a fixing, making any volatil spiritual body to endure the fire.

Fixed stars, not varying their distance from one another; and (corruptly) as

Faxed stars, Comets, from

Fax, *o.* hair,

Fiz-gig, a dart to strike fishes as they swim.

Fizon, *Foison*, *Sf.* the heart or natural juice of herbs, &c.

Flabellation, an airing with a

Flabel, *l.* a fan.

Flaccid, *l.* flagging, drooping.

Flacket, *No.* a bottle in fashion of a barrel.

Flag, *c.* a groat.

Flagellantes, *l.* Hereticks going up and down and using.

Flagellation, whipping or scourging [of themselves.]

Flagitation, *l.* earnest begging.

Flagitious, *l.* hainous, wicked.

Flagrancy, *l.* a being

Flagrant, *l.* burning, hot, vehement.

Flageolet, *f.* a small pipe.

Flags, *Nf.* turfs pared off to burn.

Flag-worm, found and bred in sedgy places, hanging to the small strings of flagroots.

Flamins, *-ens*, the old *Roman* Priests.

Flammability, aptness to be inflamed.

Flammation, a setting on fire.

Flammeous, *l.* like flame.

Flammivomous, *l.* vomiting flames.

Flammiferous, bringing or causing flame.

Flaminian way, a *Roman* high-way full of tombs and monuments.

Flanch, an Ordinary formed of an Arch-line, from the corner of the Chief, with a swelling Emboss'ment toward the Nombril of th' Escutcheon.

Flandria, *Flanders*, one great Town of 154 villages within 90 miles.

Flanchards, the nuts or knots in a Deers flank.

Flanque, the side of a company (of Soldiers) from the front to the rear.

Flaring, *Flair-*, when a ship is a little howsing in near the water, then the upper work hangs over and is laid out broader aloft.

Flash of flames, *o.* a sheaf of arrows.

Flasque, an Arch-line somewhat distant from the corner of the Chief and swelling by degrees toward the midst of th' Escutcheon, a Carriage for Ordnance, a box for gunpowder, also a bottle (or pottle) of *Florence* wine.

Flatility, uncertainty, inconstancy.

Flatulent, *-uous*, *l.* windy.

Flatuosity, windiness.

Flaunes, *o.* Custards.

Flavour, a pleasant relish and smell [in wine, &c.]

Flaw, *l.* Yellow.

Flawmes, *Sc.* flames.

Flay, *o.* flew.

Flea-bane, a whitish herb (by Ditch sides) driving away fleas.

Fleawort, whose seed resembles a flea in bigness and colour.

Fleak, *No.* a gate to set in a gap.

Flebring, *o.* a slander.

Flecked, arched like the firmament.

Flecksen, *o.* abound.

Fledwit, *Fletwit*, *Flightwite*, by some, a fine set upon Fugitives, by others, a discharging of outlaw'd fugitives from amerciaments, when they return to the Kings peace.

Fleen, *o.* to fly.

Fleet, a famous prison in *London* by the side of

Fleta, *Fleet*, *Sa.* a River, Flood, or small stream.

Flemasiree, *Sa.* the claiming a felons goods.

Fleme, a lancing or blouding instrument.

Flemed, *o.* daunted.

Fleming, *o.* Conquest.

Flemer, *o.* an expeller.

Flegmatick, as *Phlegmatick*.

Flemenesfrinthe, *-fyrinthe*, *-freicthe*,

Flemeneferd, *-frit*, *-wurde*,

Flemnenefremeth, *Flemanisfit*,

Fremenefend.t, all instead of

Flymenafyrmthe, *sa.* the receiving or relieving a fugitive.

Flemefwit. a liberty to challenge the Cattle or amerciaments of your man a fugitive.

Flemming, one of *Flanders*.

Flensborch, a Town of South *Juitland* in *Denmark*.

Flesh of Fruits or Roots, the edible part.

Fletiferous, yielding or causing weeping.

Fleure, *o.* a sweet smell.

Flexanimous, turning the mind, or of a turning mind.

Flexibility, *l.* a being

Flexible, capable of

Flexion, *l.* a bending.

Flexiloquent, *l.* speaking doubtfully or doubly.

Flick, *c.* to cut.

Flicker, *c.* a glass.

Flide-thrift, shove-groat, shovel-board play.

Fliker, *o.* to flutter.

Flint, a Castle in *Flintshire*.

Flitful, *sa.* contentious.

Flitwite, *Flitchtw-*, *Sa.* a forfeiture for

Flit, *Sa.* contention, wrangling, &c.

Flite, *Flight*, *o.* to chide.

Flittermouse, a bat.

Flitting, [a staked horse] eating up all the grass within his reach, removing from place to place.

Flizze, *No.* to fly off.

Flizzing, *No.* a splinter.

Flixweed, *Sophia Chirurgorum*, an astringent herb.

Flo, *Flone*, *o.* an arrow.

Floan, loose, not haled home to the blocks.

Floccify, *l.* to slight, or lightly esteem.

Flockmele, *sa.* in flocks.

Flodden, a hill near *Brampton in Northumberland*.

Flode, (for flowed) *o.* abounded.

Flog, *c.* to whip.

Floor of a Ship, so much, of her bottom as rests upon the ground.

Flora, *Chloris*, the Goddess of Flowers.

Florce, *f.* the blew scum of wood boyling in the dyers Lead.

Floramor, flower of Love, *Passevelours*, flower gentle.

Florein, *-rin*, a kind of coin worth about three shillings, another worth eighteen pence.

Florentine, *Fluentine*, belonging to

Florence, the chief City of *Tuscany*, in *Italy*.

Florences, a kind of Cloth brought from thence.

Florey-blew, a kind of blew for paint or limning.

Floriferous, *l.* bearing flowers.

Florilege, *l.* a gathering of flowers.

Florist, one skill'd in flowers.

Florid, *l.* flourishing.

Florulent, *l.* gay, the same as

Flosculous, *l.* flowery, or blossoming.

Flotes, pieces of Timber joyn'd, to convey burthens down a River.

Flotages, things accidentally floating on the Sea or great Rivers.

Flotson, *Flotzam*, shipwrackt goods floating on the Sea, which belong to the Lord Admiral, together with *Jetson* (things cast over-bord or on shore) and *Lagon*, *Legan*, or *Ligam* (things lying at the bottom of the Sea) and shares.

Flouke of an Anchor, that part which takes hold of the ground.

Flowry de lice, *o.* beset with Lilies.

Floting, *o.* whistling, piping.

Flower de lyse, Orrece.

It flows South, *&c.* It is high water when the Sun is in that point at full or new Moon.

It Flows tide and half tide, it will be half floud by the shore, before it begins to flow in the channel.

Fluctiferous, bringing waves.

Fluctuate, *l.* to rise in waves, also to waver or doubt

Fluctisonant, *l.* sounding with waves.

Fluctivagant, tossed or wandring on the waves.

Fluctuous, *l.* like the waves, unquiet, boisterous.

Fluellin, the herb *Speedwell*.

Fluidity, a being

Fluid, Fluent, or flowing or apt to flow, nimble.

Fluish, *No.* washy, weak, tender.

Fluminous, *l.* full of Rivers, also as

Fluvial, belonging to Rivers.

Fluvious, flowing much.

Flures, stones (resembling precious stones) coming out of Mines.

Flush fore and aft, when the Deck lies level from stem to stern.

Flushing a Town in *Zeland*.

Flux, *-xion*, *l.* a flowing, issue, or loosness of body.

Fluxing, making the patient spit up the disease.

Fluxibility, *l.* an aptness to flow.

Fly, that part of the compass where the winds are described.

Fly gross, when hawks fly at great Birds as Cranes, Geese, &c.

Focillate, *l.* to refresh.

Fodder, *Foder*, *Fother*, *sa.* 2000 pound weight of Lead, also course meat for Cattel, and a Princes prerogative of being provided by his subjects with Corn for his horses in any expedition.

Fodient, *l.* digging.

Fœmina, sulphur (in Chymistry.)

Fogage, *Fog* or *Feg*, ranck grass not eaten in summer time.

Fogo, a burning Island in *America*.

Fogm

Fogus, c. Tabacco.

Fohines, the first Monarch of the *Chinois*.

Foiles, f. l. g. leaves.

Foiling, the print of a Deers foot in the grass hardly discernable.

Foine, f. to prick or sting.

Foines, a fur (black at the top and the ground whitish) from a small beast of the same name.

Foison, f. abundance.

Fotterers, vagabonds.

Fold course, as *Faldage*.

Foliaceous, l. leavy.

Foist, a pinnace or small ship.

Folgheres, *-geres*, o. followers.

Foliage, branched work.

Foliatanes, a sort of men living only upon leaves, supprest by the *Pope*.

Foliate, l. leaved.

Folio, of two leaves to a sheet.

Folkingham, a Town in *Lincolnshire*.

Folily, o. foolishly, rashly.

Folkland, sa. copy-hold land.

Folkmoot, *Folkesmote*, *Folcmote*, sa. a general assembly of the people, the County-Court, or else the Sheriffs Turn.

Follicle, l. a small bladder, or purse.

Foe-men, o. Enemies.

Fomentation, l. a cherishing, an applying warm clothes (dipt in some liquor) to the body.

Fond, *Foond*, *Fund*, f. a bottom, or foundation, also a stock (in money or moneys worth.)

Fon'l, o. contend, labour.

Fondery, f. a stilling house, also the trade of melting metals.

Fong, sa. to take.

Fonne, o. [to be] foolish.

Fonnes, o. devices.

Fons solis, a fountain in *Lybia*, (by the Temple of Jupit r *Hammon*) boyling hot at midnight.

Fontal, belonging to *Fonts*, Fountains, springs; also Church-Baptisteries, (which were primitively Rivers.)

Fontanel, f. an issue made in the body.

Fontainbleau (for *belle eau*) a retiring place for the Kings of *France* in the Forest of *Becre*, one of the purest Fountains in the world, the *Hampton Court* of *France*, (also in dancing) a Borree so named.

Foothote, *-hute*, (q. *hot-foot*) o. straightway.

Footing-time, Nf. when the Child-bed woman gets up.

Footstal, the foot or lower part of a pillar.

Foot-hocks, *Foot-hooks*, or *Futtocks*, the compassing Timbers which give the breadth and bearing to the Ship.

Fop, o. a fool.

Forable, l. that may be peirced or bored.

Foppery, foolishness.

Forage, fodder for Cattel.

Foraminous, l. full of holes.

Foranous, belonging to the *Forum*, l. a Court or Market-place.

Forbarre, *Forebar*, to bar or deprive for ever.

Forlode, sa. to presage, also to prohibit or forbid.

Forbish, to burnish.

Forcers, an instrument to draw Teeth.

Forcheim, a Town in *Franconland*, where (they say) *Pontius Pilate* was born.

Forcipated, l. bending, hooked

Foreclose, shut out, excluded for ever.

Fordoe, o. to kill.

Fordon, *-dyd*, killed.

Forecastle, the fore part of a Ship above Decks.

Fore, o. gone.

Fore-foot, one ships lying or sailing crosse another ships w y, or with her fore-foot.

Foregoers, Purveyours going before the King in Progress.

Forein [*matter*] triable in another Court,

Foreign answer, not triable in that County.

Foreign Attachment, of foreiners goods found within any Liberty.

Forein Apposer or *Opposer*, an Exchequer Officer opposing the Sheriffs of their green wax, apposing and examining them upon their Estreats.

Forein plea, a refusal of the Judge as incompetent (the matter being out of his jurisdiction.)

Forein service, that whereby a mean Lord holds over of another without the compass of his own Fee; or else that which a Tenant performs either to his own Lord or to the Lord paramount out of the Fee.

Fore-judging, or *Forj-*, a Judgment whereby a man is deprived or put by the thing in question.

Forejudged the Court, banished or expel'd from it.

Fore-Knight and *Main-Knight*, two short thick pieces (carved with a mans head) fast bolted to the beams upon the 2d. deck.

Foreland, *Forenes*, a promontory jutting out.

Forelock-bolts, bolts with an eye at the end whereinto an iron forelock is driven, to keep them from starting.

Foreloin, when one hound going before the rest meets chace and goes away with it.

Forensal, l. used in pleading, pertaining to the Common-pleas.

Forest, a safe harbour for Deer, or any wild beasts.

Forestagium, a duty paiable to the

Forester, the Kings sworn Officer of the Forest.

Forestaller, *Regrater*, one that buyes ware before it come to Market, to enhaunse the price.

Forfare, o. forlorn.

Fore-reach upon, to Outsail.

Forfeiture, the [effect of] transgressing a penal law.

Forfeiture of marriage, a writ against one under age and holding by Knights service, who refused to marry her whom his Lord profer'd, without his disparagement.

Forfraught, o. beset.

Forgard, o. lost.

Forger of false deeds, [a writ against] one that makes and publishes false writings to the prejudice of any mans right.

Forkerve, o. cut off.

Forlaine, o. Rechased.

Forleien, o. to erre, or wander.

Forletten, o. abandoned.

Forlorn, D. lost.

Forlorn-hope, a party of Soldiers put upon the most Desperate service.

Forloyn, o. a retreat.

Forlyth, o. spoyleth.

Formalize, to form or fashion, also to play the

Formalist, one that useth

Formality, a being

Formal, punctual, precise, belonging to or giving a

Form, l. outward shew or appearance. shape or beauty, also the inward essence of a thing.

Formator, l. a former, maker, also an informer, instructer.

Formel, -mel, No. to bespeak.

Forme of a hare, the seat which she makes herself.

Former, the piece of wood on which they make the Carthrages.

Formedon, f. (the form of the gift) a writ for him who hath right to any lands or tenements by virtue of an Intail.

Formica, *Herpes*, a corroding ulcer.

Formicans pulsus, a thick and weak pulse.

Formidable, l. Dreadfull, to be feared.

Formidolous, l. the same, also fearing.

Formosity, l. beauty, fairness.

Formulary, l. a president of Law-process, &c.

Fornagium, Chimney-money, also the Landlords fee for his tenants baking in his Oven.

Forne-fader, o. first father Adam.

Fornication, l. Whoredom between unmarried persons.

Forenesss, as *Foreland*.

Forouten, o. without.

Forprise, an exception or reservation, in Leases, &c.

Forrey, o. Destroy.

Forriours, o. Fore-runners.

Forsamkill, o. Forasmuch.

Forses, *Catadupæ*, water-falls.

Forschoke, forsaken, Lands Seised by the Lord (for want of due service, &c.) and quietly possest beyond the year and day.

Forslagen, o. slain.

Forslagen, -*glen*, -*gen*, o. slain.

Forsongen, o. weary with singing.

Forspecen, o. spoken against or in vain.

Forspreak, o. an Advocate.

Forster, a Forester.

Forstraught, o. Distracted.

Forswonk and *Forswat*, o. over laboured and sweated or Sun-burnt.

Forth, l. Theft.

Forthy, -*then*, No. therefore.

Fortility, a fortifi'd place.

Forthink, o. to be grieved in mind.

Fortitude, l. valour, stoutness of mind, courage.

Fortlet, a little Fort.

Fortuitous, l. accidental, coming by Fortune or chance.

Fortuny, a kind of Tournement or running a tilt with launces on horseback.

Forvise, o. Foreshew.

Forwany, o. wanting.

Forwelked, o. Dried up.

Forwept, o. weary with weeping.

Forwysed, o. withered.

Foryede, o. overwent.

Fossatum, a Ditch, or place fenced therewith.

Fosset, *Forset*, a little long chest or coffer.

Fosse-way, the *Roman* high-way dug from *Cornwal* to *Lincoln*, Ditched on both sides, or left imperfect like a Ditch, also several other inferiour high-waies.

Fossion, l. a Digging.

Foster, Forester.

Foster-land, assigned for the finding of food.

Fostal, o. the pricking or footsteps of a hare, also a way from the high-way to a great house, *Sf.*

Fother, *Foder*, twenty hundred pound weight.

Fotheringhay, a Castle in *Northamptonshire*.

Fotion, l. a cherishing.

Fotive, l. nourishing or nourished.

Fougade, f. a kind of fire-work. a mine.

Foul, hindred or intangled with another ship, rope, &c.

Foul water, when a ship raises the sand or oaze in shallow water.

Foundemaunt, f. Foundation.

Founder, a melter and caster of metals.

Foulk, *Fulk*, *Ge.* Noble, or as *Folc*, *Sa.* People.

Founes, o Devices.

Fourche, f. (a fork) a delaying or putting off an Action.

Foutgeld, *Foot-*, an amerciament for not expeditating or cutting out the balls of great dogs feet in the Forest.

Foundered, filled (as a ship) with water by an extraordinary leak, &c.

Fowle fail o. (q. *fail fouly*,) to erre greatly.

Found, o. framed.

Fow, *Cle.* foul.

Fox-gloves, *Digitalis*, *Virga regia*, *Campanula sylvestris*, a cleansing herb.

Foxes evil, as *Alopecia*.

Foyeten, (for *Forleten*) let pass.

Foye,

Foye, a Town in *Cornwal.*

Fram, *sa.* From.

Fram-pole-fences, of the Tenants of *Writtel* Mannour in *Essex*, toward whose repair they have the Wood growing on the Fence, and as many Trees (or poles) as they can reach from the top of the ditch with their ax helve.

Fracid, *l.* rotten-ripe.

Fraction, *l.* a breaking, dissention, part of a whole number.

Fracture, *l.* the breaking [of a bone.]

Fragility, *l.* a being

Fragile, *l.* brittle, apt to break.

Fragment, *l.* a piece, or broken part of any thing.

Fragrancy, *l.* a being

Fragrant, *l.* sweet-smelling.

Fraine, *Sc.* to ask.

Fraight, *sa.* the burden of the Ship, also money paid for any thing carryed.

Frail of [*Malaga*] *Raisins*, about 70 pound.

Fraesheur, *f.* freshness, coolness, livelinefs.

Framlingham, a Town in *Suffolk.*

Frampton, a Town in *Dorcester.*

Franc, *f.* a livre, 20 pence.

Frank, *o.* free, liberal.

Franchise, *f.* freedom, exemption, priviledge.

Franchise Royale, *f.* a grant of immunity from the King.

Francigena, a native of

France, the modern name of *Gallia* conquered by the

Franci, *-cones*, *Franks*, *Germans*, under the conduct of *Pharamond*

Francis, a mans name, and (sometime) as

Frances. a womans name.

Franciscans, a strict order of *Fryers* instituted by St. *Francis* an Italian, 1198. vowing chastity, obedience, poverty, &c.

Frangible, *l.* breakable.

Frank-almoine, a tenure of Lands bestowed on such as devote themselves to the service of God.

Frank-banck, *Free-bench*, the Dower of Copy-hold-Lands which the wife (being espoused a Virgin) hath after her husbands decease.

Frank-chase, the Foresters liberty of Free-chase, whereby all (in such a compass) are prohibited to cut down wood, without his view.

Frank-fee, that which is in the hand of the King or Lord of the Mannour, being ancient Demesne of the Crown.

Frank-farm, Land wherein the nature of Fee is changed (by Feofment) out of Knights service to certain yearly services.

Frank-fold. the Lords benefit of folding his Tenant Sheep for the manuring of his Land.

Frank-law, the benefit of the free and common Law of the Land.

Frank-marriage, a Tenure in Tail-special, whereby a man hath Land with a Woman to him and the Heirs of his body doing fealty only [to the fourth descent, and thence forward service] to the Donour.

Frank-pledge, the ancient custom of the Decenniers (or freemen in each Decenna) being surety for one another (at the age of fourteen) to the King.

Frankincense, an *Arabian* gum from a tree of the same name with leaves and bark like Lawrel.

Frankendale, a Town in the *Palatinate* of the *Rhine.*

Franklin, *-colon*, a kind of red-legged bird for Hawking.

Francford, *-furt*, a famous *German* City.

Francling, a Freeholder.

Franconia, *Frankenland* in the East part of *Germany.*

Franeker, an University of *West-Friesland.*

Frape, a company or rabble.

Fraternize, to agree as Brothers, also to bring into a

Fraternity, *l.* a Brotherhood.

Frase, *Nf.* to break.

Frantick, *Phrentick*, *g.* mad.

Fraternal, *l.* Brotherly.

Fratricelli, *Fratres de paupere vita*, Hereticks following one *Hermannus* an Italian 1304. They held promiscuous beddings, Christians not to be Governours, &c.

Fratricide, *l.* the killing or killer of a Brother.

Fratruels, *l.* Brothers children, Cousin-Germans.

Fraudation, *l.* a defrauding.

Fraudulency, *l.* deceitfulness, a being

Fraudulent, crafty, full of

Fraud, *l.* guile, deceit.

F. (*Fray-maker* or *Frighter*) a mark burnt on the cheek (for want of ears to cut) for striking with a weapon in the Church or Church-yard.

Fraxinella, a plant (like a little Ash) against obstructions.

Frayes her head, [a Deer] rubs her head against a tree to renew it.

Frayn'd, *o.* refrained.

Frea, as *Friga.*

Frederick, *Ge.* rich peace, *vulgo Frery*, *Fery.*

Fredeborch, a Town of *Westphalia.*

Fredifwid, *sa.* very free.

Free the boat, cast out the water.

Freel, *f.* frail.

Freelege, *No.* privilege.

Free-bench, as *Frank-bank.*

Free-booters, Soldiers that make inroads into the Enemies Country for Cattel, &c. or that serve (for plunder) without pay.

Free-lord, a small space beyond or without the fence.

Free-Chappel, over and above the Mother-Church of a Parish, freely endowed and to which one might freely resort, or (rather) of the Kings Foundation, or at least exempted by him from the Jusrisdiction and visitation of the Diocesan.

Free-hold, free tenure, in Fee-tail, or for term of Life.

Free-warren, the power of licencing any to hunt in such or such places, also the license it self.

Freedstol, *Fridstol*, *Frithstow*, *sa.* (stool of peace) a chair of stone granted by King *Athelstan* to *John de Beverly* Arch-Bishop of *York*, as a Sanctuary for offenders.

Freidat, a Town of lower *Bavaria*, another in *Austria*, &c.

Frement, *l.* gnashing the Teeth.

Fremund, *sa.* free peace.

Frem'd, *-ened*, *o.* a stranger.

French-man, (anciently) any stranger.

Frend-less-man, *sa.* an Outlaw.

Frenigerent, *l.* guiding the bridle.

Frenith, *o.* asketh.

Frenne, (for Forein) a stranger.

Freoburgh, *Fridburgh*, as *Frank-pledge*.

Frery, *Frederick*.

Freomortel, *Frodm-*, an immunity or freedom granted for murder or man-slaughter.

Frequency, *l.* oftenness.

Frequent, *l.* often.

Frequent, *l.* to haunt or resort unto.

Frescades, *f.* cool refreshments in Summer-time.

Fresco, *I.* fresh, cool.

Walk in Fresco, in the fresh air.

Drink in Fresco, to drink cool or fresh Liquor.

Paint in Fresco, on walls newly plaistered, that it may sink in.

Fresh, *o.* refresh.

Fresh the hawse, veer out a little more or lay new plats upon the Cable.

Fresh disseisin, an arbitrary disseisin (not above 15 daies old) which a man may seek to defeat of himself, without the help of King or Judges.

Fresh-fine, levied within a year past.

Fresh force, done within fourty daies.

Fresh-gale, immediately after a calm.

Fresh-man, a novice, newly entred [in the University, &c.]

Fresh shot, fresh water (from a great river) for a mile or two in the Sea.

Fresh-spel, a fresh gang to relieve the Rowers in the long boat.

Fresh sute, an active and eager following the offender (from the time of offence) till he be apprehended.

Fret, *o.* to turn, also fraught.

Fret, *f.* a round vertil or ferril (of Iron, &c.)

Frete, *Fretten*, *o.* to devour.

Fretrots, a kind of *Adamites* (wearing a secret Crown) suppressed *Anno* 1310.

Fretted, diapered, with several lines crossing one another.

Friable, *l.* capable of

Friation, *l.* a crumbling.

Friar, *Frier*, (*f. Frere*, Brother) One that is a Regular or of some Religious Order.

Friburg, a town of *Schwaben* in *Germany*.

Friers Observant, a sort of *Franciscans*, not Conventuals but at large, yet more strictly tying themselves to the Observation of their Rule.

Friends, Quakers so called among themselves.

Fricasse, *f.* a fried dish.

Frication, *l.* a rubbing.

Fridburg, a City of the higher *Bavaria*.

Fridburge, *Frithborg*, *Friburgh*, as *Frank-pledge*.

Fridland, a town in *Germany*.

Friday, the sixth day, from

Friga, a *Saxon* Goddess in the shape of an *Hermaphrodite*

Frigate, *Sp.* a Spial ship.

Frigdores, *o.* Musick-measures (*q. Frigian* and *Dorick*.)

Frigefaction, *l.* a making cold.

Frigerate, *l.* to cool.

Frigeratory, *l.* a place to make or keep things cool.

Frigorifical, that which doth

Frigisy, *l.* to cause

Frigidity, *Frigor*, *l.* the being

Frigid, *l.* cold.

Frigmareventus, *Winchelsea*.

Frim, *No.* handsome, thriving.

Frim folks, *Li.* Strangers.

Fripery, *f.* the trade, shop, or street of

Friperers, the sorriest brokers.

Frist, *No.* to trust for a time.

Frisesmorum, a Syllogism whose first proposition is a particular affirmative, the second an universal Negative, and the 3d a particular Neg.

Frisia, *Friezland* by *Holland*.

Frising, a town of lower *Bavaria*.

Frit, salt or ashes fried or baked together with sand.

Frith, *Sa.* a wood.

Frithbrech, *Sa.* Breach of the peace.

Frithburgh, as *Fridburgh*.

Frithsocne, *-soken*, *Sa.* the liberty of having *frank-pledge*, a surety.

Fritillary. a flower in the fashion of a

Fritillus, *l.* a box out of which Dice are cast.

Fritiniancy, *-iency*, the chirping of a Swallow, &c.

Frivolous, *l.* vain, of little worth.

Frize, the garnishing at the upper end of a pillar.

Frobly mobly, *So.* indifferently well.

Fro, *o.* from.

Frodesham, a Town in *Cheshire*.

From-Selwood, a Town in *Som.*

Frondation, a taking off the leaves or branches.

Frondosity, *l.* leavinefs, a flourifhing with green leaves juft under the Architrave.

Frondiferous, bearing leaves.

Froife, a Pancake [with bacon intermixt.]

Frontal, *l.* belonging to the forehead, alfo as

Frontlet, an ornament or attire of the

Front, *l.* Forehead, alfo the forepart of any thing.

Frontals, Medicines applied to the forehead.

Frontifpiece, *l.* the fore-front of a building, alfo the Title or firft page of a book [done in picture.]

Frontier towns, ftanding on the

Frontiers, the borders of a Country.

Frontiniac, a lufcious and rich wine of that town in *France*.

Front-ftall, the forepart of a horfes bridle.

Frontones, a *Roman* name, from their high foreheads.

Frote, *f.* to rub.

Frounce, *f.* a wrinkle, alfo as

Frounches, *o. Barbillon*, *f.* a diftemper in a hawks tongue.

Frower, *So.* an edg-tool uf-ed in cleaving lath.

Froy, *o.* (*q. Fro yee*) from you.

Fructify, *l.* bring forth fruit.

Frugality, *l.* thriftinefs, good husbandry, a being

Frugal, *l.* thrifty, fparing [in expences, diet, &c.]

Fruggin, an Oven-fork.

Frugiferent, *-rous*, *l.* fruit-full.

Fruitery, *f.* a place to keep fruit in.

Frutiges, *-ices*, *l.* branched work in fculpture, as

Frucillage, in painting or tapeftry.

Frum-gyld, *Sa.* the firft payment (or recompence) made to the Kinred of a flain perfon.

Frum-ftal, *Sa.* Home-ftal, the chief feat or Manfion-houfe.

Frummagem, *c.* choaked.

Frum, *Sa.* Early, foon-ripe.

Frumentarious, belonging to corn or

Frumenty, pottage of milk and

Frument, *l.* wheat.

Frump, jeer, flout or taunt.

Fruftetum, a wood or wood-ground.

Fruffura, a breaking down or demolifhing.

Fruftraneous, *l.* done in vain.

Fruftrate, *l.* to deceive or difappoint.

Fruftulent, *l.* full of

Frufta, *l.* fmall pieces.

Fruitage, *Frut-*, as *Frutiges*.

Frutication, *l.* a fprouting or fhooting forth of young branches.

Fruticofe, *l.* full of fhoots, ftalks or fhrubs.

Fryth, *Frith*, *fa.* a wood, or a plain between woods.

Frythborgh, freedom from giving fecurity of the Peace.

Fuage, *Focage*, Herth-filver (1 s.) impofed by *Edward* 3d. (black Prince of *Wales*) on the Dukedom of *Aquitain*.

Fucator, *l.* he that doth

Fucate, *l.* paint [the face,] counterfeit.

Fugacia, *Chafea*, a Chafe.

Fugacity, *l.* aptnefs to fly away.

Fudder, *No.* a load [of lead] eight pigs or fixteen hundred pound.

Fugalia, Roman Feafts in remembrance of the expulfion of their Kings, alfo as Hock-tide.

Fugation, *l.* a putting to flight.

Fugue, *f.* when two or more parts (in mufick) chafe one another in the fame point.

Fugitive-goods, forfeited to the King from him that flies for Felony.

Fuir, *o.* fury.

Fuir, *f.* to fly, run away.

Fuir en feit, to fly corporally.

Fuir en ley, not to appear till one be outlawed.

Fukes, *Che.* locks of hair.

Fulbert, *fa.* full bright.

Fulcible, *l.* capable of

Fulciments, *l.* fupporters.

Fulgor, *-gidity*, *-gency*, a being

Fulgent, *-gid*, *l.* bright, gliftring.

Fulgural, belonging to

Fulguration, *l.* lightning, alfo a reducing metals into vapours by the help of lead (in a copel) and a violent fire.

Fulfremed, *fa.* perfect, fully framed.

Fulk, *o.* (for *Sulk*, *l.* a hollow place, or furrow.

Fullick, *o.* fully.

Fulham, *fa.* a home or habitation for Fowles.

Fullians, Monks of the order of St. *Bernard*.

Fuliginous, *l.* footy, or fmoaky.

Fullers-earth, dug up about *Brickhill* in *Bedfordfhire*, diffolved in vinegar it difcuffes Pimples, repreffes inflammations, &c.

Fullonical, belonging to a

Fuller, or fcourer of cloth.

Fulminatory, *l.* belonging to

Fulmination, *l.* a ftriking with lightning, alfo a threatning.

Fulvid, *-vous*, *l.* of a yellowifh dusky colour, lion-tawny.

Fumage, [manuring with] dung.

Fumadoes, *-thoes*, *Sp.* our Pilchards garbaged, falted, fmoakt and preft.

Fumets, the ordure of a Hart.

Fumeyed, *-mayed*, *o.* muted.

Fumidity, a being

Fumid, *l.* fmoaky.

Fumiferous, bringing fmoke.

Fumigation, *l.* a fmoaking or perfuming with fmoak, alfo calcining of bodies by the fume of fharp Spirits.

Fumitory, *Fumaria*, *l.* *Palomilla*, *Sp.* a hot biting herb.

Funambulator, *-ant*, *l.* a dancer on the Ropes.

Function, *l.* the performance or exercise of any duty or Office.

Fund, land or soil, also as Fond.

Funditour, *-tor*, *l.* a slinger, or darter.

Fundamental, belonging to

Fundament, *l.* a Foundation.

Funebrous, *-erous*, *l.* mournfull, belonging to Funerals.

Funestation, *l.* pollution by touching a dead body.

Fungosity, *l.* spunginess, a being

Fungous, *l.* full of holes, like a mushroom.

Funnel, *Tunnel*, an instrument small at one end, to convey liquor into a vessel, also the upper part of a chimney.

Furacity, *l.* a being

Furacious, pilfering, theevish.

Furbish, polish, make bright.

Furcation, *l.* a forking, making like a fork, or hanging on a gallows.

Furca, (*Calefurcia*) & *Fossa*, a jurisdiction (in ancient priviledges) of punishing felons, *viz.* men with hanging and Women with drowning.

Furies, *l.* *Alecto*, *Megera* and *Tysiphone*, daughters of *Acheron* and *Night*, tormenters of Murderers and other wicked Souls.

Furibund, *-bond*, *l.* raging, mad.

Furina, a Roman Goddess, patroness of Thieves.

Fured, *Cu.* went.

Furling-lines, *Farthelinglines*, small lines wherewith they

Furle or *Farthel the sails*, ty them up to the yards.

Furlong, the length of 40 poles, half a quarter of a mile, and sometimes of an acre.

Furlough, a licence from a Superiour to an Inferiour officer, to be absent a while from his charge in war.

Furnivals, Lords of *Fernham* in *Bucks*, whose tenure is, To find the King a righthand glove on his Coronation-day, and support his right arm while he holds the Scepter.

Furnage, as *Fornagium*.

Furole, *f.* St. *Hermes*'s fire, a little meteor appearing in the night upon the shrouds, &c.

Furr the ship, clap on another plank upon her sides after she is built, or else rip off the first planks, put other timbers upon the first, and then put on the planks again: a great (yet common) disgrace to *English* ships.

Furst sore, (*q. frost sore*) a Chilblain.

Furstenburg, a Castle of North *Schwaben* in *Germany*.

Furtive, *l.* given to stealing, or done by stealth.

Furze, whins, a prickly Bush good against the stone, Spleen, &c.

Fuscation, *l.* a clouding or darkning.

Fusibility, a being

Fusible, *l.* apt or easie to be melted, capable of

Fusion, *l.* a melting or pouring forth.

Fusil, *f.* a firelock, or a tinder box.

Fusil, *l.* a spindle, also the resemblance thereof in a coat of arms.

Fust, the trunk or body of a pillar.

Fustian, stuff made of cotton, or the down of an *Egyptian* fruit.

Fustic, a kind of wood which dyers use, from *Barbadoes*, &c.

Fustigation, *l.* a cudgelling, an ancient punishment of perjured persons.

Fusty, *Musty*, vinewed.

Futility *l.* a blabbing, babling, lightness, vanity, folly.

Futtocks, Foot-hooks, the compassing timbers scarfed upon the ground timbers and giving breadth to a ship.

Futurition, *-ty*, a being

Future, *l.* that which will be, or is to come.

Fuzen, *Fuzzen*, *No.* Nourishment.

Fyle, *Sc.* Fouled.

Fyngted, *o.* a [sore] finger tied up, alias a hawk.

Fyre levin, *o.* lightning.

Fyrte, as *Firthe*.

G.

GAal, *h.* Abomination.

Gabala, *Gibel*, *Margad*, a town of *Syria cava*.

Gab, *o.* to prate or lie.

Gabbing, lying.

Gabardine, an *Irish* mantle, rough Cassock, or Livery coat.

Gabberies, *f.* wiles, mockeries.

Gabel, *f.* tribute, custom.

Gabion, *f.* a defence made of baskets filled with earth.

Gable end of a house, the top, or (by some) the frontispiece.

Gabrantovici, *Britains* inhabiting part of *Yorkshire*.

Gabriel, *h.* the strength of God.

Gabrosentum, a frontier station of the *Romans*, supposed to be where *New-castle* and *Gates-head* now stand.

Gaddefly, a brie or brieze.

Gad, *h.* a troop or band.

Gaddi, *Gaddi*, a rare *Florentine* painter who excelled in *Mosaic* work.

Gades, two Islands westward beyond the streights, by some called *Hercules*'s pillars.

Gadling, *o.* stradling.

Gaffe, *f.* an iron hook to pull great fishes into the ship.

Gafold-gyld, *Sa.* the payment of tribute, also usury.

Gafol-land, *Gafulland*, liable to tribute, also rented.

Gage or *wage deliverance*, put in security that the thing shall be delivered.

Gage the ship, try how much water she draws, by a pole and a nail put down by the rudder.

Gage, *c.* a pot or pipe.

Gaging-rod, an instrument to measure any vessel of liquor.

a Gagle of geys, *o.* a flock of Geese.

Gaiety, *f.* gallantry, cheerfulness.

Gaitere berries, of the

Gayter tree, Prickwood.

Gainage, the instruments of tillage, also the land held by the baser sort of Soke-men or Villains.

Gainerie, the same.

Gail-dish, *Guile-dish*, *No.* the Tun-dish.

Gail-clear, *No.* a Wort-tub.

Gainsborough, a town in *Lincolnshire*.

Gainure, tillage.

Gain [*thing*] *Not.* Convenient.

Gain [*man*] active, expert.

Gain [*miles*] short.

Galactopote, *g.* a drinker of milk.

Galactite, *g.* a milky precious stone.

Galanga, an *East-India* root like ginger.

Galanthis, *Alcmena's* maid turn'd into a weasel.

Galathea, a Sea-Nymph beloved of *Polypheme*, who killed *Acis* whom she preferred before him.

Galatia, *Gallo-grecia* in *Asia* the less.

Galaxie, *g.* the milky way, made up of little stars.

Galbanum, a Syrian gum of the plant Fennel-giant.

Galeat, a kind of White-wine from a Town of that name in *France*.

Galeges, *Galages*, *Galloches*.

Galloshooes, *f.* wooden shoen all of a piece; with us, out ward shoes or cases for dirty weather, &c.

Gale, *o.* to chafe, to flout, also to yawl,

Galena, *Wallingford.*

Galenist, *-ite*, a follower of

Galen, *-nus*, a famous Physician of *Pergamus*

Galeon, *Galleon*, *f.* a great man of war.

Gallote, *f.* a small Gally, or one that rows in a Gally.

Galerion, the herb Crudwort.

Galgacus, a *British* General against the *Romans*.

Gallians, *-iens*, *f.* Galens works.

Galiard, *Gaillard*, *f.* merry.

Galilæa, *-lee*, a Region of *Syria*, North of *Judæa*.

Galingale, the Aromatick root of the rush *Cyprus*.

Galla moschata, a Confection of Musk, &c.

Galleasse, *f.* a great double Gally.

Gallego, *Sp.* an inhabitant of *Galatia*.

Gallia, *l. France.*

Galliard, *f.* Lusty, Merry, also a kind of Jovial dance.

Galliardise, *f.* liveliness, &c.

Gallie-foist, as *Foist*.

Gallicism, *l.* a *French* Idiome.

Galligaskins, *-scoines*, Breeches or slops first used by the *Gascoines* in France.

Galli-halpens. a coin forbidden by *Hen.* 5.

Gallimafry, a minced dish of several sorts of meats.

Gallion, as *Galeon*.

Galliote, as *Galiote*.

Galloglasses, *-glaghes*, Wild-*Irish* Troopers.

Galloches, as *Galege*.

Gallon, *Sp.* the same as

Gallion, or *Galeon*.

Galloway, a County both of *Scotland* and *Ireland*.

Galls, rough spurious fruit of Mast-bearing trees.

Gallulate, *l.* to begin to have a great voice.

Galli, *Cybeles* Priests inspired by drinking of

Gallus, a River in *Phrygia*, whose water made men mad; also a young man turn'd into a Cock for suffering *Sol* to discover the adultery of *Mars* and *Venus*.

Galor, *o.* for Gaoler.

Galpe, *o.* to belch.

Galnes, *Sc.* any kind of satisfaction for slaughter.

Gamahez, *A.* natural figures or images of things.

Gamaliel, *h.* Gods reward.

Gamba, *I*, a leg.

Gambado, a riding leathern leg-case, hanging in the stirrops place.

Gambalock, an Eastern riding gown, button'd under the chin.

Gamboles, *Gambades*, *f.* leg-gestures, or tumbling tricks.

Gambra, a River in *Guiny* abounding with River-horses, *Torpedos*, running-fish, &c.

Gammot, an incision-knife.

Gam' Ut, the scale of Musick, also the first or lowest note thereof.

Ganching, *f.* a *Turkish* execution of men, by letting them fall from on high upon sharp iron stakes.

Gang, *No.* to go, also a company.

Gargick, belonging to

Ganges, a great River (passing through the midst of *India*,) in some places 20 miles over, and never less than an hundred foot deep.

Gang-flower, Rogation-flower, flourishing about Rogation time.

Gangiatores, *Gaug-*, *Scotch* examiners of weights and measures.

Gangrene, *g.* a beginning of putrefaction or mortification in a member, an eating Ulcer.

Gang week, procession or Rogation week.

Gantlet, *Gauntlet*, *f.* a military glove.

Run the Gantlope, *D.* Run through the whole Regiment and receive a lash of every Soldier, from

Gant,Gaunt,Ghent, a Town in *Flanders*.

Ganymed, *Jupiters* cup-bearer, an Ingle.

Ganza, an *East-Indian* metal of gold and brass.

Garamantick, belonging to the

Garamantes, *Lybians*, subjects of

Garamas, the son of *Jupiter*.

Garbe, Gerbe, f. a sheaf of Corn.

Garbe, -bo, I. a graceful carriage, also a pleasant sharpness in Beer or Wine.

Garbe feders, o. the Feathers under a hawks beak.

Garbel, -boord, the plank next the Ships keel on the outside.

Garble [spices] purifie them from dross and dirt.

Garbles, the dust and dross that is severed.

Garbling, culling out the good from the bad of any thing.

Garboil, f. trouble, tumult,

Garbord-strake, the first seam next the keel.

Garcifer, a scotch Mill-boy.

Gardian, he that hath the

Gard, custody or care of one not able to guide himself and his own affairs.

Gard-robe, an herb, also as Ward-robe.

Gardian or Warden of the Cinque Ports, a Magistrate who in those 5 Havens hath the same jurisdiction as the Admiral elsewhere.

Gardian of the Peace, as *Conservator*.

Gardein de l'estein'ry, Warden of the stanneries.

Gardian of the spiritualties, he that hath the jurisdiction of a vacant Diocese.

Gard-manger, f. a place to keep victuals in.

Gare, a kind of very corse wool.

Garre, No. to cause or force.

Gargarism, a medicinal liquor to

Gargarize or *Gargle*, wash and cleanse the throat and mouth.

Gargarus, the top of *Ida* hill.

Garganiua, a feigned giant or monster with a

Garganta, Sp. a great throat.

Gargilon, the chief part of a Deers Hart.

Gariofilli, -phylli, Caryo- Cloves.

Garnade, o. for *Granada* a Spanish Town.

Garner, as *Granary*.

Garnet, a Tackle to hoise goods into a ship.

Garnement, Garnishment, f. a warning for one to appear, for the better furnishing the cause and Court.

Garnish, to warn, also a Prisoners fees at his admittance, both to keeper and fellow-Prisoners.

Garnishee, the party in who's hands money is attached.

Garnison, f. preparation, furniture, also as

Garrison, a place fortified and furnished with Soldiers, Ammunition, &c.

Garth, a wear for Fish, also a backside or close.

Garth-man, he that keeps or owns an open wear.

Garranty, as *Warranty*.

Garrulity, l. tatling, pratling, a being

Garrulous, full of talk, ever chatting.

Garstrange, a Town in *Lancashire*.

Garter, the chief of the 3 Kings at Arms, also half a bend.

A la Gascoignale, f. after the *Gascoigne* fashion.

Gase-hound, Agasæus, g. an admirable hunting kind of Dog.

Gastly, Ghostly, like a spirit.

Gasper, -par, one of the 3 Kings of *Collen*, see *Balthasar*.

Gastness, o, terrour.

Gaster, So. to scare or fright suddenly.

Gastromyth, g. one speaking inwardly or as out of his belly.

Gastrick, g. belonging to the Belly.

Gastroclite, -lyte, g. he that gets his living by handicraft.

Gastroepiploick vein, Gastrep-, a branch of the Port vein, spreading it self in the bottom of the ventricle.

Gastromancy, g. Divination by the Belly.

Gastrotomy, g. cutting up of the Belly.

Gat-tothed, o. Goat or Gapt-toothed.

Gather-bag, the bag that encloses a red fawn in the Hinds belly.

Gate, No. a way or path.

Ne Gate ne geyn, o. Neither got nor gained.

Gattlehead, a forgetful person, *Cambridge*.

Gaude, o. a toy or trifle, also to mock or scoff at, *f.*

Gauded, o. made gawdy.

Gaudy-daies, Colledge or Innes of Court-festivals.

Gaudiloquent, l. speaking with joy.

Gavelet, a Kentish *Cessavit*, whereby the Tenant in Gavel-kind (withdrawing his due rents, *&c.*) forfeits his Land to the Lord.

Gavel, Sa. tribute, also yearly rent.

Gavel-kind, Sa. (*Gif eal cyn*, given to all the kin) an equal division of the Fathers Lands among the Children, or of a brother (without Issue) among his Brethren.

Gavel-fester, Tol-fester, Oalegavel, Sa. Sextarius vectigalis cervisiæ, a certain measure of tribute or rent-ale.

Gaveloc, Sa. a warlike sling for stones or darts.

Gaul, La. a leaver.

Gawn, Che. a Gallon.

Gaunt, Gandavum, a chief City in *Flanders*, having 20 Islands and 48 Bridges.

Gaulonites a Jewish faction opposing the Roman Tribute.

Gawren, o. to stare.

Gaugeours, as *Gaugeators*, *Gagers*, who mark and allow vessels of Wine, oyl, Honey and Butter, before they be sold.

Gawge-

Gawge-peny, the *Gaugeors* fee.

Gayler, *o.* for *Jayler*.

Gaza, *l. g.* and *Persian*, a treasure.

Gazetta, *Gazz-*, *I.* a small *Venetian* coin (about our peny) the common price of a

Gazet, *-ette*, *f.* a News-book.

Gazul and *Suhit*, Two *Egyptian* weeds (growing in the Sands where the Nile arrives not) being burnt to ashes and sent to *Venice*, make the finest Chrystal glasses.

Geat, black amber, a sort of precious stone or solid bitumen.

Geaunt, *Geant*, *o.* a Jay.

Geazon, *E.* scarce, hard to come by.

Gedaliah, *h.* the greatness of the Lord.

Geffery, *Ge.* Joyfull peace.

Gehazi, the servant of *Elisha*.

Gehenna, *h.* the valley of *Hinnom*, where they sacrificed to *Moloch*, also hell.

Geld, *gelt*, *gild*, *guild*, *Sa.* Money, or Tribute.

Geld ne Geere, *o.* neither money nor ware or houshold-stuff.

Do Geld, *o.* raise money.

Geldable, a 3d part of *Suffolk*, the other being St. *Edmunds* and St. *Andreys* Liberties.

Geldria, *Gelderland*, a Low-Country-Province.

Gelicide, *l.* a frost.

Gelidity, frostiness, a being

Gelid, *l.* Icy, cold.

Gelo, a *Sicilian* School-boy who raised such a tumult in the School (for his book taken away by a Wolf) that the house fell and kill'd them all.

Gelones, *Scythians* who paint themselves to appear more terrible.

Gelover, *o.* a Gilloflower.

Geloum, a lake in *Sicily*, near two fountains whereof one makes women fruitfull, the other barren.

Gelous, *o.* jealous.

Gemefeder, *o.* the cheif tail-feather.

Gem, *Gemme*, a jewel, a bud or blossom.

Gement, *l.* groaning.

Gemersheim, a town in the *Palatinate*.

Gemination, *l.* a doubling.

Gemels, *l.* double, twins.

Gemini, *-nels*, *l.* twins, a sign in the *Zodiack*.

Geminous or *twin-arteries*, descending to the joynt of the knee.

Gemites, a precious stone with the resemblance of folded hands.

Gemmated, *l.* bedeckt with precious stones.

Gemmerie, a Cabinet or Jewel-house.

Gemmiferous, *l.* bearing or bringing jewels.

Gemote, the Hundred Court.

Gemmosity, an abounding with jewels, also blossoming.

Gemony, a place at *Rome*, where malefactors were cast headlong into *Tiber*.

Gemund, a town of North *Schwaben* in *Germany*.

Gemow-ring, a kind of double ring, linked with two or more links.

Gend, Gent, Neat.

Gendarme, *f.* a horseman compleatly armed.

Gens-d'armes, *f.* Soldiers.

Gender, *f.* difference of sex or kind.

Genealthud, *Sa.* approached.

Genealogie, *g.* a description of one family or pedigree.

Geneath, *Sa.* a Villain, hind, or Farmer.

Geneoglossum, *g.* the muscle that stretches out the tongue.

Generative, having the faculty or power of

Generation, *l.* an ingendring or begetting, also an age of men.

Generosa, the Title of Gentlewoman as Spinster of others unmarried.

Generosity, *l.* a being

Generous, *l.* noble in mind or bloud, bountifull.

Generical, belonging to *Genus*, or to

Genesis, *g.* birth, generation, Creation.

Genets, a kind of furr from a little beast of that name, also *Spanish* horses.

Genethliacal, belonging to

Genethliaques, Treaters or Treatises of

Genethlialogy, *l.* telling mens fortunes by casting their nativities.

Geneva, an Imperial town by the Lake *Leman* in *Savoy*, on the borders of *Switzerland*.

Gengenbach, a town of *Suevia* in *Germany*.

Genial, joyfull, festival, belonging to marriage or generation.

Geniculation, *l.* a joynting.

Genital, apt to ingender or beget.

Genitals, privities.

Geniting, a small apple soon ripe.

Genitive, of an ingendring faculty, natural.

Genitive Case, the second, formed of the Nominative, and forming all the rest.

Genitor, *l.* a Father, begetter, or beginner.

Genius, a good or evil spirit attending on particular men or places, also Nature, fancy or inclination.

Gennep, a town in *Cleveland*.

Genoa, *Genes*, a City of *Liguria* in *Italy*.

Genserick, a *Vandal*, who took *Carthage* and made stables of the Temples.

Gent, *o.* proper, handsome.

Gentian, the herb Filwort.

Gentil, a Maggot.

Gentile, *l.* Heathen, pagan.

Gentile, *f.* Gentleman-like.

Gentilesse, *f.* Gentility, Nobility.

Gentilism, *l.* Heathenism, the

the opinion or practice of Heathens.

Gentilitial, *-ious*, *l.* belonging to ancestors or kinred.

Gentiles (in Gram.) Nouns that signifie belonging to such or such a Country.

Gentleman, one that observes his

Gentility, race and propagation of bloud, by bearing arms.

Gentry Cove or *Mort*, *c.* Gentleman or woman.

Genua, *Genoua*, as *Genoa*.

Genuflexion, *l.* a kneeling.

Genuine, *l.* Natural, proper.

Genus, *l.* a kind, stock or lineage, that which contains many species or smaller kinds.

Geode, *g.* the Earth-stone.

Geodesian, one that useth

Geodesie, *Geodæsia*, *g.* the art of measuring land.

Geographical, belonging to

Geography, *g.* a descripti-of all the Regions and Countries of the Earth.

Geographer, a Describer of the Earth.

Geomanty, *g.* Divination by Circles drawn on the Earth, or opening of it.

Geometrize, to play the

Geometer, *-trician*, one skild in

Geometry, *g.* the art of measuring [the earth.]

Geometrical, belonging thereto.

Geoponical, *g.* belonging to tillage, or manuring ground.

George, *g.* Husband-man.

Georgians, Inhabitants of

Georgia, *Albania*, bordering on *Armenia*.

Georgian-hereticks, followers of *David George* (of *Delft*) who held that both Law and Gospel were unprofitable for Salvation, That He was Christ, &c. he died 1556.

Georgicks, *g.* Books treating of husbandry.

Geornlick. *Sa.* Willingly.

Gerah, the least silver coin among the Jews, worth 1 d. ob.

Gerard, *Gerald*, *Garret*, *Sa.* all towardliness.

Gerbevillier, a town in *Lorrain*.

Gerent, *l.* bearing, carrying.

Gere, *o.* Jeer, jest, frenzy.

In no Gere, *o.* at no rate.

Gerfalcon, between a Vulture and a hawk.

Gergon, *-ning*, *o.* Chattering, prating.

Gergo, *-one*, *I.* speech.

Germander, *Chamædris*, *Trissago*, *Quercula major*, the herb *English-treacle*.

Germanity, *l.* a being nearly related, brotherhood.

Germany, High-Dutchland.

St. *Germain*, the *Windsor* of *France*.

Germination, *l.* a budding.

Gernsey, *Sarnia*, an Isle about 20 miles from *Jarsey*.

Gersa, *serpentaria*, *Ceruse* made of *Aram-roots*.

Gersuma, *Sa.* *Gressume*, *Sc.* a fine or income.

Gertrude, *Gar-*, *Sa.* all truth.

Gervase, (*Sa.* all fast, or *g.* ancient, noble) a Martyr at *Millain* under *Nero*.

Gerunds, the Verbal Infinitive terminations *-di*, *-do*, and *-dum*.

Geryon, a *Spanish* King of three Countries, supposed to have 3 bodies and slain by *Hercules*.

Gery, *Geriful*, *o.* mutable, also cruel.

Gesamund, *Sa.* Assembled.

Geseke, a town in *Westphalia*.

Gessant, a Lions head born over a Chief.

Gesseram, *-ran*, *o.* a brestplate.

Gestation, *l.* a carrying.

Gesticulation, *l.* making signs, using much gesture, acting of a person, also a kind of dance.

Gestion, a doing or carriage of a business.

Gests, great actions or Exploits performed.

Getealed, *sa.* numbred.

Gethild, *sa.* patience.

Getulians, the first inhabitants of *Africa*.

Geules, a red or vermilion colour.

Gewgaws, *Gug-*, trifles for Children to play with.

Gheta, a mineral lately found in *Turky*.

Gheus, *f.* beggars, a nickname of Protestants in *Flanders*.

Ghittar, an instrument somewhat like a Cittern, only the strings are guts.

Ghittern, a small sort of Cittern.

Ghybe, *Gibe*, *No.* to scold.

Gibbon, *No.* a Nut-hook.

Gibbosity, *l.* a bunching out in the back, the Moons being 3 parts light.

Gibe, *o.* to mock.

Gibellines, a faction in *Italy* opposing the *Guelphs*.

Gibraltar, *-ther*, *Gebeltark*, *-rec*, *A.* (the Mountain of *Tarec* son to *Abdalla*) the streights of the *Mediterranean* sea, having on the North Mount *Calpe*, on the south *Abila*, with *Hercule's* pillars.

Gibsere, *o.* *f.* a pouch.

Gib-staffe, *No.* a quarter-staff.

Giddy, *No.* Mad [with anger.]

Gideon *Gedeon*, *h.* a breaker or destroyer.

Gierful, *o.* vulturine, rapacious.

Gifta, *sa.* Marriage.

Gifu, *Sa.* Grace.

Gigging, *o.* sounding.

Gigantick, *-tine*, Giant-like.

Gigantomachy, *g.* the War of the Giants [with heaven.]

Gig, *Giglet*, *-lot*, *o.* a wanton woman.

Gig-mills, for fulling and burling of cloth, prohibited.

Gigot, *f.* a leg of mutton with the whole hip-bone, also a hasche.

Gigger, *c.* a door.

Gigg, *c.* the nose.

Gigs, swellings on the inside of horses lips, also a prating, *o.*

Gilbert,

Gilbert, *Sa.* bright as gold, or as *Gislebert*.

Gilbertines, Fryers and Nuns of *Sempringham*, in *Lincolnshire*, instituted (1145) by one *Gilbert*, he lived to see 700 Fryers and 1100 Nuns of his Order.

Gild, *Sa.* Tribute, Amercement, also a Company or fraternity combined by the Princes leave.

Gildable, as *Geldable*.

Gildale, *sa.* a club, a compotation where every one paid his share.

Gildhal, *Guildhall*, the chief Hall of the City of *London*.

Gildhalda Teutonicorum, the Stilyard, hanse or fraternity of Easterling Merchants.

Gild-Merchant, a privilege whereby Merchants might hold pleas of Land within their own precincts.

Giles, *Ægidius*, *l.* *Aigidion*, *g.* a little kid, or for *Julius*, as

Gilian, for *Juliana*.

Gill, *Sf.* a small water, rivulet or beck.

Gillet. *Ægidia*, the Womans name.

Gillingham, a Forrest in *Dorsetshire*.

Gilp, *sa.* a brag or boast.

Gilt, *Jilt*, a cheat, a sly defeating ones intent.

Gilt, *c.* a picklock.

Gilt-head, a gold-coloured Fish.

Gimlet, a piercer.

Gimmal, as *Gemmow-ring*.

Gimmer-lamb, (*q. Gam-*) an Ew-lamb.

Ginglymos, *g.* (a hinge) the joining of bones, so that the same bone receives and is received by another.

Gipe, *o.* a coat full of plaits.

Gingreat, *o.* to chirp like a bird.

Ginne, *Gin*, (for engine) a snare.

Gippius, a Roman, Authour of the sentence *Non omnibus dormio*.

Gippon, *-ion*, *f.* a jump a kind of short coat or Cassock.

Gipsere, (*f. Gibbeciere*) a pouch.

Gipsous, belonging to

Gips, *l.* lime or plaister.

Giraffe, an Asian beast, under whose belly a man on horseback may ride.

Girasole, the Sun-stone of a golden splendour toward the sun, otherwise of an eye-like lustre.

Girde, *o*, to strike.

Girdle-sted, the waste or girdling place.

Girle, *Gerle*, a Roe-buck of two years.

Girthol, *sc.* a Sanctuary.

Girt, a ship is girt, when the Cable is so taught that (upon the turning of the tide) she cannot go over it.

Girvij, fen-dwellers, in *Lincolnshire*, *Cambridgeshire*, &c.

Gisarme, *Guisarme*, *Bisarme*, *Sisarme*, a kind of halberd or Battle-ax.

Gislebert, *Gilbert*, *sa.* bright pledge.

Giste, *f.* a couch or lodging place,

Gifts of the Kings progress, a writing with the names of all the places where he means to lye by the way.

Gisting, as *Agist*.

Gite, *o*, a gown.

Git, [eggs] beaten to oyl,

Glacial, belonging to

Glace, *f.* Ice.

Glaciate, *l.* freeze or turn to ice.

Gladdon, *Gladwin*, *Spatula fœtida*, Spurgewort.

Glade, an open passage in a Wood.

Gladly, (*q. leodly sa.*) commonly.

Gladiatour, *l.* a Sword-man or fencer.

Gladiature, *l.* Sword-play, or fighting.

Gladuse, *Br.* for *Claudia*.

Glaive, as *Glave*.

Glandage, *f.* mastage, or the season of feeding hogs with Mast.

Glandiferous, *l.* mast-bearing.

Glandulosity, a being

Glandulous, *l.* full of kernels.

Glanoventa, a Town upon *Venta*, *Wansbeck* or *Wantbeck*, a River in *Northumberland*.

Glare, *o.* glister.

Glastenbury, an Abby (in *Sommersetshire*) founded (they say) bp *Joseph* of *Arimathæa*, near which (in *Wiral Park*) is a hawthorn that blossoms upon Christmas day.

Glatton, *No.* Welsh flannel.

Glaucitate, *l.* to cry like a Whelp.

Glaucoma, *g.* a fiery redness in the Crystalline humour of the eye.

Glaucus, killed by *Ajax* in the *Trojan* War, also a Fisher, who (tasting of a certain herb) leapt into the Sea and became a Sea-God.

Glaver, *Glaffer*, *Chc.* Flatter.

Glave, *Glayve*, *o.* a kind of hooked Sword or Bill.

Glaymous, *o.* muddy and clammy.

Glaze, to varnish.

Glaziers, *c.* eyes, also Filchers by unripping or creeping into Windows.

Glebe-land, belonging to a Parsonage (beside the tithes.)

Gleba, *l.* a clod of Earth.

Glebosity, *l.* fulness of clods or turfs.

Glede, *o.* a burning Coal, also a Kite.

Gleden, *o.* gone.

Glee, *o.* joy, or mirth.

Glent, *o.* glanced.

Gleire, *o.* white.

Gleyre of an eye, *o.* the white of an Egge.

Glimfenders, *c.* andirons.

Glimflashy, *c.* angry.

Glimmering, a glancing or trembling light.

Glimmer, *c.* fire.

Glin, *Br.* a dale.

Glister, as *Clyster*.

Globosity, a being

Globous, *-bular*, in form of a

Globe, a thing every way round like a ball.

Glob'd, *Chc.* fond of, wedded to.

Glocester,

Gloecester, *Glevum*, the City of *Gloecestershire*.

Gloecester-hall, built by *John* Lord *Gifford* of *Brimesfield*, for Students in *Oxford*.

Glombe, *o.* to frown.

Glome, *l.* a bottom of thrid.

Glomeration, *l.* a rolling or gathering into a round lump.

Gloomy, *o.* dusky, or dark.

Withouten Glose, without deceit.

Glose, *o.* to flatter.

Glossomatical, belonging to a

Glossater, *Glossographer*, he that makes a

Gloss, *l.* a short Comment.

Glossary, a dictionary or Gloss-book.

Glossopetra, *g.* the tongue-stone (from its shape.)

Glotten, (for Cloathing) covering.

Glouted, *Che.* surprized, startled.

Glowden, *o.* shined.

Glowed, *o.* stared.

Glum, sadly, sowrely.

Glutinosity, a being

Glutinous, *l.* gluy, clammy.

Glutination, *l.* a gluing.

Gly, *Li.* to look asquint, angerly.

Glyconick [*verse*] of one Spondee and two Dactyles.

Glycerium, a Courtesan of *Thespia*.

Glyster, as *Clyster*.

Glymmer, *c.* fire.

Glym jack, *c.* a link-boy.

Glym-stick, *c.* a Candlestick.

Gmund, a Town in higher *Austria*.

Gnarity, *l.* knowledge, experience.

Gnarr, *Gnurr*, a hard knot in Wood, also a churle.

Gnast (for *Gnash*) *o.* to vex.

Gnathonical, playing or belonging to

Gnatho, *g.* a flattering parasite.

Gnathonize, to flatter or play the smell-feast.

Gnat-snapper, Fig-eater, a bird.

Gnavity, *l.* industry.

Gnew, *o.* gnawed.

Gnoff, *o.* a churle or fool.

Gnomological, belonging to the art of Dialling.

Gnomonick, *-mical*, belonging to a

Gnomon, *g.* a Carpenters square, or pin of a Dial.

Gnosticks, *Carpocratians*, *Borborite*, *Borboriani*, filthy hereticks (begun by *Carpocras* 125) pretending great knowledge, denying a future judgment, holding two Gods, one good the other bad, &c.

Gnurr, as *Gnarr*.

Goa, the best of all the *East-Indian* Cities, where the Viceroy of *Portugal* keeps his Residence.

Goaling, sending to the

Goal, or gail.

Goan, as *Gawn*.

Goam, *No.* to clasp or grasp.

Goam, *T.* to mind or look at

Goaring, cut sloping (spoken of a sayl.)

Goats-beard, *Tragopogon*, *g.* an herb with long staring leaves, good in Consumptions.

Goats-rue, with leaves like the Vetches but lighter, good against infection, &c.

Gobettyd, *a trought gob. o.* a trout drest in bits.

Goblins, as *Elves*.

Gobonated, divided into two colours, as if it were cut into small gobbets.

Go to God, *go without day*, as *Aller sans jour*, to be dismist the Court.

Go-carts, wherein Children learn to go.

Gods-good, *Nf. K. Sf.* barm, yeast.

God-bote, *sa.* an Ecclesiastical or Church-fine.

Godalming, a Town in *Surrey*.

Godard, *sa.* godly disposition.

Godfrey, (*Gods peace*) a Christian King of *Jerusalem*, who refused to be Crown'd with gold, where Christ was Crown'd with thorns.

Godiva, Wife to *Leofric*, Lord of *Coventry*, who (to gain them a release from his Impositions) rode naked through the City.

Godwin or Goodwins Sands, (on the Coast of *Kent*) heretofore the rebel Count *Godwins* Lands.

Godwin, *ge.* victorious in God.

Goes, a Town in *Zeland*.

Goëtie, *g.* witch-craft.

Gofish, *-yshe*, *o.* sottish.

Goffe, *E.* a mow of hay or Corn.

Gog, *b.* the roof of a house, covered.

A-Gog, eagerly bent upon a thing, also puft up with pride.

A-Gogue, *f.* with his belly full, frolick, lively.

Gog-magog, a (feigned) British giant (12 cubits high) whom *Corinæus*, (*Brutus's* Companion) threw down

Gogmagogs leap, a steep rock in *Cornwall*.

Golden number, (writ in golden or red letters, or of golden use in finding the changes of the Moon, &c.) it hath yearly one added till it come to 19, and then returns to one again because in 19 years the Sun and Moon were thought to finish their mutual Aspects.

Golden-Fleece, gold in grains (on the *Colchian* shore) gathered by the help of sheep-skins with the wool on.

Golden rod, a cleansing Astringent herb.

Gold-foile, leaf-gold.

Golgotha, *Syr.* a place of dead mens sculls.

Goliah, *-ath*, *h.* a Giant of the *Philistines* whom *David* slew with a sling-stone.

Goliardies, *o.* ravenously-mouthed.

Golpe, *Sp.* a flash.

A Golpe, *Sp.* at a blow.

Goman, *Gomman*, *o.* a husband or Master of a Family.

The Gome that gloseth so chartes, *o.* the man or Officer that closeth the Writs or instruments.

Gomer, *h.* (consuming) Father

Father of the *Cimbri*, also a measure somewhat above our gallon.

Gomorrhæan, one of *Gomorrha*, a *Sodomite*.

Gomphosis, *g.* the joyning of a bone together.

Gonagra, *g.* the gout in the knees.

Gonde, a town upon the *Schelde* in *Hanault*.

Gondola, *-lot*, a *Venetian* wherry-boat.

Gonfennon, *-fanon*, *f.* a little square flag at the end of a lance.

Gong (*q. Gang*) *o.* a privy.

Gonorrhæa g. the running of the reins.

Good abearing, Good behaviour, an exact carriage of a Subject towards the King and his liege people.

Good Country, a Jury of Country-men or good Neighbours.

Goodmes, *o.* Good time or mood.

Goodmanchester, a town in *Huntingtonshire*, heretofore entertaining Kings with the pomp of 180 ploughs.

Goole, (*f. goulet*) a breach in a bank or Sea-wall, also a Ditch, *Li.*

Gooly, for *Goodly*.

Goos-bill, a Chirurgeons instrument of the same use as a Crow-bill.

Goos-grass, Cleavers, cleansing and strengthening the Liver.

Goose intentos, a goose claimed of custom by the husbandmen in *Lancashire* upon the 16 Sunday after Pentecost when the old Church-prayer ended thus, *ac bonis operibus jugiter præstet esse Intentos.*

Goos-wing, a peculiar way of fitting up the mizzen-sail, so as to give the ship more way in a fair fresh gale.

Gorbelly, *-lied*, having a very great paunch or belly.

Gorce, *f.* a fish-wear.

Gorchum, a town in *Holland*.

Gor-crow, a Raven.

Gord, *f.* a whirl-pool or deep hole in the water.

Gordiæus, an *Armenian* hill where *Noahs* ark is said to have rested.

Gordius, a *Phrygian* raised from the plough to the throne he hung up his harness in the Temple (for a memorial) tied up in a very intricate manner called the

Gordian knot, Cut in two by *Alexander* (when he could not untie it) because the Monarchy of the world was promised to him that undid it.

Gore, *o.* an arbour, also a pleit or fold.

Gore, two arch lines from the sinister chief and bottom of th'Escutcheon, and meeting (in a sharp angle) in the fess-point.

Gorge, in a hawk is the Craw or crap in other fowls.

Gorget, *o.* a throat.

Gorgious, gallant, sumptuous.

Gorgons, *Medusa*, *Stenio* and *Euryale* (*Phorcys's* Daughters) who had snakes instead of hair, and killed men with their looks.

Gorlois, a Prince of *Cornwall*, whose wife *Uther-Pendragon* enchanted, and begat on her King *Arthur*.

Gorroghs, Leathern boats used by the *Romans* here.

Gormandize, to play the

Gormand, *Gour-*, *f.* a glutton.

Gormoncester, as *Goodmanchester*.

Gorst, *o.* bushes.

Gortinians, a kind of New-*England* Quakers, from *Sam. Gorton* banished thence about 1646.

Gospel, for *God-spel*, *sa.* good word or tidings.

Goss-hawk, (*q. Gross-hawk*, or rather *Goos-hawk*) a large kind of hawk.

Gossip (*q. God-sib*, *sa.* of kin before God) the God-father or God-mother.

Gossemeer, *Cossomer*, *-mor*, *Gossa-*, *Gossymear*, *Fila Virginis*, Our Ladies hair, white Cobwebby exhalations flying about in sunny weather.

Gote, a ditch, sluce or gutter.

Gothes, *Gothi*, people of

Gothia, *Gothe-land*, a Country bordering upon *Denmark* and *Norway*,

Gothlen, *o.* to grunt.

Gotish, as *Gofyshe*.

Gottorp, a town of South Juitland in *Denmark*.

Goude, a town in *Holland*.

Goule, *o.* Usury.

Gouffaucon, *o.* for *Gonfennon*.

Governail, *Gouv-*, *f.* the rudder.

Gourd, a plant somewhat like a Cucumber, also a bottle, *o.*

Goureth, *o.* stareth.

Goutes, *Som.* Common sinks or sewers.

Goutwort, *Herb-Gerrard*, *Ashweed*, Jump-about.

Gouvernante, *Gov-*, *f.* a governess or she-governour.

Goyster, *Sf.* to be frolick, ramp, or laugh aloud.

Gracchus Sempronius, a *Roman* General, who subdued the *Celtiberians*.

Graces, *Aglaia*, *Euphrosyne* and *Thalia* (daughters of *Jupiter* and *Venus*) goddesses of *Elegance*, friendship, and handsome conversation.

Grach, *o.* to behave [with a grace.]

Gracility, *l.* slenderness.

Gradatory, the ascent from the Cloyster to the Quire of the Church, also any going up by steps.

Gradation, *l. Climax*, *g.* an ascending by degrees.

Graduality, the being

Gradual, *l.* by degrees, also part of the Mass, sung between the Epistle and Gospel, also as

Graile, a book of certain Offices in the *Roman* Church.

Gradual Psalms (of degrees or steps) the 15 Psalms from 118 to 133, sung on the 15 steps

steps in *Solomons* Temple.

Graduate, *l.* haviug taken his degree.

Gradde, (*q. Grav'd*) craved.

Gradivus, *Mars*.

Græcia, *Greece*, a large part of *Europe*, the nurse of learning, prowess, and of all Arts.

Grææ, three Sisters of the *Gorgons*, they had all but one eye and one Tooth, which they used by turns.

Graffer, *Graffier*, *f.* a Notary or Scrivener.

Graffically, *g.* exactly curiously.

Graie, *Grey*, a brock or badger.

Graie-Fryer, as *Cordelier*.

Grains of Paradise, *Cardamome*.

Graith, *o.* made ready.

Grame, *o.* anger, sorrow, also mis-hap and punishment.

Gramercy, *f.* (*Grand-merci*) great thanks.

Gramineal, *-eous*, *l.* grassy, or made of grass, green.

Graminous, *l.* full of or overgrown with grass.

Grammatical, belonging to

Grammar, *g.* the Art of Speaking, Reading and Writing.

Grammatist, *-ticaster*, a young

Grammarian, one skilled in Grammer.

Grampus, a fish somewhat less than a Whale.

Grampound, a Town in *Cornwall*.

Granadil, *sp.* a small

Granado, *sp.* a Pome-granate, also a hollow bullet filled with wild-fire and shot from a morter-piece, there are also hand-granadoes.

Granary, *l.* a place to lay Corn in.

Granate, *l.* a precious stone resembling a Pomegranate-stone.

Grand, *f.* great, also as

Grandee, a great or leading man.

Grand-daies, as *Gaudy-days*.

Grandævity, *l.* greatness of age, Antiquity, Eldership.

Grand Cape, see *Cape*.

Grand-distress, of all the Lands or goods a man hath within the County or Bailywick.

Grandezza, *I.* *-deza*, *sp.* *-deur*, *f.* greatness [of state or Spirit.]

Grandiloquence, *-quy*, *l.* greatness of speech or style, a being

Grandiloquent, *-quous*, *l.* using high words.

Grandimontensers, a Religious Order erected *An.* 1076. having their Abbey on a Mountain in *Aquitane*.

Grandinous, *l.* belonging to, or full of hail.

Grand Seignior, the Great Turk.

Grandity, *l.* greatness.

Grand Sergeanty, a holding Lands of the King by service to be done him in person, as to bear his banner, spear, &c.

Grange, *f.* (a barn) a great farm with barns, &c.

Granicus, a River in *Bithynia*, where *Alexander* slew and took above 600 thousand *Persians*.

Granito, *I.* a kind of speckled Italian marble.

Grannam, *c.* Corn.

Granson, a French Poet whom *Chaucer* translates.

Graniferous, *l.* bearing grains or kernels.

Granivorous, *l.* corn-devouring.

Grantham, a Town in *Lincolnshire*.

Grans, a Town in the Earldom of *Mont-belgard*.

Granulation, *l.* a Chymical reducing of metals and minerals into

Granules, *-ules*, *l.* small grains.

Graphical, *g.* curiously described or wrought.

Graplings, *Grapnels*, a kind of Anchors with four flooks and no stock, used also in

Grapling, or fastening of Ships together in a Fight.

Grassation, *l.* a robbing, spoiling and making havock.

Grateolent, *l.* smelling gratefully or pleasantly.

Gratiæ expectativæ, Popish Bulls or Mandates for livings not yet void.

Gratch, *o.* Apparel.

Gratianople, a City of *Narbon* in *France*.

Gratianus, *Eunarius*, a Roman Emperour perfidiously slain by his Captain *Andragathius* at Lions in *France*.

Gratification, *l.* *-fying*, rewarding; making amends.

Gratings, small ledges a cross over one another (like a *Port-cullis*) in close Fights &c.

Gratis, *l.* (for thanks) freely, for nothing, undeservedly.

Gratuity, *l.* a free reward or gift.

Gration, *Sf.* an ersh or eddish;

Gratton, *k.* stubble.

Grats, a Town in *Stiria*.

Gratulatory, belonging to or full of

Gratulation, *l.* thanking, or rejoycing on anothers behalf.

Grave, *Greve*, *D.* Earl or Governour.

Grave, *o.* a ditch, also a wood.

Grave the ship, burn off the old stuff and lay on new, with train-oyl, Rosin and Brimstone boild together.

Graveling, a Town in *Flanders*.

Gravesend, a Town in *Kent*.

Graven, *o.* buried.

Gravet, *o.* a grove.

Graveolence, *l.* a rank or strong sent, a being

Graveolent, smelling rank, stinking.

Graver, a graving-steel, also an instrument to take off scales from the Teeth.

Gravidity, *l.* a being

Gravid, *l.* great with child or any young.

Graviloquence, *l.* a grave speech or speaking gravely.

Gravity, heaviness or weight, also graveness or soberness in behaviour.

Grauntee,

Grauntee, to whom is given a

Graunt, *Grant*, a gift (in writing) of such things as cannot fitly be passed by word only.

Graunt mercy, *o.* for Gramercy

Grayeth, *o.* (*q.* arrayeth) maketh trim.

Graythed, *o.* devised.

Greach-breach, as *Grith-breach*.

Grease, the fat of a Bore or hare.

Great Men, temporal Lords in Parliament, and sometimes the Commons.

Greaves, *f.* armour for the Legs.

Grecians, men of *Greece*, also (as opposed to Hebrews) Heathens.

Grecism, *l.* a greek idiom.

Gree, *Gré*, *f.* willingness, agreement, satisfaction, also (in Heraldry) a step or degree

Greek Church, differs in some things from the Roman, *viz.* in denying the Holy Ghosts proceeding from the Father and the Son, admitting only painted images, admitting none but marryed men into orders, &c.

Grede, *o.* to cry.

Green-Cloth, a Court of Justice, sitting in the Counting-house of the Kings Court.

Green-hew, *Vert*, every green thing growing within a Forest.

Green-silver, a yearly halfpeny paid the Lord of *Writtel* Mannour in *Essex* for every fore-door opening towards *Greenbury*.

Green-wax, Estreats delivered to the Sheriffs, under the Exchequer Seal (in *Green-wax*) to be levied in their several Counties.

Green-wich, a Town in *Kent*, where *Humphrey* Duke of *Glocester* built the Pallace called *Placence*.

Greece, *Grece*, *o.* gray.

Greined, *o.* made.

Greith, *o.* to remove, or bring.

Greathly, *No.* handsomely, towardly.

In Greath, well.

Greet & yowl, *Cu.* weep and cry.

Greese, *l.* a step or stair.

Gregal, *l.* belonging to a flock or company.

Gregory, *g.* watchfull.

Gregorian, [cap of hair] first made among us by

Gregory, a Barber in the Strand.

Gregorian, *Lilian*, *Forreign* or *New Account*, a correction of the Calender (through the advice of *Antonius Lilius*, and other Mathematicians) 1584 by

Pope Gregory, the XIII. who made the year to consist of 365 dayes, 5 hours, 49 minutes and 12 seconds. And that the Vernal Equinox (which was then *March* 11) might be reduced to *March* 21 (as it was at the time of the first *Nicene* Council) he Commanded the 4th. to be the 14th. of *October*.

Grenhead, *o.* [*q.* *Greenhead*] rashness.

Gresham Colledge, the house of Sir *Thomas Gresham*, who endowed it with Revenues for the maintenance of Professours of Divinity, Law, Physick, Astronomy, Geometry and Musick.

Gremial, *-ious l.* belonging to the lap or bosom.

Grest-feders, *o.* Crest-feathers.

Grete, *o.* as *Grede*, to cry.

Greves- *o.* [*q.* *Groves*] Trees, Boughs, Grass.

Greve, as *Grave*, a Lord.

Griffe graffe, *f.* by hook or by crook, any way.

Griffenberg, a Town in lower *Pomerania*.

Grigg, a young Eel.

Grills, a kind of small fish.

Grill, *o.* cold, [*q.* *gresle*, *f.* hail.]

Grilliade, *-lade*, *f.* a dish of broyled meat.

Grimace, *f.* a sour crabbed look, a wry ill-favoured face made.

Grimsbie, a Town in *Lincolnshire*.

Grim'ald, *-mould*, *ge.* power over anger.

Grinstead, a Town in *Sussex*

Grint, *o.* for grinded, ground

Grinders, *c.* Teeth.

Grise, as *Greese*.

Gripe, the sharpness of the stem under water.

The ship Gripes, when she is apt to run her nose too much to the wind.

Griph, *o.* a riddle.

Grip, *Gripe*, a little trench.

Grishild, *ge.* Grey-Lady.

Grisphe, *o.* gripe or grasp.

Grisly, *o.* fearfully, horribly,

Grith, *o* agreement.

Grit, a Gramplе-fish.

Grith breach, *Grich-*, *sa.* breach of the peace.

Grith-stole, as *Frodmortel*.

Grobianism, *f.* slovenliness, the practice of a

Grobian, *f.* a sloven.

Groffe, *Gruff*, *Growff*, *o.* Groveling.

Groine, *o.* a froward grunting look.

Groening, *-ghen*, the chief Town of

Groening-land, a Province of the *Neatherlands*.

Grommets, little rings on the upper side of the yard, to which the Caskets are fastned

Gromatick [*Art*,] of casting out the ground for quarters, fortifying a Camp, &c.

Gromel, *-mil*, the herb Pearl-plant.

Gron, *Sa.* a fenny place.

Groundsell, a threshold.

Gropers, *c.* blind men.

Groop, *o.* a pissing place.

Grosse boys, *f.* great wood, Timber.

Grosvenour, *Gravenour*, [great hunter] a noble Family of *Cheshire*.

Grossome, for *Gersuma*.

Gros, *l.* a Cave.

Grotesca, *I. -sques*, *f.* antick work, odde confused painting without any sense or meaning, also any rude misshapen thing.

Groveling, with ones face or belly on the ground.

Ground the ship, bring her on the ground, to be trimmed.

Ground-Pine, an herb creeping

ing on the ground, and resembling the pine tree.

Grout, *No.* wort of the last running, New ale, also Milker.

Groundswel, *Senecio*, an herb that quickly decayes.

Ground-timbers, which are first laid over the keel and make the ships floor.

Grouppade, *f.* a lofty kind of horse-mannage.

I Grow, *No.* I am troubled.

Growed, *o.* for *Grubbed*.

Growm, an engine to stretch woollen cloth.

Growth half-peny, paid (in some places) for tythe of every fat beast, Ox and other unfruitfull cattel.

Growz, *No.* to be chill [at the beginning of an Ague fit.]

Growne, *f.* the snowt [of a sow]

A buckGroyneth, makes that noise.

Grumosity, *l.* a curdling of liquor into a thick mass or clod, a being

Grumous, *l.* Cloddy, full of Clots or hillocks.

Gruarij, the principal Officers of the Forest.

Grunting-peck, *c.* pork.

Grunting cheat, *c.* a pig.

Gryffin, *-fon*, *g.* a fierce creature whose fore part is like an Eagle, purple coloured, and whitish wings, the hinder part like a Lion, black, by Modern Writers esteemed fabulous.

Griffith, *Grif-*, *Br.* strong-faithed.

Grymsey, a town in *Lincolnshire*.

Grys, *o.* a Partridge.

Guacatane, an *Indian* Plewort.

Guadage, as *Guidage*.

Guadelquivir, a River of *Andaluzia* in *Spain*

Guadiana, the river *Ana*, in *Portugal*, running 14 miles under ground, so that the bridge may feed 10 thousand Cattel.

Guaiacum, a *West-India* drying wood, good against the *French* disease.

Guaiavas, a kind of *Indian* apples.

Guastald, he that hath the Custody of the Kings Mansion-houses.

Guastaliens, a Religious order of men and women begun 1537 by a *Mantuan* Lady, Countess of *Guastala*.

Gubernation, *l.* a governing.

Gubernator, *l.* a Governour [of a ship.]

Gudgeons, Rudder-irons.

Guelderland, *Gel-*, one of the *Neatherlands*.

Guelphs, and *Gibellines*, two great factions in *Italy*.

Guendliana, a valiant Lady, (wife to *Gryffin* Prince of *Wales*,) slain in a battel with *Maurice* of *London*.

Guerring, *o.* (*q.* jarring) brawling.

Guerdon, *f.* a reward.

Guest-takers, *Gist-*, as *Agistors*.

Gugaws, *h.* *Gnugabb*, a jews-harp or toy for Children.

Guidage, mony for safe-conduct through a strange place

Guidon, *f.* a horse-banner, also the Cornet or bearer of it.

Guill, *Che.* to dazle [the eyes.]

Guild-hall, as *Gild hall*.

Guilford, *Geglford*, *sa.* a town in *Surrey*, the Mansion place of the *English-Saxon* Kings.

Guinethia, *Guineth*, *Venedotia*, South-*Wales*.

Guiny, *Nigritarum Regio*, a Kingdom of *Africa*.

Guise, Manner or fashion.

Gull, *Maneleta*, a certain Corn-weed.

Gules, as *Geules*.

Gule, *Goule*, or *Yule* of *August*, St. *Peter ad vincula*, Lammas day, when they say *Quirinus's* Daughter (by kissing St. *Peters* chain) was cured of a Disease in her

Geule, *f.* a Throat.

Gulick, the Chief town of

Gulick-land, a province of *Germany*.

Gulf, *Gulph*, a streight see between two lands, or the meeting of two seas.

Gulling, when the pin of a block eats or wears into the Sheever, or the yard into the Mast.

Gulosity, *l.* Gluttony.

Gulwit, for *Gyltwit*.

Gum Animi, *Indian* amber.

Gum Arabick, from the *Egyptian* thorn-tree *Acacia*.

Gummilda, she killed her self, because her Husband *Asmond* King of *Denmark* was slain in battel.

Gun, *No.* a great flagon of ale.

Gunora, a *Norman* Lady, who held the Hamlet of *Lanton* by the service of a barbed Arrow to the King when he hunted in *Cornedon* Chase.

Gunwale, the piece of Timber that reaches on either side from the half deck to the forecastle; also the lower part of any Ordnance-port.

Gurgitate, *l.* to devour or swallow up.

Gurgitive, *l.* belonging to a gulph or stream.

Gurnard, a fishes name.

Gusset, an abatement, formed of a travers line from the dexter Chief perpendicularly to the extream Bases, or Contrary-wise.

Gust, *Gest*, a Guest or stranger that lodges with us the 2d night.

Gust, *l.* a taste or relish, also a sudden blast of wind.

Gustation *l.* a tasting, also a little knowledge or experience.

Gusto, *I.* a right relish, Savour or Taste of any thing.

Gustatory,

Guſtatory, *l.* a banqueting houſe.

Gut-tide, Shrovetide.

Gutta roſacea, a præter-natural redneſs in the Face.

Gutta ſerena, a clear ſpeck [hindring the eye-ſight.]

Guttulous, belonging to or full of drops.

Guttural, *l.* belonging to

Guttur, *l.* the Throat.

Guttural letters, pronounced in the Throat.

Gutturous, *Gutter-*, having a wide throat.

Guzes, (in Her.) the ball of the Eye.

Guy, *Guido*, *Guide*, *f.* a leader or director.

Guydage, as *Guidage*.

Guye, a rope that guides gently any thing hoiſed aboard, alſo the rope that hales forward the pendant of the winding tackle.

Gwalſtow, *ſa. patibuli locus*, the Gallows or Execution-place.

Gwabr-merched, *Br.* a fine to the Lords of ſome Mannours upon the marriage of their Tenants-daughters, alſo as *Lair-wite*.

Gy, *o.* a guide.

Gybe, *c.* any writing or paſſe.

Gyges, a *Lydian* Shepherd who kil'd the King *Candaules* (his Maſter) and enjoy'd his Crown and Wife (whom he had ſhown him naked) by the help of

Gyge's ring, taken from a dead Giants finger found in the belly of a braſen horſe in the earth, who's collet (turned inward) made him inviſible.

Gyltwite, a compenſation or amends for treſpaſs or fraud.

Gymnaſtick, *g.* belonging to a

Gymnaſe, *g.* a place for exerciſe (of body and mind) a School.

Gymnaſticks, books treating of Exerciſe.

Gymnaſiarch, the head Maſter of the place where the Champions did exerciſe, the chief Maſter of a School.

Gymnoſophiſts, *g.* Indian Philoſophers of a naked and ſolitary living.

Gyndes, a river cut by *Cyrus* (in his ſiege of *Babylon*) into 46 channels.

Gynecocracy, *Gynocraty*, *g.* a Feminine Government.

Gypſation, *l.* a plaiſtering with Mortar.

Gyration, *l.* the fetching of a large compaſs, a wheeling about, dizzineſs.

Gyre, *g.* a circuit, compaſs or cariere, the bound or end of a courſe or race, alſo a traunce, dump or fit, *o.*

Gyron, *Guyron*, *f.* a geron, half a ſquare or quarter in an Eſcutcheon cut off by an oblique or diagonal line.

Gyſarme, as *Giſarme*.

H.

H*Aam*, *ſa.* an *Albe*, a Prieſts linnen veſtment.

Habakkuk, *h.* a wreſtler.

Haberdaſher, (*q. Habt ihr dies? ge.* have you that? or *Avoir d'acheter*, *f.* having to buy? or *Kooper-Daeſer*, *D.*) a Merchant of toyes or ſmall wares.

Hab-, *of Hats*, a Hat-ſeller.

Habere facias ſeiſinam, a Writ commanding the Sheriff to give a man ſeiſin of Lands recovered in the Kings Court.

Habere facias viſum, a writ for the veiwing of Lands or Tenements.

Habeas Corpus, a writ from the King-Bench, for a Priſoner to remove himſelf thither, and anſwer the cauſe there.

Habeas Corpora, a writ for the bringing in a Jury, or ſo many of them as refuſe to come upon the *venire facias*.

Habendum, the latter principal part of a conveyance, limiting and qualifying the eſtate paſſing in the premiſſes.

Haberdupois, as *Averdupois*.

Habergion, *Haub-*, *f.* a diminutive; Haubert, a little coat of mail, or ſleeves and gorget only.

Habiliment, *f.* cloathing, alſo Armour.

Habilitation, a making one able or capable.

Hability, *l.* an aptneſs or capacity.

Habit, *l.* cloathing, alſo cuſtom of doing any thing.

Habitable, *l.* that may be inhabited or dwelt in.

Habitacle, *-ation*, *l*, a dwelling.

Habitual, *l.* grown to a

Habit or cuſtome.

Habituate, *l.* to accuſtome.

Habitude, *l.* the habit, ſtate or diſpoſition of body or mind.

Hables, *f.* a Haven or Port.

Hab-nab, (*q. hap n'hap*,) at a venture, whether it happen (ſucceed) or no.

Hack, *Li.* a hay-loft.

Hack, *Tu.* Truth, and

Hacktawlaw, *Tu.* high truth, a Divine Attribute.

Hace, *o.* for have, alſo hoarſe.

Hach, *Hache*, *Hachis*, *f.* a diſh of ſliced ſteeved meat.

Hadad, *h.* rejoycing.

Hades, *g.* hell, or the ſtate of the Dead.

Hadarezer, *Aderezer*, *h.* beautiful help.

Hadleigh, a Town in *Suffolk*.

Hadbote, *ſa.* ſatisfaction for the violation of holy Orders, or for violence offered to perſons in holy Orders.

Hadock, *Hadd-*, a ſmall kind of Cod-fiſh.

Hadrian, a great Roman Emperour.

Hadersleve, a Town of South *Jutland*.

Hadrianople, *g.* a City of *Macedonia* in *Greece*.

Hæmatopodes, *g.* Birds with

feet red as blood.

Hæmon, a *Theban* youth who killed himself over the tomb of *Antigone*, put to death by *Creon*.

Hæmoptois, -*sis*, *g*. spitting of bloud from the vital parts.

Hæmorrhagy, *g*. a violent bursting out of blood.

Hæmorrhoides, *g*. the Piles a distention of the Fundament veins by too much melancholy blood.

Hæmus, a Mountain dividing *Thrace* and *Thessaly*.

Hærede deliberando alij, a writ for the Sheriff to command the delivery of the body of anothers ward to him who's ward he was, by reason of his Land.

Hærede abducto. a writ for the Lord who having by right the Wardship of his Tenant under age, hath him conveyed away.

Heresy, *g*. (a sect) a doctrine contrary to the fundamentals of Religion.

Hæretico comburendo, a writ that lay against one who (being convict of Heresie and abjuring it) fell into it again.

Hæsitation, *l*. a doubting, a sticking at any thing.

Hafne, *sa*. a Haven or Sea-Port.

Haga, *sa*. a house.

Hagbes, *No*. haws.

Hagar, *h*. a stranger, or chewing the cud.

Hagester, *K*. a Mag-pie.

Hagard, *f*. wild, untamed.

Hagard Faulcon, which for some time preyed for her self.

Haggai, *h*. pleasant.

Haggase, a kind of pudding made of hogs flesh.

It Haggles, *No*. it hailes.

Haggs, vapours (like flame) about the hair or horses manes, not so much flaming as reflecting light.

Hagiographer, *g*. a writer of holy things.

Haguenaw, a Town in lower *Elsass* or *Alsatia*.

Hague, the best village in *Europe*, where the States of *Holland* keep their Court.

Haie, *f*. (hedge) a net to catch Conies.

Haile, *sa*. health, whole.

Hain, a River in

Hainault, one of the *Netherlands*.

Hailes, *o*. happiness.

Haine, *f*. hatred.

Haire, when a Masculine diurnal Planet appears in the day time.

Haimburgh, a Town (in higher *Austria*) where there grows some store of Ginger.

Haimhaldatia Catallorum, (in *Scotland*) a seeking restitution for goods wrongfully taken away.

Hakals, large pikes taken in *Ramsey* Moor.

Haketon, *o*. a sleeveless jacket

Halcyonian, peaceable, belonging to

Halcyon, *Alcyon*, a Kingfisher, which (in calm weather) builds and breeds on the sea-shore.

Hale, *Ss*. a trammel, *Ess*. an iron to hang pots on over the fire.

Halcbrede, a lout or lubberly Man or Woman.

Haledon, *Heaven-field* in *Northumberland*, where King *Oswald* (having erected a cross unto Christ) vanquished the Brittish King *Cedwal*, and became a devout Christian.

Halesworth, a Town in *Suffolk*.

Half-lord, *c*. six-pence.

Half-mark, a Noble, 6 and 8 pence.

Half-seal, the sealing of Commissions to Delegates, appointed upon any appeal in Ecclesiastical or marine causes.

Halicarnassus, the chief City of *Caria*, where the famous tomb of *Mausolus* was built by his Queen *Artemisia*.

Halidome, *sa*. holy judgment.

Halieuticks, *g*. treatises of the art of fishing.

Halifax, (*sa*. holy hair) *Horton*, a Town in *York shire*, from a Maids head cut off by a Priest and hung upon a Yew-tree there.

Haliography, *g*. a description of the Sea.

Halitnous, *l*. thin, vaporous, passing easily through the pores.

Halinitre, *g*. Salt-petre.

Halitz, a Town of *Russia nigra* in *Poland*.

Hall the ship, call to her, to know whence she is, and whither bound.

Haliwerk-folk, *sa*. Priests and Religious persons.

Hallage, toll to the Lord of a fair or market for commodities vended in that Common-Hall, also for cloaths brought for sale to *Blackwell-hall*, *London*.

Hallam-shire, was part of *York shire*.

Hallelujah, *h*. praise the Lord.

Halle, a Town on the *Sein* in *Hainault*.

Hallucination, *l*. an erring or mistaking.

Hallandia, part of *Scandia*.

Halm, the stalk (of Corn) from the ear to the root.

Halsier, he that draws the

Halser, the rope next to a Cable.

Hal fang, *Healfang*, *sa*. a Pillory.

Halo, *g*. a Circle about the Moon or other Star.

Halse, *o*. to embrace.

Hals, *sa*. a neck.

Halstead, a Town in *Essex*, and a village in *Kent*.

Halonesus, an *Ægean* Isle defended by women when all the men were slain.

Halteth, *o*. holdeth.

Halt, a stop or stay [in marching.]

Halyardes, the ropes that hoise up the yards.

Hallyattes, a King of *Lydia* Father to *Crœsus*.

Halymote, as *Heal-gemote*.

Ham, *h*. crafty or heat.

Ham, *sa*. a house or village.

Hamadryades, *g*. wood-Nymphs.

Haman, *h*. making an up roar.

Hambles, (for *Hables*) havens.

Hamburgher, one of

Hamburgh, the chief City of *Lower-Saxony*.

Hames, two crooked pieces of Wood encompassing a horse-collar.

Hamkin, a kind of pudding made upon the bones of a shoulder of Mutton.

Hameling, *Hambling of Dogs*, the same as expeditating.

Hameled, *o*. abated.

Hamlet, *hamel*, *hampsel*, a little village sometimes the seat of a free-holder.

Hammocks, hanging ship-beds.

Hammon, *g*. (sandy) a name of *Jupiter*.

Hammone, *Ham*, a Town in the Erldom of *Mark*.

Hamor, *h*. an asse, or dirt.

Hampton, *Southampton* in *Hantshire*, and above 20 villages elsewhere.

Hampton-Court, a Royal Palace on the *Thames* in *Middlesex* built by Cardinal *Wolsey*, finisht by *King Henry* the 8*th*.

Hamsoken, *sa*. the liberty or freedom of ones own house.

Han, *o*. to have.

Hanjar, a rich dagger worn by the *Bashaws* Wives.

Hand-cloth, *sa*. a handkerchef.

Handfull, four inches.

Han-speek, a wooden leaver.

Handy-warp, a kind of cloth made at *Cokfal*, *Bocking* and *Braintree* in *Essex*.

Hanceld, *o*. cut off.

Hanaper, *Hanper*, seems to be the same as originally) the Latin *Fiscus*. See Clerk of. &c.

Hanlerct, part of *England*

Diocess in *Denmark*.

Hankwit, *Hangwit*, *sa*. [-being acquited of] a fine for the the unjust hanging or escaping of a Prisoner.,

Hankyn, *Hall*, *Henry*, or little Hans.

Hannah, *h*. gracious, merciful.

Hannaw, part of *Wetraw* in *Germany*.

Hannibal, (Gracious Lord) a *Carthaginian* General, who was beaten by the Roman, *Scipio*; and poison'd himself.

Hand boven bread, *La*. with little leaven, stiff.

Hanno, a *Carthaginian* rebel who had his eyes put out.

Hannonia, *Haynault*, one of the Low Country-Provinces.

Hans, *D*. a Companion or fellow.

Hansz, *ge*. John.

Hans-in-kelder, *D*. Jack or the fellow in the cellar, also the child in the mothers Womb.

Hanse, (a Gothish word used also in the Ordonnances of *Paris* for) a society of Merchants combined for the good usage and safe passage of Merchandize from Kingdom to Kingdom.

Hanse-towns, (in *Germany*) about 72 joyn'd in a league offensive and defensive against all enemies whatsoever, *Heyl. Cosm.* the principal seats of the Dutch Merchants.

Hansiatick, free of, or belonging to the Hanse-towns or Merchants.

Hansholm, an Island in *Denmark*.

Hansel, (*q*. hand-sale) the first money taken in a morning.

Hanylowres, *o*. subtilties cunning tricks.

Hanselynes, *o*. short breeches.

Hanten, *o*. to use or accustom.

Hanty [-orse,] *No*. wanton.

Hap, *f*. to catch or snatch.

Hapharlet, *Happarlet*, a course coverlet for a bed.

Happa, *hap ye*, *No*. think you,

Happe, *No*. to cover or heap cloaths on.

Haque, a hand-gun about three quarters of a yard long.

Haquebut, *f*. the same as *Harquebuse*.

Haracana, *Herocane*, *Hurricane*, a violent whirlwind or tempest overturning all.

Harald, *Herauld*, an Officer proclaiming War or Peace, examining coats of arms, &c.

Haran, *h*. anger.

Harangue, *f*. an Oration or speech.

Haraphah, *h*. a medicine.

Harasse, *f*. to tire or wear out, to trouble, or disquiet and torment.

Haratium, the breed or stock of Swine.

Harbinger, (*q*. *Herberger*, *D*.) he that goes before and provides lodging.

Harbours, [a Hart] goes to rest.

Herderwick, an University in *Gelderland*.

Hardiment, *o*. boldness.

Hardly, *o*. verily, seriously.

Hare lip, cloven like a Hares.

Hare-pipe, a snare made of cane (or Elder) to take Hares.

Hariant, *Hauriant*, [a fish] represented standing upright (in Heraldry.)

Haried, *o*. pulled.

Hariolation, *l*. a sooth-saying.

Heriot, as *Heriot*.

Harlotrise, *o*. for Harlotry.

Harlem, a City in *Holland* where (they say) Printing was first invented, *Anno* 1440.

Harling, a Town in *Norfolk*.

Harlingen, a Town in *West-Friezland*.

Harlet, (*q*. *Hotelet*,) a little whore.

Arlotta, *l*. a proud whore.

Arlotta,

Arletta, *Arlotha*, Duke *Roberts* Concubine Mother to Duke *William* the Conquerour.

Harman, *D.* the general of an army.

Harmans, *c.* the stocks.

Harman-beck, *c.* the Constable.

Harmodius, *Aristogeiton's* fellow conspiratour against the *Athenian* Tyrant *Hipparchus*.

Harmonia, the wife of *Cadmus*, Daughter of *Mars* and *Venus*.

Harmonides. a *Trojan* beloved of *Minerva* and inspired with all kind of Manufacture.

Harmonious, -*ick*, -*ical*, full of

Harmony, *g.* Musical consent or agreement.

Harns, *Cu.* brains.

Harnet, *o.* for *Hornet*.

Haro, *Harol*, as *Hue* and *Crie*.

Harold, as *Harald*.

Harowed hell, *o.* Conquered, spoiled.

Harpalice, a great huntress, who (by force of arms) rescued her father *Lycurgus* from the *Getans*.

Harpe, the Fauchion wherewith *Mercury* slew *Argus*, & *Perseus Medea*.

Harping irons, barb'd at the end, to strike great fish with.

Harpings, the breadth of a ship at the bowe, also the end of the bends fastened into the stem.

Harpocrates, the *Egyptian* god of silence, with one hand upon his mouth.

Harpyes, 3 filthy, monstrous and ravenous birds (of the lake *Stymphalis* in *Arcadia*) with Womens faces, Vultures claws &c. *Aëllo*, *Celero*, and *Ocypete*.

Harquebuse, as *Arquеb*-.

Harrow, *o.* fie! away! alas!

Harre, *o.* hearkning, obedience.

A Sea harr, *Li.* a tempest coming from the sea.

Hart, a stag full five years old.

Hart-Royal, having been hunted by the King or Queen.

Hart-Royal proclaimed, when (being chased by the King out of the forest) Proclamation is made that none shall hurt him or hinder his return.

Hart-hall in *Oxford*, built (together with *Exeter* Colledge) by *Walter Stapleton* Bishop of *Exeter*.

Hartle-pool, a town in *Durham*.

Harts-tongue, a long-leaved herb good for the Liver, Spleen, and passions of the heart.

Hartwort, a plant good for Harts or stags to feed on.

Harth-penny, -*silver*, Chimney-money.

Harwick, a town in *Essex*.

Haspat or *Haspenald-lad*, *No.* a stripling, between man and boy.

Hasel-nut, good only after fish (to hinder the ingendring of flegme.)

Hassord, a Town in the Bishoprick of *Mentz*.

Haske, *Li.* harlh, also a sign o Fishes *Haske*, the sign *Pisces*.

Hale, a town in the lower *Elsasz* or *Alsatia*.

Hassia, a Province of *Saxony*.

Hastings, a town in *Sussex*.

Hastilude, *l.* spear-play, a running at Tilt or Tournament.

Hatering, *sa.* Cloathing.

Hatches, the Overtures or Trap-doors of the deck, to let things down into the hold.

Hatch-way, the place perpendicular over the hatches.

In the Hatch-way, On the hatches.

Hate, *o.* for heat.

Hatfield, a town in *Hertfordshire*, a Village in *Hereford* and *Yorkshire*.

Hatfield-Brodock, a town in *Essex*.

Hatherley, a town in *Devon*.

Hattle Ky, *Che.* wild, Skittish Cow.

Hattock, *No.* 12 sheaves of corn.

Hauberg, -*ert*, *f.* a coat of mail.

Haubergeon, *f.* a little one.

Haubergets, *Haberjects*, a kind of Cloth mentioned in *Magna Charta*.

Haverjannock, *No.* an Oaten Cake or loaf.

Hauback, *o.* (*q.* have or held back] return.

Havelock, a *Danish* foundling, and Scullen in the Kings kitchen, preferred by degrees to the marriage of the Kings Daughter.

Havelburg, a town in *Germany*.

Haven, a port or safe riding for ships.

Have, *o.* heaved.

Haver, *Cu.* Oats.

Haveril, a town in *Suffolk*.

Havering, a town in *Essex*, from a ring supposed to be sent from St. *John Baptist* (by a pilgrim) to King *Edward* the Confessour.

Haulstead, a town in *Essex*.

Haunce, *o.* for *Enhaunce*.

Haunt, the walk of a Deer.

Haulm, *Helm*, *So.* Stubble

Hauriant, as *Hariant*.

Hause, *Hose*, *No.* the throat.

Hauselynes, *Hans*-, *o.* breeches or flops,

Hausible, *l.* that may be drawn or emptied.

Haust, *l.* a soop or draught in drinking, also (*No.*) a dry cough.

Haut-goust, *ho-goo*, *f.* a high tast, or relish.

Haw (*f. hay*) a hedge, also a Disease in the eye, also black, *o.* also to have.

Haws, *K.* little pieces of land adjoyning to the housen, also by some the houses themselves.

Haward, *Hayw*-, the keeper of the Town herd [from breaking or cropping hedges]

Haugh, *Howgh*, *No.* a green plat in a valley.

Hawise as *Avice*.

Haw-

Hawkers, deceitful fellows wandring up and down to buy and sell brass, pewter, &c. which ought to be utter'd in open market, also those that sell News-books about by retail, as the Mercury-women do from the press by whole sale.

Hawk-weed, with thick and dark jagged leaves, good for the eyes and all inflammations.

Hawlkes, *o.* corners.

Hawser, as *Halser*.

Hawses, the holes under the ships head through which the Cables come.

Hawten, *o.* (*f. hautain*,) insolent.

Haws, the fruit of the

Haw-thorn, Hedg-, or white-thorn.

Haylse, *o.* to charge or command.

Haylsham, a Town in *Sussex*.

Hazarders, players at

Hazard, *f.* chance, the play at dice, &c. also a place into which if the Tennis-ball be strucken, it is a loss.

Hay, *Trecketble*, in *Brecknockshire*.

Hay-boot, a permission to take thorns, &c. to make or repair hedges.

Haydegines, *o.* a Country dance.

Haylayks, *Tu.* the women-slaves.

Hayn, *o.* hatred.

Hazael, *h.* seeing God.

He, *hoo*, *No.* She.

Headborow, *Burrow-head*, *Borow-elder*, *Burs-holder*, *Chief-pledge*, *Third-oorow*, *Tithingman*, chief of the frank-pledge, or Governour of those within his own pledge, now a Constable.

Head-land, a point of Land lying farther out (at Sea) than the rest. also that which crosses the ends of the plough'd Lands.

Head-lines, the ropes that fasten the sails to the yards.

Head-sailes, those of the fore-mast and Bolt-sprit, which make the ship fall off from the Wind, and (in quarter-Winds) are the chief drawing Sails.

Head-sea, that which after a storm [and sometimes before] runs contrary to the present wind, here long ships go easiest, because they'l ride upon two waves at once.

Head-silver, as *Common-fine*.

Head-pence, about 40 pounds collected every 3d. and 4th. year by the Sheriff in *Northumberland* without any account to the King, and therefore put down by *Henry the sixth*.

Heafsling, *sa.* a Captive.

Heafod, *sa.* a head.

Healsfang, as *Halsfang*.

Healed, *o.* for heared.

Healing, *Der.* a hylling, or coverlet.

Heal, *ss.* to cover.

Healgemote, *halymote*, *sa.* a Court Baron, or the meeting of all the Tenants of one hall or Mannour.

Heam, the same in Beasts as the secundine in Women.

Hearse, [a husk,] an empty tomb or Monument for the dead, also the funeral Cloth or litter, wherein the Corps is carryed.

Hearth-money, Chimney-money.

Hearts-ease, *Pansie*, *Pances*, *Jacea*, *herba Trinitatis*, good for Ruptures and the falling sickness.

Heath-poult, a bird resembling a Pheasant.

Heave-offerings, First fruits paid to the Jewish Priests.

Heave the booth, *c.* rob the house.

Heaver, *c.* a breast.

Hebdomade, *g.* the number of seven [years, ages, months, but most commonly] daies.

Hebe, Goddess of youth, Daughter of *Juno* without a Father, *Jupiters* Cup-bearer till she fell and was removed.

Hebbermen, Fishers below *London-bridge*, (commonly at Ebbing water) for smelts, whitings, &c.

Hebbing-wears, laid for Fish at ebbing water.

Hebetude *l.* a bluntness of point or edge, also dulness of wit.

Hebraïsm, a dialect or idiom proper to the

Hebrew [*tongue*,] belonging to the

Hebrews, Jews, the posterity of

Heber, *h.* a Companion, inchanter, &c. in whose Family (they say) the old language alone remained pure.

Hebrides, *Ebudæ*, *Ebudes*, *Habudes*, *Ebuniæ*, *Mevaniæ*, the Western Islands 44 in number.

Hebrus, a River of *Thrace*.

Hecalius, an Attribute given *Jupiter* by *Theseus*, from

Hecale, an old Woman and *Theseus*'s Land-lady, who had devoted herself for his safe return from the Wars.

Hecate, *Apollo*'s sister, *Luna*, *Diana*, *Proserpina* [with three heads,) also a *Thracian* Witch.

Hecatomb, *g.* a sacrifice of an hundred Beasts at once.

Hecatompolis, *g.* *Creete*, which had an hundred Cities in it.

Hecatompylæ, *-pylos*, the Egyptian *Thebes*, which had an hundred gates.

Heck, an engine to take fish withal in *Yorkshire*, also a rack to feed at, *No.* see *Hack*.

Heckled, *o.* wrapped

Hectick, *g.* (habitual) a feaver inflaming the heart and soundest parts.

Hecla, a Mountain in *Island* sending forth a noise like the cries of tormented persons.

Hector, *Priam*'s son, slain by *Achilles* before *Troy*.

Hecuba, *Priam*'s wife, who is feigned [after the taking of *Troy*] to be turned into a bitch.

Heda, a Haven or Port.

Hederal [Crown] made of *Hedera*, *l.* Ivy.

Hederiferous, *l.* Ivy bearing.

Hederiform vein, passing a-long the sides of the womb.

Hedonick, *Cyrenack* [Philosophers.]

Heels [to starboard, &c.] the ship leans to that side.

Heep, *o.* help.

Heer and Hace, *o.* hoarse and harsh.

Heer and Houne, *o.* hare and hound.

Hegesians, Philosophers following

Hegesias, disciple to *Parabates*.

Hegesistratus, the founder of the City *Elea* in *Asia*.

Hegira, *A.* the flight [of *Mahomet* from *Mecca*] the *Turkish Epoche*, or Computation of time, beginning *July* 16. 622. by some 6 7.

Hegow, part of *Suevia* or *Schwaben* in *Germany*.

Heidelberg, a town in the *Palatinate* of *Rhine*.

Hainfare, *Hinefare*, *Sa.* a Servants departing from his Master.

Heiminckstede, a town of *Holstein* in *Germany*.

Heir, he that succeeds by right of bloud in any mans lands or tenements in fee.

Heir, *o.* their.

Heire, *o.* hair-cloth.

Heir-lome, *-loom*, Houshold stuff as Tables, presses, &c. which having belonged to the house for certain descents, do (by custom, not Common law) accrew to the heir.

Heisa, service.

Heisugge, *o.* an hedg-sparrow.

Helaw, *-loe*, *No.* bashfull.

Helbecks, certain solitary rivolets in *Richmondshire*.

Helchesaites Hereticks that followed one

Helchesaus, he held that it was no sin to deny Christ in time of persecution.

Helcysm, *g.* the dross or scum of silver or any metal.

Helder, *No.* rather, before.

Hell, *o.* an account or total summe.

Helded, for held.

Hele, *o.* to cover, or hold.

Helena, Wife to *Menelaus*, stolen by *Paris*, occasioned the *Trojan* wars.

Helenites, white Friers wearing a yellow cross on their breasts.

Helenopolis, *Frankfurt* in *Germany*.

Heliacal, *g.* belonging to the sun.

Heliacal emersion, when a star which was hid by the light of the Sun, appears.

Heliades, Daughters of the sun, and Sisters to *Phaeton*, who for his death wept themselves into poplar trees.

Helias, as *Elias*.

Helical, belonging to *Ursa major* or *Charles-wain*.

Heliconian, belonging to

Helicon, a hill in *Phocis*, sacred to *Apollo* and the

Heliconiades, the Muses.

Helioscopie, *g.* the furthest point of the suns course, also a kind of Spurge.

Heliotropian, belonging to the

Heliotrope, *-py*, *g.* the plant Waterwort or Turn-sole, also a kind of precious stone.

Helispherical, round as the Sun.

Helix, *g.* a spiral line, rowling in several circles.

Helle, Daughter to *Athamas* King of *Thebes*, falling from the back of a golden ram into the *Pontick* sea, occasioned the nameing of it

Hellespont, *Brachium Sti. Georgii*, the narrow sea by *Constantinople* dividing *Asia* from *Europe*.

Hellebore, *Melampodium*, Christwort because it flourisheth about Christmas, an herb good against madness.

Hellenism, *g.* as *Grecism*.

Hellenistical, belonging to *Hellas*, *g. Greece*.

Hellenize, to play the

Hellenist, *g.* a *Grecian*, also a *Greekizing Jew*, born out of *Judea* and using the *Septuagint* translation.

Helm, *Ge.* a handle, the piece of wood that guides the rudder, also as *Haulm*.

Helmeley, a town in *Yorkshire*.

Helmed in stark stowers, *o.* defended in sharp assaults.

Helstone, a town in *Cornwall*.

Helter-Skelter, *q. Heel-ter-Schetter*, *D.* all to shatter, violently, rashly, confusedly.

Heluation, a gluttonous devouring.

Helve, *o.* the handle.

Helvetian, belonging to

Helvetia, *l.* *Swizzerland* or *Switzerland*.

Hem, *o.* Them.

Hemerobaptists, *g.* daily Baptists, a Sect that baptized themselves every day.

Hemerologe, *g.* a Calendar or day-book.

Hemicade, *g.* half a hogshead.

Hemicircular, half round.

Hemicranick, belonging or subject to the

Hemicrain, *-cranie*, *g.* the Megrim.

Hemicycle, *g.* a half circle

Hemingham Castle, in *Essex*.

Hemingston, a Town in *Suffolk*, held formerly by *Baldwin le Petteur*, *per saltum, sufflum et pettum, sive sufflatum et bumbulum*. (a jump, a puff, and a fart) before the King upon Christmas day.

Hemiplexy, *-xia*, *g.* the Palsie on one side only.

Hemisphere, *g.* the visible half-compass of the Heavens.

Hemistick, *g.* half a verse.

Hemorrhagy, *g.* a large flux of bloud.

Hemorrhoides, *g.* Emrods, the piles like teats in the fundament.

Hemorrhoidal vein, the first branch of the Mesenterick, ending at the Colon & strait gut.

Hemlock, a venemous herb.

Hemule, a Roe-buck of the third year.

Hempstead, a town in

Hertfordshire, and other villages elsewhere.

Henares, a river in *Spain*.

Henbane, a venemous herb.

Henchman, (q. *Hengst-man* *Sa.* a horsman or Groome) and

Heinsman (q. *Hine-man*, *Sa.* a serving-man or Manservant) a page of honour.

Hend, *Hende*, *o.* (q. handy or handsom) Feat, fine, gentle.

Hendecasyllable, *Phaleucium*, a verse of eleven syllables, as, *Quoquo diffugias pavens Mabili*.

Hengston-hill, in *Cornwall*, where King *Egbert* defeated the *British Danmonii* and *Danes* conspiring against the *English*.

Hengwit, as *Hankwit*.

Hengest, *-gist*, (*Sa.* a stonehorse) he led the first *English* men hither.

Henghen, *Sa.* a prison or house of Correction.

Heniochus, *g.* as *Auriga*.

Henoch, *h.* taught or dedicate.

Henley, a town in *Oxfordshire*, *Warwickshire*, and other Villages.

Henry, (q. *Heymrick*) *Sa.* of a rich home or house.

Hent, *o.* to catch.

Hepatical, *-tarian*, *g.* belonging to the liver.

Hepaticks, treatises or obstructions of the Liver.

Hepatick vein, the great carrying vein.

Hephæstian [Montains] in *Lycia* alway burning.

Heppen, *Heply*, *T.* neat, handsome

Heptaëdrical, belonging to

Heptaëdron, *g.* a figure of seven sides.

Heptagonal, belonging to a

Heptagon, *g.* a figure of seaven angles.

Heptaphony, the having seven sounds.

Heptarchy *g.* a seaven-fold government, as of *England* by 7 *Saxon* Kings.

Heptameron, *g.* a work of seven daies.

Haraclea, St. *Giles* in *France*.

Heraclitus, the weeping Philosopher of *Ephesus*.

Herald, as *Harald*.

Heraude, *o.* to proclaim.

Herawdes, *o.* feats of activity.

Herbage, the natural food for Cattel, also a liberty to feed ones cattel in the Forrest or another mans ground.

Herbert, *sa.* the light or glory of an army, a good Commander.

Herbigage, *o.* lodging, and

Herborow, *o.* harbour.

Herbalist, *Herbist*, *-bary*, *l.* one skilled in herbs.

Herbal, a treatise of herbs.

Herbegeours, *Herberjours*, *o.* Herbergers, Inn-Keepers.

Herbenger, as *Harbinger*.

Herber, *o.* arbour.

Herbiferous, *l.* bearing herbs or grass.

Herb Christopher, a kind of *Aconite*, with berries like beads.

Herb Paris, True love, Oxeberry, the leaves like a true lovers knot with a berry in the midst, good against poison, inflammation, &c.

Herb Robert, a kind of Cranes-bill with reddish stalks, helps the stone, stops bloud, &c.

Herbipolis, *Wirtzberg*, in *Germany*.

Herbred, (q. *haer broed*) their bread.

Herbosity, plenty or fulness of herbs, a being

Herbulent, *l.* grassy or full of herbs.

Herciebant, they harrowed.

Hercinia, a *German* forest of 60 daies journey in length and 9 in breadth.

Herculean, *-lane*, belonging to

Hercules, the son of *Jupiter* and *Alcmena*, therefore engaged by *Juno* in 12 dangerous enterprises, which he overcame.

Hercules pillars, raised on Mount *Calpe* and *Abila*, at the streights mouth.

Herculeus morbus, the

Herculean or falling sicknes which (they say) he got by eating too many quails.

Herdelenge, the dressing of a Roe, as the undoing of a Bore.

Here, *sa.* an army [of rebels.]

Here de Cæsar, for *Æra* &c. an account of time, in *Spain* and *Arabia*, taking date 38 years before Christ and lasted in *Spain* till the year 1383.

Hereditary, *Hær-*, *l.* coming by inheritance.

Hereditaments, all things that descend by way of inheritance, and fall not as Chattels, within the Compass of an Executor.

Heresare, *sa.* [subsidy towards] warfare.

Hereford, the City of *Herefordshire*, where *Ethelbert* King of East *England*, going to woo the Daughter of *Offa* King of the *Mercians*, was murthered.

Heregeat, as *Hariot*.

Heregeld, a subsidy for carrying on the war.

Heremitage, *Erem-*, a solitary dwelling of

Heremites, *Erem-* persons devoted to religious solitude.

Heresie, as *Hæresie*.

Heresiarch, *Hære-*, *g.* the principal authour of any Sect or Heresie.

Hereslita, *-slia*, *sa.* a Soldier departing without Licence.

Heretogh, *D.* a Duke or Leader of an army.

Hericane, as *Haricane*.

Herility, *l.* Master-ship.

Heriot, *Hariot*, a tribute given to the Lord of a Mannor for his better preparation toward the war, now the best chattel that a Tenant hath at his death, due to the Lord by Custom or service.

Herlaxton, a town in *Lincolnshire* where was ploughed up a brazen vessel with a golden helmet set with precious stones, presented to *Catharine* of *Spain* wife to King *Henry* 8.

Herman, as *Harman*.

Hermaphrodite, *g*. (*Mercury-Venus*) one of both sexes, man and woman.

Hermetical, belonging to

Hermes, *g*. *Mercury*.

Hermes Trismegistus, a great *Egyptian* Philosopher.

Hermes fire, as *Furole*.

Hermione, the Daughter of *Menelaus*.

Hermite as *Heremite*.

Hermitage, as *Heremitage*.

Hermitorium, an Hermitage, or Chappel belonging thereto.

Hermitress, a woman Hermite or Eremite.

Hermodactyles, *g*. *Opprobrium Herbariorum*, certain roots like fingers, but of what plant is uncertain.

Hermopole, *g*. a place where Images are sold.

Hermotimus, a *Lydian* whose soul was wont to wander far from his body and return with foreign news, till once his enemies to k his body and burnt it the mean while.

Hern, *o*. Corner.

Herniosus, *l*. bursten-bellied.

Hernsucs, *Li*. an heron.

Herodian, belonging to

Herod, King of the Jews under the *Roman* Emperour.

Herodian disease, a being eaten up of lice, as He was.

Heroick, *-cal*, noble, lofty, belonging to or becoming an

Hero, *g*. a Noble or valiant man.

Heroick [*verse*] *Hexameter*.

Heroine, *g*. a Noble or Virtuous woman.

Heroner, *o*. a hawk that flies at a

Heron, *Ardea*, a bird whose dung burns what it touches.

Herophila, the *Erythræan* Sibyl, who being (by *Tarquin*) denied the price of her 3 books of prophecies, burnt 2, and received the whole price for that which was left.

Herostratus, to purchase fame, burnt the Temple of *Diana*.

Herpsac, as *Fredmortel*.

Hersilia, the wife of *Romulus*, worshipped by the name of

Hera, the Goddess of youth.

Herry, *Hery*, *o*. to praise.

Hertford, *Herueford*, the chief town of *Hertfordshire*.

Herthus, a *Saxon* Goddess, like the *Latin Tellus*.

Herwarden, a free City of *Westphalia*.

Hesione, Daughter of *Laomedon* King of *Troy*, whom *Hercules* delivered from a great whale.

Hesperian Gardens, whose trees bare golden apples kept by a watchfull dragon which *Hercules* slew. Here dwelt the

Hesperides, the 3 Daughters of

Hesperus, the brother of *Atlas*, changed (after his death) into the Evening-star.

Hesta, *-tha*, a Capon.

Hests, *o*. Commands or decrees.

Heteroclitical, belonging to

Heteroclites, *g*. nouns irregular in their declinings.

Heteriark, *g*. the General of the Allies, also an Abbot.

Heterodoxy, *l*. a being

Heterodox, *g*. of another judgment or opinion than what is generally received.

Heterogeneity, the being

Heterogene, *-neal*, *-neous*, *g*. of another or different kind.

Heteroscians, *g*. inhabitants of either temperate Zone, whose shadows are to one side and contrary to those of the other temperate Zone.

Heth, *h*. fear or astonied.

Hethen, *o*. mockery.

Hetheneffe, the Heathen world, opposed to Christendom.

Hetruria, *Tuscany* in *Italy*.

Hette, *o*. to vow, promise or command.

Hete, *hight*, *o*. promised.

Hetter, *No*. Eager, earnest, keen.

Heva, *-ah*, as *Eva*, *Eve*.

Heveningham, *Henn-*, a town and a family in *Suffolk*.

Heven, *hafe*, *o*. to rise up.

Hew, *o*. colour, also welfare, also to hover.

Hewmond, *o*. shining.

Hewte, a little Copse or Grove.

Hexaëdron, *g*. a figure consisting of six sides.

Hexagonal, belonging to

Hexagon, *g*. a figure having six corners.

Hexam and Hexamshire, are now within the County of *Northumberland*.

Hexameter, *g*. consisting of six feet, whereof the last is a Spondee, the last but one a Dactyle, the rest indifferent.

Hexapedes, *g*. a fathom.

Hexaptote, *g*. having 6 cases.

Hexastick, *g*. a Stanza or Staff of six verses.

Hext, *o*. perhaps for highest, as Next for nighest.

Heydelberg, a City of *Germany*.

Hezekiah, *Ezechiah*, *Hizkiah*, *h*. the strength or apprehension of the Lord.

Hiation, *l*. a gaping.

Hibernian, *Irish*.

Hibernia. *Ireland*.

Hibride, mongrel, of a mixt generation.

Hicbel, *Hatchel*, an instrument to combe hemp or flax.

Hickling, a town in *Norfolk*.

Hickway, a Woodpicker or Wryneck.

Hictius doctius (*q. Hic est doctus*) a canting word among Juglers, to amuse the people.

Hidage, *Hyd-*, an extraordinary tax upon every

Hide of Land, *familia*, a plough-land, or as much as one plough yearly ploughs, about an hundred acres.

Hidous,

Hidous, *o.* for hideous.

Hide-bound, when the skin cleaves to the sides of Cattel, or the bark is too straight for the body of the Tree.

Hide and Gain, Arable land, see *Gainage*.

Hidel, *o.* a Sanctuary, protection, or hiding place.

Hidromel, as *Hydro-*.

Hiera picra, a Confection of *Aloes Succatrina*.

Hierarchie, *g.* a holy spiritual or Church Government.

Hierarchie of Angels, their supposed order of nine degrees, viz. 1. *Seraphims*, *Cherubims*, *Thrones*, 2. *Dominations*, *Principalities and Powers*, 3. *Vertues*, *Archangels*, and *Angels*.

Hierarchical, pertaining to a holy Governor, or Government.

Hieratick, *-cal*, *g.* sacred, consecrated to a holy use.

Hieratick paper, dedicated only to Religious books.

Hierd, *Hyerd*, *Herde*, *sa.* a Shepherd.

Hieroglyphicks, mystical, Egyptian, sacred Characters or Images (instead of writing) expressing a thing, word or sentence, as that of *Diosp-lis*, a Child, an old Man, a Hawk, an *Hippopotamus* and a Crocodile, for, Oh ye that come into the World, and that go out of it! God hates impudence.

Hierograms, *g.* sacred writings.

Hierography, divine writing, or a description of divine things.

Hieronymians, Monks of the order of St.

Hierome, *Hieronymus*, Jerome, one of the chief Fathers of the Latin Church, he translated the Bible into Latin.

Hierosolymitan, belonging to *Hierosolyme*, *g.* Jerusalem, the chief City of *Judæa*.

Hierothius, *g.* (holy God) a mans name.

His testibus, added (in ancient deeds) after, *In cujus rei testimonium*.

Higham-ferries, a Town in *Northamptonshire*.

Higham, a Town in *Suffolk*, and other Counties.

Higra, an encounter of contrary waters.

Hight, *heete*, *o.* named, called.

Hight, *Cu.* to promise or vow: *Ps.* 116 14.

Hilarion, a Syrian hermite famous for many great miracles.

Hill, *sc.* to cover.

Hilarity, *l.* mirth chearfulness.

Hilarius, Bishop of *Poictou* in *France*, persecuted by the *Arrians*.

Hilary or *Hillary term*, begins January the 23d. (except it be Sunday) and ends *February* the 12th.

Hildeth, *o.* giveth.

Hildebert, *ge.* famous Lord.

Hillulim, *h.* praises, a Jewish wedding-song.

Hilkiah, *h.* the Lords gentleness.

Himple, *No.* to halt.

Hin, *h.* twelve sextaries or Logins, which contain about 6 egg-shels each.

Hindberries, *No.* Raspberries.

Hinkley, a Town in *Leicestershire*

Hine, *hinde*, a servant at husbandry, also (*Cu.*) hence.

Hinefare, as *heinfare*.

Hinnible, *l.* apt or able to neigh.

Hinton, the name of several small Towns.

Hippace, *f. l.* Cheese made of Mares milk.

Hipparchus, *g.* Governour or master of the Horse, also an *Athenian* Tyrant slain upon his deflouring a Maid.

Hippe, Daughter of *Chiron*, a great huntress, got with Child and turn'd into a Mare.

Hippiades, *g.* Images of Women on horse-back.

Hippiatrie, *g.* horse-physick.

Hippiaticks, *g.* books treating of horses.

Hippicon, *-cum*, eight miles, or rather four furlongs.

Hippocentaurs, as *Centaurs*.

Hippocras, *Hipo-*, a compounded and spiced wine from the supposed inventor

Hippocrates, a famous Physician of *Coos*, who lived 104 years.

Hippocrate's bag, made of white Cotton, pointed at the bottom like a Sugar-loaf.

Hippocrene, a Fountain in *Bæotia*, sacred to the

Hippocrenides, the *Muses*.

Hippodame, *-mia*, Daughter to *Oenomaus* King of *Elis*, whom *Pelops* won at a race with her Father by corrupting his Chariot-driver.

Hippodrome, *g.* a tilt-yard, or horse-race.

Hippo-gryph, *g.* a feigned beast, half horse, half Griffin.

Hippolyta, a Queen of the *Amazons*, whom *Hercules* gave *Theseus* to wife.

Hippolytus, their Son, torn in pieces by his Chariot-horses as he fled, being accused of adultery by his Wives mother *Phædra* whose sollicitations he refused.

Hippomachy, *g.* a justing or fighting on horse-back.

Hippomenes, and *Atalanta* (won by his golden apples thrown in her way) were turn'd to a Lion and Lioness for lying together in *Cybele's* Temple.

Hippo, *on*, an *African* City whereof St. *Austin* was Bishop.

Hippona, the Goddess of horses and horse-coursers.

Hipponax, an Ephesian Poet, whose sharp writings made his Enemies hang themselves.

Hippophæston, *g.* an herb on the Fullers thorn, good for the falling sickness.

Hippotades, *Æolus*, King of the Winds.

Hypsicratea, followed her husband *Mithridates* in all his wars and dangers.

Hircifcunda, the division of an inheritance among heirs.

Hircine, *l.* belonging to

Hircus, *l.* a Goat, also the left shoulder of *Auriga*.

Hirculation, *l.* a disease in Vines making them barren.

Hirsute, *l.* rough, hairy, bristly.

Hirundinous, belonging to a swallow.

Hispalis, *Sevil* on the River *Bætis* in *Spain*.

Hispania, *l. Spain.*

Hispanian, a Spaniard or Spanish.

Hispaniola, *Hayti*, the fairest of all the *American* Islands.

Hispid, *l.* as *Hirsute*.

Historian, one read or skild in History, also as

Historiographer, one practising

Historiography, *g.* a writing of Histories.

Historiologie, *g.* a discourse of History.

Histrionick, *-cal*, belonging to, or fit for an

Histrio, *l.* a stage-player.

Hitch, to catch hold of any thing (with rope or hook.)

Hitching, a Town in *Hertfordshire*.

Hithe, *Hythe*, (as Queenhythe, Lamb-hythe, &c.) a little Port or Haven to imbark or land wares.

Hithe, a Town in *Kent*

Hlaford, *Laford*, *sa.* a Lord.

Hleafdian, *Le-*, *sa.* a Lady.

Hlafordsocna, *sa.* the protection of a Lord.

Hlasocna, *sa.* the benefit of the Law.

Hoan, *sa.* a fine whetstone.

Hoast-men, an ancient guild or fraternity (trading in Seacoal) at *New-castle*.

Hoat, as *Hot*.

Hob, *o.* a clown, also (*No.*) the back of the Chimney.

Hobgoblins, (*q. Rob.*) Robin-good-fellows.

Hobbie, a hawk less than a Sparrow-hawk, also a little Irish nag, for the service of

Hobilers, *Hoblers*, a kind of Irish Knights, light horsemen, also those (with us) whose tenure was by maintaining a light nag, to certifie an invasion or any peril by the Sea-side.

Hock and *Hocks*, *o.* Mire and dirt.

Hoch-berg, a Town in *Brisgow*, part of *Schwaben* in *Germany*.

Hockettour, *Hoquetour*, *f.* a Knight of the post, decay'd man, basket bearer.

Hock-tide, *Hocks-tide*, (*q hogh tijd*, *D.* a high time or day) blaze tide or St. Blazes day, observed for the sudden death of *Hardicnute* the last King of the *Danes* and their fall with him.

Hoc-munday, the Munday seven-night after Easter-week

Hock tuesday money, paid the Landlord for giving his Tenants and Servants leave to celebrate.

Hock-Tuesday, the second tuesday after Easter-week, whereon the *Danes* were mastered.

Hocus Pocus, a jugler shewing tricks by sleight of hand.

Hodge-podge, *Hotch-pot*, a *Gallimaufry* or mixt dish of flesh cut in pieces and herbs boild together, also a putting together of Lands of several tenures for the better division of them.

Hodgee, *P.* a holy man or Priest.

Hoddy, *so.* well, pleasant, in good humour.

Hodiurnal, *l.* belonging to the present day or time.

Hodmandod, *Nf.* a shel-snail.

Hoday, *P.* God, a word much used by the Turks.

Hog, a young sheep, also (*c.*) a shilling.

Hogan, *Mogan*, (*Hoghen Moghen*, *D.*) High and Mighty, the Title of the Estates of the United Provinces.

Hogenhine, *Third night awn hine*, a guest that lies in the house the third night, who was then accounted one of the Family, and the Host was responsible for his mis-behaviour.

Ho-goo, as *Haut-goust*.

Hogs head, 63 gallons or the fourth part of a tun.

Hog-steer, a wild Boar of 3 years old.

Hoistings, as *Hustings*.

Hoker, *o.* peevishness.

Hokerly, *o.* aukwardly, hookedly, crooked, crossly.

Hold, as Covert.

Hold off, hale away the Cable (as it is heaved in from the Capstain) to keep it from slipping back.

Holland, the chief of the seven united Provinces, also a third part of *Lincoln-shire*, the other being *Kesteven* and *Lindsey*.

Hollow-root, an herb somewhat like Fumitory.

Holly, *o.* for whole.

Holm, the holly-tree, also a River Island.

Holocaust, *g.* a whole burnt offering.

Holographical, *g.* wholly writ with his hand that sent it.

Holofernes, *Holoph-*, *h.* (profane, or mad) *Nebuchadnezzars* General.

Holour, *o.* a Whore-monger.

Holstaines, *o.* hail-stones.

Holsatia, (*q. Holt Sassia* or *Saxony*) *Holstein*, woody *Germany*, a Dukedom.

Holte, a Town in *Norfolk*,

Holly-hocks, a kind of Mallows with beautiful Flowers.

Holy-rose, the leaves are like Sage (but whiter) and the blossomes presently fall.

Holy-thistle, *Carduus Benedictus*, a very wholsome Root.

Holy Thursday, Ascension-day, ten dayes before Whitsunday.

Homage, the Jury of a Court Baron, of such as owe to that Lord

Homage, (*f. Hommage*,) service, fidelity, sworn by the Tenant (on his knees) to the Lord, in these words, I become your man from this time forth, for life, for member, & for worldly honor, &c.

Hommageable, subject or belonging thereto.

Homage Ancestrel, done by his Ancestours time out of mind.

Homager, one that doth (or is

is bound to do) homage to another, as the Bishop of *Man-Isle* is said to be homager to the Earl of *Derby*.

Homagio respectuando, a writ for the Escheator to deliver land to the Heir (of full age) notwithstanding his homage not done.

Hombre, *sp.* a man, also a game at cards.

Homberg, a Town in *Westphalia*.

Homerical, after the manner of

Homer, (*q. Haömer*, *h.* the Eloquent) the most famous Greek Poet.

Homesoken, *Hamsoken*, *-soca*, *sa.* [an immunity or liberty of] entring violently into an house.

Homicide, *l.* the Commission or Committer of Murder, Manslaughter or Chance-medley.

Homiletical Vertues, which concern mutual conversation.

Homily, *g.* a speech or Sermon, common discourse or Communication.

Homine eligendo ad custodiendam peciam sigilli pro Mercatoribus editi, a writ for a Corporation to choose a new man to keep one part of the seal appointed for statutes-merchant.

Homine replegiando, a writ for the bailing a man out of Prison.

Homine capto in Withernamium; a writ to take him that hath conveyed a bondman or woman out of the County, so as they cannot be replevyed according to Law.

Hominatio, may be called *Dominatio*, as many use

Hominium, *l.* for *Homagium*.

Homæology, *g.* likeness of

Homæomerie, *g.* a likeness of parts.

Homæon, *g.* a similitude taken from the parts of a thing.

Homæoptoton, *g.* when divers clauses end with the like cases.

Homæoteleuton, *g.* when divers clauses end alike or with the same cadence.

Homodox, *g.* of the same opinion.

Homogeneal, *-eous*, *g.* of the same kind.

Homography, *g.* alike writing or painting.

Homologie, *g.* a confessing or agreeing.

Homologation, an admission, allowance or approbation

Homonymie, *g.* likeness of name, a being

Homonymous, *g.* having the same name, though the things be of several kinds, also doubtful, ambiguous.

Hondfangenethef, *Hontfon-*, a thief taken with

Hond-berend, *-habend*, a circumstance of manifest theft, when one is taken with the thing in his hand.

Hond-fish, *o.* dog-fish.

Honie comb'd, [a piece] ill cast, over-worn and rugged within.

Hony-suckle, Wood-bine.

Honi soit qui mal y pense, *f.* (let him be berayed who things any harm of it) the Motto of the Garter.

Honitone, a Town in *Devon*.

Honours Courts, held within

Honors, the more noble sort of seigniories, on which the inferiour Lordships or Manners do depend.

Honour point, the upper part of an Escutcheon, between the chief and the Fesse-point.

Honorary, *l.* belonging to, or done in token of honour.

Honorificabilitudinity, *l.* honorableness.

Honorifical, *l.* bringing or causing honour.

Honorius, Son to *Theodosius* the first, he divided the Empire between his two Sons *Arcadius* (in the East) and *Theodosius* (in the West.)

Hony-moon, the sweet-month next after marriage.

Hood-wink't, *c.* benighted, belated.

Hooks of the ship, all the forked timbers placed upright on the keel.

Hook-norton, a Town in *Oxfordshire*.

Hoonkeawr, *P.* (a man of blood) King, a title of the Grand-Signiors.

Hoop, *T.* a peck.

Hope, the side of a hill, also (*No.*) a low ground amidst the tops of hills.

Hope-Castle, in *Flint-shire*.

Hope-steres, Pilots.

Hophas, a River in *Bæotia*.

Hoplochrism, *g.* the anointing a sword (or other arms) with weapon-Salve.

Hoplochristical, belonging to the weapon salve.

Hopple, (*q. Couple*) *the horse*, tie his legs together.

Hoqueton, *f.* a short sleeveless coat. (sket.

Hoppet, *No.* a little hand-ba-

Horary, *l.* hourly, belonging to

Horæ, *l.* hours, Goddesses, Daughters of *Jupiter* and *Themis*. (name.

Horace, *-atio*, *-tius*, a mans

Hord, *l.* a Cow great with Calf.

Horcentrick, *f.* out of the Centre, quite without the compass, when the Sun is farthest from the Centre of the Earth.

Horismos, *g.* the definition of a thing (to the best advantage.)

Horizontal, belonging to the

Horizon, *g.* the Circle bounding our sight and dividing the upper hemisphere from the lower, the line in which the Sun alway rises and sets.

Hornbeam, a tree of very hard fire-wood.

Hornbeam-pollengers, Trees that have usually been lopped, are above 20 years growth, and therefore not tythable.

Horn-Castle, in *Lincolnshire*.

Hornet, a large kind of wasp

Hornicle, *Sf.* the same.

Horn-geld, a Forrest-tax for horned beasts.

Horodix, *g.* a Dial.

Horological, belonging to an

Horologe, *g.* an hour-teller, Clock, Dial, Glass or watch.

Horolo-

Horologiography, g. a treatise of Clocks or Dials.

Horometry, g. the measure or measuring of hours.

Horoscope, g. a marking of hours, or the thing whereon they are marked, so much of the firmament as ariseth every hour, also the Ascendant of ones Nativity, or the Calculation thereof by observing that Hour.

Horridity, l. a being

Horrid, l. frightfull, dreadfull.

Horripilation, l. a growing rough with hair, also a sudden quaking or standing up of the hair for fear.

Horrisonant, l. making a terrible and roaring noise.

Horror, l. a quaking for fear or cold, astonishment.

Horrow, o. nasty, base.

Hors de son fee f. (out of his fee) an exception to avoid an Action (brought by the pretended Lord) for Rent or other service.

Horse, a rope fasten'd to the fore-mast shrouds, to keep the Sprit-sail sheats clear of the anchor-flooks.

Horse-ballet, a horse-danse.

Horsham, a town in *Sussex*.

Horse-heal, Elicampane.

Horse-tail, an herb good for inward Wounds or Ulcers.

Hortative, -*tatory*, belonging to

Hortation, l. an exhorting.

Hortensius, an Eloquent *Roman*, Father of

Hortensia, she so pleaded her cause before the *Triumviri*, that they took off a great tax from the people.

Hortensian, l. belonging to a garden.

Hortolages, f. Garden-stuff, things growing in gardens or Orchards.

Hort-yards, Garden-yards.

Horwood, a Town in *Gloucestershire*.

Hosanna, *Os-*, *b.* Save now, O Lord! I beseech thee save! a solemn acclamation at the feast of Tabernacles.

Hose, as *Hause*, also to hug or carry in the arms, *No.*

Hospitalers, an Order of Knights having the care of

Hospitals, 'Spitles, houses erected for the relief of Pilgrims, poor, sick, and impotent people.

Hospitality, l. a being

Hospitable, -*tious*; l. kind to the poor, strangers &c.

Hospiticide, l. he that kills his guests.

Host, an army, also the sacramental sacrifice or body of Christ, also the Landlord entertaing guests, f.

Hoste, *No.* Cough: see *Haust*.

Hostage, f. a pledge in war.

Hosters, o. they that take in Lodgers.

Hostey, o. to Besiege.

Hostilements, o. Necessaries.

Hostle, (f. *Hostel*) a great house, Hall, Inne, &c.

Host'ler, the Horse-Groom, but properly the keeper of an

Hostery, *Hostelry*, (f. *Hostellerie*) an Inne.

Hosticide, l. a killer of his enemy.

Hostile, l. belonging to or like an enemy.

Hostility, l. enmity.

Hotagoe the tongue, *Sf.* move it nimbly.

Hotch-pot, -*potch*, as *Hodgpodge*.

Hote, *hate*, *hat*, o. called.

Hote the knot, o. made fast.

Hoten, o. they promise, or command, also as *Hot*.

Hoti & Dioti, g. That [the thing is] and How or Why [it is so.]

Hounds, holes in the Cheeks of the masts, wherein the Ties run that hoyse the yards.

Hounds-tongue, the leaves are like the tongue, and the smell like the piss of hounds.

Hovingham, a Town in *Yorkshire*.

Hover ground, *So.* Light ground.

Houp, f. a Lapwing.

Housage, paid for setting up any stuff in a house.

House, the twelfth part of the Zodiack, also (*No.*) the Hall.

Housleek, Sengreen, a cooling herb.

House-bote, Estovers, an allowance of Timber from the Lords wood for the repairing or upholding a tenement.

Housse, f. the cloth which the Kings horse guards wear behind the saddle.

Gill-Howter, *Che.* an Owl.

Houton, o. hollow.

How, *Hoo*, an high place.

Howden, a town in *Yorkshire*.

Howgates, o. how or which way.

Howld, *Hold*, the room between the Keilson and the lower deck.

Howfe, o. for hoof.

Hownds, as *Hounds*.

Howlsom [*ship*] that will hull, trie and ride well at anchor, without much rowling.

Hown, o. for Gown.

Howsel, to administer the sacrament to one on his death-bed.

Howse-in the ship, bring her in narrow to her upperworks, after she is past the breadth of her bearing.

Hozing of dogs, as Expeditating.

HS. (for *LLS.*) the *Roman* coin *Sestertius*, or two Asses and a half.

Hubba, a *Danish* Captain who once invaded this Island.

Hudegeld, supposed to be mistaken for *Hinegeld*.

Hue and Cry, the pursuit of a Felon by the High-way, by describing the party and giving notice from Constable to Constable.

Huers,

Huers, as *Conders*.

Hugh, *D.* a Cutter or Slasher, or else (*q. hogh*) high.

Huguenotism, -*terie*, *f.* the doctrine or profession of the

Huguenots, *Hugonots*, a Nick-name of the *French Calvinists*, from

Hugo, a great leader and writer among them, or from

Hugon, a gate in *Tours* near which they assembled, or from

Huc nos venimus, (Hither we come) the beginning of their Protestation.

Huick, *Huke*, a *Spanish* and *German* mantle covering the whole body.

Huissiers, *f.* Ushers.

Hulk, a kind of great and broad ship.

Hulfeere, *Hulver*, Holly.

Hull, *Kingston* upon

Hull, a river in *Yorkshire*.

Hull, the Body of a ship without the rigging.

The ship Hulls, when she is at sea and (in a calm or storm) takes in all her sailes.

Hullock, part of a sail loosed (in a storm) to keep the ships head to the Sea.

Hulm, as *Holm*.

Hulstred, *o.* hidden.

Humane, belonging to man, Courteous, having

Humanity, Man-hood, or mans nature, also kindness or Courtesie.

Humane Signs, Gemini, Virgo, Libra and Aquarius.

Humber, a great River (or arm of the Sea) in *Yorkshire*.

Humbles, *o.* for humbleness.

Humectation, *l.* a moistening, a softning hard bodies by sprinkling moisture on them.

Humeral, *l.* belonging to the shoulder.

Humerous, *l.* having large shoulders.

Humicu'ation, *l.* a lying on the ground.

Humiliates, a Religious Order instituted 1166. who did

Humiliate, or keep themselves low and humble.

Humidate, *l.* to make

Humid, *l.* wet, moist or liquid.

Humiferous, *l.* waterish, wetting.

Humourist, fantastick, full of humours, or odde fansies.

Humoursom, the same, also obstinate, that will have his own way or humour.

Humorosity, *l.* moistness, fullness of

Humour, *l.* moisture, juice or sap; also a mans disposition or fansy.

Humours in the Body, Bloud, Choler, Phlegme, and Melancholy.

Humfrey, -*phrey*, -*fred*, *Sa.* house-peace.

Humling, *o.* sounding like a humble bee.

Hundred, ten Tithings.

Hundreders, a Jury of men dwelling in the hundred where the Land in controversie lies.

Hundredlagh, *sa.* the Hundred-Court.

Hundred-penny, raised heretofore by the Sheriffs, out of the hundreds.

Hundred-setena, *sa.* the Inhabitants or constitution of a hundred.

Hungerford, a town in *Barkshire*.

Hungaria, -*ry*, *Pannonia*, divided by the *Danaw* into two parts, subject partly to the Emperour and partly to the *Turk*.

Hunnes, *Scythians* that over-ran all *Gallia* and *Italy*, but at the entreaty of Pope *Leo*, retired themselves into *Hungary*.

Huntersdune, *Huntington*, the Chief Town in that shire.

Hurclys, *o.* sits (as a hare.)

Hure, *No.* hair.

Hurlebats, as Whirl-bats or Whorl-bats.

Hurleth, *o.* makes a noise.

Hurlers, Great stones in *Cornwall*, so tranformed [as the People think] for prophaning the Sabbath by hurling of the Ball.

Hurn, *Hyrn*, *sa.* a Corner.

Hurricane, as *Haracane*.

Hurts, *Heurts*, round blew figures in Heraldry.

Hurtle, *o.* to skirmish.

Hurtleth, *o.* carries, throws.

Hurst, *sa.* a little wood or plump of trees.

Huscarl, *sa.* a houshold servant.

Huseans, buskins.

Husem, *Hussum*, a town of South *Juitland* in *Denmark*.

Husfastne, he that holdeth house and land.

Husky lour, *c.* a guinny.

Hussars, *Hu'ares*, *Hungarian* Horsmen, from

Husa, the cry which they make at their first charge.

Husseling people, Communicants, partakers of the

Hussel, *sa.* the Holy Eucharist.

Hussite, a *Bohemian* Coin in memory of

John Husse, the first Reformer in *Bohemia*.

Hussites, his followers.

Hustings, *sa.* (house of causes) the principal and highest Court in *London*, held before the Lord Mayor and Aldermen; the same was at *Winchester*, *Lincoln*, *York*, &c.

Hutton, about 20 small towns.

Huy, a town, in the Bishoprick of *Liege*.

Hyacinthine, belonging to

Hyacinth, *Jacinth*, a precious stone of a waterish colour, also the purple flower Crowtoes, made of

Hyacinthus, playing at quaits with *Apollo* was killed by his quait blown upon his head by *Zephyrus* whom he had slighted,

Hyades,

Hyades, Atlantides, Suculæ, the seven stars Daughters of *Atlas*, lamenting of

Hyas, their Brother devoured by a Lion.

Hyaline, *g.* of glass.

Hybernial, *-nian*, *l.* of Winter.

Hybla a Sicilian Mountain, famous for Thyme and Bees.

Hyblæan, belonging thereto.

Hybreas, Governour of *Nylasis* (a City of *Caria*) destroyed by *Labienus*, because he called himself Emperour of *Caria*.

Hyde-gyld, as *Hidage*, also a price or ransome to save ones skin [from beating.]

Hydra, a monstrous Serpent with a great many heads, whereof when *Hercules* had cut off one, there came up two in the room.

Hydragogues, *g.* medicines to draw forth water from hydropical parts.

Hydragogy, *g.* a conveying of water by furrows and trenches.

Hydrargyrous, *g.* belonging to quicksilver.

Hydraulicks, *g.* musical water-works.

Hydrogogon, *g.* a purge against watery humours.

Hydrographer, a describer of Waters, Sea-Charts, &c.

Hydrographical, belonging to

Hydrography, *g.* a description of water, Seas, Creeks, Promontories, &c.

Hydromantick, belonging to an

Hydromancer, one that useth

Hydromancy, *-tie*, *g.* divination by water, or raising Spirits in the Water.

Hydromel, *g.* Metheglin, a drink of water and hony.

Hydrophoby, *g.* a melancholy dread or fearing of waters, caused (sometimes) by the biting of a mad dog.

Hydrophobical, belonging thereto or troubled with that fear.

Hydropick, *-cal*, *g.* belonging or subject to the

Hydropsy, *g.* the Dropsy.

Hydropotist, *g.* a continual drinker of water.

Hydroscope, *g.* a modern instrument to discern the watery volatil streams in the Air.

Hyemal. *l.* winterly.

Hyemation, *l.* a wintering.

Hyena, a beast like a Wolf (with a mane and long hairs) accounted the subtilest of all Beasts, changing sex often, and counterfeiting mans voice.

Hyerds, *o.* [hired] guides, leaders.

Hygiastick, *g.* tending to the preservation of health.

Hylas, going to fetch *Hercules* some water, fell into the River, or (poetically) was pulled in by the Nymphs in love with him.

Hyleg, that Planet or place in the heavens by whose digression they judge of the life or state of a person.

Hylled, *o.* hid.

Hyllus, *Hercules*'s Son, who built a Temple (at *Athens*) to *Misericordia*, the Goddess of pity.

Hylopathy, *g.* the power or faculty of a Spirit to fill the whole capacity of a body; to become so firmly and closely united to it, as both to actuate and be acted upon, to affect and be affected thereby.

Hymenean, belonging to

Hymen, *-næus*, Son of *Bacchus* and *Venus*, the God (or first instituter) of Marriage, also a nuptial or wedding Song.

Hymn, *g.* a Psalm or sacred Song.

Hymniferous, bringing or making hymns.

Hymnigrapher, a writer of hymns.

Hymnist, a singer of hymns.

Hyngham, a Town in *Norfolk*.

Hyothyroides, one of the two muscles lifting up the *Larynx*.

Hype at one, *No.* to pull the mouth awry, to do one a mischief.

Hypallage, *g.* an order of words contrary to their meaning in construction.

Hypanis, a Scythian River, whence daily arise bubbles with small insects, quickened at morning, flying at noon, and dead at night.

Hyperbaton, *g.* a transposing of words from the plain Grammatical order.

Hyperbolical, belonging to, or spoken by way of an

Hyperbole, *g.* an expression beyond the Truth, either in excess (called *Auxesis*) or diminution (called *Meiosis*.)

Hyperboreans, very Northen people.

Hypercathartica, *g.* purges that work too violently.

Hypercritical, belonging to

Hypercriticism, the judgment or censure of an

Hypercritick, *g.* a Master Critick, or over Critical.

Hyperdissyllable, [a word] of more than two syllables.

Hyperion, the [Father of Sun, the Son of *Cœlus* and Brother of *Saturn*, he first found out the motion of the stars.

Hypermeter, *g.* [a verse] having a syllable above its ordinary measure.

Hypermnestra, one of *Danaus* 50 Daughters commanded to kill their husbands (the 50 Sons of *Ægyptus*) she only saved her husband *Lynceus*, who afterwards killed *Danaus*.

Hyperphysical, *g.* supernatural.

Hyphen, *g.* a note of union, the stroke between two words or syllables.

Hypocaust. *g.* a stew, stove or hot-house.

Hypocistis, *Erythanon*, an excrescence of the Plant *Cistus*, whose juice stops fluxes.

Hypocondriack, *-cal*, belonging to the

Hypocondria, *g.* the sides of the upper part of the belly (about the short ribs) under which

which lie the Liver and Spleen the seats of Melancholy.

Hypocritical, belonging to

Hypocrisy, the practice of an

Hypocrite, g. an Actor in a play, also a dissembler or Counterfeit.

Hypogastrick, belonging to the

Hypogastrium g. the groin or lower part of the belly.

Hypoge, g. a cellar or vault under ground.

Hypogion, g. a great swelling inflammation of the eyes.

Hypoglottian [*medicines*] g. lying under the tongue and melting.

Hypogram, g. a subscription, or any writing subscribed.

Hypomone, as *Paradox*.

Hypophora, a branch of the figure *Prolepsis*.

Hypospadican, -*dian*, -*diæan* whose water comes out of the midle of his yard, an *Hermaphrodite*.

Hypostatical, belonging to

Hypostasis, g a personal subsistence.

Hypostatical union, of Christs humane nature with his Divine person.

Hypothecary, g. belonging to a pledge or gage

Hypothenusal line, that side of a right-angled triangle, as is subtended or opposite to the right angle.

Hypothetical, conditional, belonging to an

Hypothesis, g. a supposition upon which an argument or dispute is grounded.

Hypothetical Syllogism, beginning with the Condition If.

Hypotyposis, g. a rhetorical and most lively description of a person or thing.

Hypsicratea, as *Hipsi*-.

Hypsipile, Queen of *Lemnos* banished thence for saving her Father *Thoas*, when all the men of the Island were killed by women.

Hyrcania, part of *Asia*, bordering South on *Armenia*.

Hyreus, a Countryman of *Bæotia*, to whom was born *Orion* of an Oxes dung watered by *Jupiter*, *Mercury*, and *Neptune* whom he had entertained.

Hyrn, as *Hurn*.

Hyrse, the plant Millet.

Hyspaan, a City of *Persia*.

Hysterical, belonging to the

Hystera, g. the womb, also the after-birth.

Hysterical passions, fits of the Mother.

Hysterology, g. a placing that last (in Discourse) which should be first, *& e contra*.

Hysteron-proteron, g. (last-first) a speaking or doing præposterously, putting the Cart before the horse.

Hyth, as *Hithe*.

Hyttenia, *Tetrapolis*, part of *Attica*, having 4 chief Cities.

I.

JAacob, as *Jacob*.

Jabber, to pratle or chat.

Jabesh, h. Confusion.

Jabin, h. Understanding.

Jack, *Wambasium*, a horsemans defensive coat in war.

Jack by the hedg, Alliaria, an Herb with broad leaves, smelling like garlick.

Jack with a Lanthorn, *Ignis fatuus*.

Jackall, the lions provider, following his prey with open cry gives notice thereby to the Lion who follows him; the beast that is shewn in *England* under that name resembles a fox in all things save the smell.

Jacca, a City of *Arragon* in *Spain*.

Jacchus, one of the names of *Bacchus*.

Jacent, lying along, sluggish.

Jacynth, as *Hyacinth*.

Jacob, h. (a tripper, supplanter or beguiler) *Israels James*.

Jacobins, *Dominicans*.

Jacobites, Hereticks (An. 530.) following one

Jacobus-Syrus, he held but one will, nature and operation in Christ, Circumcised both sexes &c.

Jacobus, a broad piece of gold coined by

Jacobus, l. *James*, the first King of Great *Britain*.

Jacobs-ladder, reaching from earth to heaven, *Gen.* 28.

Jacobs-staff, a certain Geometrical instrument, a staff with a sword in it, also a pilgrims staff wherewith they walk to

St. Jago, Sp. *Jaques*. f. *James* of *Compostella* in *Spain*.

Jactancy, -*titation*, l. a vain boasting.

Jactator, l. a boaster.

Jaculable. capable of

Jaculation, l. a shooting or darting.

Jaculatory, suddenly cast forth (like a dart.)

Jactivus, *Je*-, he that loseth by default.

Jael, h. a Doe.

Jaen, a town in *Spain*.

Jalap, a black *West-India* root purging waterish humours.

Jallamaka, a place (in the *Moguls* Country) to which they go in pilgrimage.

Jamaica-wood, *Granadillo*, a fine-grain'd speckled wood, from

Jamaica, an *American* Island taken from the *Spaniard*, 1655.

Jambes, f. (legs) the side-posts of a door

Jague, c. a ditch.

Jambeaux, -*ux*, f. armour for the legs.

Jambick verse, whose feet are

Jambick, the first syllable short and the other long.

Jamblicus, a *Syrian Pythagorean* Philosopher, the Disciple of *Porphyrius*.

Jamb-stone, the Mantle-tree-stone.

James, as *Jacob*.

Jamoglaw, a Turkish Officer.

Jampnum, Furze, *Gorse*.

Jane, o. half-pence of *Genoua*.

Jangerlesses, o. brablers.

Janizaries, *Tu.* (the new Militia) the principal foot-soldiers of the Turks Guard.

Janewits, a Town in *Bohemia*.

Jannes and Jambres, the *Egyptian* Sorcerers withstanding *Moses*.

Jannocks, *No.* oaten bread.

Jansenism, *-ianism*, the Doctrine of

Corn. Jansenius, Bishop of *Ypres*, an opposer of Universal redemption, and an enemy to the Jesuits.

Janthe, the Daughter of *Telessa*, who (on her wedding day) was transformed to a man.

Janicula, *Italy*, from

Janiculum, a town built by

Janus, an ancient King of *Italy*, painted with two (and sometimes four) faces.

Janus's Temple, built by *Numa*, in peace shut, and in war open.

Jape, o. jest, play.

Japed, o. cheated.

Japan, an Island in *Asia*.

Japetus, Son of *Titan* and *Terra*, Father of *Prometheus* and *Epimetheus*.

Japygia, *Calabria*, *Magna Grecia*, on the borders of *Italy*.

Jarbas, King of *Getulia*.

Jargon, *f.* gibrish, pedlers French.

Jark, *c.* a Seal.

Jarnac, a Town in *France*.

Jaroslaw, a Town and Dutchy belonging to the eldest Son of *Muscovy*.

Jarro, *sp.* an earthen pot or pitcher.

Jarre of Oyl, twenty gallons.

a Jarre, *Nf.* [the door stands] half open.

Jarrock, a kind of Cork.

Jarsey, a French Island subject to *England*.

Jasion, *-ius*, Son of *Jupiter* and *Electra*, to him *Ceres* brought forth *Pluto*.

Jasmin, *Jesemin*, a tree whose flowers (with other mixture) make *Jesemin*-butter.

Jason, Son of *Eson* King of *Thessaly*, he fetcht the golden fleece from *Colchos*.

Jasper, a green precious-stone with red veins, also *Gasparus*, a mans name.

Jasponyx, *g.* a white Jasper with red strakes.

Jatraliptick, *g.* one that cures by outward application of ointments, frications, &c.

Jathromathematique, a Physician and Mathematician, or that cures in a Mathematical way.

Java, an Island of *Asia*.

Javan, *Jon*, founder of the *Jonian* or Greek Nation.

Javarine f. the Fort *Raab* in *Hungary*.

Javelin, *f.* a dart or launce, between a Pike and Partisan.

Jaundice, a disease properly yellow, yet the worst kind is also black.

J'ay tout perdu mon temps & labeur, *f.* I have quite lost my time and pains.

J'ay en vous toute ma fiance, *f.* I have all my confidence in you.

Jazul, a blew precious stone.

Jaycza, the chief Town of *Bosnia* in *Turkie*.

Iberia, *Spain*.

Ibete, *o.* set forth, went.

Ibex, *Evick*, a kind of mountainous Goat.

Ibis, a *Lybian* bird feeding on Serpents, which (they say) taught *Hippocrates* the use of glisters.

J. C. Juris-Consultus, a Lawyer.

Icarus, Son of *Oebelus*, he was slain by a Shepherd of *Athens* whom he had made drunk.

Icarian, belonging to

Icarus, the Son of *Dædalus*, who (flying too high) melted the wings his Father made him, and fell into the Sea.

Ice-bone, *Nf.* a rump of Beef.

Iceni, the antient inhabitants of *Suffolk*, *Norfolk*, *Cambridge*, and *Huntingtonshire*.

Iche, o. I.

Ich Dien, *Ge.* (I serve) the motto of the Princes-arms (three Ostrich feathers) won by *Edward* the black Prince from *John* King of *Bohemia*.

Ichabod, *h.* where is glory?

Ichneumon, *g.* an Indian Rat.

Ichnography, *g.* a platform or ground-work of any building.

Ichthyocolla, Isinglass, glew made of the skin of Fishes.

Ichthyologie, *g.* a discourse or description of Fishes.

Ichthyonomancy, *g.* a divination by Fishes.

Ichthyophagi, *g.* Fish-eaters.

Ichthyophagy, *g.* Fish-eating.

Icleped *o.* called, named.

Icond, *o.* learned.

Iconical, *-nomical*, belonging to an

Icon, *g.* an Image or picture.

Icon Basilike, *g.* the picture of the King.

Iconism, a true and lively description.

Iconoclast, *-tes g.* a demolisher or breaker of Images.

Iconography, *g.* the platform or model of a house, a description by cuts, &c.

Icorven, *o.* cut or carved.

Icterical, belonging to or troubled with

Icterus, *l.* the Jaunders, Jaundise, or overflowing of the gall.

Ida, a *Trojan* Mountain, where *Paris*, gave judgement against *Juno* and *Pallas* for the

Idalian Queen, *Venus*.

Idas, the Son of *Neptune*, who (by force) carryed away

way *Marpesia* the Daughter of *Mars*, as she was dancing in a wood.

Ideal, belonging to an

Idea, *g.* the form or representation of any thing in the mind.

Ideated, made by or for a pattern in the imagination.

Identification, a causing of

Identity, sameness, or being the very same.

Identitate nominis, a writ for him that is imprisoned for another of the same name.

Ides, the eight daies next to the nones in every moneth.

Idiograph, *g.* a private writing, or of ones own handwriting.

Idiom, *g.* the peculiar phrase of any language.

Idiopathy, *g.* a peculiar passion, or affection.

Idiosyncrasy. *g.* the natural property, or peculiar temper of a thing.

Idiotism, as *Idiom*, also as

Idiocie, simplicity, the being an

Idiot, *g.* a natural fool, of whose estate the King (by his prerogative) hath the disposal.

Idiotical, belonging to fools or private men.

De Idiota inquirendo vel examinando, a writ to examine (by Jury, &c.) the party suspected of Idiocy.

Ido, *o.* undone.

Idolatrous, given to

Idolatry, *g.* a worshipping of

Idols, images, false Gods, or the true God by images.

Idolaster, *o.* Idolater.

Idolet, a little Idol.

Idomeneus, *Deucalions* Son, and *Minos's* Grand-child, driven from his Kingdom for offering to sacrifice his Son (according to his vow) being the first that met him at his return from *Troy*.

Idoneity, fitness, a being

Idoneous, *l.* fit, convenient.

Idyl, *g.* a kind of Eclogue or short Poem.

Jear-capstain, holds off the cable from the main Capstain and serves to heave the

Jear [*rope*], a piece of a hauser (in great ships) fastend to the main yard and foreyards, to help to hoyse up the yard and succour the ties.

Jeat, as *Geat*.

Jebbe-aekchisee, the Grand Signiors pocket-mony which he throws to his Buffoons, &c.

Jebusites, inhabitants of

Jebus, *h.* (the fire of the Lord) the old name of *Jerusalem*.

Jeconiah, *h.* stability of the Lord.

Jeer, as *Jear*.

Jeeret, a Turkish exercise of darting launces on horseback.

Jegen, an Isle in North *Juitland*.

Jegerndorf, a Town in *Silesia*.

Jehoahas, *h.* the Lord seeing.

Jehoash, as *Joash*.

Jehojakim, as *Joakim*.

Jehoram, as *Joram*.

Jehosaphat, *h.* the Judgement of the Lord.

Jehovah, *h.* (which was, and is, and is to come) Gods proper name of his own imposing, never pronounced by the Jews on pain of death, only by the High-Priest in the holy of Holies on the day of expiation.

Jehu-march, furious, like that of the Captain

Jehu, *h.* being.

Jejunation, *l.* a fasting.

Jejunity, a being

Jejune, *l.* hungry, empty, barren.

Jemmingen, a Town in *Westphalia*.

Jeman, for Yeoman.

Je ne sçay quoy, *f.* [sick of] I know not what.

Jennets, Barbary-horses.

Jenticulation, *l.* a breaking ones fast.

Jeofailes, (*f. J'ay faillé*, I have failed) an oversight in pleading or other law proceedings.

Jeopard, *f.* to endanger or run the

Jeopardy, danger or hazard.

Jeremiah, *h.* high of the Lord.

Jeroboam, *h.* fighting against.

Jerusalem-Artichoaks, Batatas, (Potatoes,) of *Canada*.

Jerby, a Town in *Cumberland*.

Jesses, short straps fasten'd to the hawks legs and varvels.

Jesu, the Genitive, Dative, Vocative and Ablative case of

Jesus, the same as

Jesuah. *Josuah*, *Jehosuah*, a Saviour.

Jesuati, *Apostolici*, Monks begun (by *John Columbanus* and *Francis Vincent*) at *Siena* in *Italy* *An.* 1365.

Jesuites, (of the society of Jesus) instituted by St. *Ignatius Loyola* a Spaniard, and confirm'd by Pope *Paul* III. *An.* 1540. *Sep.* 15. To the common Vows of Poverty, Obedience and Chastity, he added Mission, to go whithersoever the Pope should send them.

Jesus Colledge, in *Oxford*, built (for Welshmen) by *Hugh Price* Dr. of the Laws.

Jet, *o.* a device.

Jethro, *h.* excelling.

Jetzeba, *Itz.*, a Town in *Holstein*.

Je vouldray, *f.* I would.

Je vous die sans doute, *f.* I tell you without doubt, for certain.

Jetson, *Jetzon*, *Jotson*, see *Flotson*.

Jews-ears, (*q. Judas's Ears*) an excresence about the root of Elder, on which *Judas* is supposed to hang himself.

Jewise, *o.* reward by revenge, also a gibbet, or (as *Juise*) Judgement.

Jews-stone, a Marchesite.

Ifare, *o.* gone.

Ifere, *o.* together.

Ifete, *o.* an effect.

Ifette, o. fetched.
Ifretten, o. devoured.
Ificched, o. fixed.
Ifounded, o. sunk.
Ignaro, I. a foolish ignorant fellow.
Ignifluous, l. running or flowing with fire.
Ignifie, l. to set on fire.
Ignipotent, l. powerful in fire.
Ignis fatuus, l. (a foolish fire,) Will with a wisp, a slight exhalation set on fire; it follows one that follows it, because the air doth so, also a foolish fancy.
Ignivomous, l. spitting or vomiting fire, as *Etna*, &c.
Ignitegium, as *Curfeu*.
Ignitible, l. capable of
Ignition, a being or making
Ignited, set on fire, made hot or fiery.
Ignoble, l. base (in birth, spirit, &c.)
Ignominious, l. full of
Ignominy, l. disgrace, reproach, slander, &c.
Ignoramus, l. (we are ignorant) written (by the Grand Inquest) upon bills whose evidence is weak, and the party (thereupon) delivered, also as *Ignaro*.
Igraven, o. buried.
Igurde, *Igourd*, o. in a round, or to fly [round.]
Ignoscible, l. pardonable.
J. H. S. taken and used (by ignorant Papists, &c.) for *Jesus Hominum Servator*, but proved by Antiquaries to be only a contraction of the greek, ̓ΙΗΣΟΥ͂Σ Jesus.
Ihird, *Ihiried*, o. praised.
Iholpe, o. helped.
Ihight, as *hight*.
Jilt, o. to deceive or defeat ones expectation especially in the point of Amours.
Ikend, o. known.
Ik, D. *Ich*, ge. I.
Ikenild-street, (from *Iceni*) one of our four famous Roman High-waies from *Southampton* to *Tinmouth*.
Ilchester, *Ivelcester*, a Town in *Somerset-shire*.
Ilfarcombe, a Town in *Devonshire*.
Ilia, Daughter of *Numitor* King of the *Albanes*, a Vestal Nun, but Mother of *Romulus* and *Remus* by *Mars*.
Iliades, *Homer's* books of the destruction of
Ilium, *Troy*, from
Ilus, a King thereof, the Son of *Dardanus*.
Iliaque, -*acal*, belonging to the
Iles, *Ilia*, g. the flanks or three small guts.
Iliac-passion, wind in the small guts.
Ilike. o. like.
Ilimed, o. taken.
Ilk, o. each, the same.
Ilioneus, a Companion of *Æneas* into *Italy*.
Illaborate, l, without labour or pains, plain.
Illaccrable, l. that cannot be torn in pieces.
Illachrymable, without pity, uncapable of
Illachrymation, l. weeping.
Illaqueate, l. to entangle.
Illatebration, l. a hiding or seeking of corners.
Illative, belonging to
Illation, l. an inference or conclusion.
Illatration, a barking at.
Illecebrous, l. enticing.
Illegitimate, l. unlawful, baseborn.
Illepid, l. dull, unpleasant.
Illeviable, which may not be levied.
Illiberal, l. niggardly.
Illicit, -*tous*, l. unwarrantable.
Illigation, l. an enwrapping or entangling.
Illimitable, that cannot be limited.
Illimitate, l. unbounded.
Illiquation, l. a mingling earthly bodies with mettalline.
Illiterate, l. unlearned.
Illogical, not according to the rules of Logick.
Illoques, o. (q. *illuc*) the place whither the dogs are to run.
Illucidate, l. the same as
Illuminate, l. to enlighten, explain.
Illuminous, l. without light.
Illusion, l. deceit.
Illustrate, l. to make clear, or set forth.
Illustrious, l. famous, renowned.
Illude, to mock or deceive.
Illusory, l. mocking.
Illutible, that cannot be purged from filth.
Illyricum, *Sclavonia*, or *Windenland*.
Ilmister, a Town in *Somersetshire*.
I mete, o. I might.
Imagery, f. painted or carved work of Images.
Imagination, l. feigning, also the phansie.
Imasked, (for masked) o. wrapped.
Imaus, a Mountain dividing *Scythia* into two parts.
Imbargo, *Emb-*, *Sp.* an arrest or stop of Ships or Merchandise.
Imbark, l. to go aboard.
Imbecillity, l. weakness.
Imbellick, l. unwarlike, cowardly.
Imbellish, f. adorn, beautifie.
Imberweek, as *Ember-*,
Imbering-daies, the Wednesday, Fryday and Saturday in Ember-week.
Imbezle, -*esil*, to steal, pilfer or purloyn.
Imbibe, l. to drink-in, receive greedily.
Imbibition, a drinking-in, &c.
Imbordring, making the Field and circumference (in Heraldry) both of one metal, colour or fur.
Imbosk, f. to hide or shroud ones-self in a wood.
Imbossment, the manner of
Imbossed work, with bosses or bunches in metal or stone.
Imbracery, as *Embra-*,
Imbricate, squared and bent like unto, also carved with an
Imbrex, l. a gutter-tile.
Imbrication, l. a covering with tile.

Imbrocado, *Sp.* Cloth of Gold or Silver.

Imbroyl, *f.* to put into a combustion, or set together by the ears.

Imbuition, *l.* a thorow moistening, seasoning or staining.

Imeint, *Imenit*, *Immenged*, *o.* mingled.

Imitatives, verbs expressing.

Imitation, *l.* following or doing like another.

Imitatrix, she that imitateth.

Immaculate, *l.* spotless.

Immanity, *l.* outragious cruelty, excess, hugeness.

Immansuete, *l.* untractable, wild.

Immanuel, *h.* God with us.

Immarcescence, *l.* a not fading or withering, incorruptibleness.

Immarcessible, incorruptible, immortal.

Immaturity, untimeliness, unripeness, a being

Immature, *l.* unripe, unseasonable.

Immediate, *l.* next and presently following, with nothing between.

Immedicable, *l.* incureable.

Immemorable, *l.* not worth the remembering, unremarkable.

Immensity, *l.* hugeness, vastness, a being

Immense, *l.* exceeding large, unmeasurable.

Immersible, which cannot be drowned, uncapable of

Immersion, *l.* a dipping, ducking or plunging-in.

Imminency, a being

Imminent, *l.* hanging over, ready to fall.

Imminution, *l.* a making less.

Immission, *l.* a sending, putting, graffing or glanting-into.

Immobility, *l.* unmoveableness.

Immoderate, *l.* without measure.

Immolate, *l.* to offer in sacrifice.

Immolation, *l.* a sacrificing.

Immorality, prophaneness, want of morality or common honesty.

Immorigerous, *l.* disobedient.

Immortalize, to give or cause

Immortality, *l.* a being

Immortal, which cannot dye.

Immunity, *l.* freedom, priviledge.

Immure, *l.* to inclose with, or between walls.

Immusical, having no musick or harmony.

Immutability, *l.* Constancy, a being

Immutable, *l.* unchangeable.

Impacable, *Impla-*, which cannot be appeased.

Impacted, *l.* driven in.

Impair, as *Empair*.

Impale, *l.* to spit on a stake, to crown or adorn, also to fence about with pales, and (in Heraldry) the halfing a Coat of Arms.

Impanation, the turning of another substance into bread.

Imparisyllabical, not having a like number of syllables in every case.

Imparity, *-ility*, *l.* unevenness, inequality.

Imparlance, as *Emparlance*.

Imparsonee, in actual possession of a parsonage.

Impassibility, a being

Impassible, not moved with passion or affection.

Impe, *Ympe*, *Du.* a shrub.

Imp, *Br.* a young shoot or twig.

Imp, (*f. ente*,) a graff,

Imps, witches little familiars.

Imp a [hawks feather,] graff a new piece on an old broken stump.

Impeach, *f.* to hinder, also to accuse one as guilty of the same crime with himself.

Impeachment of waste, a restraint from committing waste upon lands or Tenements.

Impeccability, a being

Impeccable, uncapable of sinning or offending.

Impedition, *l.* a hindring.

Impediment, *l.* a hindrance.

Impedient, *-itive*, *l.* hindering.

Impel, *l.* to drive or thrust on.

Impend, *l.* to bestow or spend.

Impendency, a being

Impendent, *-ding*, *l.* hanging over ones head.

Impendious, over-liberal.

Impenetrable, which cannot be pierced.

Impenitent, hard-hearted, not repenting.

Impennous, *l.* without feathers.

Imperative, *l.* commanding.

Imperceptible, which cannot be perceived.

Imperfect, [or *Præterimperfect*] *tense*, hath (in English) the sign did before it.

Imperial, belonging to an

Imperator, *l.* a Commander, General or Emperour.

Imperil, to hazard or endanger.

Imperious, Domineering, insulting.

Imperforable, *l.* not to be bored thorow.

Imperforation, a closing up for want of boring or pierceing.

Impersonal [verbs] without the distinction of persons.

Impertinence, a thing not belonging to the matter in hand, a being

Impertinent, nothing to the purpose.

Impervestigable, *l.* impossible to be found or searched out.

Impervious, *l.* which cannot be gone or passed through.

Impetiginosity, a being

Impetiginous, full of, or troubled with an

Impetigo, *l.* an Itching scab.

Impetrable, which one may

Impetrate, *l.* obtain by request.

Impetren, *o.* to entreat.

Impetuosity, a being

Impetuous, boisterous, furious, violent.

Impiated, defiled, not purged from sin.

Impierment, impairing or prejudicing.

Impicate, l. to cover with pitch.

Impiety, wickednesse, a being

Impious, l. ungodly.

Impignorate, l. to pawn.

Impigrity, quicknesse, a being

Impigrous, l. diligent, ready.

Impinge, to throw, dash, or run against a thing, also to drive or fasten a nail, &c.

Impinguate, l. to make fat.

Impinguation, a fatning.

Implacability, obstinacy, a being.

Implacable, l. not to be appeased or reconciled.

Implantation, l. a planting or fastening into.

Implead, to sue one at law.

Implement, l. a filling up.

Implements, tools, and other ecessaries belonging to a ouse or trade.

Implication, l. a folding or wrapping within, an entangling, also a necessary consequence, and as *Ploce*.

Implicitly, intricately, not in express terms but as included and mixt with another.

Implicit faith, upheld by the judgement and authority of many agreeing together.

Implore, l. to beseech humbly and (as it were) with tears.

Implume, l. bald, without feathers.

Impluvious, l. wet with rain.

Impolite, l. rough, unpolished.

Imporcation, the making of a balk in ploughing.

Imporous, l. without pores or holes.

Importance, [a carrying in it] great weighty or consequence.

Importunity, a being

Importunate, troublesome [with two often and unseasonable requests.]

Importune, l. to request earnestly and often.

Importuous, without port or haven.

Impositive, unnatural, imposed or given to.

Impositour, he that imposeth the pages into a Form for the press; also a School-Monitor.

Impostitious [names] primitive or radical.

Impossibility, a being

Impossible, which cannot be done.

Imposition, l. an imposing or laying on, a strict injunction, also as

Impost, f. tribute or tax, properly for Merchandise imported, as Custom is for wares shipped out of the Land, but they are confounded.

Imposture, the Practice of an

Impostour, l. a Cheat.

Imposthume, *-tume* (for *Aposteme*, g.) a gathering together of bad humours in any part of the body.

Impotence, *-cy*, a being

Impotent, l. unable, weak, lame.

Impoundage, a putting into a pound.

Imprecate, l. to curse, or call down mischief.

Imprecation, a Curse or Cursing.

Imprecivble, unvaluable,

Impregnable, l. not to be won or taken by force.

Impregnate, to make fruitfull or cause to swell.

Impregnation (in Chymistry) when a dry body hath drunk in as much moisture as it will admit.

Imprescriptible, without the compass of prescription, which by no length of time can be aliened or lost.

Imprese, I. a Devise with a Motto, signifying some particular design or undertaking.

Imprest-money, Imprest, or Prest-money, ready money given (as earnest) to Soldiers obliging them to be ready upon all occasions.

Impression, l. a printing, stamp or mark.

Impression of Books, usually 1500, but in *France* 1250 is the usual *journée* (or dayes-work.)

Imprimery, f. a print or impression, also a printing-house or the art of printing.

Imprimings, beginnings, first essaies.

Imprimis, l. first of all.

Improbation, l. a disallowing, contrary to Approbation.

Improbability, a being

Improbable, l. unlikely, which cannot be proved.

Improbity, l. Dishonesty.

Improcerous, low, not tall.

Improcreability, barrennesse, an unaptness to procreate.

Improlifical, not begetting nor apt to have issue.

Impromiscuous, unmingled, not confused.

Improperate, l. to upbraid one with a fault, to Nick-name, also to make haste to go in.

Impropriation, as Appropriations about 3845 Parsonages passing by inheritance.

Improvidence, want of fore-sight, a being

Improvident, careless or forgetfull to provide.

Improvement, a making better and more profitable, a thriving or benefitting.

Imprudence, want of discretion, a being

Imprudent, l. unwise, indiscreet.

Impudence, a being

Impudent, l. shameless.

Impugn, l. to fight against, contradict or resist.

Impuissance, f. weakness.

Impulse, *-sion*, l. a motion, driving or thrusting forward.

Impunitively, without punishment, unpunishably.

Impunity, l. freedom from punishment.

Impurity, l. uncleanness.

Imputation, l. a laying to ones charge.

Imputative, *l.* reckoned as done by or belonging to another.

Imputrescence, *l.* a keeping it-self from putrifying or rotting.

Imputrescible, *l* incorruptible.

Imrobor (Emeer-Ahor) Basshaw, *Tu.* Lord of the stable, chief Master of the Grand Signiors horse, Mules, Camels, and all his Cattel.

In alto & imo, as *Alto & basso*.

Inaccessible, *l.* not to be com'n at.

Inadvertence, *-cy*, carelesness, inconsideratenesse.

Inadulable, that will not or cannot be flattered.

Inachus, the most ancient King of the *Argives*.

Inaffability, a being

Inaffable, discourteous, unpleasant in conversation.

Inaffectation, a carelesness, or freeness from vain-glory.

Inalimental, without nourishing.

Inambulate, *l.* to walk, up and down.

Inamiable, *l.* unlovely.

Inamissible, which cannot be lost.

Inamorato, *I.* a lover.

Inaniloquent, *l.* speaking vainly, or emptily.

Inaniloquution, a vain or idle speaking.

Inanimate, *l.* without life or Soul.

Inanity, *l.* emptiness, vanity.

Inappetency, want of appetite.

Inarable, *l.* not to be ploughed.

Inarticulate, confused, not articulate or distinct.

Inargentation, *l.* a covering with silver.

Inaspicuous, invisible, or hard to be seen.

Inaudible, not to be heard.

Inaugurate, *l.* to ask counsel of the Augurs or Soothsayers, also to confer honour, to invest with an office or place of dignity, also to consecrate.

Inaurated, *l.* guilded over

Inauspicious, *l.* unlucky, boding mischief.

Inborh & Outborh, *Inborow & Outborow*, he that gave passage to (or was surety for) those that travelled between the two Realms of *England* and *Scotland*.

Incandescence, *l.* a growing hot or angry.

Incalescence, *l.* a growing warm or lusty.

Incanescence, *l.* a growing gray or hoary-headed.

Incantator, *l.* he that useth

Incantation, *l.* inchanting or charming.

Incapacity, unableness, uncableness, unfitness.

Incarcerate, *l.* to imprison.

Incarnadin, *f.* a deep rich or bright carnation colour.

Incarnate-colour, a flesh-colour, or colour of a damask Rose.

Incarnation, *l.* a making flesh to grow, also an assuming or being made flesh.

Incarnative, a salve or medicine to cause flesh to grow.

Incastellated, *f.* narrow-heeled as a horse.

Incendiary, *l.* *Boute-feu*, *f.* one that sets houses on fire, or sows dissention among men,

Incense, *l.* to inflame or provoke.

Incense, a perfume of the best frankincense.

Incension, *l.* a setting on fire, also Musick in Consort.

Incensory, *l.* a Censor, Censing or perfuming pan.

Incentive, *l.* stirring, provoking, inflaming ; also a provocation, motive, or thing that will quickly take fire.

Incentor, as *Incendiary*, also a singer of descant, between Succentor and Accentor.

Inception, *l.* a beginning or undertaking.

Inceptour, *l.* a beginner, he that is taking or hath newly taken his degree.

Incessantly, Continually, without intermission or ceasing.

Incerning, *l.* sifting, examining.

Incession, *l.* a going or walking.

Incestuous, he that committeth

Incest, *l.* (untying the Cestus or virgin-girdle) defiling one that is near of blood or kinred.

Inchantment, a Charm or Conjuration.

Inchipin, the lower gut of a Deer.

Inchoative, beginning, apt to

Inchoate, *l.* begin, or take a beginning.

Inchoative verbs, signifie to begin to do that which the primitives signifie.

Incident, *l.* cutting off or hindring.

Incident, *l.* happening, also an accident or circumstance, and (in law) a thing necessarily depending on another, as a Court Baron is so incident a Mannor, that it cannot be separated from it.

Incidentally, indirectly, collaterally or by chance.

Incineration, a reducing to ashes.

Incipation, a beginning.

Incision, *l.* a cutting or lancing, also a short pointing of a sentence.

Incisure, *l.* a cut or gash.

Incite, *l.* to stir up or provoke.

Inclamitation, *l.* a frequent calling upon.

Inclemency, *l.* rigour, unkindness.

Inclination, *l.* a bending or leaning towards, a disposition.

Include, to shut or take in.

Inclusion, an inclosing or shuting in, also as *Epanadiplosis*.

Inclusive [*of*,] containing, comprehending.

Inclusively, by taking-in the extreams.

Incoacted, *-ted*, *l.* uncompelled.

Incogitable, *l.* not thought of, or which cannot be compreprehended by thought, also rash.

Incogitancy, l. rashness, unadvisedness, inconsiderateness.

Incognito, l. unknown, in private.

Incohible, l. which cannot be restrained.

Incolumity, l. healthfulness, safety.

Incomity, l. unsociableness, want of civility in Conversation.

Incommeable, l. unpassable.

Incommensurable, l. holding not the same proportion, or not to be measured with another thing.

Incommiscibility, a being

Incommiscible, uncapable of being mixt or mingled together.

Incommodate, to hurt or endammage.

Incommodious, l. inconvenient, unfit or unprofitable.

Incommunicable, which cannot be made common or imparted to another.

Incommutative, not to be changed or altered.

Incompact, l. not well jointed or joyned.

Incomparable, l. without compare, not having the like.

Incompatibility, a being

Incompatible, l. not agreeing together or enduring one another.

Incompensable, uncapable of being recompensed.

Incompetency, a being

Incompetent, unfit, unsufficient.

Incompossible, [proposition] affirming what another denies.

Incomprehensible, l. which cannot be comprehended or conceived.

Incomputrible, which will not rot or decay.

Inconcinnity, l. unfitness, unhandsomness, a being out of order.

Incongelable, not to be congeled or frozen.

Incongruity, a being

Incongruous, l. disagreeable, unmeet.

Inconnexion, l. a not holding together.

Inconsiderable, not worth considering or taking notice of.

Inconsiderate, rash, giddy.

Inconsideration, rashness, unadvisedness.

Inconsistency, a being

Inconsistent, which cannot consist or stand together.

Inconsolable, l. not to be comforted or appeased.

Inconstancy, unstableness, fickleness.

Incontinency, want of moderation in affections & desires.

Incontinent, unchaste, also by and by.

Incording, Bursting, the faling down of the guts into the horses Cod.

Incordiate, to perswade or put into ones heart.

Incorporate, l. to mix bodies or substances together.

Incorporeal, Spiritual, without a body.

Incorrigibility, a being

Incorrigible, head-strong, past correction.

Incorruptible, l. never decaying, free from corruption.

Incrassate, l. to make thick, or gross.

Increate, Uncreate, not made.

Incredibility, a being

Incredible, l. not to be believed.

Incredulity, l. a want of believing, a being

Incredulous, hard or slow of believing.

Increment, l. an increase or waxing bigger, also as *Climax*.

Increpation, l. a chiding.

Incressant [*Moon*] between the prime and full.

Incroche, as *Encroach*.

Incrustation, l. a rough casting or pargetting, a making or becoming Crusty on the outside.

Incubation, l. a lying down, sitting, brooding, or hatching.

Incubus, l. the Devil (in mans shape) lying with women, as *Succubus* with men, also the Night-mare, or raw humours from the stomach troubling the brain and animal spirits, that the body cannot move.

Inculcate, l. to tread or thrust in, to beat into the memory by frequent repetition,

Inculpable, l. unreprovable, blameless.

Incumbent, l. lying or leaning upon, also he that is in present possession of a Benefice.

Incumbrance, as *Encumbr--*.

Incurable, l. not to be cured.

Incurr, l. to run upon.

Incursion, l. a running upon, a meeting or hitting against one another, also an inroad.

Incurvation, l. a bending or Crooking.

Incussion, l. a violent shaking or dashing against.

Indacus, a servant of the Emperour *Leo*, who could outrun any horse.

Indagable, which may be searched after.

Indagation, l. a diligent searching or hunting out.

Inde, f. Indico, a mineral used in dying blew.

Indecent, l. unbecoming, unfitting.

Indecimable, not to be tythed.

Indeclinable, l. which cannot be declined or shunned, also (in Gram.) not varying the termination.

Indecorum, l. unseemliness, unhansom carriage.

Indefatigable, l. which cannot be wearied or tired.

Indefeisible, which cannot be defeated or made void.

Indefensus, one that is impleaded and refuseth to answer.

Indefinite, l. not defined, determined, limited or bounded.

Indelible, l. which cannot be razed or blotted out.

Indemnify, to save harmless

Indemnity, l. freedom from dam-

damage or danger, pardon.

Indenization, the Act or Patent which doth

Indenize, make a stranger a free Denizen.

Indented, *f.* resembling the teeth of a saw.

Indenture, a writing (indented at the top) containing some mutual Contract, Conveyance or Covenant.

Independency, a being

Independent, absolute, not depending on another.

Independents, Congregationalists, appearing in *England* about the year 1643, their Churches are not subordinate (as Par. chial to Provincial and they to National) but Coordinate without superiority.

Indeprecable, *l.* that will not be perswaded or entreated.

Indeprehensible, *l.* which cannot be taken.

Indefinent, *l.* continual, without ceasing.

Indeterminate, not precisely determined, but left indifferent.

Index, *l.* whatsoever shews or directs, the fore-finger, hand of a Clock, table of a book, &c.

India, the Indies, a famous, vast and rich Eastern Country.

West-Indies, *America* or The new World.

Indian-mouse, *Ichneumon*, which creeping into Crocodiles mouths, eats up their Entrails and kills them.

Indicative, shewing, declaring, which doth

Indicate, *l.* direct, make manifest.

Indicative-mood, wherein the verb plai. ly affirms, denies or asketh a question.

Indication, a shewing, also a mark directing to the right way of prescribing medicines.

Indicavit, a writ whereby the Patron may remove an action of tythes (against his Clerk by another and extending to the 4th. part of the tythes) from the Court Christian to the Kings Court, whereto it belongs.

Indiciduous, shewing, detecting, discovering, also not apt to fall.

Indico, as *Inde*.

Indiction, a tribute or tax, also the space of fifteen years, which computation began at *Rome* (instead of the Heathenish *Olympiades*) at the dismission of the *Nicene* Council.

Indictive, solemnly declared or uttered, whereto the people were called by Proclamation.

Indictor, he that indicteth another.

Indictee, he that is indicted.

Indifference, *l.* a careless and unconcerned affection.

Indigence, *l.* penury, want, a being

Indigent, poor, or needy.

Indigenous, *-nital*, natural, born in the same Town or Country.

Indigestible, *l.* which cannot be digested, or concocted.

Indigestion, a crudity or want of digestion in the Stomach.

Indigitate, *l.* to signifie or shew by pointing.

Indignation, disdain, wrath.

Indignity, *l.* unworthiness, also an affront or unworthy dealing.

Indiscernable, not to be perceived.

Indiscerptible, not to be rent or divided.

Indiscretion, want of discretion or prudence.

Indiscriminately, without making any separation or difference.

Indissolvable, not to be dissolved.

Indissoluble, *l.* which cannot be untied, loosed or undone.

Indistinct, not distinguished or known a sunder.

Indistinctly, without distinguishing one from another, promiscuously, confusedly.

Inditement, as *Enditement*.

Inditiate, to give a mark or sign.

Individuity, *-uality*, a being

Individual, *l.* inseparable not to be divided.

Individuum, *l.* an individual, singular or particular body or thing, as *Peter*.

Individuum vagum, an indiv dual at large, a singular thing but not determined to be this or that in particular, as a man.

Indivisible, *l.* which cannot be divided.

Indivisum, *l.* that which two hold in common without partition.

Indocility, *-cibility*, *l.* unteachableness, unaptness to be taught.

Indocked, put into a Dock.

Indoctrinate, *l.* to teach or instruct.

Indolency, *l.* a not feeling (or want of) pain.

Indomable, *l.* untameable.

Indorse, to write on the backside, to lay on the back.

Indorsed fish (in *Her.*) born with their backs to each other.

Indorsement, the Sealed and delivered, &c. on the back of an Indenture; a Condition on the back-side of an Obligation, &c.

Indostan, that part of *India* which belongs to the Great *Mogul*.

Indubitate, *l.* not doubted of, taken for certain.

Indubitation, a not doubting.

Indubitably, undoubtedly.

Inducement, *f.* a perswasion, enticing or drawing on.

Induciary, belonging to a truce or league.

Induciat heir of this Imperial Crown, King *James* (then King of *Scotland* only.)

Inductile, which may be brought into or perswaded.

Induction, as *Inducement*, also a form of argument enumerating the particulars, also a giving livery and seisin of a Church to the Incumbent.

Indue, *l.* to put on.

Indulcate, *-ciate*, *l.* to sweeten.

Indulge, *-giate*, *l.* to bear with, to cocker or make much of.

Indulgence, pardon, favour, toleration, gentleness in suffering, also as

Indult, a special act of Grace, pardon or favour (in a written Instrument) from the Pope or other Prince.

Indument, *l.* a garment or cloathing.

Indurate, to harden, also hardened, unrelenting.

Indus, a River in the *East-Indies*.

Indusiated, *l.* cloathed with an

Indusium, *l.* a shift, or any under-garment,

Induustan, an *Indostan*.

Industrious, full of

Industry, *l.* labour, diligence.

Inebriate, *l.* to make drunk.

Inecbed, *o.* put in (*q.* eked in.)

Ineffable, *l.* unspeakable, not to be uttered or expressed.

Ineffugible, *l.* as *Inevitable*.

Inelaborate, not laboured or taken pains for.

Inelegant, rude, without elegance.

Ineluctible, not to be overcom'n by wrestling or taking pains.

Inept, unapt, foolish, out of season.

Ineptitude, unaptness, also fondness, foolishness, vainness.

Inequitable, not to be rid through.

Inequality, unevenness.

Inertitude sloathfulness, dulness, ignorance.

Inescation, a baiting, deceiving, inveigling.

Inescutcheon, an ordinary of a three-fold-line, representing the shape of th' Escutcheon.

In esse, in actual being.

Inestimable, *Inest-*, which cannot be valued (to the worth.)

Inestuate, to be very hot or boil much.

Inevitable, which cannot be shunned or avoided.

Inexaturated, *Inexsat-*, not filled or satisfied.

Inexaturable, which cannot be filled or satisfied.

Inexhauribility, a being

Inexhauri le, *-haustible*, not to be drawn dry or emptied.

Inexorable, which cannot or will not be perswaded or intreated.

Inexpedient, not expedient or fit.

Inexperience, want of experience.

Inexpiable, *l.* which cannot be purged from guilt, or satisfied for.

Inexpleble, not to be filled.

Inexplicable, which cannot be explained or unfolded.

Inexpugnable, invincible, impregnable, which cannot be taken by force.

Inextinguible, which cannot be put out, unquenchable.

Inextirpable, not to be rooted out.

Inextricable, so intricate and difficult, that one cannot wind ones self out of it.

Inexsuperable, *Inexup-*, which cannot be overcom'n.

Infallible, never failing, never deceived or deceiving.

Infame, to defame or slander.

Infamous, scandalous, full of

Infamy, slander, reproach or ill report.

Infancy, (properly speechless age but commonly) mans first age (from one to seven years.)

Infandous, (not to be spoken) very wicked, heinous.

Infangthef, *-theof*, *-geneth-*, [a liberty of trying] a thief stealing and taken in a mans own Jurisdiction.

Infanta, any Daughter of the King of *Spain* except the *Princesa* (the eldest.)

Infante, any Son of the King of *Spain* except the *Principe* (the Eldest.)

Infanterie, *Sp.* the Foot-Souldiery.

Infanticide, *l.* a killing of Infants.

Infatigable, as *Indefat-*.

Infatuate, to besot or make foolish.

Infaust, *-tous*, unlucky.

Infelicity, unhappiness.

Infeodation, a granting in fee.

Infeof, *Infeoffe*, to grant in fee.

Inferial, belonging to funerals or funeral rites.

Inference, a conclusion (from premisses.)

Inferiour, lower.

Inferiour Planets, below the Sun.

Infernal, belonging to hell or the Deep.

Inferrible, which one may

Inferre, bring-in or conclude (from premisses.)

Infertil, barren, unfruitful.

Infest, to trouble or molest.

Infestive, unpleasant, without sport, joy or solemnity.

Infibulate, to button or buckle-in.

Inficial, *-atory*, belonging to

Inficiation, a denial.

Infidelity, unfaithfulness, the being an

Infidel, unbeliever, heathen.

Infidous, false, unfaithful, not be trusted.

Infimous, *l.* lowest, meanest.

Infinitive, *Infinite*, *Indefinite*, without end, number or measure.

Infinitive mood, not determined

mined or limited (by number or perſon.)

Infinity, endleſsneſs, unmeaſureableneſs.

Infirmary, Fermory, a place for the ſick in a Monaſtery, alſo an Hoſpital.

Infirmity, a being

Infirm, weak, indiſpoſed.

Infix, to faſten-in.

Inflame, to ſet on fire.

Inflammation, an inflaming, alſo a paſſive burning or ſwelling with heat.

Inflate, puft-up, ſwoln.

Inflation, *f.* a puffing-up or windy ſwelling.

Inflexible, which cannot be bent or bowed, unruly.

Inflict, to lay [a puniſhment] upon.

Influence, a flowing in or upon, a ſending forth vertue, power or operation upon inferiour things, alſo to cauſe action or motion.

Influx, a flowing in.

Infœcundity, unfruitfulneſs, barrenneſs.

Infoliate, to be full of (or wrapt in) leaves.

Information, a faſhioning, inſtructing or making known.

In forma pauperis, having Council and Clerks aſſigned without fees, upon Affidavit made that (your debts being paid) you are not worth five pounds.

Informatus non ſum, non ſum informatus, an Atturneys formal anſwer in Court, when he hath no more to ſay in defenſe of his Client.

Information for the King, (which,) for a Common-perſon, is called a Declaration) by one who proſecutes as well for the King as for himſelf.

Informers, Promoters, Delatores, who complain in Court, of any that offend againſt the Laws or penal Statutes.

Informity, Deformity, a being

Informous, without ſhape or faſhion, ill favoured.

Infragible, Infran-, not eaſily broken or diſcouraged.

Infriction, *-cation*, a rubbing or chafing-in.

Infringe, to break in pieces, to endammage or diminiſh.

Infucate, artificially to colour or paint (the face, &c.)

Infuſcate, to make dark or dusky.

Infuſe, to pour in, to inſpire with.

Infuſion, a pouring-in; the giving of a Glyſter, alſo the ſteeping of things in liquor, that their virtue may paſs into it, and alſo the liquor in which they have been infuſed.

Ing, Da. a meadow or low ground.

Ingage, to pawn, to adventure.

Ingannation, *I.* deceit, couſenage.

Ingeminate, *l.* to double or repeat often.

Ingenerable, *l.* not to be begotten.

Ingeniculation, *l.* a kneeling.

Ingenio, the Sugar-houſe or mill in *Barbado's*.

Ingeny, Ingenioſity, wit, witineſs.

Ingenious, *l.* witty.

Ingenuity, good or free nature, a being

Ingenious, good-natured, well-born and bred.

Ingenious and Ingenuous, are too often confounded.

Ingeſt, *l.* to carry or pour in.

Ingeſtion, *l.* a carrying or conveying-in.

Ingle, as *Catamite*, alſo a fire or a blaze, *Cu.*

Inglorious, without glory, obſcure.

Ingluvious, *l.* gluttonous, ravenous.

Ingolſtad, a Town in lower *Bavaria*.

Ingot, (*q. Lingot*, *f.*) a little [tongue or] wedge of gold, alſo the trough wherein it is molten.

Ingrailed bordure made of a line bending inward toward the field.

Ingratitude, unthankfulneſs, a being

Ingrate, ungrateful, unthankful, alſo unacceptable, unpleaſant.

Ingratiate, to get into ones favour.

Ingredient, one part of a compound medicine, &c.

In gree, *f.* in good part.

Ingreſs, *-ſion*, *l.* an entring or walking into, alſo a beginning.

Ingreſſu, a writ of entry, whereby a man ſeeks entrance into Lands or Tenements.

De Ingreſſu ſine aſſenſu Capituli, &c. a writ for his Succeſſour who alienated without conſent of the Chapter.

Ingria, a Province in *Swedeland*.

Ingroſſator magni Rotuli, Clerk of the Pipe.

In groſſe, belonging to the perſon of the Lord.

Ingroſſer, a foreſtaller, he that buys bread-corn growing, or dead victuals to ſell again, &c. alſo a Clerk that writes Records or Inſtruments in Parchment-skins.

Ingroſſing of a fine, the Chirographers making the Indentures and delivering them to him to whom the Cogniſance is made.

Ingruent, approaching, unlookt-for.

Ingurgitate, Ingulph, to devour or ſwallow like a gulf or bottomleſs pit.

Inguſtable, which may not or cannot be taſted.

In hie, *o.* in haſte.

Inhabitant, a dweller.

Inhabited, dwelt-in.

Inhabitable, not to be dwelt in.

Inhalation, a breathing in or upon.

Inherent, ſticking to or abiding in.

Inheritance, a perpetuity

 of

of Lands or Tenements to a Man and his Heir.

Inhesion, *Inhæs-*, a sticking or cleaving to.

Inhibition, a forbidding or stopping, a writ forbidding the Judge to proceed any farther in the cause before him, and (most commonly) a writ from a higher Court-Christian to an inferiour, upon an appeal; as Prohibition is from the Kings Court to any Inferiour.

Inhild, o. to infuse.

Inhonestation, a disgracing, shaming, or making dishonest.

Inhospitality, *-ability*, a being

Inhospital, *-able*, not affording or unfit for entertainment.

Inhumanity, cruelty, a being

Inhumane, barbarous, not like a man.

Inhumation, a burying or putting into the ground.

Inhume, to bury.

Inidoneus, unfit, improper.

Injection, a casting, squirting or conveying in.

Inimical, *-citial*, like an enemy.

Inimitable, which cannot be imitated.

Iniquity, injustice, want of equity.

Iniswen, *Albion*, the white Island, an ancient name of *Britain*.

Initiate, to enter or begin.

Initiative, which doth initiate.

Initiated, entred or admitted to any Art or Faculty.

Injucundity, unpleasantness.

Injunction, a Command, also a writ or decree of Chancery, sometimes to give possession to the Plantiff (upon the Defendants not appearing,) sometimes to stop the rigorous proceedings of another Court.

Injurious, wrongful, against right.

Inkling, (q. tinkling, a little sound, or else q. *Eenckelinghe*, D. a running of division) a small and uncertain report.

Inlagh, *Inlaughe*, under the law, one that is not out-lawed.

Inlagary, *-ation*, a restitution of an Out-law to the protection of the Law and Liberty of a Subject.

Inlay, to lay in, to lay coloured Wood in Wainscot-work, Cup-boards, &c. *See* Marquetry.

Inland, far in the Land.

Inleased, (*f. enlaßé*) intangled or insnared.

Inmate, one who (not being able to maintain himself) is admitted (for money) to dwell joyntly with another.

Innable, *-atable*, which cannot be swimmed in.

Innarrable, not to be declared.

Innate, natural, imbred.

Innavigable, which cannot be sailed in or upon.

Innerest, o. innermost.

Innes of Chancery, Houses for Attorneys and young Students in the Law, viz. *Cliffords*, *Lyons*, *Clements*, *Bernards*, *Staple*, *Furnivals*, *Davies* (or *Thavies*) and *New-Inn*.

Innes of Court, Colledges for Counsellours and Students at law, viz. The *Inner Temple* (to which belong the three first houses of Chancery) *Grays-Inne*, (to which belong the next two.)

Lincolns-Inne, (having the two next) and the *Middle Temple*, (with the last.) The *Outer-Temple* is converted to *Essex-house*.

Serjeants-Innes, two higher Houses for the Judges, Barons of the Exchequer and Serjeants at Law. These altogether (saith Sir *Edward Coke*) make the most famous University (for profession of Law only, or of any one humane Science) in the world.

Innitent, endeavouring, leaning on.

Innocents or *Childermas-day*, *December*, the 28th. in memory of the Innocent Children slain by *Herod*.

Innocuous, harmless or free from hurt.

Innominable, not to be named.

Innotescimus, *Vidimus*, Letters Patent.

Innovate, to make or become new.

Innovator, the author of

Innovation, a bringing up of new customs, opinions, &c.

Innoxious, harmless, also safe.

Innubilous, without clouds.

Innuendo, *l.* by meaning or signifying [such a particular person,] as to say that he (*Innuendo*, the Plantiff) is so or so.

Innutrition, a nourishing.

Ino, Daughter of *Cadmus*, nurse to *Bacchus*, and wife to *Athamas* King of *Thebes*, who (in his madness) supposing her to be a Lioness, drove her headlong into the Sea.

Inobservable, not to be observed.

Inocciduous [*stars*,] never setting or going down.

Inoculate, to engraff a bud or kernel.

Inodoration, a perfuming.

Inome, *-ed*, o. taken, obtained.

Inominal, unlucky.

Inopacous, open, not shadowed.

Inoffensive, giving no offence.

Inofficious [*will*,] which omits or slightly provides for those that ought chiefly to be considered.

Inopinate, unthought of, unlookt-for.

Inopious, poor, needy.

Inoptable, not to be wished.

Inordinate, out of order or measure.

Inorganity, a being

Inorganical, wanting Organs or instruments of motion or operation.

Inprision, an attempt.

Inquietude, restlesness.

Inquiline, a native, born where he dwells.

Inquination, a defiling.

Inquirendo, an authority (given) to enquire into something for the Kings advantage.

Inquisition, a diligent search, inquiry or Examination.

Spanish Inquisition, Sacred Council of the *Inq-*, erected by *Ferdinand* the Catholick about 1492. to see that all *Moors* (whose Empire then determined in *Spain*) were baptized.

Inquisitive, making a diligent search, prying into.

Inquisitors, Searchers, Coroners, Sheriffs, &c.

Inrise, *o*. in [his] beauty.

Inrollment, a Registering of things [in the rolls of Chancery.]

Insanity, a being

Insane, *l.* unsound (in body or mind.)

Insanguin'd, dipt in bloud.

Insative, not sown or planted, growing of its own accord.

Insaturable, Insatiable, not to be satisfied or filled.

Inscient, *-ious*, ignorant.

Inscribe, to write upon, to make an

Inscription, a name or title written or engraven upon.

Inscrutable, unsearchable, not to be found out.

Insculption, a carving or engraving.

Insecable, which cannot be cut or divided.

Insects, small fleshless and bloudless vermine, either not divided into joynts as other creatures, or as it were divided between the head and body, as flies, &c.

Insectation, a railing against, a prosecuting or following [with ill language.]

Insectile, cut, or which cannot be cut.

Insection, *l.* a cutting into, also a Declaration, treatise or long Discourse.

Insemination, a sowing into.

Insense, *Y.* to inform (an elegant word.)

Insensate, Mad, foolish, senseless.

Insensible, senseless, also not to be perceived.

Insertion, a putting, planting or graffing in.

Insiccation, a drying.

Insident, siting or setling upon.

Insidiation, a lying in wait to ensnare.

Insidiatores viarum, Waylayers.

Insidious, deceitfull, crafty, wily.

Insimulation, an accusing.

Insimul tenuit, one species of the writ of partition.

Insinuation, a winding ones self in by degrees, also an intimation or slight touch of a thing.

Insipid, unsavory, foolish, without taste or judgment.

Insipience, ignorance, foolishness.

Insist, to urge or stay upon.

Insition, a graffing or putting into.

Insociable, not fit for company.

Insolation, a bleaching or laying in the sun.

Insolency, a being

Insolent, proud, arrogant, contrary to common custom.

Insoluble, as *Indissoluble* or *Indissolvable*.

Insomnious, wanting sleep, also dreaming much.

Inspection, a looking narrowly into, an overseeing.

Insperable, not to be hoped for.

Inspersion, a sprinkling upon.

Inspeximus, Letters patent.

Inspire, *l.* to breath into.

Inspiration, a breathing into, a being affected with the Spirit [of God.]

Inspruck, the chief town of *Tirol* in *Germany*.

Inspissate, to make thick or massy.

Instability, unconstancy, ficklenes.

Instalment, a setlement or sure placing in, and sometimes as Abatement.

Instancy, a being

Instant, near at hand, earnest or urgent, also an indivisible moment of time.

Instance, an example, importunity.

Instauration, a renewing or repairing.

Instigate, to prick, provoke or egg on.

Instillation, a gentle infusion, a letting or falling in by drops.

Instimulate, to spur-on.

Instinct, inward motion or prompting (usually natural.)

Instrumental, serviceable as a means.

Institutes, Ordinances, Instructions [in the Law, &c.]

Institution, an Order or appointment, also the Bishops investing a Parson with Cure and Spiritualty (as Induction doth with the Temporalty) of a living.

Insubid, rash, inconsiderate.

Insubria, *Gallia Cisalpina*, *Lombardy* or *Lumb-*, in *Italy*.

Insular, belonging to an Island.

Insulsity, unsavorines, folly.

Insult, to leap upon or triumph over.

Insultation, *-lture*, a leaping, boasting, &c.

Insuper, upon.

Insuperable, which cannot be overcom'n.

Insupportable, Intolerable, not to be born or endured.

Insurrection, a rising against.

Intabulate, *l.* to write in tables.

Intabulation, a boarding or planking.

Intactible, not to be touched.

Intakers, Thieves (on the borders of *Scotland*) who received such booties as their Complices (the Out-parters) brought them.

Intaminate, to defile.

Intangible, as *Intactible*.

Integral, entire, whole.

Integration, a restoring or making whole.

Integrity, sincerity, soundness, uprightness.

Integument, a covering, also a thing spoken covertly or darkly.

Intellectual, belonging to the

Intellect, the faculty or act of understanding.

Intellectualist, one quick of apprehension or

Intelligence, understanding, also notice or information.

Intelligible, which may be understood.

Intemperance, a being

Intemperate, immoderate in desire, diet, *&c.*

Intempestivity, a being

Intempestive, unseasonable, out of order, also unlucky.

Intendment, *f.* understanding, meaning.

Intenebrate, to darken.

Intenerate, to make tender, soft, merciful or pliant.

Inteneration, a softening.

Intense, *-sive*, set, fixed, bent upon a thing.

Intensly, to the utmost, in the highest degree.

Intensively, as *Appreciatively*.

Intent, *-tion*, a purpose, meaning or design.

Intent, *-tive*, as *Intense*, *&c.*

Intentable, which cannot be tempted.

Intentation, a threatning.

Intenuate, *o.* slender or sliced.

Inter canem & lupum, *l.* (between Dog and Wolf) by twylight.

Intercalarity, the burden of a Song, or as

Intercalation, a putting in or between, particularly that

Intercalaris dies, the odde day in *February* every Leap-year.

Interchangeably, by turns.

Intercede, to come between, to play the

Intercessour, Mediatour, he that maketh

Intercession, mediating or praying for another, or helping him to pray.

Intercident, falling between.

Intercident (or *-tal*) *day*, an extraordinary or critical day, forced by the malice of the disease.

Intercision, a cutting off in the midst.

Interclusion, a stopping the passage between.

Interclusive, stopping or stopped, enclosed, shut-in.

Intercolumniation, the distance (or work placed) between two columns or pillars.

Intercommoning, feeding Cattle promiscuously in two contiguous Commons.

Intercostal, *l.* between the ribs.

Intercourse, a passing or passage between.

Intercurrent, running or passing between.

Intercutaneous, between the skin and Flesh.

Interdict, to forbid, also as

Interdiction, a forbidding, also a Church-censure prohibiting the administration of Divine Rites.

Interdicted of water and fire, banished, excommunicated.

Interduct, a space left between full sentences (in writing.)

Interemption, a killing.

Interequitate, to ride between.

Interessed, concerned, having an

Interest, concernment, part or share, right and title; also the use of money lent.

Interfaction, an interrupting one in his discourse.

Interfection, a killing.

Interfectour, an interficient or destructive Planet, placed in the eighth house of a Nativity.

Interfeir, as *Enterfeir*.

Interfluent, *-uous*, flowing or running between.

Interjacency, a being

Interjacent, lying between.

Interject, cast or placed between.

Interjection, a particle expressing a sudden passion, as Oh! &c. also as Parenthesis.

Interim, [In] the mean while.

Interiour, *l.* inward, on the inside.

Interition, a perishing or decaying.

Interlocution, a speaking between.

Interlocutory, Order, not final but for the present, till the cause can he heard.

Interlopers, (*q. Interleapers*) *D.* those that intercept the trade of a Company, and are nat legally authorised.

Interlucation, a letting in of light by cutting away Boughs.

Interlude, a Comedy or that which is play'd (or done) between the Acts.

Interlunary, belonging to the

Interlunium, the space between the old and new Moon.

Intermean, a mean between two.

Intermeation, a passing between.

Intermedian, lying or being between.

Intermeteth, *o.* medleth.

Intermicate, *l.* to shine between or amongst.

Interminant, boundless, uncertain.

Intermission, a putting between, a ceasing or leaving off for a while.

Intermissions, spaces between the wall and pillars, or pillars and pillars.

Intermit, to discontinue or leave-off for a time.

Intermitting [*pulse*,] discontinued for a while by the fit, an ill symptome.

Intermixtion, a mingling between or amongst.

Intermural, between the Walls.

Internal, inward.

Internecion, *l.* an utter slaughter or killing all.

Internunciate, to go on a message between party and party.

Interpel, to interrupt or disturb.

Interpellation, an interrupting, or being interrupted in ones business.

Interpleder, as *Enterpl-*.

Interplication, a folding between.

Interpolation, a new dressing or polishing of a thing.

Interpose, to put or set between.

Interposition, a medling or putting between.

Interpretation, an expounding or explaining.

Interpunction, a distinguishing by points.

Interr, to bury.

Interrex, he that ruleth during the

Interreign, *-regency*, *-regnum*, the space between the death or deposition of one King or Governour, and the Succession or election of another.

Interrogation, a question.

Interrogation-point, in Latin thus (?) in Greek thus (; .)

Interrogative, used in asking of questions.

Interrogatory, belonging to questioning, also a question in legal examinations.

Interruption, a disturbing one in the midst of business, also a Parenthesis.

Interscident, *l.* cutting or hewing in two.

Interscript, *-tion*, an interlining, or writing between the lines.

Intersecants, pertransient lines crossing one another.

Intersection, a cutting in the midst.

Intersertion, a graffing or putting in between.

Intersonant, sounding between, or in the mean while.

Interspersed, bestrewed, scattered or sprinkled between.

Interspersion, a sprinkling or scattering between.

Interspiration, a breathing between.

Interstitial, having an

Interstice, distance or space between.

Intertexture, a weaving between.

Interval, any distance or space either of place or time.

Intervene, to come between.

Intervenient, coming between.

Intervert, to deceive or falsly to convey away a thing committed to ones charge, also to turn upside down.

Interview, a meeting of great persons, a sight of one another.

Intervigilate, watching now and then or between whiles.

Intestable, uncapable (by law) to make a will, or to be taken for a witness.

Intestate, [dying] without a will, also one that hath lost his credit.

Quasi intestate, whose Executors do refuse.

Intestine, *-nal*, inward, hidden, belonging to the

Intestina, inwards, entrails.

Intestina gracilia, the little guts.

Intestina terræ, Earth-worms.

Intestinum duodenum, the gut next to the stomack.

Intestinum cæcum, the fourth or blind gut.

Intestinum jejunum or *tenue*, the hungry or empty gut.

Intestinum quintum vel crassum, the same as Colon.

Intestinum rectum, the strait or Arse-gut.

Inthronize, to place on a throne.

Intiertie, as *Entiertie*.

Intimacy, great familiarity, a being

Intimate, inwardly acquainted; also to shew or signifie privately.

Intimidate, to affright or make fearful.

Intinction, a dying or colouring.

Intire, whole or sound, as Entire

Intituled, having this title.

Intitulation, an intitling or adding a title.

Intolerable, not to be born or endured.

Intone, to thunder or speak aloud.

Intonation, a thundering or making a terrible noise.

Intoxicate, to poison or make drunk.

Intractable, *l.* not to be handled or managed.

Intrado, *En-*, *Sp.* an entrance, also an yearly revenue.

Intraneous, *l.* inward.

Intress, *o.* lining (perhaps for living.)

Intribution, Contribution, or lot-money paid for lands.

Intricacy, a being

Intricate, intangled, perplexed.

Intrigue, *-que*, *f.* Intricacy, incumbrance, labyrinth, secret working.

Intrinsecal, inward, secret.

Introclude, to shut within.

Introduce, to bring in.

Introduction, a leading in, a preface or beginning.

Introgression, a going in.

Introit, an Entry or Entrance, the first part of the Mass beginning *Introibo ad altare-*.

Intromission, a letting in.

Introruption, a breaking in by violence.

Introvenient, coming in.

Introversion, a turning [ones thoughts] inward.

Intrude, to thrust in rudely

ly and violently.

Intrusione, a writ against an

Intruder, he that commits

Intrusion, unlawfull thrusting himself into anothers right.

Intuitive, belonging to

Intuition, a clear and distinct beholding of a thing.

Intumescence, *l.* a swelling.

Intumulate, to bury or throw an heap upon.

Invaginate, to put into a sheath or scabbard.

Invadiationes, Morgages or pledges.

Invalidate, to make

Invalid, weak, of no force or value.

Invadible, capable of

Invasion, Invading, setting upon another mans right.

Invecked [*bordure*] inverting its points into it self.

Invection, a carrying in or against.

Invective, a railing, reproaching, biting and bitter speech.

Inveigh, to rail against.

Inveigle (*f.* aveugler. to blind, or *I. Vagolare*) to allure or draw in.

Invelope, as *Envelope*.

Invention a finding out, a devise.

Inventory, -*tary*, a repertory or Catalogue of Dead mens goods, to be valued by four credible men (at least) and exhibited to the Ordinary.

In ventre sa mere. *f.* In his Mothers belly, the name of a writ.

Inversion, Inverting, a turning the inside out, or upside down.

Invest, to cloath, compass or besiege, also to give one possession of a thing.

Investigable, which cannot be searched or found out.

Investigation, a diligent search or enquiry.

Investiture, *l.* a giving possession, or endowing.

Inveterate, grown old, rooted, setled.

Invid, spightfull, malicious.

Invigilate, to watch carefully.

Invigorate, to give vigour, life, and courage.

Invincible, not to be conquered.

Inviolable, not to be violated or broken.

Inviron, as *Environ*.

Invious, without way or path.

Invisible, not to be seen.

Invitatory, belonging to

Invitation, a bidding or calling to.

Invitiate, to spoil or defile.

Inumbrate, to shade or cast a shadow upon.

Inunction, an annointing thorowly.

Inundation, an overflowing, a floud.

Invocate, to call upon.

Invoice, a particular of the value, custom & Charges of any goods sent by a Merchant (in another mans ship) and consigned to a Factor or Correspondent in another Country.

Involate, to fly in or upon.

Involve, to wrap or fold in, intangle or overwhelm.

Involvent, wrapping, &c.

Involuntary, unwilling.

Inurbanity, *l.* incivility, Clownishness.

Inure, *Enure*, *l.* to accustom, also (in Law) to take effect or be available.

Inusitate, *l.* not accustomed, seldom used, unusual.

Inutility, *l.* unprofitableness.

Invulnerability, a being

Invulnerable, *l.* not to be wounded.

Jö, Daughter of *Inachus*, turn'd into a Cow by *Jupiter*, that she might not be known of *Juno*, who drave her into *Egypt*, where she recovered her former shape and was made a Goddess.

Joab, *h.* Father-hood.

Joachim, *Jehoiakim*, *h.* preparation of the Lord.

Joan, the feminine of *John*.

Joannites, Knights of St. *John* of *Jerusalem*.

Joannitiques, Red Monks with the figure of a Chalice on their breasts.

Joash, *Jehoash*, *h.* the fire of the Lord.

Job, *c.* a guinny.

Job, *h.* sighing, sorrowing.

Jobelin (*f. Gobelin*) a sot or fool.

Jocalia, Jewels.

Jocarius, a buffoon or jester.

Jocasta, Daughter of *Creon* King of *Thebes*, after the death of her husband *Laius*, she unwittingly married her own son *Oedipus*.

Jockumgage, *c.* a chamber-pot.

Joclet Yoklet, a little farm, requiring a small Yoke of Oxen to plow.

Jocosity, *l.* merriness, a being

Jocose, *Jocund*, *Jocatory*, *Jocular*, *Joculary*, *Joculatory*, *l.* merry, jesting.

John, *h.* Gracious.

Joilite, *o.* for Jollity.

Joinder, *Joyn-*, the coupling of two in a suit against one another.

Join issue, put the cause to the trial of a Jury.

Joint Tenants, that hold lands or Tenements jointly, by one title or without partition.

Jointure, a settlement upon the wife in respect of marriage.

Join-ville, a Town of *Champagne* in *France*.

Jolaus, being old, was restored to youth by the Prayers of his Uncle *Hercules*, whose chariot he drove.

Joly & *Jolanus*, for *Julius* and *Julianus*.

Jollitrin, *f.* a Youngster, or young Gallant.

Jombre, *o.* to joyn.

Jonah, -*as*, *h.* a Dove.

Jona-

Jonathan, *h.* the gift of God.

Jongleric, *f.* Jugling.

Joncade, *f.* a Spoon-meat of Cream, rose-water and Sugar.

Jonism, -*ick*, belonging to

Jonia, a Country of *Asia* the less.

Iö Pæan, a voice or song of rejoicing [to *Apollo*.]

Jopas, a musical King of *Africa*, one of *Dido*'s Suiters.

Joram, *Jeho-*, *h.* the height of the Lord.

Jor and Dan, the two heads of

Jordan, *h.* the River of Judgment.

Joscelin, *Justulus*, a Diminutive of

Jost, *Justus*, or Jodocus. Joyce.

Joseph, *h.* Encrease.

Josias, *h.* the fire of the Lord.

Josuah, *Jesus*, *h.* Saviour, a Name common to the Generals of Armies.

Iöta, *g.* Jod, *h.* the letter I, (being the smallest of them all) a thing of little or no value.

Iotacism, a frequent beginning with the letter I; also a fault in pronouncing it too broad. All (but Englishmen) pronounce it *ee*.

Jove, (*q. Jehove*) *Jupiter*.

Jovial, (like *Jupiter*) Noble, also pleasant or merry.

Jouketh, [the hauk] sleeps.

Journal, *f.* a diary or day-book, also as much land as a team of Oxen can plough in one day.

Jouissance, *f.* mirth or jollity.

Journ choppers, regraters of yarn.

Journé, *f.* a day, a daies journey or work, a day of battel.

Journy-man, working [properly by the day, but now] by the year.

Joyce, *Jocosus*, -*sa*, merry.

Joyes of Planets, when they are in those houses where they are most powerful.

Jowe, *o.* for jaw.

Joyeux, *f.* joyful.

Joyleyning, *o.* the same.

Ipent, *o.* pin'd or pen't.

Iphianassa, *Iphinoe* and *Lysippe*, Daughters of *Prœtus* King of *Argos*, preferring their beauty to *Juno's* were by her struck with madness, imagining themselves to be Cows.

Iphicles, -*clus*, Son of *Amphitryo* by *Alcmena*, who bore him with *Hercules* (by *Jupiter*.)

Iphicrates, an *Athenian* Captain, who banished himself because they would not be guided by him.

Iphigenia, *Agamemnons* Daughter, which should have been sacrificed to *Diana* because her Father had slain a Hart of hers, but the Goddess pityed her and sent an Hart to be offered in her stead.

Iphimedia, ravished by *Neptune*, brought forth *Ephialtes* and *Otus*, who grew (every moneth) nine fingers in length, till (helping the Gyants against the Gods) they were slain by *Apollo*.

Iphis, a young man who hang'd himself for the love of *Anaxarete*, who was also turn'd into a stone.

Iphis, a Cretan Virgin turn'd into a man on her wedding day (at the prayers of her Mother) to avoid the anger of her husband *Lygdus*, who supposed her to be a man and had provided her a wife, he having commanded her Mother, if she brought forth a girl, to destroy it.

Ippocrass, as *Hippocras*.

Ipriued, *o.* searched, pryed into.

Ipsissime, *l.* the very same.

Ips, a Town on the River *Ips* in the higher *Austria*.

Ipswich, the chief Town of *Suffolk*, where Cardinal *Wolsey* (a Butchers Son) was born.

Ipulled, *Ipolid*, *Ipolish:d*, *o.* smoothed.

Iracundious, teasty, soon angry.

Iradde, -*rad*, *o.* readd.

Irascible, subject to or capable of anger.

Irayled, *o.* covered.

Irayed, *o.* arrayed.

Irching, *o.* Urchin.

Irchinfield, *Archenfield*. Where *Hereford* now doth, and the old *Ariconium* did stand.

Ire al largum, to go at large, escape, or be set at liberty.

Ire, *f.* anger, wrath.

Ireland, Western Island and Kingdom subject to *England*.

Irene, the Mother of *Constantine* he seaventh, reign'd with him 9 years, he expelled her and reign'd alone 7 years again she took him by craft, put out his eyes, cast him into prison (where he died) and reigned alone 4 years.

Iris, *Juno's* messenger, the rain-bow, also an hexagonal precious stone.

Irmunsul, *Ermisul*, (supposed to be *Mercury*) worshipped by the ancient Britains.

Ironical, belonging to an

Ironie, *g.* a speaking by contraries or mockingly.

Iron-sick, leaky, by reason of the Irons being rusty and hollow in the planks.

Iroquois, a people of *Canada* in *America*.

Irradiate, *l.* to enlighten or shine upon.

Irrational, *l.* unreasonable.

Irrecordable, not to be remembred.

Irrecuperable, *Irrecoverable*, *unre-*, not to be recovered, utterly lost.

Irredivivous, which cannot be revived or repaired.

Irrefragable, unbreakable, undeniable.

Irregularity, a being

Irregular, disorderly, out of rule,

rule, also uncapable of taking holy Orders, as being maimed, base-born, criminal, &c.

Irreligious, ungodly, prophane.

Irremeable, from whence there is no returning.

Irremediable, *l.* not to be remedied.

Irremissible. *l.* not to be remitted or pardoned.

Irremunerable, *l.* which cannot be rewarded or recompensed.

Irreparable, *l.* which cannot be repaired or made up again.

Irreplevisable, *-isable*, not to be replevied or set at large upon sureties.

Irreposcible, *l.* not to be required again.

Irreprehensible, *l.* unreprovable, blameless.

Irresolute, unresolved, doubting.

Irreverent, rude, without reverence.

Irrevocable, *l.* not to be revoked or called back.

Irrigate, *l.* to water or moisten.

Irriguous, *l.* that is or may easily be watered or washed.

Irrision, *l.* a laughing at.

Irritate, *l.* to provoke or stir up.

Irrite, *l.* void, of no effect or weight.

Irroborate, *l.* to make strong.

Irrogation, *l.* imposing a tribute, penalty, &c.

Irrorate, *l.* to bedew, besprinkle or moisten.

Irruent, *l.* rushing-in.

Irrugation, *l.* a wrinkling.

Irrumpent, *l.* breaking in.

Irruption, *l.* a violent breaking-in or forced entrance.

Irus, a beggerly messenger between *Penelope* and her suiters, whom *Ulysses* kill'd with his fist.

Isaac, *h.* laughter.

Isaca, *Isca*, the River *Ex*.

Isagogical, belonging to

Isagogue, *g.* an introduction.

Iseland, the utmost Northern Island.

Isca Dunmoniorum, *Excester*,

Isca Silurum, *Caerleon* in *Monmouthshire*.

Iscariot, (*q. Ish Carioth*) *h.* one of *Carioth* a Town in *Judaea*.

Ischia, an Island near *Naples*.

Ischiatick, *g.* troubled with the Sciatica or Hip-gout.

Ischnotes, *g.* a slender, childish or Foeminine pronunciation.

Ischuria, *g.* a stoppage or difficulty of Urine.

Isembourg, a County of *Veteravia*.

Ishmaelite, *Ism-*, one descended from, or like to

Ishmael, *Ism-*, *h.* God hath heard, or the hearing of God.

Ishad, *Ished*, *o.* scattered.

Ishet, *o.* shut.

Ishorn, *o.* (for shorn) docked.

Ishove, *o.* set forth, shown.

Isicle, (*q.* Icicle, or small ice) hanging at the house-eaves, &c.

Isis, an Egyptian Goddess made of *Iö*.

Isis, the River *Ouse* in *Wiltshire*.

Islip, *Gislipe*, a Town in *Oxfordshire*, where King *Edward* the Confessour was born.

Isonomy, *g.* equality of Goverment under the same Laws.

Isonglass, *Isin-*, as *Ichthyocolla*.

Isosceles, *g.* [a triangle] with two equal sides and opposite angles.

Isota de Nugarolis, a virgin of *Verona*, famous for Philosophy, Philology and Poetry.

Ispahan, the Metropolis of *Persia*.

Isped, *o.* dispatched.

Ispended, *o.* considered.

Isperi, *o.* (*q.* Vespers) Orison.

Israelites, the Children of *Israel*, *h.* (prevailing with the Lord) *Jacob*.

Issachar, *h.* Wages.

Issue, an effect, Children, profits of fines or lands, the matter depending in suit.

Istalled, *o.* placed.

Isthmian, belonging to the

Isthmus, *-us*, *g.* Neck of land between two Seas [whereon *Corinth* stands.]

Istrained, *o.* (for strained) tied close.

Istria, part of *Italy* joyning to *Illyricum*, and subject to *Venice*.

Isurium Brigantum, an ancient City in *Yorkshire*, out of whose ruines was raised *Ealdburg* or *Aldborow*.

Iswent, *o.* swinged, tossed.

Italianated, which doth

Italianize, play the

Italian, one of (or belonging to)

Italia, *-ly*, one of the most famous Countries in *Europe*, whose chief City is *Rome*, where the Pope hath his seat.

Italiana, a kind of Mercers stuff.

Iterate, *l.* to repeat, do or say a thing over again.

Ithaca, an *Ionian* Isle (where *Ulysses* was Prince) full of Goats, but no hare can live there.

Ithee, *o.* to thrive.

St. *Ithies*, a Town in *Cornwall*.

Itinerant, *l.* traveling up and down.

Itinerary, belonging to a journey, also a Calender of miles, lodging and other passages on the way.

Itinerate, *l.* to travel or take a journey.

Itwight, *o.* (*q.* twitched) drawn.

Itylus, slain by his own mother *Aedon* instead of *Amaneus* the Son of *Amphion*.

Itys, slain by his Mother *Progne* and set before his Father *Tereus* (King of *Thrace*) at a banquet, for deflowring her sister *Philomel*; he perceiving the murder, with his naked

naked sword pursued them, but (in their flight) they were changed, *Progne* into a Swallow, *Philomel* into a Nightingale, and *Itys* to a Pheasant.

Jub (*q. Jug.*) *o.* a bottle.

Juba, King of *Mauritania*, a Constant friend to *Pompey* and his party.

Jubal, *h.* fading, or a trumpet.

Jubarb, (*q. Jovis barba*) houseleek.

Jubeb, *Jujubes*, *Sericum*, (*A. Zufalzef*) a kind of prune, used much in Physick.

Jubilation, *l.* a shouting for joy.

Jubilate Lector, having read Divinity fifteen years.

Year of Jubile, *-lee*, among the Jews every fiftieth year, when with Jobels (Rams-horns) and trumpets they signified their rejoycing and remission. Among Christians ordained by Pope *Boniface* the Eighth (1300) to be kept every hundredth year, by *Clement* the sixth, every fiftieth year, and by *Sixtus* the fourth (as it now stands) every 25 year, beginning it first *Anno* 1475.

Jucatan, a *Peninsula* of New *Spain*.

Jucundity, *l.* pleasantness.

Judah, *Jehudah*, *h.* Confession.

Judæa, *Chananæa*, *Canaan*, part of *Syria*, the holy land or land of promise.

Judaick, *-cal*, Jewish.

Judaism, the Faith, Custom or Religion of the Jews; also a Mortgage.

Judas, *Jude*, as *Judah*.

Judas tree (with broad leaves) whereon he is supposed (by some) to hang himself.

Judgement. *Judicium*, the second part of Logick disposing Arguments, as the first part (Invention) finds them out.

Judicabl, which may be judged.

Judication, the giving of judgment.

Judicatory, *-ture*, *l.* a place of judgment.

Judicial, *-ary*; belonging to a

Judge or Judgement.

Judicious, full of judgment, wise.

Judicium Dei, tryal of *Ordel*.

Judith. *h.* praising.

St. Ives, a town in *Huntington*.

Ivetot, a town of lower *Normandy* in *France*, whose governour was called

King of *Ivetot*, one of a great Title and small inheritance.

Jugal, *l.* belonging to a Yoke or Wedlock.

Jugament, *l.* a yoking or coupling.

Jugular, *-arie*, belonging to the throat.

Jugulation, *l.* a killing or cutting ones throat.

Jugum terræ, half a ploughland.

Jugurth, *-tha*, King of *Numidia*, taken by the *Romans* (after a long war) and brought to *Rome*, where he died in prison.

Ivingoe, a town in *Bucks*.

Juise, *o.* Judgement, trial, examination.

Jujubes, *-uves*, Jubeb-fruit, *Italian* plums like Olives.

Juitland, *Jut-*, North and South, parts of *Denmark*.

Juke, to pearch or roost as a hawk.

Julep, *A.* a preparative (of Syrups &c.) to open the inward parts and prepare for a purgation. from

Julap, *P.* a kind of Rose-water.

Julian, *-nus*, a *Roman* Emperour who apostatized from Christianity to Heathenism.

Julian, *-na*, *Gilian*, a Womans name.

Julian Law (among the *Romans*) made Adultery death.

Julian Account, Old, *English* account, whereby the year consists of 365 dayes and 6 hours, a Correction of the Calendar made (44 years before the birth of Christ) by

Iulius Cæsar, the first *Roman* Emperour, he subdued *France*, *Spain*, *Britain*, and the greatest part of *Germany*, reigned 3 years, and was stab'd in the Senate-house.

Iuliers, an Imperial town and Dukedome.

Iulio, an *Italian* coyn (about 6 d. value) in the papacy of Pope *Iulius*.

Iulus, *g.* (soft-haired or mossy-bearded) *Ascanius*, the son of *Æneas*, also a son of *Ascanius*.

Iullaber, a little hill in *Kent*, where (they say) *Iullaber* (a Giant or Witch) was buried, or where *Laberius Durus* (a Captain of *Iulius Cæsars*) was slain.

Iuly, *Quintilis*, the fifth Moneth from March, so called in honour of *Iulius Cæsar*.

Iumbals, certain sweet-meats

Iumentarious, belonging to a

Iument, *l.* a horse or any labouring beast.

Iument, *f.* a mare.

Iuncaria, a soil where rushes grow.

Iuncto, (*Iunta*, *Sp.*) a Cabal, Combination of particular persons.

Juncture, *l.* a joynt or joyning.

Juncture [*of time*] the very nick or moment.

Juncture [*of affairs*] the present posture.

Jungible, which may be joyned.

Junk, any piece of an old Cable.

Junonian, *-ick*, belonging to

Juno, Twin-sister and Wife to *Jupiter*.

Juno's tears, the plant *Vervain*.

Juniority, a being

Junior, *l.* Younger.

Junto, *Sp.* as *Juncto*, a meeting of men to sit in Council.

Juon, o. John.
Ivory, f. Elephants Teeth.
Jupart, o. Jeopardy.
Jupiter, Son of *Saturn* and *Ops*, he conspired against his Father, expelled him and divided the Empire between Himself, *Neptune* and *Pluto*.
Jupiter Belus, second King of *Babylon*, Son of *Nimrod* (or Saturn.)
Jupiters distaffe, *Mullein*, *Candelaria*, a kind of Clary.
Jura Regalia, as *Regalia*.
Juration, l. a swearing.
Jurate, l. sworn.
Jurates, Aldermen, or Sheriffs.
Jurden, *Jurdan*, *Jordan*, *Jourdon*, (q. *Gor-den*, *sa. stercus cubilis*) a Chamber-pot.
Juridick, *-cal*, l. belonging to the Law, lawful, actionable.
Juridical day, a Court-day.
Jurisdiction, l. authority, also the compass or extent thereof.
Juris prudence, l. knowledge or skill in the Laws, also the stile or form of the Law.
Jurist, a Lawyer.
Jurn-choppers, as *Journ-*.
Juror, one of the
Jury, a Company of men sworn to deliver a truth upon such evidence as shall be delivered to them.
Grand Jury, twenty four grave and substantial men.
Petit Jury, twelve men (at least.)
Juris utrum, a writ for the incumbent whose Predecessour hath alienated his Lands or Tenements.
Jury-mast, made at Sea, in case of necessity.
Ivry, a Town in *Normandy*.
Jus Coronæ, (Crown-Right) part of the Law of *England*, and (in many things) differs from the General Law.
Jus Curialitatis Angliæ, the Courtesie of *England*.
Jus Patronatus, the right of Patronage or presenting a Clerk to a Benefice.
Jussel, a minced dish of several meats.
Jussulent, l. full of, or stewed in broth.
Justes, f. Turnaments or Tiltings on horse-back with spears and lances.
Justice, *-cer*, *-cier*, f. a Judge or Administrer of Justice.
Lord Chief Justice of the Kings Bench, he hears and determines all Pleas of the Crown, Treasons, Felonies, &c.
Lord Chief Justice of the Common-Pleas, he hears and determines all causes at the Common-Law, that is, all Civil causes (personal and real) between common persons.
Lord Justice of the Forest, Justice in eyre of the Forest, one which hath Jurisdiction over all the Forest on this side *Trent*, and another over all beyond.
Justices of Assise, sent (by special commission) into this or that (but not his own) County, to take Assises for the Peoples ease.
Justices of Oyer and Terminer, deputed (upon special and extraordinary occasions) to hear and determine some particular causes.
Justices errants or in Eyre, were sent with Commissions into the Country to determine the Pleas of the Crown; for the ease of the Subject, who must else have com'n to the Courts at *Westminster*.
Justices of Gaol-delivery, sent with Commission to hear and determine all causes belonging to any cast into Gaol.
Justice of the hundred, the Lord or Alderman of the Hundred.
Justices of Labourers, appointed to redresse their frowardness, who would either not work or have unreasonable wages.
Justices of Nisi prius, are (now) the same with Justices of Assises. Some make this difference, that the first have jurisdiction in causes personal as well as real, and these (in strict acception) deal only in Possessory writs.
Justices of Trail-baston, (f. draw-staff,) Inquisitours appointed by King *Edward* the first, on occasion of great disorders in the Realm, during his absence in the Scotish and French wars.
Justices of the Pavilion, authorised by the Bishop of *Winchester* (at a fair held near that City) by virtue of a grant from King *Edward* the fourth.
Justices of the Peace, appointed (by the Kings Commission) to attend the peace of the County where they dwell.
Justicements, all things belonging to Justice.
Justicies, a writ for the Sheriff to dispatch some special cause above the ordinary reach of his County-Court.
Justiciable, subject to authority or Law.
Justicium, *Lawsteed*, vacation, a stay or ceasing from ministration of Justice.
Justifical, executing or doing Justice.
Justification, a justifying, clearing, maintaining, making good or shewing a good reason for.
Justificators, Compurgators, which (by oath) justifie the Innocency, report or oath of another.
Justinians, Fryers and Nuns instituted 1412 in
St. *Justines*, an Abbey at *Padua*.
Justinianists, *Civilians*, Students of the Civil Law, reduced into the *Code* and *Pandects* by
Justinian, *-nus*, an Emperour of *Rome*.
Justinopolis, *Calo d' Istria*, a City of *Istria*, built by the Emperour *Justine*.

Jutties,

Jutties of houses, those parts that jut or stand out beyond the rest.

Juturna, the Daughter of *Daunus*, made by *Jupiter* (for the loss of her maidenhead) the immortal Nymph of the River *Numicius*.

Juvenal, a Roman Satyrist.

Juvenility, a being

Juvenile, *l.* youthful, lusty.

Juventas, *Hebe* Daughter of *Juno* without a Father, the Goddess of Youth, also young age.

Juverna, *Hibernia*, *Ireland*.

Iwimpled, *o.* muffled.

Iwis, *o.* certainly.

Ixions wheel, (a feigned punishment in hell) continually turning about, having fastened on it

Ixion, Son of *Phlegyas*, thrown to hell for boasting that he had lien with *Juno*, in whose stead *Jupiter* had placed a Cloud, on which he begat the Centaures.

Iwroke, *o.* wreaked.

Iwry, *-yen*, *o.* hidden.

Iven, *o.* eyes.

Izhak, as *Isaac*.

K

K*Ab*, as *Cab*.

Kabballa, as *Cabala*.

Kale, *Cale*, *Che.* a turn (*vicem.*)

Kalends, (as *Calends*) beginning [of the Moneth.]

Kali, Glass-wort, the herb whose ashes make Chrystal glasses.

Kallo, a Town in North-*Juitland*.

Kaminieck, the chief Town in *Podolia*.

Kamp fight, as *Camp-fight*.

Kantref, as *Cantred*.

Karavan, *Kacabar*, as *Caravan*.

Kardiognostick, as *Cardiogn-*.

Karena, (in Chymistry) the twentieth part of a drop.

Karle, *Sa.* a man or Clown.

Karle-cat, *Li.* a he, or bore-cat.

Karnten, a Province of lower *Austria* in *Germany*.

Karobe, *Ca-*, *Karoble*, the Fruit of the Carobe-tree, also the herb St. *Johns bread*, also the 24 part of a grain.

Karos, *Ca-*, *g.* head-ach, drowsiness.

Karrata fœni, a load of hay.

Karyn, *o.* Lent.

Katharine, as *Catharine*.

Katzen silver, a stone said to be invincible by fire or water.

Kayage, Wharfage, see *Key*.

Kazzardly [*Cattel*,] *No.* subject to dye or to Casualties.

Keale, *Li.* a cold.

Keals, as *Kiles*.

Keckle, the Cable or bolt-rope, serve them with a small rope, to keep them from galling.

Kedel, as *Kiddle*.

Kedge, *Sf.* brisk, lively.

Kedger, *Kedger-Anchor*, used in bringing a ship up a narrow place.

Keel, the lowest Timber or bottom of a ship, also a vessel to cool new drink in.

Keels, *Keyls*, *Cyulæ*, a kind of long boats, used by the Saxons.

Keelson, the Timber (fastened to the keel) above the ground-timbers.

Keen, *Kene*, *o.* sharp.

Keep, a place to keep fish in the water, and meat from flies.

Lord Keeper [*of the great Seal of England*,] through whose hands pass all Charters, Commissions and Grants of the King under the great Seal, the place and authority (since 5 *Elizabeth*) is the same as the Lord Chancellours, and therefore they cannot properly be both together.

Keepers of the Liberties of England, *Custodes Libertatis Angliæ*, &c. the style or title of all judicial proceedings, from the beheading of the King till *Oliver* was declared Protector, called the Rump-time.

Lord [*Keeper of the*] *Privy Seal*, through whose hands pass all Charters before they come to the Great Seal, and some things which do not pass the great Seal at all.

Keeper of the Touch, Master of the Essay in the Kings Mint.

Keeper of the Forest, Chief Warden of the Forest, the principal Governour thereof.

Keenk, a little turn or doubling of a rope hindring the running smooth.

Keeve [*a Cart*,] *Che.* overthrow it, or turn out the dung.

Keeve, *Dev.* a brewers fat.

Keiked, *o.* stared.

Keisersberg, a Town in upper *Alsatia*.

Keisers-Lautern, a Town in the *Palatinate* of *Rhine*.

Kele, *o.* to cool, also pottage, *No.*

Kelewart, pottage-herb, Coleworts.

Kellow, *No.* Black-lead.

Kell, the Caul about the paunch.

Kelter, *Kilter*, *So.* frame, order.

A Kembo, (*I. Aschembo*, a-cross, or Ghembo) crooked.

Kemeling, *o.* a brewers vessel.

Kemmet, *Shrop.* foolish.

Kempt, (for kembed) *o.* trimmed.

Kempten, a City of *Schwabia* in *Germany*.

Ken, *c.* a house.

Ken, *sa.* to see or know, also view or sight, also to teach, *o.*

Kenchester, a Town in *Herefordshire*.

Kendal, a Town in *Westmorland*.

Kenkelm, *sa.* defence of his kinred.

Kenelworth, a Town in *Warwick-shire*.

Kennel, a pack [of hounds,] or the place where they are kept, also a foxes Earth or hole.

Kennets, a sort of course *Welsh* cloth.

Kenodoxy, *Ce-*, *g.* vainglory, or a being vainglorious.

Kenotaph, as *Cenotaph*.

Kenspecked, *No.* Markt or branded.

Kepen, *No.* to keep or care-for.

Kepe, *o.* care, also a fort.

Keppen, *o.* to hood-wink.

Kerchief, (*f. Couvrechef.*) a linnen dress of [old] womens heads.

Kerf, *o.* a great Company.

Kerfe, *Sf.* the furrow made by the saw.

Kerfte, *o.* carved.

Kerk, *Kirk*, *Sc.* a Church.

Kerle, *Dev.* a loyn [of veal, &c.]

Kermes, the grain of the Scarlet Oak.

Kern, *Br.* a horn.

Kern, to corn or salt.

Kern, an *Irish* Rogue, or light-armed footman; also a plain Country Farmer.

Kernels, *o.* Corners or holes in battlements.

Kernel, *o.* to fortify and embattel an house.

Kernel-wort, good against

Kernels, hard knots in the neck, &c.

Kerry, a County of *Munster-Province* in *Ireland*.

Kerse, as *Cresses*. *o.*

Kersey, (*D. Kersaye*, and *Karsaye*) a kind of stuff or slight Cloth.

Kerveth, *o.* grieveth.

Kesar, *B. Keisar*, *D. Cæsar*.

Kest, *o.* for *Cast*.

Kesteven, a third part of *Lincolnshire*.

Keswick, a town in *Cumberland*.

Ketch, a small kind of ship.

Kettering, a town in *Northamptonshire*.

Kever, *o.* Recover.

Key, *Kay*, (*D. Kaeye*, *f. Quay*) a Wharf, to land or Ship goods or wares at.

Key (in Musick) as *Cliff*.

Keyles, *o.* as *Keeles*.

Keynard, *o.* a micher, hedg-creeper or Truant.

Keyserswerd, a town of *Berg* in *Germany*.

Kibris, as *Abric*.

Kichel, *o.* a kind of cake.

Gods Kichel, a Cake given to Godchildren at their asking blessing.

Kid, *No.* a small brush-fagot.

Kid, *Kith*, *o.* known.

Kiderow, *Che.* a place for a sucking Calf to lie in.

Kidder, *Kiddier*, a Badger, or Carrier of Victuals to sel.

Kidderminster, a town in *Worcestershire*.

Kiddle, *Kidle*, *Ke-*, an open Wear to lay Weels in.

Kidnapper, *c.* a stealer or enticer away of Children, &c.

Kildare, a County of *Ireland*.

Kilderkin, (*q. Kinderkin*, *D.* a little child) the eigthth part of a Hogshead.

Kiles, *Keales*, *Kettle-pins*, (*f. Quilles*) Nine-pins.

Kilketh, an old servile kind of payment.

Kilkenny, a County in *Ireland*.

Kimbolton, a town in *Huntingtonshire*.

Kime, (*sa. Guma*) a man.

Kim-Kam, as *Camoise*.

Kimling, *Li.* a brewing-vessel.

Kimmel, *Kemlin*, *No.* a poudring tub.

Kinburgh, *Sa.* strength and defence of kindred.

Kinchin, *c.* a little child.

Kinchin-Cove, *c.* a little man.

Kinds, *-dels*, *o.* Young-ones.

Kinder, a great company [of Cats.]

Kineton, a town in *Warwickshire*.

*King of Herauld*s, King at arms, *Pater patratus*, the cheif of that society.

King of Ivetot, see *Ivetot*.

King of the minstrels, to see that the minstrels did their duty yearly (at *Tutbury* in *Staffordshire*) at our Ladies Assumption.

Kings Bench, where the King was wont to sit in person.

Kngs-cleer, a town in *Hantshire*.

Kings-Evil, a disease or swelling cured by the stroking of the Kings of *England* ever since King *Edward* the Confessor.

Kings silver, due to the King in the Court of Common-pleas for licences to levy fines.

Kings-bridg, a town in *Devonshire*.

Kings-spear, a flower good against the poison of asps.

Kings Swan-heard, keeper of his Swans. No fowl can be a stray but a Swan.

Kingstone [*upon Thames*] in *Surrey*, where *Athelstane*, *Edwin* and *Ethelred* were crowned in the open Market-place, also above 20 small towns.

Kingsale, *Kinsale*, an *Irish* port-town.

Kinrest, *o.* quiet (or kindly) rest.

Kintal, (*Sp. Quintal*) about an hundred pound weight.

Kirat, *a.* three grains.

Kirk, *Sc.* a Church.

Kirked, *o.* turning upwards.

Kirkby, above 20 small towns.

Kirkby-Morside, in *Yorkshire*.

Kirkby Steeven, and

K-Landall, in *Westmorland*.

Kirkbys-Quest, of all the lands in *England*, made by *John Kirkby* Treasurer to *Edward* the first 1277.

Kirkham in *Lancashire*.

Kirkton, in *Lincolnshire*.

Kitt, *No.* a Milking-pail like a churn.

Kit-kaies, the fruit of the ash-tree.

Kite, *Cu.* a belly.

Kitchiness-bread, *La.* thin soft oat-cakes.

Klick up, *Li.* Catch up.

Knap, a little hillock, also to browse.

Knap-sack, *Snap-*, a bag at a Soldiers back.

Knap-,

Knape, D. *Cnawa*, *Sa* Knave, a boy or Servant, also (as they often are) an unlucky or dishonest fellow.

Knares-brough, in *York shire*.

Knap-weed, *Iacea nigra*, an herb somewhat like *Scabious*.

Knarri, o. (q. *Knurry*) stubby, knotty.

Knave-line, a rope (from the Ram-head) to keep the new ties and halliards from turning about one another.

Knedde, o. for knit.

Knees, partitions (in plants) like knees or joynts; also crooked timbers that bind the ship-beams and futtocks together.

Knetles (q. *Knottles*) two rope-yarns twisted together (with a knot at each end) to sease a rope, block, &c.

Knet, o. (q. *Ghenett*, D.) neatness.

Knight, *Sa.* a Servant, Soldier or Horsman, a title of dignity (now) above an Esquire; also a timber (carved with some head) wherein are four sheevers, three for the halliards and one for the top-rope to run in.

Knights of Alcantara in *Leon*, as Knights of the Pear-tree.

Knights of the Annunciada or *-ation*, a Savoy-Order of fourteen, who wear a Collar of Gold and the Virgin *Maries* Medal.

Knights of St. Andrew or the Thistle, by *Achaius* King of *Scots*, *An.* 809.

Knights of Austria and *Corinthia* or St. *George*, instituted 1470 by the Emperour *Frederick* the 3d first Arch-Duke of *Austria*.

Knights Batchelour, our simple or plain Knights, the lowest but most ancient Order.

Knights of the Band or red Scarfe, instituted by *Alphonso* the 11th. King of *Leon* and *Castile*, An. 1330.

Knights Bancret or *Bann-*, made in the field by cutting off the point of their Standard and making it a Banner, and who may display their arms in a Banner in the Kings army. They that are created under the standard of the King personally present take place of Baronets.

Knights Baronets, erected by King *Iames*, and take place of *Knights Batchelours*, Ordinary Bannerets, and

Knights of the Bath, who bathed themselves (and used many religious ceremonies) the night before their Creation.

Knights of the Broom-flower, erected by St. *Lewis*, with this Motto, *Exaltat humiles*.

Knights of Calatrava in Spain, with a red cross on their left breast.

Knights of la Calza (the stockin) a *Venetian* Order.

Knights of the Chamber, made in the kings Chamber, in time of peace, not in the field.

Knights of the Carpet, who kneel on a Carpet in receiving their Order.

Knights of Christian Charity, made by *Henry* 3d of *France*, for the benefit of poor Captains and maimed Soldiers, whom he provided for.

Knights of the Crown Royal, instituted by *Charlemaigne* in favour of the *Frisons* who aided him against the *Saxons*.

Knights of Cyprus or the sword, by *Guy* of *Luzignan*, king of *Ierusalem* and *Cyprus*, 1195.

Knights of the Dane Broge, instituted by the king of *Denmark*, 1671 in memory of a victory over the *Swedes*, when the *Danish* Colours were seen (as they say) in the heavens.

Knights of the Dog and Cock, instituted by *Philip* the first of *France*.

Knights of the Dove, by *Iohn* the first of *Castile*, 1379.

Knights of the Dragon, Erected by *Sigismund* the Emperour, 1417.

Knights of the white Eagle, Erected in *Poland* by *Ladislaus* 5. 1325.

Knights of the Elephant, a *Danish* Order.

Knights de l' Espice, of the Ear of corn or the Ermine (which hung at a Collar of golden Ears) by *Francis* the first, 1450. in *Bretaigne*.

Knights of St. Gall or the Bear, by *Frederick* 2. Emperour 1213.

Knights of the Garter or St. George, the most Noble Order of *England*, instituted by King *Edward* the third, after many notable Victories. Under the Soveraign of the Order (the King) are five and twenty Companions. They alwaies wear their *George* and Star (or rather the Sun.)

Knights of the Gennets, the most ancient Order in *France*, created by *Charles Martel*, (after the discomfiture of the *Saracens* at *Tours*) 783. When many of those Gennets (like Spanish or Civit Cats) were found in the Camp.

Knights of St. George, an Order in *Genoa*.

Knights of the Golden Fleece, by *Philip* Duke of *Burgundy* at his marrying *Isabel* the Daughter of *Portugal*, of Thirty the King of *Spain* is chief.

Knights of the Golden shield, by *Lewis* the second, with this Motto, *Allons*, (Let us go.)

Knights of the Half-moon or Crescent, by *Renier* Duke of *Anjou* at his conquering *Sicily* (1462) whith this Motto, *Los* (praise.)

Knights of the Hare, fourteen Gentlemen knighted by king *Edward* the third in *France*, at the shouting of the *French*, which he thought was the onset of the Battel, but was only occasioned by the starting of a Hare at the head of their army.

Knights of the Holy Ghost, by *Henry* the *third*, born and crown'd

Crown'd King of *France* on Whit-sunday, this Order (though modern) is most used now in *France*.

Knights Hospitallers, the same as

Knights of St. John of Jerusalem, *Ioannites*, erected at *Jerusalem*, about the year 1104. by *Baldwin* the first, supprest in *England* (by *Hen.* the 8th.) for adhering to the Pope.

Knights of St. Iago, (*Iames*) a Spanish Order instituted by Pope *Alexander* 3d. they observe St. *Austins* rules, and their great Master is next to the King in State, having 150 thousand Crowns yearly Revenue.

Knights of the Iarre, instituted by *Don Garcia* King of *Navarre*.

Knights of Iesus Christ, a *Portugal* Order.

Knights of St. *Lazarus*, expelled *Jerusalem* and entertained by St. *Lewis*.

Knights of the Lilly or of Navarre, a French Order, by Prince *Garcia the 6th*. 1048.

Knights of the Virgin Maries Looking-glass, by *Ferdinand* Infant of *Castile* 1410.

Knights of St. Magdalene, by St. *Lewis*, to reclaim quarrels and Duels, and to mind them of Repentance.

Knights of Maltha, given them by the Emperour *Charles the* 5th. 1529. paying an yearly Heriot of a Faulcon (which is now paid to the King of *Spain*) when the Turk drave them from *Rhodes*, whither they came from *Jerusalem*.

Knight Marshal, he takes Cognizance of all transgressions and Contracts within the Kings House and Verge thereof.

Knights of the Virgin Mary in Mount Carmel, (by *Henry* the 4th. of *France* 1607.) an hundred French Gentlemen.

Knights of St. Mark, a Venetian Order.

Knights of San Maria de Mercede, a Spanish Order.

Knights of St. Maurice and Lazaro, instituted 1119. and the Duke of *Savoy* confirmed their great Master by the Pope.

Knights of St. Michael th' Archangel, 36 French Knights (instituted by *Lewis* 1469) whereof the King is chief.

Knights of the Militia Christiana, erected lately in *Poland*.

Knights of Montesia, in the Kingdom of *Valentia*, by *James* 2d. King of *Arragon*, at the extirpation of the Templars, 1317.

Knights of nova Scotia in the West-Indies, erected by King *James*, they wear an Orange-tawny ribban.

Knights of Orleance or the Porcupin, a French Order, with this devise, *Cominus & Eminus*.

Knights of the Post, whom you may hire to swear what you please.

Knights of the Pear-tree, or St. *Julian*, instituted 1179. called afterwards Knights of *Alcantara* in the Kingdom of *Leon*.

Knights of the Precious blood of Christ, (1608) by the Duke of *Mantua*, where some drops are said to be kept.

Knights of Rhodes, Hospitallers driven out of the Holy Land, and holding this Isle two hundred years, were forced from thence also by *Solyman*, and seated themselves in *Maltha*.

Knights of the Round-Table, King *Arthurs* Knights, a British Order, the most ancient (they say) of any in the World.

Knights of San Salvador in *Arragon*, instituted by *Alphonso* 1118. succeeding the Templars in *Montreal*.

Knights of St. *Sepulchre*, instituted by St. *Hellen* (a British Lady) after she had found the holy Cross, and confirmed by the Pope.

Knights of the Ship, by St. *Lewis* in an expedition against the Saracens.

Knights of the Shire or Parliament, two Knights (or Esquires) chosen (upon the Kings writ) by the Freeholders of every County, to consult in Parliament (on behalf of the Commons of *England*) touching the publick affairs of the Realm.

Knights of the Seraphims, by *Magnus* the 4th. King of *Sweden*, 1324.

Knights of the Star, a French Order with this motto, ——— *Monstrant Regibus astra viam.*

Knights of St. Stephen or Florence created by *Cosmo* Duke of *Florence*, *An.* 1591. in honour of Pope *Stephen* the 9th.

Knights of the Swan, the Order of the house of *Cleve*.

Knights of the Sword and Baudric, a *Swedish* Order.

Knights of Livonia or Sword-bearers, by *Albert* a Monk (and some rich Merchants) of *Breme*, 1203.

Knights of the Temple, Templaries, or

Knights Templars, instituted by Pope *Gelasius* or (as some say) *Baldwin* the 2d. about the year, 1119. Their Office and Vow was to defend the Temple, Sepulchre, and Christian Strangers, but growing vicious (after two hundred years) were supprest by *Clement* the V. and their Lands bestowed on the *Joannites*, of whom the Lawyers purchased the Inne founded by the said Templars in *Fleet-street*.

Knights Teutonick, *Mariani*, a mixt Order of Hospitallers and Templars, to whom the Emperour *Frederick* the 2d. gave *Prussia*, on condition to subdue the Infidels, which they did. Th' Elector of *Brandenburgh* was (at last) sole Master of their Order, for at at first they had three.

Knights of the Thistle, a French Order (in the house of *Bourbon*) constantly bearing this Motto, ——— *Nemo me impunè lacessit*, also the same as Knights of St. *Andrew*.

Poor Knights of Winsor, twenty six (old Soldiers, &c.) depending on the Order of the Garter.

Knights-fee, Inheritance sufficient to maintain a Knight, by some 800, by others 680 Acres, such as had 20 pound *per annum* (in fee or for life) might have been (till 17 *Car.* 1.) compelled to be made Knights.

Knights-fee, is also the rent that a Knight paies (for his fee) to the Lord of whom he holds.

Knight-service, a Tenure (abolished by 12 *Car.* 2.) obliging a man to bear arms in defence of his Country.

Knighten-Gyld, a Guild or Company of 19 Knights in *London* founded by King *Edgar*, giving them some void ground (without the walls) called Portsoaken Ward.

Knightle, *No.* active, skilful.

Knipperdolings, Hereticks (in *Germany*) following one *Bern. Knipperdoling*, contemporary and Companion with *John* of *Leyden*.

Knittlidg, the ballast of a Ship.

Knit-back, *Bone-fit*, consound, Cumfrey.

Knock fergus, (the Rock of *Fergus*.) an Irish Port town.

Knoll, a little hill, also a Turnep, *k*.

Knolls of Peace, *Duni pacis*, cast up by mans hand, near *Sterling* in *Scotland*.

Knopped, *o.* tied, laced.

Gold-knops, Crowfoots.

Knots (*q.* knuts [birds) a small delicious foul beloved of *Canutus* the Danish King.

Knot-grass, *Polygonum*, an herb (with long and narrow leaves) lying on the ground, good against the Stone, fluxes and inflammations.

Kolding, a Town in North-*Jutland*.

Koningsberg, a Town of *Mentz* in *Germany*, also a *Polish* University.

Korban, as *Corban*.

Krain, a Province of lower *Austria* in *Germany*.

Kunigunda, *Cu-*, wife to the Emperour *Henry* the 2d. to clear her self from the imputation of unchastity, went bare-foot and blind-fold on red hot irons.

Kydde, *o.* for kid.

Kyddier, as *Kidder*.

Kye, *No.* for kine.

Kyle, a County in the South of *Scotland*.

Kylham, a Town in *Yorkshire*.

Kylyw, an exaction (perhaps some kind of pottage) exacted by Forresters and other Bailiffs.

Kynyl, *o.* a litter [of Cats.]

Kyneton, a Town in *Herefordshire*.

Kyrk, (*g.* Κυριακὴ) a Church.

Kyrie Eleëson, *g.* Lord have mercy [upon us] used both in the Greek and Latin Liturgies, as (in like manner)

Christe Eleëson, Christ have mercy [upon us.]

Kyth, *Sa.* kindred or alliance, whence we say (though corruptly) neither kit nor kin, also to shew, see *Kid*.

Kytte, *o.* for cut.

L.

L*aas Latch*, *Lace*, *o.* a net, gin or snare.

Laban, *h.* white or shining.

Labarum, *g.* a banner or ensign, particularly that of *Constantine* the Emperour, having the picture of himself and Children, the two first Greek Capitals of Christs name wrought in gold and precious stones, in honour of his miraculous conversion by the apparition of the Cross.

Labda, the lame Daughter of *Amphion*, despised by the rest of the *Bacchidæ*.

Labdacism, as *Lamdacism*.

Labdanum, *Lad-*, *Land-*, a sweet transparent gum, from the leaves of the shrub *Cistus Ledon*.

Labefaction, *l.* a weakning or loosning.

Labels, ribbans hanging at Garlands, Mytres, &c. slipps of Parchment hanging at Indentures, &c. also the three lines which hang from the file of an Escutcheon, denoting the Elder brother.

Labeones, *l.* blabber lipp'd persons.

Labial, *l.* pertaining to the lips.

Labienus, one of *Cæsars* Captains in *Gallia*, who (in the Civil wars) clave to *Pompey*.

Lability, *l.* instability, a being

Labile, *l.* apt to slip or fall.

Laborarijs, a writ against those that cannot live, and yet refuse to serve, or that refuse to serve in summer, where they served in winter.

Laboriferous, *l.* enduring or taking pains.

Laboriosity, *Laborosi-*, a being

Laborious, of great pains and labour.

Labours, [the *Ship*] rowles and tumbles very much.

Labrador, *Sp.* a Labourer.

Labrous, *l.* having a brink or brim, or great lips.

Labyrinth, a maze, made with so many windings and turnings that one cannot easily get out, also any intricate business.

Lacca, a red gum from certain Arabian trees.

Lacedæmonians, people of *Lacedæmon*, *-nia*, *Sparta*,

Mastibrea, *Ebeda*, *Zaconia*, the chief City of *Laconia*.

Lacerable, *l.* which one may

Lacerate, *l.* tear in pieces.

Lacert, *l.* a Lizard, Ewt, Evet, Eft.

Lacession, *l.* a provoking to anger.

Lachanopolist, *g.* a seller of herbs.

Lache, *f.* Lazy.

Laches, *-esse*, *f.* Negligence.

Lachesis, one of the 3 Destinies.

Lachrymable, *l.* to be bewailed.

Lachrymate, *l.* to weep, also to drop with moisture.

Lachrymatory, a weeping-place, also a Tear-botle sometimes buried with ancient urns.

Lachrymæ Christi, Wine made near the Mountain *Vesuvius*.

Lack, an *East-India* gum (gathered by Ants) which makes the best wax.

Lacken, *o.* contemned, lessened.

Lacker, a varnish (whose chief ingredient is gum-lack) used in imitation of Gilding.

Laconick, *-cal*, belonging to

Laconia, *Zaconia*, a Country of *Peloponnesus*.

Laconize, to use

Laconism, the *Lacedæmonian* (short and pithy) speech, or hard life.

Lactary, *l.* a Dairy-house or man.

Lacte, *o.* an Offense.

Lacteal, *-eous*, *l.* milky.

Lactifical, *l.* breeding milk.

Lactucina, a *Roman* Goddess over Corn, when the ears began to fill.

Lacunation, *l.* a making of holes.

Ladanum, as *Labdanum*.

Ladas, *Alexanders* page, who ran so swiftly that the print of his foot could not be discerned in the sand.

Lad, *o.* fed.

Ladde, *o.* (*q. leaded*) led.

Lade, to load, also a passage of waters.

Ladenberg, a town in the Palatinate of the *Rhine*.

Laden, another.

Ladies-bedstraw, an herb in dry pastures, with small leaves and yellow flowers.

Ladies-bower, a plant with abundance of small branches and leaves, fit to make Arbours for Ladies.

Ladies-mantle, with a neat indented leaf almost like a star.

Ladies-smocks, a kind of water Cresses.

Lady traces, a kind of *Satyrion* or *Orchis*.

Ladogo, a town (and a large Lake) in *Moscovy*.

Ladon, an *Arcadian* River, where *Syrinx* was turn'd into a reed.

Laft, (for *left*) *o.* left off, also enclosed.

Lafordswick, *sa.* a betraying ones Lord or Master.

Laga, *sa.* Law.

Lagan, See *Flotson*.

Lagemen, *Lahmen*, *sa.* Good men of the Jury.

Lage, *c.* water.

Lagen, (*q.* flagon) a measure of six Sextaries.

Laghslite, *sa.* a [mulct for] breach of the law.

Lagophthalmie, *g.* a sleeping like a hare, with the eyes open.

Laguibray, a town in *Normandy*.

Lahor, a town and Kingdom under the *Mogul*.

Laiazzo, a Town in *Anatolia*.

Laick, *-cal*, belonging to the

Laity, (opposed to Clergy) the people not in holy Orders.

Laid-sterne, *sc.* (*q. Lead-star*) the pol-star.

Laines, (*q.* Layings) Courses or ranks of stone or brick in building.

Laire, the place where a Deer harbours by day.

Lairwite, *Lechirwite*, *Leger-geldum*, an ancient custom of punishing Adultery and fornication, by the Lords of some Mannors.

Lais, a *Sicilian* harlot living at *Corinth*, whose excessive rates made *Demosthenes* say, He would not buy Repentance so dear. By her instigation *Alexander* burnt *Persepolis*. She was killed by the women of *Thessaly* in the Temple of *Venus*.

Lait, *o.* allure.

Laius, *Jocasta's* husband, after whose death she married his son *Oedipus*.

Lake, *No.* to play.

Lake, a purple-colour paint, see *Lacca*.

Lake, (*D. Laecken*) *o.* fine cloth, Lawn.

Lamanny, (*f. l'aimant*) *o.* a lover.

Lambdacism, an insisting too much upon

Lambda, *g.* the Letter *L.*

Lambdoides, *Lamd-*, *Labd-*, the hindmost seam of the skull.

Lambeth, *-hith*, *Lomehith*, a town in *Surrey*.

Lambeth-house, a Palace belonging to the Arch-bishops of *Canterbury*, built by the Arch-bishop *Baldwin* 1183. where *Hardy-Cnute* the *Dane* died suddenly in the midst of his excessive luxury.

Lambert, *Sa.* Fair lamb, or far famous.

Lambition, *l.* a licking or light touching of a thing.

Lambitive, licking or lapping.

Lamborne, a town in *Berkshire*.

Lamech, *h.* poor or humbled.

Lamel, *l.* a little thin plate.

Lamers, *o.* thongs.

Lamia, a harlot to whom the *Thebans* built a Temple.

Lamiæ, *l.* fairies or female Spirits.

Lamination, *l.* a beating into a

Lamina, *l.* a thin plate of metal.

Lammas-day, (*q.* Lambmass or Loaf-mass) the first day of *August*.

La Mothe, a town in *Lorrain*.

Lampass, -*preys*, a Disease in a horses mouth, cured by burning with a hot Iron.

Lampadias, a constellation in the head of *Taurus*.

Lampetia and Phaëthusa, kept the Sheep of their Father *Phœbus* in *Sicily*.

Lampoon, a libel in verse.

Lamprey, Suck-stone, a fish with holes on the sides like eyes.

Lamsacus, a town upon the *Hellespont*.

Lanarious, *Laneous*, belonging to wool.

Lancaster, *Lon-*, the chief town (upon the River *Lone*) in *Lancashire*.

Lancelot, (a lance-knight) one of king *Arthurs* knights.

Lance-pesado, *Launce-*, *Lance-presado*, (*f. Lance-pessade*,) the lowest Officer in a foot-Company, Commander of ten.

Lancet, a Chirurgeons instrument in letting bloud.

Lanciano, a City of *Naples*.

Lanch, to put [a ship] a flote.

Lanciferous, *l.* Lance-bearing.

Landa, *Lawnd*, an open field without wood.

Landboc, a Deed whereby lands are holden.

Landegandman, One of the inferiour tenants of a Mannour.

Landcheap, a Customary fine to a Town, &c. at every alienation of Land in the same.

Landaffe (a Church on the River *Taff*) a City in *Wales*

Land, *La.* Urine.

Land-cape, an end of Land reaching farther into the sea than other parts of the Continent.

Good Land-fall, when we see the Land, according to the day of our own reckoning.

Landgable, a tax or rent issuing out of land.

Landgraviate, the Country which belongs to a

Land-Grave, *Lands-*, *Land-drossard*, *D.* a Count or Earl of a Province, whereof in *Germany* there are four,

Landes, a County of *Gascoigne*.

Landimers, Measurers of Land.

Land-locked, having the land round about us, and the Sea no where open upon us.

Landrecy, a town in *Hainault*.

Land-loper, *D.* a Vagabond that runs up and down the Country.

Landman, *Land-tenant*, the same as *Terre-tenant*.

Land-mark, whereby the Pilot knows how they bear by the compass.

Land-mate, *Heref.* He that reaps with another on the same ridge of ground.

Land-pirates, High way men.

Landskip, *Lantskip*, *D. Païsage*, *f. Parergon*, *g. By-work*, All that in a picture which is not of the Body or Argument, also a description of a fair prospect.

Landsperg, a City of *Brandenburgh* and of the higher *Bavaria*.

Landshut, a City of lower *Bavaria*.

Land-to, just so far off at sea, as one may discern the land.

Land-turn, the same from off the land by night, as a Brieze is off the Sea by day.

Lanfrank, an *Italian* Arch-Bishop of *Canterbury*, 1060

Langate, *Languet*, *f.* a long and narrow piece of Land &c.

Langot, *No.* Latchet [of the shoe.]

Lang de beuf (*f. Langue de bœuf*) a kind of yellow-flower'd buglos.

Langemanni, having *Soc* and *Sac*.

Langrel, a loose-shot going into the piece with a shackle and shortned, but flying out at length with half-bullets at the ends.

Langporte, a town in *Somerset*.

Langland, an Island in the *Baltick* Sea.

Langres, a City of *Champagne*.

Langued, *tongued*, having the tongue (*Gules*, *Azure*, &c.)

Languedoc, part of *France*, where the *Goths* continued long, and who say *Oc* instead of *Ouy*.

Languerth, -*goreth*, *o.* languisheth.

Languid, *l.* weak, faint.

Languifical, *l.* causing

Languor, *l.* a languishing, decaying, drooping.

Laniation, *l.* a tearing like a Butcher.

Laniferous, *l.* bearing wool or Cotton.

Lanifical, *l.* making wool or woollen Cloth, pertaining to such work.

Lanionious, *l.* belonging to a Butcher.

Lanipendious, *l.* weighing wool, spinning or making yarn.

Lanis de crescentiâ Walliæ, &c. a writ for the passing over of wool without custom being paid in *Wales*.

Lank, *o.* slender, weak.

Lanner, -*ret*, (*f. Faulcon Lanier*) a kind of hawk.

Lanniers, small ropes reeved into the Deadmens eyes of all the shrowds, to loosen them or set them taught.

Lanthony, an Abbey in *Monmouthshire*, enclosed with such

ſuch high Hills that the Sun is not to be ſeen there but between the hours of twelve and three.

Lamgrave, as *Landgrave*.

Lantskip, as *Landskip*.

Lanuginous, belonging to, or covered with

Lanuge, *l.* ſoft thin down.

Laocoon, Son of *Priam* and Prieſt of *Apollo*, he diſſwaded the *Trojans* from receiving the Horſe.

Laodamia, Daughter of *Bellerophon*, ſhe brought forth *Sarpedon* (King of *Lycia*) to *Jupiter*, and was ſhot with her own Arrows by *Diana*.

Laodamia, Daughter of *Acaſtus*, deſiring to ſee the Ghoſt of her Husband *Proteſilaus* (ſlain by *Hector*) died in his arms.

Laodiceans, the people of

Laodicea, a City in *Aſia*, where was held the

Laodicean Council, under *Pope Silveſter*, *Anno* 320.

Laodochus, Son of *Antenor*, in his ſhape *Minerva* came to perſwade *Pandarus* to break the league by darting at *Menelaus*.

Laomedon, Father of *Priamus*, and King of the *Trojans*, ſlain by *Hercules* for not performing his promiſe made for his preſerving his Daughter *Heſione* from the Sea-monſter, to which he was forced to expoſe her for defrauding *Neptune* and *Apollo* of their wages for building the City-walls.

Laon, a City of *Picardy*.

Lap, *c.* Pottage.

Lapicide, *l.* a Stone-cutter, or hewer of Stone.

Lapidable, which may be ſtoned.

Lapidary, a Jeweller.

Lapidarious, *-deous*, ſtony, like or belonging to ſtones.

Lapidation, *l.* a ſtoning to death.

Lapideſcence, *l.* a waxing hard like ſtone.

Lapideſcent, waxing hard, &c.

Lapidifical, making or breeding ſtones.

Lapidification, a making ſtony.

Lapis Calaminaris, as *Cadmia*.

Lapis Contragerva, a ſtone good againſt the biting of Serpents.

Lapis Hæmatites, a blood-ſtone.

Lapis Infernalis, a ſtone made of the ſame lye that black ſoap is.

Lapis Judaicus, a white ſtone (found in *Judæa*) about the bigneſs of an acorn.

Lapis Lazuli, as *Lazule*.

Lapis Nephriticus, a ſtone (good againſt the ſtone in the Kidneys) coming from new *Spain*.

Lapis Opprobrij, the ſtone of diſgrace at *Padua*, on which whoſoever ſits (acknowledging himſelf *Non-ſolvent*) cannot be impriſoned for debt.

Lapis Tutiæ, as *Tutie*.

Lapithæ, a people of *Theſſaly*, the firſt inventers of bridles and Saddles.

Lapland, *Laponia*, part of *Swethland*.

Lappaccan, belonging to a bur.

Lappiſe, when Grey-hounds open in their courſe, or hounds ſpend their mouths in the leam or leaſh.

Lapſe, *l.* a ſlip or fall.

Lapſed, let ſlip.

Lapſed Benefice, to which the Patron neglects the preſentation for ſix moneths.

Lap-wing, (*q. Cap-wing*) a bird well known.

Laquery, *l.* the roof of a Chamber vaulted.

Lar, the chief City of

Lareſtan, a Province (bearing the faireſt Dates, Oranges and Pomegranats) in *Perſia*.

Lara, *-runda*, one of the *Naiades*, on whom *Mercury* (inſtead of carrying her to hell for revealing to *Juno* the Love of *Jupiter* to *Juturna*) begat two twins called

Lares, *Penates*, the houſhold-Gods.

Lar-board, Port, the left ſide of a Ship.

Larceny, *f.* theft of perſonal goods or Chattels in the owners abſence.

Great Larceny, when the theft exceeds the value of 12 pence.

Petit Larceny, when it exceeds not that value.

Larch-turpentine, a kind of Roſin growing on the

Larch-tree, it hath leaves like a Pine and bears the drug *Agaricum* from

Lariſſa, a City of *Theſſaly*, and ſeveral other places.

Larding-money, paid the Marqueſs of *Wincheſter*, for his Tenants hogs feeding in his woods.

Larcow, *ſa.* a Maſter.

Lare, *ſc.* learning.

Large, (in Muſick) eight Sem'briefs.

Large, with a quarter-wind neither by nor before a wind, but betwixt both.

Laredo, a Port-Town of *Biſcay*.

Largeſſe, *f.* a boon, bounty or liberality.

Largifical, *l.* beſtowing bountifully and frankly.

Largiloquent, *l.* full of words.

Largitional, an Officer that overſees the beſtowing of gifts.

Larius, *Lago di Como*, the greateſt lake in *Italy*, containing (from North to South) ſixty miles.

Larmiro, a Port of *Theſſaly*.

Larta, a Town of *Epirus*.

Lark-ſpur, a flower (of ſeveral ſorts) much regarded of Floriſts.

Larons, *f.* theevs.

Lar-ſpel, *ſa.* a leſſon or Sermon.

Larval, belonging to a

Larva, *l.* a Ghoſt or Spirit.

Larvated, maſqued, for the repreſenting a Ghoſt or Goblin.

Larunda, the ſame as *Lara*.

Larus, a ravenous devouring bird.

Larynx, g. the head of *Arteria Aspera*, the instrument by which we speak.

Lasciviate, to give one self to

Lasciviousness, a being

Lascivious, l. wanton.

Lashlite, the Danish common forfeiture, *viz.* 12 Ores, (about sixteen pence each Ore.)

Lask, *Laxitas*, l. *Diarrhœa*, g. the wherry-go-nimble or looseness of the belly.

Lasking, *Veering*, quarter-winds, Large and Roomer, are (in a manner) all one.

Lassed, o. left.

Lassitude, l. weariness.

Last, D. a burden or weight, also (in the Marshes of *East Kent*) a Court of 24 Jurats.

Last of unpackt Herrings, 18 barrels.

Last of Codfish, 12 barrels.

Last of Wool, 12 sacks.

Last of Leather, 20 Dickers.

Last of Osmonds, 4 thousand weight.

Last of Herrings, ten thousand.

Last of Pitch, *Tar* or *Ashes*, fourteen barrels.

Last of Hides, twelve dozen.

Last of Corn or *Rapeseed*, 10 quarters.

Lastage, *Lestage*, *Lesting*, a Custom challenged in Markets and Fairs for ones carrying of things, or for wares sold by the Last, also the ballast of a Ship.

Last heir, the Lord or King, to whom the Land comes by Escheat, for want of a lawful heir.

Lase on, the bonnet to the course or drabler to the bonnet, &c.

Lash, bind any thing up to the Ship sides or Masts.

Lashers, the ropes that bind together the tackle and breechings of great Ordnance.

Lateh, o. release, let go.

Latchets, small lines (like loops) sown into the bonnet or drabler (to lase them together.)

Latching, *No.* catching, infecting.

Late, *Cu.* to seek.

Latebrous, full of

Latebræ, l. dens or hiding-holes.

Latent, l. lurking, lying hid.

Lateral, l. belonging to the side.

Laterality, a being side-wayes.

Laterane [Palace,] given to the Pope by *Constantine*, and belonging formerly to

Lateranus, a Roman Patrician who hid himself from business, and (being designed Consul) was slain by *Nero's* Command.

Lateritious, like or made of brick.

Lathe, *Lethe*, *Sa.* a great part of a County, 3 or 4 hundreds, &c.

Lathe, *Li.* a barn, also ease or rest.

Lathing, *No.* entreaty, invitation.

Latible, l. a hiding-place.

Laticlave, [a purple cloak] with broad nails or studs, a badge of the Senatorian Order.

Latifolious, l. having broad leaves.

Latimer, (q. *Latiner*, f. *Latinier*,) an interpreter or Translator [into Latin.]

Latinism, *-ity*, a speaking after the Latin Idiom.

Latinus, an ancient King of *Italy*, who marryed his Daughter *Lavinia* to *Æneas*.

Lation, l. a bearing or carrying.

Latirostrous, having a broad or flat bill.

Latitancy, *-ation*, l. a being

Latitant, lurking or lying hid.

Latitat, a writ whereby all men in personal actions are called originally to the Kings-bench, upon supposition that he lurks or lies hid.

Latitude, l. breadth, wideness.

Latitude of a place, the Arch of the Meridian between the Equinoctial and the *Zenith*.

Latitude of a Star, the Arch of a great circle (drawn by the poles of the Ecliptick) between th' Ecliptick and the Star.

Latitudinarians, the moderate Divines of the Church of *England*, abusively so called.

Latomy, g. a stone-quarry.

Latonian, belonging to

Latona, Daughter of *Cœus*, one of the *Titans*, on whom *Jupiter* begat the

Latonian-lights, *Apollo* and *Diana*, the Sun and Moon.

Laton, *-oun*, o. for Latten.

Lator, l. a bearer or messenger.

Latration, l. a barking.

Latred, o. for *Leytred*.

Latrie, g. worship or service.

Latrocination, l. a committing of robbery.

Latte, o. for led.

LatWeather, wet or otherwise unseasonable. *No.*

Lavare, *-atory*, l. a vessel or place to wash in.

La Val, a Town of *Anjou* in *France*.

Lavatrine, l. a sink or washing place in a kitchin.

Lau, a Town in the Dukedom of *Mecklenburgh*.

Laubach, the chief Town of *Carniole* in *Germany*.

Laudable, l. commendable, praise-worthy.

Lauds, praises, also part of the Roman service containing certain Psalms beginning with *Laudate Dominum*.

Laudanum, as *Labdanum*.

Laudative, [belonging to] a commendation.

Lauden, *Lothen*, part of *South-Scotland*.

Lave, l. to wash or Purge.

Lavamandt, a Town of *Carinthia* in *Germany*.

Th

The Lave, Cu. all the rest.

Lavedan, an Iron-grey Gennet bred upon

Lavedan, a *Pyrenean* Mountain, breeding the best horses of *France*.

Laven, (hive-out) o. draw empty.

Lavender, Spiknard, a common plant, also a Laundress, *o*.

Lavenham, a town in *Suffolk*.

Laver, a place or vessel to wash in.

Laverd, Loverd, Laford, o. Lord.

Laverne, a *Roman* Goddess, Patroness of the

Laverniones, Theeves.

Laverock, a kind of bird.

Lavinia, Æneas's wife, who gave name to

Lavinium, a City in *Italy*.

Launcegays, Offensive weapons prohibited and disused.

Launcelot, Lan-, Launcette (I. Lancetta) a fleam to let bloud, also a mans name.

Launcepesado, as *Lancepesado*.

Laund, Lawn (Sp. Landa) plain untilled ground (in a park.)

Launston, a town in *Cornwall*:

Lavolta, I. a kind of dance, also a course held in sailing.

Laureate, -ted, l. crowned with

Laurel, Baies, worn by the ancient *Roman* Triumphers.

Laurel and *Bay-tree* are confounded in Latin, but with us known to be two distinct trees.

Laureated letters, sent by the *Roman* Generals to the Senate (and bound up in Laurel) to give them notice of their victories.

St. *Laurence*, a *Roman* Deacon and famous Martyr, broyled to death for producing the poor (as the Treasure of the Church) to *Valerian* the Prefect.

Laurentalia, Feasts in honour of *Acca Laurentia*, Wife to *Faustulus*, who nursed *Romulus* and *Remus*, when exposed by command of *Amulius* King of the *Latins*.

Laurer, o. for Laurel.

Lauriferous, l. bearing bays or laurel.

Laustein, a town of *Mentz* in *Germany*.

Lausus, Son of *Numitor*, slain by his Uncle *Amulius*, also the son of *Mezentius* King of the *Hetrurians*, slain by *Æneas*.

Lausanna, a City of *Switzerland*.

Law, Sc. a hill.

Law of Arms, Martial law which directs how to proclaim and make war, to make and observe leagues, &c.

Law of Maneleta (a Cornweed) ordained by King *Kenneth* of *Scotland*, that if any suffered his land to be over-run with weeds, he should forfeit an Oxe.

Law of Marque, Mart or Reprisal, whereby men take the goods of them from whom they have suffered wrong (and cannot get ordinary Justice) when ever they catch them within their Marches or limits.

Law-Merchant, proper to Merchants, and differing from the Common Law of *England*. If one (of any two Joint- Merchants) die, The Executor shall have the Moiety.

Law Spiritual, the Ecclesiastical Law allowed by the Laws of the Realm.

Law of the Staple, as *Law-Merchant*.

Law day, View of Frankpledge, or Court-Leet, also the County Court.

Lawenburg, a town in *Saxony*.

Lawing of dogs, cutting off three claws of the fore-foot, or as Expeditating.

Mastiffs must be Lawed every three years.

Lawingen, a Town in *Schwaben* on the *Danaw*.

Lawland, an Island in the *Baltick* Sea.

Lawless-Court, held on *Kingshil* at *Rochford* in *Essex*, the Wednesday after *Michaelmas* at Cockcrowing; They whisper and have no Candle, and write with a coal. He that ows suit or service and appears not, forfeits double his rent every hour he is missing.

Lawless-man, an Outlaw.

Lawn, as *Laund*.

Lax, a certain fish without bones.

Laxation, l. a releasing, easing, or freeing.

Laxitomne, a town in the Isle of man.

Laxity, l. loosness, liberty.

Lay, f. a song, also as *Ley*.

Lay branches, bend them down and cover them, that they may take root.

Lay a land, Sail out of its sight, but if another point of land interpose, it is shut into it.

Layer, Bed, the Channel of a Sea-Creek, wherein Oysters are thrown to breed, and not to be taken till a large shilling may be ratled between the shels.

Lay-land, which lies untilled.

Lay-man, following Secular Employments, not of the Clergy.

Laystall, sa. a Dunghill.

Laystoff, a town in *Suffolk*.

Lazar, a poor man full of sores, &c.

Lazaretto, I. an hospital or Pest-house. At *Milan* is one 1800 yards in Compass with as many Chambers as are daies in the year.

Lazarus, h. Lords help.

Lazule, a blewish kind of marble of which they make the colour Azure, and much used in Physick.

Lazy, No. Naught, bad.

Leach,

Leach, o. a Physician.

Leaden, *Lidden*, *No.* a noise or din.

Leafdian, *Hle-*, *sa.* a Lady.

League, a Covenant or agreement, also the space of three miles.

French League, about two miles and an halfe.

Spanish League, somewhat more than three miles.

Leah, *b.* painfull.

The ship Leaks, is Leak, springs a Leak, makes (or takes in) water.

Leam, *Liam*, *Leash*, a line to hold a dog or hawk in.

Leander, a Young man of *Abydos*, who was wont (in the night) to swim over the *Hellespont* to *Hero* (one of *Venus's* Nuns) at *Sestos*, till at length he was drowned.

Lean nothing, *No.* Conceal nothing.

Leap, *Lib*, *Sf.* half a bushel.

Leap-year, as Bissextile.

Lear, *No.* to learn.

Learches, slain by his Father *Athamas* King of *Thebes*, who (in a raging madness) took him for a Lions whelp.

Lease, *o.* praise (*l. laus.*)

Lease, *f.* a demising or letting of lands or any Hereditament to another (for a certain term of years or life) for a rent therein reserved.

Lease parole, made by word of mouth.

Leassee, to whom the lease is made.

Leassor, he that lets it.

Leash, as *Leam.*

Leash of hares, hounds, &c. Three.

Leasing, *Sf. K.* Gleaning.

Leasings, *-ungs*, *sa.* Lies.

Leaven, a piece of dough salted and sowred, to ferment and relish the whole lump.

Leaveret, *Lev-*, *f.* a young hare.

Leauty, *o.* Loyalty.

Lecanomanter, he that useth

Lecanomancy, *g.* Divination by [water in] a bason.

Leccator, a riotous debauched person.

Lecca, a City of *Naples.*

Lech, *o.* for Like and Leech.

Lechnus, an *Arcadian* spring good against abortions.

Lectern, *-orn*, (*f. Lectrin*) a Reading-Desk.

Leck-on, *No.* pour on more [liquor.]

Lectistern, *l.* the adorning of a bed for a banquet (with the Images of the Gods, &c.)

Lector, *-tour*, *l.* a Reader.

Lecture, *l.* a Reading or lesson, also the place and Office of a

Lecturer, a publick Reader or Professour, an Extraordinary Preacher.

Leda, being deceived by *Jupiter* in the form of a Swan, she brought forth two egges, whereof one produced *Pollux* and *Helena*, the other *Castor* and *Clytemnestra.*

Leden, *o.* to languish, also (for Latin) Language.

Ledors, *o.* instead of

Ledoires, *f.* reproaches, revilings.

Ledges, small Timbers coming thwart ships (from the wast-trees to the Roof-trees) to bear up the Nettings.

Ledge, *o. Leg*, *Li.* to lay.

Lee, opposite to the Wind or Weather-gage.

A-lee the helme, put it to

Lee-side (not to the Weather-side) of the ship.

Look to the Lee-latch, that the ship go not to lee-ward of her Course.

Lay her by the Lee, with all her sails flat against the Masts, and the wind on her broad-side.

Le, *Br.* a place.

Lee, *Lew*, *Sf.* Calm, under the Wind.

Lee-fang, a rope reeved into the Creengles of the courses, to hale in the bottom of a sail

Lee-ward tide, when the wind and tide go both one way.

Leech, the outside or skirt of a sail from the Earing to the Clew.

Leech-lines, fasten'd to the leech of the top-sails.

Leechyd, *o.* dressed, seasoned.

Leed, *Lid*, *o.* March *q. Loud* [*month.*] Hence

Lide-pills, *o.* Cow-hides.

Leeds, a Castle in *Kent*, also a town in *Yorkshire.*

Leek, a town in *Staffordshire.*

Leer, the place where a Deer lies to dry himself from the dew.

Leero-way, *Lyra-way*, a tuning or playing on the Viol, differing from that of *Alphonso.*

Lees, *o.* to release.

Lees, Dregs [of wine, &c.] also, for *Leesing*, *o.* Lying.

Leeten you, *Che.* Make your self, pretend to be.

Leet, a Law-day.

Court-Leet, a Kings Court of Record (in whose mannor soever it be kept) it Enquires of all offenses under High Treason, punisheth some and certifies the rest to the Justices of Assise.

Lefe, *o.* (*q.* loveth, answering the Latin and Greek) is wont, also willing, and as

Leve, *Liefe*, *o.* dear, beloved.

Leethwake, *No.* limber, pliable.

Legacy, a particular thing given by a last Will and Testament.

Legality, *l.* lawfulness, keeping the law, the condition of a

Legalis homo, *Rectus in Curia*, Not out-lawed, Excommunicated or Defamed.

Legation, *l.* an Embassy, the office of a

Legate, *l.* an Ambassadour, or Oratour.

Legatee, *-tary*, *-tory*, he or she to whom any thing is bequeathed.

Leged, *o.* (*q. legged, layed*) resident.

Leggen, *o.* to allay, asswage.

Legging, *o.* lodging.

Legend

Legend, *l.* a writing [about the edge of a piece of Coin.]

Golden Legend, *-dary*, a Popish book of the lives of Saints, very fabulous.

Legeolium, *Castle-ford* in *York-shire*.

Leger-book, a register belonging to Notaries or merchants.

Legerdemain, *f.* slight of hand.

Legergild, as *Lairwit*.

Legiaunce, *o.* Allegiance.

Legible, *l.* which may be readd.

Legiferous, *l.* making or giving Laws.

Legionary, belonging to a

Legion, *l.* a Brigade or part of a Roman Army, consisting at first of 3000 Foot, and 300 Horse; encreased by degrees to 6000 Foot, and 3000 (or, as some say, 730) Horse, by some it is said to be an Army of 6666.

Legislative, belonging to the making of Laws.

Legislatour, *l.* a Law-giver.

Legist, *-ter*, *l.* a Lawyer.

Legitimation, a making

Legitimate, *l.* lawfull.

Leguminous, *l.* belonging to pulse.

Legs [*of the Martnets*,] small ropes (a foot long) put through the bolt-ropes of the main and fore-sail in the Leech, and (being splised into themselves) have a little eye whereinto the Martnets are made.

Leicester, *Legeocester*, *Legecestria*, *Leogora*, the cheif Town in *Leicester-shire*.

Leid, *sc.* a Language.

Leiden, *Leyden*, an University in *Holland*, erected by *William* Prince of *Orange*, 1575.

Leigh, *Ley*, a pasture, or as *Le*.

Leighton-Buzzard, a Town in *Bedfordshire*.

Leipsick, a Town in *Misnia*.

Leinster, *Lemster*, *Leighnigh*, a Province in *Ireland*.

Leit, *o.* Light.

Leith, a Town by *Edenburgh* in *Scotland*.

Lele, *o.* (*q.* lawly) lawful.

Léman, (*q.* lead-man, or rather *L' Aimant-te*, *f.*) a Sweet-heart or Lover (He or She) but vulgarly, the Concubine of a Priest or married man.

Lemán, *-nus*, the Lake upon which *Geneva* stands.

Lemes, *o.* lights, flames.

Lemnian, belonging to

Lemnos, an *Ægean* Isle into which fell the

Lemnian God, *Vulcan*, thrown out of Heaven by *Jupiter*.

Lemnian Earth, Vermillion or red Earth.

Lemburgh, a Town in *Podolia*.

Lemgow, a free City of *Westphalia*.

Lemster Ore, famous wool of

Lemster, *-tir*, *Leonminster*, a Town in *Herefordshire*.

Lemures, *l.* Hobgoblins.

Lends, *o.* the loyns.

Lene, *o.* to lend.

Lenitive, *Lenient*, softening, asswaging, causing

Lenity, *-tude*, *l.* softness, meekness, gentleness.

Lenham, a Town in *Kent*.

Lennox, a County in South-*Scotland*.

Lenonian, *l.* belonging to a bawd.

Lentiginous, full of freckles or pimples like

Lentils, small round and flat pulse growing in hot Countries.

Lent, *D.* (the Spring) the forty dayes of abstinence next before Easter, appointed here first by *Ercombert*, King of *Kent*, *An.* 641.

Lentiscine, belonging to the

Lentisk, the Mastick-tree.

Lentour, *l.* stiffness, clamminess.

Lentous, *l.* pliant, tender, limber, also idle.

L' envoy, *f.* the message, also the conclusion of a Poem, serving for dedication or short repetition.

Leonine, belonging to

Leo, *l.* a Lion, one of the 12 signs, also the Names of several Emperours and Popes.

Leocorion, a Monument erected by the *Athenians* in honour of

Leo, the Son of *Orpheus*, who sacrificed his three Daughters, to appease the Gods and divert a great Plague.

Leodegar, *Leodgard*, keeper of the people.

Leodium, *Liege*, a City in *Germany*.

Leofstan, *sa.* most beloved, or precious-stone.

Leofwin, *sa.* win-love.

Leoh, *sa* Light.

Leon, a Spanish Province and City.

Leonard, *sa.* of a Lion-like nature.

Leonidas, a famous Captain and King of the *Lacedemonians*.

Leopard, *Libbard*, an Affrican spotted beast begotten between a Pard and Lioness.

Leopold, *Leodpold*, *sa.* defender of the people.

Leopolis, *Lewenberg*, a town in *Russia nigra*.

Leorning-Cnight, *sa.* a disciple or Scholer.

Lepande, *o.* leaping.

Lep and lace, four pence paid the Lord of *Wittel* Mannour in *Essex*, for every cart (except a Noblemans) that passes over *Greenbury* (part thereof.)

Lepanto, *Naupactum*, a City of *Locris*.

Lepidity, a being

Lepid, *l.* neat or pleasant.

Leporean, *-rine*, *l.* belonging to a hare.

Leporarius, a Grey-hound.

Leprosity, a being

Leprous, full of

Lepry, *-rosie*, a white scurf all over the body.

Leproso amovendo, a writ for the removing of a Leper.

Leptology, g. a description of minute and sordid things.

Lere, o. for leather, also (*l'air*. f.) the air of the face or complexion.

Lerida, a Town in *Catalonia*.

Lernean, belonging to

Lerna, g. a water-serpent, also the Lake where *Hercules* slew the Serpent *Hydra*.

Lerpool, a Town in *Lancashire*.

Without Les, o. incessantly.

Lesbian, belonging to

Lesbos, an *Ægean* Isle, very exact in their buildings.

Lescar, a City of *Bearne* in *France*.

Lesinage, Lthriftiness, good husbandry, from

Lesina, I. a Coblers awl.

Lesingour, o. a Lyar.

Lesion, l. a hurting.

Lespegend, *Sa*. Youngmen.

Lessee, to whom the Lease is made.

Lesser, -*sor*, who lets the Lease.

Lesses, the dung of a Bear, or any ravenous beast.

Lessel, o. a shady bush or hovel.

Lessian diet, very moderate, prescribed by

Lessius, a famous modern Physician.

Lest, o. for lust.

Lestage, as *Lastage*.

Lestrigones, a barbarous and Giant-like people of *Italy*, whose King *Antiphates* tore one of *Ulysses*'s Companions in pieces with his Teeth.

Letchland, a Town in *Glocestershire*.

Letany, as *Litany*.

Leth, as *Lathe*.

Lete, o. to cease or leave.

Letest fare, o. (lettest go) makest a shew.

Lethality, l. a being

Lethal, l. deadly, mortal.

Letherwite, corruptly for *Lecherwite*, or *Lairwite*.

Lethargick, sick of, or belonging to the

Lethargy, g. the Drousie evil, a cold distemper causing excessive sleeping, the loss of sense and memory.

Lethæan, belonging to

Lethe, g. [a supposed River of Hell causing] forgetfulness.

Lethiferous, l. deadly.

Lethy, o. as *Lither*.

Letifical, *Laet*-, l. making glad.

Letter-missive, an Epistle or letter sent.

Letter of Atturney, Authorising an Atturney, that is, a man appointed to do a lawfull act in our stead.

Letters of Marque or Mart, authorising one to take by force of Arms those Goods which are due by the Law of Marque.

Letters Patent, Open writings sealed with the broad-seal of *England*, enabling a man to do or enjoy what otherwise of himself he could not.

Lettice, *Lactuca*, a plant breeding Milk.

Letice, *Lætitia*, Joy.

Lettowe, *Littaw*, *Lituania*.

Lettrure, *Literature*, book-learning.

Levament, -*ation*, a lifting up, easing or comforting.

Levant, f. the East [wind, Countrey, Sea, &c.]

Levant and Couchant, when Cattel have been so long in another mans ground, that they have lain down, and are risen again to feed.

Levari facias, a writ directing the Sheriff to levy mony upon the Lands and Tenements of him that has forfeited his Recognisance.

Levari facias damna de Disseisitoribus, a writ directing the Sheriff to levy dammages wherein the Disseisor has been condemned to the Disseised.

Levari facias quando Vicecomes returnavit quod non habuit emptores, a writ commanding the Sheriff to sell the Goods of the Debtor, which he hath already taken and returned, that he could not sell.

Levari facias residuum debiti, a writ for the Sheriff to levy the remnant of a debt that hath been in part satisfied.

Levatory, l. an instrument to elevate the depressed *Cranium*.

Leucophlegmatick, troubled with a

Leucophlegmatie, g. a dropsie caused by the abounding of white flegme.

Leucothea, *Ino*, *Matuta*, *Aurora*.

Leucothoe, turn'd into a Frankincense-tree by *Apollo*, who had gotten her with Child, for which she was buried alive by her Father *Orchamus* King of *Babylon*.

Leuctra, a Town in *Bœotia*.

Leud, *Lewit*, *sa*. ignorant.

Leve, o. for leave.

Level-Coil, I. (*Leva il Culo*) hitch-buttock, when one (having lost the game) sits out, and gives another his place.

Levellers, a factious part of the Parliament-Army (about the year *1649*.) who would have had all things common.

Lever, o. better.

Levessel, as *Lessel*.

Leveth, o. beareth.

Levi, h. joyned.

Leviathan, h. a Whale, or (by some) a great water-Serpent, also the Devil.

Levie, (*f*. *lever*) to raise, to gather or exact [money, &c.] to cast up [a ditch,] to erect [a mill, &c.]

Levigation, *Læv*-, l. a levelling, smoothing or making plain.

Levisomnous, l. watchfull, soon waked.

Levissa, *Lewis*, the largest Isle of all the *Hebrides*.

Levitical, belonging to the

Levites, those of the Tribe of *Levi*, whose inheritance the Priest-hood was.

Leviticus, a book describing the whole Levitical Order.

Leewarden, a Town in *West-Friezland*.

Levity, *l.* lightness.

Lewis, -*wes*, the chief Town of *Sussex*.

Lewis, (*f. Lovis*) *Lodowick*, *Ludwig*, *sa.* the defense of the people.

Lewlin, *Lewellin*, *Llew*-, *Br.* Lion-like.

Lex Bretoyse, -*oise*, *Lex Marchiarum*, the law of the *Britains* or Marches of *Wales*.

Lexicon, *g.* a vocabulary or Dictionary.

Lex talionis, a law returning like for like.

Lex deraisnia, or rather *Deraisina*, the proof of a thing which one denies to be done by him, and his Adversary affirms it.

Ley, *f.* (*ly*) the law.

Ley-gager, Wager of Law.

Leyden, as *Leiden*, built on one and-forty Islands.

Leyes, *o.* perhaps *Libyssa*, a City of *Bithynia*, or else *Levissa*.

Legerwit, as *Lotherwit*.

Leyton, a Town on the River *Ley*, about 5 miles from *London*.

Lhan, *Br.* a Church.

Liam, a leam or leash.

Liard, *o.* nimble.

Liart, *or* (*q.* pliant for pliant) gentle, lithe.

Libament, -*ation*, *l.* a [liquid] sacrifice.

Libanomancy, *g.* Divination by

Libanus, *g.* Frankincense

Libb, *o*, to geld.

Libbards-bane, *Doronicum*, a kind of herb.

Libben, *c.* a private dwelling house.

Lib edge, *c.* a bed.

Libel, *l.* (a little book) an original declaration of any action in the civil Law, also as *Infamous Libels*, an invective or slanderous Writing.

Libellatici, some primitive Christians having bought Libels or Testimonies of the Roman Magistrate, falsly declaring that they had been assistant at the Pagan sacrifices.

Liberate, a Chancery writ or Warrant to the Treasurer, Chamberlain and Barons of the Exchequer, to pay out any summe granted under the broad-Seal, or to the Sheriff to deliver possession of Lands and Goods extended.

Liberation, *l.* a freeing or delivering.

Libera batella, a free boat.

Libera Chasea habenda, a writ granting a free Chase proved to belong to the Mannour.

Liber [*Pater*,] Bacchus.

Liber taurus, a free Bull.

Libertas, *l.* a priviledge (by grant or prescription) to enjoy some extraordinary benefit, also a Roman Goddess whose Temple was on the hill *Aventinus*.

Libertate Probanda, a writ for such as were challenged for slaves, and offerd to prove themselves free.

Libertatibus allocandis, a writ for a Citizen (impleaded contrary to his liberty) to have his priviledge allowed

Libertatibus exigendis in itinere, a writ for the Justices in Eyre to admit of an Atturney for the defense of another mans Liberty before them.

Libertinage, -*inism*, -*nity*, sensuality, licentiousness, the state and condition of a

Libertine, *l.* one born or made free, also a loose and dissolute Epicure.

Libertinism (in Divinity) is defined to be, a false liberty of belief and manners, which will have no other dependance but on particular fancy and Passion.

Libethra, a Town on the Mountain *Olympus* destr ed by a violent flood.

Libethra, a Fountain of *Magnesia*, sacred to the

Libethrides, the Muses.

Libidinist, a sensualist, one that gives himself up to

Libidinosity, lasciviousness, a being

Libidinous, *l.* lustful, incontinent.

Libitina, the Goddess or superintendant of Funerals, Sepulchres and funeral Rites.

Libitinarians, *l.* bearers.

Libitude, *l.* will, pleasure.

Ad Libitum, at will or pleasure.

Libourne, a Town of *Guienne* in *France*.

Libral, belonging to

Libra, *l.* a pound weight, also the balance, one of the 12 Signs of the Zodiack.

Librarious, belonging o to books or to a

Library, a study or place where books are kept.

Libration, *l.* a weighing or balancing.

Librata terræ, contains four Oxgangs, and every *Oxgang* thirteen Acres.

Libya, *Africa*.

Licanthropy, as *Lycan*-.

Licand, *o.* well-liking.

Licaon, a King of *Arcadia* turn'd into a Wolf.

Licence to arise, a liberty or space given by the Court to a Tenant in a real action (Essoyned *de malo lecti*) to arise or appear abroad.

Licentia transfretandi, a Licence (from the King) of passing over-sea.

Licentiate, one that hath license or Authority to practice in any Art.

Licentious, loose, disorderly, unruly.

Lichas, a boy whom *Hercules* threw into the Sea (where he was turn'd into a Rock) for bringing him the poisoned shirt from *Deianira*.

Liche,

Liche, *o.* for like.

Lichfield, *Licidfield*, (field of Carcases) a Town in *Staffordshire*, where many (they say) were martyred in the time of *Dioclesian*.

Lich fowles, *sa.* (carcase-birds) Scrich-Owls, Night-Ravens.

Licitation, *l.* a cheapning or prizing, also a setting out to Sale and enhauncing the price.

Licite, *l.* lawful.

Lictorian, belonging to the

Lictors, *l.* Sergeants.

Liddesdale, part of South-*Scotland*.

Lidford-law, (in *Cornwall*) the course whereof is very summary, and is commonly taken for hanging men first and inditing them afterwards.

Lief, *Leof*, *sa.* rather.

Lief-hebber, *sa.* a Lover.

Lieftenant, *Lieut-*, *f.* holding the place or doing the office of another, a Deputy.

Liege, *Luykland*, a Bishoprick (in the *Netherlands*) called the paradise of Priests, where there is Coal (they say) kindled with water and quenched with Oyl or Salt.

Liege [*Lord*] *Soveraign*, owning no Superiour.

Lieges, *Liege people*, the Kings Subjects.

Liege-man, he that oweth

Liegeancy, (*l. Liga*, a league or bond) allegiance, fealty, faithful obedience.

Ligeance, the same, also the Dominion or territory of the Liege-Lord.

Lieue, *f.* a french league.

In Lieu, *f.* in place or stead.

Lientery, *g.* a flux of the Stomach or belly, presently voiding things undigested.

Liesse, a Town in *Picardy*.

Life-gard, *D. Gard du Corps*, *f.* the gard of the body.

Life-rent, an exhibition received for term (or sustentation) of life.

Lift hause, *o.* left hand.

Lifts, ropes serving to top the yard-arms or make them hang higher or lower, &c.

Lift, *Nf.* a stile to be opened like a gate.

Lifter, *Plyer*, *c.* a crutch.

Lig, *No.* to lye.

Ligament, *l.* a string or tyband, especially that wherewith the joynts of bones and gristles are fastened together.

Ligature, the same, also as

Ligation, a tying or binding.

Light-horse, lightly armed.

Light-mans, *c.* [break of] day.

Ligne, *f.* (corruptly lime) to couple as Dogs with Bitches.

Lignation, *l.* a providing or fetching of wood.

Lignes, *o.* liketh, yieldeth, or rather pleasure or liking.

Lignean, *-eous*, full or made of Wood, wooden or Woody.

Lignicide, *l.* a Wood-cutter.

Lignum Asphaltum, a kind of Bituminous Wood, supposed to grow by the Dead-sea.

Lignum Nephriticum, Wood brought from *Hispaniola*, good for the Stone in the Kidneys.

Lignum Rhodium, *Aspalathus*, a sweet Wood, of which is made the Oyl of *Rhodium*.

Lignum vitæ, the Wood called *Aloes*, by the *Arabians Calam u:o*.

Ligorne, *Livorne*, a Port-Town of *Tuscany*.

Ligue, *f.* a league, or alliance.

Ligula, *Uvula*, a little piece of flesh in the roof of the mouth.

Liguria, a hilly part of *Italy*.

Ligurion, *l.* a glutton or devourer.

Liguritiom, *l.* a Ravenous or gluttonous devouring.

Lily, the rose of *Juno*, a specious Flower,

Lilith, a kind of She-Devil, destructive to Children (as the Jews imagined.)

Lilium Paracelsi, the tincture of Antimony.

Lilliers, a Town in *Artois* one of the *Netherlands*.

Lillo, a Fortress in *Brabant*.

Lilybæum, a Sicilian Promontory, with a Town of the same name.

Lima la Ciudad de los reys, *Sp.* the City of the Kings or Twelf-day (because then the first stone was laid by *Pizarro*, 1553) the Metropolis of *Peru* in *America*.

Limagne, a Province in *France*.

Limaceous, belonging to a Snail.

Limail, *o.* *-aille*, *f.* Filings, steel-dust, &c.

Limation, *l.* a filing or polishing.

Limatura Martis, the filings of Horn, for the making of *Crocus Martis*.

Limb, part of a quadrant, &c. also the eclipsed part of the Sun or Moon.

Limbeck, an Alembick or Still.

Limbers, *Limber-holes*, square holes in the bottom of all the ground-timbers to let the water pass to the well of the pump.

Limburgh, a Town and Dukedom in the *Netherlands*.

Limbus Patrum, a place (on the borders of Hell) where the Holy Fathers were supposed to reside till the coming of our Saviour.

Limed, *o.* polished.

Lime-hound, *Limer*, bloud-hound, a great Dog to hunt the wild Boar.

Limenarch, *g.* the Governour of a Port.

Limerik, a Town and County in *Ireland*.

Liminarie, *f.* set at the entry or beginning of any thing.

Limitation, a stinting or

or setting of bounds.

Limitation of Assize, a certain time set down by Statute, wherein a man must alledge himself or his Ancestor to have been seized of Lands sued for by a writ of Assise.

Limning, a kind of painting in water-colours.

Limosin, a Province in *France*.

Limosity, a being

Limous, *l.* muddy.

Limpidity, -*pitude*, a being

Limpid, *l.* pure, bright, transparent.

Limpin, a muscle [fish.]

Linage, kindred or stock.

Linament, *l.* linnen thread, also a tent or lint for a wound.

Linarium, a flax-plat.

Linch, *sa.* a bank, wall or Causey, to distinguish bounds.

Linch-pins, *Lins*-, at the end of the Axle-trees.

Lincoln, *Lindum*, *Lindecoit*, *Lindecollina Civitas*, the chief Town in *Lincolnshire*.

Lincoln Colledge (in *Oxford*) founded by *Richard Fleming* Bishop of *Lincoln*.

Lincolns-Inne, one of the four Innes of Court, the house (heretofore) of Sir *Henry Lacy* Earl of *Lincoln*.

Lindaw, a City of *Schwaben* in *Germany*.

Lindsey, a third part of *Lincolnshire*.

Linde, *o.* the same as

Line-tree, *Tilea*, a tall tree with broad leaves and fine Flowers.

Lineal, -*ar*, belonging to a line.

Lineament, a line in painting, also the feature or proportion of any thing drawn out in lines.

Ling, *Erix*, heath.

Lingel, a little tongue or thong.

Linghen, a City of *Westphalia*.

Lingot, as *Ingot*.

Linguacity, *l.* talkativeness, a being long-tongued.

Linguist, one skilled in tongues or languages.

Linigerous, *l.* bearing flax.

Liniment, *l.* a thin Oyntment.

Linlithquo, *Lindum*, a town in *Scotland*.

Linosity, *l.* a bundance of flax.

Linsey-woolsey, cloth mixt of linnen and Woollen.

Lintearious, *l.* belonging to Linnen.

Lintz, a Town in *Colenland*, and another in higher *Austria*.

Lintel, the head-piece or upper post of a door, also as Lentil.

Lint-stock, a carved stick (about half a yard) with a cock at on end to hold the Gunners match, and a sharp Pike at the other, to stick it any where.

Linus, the Son of *Apollo* and *Psammas*, hiding himself among the bushes (for some fault) was torn in pieces by the Dogs, also a famous Musician who taught *Orpheus* and *Hercules*, who knockt him (they say) on the head for laughing at his unhandsom playing.

Linx, an ounce, a kind of spotted beast.

Lionel, *f.* a little lion.

Lioncel, *l.* the same.

Lions paw, *Leontopodium*, an herb.

Lipara, a Mediterranean Island.

Lipothymie, *g.* a swooning or fainting away by the failing or oppression of the vital Spirits.

Lippe, a Dukedom of *Westphalia*.

Lippitude, *l.* waterishness, bloud-shot or bleeredness of the eyes.

Lippen, *Sc.* to trust to, to rely on.

Liquable, *l.* which may be melted.

Liquation, *Liquefaction*, *l.* a melting, dissolving or making soft.

Liquefie, *l.* to melt.

Liquescency, a melting or growing soft.

Liquidate, to make

Liquid, *l.* soft, moist or clear.

Liquids, the letters, l, m, n, r, which are soft and melt (as it were) in pronouncing.

Liripoop, *Liripipium*, *Cleropeplus*, a Livery-hood.

Lisard, as *Lizard*.

Lis, *o.* for less and Release, also for list or border.

Lissed, *o.* bounded.

Lisle, a Town in *Flanders*.

Lisbone, a City in *Portugal*.

Lisieux, a City of *Normandy*.

Litany, *g.* an humble supplication or prayer, also a particular part of the Liturgy, to be used on certain dayes.

A Lite, *No.* a few or little.

Lite on, *No.* rely upon.

Liten, *No.* a garden.

Litation, *l.* a sacrificing, or atoning by sacrifice.

Literal [*meaning*] plain, common, according to the words.

Literality, the same as

Literature, *l.* learning, skill in Letters.

Lith, *o.* a limb, also plain or smooth.

Lithanthrax, *g.* a stony coal, a kind of Gagate.

Lithargie, *Litargy*, *l.* the foam that ariseth in the trying of Silver or Lead.

Lithe the pot, *Che.* Thicken it.

Lither, *o.* lazy, sluggish.

Lithy, *o.* humble.

Lithiasis, *g.* the stone engendred in Mans body.

Lithoglyphick, *g.* a graver or cutter in stones.

Lithomancy, *g.* Divination by casting pebble-stones, or by the load-stone.

Lithontribon, *g.* a confection that breaks and drives away the stone.

Lithontriptick, g. wearing or breaking the stone.

Lithontriptica, g. such medicines.

Lithotomy, g. a cutting of stones, also a place where they are cut or dug.

Litigation, l. a strife or wrangling, a suit or pleading.

Litigious, l. contentious, quarrelsome.

Litispendence, l. the hanging or depending of a suit till it be decided.

Litletons Tenures, a book of sound exquisite learning (saies Lord *Coke*) comprehending much of the marrow of the Common Law, written by *Tho. Littleton* (alias *Westcote*) Justice of the Kings bench in King *Edw.* 4.

Litmose bule, a kind of blew paint.

Litoral, *-rean*, l. belonging to the shore or Sea-side.

Littlebrough, a Town in *Nottinghamshire*.

Littleport, a town in *Cambridgeshire*.

Litleworth, a Town in *Leicestershire*.

Litotes, g. a figure, whereby more is signified than is expressed.

Littera, litter or straw.

Lituania, *Lith-*, a Province of *Poland*.

Liturate, l. to blot out.

Liturgick, belonging to

Liturgie, g. a publick office or service, particularly the public form of Divine service

Liven, o. to believe.

Livery, a Noble or Gentlemans cloth or colours worn by his Servants, with Cognizance or without, also a writ whereby the Heir did obtain possession of his lands at the Kings hands.

Livery of Seisin, a delivery of Possession of Lands, Tenements (or other corporeal thing) to one that has right (or probability of right) thereto.

Livery-stable, where the Horses of Strangers stand at

Livery (*for delivery*, or *Livrée*, *f.*) allowance (by week, day, &c.)

Liverwort, (*Lichen*, *Hepatica*, *Jecoraria*, helps all distempers of the Liver.

Lividity, l. a being

Livid, l. black and blew, of a leaden colour.

Livonia, *Liefland*, a Province in *Poland*.

Livor, l. a black and blew mark from a blow or humour, also envy spight and malice.

Lixiviated, of, like or washed with

Lixive, *-via*, *-ium*, l. lee or lye made of ashes.

Lixor, l, a water-bearer.

Lizard, a little greenish beast (in *Italy* and other hot Countries) like our evet, but bigger and without poison, a lover of men and very medicinal.

Lizard-point, the utmost South-west point of *Cornwall*.

Lizen'd Corn, (q. lessened) *Sf.* lank or shrunk.

Llys, Br. a place.

Loach, as *Lohoc*.

Loads, trenches to drain fenny places.

Lobbe, *Lobling*, a great Northern Sea-fish.

Lobby, (*ge. Lau'e*,) a gallery or walking-place, also a bed-room.

Local, belonging to a place.

Locality, the being of a thing in a place.

Location, l. a placing, also a letting out to hire.

Lock, a place where Rivers are stopped, also a lake, *No.*

Locarne, a Town in *Italy* belonging to the *Switzers*.

Lockers, little cup-boards at the Ship-sides for shot, &c.

Lochen, a Town in *Zutphen*.

Loco-cession, l. an yeilding or giving place.

Loco-motion, l. a moving out of the place.

Locri, *-ians*, people of

Locris, a City in *Greece*.

Loculament, l. a little place apart by it self.

Locupletity, a being

Locuplete, l. Wealthy.

Locus partitus, a division between Towns or Counties.

Locust, l. a kind of beetle, a winged insect, and another not winged, edible.

Locution, l. a speaking.

Loddon, a Town in *Norfolk*.

Lodemanage, the art or hire of a

Lodesman, a Pilot, guiding the ship with a

Lode-stone, (q. Lead-stone, from the colour and use) turning it self to the

Lode-star, the north-star, a guide to Marriners.

Lode-ship, a kind of Fishing vessel.

Lode-works, certain works in the Stannaries of *Cornwall*.

Lodges, [a buck] goes to rest.

Loe, *No.* a little round hill or great heap of stones.

Log, an hebrew measure of six egg-shels or half a pint.

Logarithmes, g. numbers, which being fitted to proportional numbers, alwaies retain equal differences.

Logating, an unlawful game disuled.

Log-line, *Minute-line*, with a piece of board at the end and lead to keep it edg-long in the water, to shew (by the fathoms which this runs out in a minute) how many leagues the ship will run in a watch (14 fathom to a mile.)

Logician, one skilled in

Logick, g. the art of Reasoning or disputing.

Logism, a due, judicious and rational understanding a thing.

Logist, g. one skilled in the

Logistick Art, the Art of reckoning or casting account.

Logists, ten Athenians who took the accounts of all Magistrates within thirty dayes after their determining, lookt to the publick Revenue, &c

Londenburgh, a town in South-

South *Juitland*, over against *De Strands* an Isle in the *German* Ocean.

Logographers, *g.* Lawyers Clerks.

Logomachy, *g.* Contention in or about words.

Log-wood, *Block-wood*, *Compechio*, brought from *Compeche* and other remote parts and used in dying of Black Hats.

Loire, a principal River of *France*.

Lohoe, *Lohock*, *Loche*, . a Confection to be melted in the mouth.

Gualter Lolhard, a *German* Authour of the

Lollards, Hereticks abounding here under *Edward* 3d. and *Henry* 5th. and (in general) those that oppose the setled Religion of the Land.

Lollardy, Lollery, their Doctrine.

Lombard, *Lombar*, *Lum-*, D. a bank for usury or pawns, also as

Lombardeer, an Usurer or Broaker, so called from the

Lombards, *Longobards*, Inhabiting the hither part of *Italy*, and much addicted to Usury.

Lombes, o. for Lambs.

Lombarie, belonging to the loins.

Lome, o. Clay, Mortar.

Londenoys, o, one of

London, (*Br.*Lundayn.) *Augusta*, *Nova Troja*, *Lindonion*, *Londinum*, *Longidinium*, *Londinium Lundinium* (from *Llwyn* a wood, *Llong* a Ship, or *Llawn* full, populous, and *Dinas*, *Br.* a City) the Metropolis and Epitome of *England*.

Londles, (*q. Landless*) *o.* a banished man.

London-Derry, a town in *Ireland*.

Longævity, *l.* length of daies or long life.

Longhbraw, a town in *Leicestershire*.

Longen, *o.* for belong.

Longanimity, *l.* Long-suffering, patience, forbearance.

Longinquity, *l.* length of place or time.

Long it hither, *Sf.* reach it.

Longitude, *l.* length.

Longitude of a place, the distance of it East, numbred in the Equinoctial by Meridians, from the first general and fixed Meridian.

Longitude of a Star, the arch of the Ecliptick, between the beginning of *Aries* and the Circle of the stars Latitude.

Long-Meg's Daughters, Seventy seven stones erected round about

Long-Meg, a stone fifteen foot high, near *Salkeld* in *Cumberland*.

Long-primer, one of the Printers Characters.

Loof-peeces, the Ordnance which lies at the

Loof of the Ship, that part aloft which lies just before th eChes-trees, as far as the bulk-head of the Castle.

Loof-up, Keep your Loof, keep the Ship close to the wind.

Spring your Loof, From going large, Clap close by the wind.

Loof-hook, to succour and secure the Tack.

Loom, *Che.* an instrument or tool.

Loom-Gale, the best fair Gale to sail in.

She Looms a Great Sail, seems to be a great Ship.

Loose-strife, Willow-herb, which (they say) parts Cattel fighting.

Loode, *o.* led.

Loos, *Lose*, *o.* praise.

Loot, *D.* Lead. Hence

Lootsman, as Lodesman.

Loover, as Louver.

Lope, *Li.* to leap.

Loppe, *o.* a Spider, or rather (as in *Lincolnshire*) a flea.

Lopum, a desert in *Bactria*, where Passengers (they say) are seduced and destroyed by Evil Spirits.

Loquacity, *l.* talkativeness.

Loquabre, part of North-*Scotland*.

Lorament, *l.* a bond made of thongs.

Loray or *Lorry-law*, whereby if a Combat be accepted, and after taken up by consent of the Lord of the Fee (in *Orleans*) each party payes 2 *s.* 6 *d.* but if performed, the party vanquished payes 112 shillings.

Lord in grass, he that is Lord having no Mannor, as the King in respect of his Crown.

Lordane, as *Lourdane*.

Lore, *sa.* learning, skill.

Loretto, a Town in *Italy*.

Loricated, *l.* armed with a coat of mail.

Lorimers, *-iners*, *Lormiers*, *f.* a trade and Company in *London* that make Bits, Spurs, and all small Iron-work.

Lorion, *-ot*, *f.* a Witwal, Yellow-peck or Hickway.

Lorn, part of South-*Scotland*.

Lorne, *o.* for Forlorn, lost.

Lorrel, *o.* a Devourer.

Lorrain, a *German* Dutchy.

L'Orty, a Great and ancient family in *Somersetshire*.

Losel, *o.* a lout, or as

Lossel, *o.* a crafty fellow.

Losengs, (*q.* leasing or glozing) a Nickname of *Herbert* Bishop of *Norwich*, and signifies as

Losenger, *o.* a flatterer.

Lotle de, *sa.* a pot containing the names of those that were to be chosen into Office by Lot.

Lot, *b.* wrapped or joyn'd together.

Lotharius, a *German* Emperour who betook himself to a Monastery.

Lothebrook, (*q.* Leather-breech) a *Dane*, whose Daughters were so skild in Needle-work that the *Danes* bare a Raven of their working, as an invincible Ensign.

Lot,

Lot or *Loth*, the thirteenth dish of Lead (in the *Darby-shire* mines) . which belongs to the King.

Lotherwit, as *Leyerwit*.

Lotion, *l.* a washing or cleansing, and (in Physick) a taking away the superfluous quality of a medicament, or the bringing-on a new one.

Loteby, *o.* Companion or love.

Lotis, *-tus*, the Daughter of *Neptune*, who flying from *Priapus* (to save her Chastity) was turn'd into a Lote-tree.

Lotophagi, *Africans* feeding much on the Lote tree, which *Vlysses's* Companions (having tasted) could hardly be drawn from.

Love-daies, whereon *Arbitrements* were made, and controversies (among Neighbours) determined.

Love-apple, a *Spanish* root of a Colour near *Violet*.

Lovel, *De Lupello*, an ancient family in *Northampton-shire*.

Lour, *c.* Money.

Lound, as *Laund*.

Loverd, *Lav-*, *o.* a Lord.

Lovingis. *sc.* (*Louanges*, *f.*) praises.

Lourdan, *Lordane*, *Lurdan*, (not from the *Danes* Lording it here idly while others laboured, but from the *French* *Lourd*, *Lourdant*, *-din*) a Dunce or Block-head.

Lourdy, *Sf.* sluggish.

Lourgulary, (*f.* *Lourderie*, incivility) casting any corrupt thing appoisoning the water, is *Lou-*, and Felony.

Louvaine, an University of *Brabant*.

Louver, *Loover*, (*f.* *l' Ouverte*) an open place at the top of the house (for air, smoak, &c.)

Louvre, (*f.* *L' Oeuvre*, the Work) the Royal Palace at *Paris* (answering our *Write-Hall*) augmented with a long and stately Gallery by *Henry* the fourth.

Lowbellers, such as go with a *Lowbel*, *Lough-bel*, used in the catching Larks, &c.) with a

Lough, *Luff*, (*Da.* *Loge*) Light or flame, also the vessel wherein the light is put (in *Lowbelling*)

Low-Countries, see *Neatherlands*.

Lower-Counter, the hollow arch between the lower part of the Ships Gallery and the Transome.

Louke, *o.* an Overseer of Accounts.

Louthe, a town in *Lincolnshire*.

Louting, (*q.* saluting) *o.* honouring.

Low-masted or *Under-masted* [*ship*,] when the Mast is too small or too short.

Low, *o.* fire, heat; also to praise.

St. *Loye*, *o.* St. *Louis*.

Low-land-men, the off-spring of the *English* *Saxons*, in the East part of *Scotland*.

Lowk, *No.* to weed corn.

Lozenge, *f.* a little square cake of preserved flowers, herbs, &c. also (in Heraldry) a quarry of glass, or any thing of that form.

Lua Mater, the ancient goddess of *Lustrations* or purgings.

Lubeck, a town in lower *Saxony*.

Lublin, a Town in *Poland*.

Lubrefaction, a making slippery or stirring.

Lubricity, *l.* slipperiness, a being

Lubrical, *-cious*, slippery, uncertain, wanton.

Luca, a town in *Tuscany*.

Luce, *Livonia*, *Leef-land* by upper *Germany*.

Lucernes, a beast (almost as big as a Wolf) of a very rich fur in *Rusia*.

Lucent, *-cy*, *l.* Lightsome.

Lucible, *l.* light of it self or apt to shine.

Lucida Lancis, a star in *Scorpio*.

Lucidity, *l.* a being

Lucid, *l.* shining, bright.

Lucifer, *l.* the morning-star, also *Nebuchadnezzar* King of *Babylon*, and an Arch-Devil.

Luciferous, *l.* bringing light.

Luciferians, Hereticks that followed one

Lucifer, Bishop of *Calaris* in *Sardinia* (Anno 365) who held that the soul was propagated out of the substance of the flesh, &c.

Lucina, *Juno*, as Patroness of Child-birth.

Lucher, (*q.* *Luckilyer*,) *o.* more likely or rather.

Lucius (*bright*) a *Roman* name of men.

Lucrative, *l.* gainfull or taken with gain.

Lucration, a gaining or winning.

Lucre, *l.* gain or profit.

Lucrece, *-retia*, being ravished by *Sextus* the son of *Tarquinius Superbus*, caused the banishment of him (and Kingly Government) from *Rome*.

Lucrous, *l.* gainfull, profitable.

Luctation, *l.* a striving or wrestling.

Luctatius Catulus, a *Roman* Commander who with 300 ships beat 600 of the *Carthaginians*, and put an end to the war.

Luctiferous, *l.* causing sorrow.

Luctisonant, *l.* signifying or expressing sorrow.

Lucubration, *l.* a studying (or working) by Candle-light.

Lucubratory, belonging thereto.

Luculency, *l.* a being

Luculent, clear, bright, famous.

Lucullus, an eloquent *Roman*, grown very rich by the War with *Mithridates*, gave himself up to ease and pleasure, till (growing mad) he was committed to the care of his Brother *Marcus*.

Ludgate, *q.* *Fludgate* (from the river near it) or *Leodgate* (the peoples gate) and not of any Fabulous King *Lud*.

Ludi-

Ludible, *l.* sportive, apt to play.

Ludibrious, *l.* shameful, reproachful.

Ludicral, *-crous*, in (or full of) sport, mockery or jesting.

Ludification, *l.* a mocking or deceiving.

Ludlow, a Town in *Shropshire*, with a fair Castle.

Ludovicus Pius, he succeeded his Father (*Charles* the great) in the Empire and the Kingdom of *France*.

Lues Venerea, the Venerean murrain or French Pox.

Luse, *sc.* love, or the open hand.

Lugdunum, *Lyons* in *France*.

Lugdunum Batavorum, *Leyden* in *Holland*.

Lugent, *l.* mourning.

Lugubrous, *l.* mournful.

Luition, *l.* paying a ransome, or making satisfaction for any offense.

Luke, (*h.* taken,) a Physician of *Antioch* and an Evangelist, hanged (saies *Nicephorus*,) on a green Olive-tree.

Lumbar, as *Lombar*, also belonging to the Loins.

Luminaries, *l.* lights, also (in the Western or Latin Church) the Feast of Christs Nativity.

Luminous, *l.* full of Light.

Luneburgum, *Lunenburgh* in *Germany* (built by *Julius Cæsar*) where the Image of the Moon remained till the daies of *Charles* the great.

Lunar, belonging to

Luna, *l.* the Moon.

Lunatick, troubled with a

Lunacy, *l.* [Moon-]madness.

Lunden, a City in *Denmark*.

Lunenbourg, a Saxon Dutchy.

Lunes, leashes or long lines to call in Hawks.

Lungis, (*f. Longis*,) a slim slowback, dreaming lusk or drowsie gangril.

Lungwort, an herb good for the distempers of the Lungs.

Lupa, a she-wolf (or Harlot) which nourished *Romulus* and *Remus* in the

Lupercal, a place about *Rome*, where (upon the 15 of *February*) were celebrated the

Lupercalia, Feasts in honour of *Pan* (whom they invoked to drive away Wolves) performed by the

Luperci, the Priests of *Pan*, who ran up and down naked and (with a Goat-skin) strook or stroakt the Women, to cause fruitfulness and easie deliverance.

Lupines, flat pulse like small beans, bitter and Physical.

Lura, *l.* the mouth of a Sack or botle, hence

Lurcation, *l.* a greedy or gluttonous devouring.

Lurdan, as *Lourdan*.

Lure, for allure.

Hawks Lure, a device of Leather stuck with Feathers and baited with flesh.

Lurries, *c.* all manner of cloaths.

Lurid, *l.* pale, wan.

Lusatia, a German Province.

Luscition, *l.* a being dimsighted or purblind.

Lushborow, *-burg*, a base coyn (counterfeiting the English) brought from beyond-sea (perhaps from *Luxenburg*) and forbidden, in the daies of King *Edward the 3d*.

Lusitania, the Kingdom of *Portugal*.

Lusion, *l.* a playing or pastime.

Lusk, a slug or sloathful fellow.

Lust of a ship, her inclination to one side more than another.

Lustration, a going about in procession, or purging by Sacrifice (every fifth year.)

Lustrifical, purging or making holy.

Lustre, *f.* shinning, also as

Lustrum, *l.* the space of fifty moneths.

Luted, *-eous*, *l.* clayie, muddy.

Lutheranism, the doctrine of the

Lutheranes, followers of

Martin Luther, who (from an *Augustin* Fryer) forsook the Church of *Rome* and wrote against the errours of it, *Anno* 1515.

Lutherans, (though sometimes confounded with, yet really) differ from Calvinists, in holding predestination from foreseen Faith and good works, &c.

Luton, a Town in *Bedfordshire*.

Lutulent, *l.* miry, dirty.

Lutzelstein, a County in *Lorrain*.

Luxenburgh, a Dutchy in the Low-Countries.

Luxate, *l.* to loosen or put out of joynt.

Luxuriate, *l.* to abound, exceed or grow rank.

Luxuriant, growing to excess and superfluity, also as

Luxurious, *l.* wanton, given to

Luxury, *l.* riot, riotousness.

Lying under the Sea, when in a storm the Ship is a-hull, and the helm so fastened a-lee, that the sea breaks upon her bow and broad side.

Lycanthropy, *g.* a Melancholy frenzy causing a man to think himself a Wolf, and avoid the company of men.

Lycaon, a king of *Arcadia*, turn'd into a Wolf by *Jupiter* whom he entertain'd with Mans-flesh.

Lycaonia, *Arcadia*, and another Country near *Phrygia*.

Lychan, a Town in *Norfolk*.

Lyceum, a famous School of *Aristotles* near *Athens*, and another of *Cicero's* at his mannor of *Tusculum*.

Lycium, *g.* a decoction of bramble or box-thorn.

Lyco-

Lycomedes, King of the Island *Scyrus*, among whose Daughters *Achilles* lived in womans apparel, to keep himself from the *Trojan* Wars.

Lycurgus, King of *Sparta*, having made them many good Laws, resigned the Crown to his Nephew and kild himself, also a King of *Thrace* who rooted up the vines to keep his people sober.

Lycus, a King of *Bœotia*, who married *Antiope*, and put her away when gotten with Child by *Jupiter* in form of a Satyr, also a King of *Lybia*, who used to sacrifice his guests.

Lydbury, a town in *Herefordshire*.

Lydia, a womans name from the Country

Lydia, *Mæonia*, a Kingdom of *Asia* the less, so called from

Lydus, who succeeded his Father *Atys* in that Kingdom.

Lyer in a ship, is under the Swabber and keeps clean the beak-head and Chains, is proclaim'd at Main-mast on Monday aud holds his place for that week.

Lydian Musick, dolefull.

Lydian Spinster, a Spider.

Lydford-law, see *Lidford*.

Lykam, *o.* (*Lichaem, D.*) a body.

Lykerous, *o* Letcherous.

Lympha, *l.* Water.

Lymphatick, *l.* Distracted, by seeing (as it were) a Nymph in the water.

Lymbergh, a town in *Lincolnshire*.

Lyn Regi, a town in *Norfolk*.

Lynchet, a green bulk dividing land.

Lyccan, *-eous*, belonging to

Lynx, a spotted beast like a Wolf, quick-sighted, made of

Lyncus, King of *Scythia*, so changed by *Ceres*, for going about to kill his guest *Triptolemus*.

Lyncuris, a bright stone congealed of the *Lynxes* Urine.

Lynceus, a quick-sighted *Argonaut*, reported to see the new moon at her change, to see through stone walls, &c.

Lyndus, a City of *Rhodes*, famous for sacrifices to *Hercules*.

Lyons, a fair and wealthy City of *France*.

Lypothymy, as *Lipothymy*.

Lyra, [*Arion's*] harp, a constellation.

Lyrick. belonging to an harp.

Lyrist, he that plaies on, or sings to the

Lyre, *l.* a harp.

Lyrick-poets, (as *Pindar* and *Horace*) who make

Lyrick-verses, (not Heroick) composed to the Harp or Lute.

Lysander, a *Lacedemonian* who beat the *Athenians*.

Lysidice, Daughter of *Pelops*, Mother of *Alcmena*, and Grandmother of *Hercules*.

Lysimachus, one of *Alexanders* Captains thrown to a Lyon which he kill'd by pulling out his tongue.

Lysius, a name of *Bacchus*.

Lyskerd, a town in *Cornwal*.

Lystwythiel, a town in *Cornwal*.

M.

M. (For Murder or Man-slaughter) on the brawn of the Thumb of every one admitted to his Clergy.

Mab. Br. a Son.

Mabel, *Mabilia*, (*q. amabilis*, *l.* lovely, or *Mabelle*, *f.* My fair one) a Womans name.

Mac, *Ir.* a Son.

Mac-beth, a *Scotch* Usurper who kild *Duncom* the King.

Macaleb, a Pomander or bastard-coral, whose sweet and shining black berries serve for bracelets.

Macareus, the son of *Æolus*, who got his sister *Canace* with child, whereupon her Father sent her a sword with which she killed herself.

Macao, a Portugall Isle on the North of *China*.

Macaronique, *f.* a confused huddle of many things together.

Macarons, *f.* Sweet-meats made of Almonds, Sugar, Rosewater and Musk.

Maccaroni, *I.* lumps of boild paste, served up in butter and strew'd with spice and grated cheese.

Maccabees, Two Apocryphal books containing the History of *Judas*

Maccabæus, son of *Matathias*, from

Macabi, the initial letters of *Mi Camoca Belim Jehovah* (*Who among the Gods is like unto thee O Lord?*) which (they say) was in his banners against *Antiochus*.

Macedonians, people of

Macedonia, *Æmathia*, *Æmonia*, *Romelli*, a large country in *Europe*, whereof *Philip* and *Alexander* were Kings.

Macegrefs, those that wittingly buy and sell stollen flesh.

Macellarious, *l.* belonging to the Shambles.

Macellator, *l.* a Butcher.

Macerate, *l.* to soak in liquor, also to make lean, mortify or weaken.

Machaon, a famous Physician, who went (with the *Grecians*) to the *Trojan* Wars, and was slain.

Machevalize, the same as *Machiavelianize*, to play the

Machiavelian, *-villian*, he that practiseth or studieth

Machiavelianism, State-policy, the Doctrine of *Nicholas*

Machiavel, a famous Historian and Recorder of *Florence*, whose politicks have poison'd almost all *Europe*.

Machil, *Meghil*, *h*. the rich robe of the Ephod, *Exodus* 28, 34.

Machine, *g. l. f.* an Engine or instrument.

Machination, *l.* a plotting or contriving.

Machlin, a City and Territory (of 9 Villages) in *Brabant*.

Macilent, *l.* lean or thin.

Mackaroons, as *Macarons*.

Mackenboy, *Makimboy*, an *Irish* Spurge, which purgeth one much, only by being born about one.

Mackerel, *Maquerel*, *f.* a spotted fish well known, also a Pander or Procurer.

Macclesfield, a town in *Cheshire*.

Macritude, *l.* leanness.

Macrobij, *g.* Certain Long-lived *Æthiopians*.

Macrocosm, *g.* the Great World, contradistinct to *Microcosm*.

Macrology, *g.* a figure using more words than are Necessary.

Mactation, *l.* a killing.

Mactator, *l.* a killer or murderer.

Maculate, *l.* to stain or spot.

Maculatures, waste or blotting-papers.

Mad, E. an Earth-worm.

Madagascar, St. *Laurence*, an *African* Isle, (the greatest in the World) a thousand mile in length and about 4 hundred in breadth.

Madder, a plant with a red root, serving to dye Wool.

Madefaction, *l.* a moistening.

Madify, *Madidate*, *l.* to wet.

Mader, a Town in *Zealand*.

Madera, an Isle on the West of *Barbary*.

Madidity, *Madour*, *l.* moisture

Madid, *l.* wet, washed, also drunken.

Madning-money, old *Roman* Coins found about *Dunstable* are so call'd by the Country people.

Madoc, a *British* name, from

Mad, *Br.* Good.

Madrid, *-il*, the Metropolis of *Castilia Nova*, where the King of *Spain* keeps his Court.

Madrigal, an *Italian* air, of one single rank of Verses.

Maegbote, *Mag-*, *sa.* a recompense for the murder of ones Kinsman.

Mæonides, *Homer*, the son of *Meon*.

Mæonia, *Lydia*.

Mæotis, *Marbianco* or *Mardella Tana*, *Garpaluc*, a Lake in the North part of *Scythia*.

Maeremium, Timber.

Maestricht, a town in *Brabant* subject to the *French*.

Magazine, *f.* a store-house [of Warlike ammunition, &c.]

Magdalen, *h.* magnified or Exalted.

Magdalen Colledge in Oxford, built (with a Hall adjoyning) by *W. Wainflet* Bishop of *Winchester*.

Magdalen Colledge in Cambridge, converted from an Hostel for Monks by the Duke of *Bucks*, about the beginning of K. *H.* 8.

Magdaleon, *l.* a Langate or long plaister like a rowler.

Magdeburg, *Parthenopolis*, (*Maids-town*) the Chief City of *Saxony*, half free, half subject to the Elector of *Brandenburg*.

Magellanick, belonging to, or discovered by *Ferdinando*

Magellanus, a Noble *Portugal* whose ship (the *Victoria*) said round the world in the years 1520 and 1521, though he himself perished in the Atchievement.

Magellanica, part of South *America*.

Magellan's clouds, two small clouds (near the South pole) of the same colour as the *Via lactea*.

Magi, P. (Philosophers) the Wisemen mentioned *Math.* 2.

Magician, one that studies or practiseth the

Magick [*Art*] Wisdom, Philosophy, also as

Diabolical Magick, the black Art or dealing with familiar Spirits.

Natural Magick, the Science of Nature, which is lawfull, and the ground of all true Physick.

Magical, belonging to *Magick*.

Magintum, *Dunstable*, in the Emperour *Antonines Itinerary*.

Magistery, *l.* Mastership, also the total substance of a thing reduced to its primitive juice.

Magistral, *-terial*, like or belonging to a Master.

Magisterial pill, *plaister* &c. prepared after the best manner.

Magistracy, *l.* the office of a

Magistrate or Chief Ruler.

Magna Assisa Eligenda, a writ for the Sheriff to summon four lawfull Knights, to chuse twelve Knights of the Vicinage, to pass upon the Great Assise between the Plaintiff and Defendant.

Magna Charta, (The Great Charter) the most ancient of our written Laws, Granted by King *Henry* 3. confirmed by King *Edward* the first, and other Kings.

Magnalia, *l.* Great things or works.

Magnality, an admired greatness.

Magnanimity, *l.* a being

Magnanimous, *l.* Couragious, of a generous, great or stout Spirit.

Magnes, a beautifull youth of *Smyrna*, beloved of *Gyges* King of *Lydia*.

Magnetick, attractive, belonging to the

Magnete, *l.* the loadstone, which draws iron to it.

Magnificat, [My Soul] doth magnifie, the Song of the Virgin *Mary*, (*Luke* 1. 46.)

Correct the Magnificat, Attempt to amend the Scripture, or that which is beyond correction.

Magnifical, -*cent*, Noble, atchieving worthy acts.

Magnificence, *l.* statelinesss, sumptuousness.

Magnifici, *l.* the Governours of the German Academies.

Magnifico's l. the chief Noblemen of *Venice*.

Magnifie, *l.* to greaten, extol, or make great account of.

Magniloquence, *l.* a discourse of great matters, or being

Magniloquent, *l.* speaking loftily, or in a great style.

Magnitude, *l.* greatness.

Mago, the chief of this name encreased very much the wealth and discipline of *Carthage*.

Magog, *h.* (of Gog or the house top) *Gen.* 10. 2. founder of the

Magogi, the Scythians or Tartars.

Gog and Magog, (*Ezek.* 38. 2.) generally expounded of *Antiochus* the great, King of *Asia* and Syria.

Gog and Magog, (*Rev.* 20. 8.) the Enemies of the Church, either secret and open, or Hereticks and Tyrants, or the *Ottoman* Family, &c. Opinions are various.

Mahamorra, a *Portugal* fort on the Coast of *Fez*.

Magonel, as *Mangonel*.

Mahim, *Maim*, (*f. Mehaing*) the loss [of the use] of any member, which may be usefull or defensive in battel.

Mahone, a large Turkish ship

Mahound, *o.* Mahomet or Muhammed.

Mahumetism, *Mahumetry*, *Mahumetanism*, the Religion and Law of the

Mahumetans, *Mahoms*, Turks, followers of

Mahumet, *Maho-*, an *Arabian* born 572. his Father a Pagan and his Mother a Jew Captain of a rebellious crew, among whom (by the help of *Sergius* a Monk) he introduced the Turkish Religion contained in the *Alchoran*.

Maia, Daughter of *Atlas* and one of the *Pleiades*, on whom *Jupiter* begat *Mercury*.

Maid-Marrian, (or *Morion*) a boy drest in Maids Apparel, to dance the *Marisco*.

Maiden-hair, *Adiantum*, *Capillus Veneris*, a plant.

Maiden-head, or -*hood*, Virginity.

Maiden-head, -*hith*, *South-Ealington*, a town in *Berk-shire*.

Maid, *Skate-Damzel*, *Li.* a small kind of raye.

Maiden-rents, a Noble paid by every Tenant (in the Mannour of *Builth* in *Radnorshire*) at their Marriage, at first (perhaps) a fine for a licence to marry a Daughter, or as in *Marcheta*.

Maifaie, *Mafey*, (*f. Ma foy*) by my faith,

Maidstone, *Medweagesion*, a pleasant Town on

Medway, a River in *Kent*

Majestative, the same as

Majestical, full of or belonging to

Majesty, *l.* Royal State or gravity.

Maignagium, a Brasiers shop.

Maile, (*f.* an half-penny) an old small piece of money.

Maim, as *Mahim*.

Main-Knight, that which is placed aft the Main-sail.

Maina, part of *Morea*.

Mainamber, a strange rock in *Cornwall*.

Main-hamper, a basket wherein they carry grapes to the press.

Maienne, a Town in

Main, a French Province.

Mainour, *Minour*, *Manour*, (*f. Manier* to handle) the thing stolen, and wherewith the thief is taken.

Mainpernable, bailable which may be bailed.

Mainpernors, they that bail, take into their hands and are sureties for any one to appear at a certain day.

Mainprize, *f.* the taking a man into friendly custody, and being security for his appearance.

Main-porte, a certain tribute (commonly of loaves) paid in some places instead of Tythes.

Mainsworn, *No.* forsworn or perjured.

Maint, *fa.* mingled.

Maintenance, *f.* holding [a child that learns to go] by the hand, also the upholding or maintaining a cause or person by word or deed, also (*q. Menasance*) *o.* threatning

Mainsainor, he that seconds a cause depending by money, friends, &c.

Majo, an *Irish* County.

Major, *l.* Greater, a Regiment-Officer, next the Lieutenant-Colonel.

Major-General, next the Lieutenant-General.

Major, Mayor, the Governour of a City or Corporation-town.

Major-proposition of a Syllogism, the first.

Majorque, -*rca*, an Isle on the *Spanish* Coast.

Majoration, *l.* a making Greater.

Maisnilwarings, *Manwarings*, a great and ancient Family in *Cheshire*.

Maisthleb, *o.* Maslin.

Maison-Dieu, (for *Maison de Dieu*, *f.* Gods house) an Hospital or Alms-house.

Make, *Li.* a Consort.

Make, *c.* an half-peny.

Make, to perform or execute.

Make his beard. *o.* deceive him.

Make, *o.* to hinder.

Make-hawk, an old staunch flying

flying hawk, to make or teach a young one.

Makeless, *No*. Matchless.

Malabar, a very populous *East-India* kingdome.

Malaca, a Town in *India*.

Malachias, *h*. the Angel or Messenger of God.

Malachite, *g*. a precious stone of a dark mallow-green.

Malacissation, a kneading or making soft.

Malacy, *g*. a calm at sea, also the longing of women with child.

Maladie, *f*. disease or sickness.

Malaga, -*ago*, -*aca*, a Port-town of *Andalusia* in *Spain*.

Malanders, a disease in horses, causing them

Mal-andare, *I*. to go ill.

Malapert, -*pert*, (*f*. *Mal-appert*, ready for mischief, or *Mal-appris*, ill-taught) impudent, saucy.

Malchow, a town of *Mecklenburg* in *Germany*.

Mal disant, *f*. an Evil-speaker or back-biter.

Maldives, *Asian* Islands.

Maldon, *Camalodunum*, a town in *Essex*.

Male, *D*. a sack or budget.

Male bouche, *f*. a wicked mouth.

Malecontent, *f*. [one that is] discontented.

Malediction, *l*. an evil-speaking or cursing.

Malefactour, *l*. an Offender or Evil doer.

Malefesance, a transgressing.

Maleficiate, to be

Maleficent, doing a

Malefice, *l*. an evil deed, displeasure or shrewd turn.

Malespine, a Marquisate of *Tuscany*.

Maletalent, *o*. ill-will.

Maletent, *Malet t*, -*o'te*, (*f*. -*este*) an ancient toll of fourty Shillings for every sack of Wool.

Malevolence, *l*. ill-will, a being

Malevolent, unkind, ill-natured, of ill effect or influence

Mal-grace, *f*. Dis-favour.

Malign, to Spite, to bear

Malignity, *l*. Malice or Grudge.

Malines, a town in *Brabant*.

Malison, (*f*. *Maudisson*) a curse.

Malkin, *Maukin*, a Scovel (of old clouts) to cleanse the Oven.

Mallard, a Wild Drake.

Malleable, which may be

Malleated, *l*. hammered or beaten out.

Malleguetta, a Country on the Coast of *Guiny*.

Malleverers, *Mali Leporarii*, an ancient family in *Yorkshire*.

Mallows, a plant of a loosening quality.

Malmsey, (*f*. *Malvaisie*) wine from

Malvisia, *Marvisia*, a promontory of *Chios*, or (rather) from *Monembasia* (or *Epidaurus*) in *Morea*, whence comes the best.

Malmesbury, *Maidulphsburgh*, a town in *Wiltshire*.

Malpas, a Town in *Cheshire*.

Malt, *o*. melted.

Maltesian, belonging to

Malta, *Melita*, a Rocky and Barren Isle some sixty miles from *Sicily*, belonging to the Knights of *Rhodes*.

Malton, a town in *Yorkshire*.

Malveis Procurors, packers of Juries by Nomination or other procurement.

Malversation, *f*. ill conversation or Misdemeanour.

Malure, *o*. (*f*. *Malheur*) Mischance.

Mamalukes, *Mamm*-, (*A*. light-horsemen) an Order of valiant Soldiers in the last Empire of *Egypt*.

Mamercus, a Bishop of *Vienna*, who instituted Litanies.

Mamitus, an *Assyrian* King, a terrour to the *Egyptians* and other Nations.

Mammeated, *l*. having paps or teats.

Mammet, *o*. a puppet, (*q*. little

Mam or Mother.)

Mammillary processes, certain bones in the Temples representing the teats of a Cow.

Mammocks, fragments or pieces.

Mammonist, a worldling, one that worships or seeks after

Mammon, *Sy*. [The God of] Riches.

Mammon of unrighteousness, False Riches, This Worlds Goods.

Mammooda, an *East-India*-Coyn, the value of our Shilling.

Mammalucks, as *Mamalucks*.

Man the Ship, store it with a sufficient number of men, also call them all up aloft.

Man the Capstain, heave at it.

Man the top well, take in the Top-sails with hands enow.

Manation, *l*. a flowing or running (of water.)

Manage, *I*. to handle or govern.

Manar, an *Asian* Isle.

Manasses, *h*. forgotten.

Manbote, *sa*. a pecuniary compensation for killing of a man.

Man, an Isle between *Lancashire* and *Ireland*.

Manche, *f*. a sleeve, or any thing in such a form.

Manchester, a Town in *Lancashire*.

Manchet, (*f*. *Michette*) the smallest and finest sort of bread.

Manch present, a bribe or present from the Donours own hands.

Mancipation, *l*. an ancient manner of selling and delivering possession before witnesses with several circumstances, also as *Emancipation*.

Manciple, *l*. a Clerk of the Kitchin, or Caterer, that buys the

the provisions for a Colledge or Hospital.

Manca, a square piece of Gold, commonly valued at 30 pence.

Mancuse, -*sa*, (q. *Manu cusa*) the value of a mark in silver.

Manca, is sometimes rendered, The fifth part of an ounce.

Manca and *Mancusa*, are sometimes both translated by *Marca*.

Mandamus, a writ that lay after the year and day, where (in the mean time) the writ called *Diem clausit extremum* had not been sent to the Escheatour, also a Charge for the Sheriff to take into the kings hands all the lands of a kings widow, who (contrary to her Oath) had married without his consent.

Mandatary, he to whom a command is given, also he that comes into a Benefice by a *Mandamus*.

Mandate, a Command of the King (or his Justices) to have any thing done for the dispatch of Justice.

Mandevils, *de Magna Villa*, an ancient family in *Essex*.

Mandible, *l.* which may be eaten.

Mandilian, -*lion*, *I.* a Soldiers loose Cassock.

Mandingo's, Inhabitants of *Guiny* (on the river *Gambra*) who take Tobacco in large and short bowls, through a reed of a yard long.

Mandonius and Indibilis, two famous *Spanish* Captains who assisted the *Romans* against the *Carthaginians*, but beginning to revolt, they were only discharged.

Mandragora, -*goras*, -*drake*, -*drage*, *g.* a plant bearing yellow apples, the root cold in the fourth Degree and used by Chirurgeons to cast men into a deep sleep.

Mandrakes (*Can.* 7. 13, *b.* lovely) pleasant flowers, or something else smelling sweet which the Common Mandrakes do not.

Mandrakes shewn in the perfect shape of men, &c. are perfect Cheats (of Briony roots, &c.)

Manducable, *l.* eatable, capable of

Manducation, *l.* a chewing or eating.

Mandy-Thursday, as *Maundy*-.

Maneh. *h.* Mina, a pound.

Maneh of Gold, an hundred shekels or 75 pound sterling.

Maneh of Silver, sixty shekels or 7 pound 10 shillings.

Manentes, Tenants, also *Manses* or Hides of land.

Manfredonia, a City of *Naples*, on the Gulph of *Venice*.

Manganese, (in colour and weight like the loadstone) the most general ingredient of glass.

Manger, a place to receive the water that comes in at the Hawses.

Mangin, *China* so called by the *Tartars*.

Mangonel, *Mangon*, *I.* an old warlike engine, to cast great stones or darts.

Mangonism, *l.* the Craft or trade of

Mangonizing, -*zation*, trimming-up things for sale.

Manheim, a fort in the lower Palatinate.

Maniable, *f.* tractable, to be managed or wielded.

Maniack, *g.* Mad.

Manichees, Hereticks following one

Manes, a *Persian*, who affirmed himself to be Christ and the Paraclete, held a fatal Necessity of sinning, &c.

Manicles, *f.* Hand-cuffs or Fetters.

Manifesto, *I.* an open or publick Declaration, concerning State-affairs, &c.

Maningtree, a Town in *Essex*.

Manipular, belonging to a *Maniple*, *l.* a handfull, a band of Soldiers, also a Fannel or Scarf-like Ornament on the left wrist of Priests at Sacrifice.

Manlius, a *Roman* name.

Man, *Manna* (q. *Man hu*, *Ch.* what is this?) the dew or bread of heaven which the *Israelites* ate in the Desert; also (at this day) a Physical congealed dew gathered in the morning (from the leaves of Mulberries, &c.) in *Calabria* and other hot countries, also a sweet extract out of any matter.

Mannaty, *Manati*, an Amphibious *West-India* beast between a Fish and a Cow.

Mannish, *sa.* Wicked.

Mannour, *Manor*, a Jurisdiction and Royalty incorporeal, also the Land or Seat.

Manor in gross, the right of a Court-Baron (and its perquisites) while another enjoyes the Land.

A Manor cannot be without a Court-Baron and two Suiters.

Man of War, a valiant Soldier or Warrior, also a Ship of War.

Manpygarnon, a kind of pottage

Manqueller, *sa.* a murderer.

Le Mans, the Chief town of *Maine*.

Mansion, *l.* an abiding, a dwelling-place, also a Mannor-house, Capital Messuage, or the Lords chief dwelling-house within his fee.

Mansfield, a town in the upper *Saxony*.

Mansfield, a town in *Nottinghamshire*.

Man slaughter, the unlawfull killing of a man without premeditated malice. It is Felony (because wilfull) but admits Clergy for the first time.

Mansura, *Mas*-, Farmers houses.

Mansus, a Farm.

Mansuetude, *l.* meekness, a being

Mansuete, *l* gentle, tractable.

Mantels, *-tles*, [the Beer] Flowers, also [the hawk] stretches her wings along after her Legs.

Manticulate, *l.* to pick a purse, or do any thing closely.

Mantiore, *-corn*, *I.* a ravenous Indian beast, with three ranks of Teeth, a face like a man, and body like a Lyon.

Mantile, *Mantle*, *f.* a Cloak or long robe, also the flourish proceeding from the wreath and helm, and descending on each out-side of th' Escutcheon.

Manto, a Theban Prophetess Daughter of *Tiresias*, and Mother of *Ocnus* the Founder of

Mantua, a City of *Italy* on the River *Po*.

Mant-wine, brought from thence.

Manual, *-ary*, *l.* filling or belonging to the hand.

Manual, a small volume portable in the hand.

Manualist, a handi-craftsman.

Manubial, *-ary*, *l.* belonging to a prey or booty.

Manucaptio, a writ for him that offers sufficient bayl, and cannot be admitted.

Manucaption, *l.* a taking with or by the hand.

Manucaptors, bails or sureties.

Manuduction, *l.* a guiding or leading by the hand.

Manuel, that whereof present profit may be made.

Manufacture, *l.* handywork.

Manumission, *l.* an enfranchizing or making free.

Manumitt, *-miss*, *l.* to make a bondman free, by turning him round, giving him a cap, and other Ceremonies.

Manure, (*Main-ouvrier*, *f.* to till [the ground.]

Manus Christi, Sugar boild with Rose-water, (sometime violet or Cinnamon Water.)

Manuscript, *l.* written with the hand, not printed.

Manutenentia, a writ used in case of [corrupt] Maintenance.

Manutention, a holding with or by the hand.

Manworth, *sa.* the price of a mans head.

Manzed shrew, *o.* wicked scold.

Maple, a wood much used by Turners.

Mar, *-rria*, part of North-Scotland.

Maran-atha, *Sy.* *Schammatha*, *h.* (the Lord cometh) the third and highest degree of Excommunication.

Marathon, a Grecian Town, about 10 miles from *Athens*.

Maravedis, a small Spanish coyn, thirty four of them go to a Ryal or six pence.

Marcab, the pinion of the wing of *Pegasus*.

Marcellus, a great Roman General, circumvented by *Hannibal*, and slain, also a Roman Bishop, who instituted the Order of Cardinals.

Marcessible, *l.* apt to rot or putrifie.

Marc-grave, *Mart-grave*, *D.* a Count or Earl of the

Marches, *D.* the borders or Frontiers of a Country.

Marchasite, *Marchesite*, *Marquesite*, a fire-stone, a stone partaking of the nature and colour of some metal, not to be separated but into smoak and ashes.

Marche, a Province of *France*.

Lords Marchers, Noblemen inhabiting (and securing) the

Marches of Wales or Scotland, the bounds between us and them.

Marcheta, *Mer-*, (by Skene, the rai'd or first carnal knowledge of a woman) a Scotch law by *Eugenius* 3d. that the Lord should have the first nights lodging with every woman marryed within his fee, abrogated by *Malcolm.* 3d. for which they pay a Mark.

Marchioness, the Wife of a Marquiss.

March-pane, *Massepain*, *f.* *q.* *massa panis*,) Sugared paste made into little cakes.

Marcidity, *-cour* *l.* a being

Marcid, *-dious*, *l.* rotten, withered, feeble.

Marcionists, *-ites*, Hereticks following one

Marcion, a Stoick Philosopher, who held that Christ was not the Son of God.

Marcus, *Mark*, a proper name.

Marcus Curtius, for his Countries good rode arm'd into a gaping of the Earth.

Cry the Mare, (in *Herefordshire*) the reapers tye together the tops of the last blades, and at a distance throw their sickles at it, and he that cuts the knot hath the prize, with shouting and good cheer.

Maremaid, as *Mermaid*.

Night Mare, as *Incubus*.

Mareotis, a large Egyptian lake on the South of *Alexandria*.

Mareshal, as *Marshal*.

Margaret, (*Marget*, *Meg*, *Peg*) *g.* a Pearl.

Margarets, *o.* Daisies.

Margaritiferous, *l*, bringing forth or having plenty of

Margarites, *g.* Pearls found in Oysters and other shel-fish.

Margelain, *o.* *Marjerom.*

Margery, (*Madg*) by some the same as *Margaret*, by others as

Majorana, Sweet Marjerom.

Margery Prater, *c.* a hen.

Marginal, *-neal*, belonging to a

Margin, *-gent*, *l.* the brink or brim, also the uttermost part of a page.

Mariandunum, part of *Asia*, where is the *Acherusian* cave

cave by which *Hercules* (they ſay) went down to hell.

Mariembourg, a Town in *Hainault*.

Mariets, *f.* Marian-Violets.

Marinate fiſh, fry them in Sallet oyl and then pickle them.

Marinated, pertaining to the Sea, taſting of Salt water, alſo (*c.*) tranſported into ſome forreign plantation.

Marine, *Maritan*, *-time*, *l.* belonging to, near or from beyond the Sea.

Marjoram, *Majorana*, *Amaracus*, a comforter of the Brain and Nerves.

Maritagio amiſſo, &c. a writ for a Tenant in frank-marriage to recover Lands whereof he is deforced.

Marital, *l.* belonging to an Husband or Marriage.

Marius, a valiant Roman choſen Conſul ſeven times.

Mark, an Earldom in *Germany*.

Mark of Adam, *o.* mark of manhood.

Mark [*of Silver*,] thirteen ſhillings and four-pence.

Mark [*of Gold*,] thirty three ſhillings and four pence.

Scotch Mark, thirteen-pence half-penny.

Marketzeld, or rather

Marketgeld, toll of the Market.

The Market hardens, *No.* things grow dear.

Mark-penny, paid at *Maldon* for laying pipes or gutters into the ſtreets.

Markab, as *Marcab*.

Marle, *Malin*, a chalky earth uſed in ſoiling of Land.

Marleborough, a Town in *Wiltſhire* (ſeated on a chalky ground) where a Parliament made the

Statute of Marleborough, for appeaſing of tumults.

Marlerium, *-etum*, a Marle-pit.

Marlin, *Merlin*, (*f. Eſmerillon*) a ſmall kind of Hawk.

Marle the Sail, faſten it to the bolt-rope, with

Marling, a ſmall tarr'd line of untwiſted hemp, to ſeaſe the ends of ropes from ſarſing out, &c.

Marling-ſpeek or ſpike, a ſmall iron for ſpliſing of ſmall ropes and opening the bolt-rope (to ſew in the Sail.)

Marlow, a Town in *Bucks*.

Marmaduke, (*q. Mehr-machtig*, *Ge.* more powerfull) a mans name.

Marmelade, *f. l.* conſerve (of Quinces, &c.)

Marmoration, *l.* a building with marble.

Marmorean, like (or made of) Marble.

Marmoſet, a kind of black Monkey with a ſhaggy neck, (as they are ſhown in *England*.)

Marmot, *f.* a Mountain-rat.

Marne, a River of *Champagne* in *France*.

Maronea, *-ogna*, a City of *Ciconia*, whence

Maronean wine, ſo ſtrong, that if twenty times ſo much water be mixt with it, it ſtill retains its virtue.

Marocco, an African Kingdom Weſt of *Barbary*.

Maronites, (a branch of the *Jacobites*) Chriſtians of Mount *Libanus*, whoſe Patriarch is alwayes called *Peter*.

Marpiſſa, *Alcyone*, the beloved Wife of *Idæus* (the comlieſt man of his time.)

Marpurg, a Town of *Heſſen* in *Germany*.

Marques, as *Repriſals*.

Letters of Marque, See *Lett-*,

Marquenterre, part of *Picardy*.

Marqueſite, as *Marchſite*.

Marquiſate, the title and juriſdiction of a

Marqueſs, *-quiſs*, (*q.* Lord Marcher) a Noble-man between a Duke and Earl.

Marquiſate of the Empire, part of *Brabant*, conteining *Lovaine*, *Bruxells*, *Nivell* and *Antwerp*.

Marquetry, *f.* a Joiners checquer'd in-laid work with wood of divers ſorts and colours, and ſometime confounded with Moſaique.

Marrow, (*f. Maraud*,) a fellow, knave or beggerly raſcal.

Marrows, *No.* fellows (ſpoof Gloves, Shoes, &c.)

Mars, the Son of *Juno* (without the help of *Jupiter*) War or the God of War, alſo the Planet next above the Sun.

Marſeilles (in *Provence*) the moſt ancient City of *France*.

Marſa'quivir, a Spaniſh Port in the Kingdome of *Algiers*.

Marſhal, *Ge.* (Maſter of the Horſe) the name of ſeveral Officers, whereof the chief is the

Earl Marſhal of England, his Office conſiſts (eſpecially) in matters of War and Arms.

Marſhal of the Kings Houſe, he hears and determines all Pleas of the Crown, &c.

Marſhal of the Exchequer, to whom the Court commits the Cuſtody of the Kings Debtors, &c.

Marſhal of the Kings Bench, who hath the Cuſtody of the priſon called the Kings-Bench in *Southwark*.

In every Regiment there is a *Marſhal*, who Executes all Orders of the Council of War.

Marſhalſee, the Court or ſeat of the *Marſhal*, alſo the Priſon in *Southwark* ſo called.

Marchfield, a Town in *Gloceſterſhire*.

Marſyas a Phrygian Muſician, who chalenged *Apollo*, and (being overcom'n) was flead for his preſumption.

Mart, a great Fair or Market.

Martagon, a ſort of Lilly.

Martane, a River of *Lorraine*.

Martens, ſables, a rich furr of a little beaſt of that name.

Martes mark, *o.* Mars's mark.

Martia, *Cato's* wife, whom he gave to his friend *Hortensius*, after whose death he took her again.

Martial, Warlike, belonging to (or born under the Planet) *Mars*.

Martial-Law, which depends on the voice of the King or of his Lieutenant, or of the General or his Officers in wars.

Marticbore, as *Mant-*.

Martin, *-nus* (*q. Martius*) a mans name.

St. *Martin*, a Military Saint, Bishop of *Tours*.

Martinet, *Martlet*, *Apus*, a Swift, (the word is diminutive, but the bird is bigger than the Common *Martin*.)

Martingale, *f.* a leather passing from the horses chaps to his fore-girth, to make him reign well, and hinder the casting-up of his head.

Martnets, small lines fastened to the Legs on the leetch of a sail, to bring it close up to the yard in fartheling.

Top the Martnets, hale the martnets of the top-sails.

Martock, a town in *Sommersetshire*.

Martyria, *g.* testimony, a confirming what one speaks, by ones own experience.

Martyrologie, *g.* a discourse or Book of

Martyrs, *g.* Witnesses sealing the truth of Christianity with their bloud.

Martyrdom, their Suffering.

Marvel of Peru, an *American* Nightshade, with flowers of wonderfull variety.

Marullus Pomponius, a great Grammarian and Critick, who reproved *Tiberius* for speaking improper Latin.

Mary, *h.* Exalted, or from

Marah, *h.* bitternesf.

St. *Mary Cray*, a town in *Kent*.

Mascarade, *f.* a Mask or Mummery.

Mascon, a City in *Burgundy*.

Mascle, (*f. Maale*) a short lozenge (in Blazon) with a square hole in the midst.

Masham, a Town in *Yorkshire*.

Masculine, *l.* Manly, of the Male-kind.

Maskewd, *o.* fenced, fortified.

Mass, (*f. Messe*, *l. Missa*, *h, Missah* an Oblation) the Popish Liturgie or Church-service.

Mass-daies, *Sa.* Holy-days.

Massa, a Countrey between *Tuscany* and *Genoa*.

Massanello, (for *Thomas Anello*) a Fisher-man of *Naples* who headed the tumultuous people against their Governours, arose to great dignity and (in a moment) slain.

Massicot, *f.* (*q. Massa cocta*) Oaker made of Ceruse or white-lead.

Massacre, *f.* (*I. Mazzare* to kill with a *Mazze*, a mace or club) a General Slaughter.

Massilia, *Marseilles* in *France*

Massilians, as *Messalians*.

Massinissa, a King of *Numidia*, first an Enemy, afterwards a faithfull friend to the *Romans*.

Mass-Munster, a town in *Alsatia*.

Massovia, a Province of *Poland*.

Massorets, Jews that corrected (in the Margent) the false-written words of the Scripture-text.

Mast, the fruit of the Oak, Beech, Chesnut, &c.

Main-mast, four fifths of a ships breath, multiplied by 3 [feet,] and (for thickness) one inch to a yard.

Fore-Mast, (and *Bolt-sprit*) four fifths of the Main mast.

Missen-Mast, half the Main-Mast.

Top-Mast, half the length of its own mast.

Master of the Armory, having the Care and over-sight of his Majesties Armour.

Master of the Ceremonies, the Kings Interpreter, introduceth Ambassadours, &c.

Masters of the Chancery, Assistants to the Lord Chancellour and Master of the Rolls.

Master of the Horse, he that hath the rule and charge of the Kings stable.

Master of the Kings Houshold, *Grand Master-*, Lord Steward-, under whom is the

Master of the Houshold, a Principal Officer of great authority and antiquity.

Master of the Jewel house, hath charge of all plate for the King or Queens Table, or in the Tower, Chains, loose Jewels, &c.

Master of the Mint. *Warden-*, he receives the Silver of the Goldsmiths, &c.

Master of the Kings Musters, or

Muster-Master General, sees that the Kings forces be compleat, well armed and trained.

Master of the Ordnance, who hath care of all the Kings Ordnance and Artillery,

Master of the Posts, was an Officer of the Kings Court, who appointed all that provided Post-horses, &c.

Master of the Rolls (till 11 *Henry* 7. called *Clerk of the Rolls*) *Magister vel Custos Rotulorum*, *Clericus parvæ bagæ*, &c. Assistant to the Lord Chancellour of *England*, and (in his absence) hears Causes and gives Orders.

Master of the Court of Wards and Liveries, the Chief Officer of that Court, abolished 12 *Car.* 2.

Master of the Wardrobe, (an Office near puddle-Wharf) He has the Charge of all former kings and Queens ancient Robes in the Tower, all hangings, bedding, &c. for the kings houses, delivers Velvet or Scarlet for Liveries, &c.

Maſterie, q. *Maiſtrete* (for *Maiſtriſe*) Maſterſhip, or elſe for maſtereth.

Maſterwort, *Imperatoria*, it provokes ſweat, and (being held between the Teeth) draws rheum very much.

Maſtication, l. a chewing.

Maſticatory, a medicine to be chewed.

Maſticine, belonging to

Maſtick, a clear ſweet-ſmelling gum of the Lentisk tree in *Chios*.

Maſticot, a fine yellow powder for paint.

Maſty, q. *Naſty*, or fatted with Malt.

Maſtigophore, g. one deſerving ſtripes, or the Officer that (with blows) makes way in a croud.

Maſtling, (q. *Meſsing*, ge. braſs.) o. ſhining.

Maſtrake. f. a winter-garment of Wolves and Deer-skins.

Maſura terræ, about four *Oxgangs*.

Maſtuerco, an Indian healing herb.

Mats, broad clowts (of ſynnet and thrums) to ſave any thing from galling.

Matachin, f. an antick or morrice dance.

Matagot, a kind of Ape, alſo a Hypocrite.

Matapan, (in the *Morea*) the moſt Southern Cape of *Europe*.

Match, when a Wolf deſires copulation, he goes to his Match or Mate.

Mate, ſa. daunted, alſo conſumed, dead.

Check-mate, when (at Cheſs) there is no way left for the King to eſcape, and the game is ended.

Blind-mate, when he that mates the King (not perceiving it) cries only Check.

Matelotage, f. the hire of a ſhip or boat, from

Matelot, f. a ſeaman or boatman.

Mateology, g. a vain over-curious enquiry into things.

Mateotechny, g. a vain art, or the vanity of any ſcience.

Materia prima, the firſt matter, or ſubject of all ſubſtantial formes.

Material, l. conſiſting of matter or ſubſtance, alſo weighty or important.

Materiation, l. felling of Timber for building, or preparing it for war.

Mater Metallorum, Quick-ſilver.

Maternal, l. Motherly.

Maternity, mother-hood.

Mathematical, belonging to a

Mathematician, one skil'd in the

Mathematicks, g. Sciences taught by Demonſtration, viz. Arithmetick, Aſtronomy, Geometry and Muſick.

Matthew, h. reward.

Mathurins, Fryers of the Holy Trinity, who are to employ the alms they beg, in redeeming Chriſtian ſlaves from the Turks.

Matines, f. Morning-Prayers at three a Clock.

Matire, o matter.

Matricide, l. a killing or killer of his Mother.

Matricious, belonging to the

Matrice, -*ix*, l. that part of the womb, where the Child is conceived; alſo a mould for Printers Letters.

Matriculation, l. a being

Matriculated, ſworn and regiſtred into the ſociety of our Mother the Univerſity.

Matrimonial, l. belonging to

Matrimony, l. Marriage.

Matron, a grave motherly Woman.

Matta, an Indian Idol which they viſit yearly, and to whom they ſacrifice a piece of their tongues.

Mattathias, *Matthias*, h. the Gift of the Lord.

Matted plants, growing as if they were plaited together.

Mattins, as *Matines*.

Mattock, (q. *Met haeck*, D. with a hook) a kind of pick-axe.

Mattreſs, ſ. a quilt or flock-bed.

Matura, the Goddeſs of Corn when it began to ripen, as *Patalena* was, when the cups began to open.

Maturated, l. ripened, haſtened.

Maturation, a ripening.

Maturative, belonging to, helping or cauſing

Maturity, l. ripeneſs, perfection.

Matutine, -*nal*, l. belonging to

Matuta, the morning.

Maud, *Matilda*, *Mathildis*, Ge. Lady of Maids.

Maudlin, *Coſtus hortorum*, like Tanſey in ſight, and Alecoaſt in vertue.

Mauger, *Malgerius*, a proper name.

Maugre, (f. *Mal gré*) in ſpight of ones Teeth.

Thou canſt (*kenneſt*) *me Maugre*, o. oweſt me a ſpight.

Mavis, a thruſh, alſo a buſhel, o.

Maumet, o. Mahomet.

Maund, f. a hand-basket with two lids, or hamper, (to carry victuals, &c.) whence

Maundy-Thurſday, ſhore or Sheer-Thurſday, next before Eaſter, when the King (or his Almoner) waſhes the feet of certain poor men and gives them Doles.

Maunding, c. begging.

Mavors, as *Mars*.

Mauritania, the utmoſt Region of *Africa* toward the *Gaditan Bay* or the ſtreights of *Gibralter*.

Mauſolæum, a famous marble Sepulchre (one of the ſeven wonders of the world) 25 cubits high, 411 foot about, ſupported with 36 curious pillars, built by *Artemeſia* for her Husband

Mauſolus, King of *Caria*.

Maxentius, the Son of

Maximinus, a Roman Ty-

 rant

rant, persecutour of Christianity.

Maxillar, -ry, *l.* belonging to the Jaw-bone.

Maxime, an axiom, rule, or undeniable principle in any Art.

Maximilian, (composed of *Maximus* and *Æmilianus*, *Q. Fabius* and *Scipio*) a German Emperour Son to *Fredrick* 3.

Maximinus, a Roman Emperour Author of the sixth persecution.

May, the Moneth dedicated to

Maia, the Mother of *Mercury*.

May-fly, bred (in *May*) of a Water-cricket crept out of the water.

May games, *Floralia*, beginning (probably) from such a Roman custom, according to *Ovid*.

Exit & in Maias Festum
Florale Calendas, *Fast.* 4.

Maynour, as *Mainour*.

Mayor, *Meyr*, as *Maior*.

Maystrye, *o.* a Master-piece.

May-weed, resembling Cammomel, but of a stinking savour and odious to Bees.

Mazagan, a *Portugal* fort on the coast of *Morocco*.

Maze, an astonishment, also as

Miz-maze, a labyrinth or place full of intricate turnings.

Mazara, a town in *Sicily*.

Mazer, -*zar*, -*zeline*, a beker or standing-cup to drink in, commonly made of

Maeser, *D.* Maple.

Mazzards, *West.* black-cherries.

Mazzo, a Town in the *Valteline*.

Meaco, the chief City in *Japan*.

Mead, *Mede*, (*Br. Medd*) as *Hydromel*.

Mead, a Meadow.

Meadow-sweet, *Regina prati*, with crumpled leaves, stops bleeding, &c.

Meag *Meak*, *E.* a peas-hook.

Meagre, *f.* lean.

Meal-Rents, payable by some Tenants in the Honour of *Clun*, to make meat for the Lords hounds.

Mean, *midle*, in the midle, between two extreams.

Mean part (in Musick,) the Tenour, between treble and Basse.

Meander, *Mean-*, *Madre*, *Palazzia*, a Phrygian River with many turnings.

Meandrous, full of

Meanders, [things full of] intricate turnings and windings.

Mear-stones, placed for bounds between land and land.

Mease, (*q. Maison*) *f.* a mansion-house, also a measure of 500 Herrings.

Measles, a disease somewhat like the small pox.

Measn, as *Mesne*.

Measondue as *Maison Dieu*.

Measure of length, three barly corns (from end to end) make an inch, twelve inches a foot, two foot and a half a step, 3 foot a yard, 3 foot and nine inches an ell, 6 foot a fathom, five yards and a half a Rood, (pole or pearch) forty Roods a Furlong, and (with the breadth of four Rods) an Acre, eight Furlongs an English mile.

Meath, *Ir.* choice or liberty, also a Province of *Ireland*.

Meaux, a City in *France*.

Mecænas, a Noble man of *Rome*, who favour'd *Virgil*, *Horace*, and other learned men.

Mecha, *Meccha*, a City of *Arabia fælix*, not far from *Medina*, but of far greater resort and traffick.

Mechanick, -*cal*, *g.* belonging to an Handy-craft.

Mechanick, a Trades-man.

Mechanick Arts, (chiefly seven) Agriculture, Architecture, Clothing, Hunting, Medicine, Military Discipline, and Navigation.

Mechlin, a City of *Brabant*.

Mechoachan, a root of great efficacy in the Dropsie.

Mechation, *l.* Whoredom.

Mecklenburg, a German Dukedom.

Medal, -*lia*, (*f. Medaille*) an ancient flat jewel or coyn, (not current money, but, representing some effigies or other ingenious device.

Mede, *Sa.* a desert or merit.

Medea, a sorceress feigned to have the power of renewing youth, &c.

Medes, *o.* to boot.

Medembleck, a Town in *Holland*.

Medewife, *Sa.* a woman of merit.

Medfee, *Sa.* a bribe or reward, also the bote or compensation given in an exchange.

Media, a large Country in *Asia*.

Median, *l.* mean, midle, indifferent.

Median vein, the midle, common or black vein.

Mediastine, *l.* the thin skins dividing the whole breast (from the throat to the Midriff) into two hollow bosoms, also a drudge or kitchin-slave.

Mediation, *l.* a dividing in two, also coming between, the work of a

Mediatour, *l.* he that doth

Mediate, intercede or entreat for another.

Medicable, *l*, able to heal, or easy to be healed.

Medicament, *l.* a medicine.

Medicaster, *l.* a Quack or pedling Physitian.

Medicated [meats, &c.] mingled with medicinal ingredients.

Medication, *l.* a curing.

Medicinable, curable.

Medicine, *l.* Physick, of five kinds, Nosognomick, discerning diseases; Boethetick, removing them; Pharmaceutick, curing them by application of Medicaments; Chirurgick, by incision or cau-

cauterising, *Diateri k*, by Diet.

Mediok, *l.* a Physitian.

Mediety, *l.* the midle or half.

Meditas linguæ, a mixt inquest of Denizens and Strangers.

Medimne, *-num*, *l.* 6 Bushels.

Medina, a City of *Arabia* where Mahomets Tomb stands.

Mediocrity, *l.* indifferency moderation, a mean.

Medio acquietando, a writ to distrain a Lord for acquitting a mean Lord from a Rent which another claims.

Mediolanum, *Millain*, the Chief City of *Lombardy*, so called (they say) from a sow half covered with Wooll, found in digging the foundation.

Medisance, *f.* evil-speaking, reproach.

Meditative, belonging to

Meditation, *l.* a studying or devising.

Mediterranean, *l.* in the middle of the Earth.

Mediterranean Sea, the Midland Sea, Dividing *Europe* from *Africa*, and part of *Asia*.

Medle, *o.* mingle.

Medlar, a fruit (if rotten-ripe) gratefull to the stomach.

Medlefe, *-letum*, quarrelling, scuffling.

Medrinacles, Pouledavies, a Course kind of Canvas.

Medullar, belonging to the marrow.

Medusean, belonging to

Medusa, *Phorcys's* Daughter with golden hair, turn'd into snakes by *Minerva*, for lying with *Neptune* in her Temple.

Meed, *o.* Merit or reward.

Meedless, *No.* unruly.

Meegre Larbre, *o.* (*q. Maigre en arbre*) as Lean as a tree.

Meen, *Mine*, *f.* the Countenance, or posture of the face.

Meer, for *Meer Right*.

Mees, *sa.* meadow.

Meet, *Mete*, *No.* measure.

Meet now, *No.* Just now.

Meeter, *-tre*, Verse or measure.

Meeterly, *Meeth-*, *Meed-*, *No.* handsomely, modestly.

Megaclo, Daughter of

Megares, King of *Lesbia*, who hired the muses to be her maids and (with their singing) to pacifie his frowardness towards her mother.

Megacosm, *g.* *Macrocosm*, the great world.

Megæra, one of the Furies.

Megalensian, or *Megalesian* Games, in honour of the great Goddess *Cybele*.

Megalopsychie, *g.* Magnanimity, greatness of Soul.

Megalysus, A *Persian* Noble, who (for *Darius*) overthrew the tyranny of the *Magi*.

Meganologie, *g.* a discourse of Greatness

Megarick Phylosophers, instituted by *Euclid*, born at

Megara, a Town near the *Isthmus*, also the daughter of *Creon* King of *Thebes*, slain by her own husband *Hercules*.

Megbote, as *Mag-*.

Megrim, *Migrame*, (*Hemicrania*) a pain (by fits) in the Temples or fore-part of the head.

Meine, *o.* the same as

Meiny, *Mesnie*, *f.* a Family.

Meiosis, *g.* a diminution, making a thing less than it is.

Meke, *o.* meek.

Meladine, a king of *Egypt*, courteous to the Christians when they were half drowned.

Melampode, *g.* *Hellebore*.

Melampus, (black-foot, by being laid in the Sun) a Physician that understood the voices of Birds and Beasts.

Melancholick, troubled with

Melancholy, *g.* black choler, one of the four humours, also a pensive distemper from the abounding thereof.

Melantho, Daughter of *Proteus*, being desirous to ride on a Dolphin, *Neptune* (in that shape) deceived her and ravished her.

Melanthus, a banished *Messenian*, who having holpen the *Athenians* against the *Bœotians*, was by them chosen king.

Melborn, a Castle in *Darbyshire*, where the Duke of *Bourbon* was prisoner 19 years.

Melchior, one of the *Magi*, or 3 kings of *Colen*, also an Heretick, founder of the *Melchiorists*.

Melchites, a *Syrian* Sect Subject to the Patriarch of *Antioch*, of the same Tenents with the *Grecians* (save that they observe both Saterday and Sunday:) in Religion they follow the injunctions of the Emperour or

Melchi, *Sy.* king.

Melchizedeck, *h.* King of Righteousness.

Meldfeoh, *Sa.* the Informers fee.

Meleager, son of *Oneus* king of *Calidonia*.

Melechsala, the son of *Meladine*, king of *Egypt*, he won the peoples hearts from his Father, who (therefore) lived unbeloved and died unlamented.

Melilote, *Mill-*, *Corona Regia*. (*q. Honey-Lote*) an herb with round leaves and slender branches.

Meliorate, *l.* to wax or make better.

Meliority, Betterness.

Melissa, *Mellona*, *-nia*, the Patroness of bees.

Melite, *o.* power.

Melius inquirendo, a writ for a second (more impartial) enquiry of what lands a man died seized.

Melasses, Treacle, the dross of Sugar.

Mellation, the [time of] taking the honey out of hive.

Mell, *o.* medle.

Mellean, *-eous*, of or like Honey.

Mellifrous, *l.* bringing or bearing Honey.

Mellification, a making honey.

Mellifluent, *-uous* flowing with honey, eloquent.

Melliloquent, Sweet-spoken.

Mellisent, (hony-sweet) a womans name.

Mellitism, honeyed wine.

Mellitergie, *g.* Bees-work, making of honey.

Mellona, see *Mellissa*.

Melody, *g.* harmony, a sweet-song.

Melowne, (*f. Milan*) a kite.

Melpomene, one of the Muses, Authour of Tragedies.

Melton-Mowbray, a Town in *Leicestershire*.

Membranatick, belonging to a

Membrane, *l.* a thin skin, rind or parchment.

Pleuritique Membrane, through whose doubles pass all the Sinews, Veins and Arteries, which are between the Ribs.

Membrature, *l.* a setting or ordering of Members or Parts.

Membrino, a fam'd Knight errant in *Don Quixot*, whose helmet was said to be impenetrable.

Memnonian birds, reported to have flown out from the funeral pile of

Memnon, Brother of *Laomedon*, slain by *Achilles* in the *Trojan* war.

Memorable, *l.* easie or worthy to be remembred.

Memorandum, *l.* [a note or token of] something to be remembred.

Memoires, *f* remarkable observations.

Memorial, *l.* that which puts one in mind, or makes one to be remembred.

Memories, obsequies or Remembrances for the dead.

Memorious, *l.* having a good Memory.

Memento mori, *l.* remember dying.

Of blessed Memory, happy or honoured in being thought upon.

Memphians, *-ists*, Egyptians, inhabitants of

Memphis, *Alcairo*, the chief City of *Egypt*.

Menage, *f.* a leading or handing.

Menahim, *h.* a comforter.

Menalippus, a Theban, slain by the friends of *Tydeus*, to whom he had first given a mortal wound.

Menasseh, *Manassah*, *h.* forgotten.

Mendaciloquent, *l.* speaking lies.

Mendicant, *l.* begging.

Mendicants, begging Fryers.

Mendication, a begging.

Mendicity, beggery.

Mendience, *f.* the same

Mendlesham, a Town in *Suffolk*.

Menelaus, the Son of *Atreus*, and Husband of *Helena* the Daughter of *Jupiter* and *Leda*.

Menestheus, the Son of *Peleus* and King of *Athens* who died at the siege of *Troy*.

Mene, *o.* meditate.

Menged, *o.* mingled.

Mengrel, *o*, mongrel.

Mengrelians, *Circassians*, (next neighbours to the *Georgians*) of the Greek Religion, save that they baptize not their Children till eight years old.

Menial-servants, Family servants.

Menials, the same

Meninges, *g.* the two thin skins about the Brain, *viz.* *Dura mater* between the skul and the *Pia mater*, next the Brain.

Menivew, the fur of a small *Muscovia* beast.

Menker, the Whales jaw, a star.

Mennow, (*f. Menu*, small) *Minimus*, a Cockrel, a very little fish.

Menachius, the Son of *Creon* and the last of *Cadmus*'s race, who slew himself for the safety of his Country promised by the Oracle on that account.

Menologe, the greek Martyrology, Calendar or Collection of Saints-days in every moneth.

Mensal, *l.* belonging to a Table.

Menseful, *Y.* comely, creditable.

Mension, *-suration*, *l.* a measuring.

Menstrual, *l.* monthly.

Menstruosity, a being

Menstruous, *-uant*, *l.* abounding with or belonging to monthly Terms or Flowers.

Mensurate, *l.* to measure.

Mensura Regalis, the Kings standard of th' Exchequer.

Mental, *l.* thought or kept in the mind.

Menteith, part of South *Scotland*.

Mentition, *l.* a lying or telling of lies.

Mentz, *Mænus*, *-Mogus*, a free City on the *Rhine* in *Germany*.

Meny, *No.* a Family.

Meotides, Lakes and Marshes between *Europe* and *Asia*.

Mephibosheth, *h.* shame of mouth.

Mephistophiles, Dr. *Faustus*'s familiar spirit.

Mephitick, stinking, dampish [savour of the earth.]

Mera, a great huntress ravisht by *Jupiter* in the shape of *Diana*, who shot her to death and turn'd her to a Celestial Dog.

Meracity, *l.* pureness without mixture.

Meraud, (*q. Esmeraude*) a Womans name.

Mercative, belonging to

Mercature, *l.* the Trade of Merchandize.

Mercedary, *l.* he that hireth, also as

Mercenary, he that is hired

hired for reward or wages.

Merch, part of South *Scotland*.

Merchenlage, the law of the

Mercian, Inhabitants of *Cheſter*, *Glocester*, *Hereford Oxford*, *Salop*, *Stafford*, *Warwick*, and *Worceſter*. This was one of the three ſorts of laws out of which the Conqueror framed ours, mixt with thoſe of *Normandy*; the other two being *Danelaege*, and *Weſt-Saxenlaeg*.

Mercimoniatus Angliæ, the Cuſtom or Impoſt of *England*.

Mercurialize, to play the

Mercurial, *-liſt*, fantaſtical, talkative, theeviſh, Eloquent, one born under

Mercury, the Planet next above the Moon, alſo Quick-ſilver, the Son of *Jupiter*, and *Maia*, the meſſenger of the Gods, alſo a News-book.

Mercurian, eloquent &c.

Mercurius Triſmegiſtus, as *Hermes*, *&c.*

Mercury-women. See *Hawkers*.

In the grievous Mercy of the King, in hazard of a great fine or penalty.

Merdiſerous, *l.* carrying dung.

Mere, a ſtanding water which cannot be drawn dry, alſo as *Lynchet*.

Mere, a Town in *Wilts*.

Meritricious, *l.* whoriſh.

Mergen, *ſa.* the morning.

Merell, *o.* (for *Wereld*, *D.*) the World.

Meridian, an imagined circle (paſſing through the Poles and the Zenith) which being touched by the centre of the Suns body, maketh Noon-tide, alſo as

Meridional, belonging to the South or to mid-day.

Meridiation, *l.* a ſleeping at Noon.

Meriſmus, *g.* diviſion, a diſpoſing things in their proper places.

Meritot, *Oſcillum*, a childiſh play of ſitting and ſwinging in a rope.

Meritorious, full of

Merit, *l.* deſert, alſo to deſerve.

Merk, *o.* Dark. Se *Murk*.

Merkin, (*f. la mere*, Matrix) *pubes* [*ementita*] *mulieris*.

Merle, *f.* a blackbird.

Merlin, a *Britiſh* Conjurer.

Mermaides, *Syrens*, (*Ligæa*, *Leucoſia* and *Parthenope*,) Sea-maids (with their neather parts fiſhy) who were ſaid with their muſick to entice Seamen & then deſtroy them.

Mern, part of North-*Scotland*.

Merodach-Baladan, *h.* bitter Contrition without judgment.

Meroden, a town in *Gulickland*.

Dia Meroes, the fartheſt of the Northern Climates, whoſe parallel runs through

Meroe, a City in an Iſland of that name encompaſſed with *Nilus*, from

Meroe, the Siſter of *Cambyſes* founder thereof.

Merope, one of the *Pleiades*.

Merrick, an ancient *Britiſh* name of a man.

Merry banks, *Der.* a cold poſſet.

Merſion, *l.* a Ducking, drowning or over-whelming.

Mertlage, for *Martyrologie*.

Merton Colledge (in *Oxford*) founded by one *Walter* of

Merton, a town in *Surrey*.

Meroil, a town of *Luxemburgh*.

Meſe, half a thouſand of herrings, alſo the mean or midle-ſtring of an inſtrument.

Meſel, *Sa.* a Leper.

Meſenterick, *Meſeraick*, belonging to the

Meſentery, *g.* (mid-bowels) the Double skin faſtening the bowels to the back and one another, encloſing a number of veins which nouriſh the guts, conc[oct] the juice of meat, and convey it to the liver to be made bloud.

Meskite, a ſynagogue among the *Turks* and *Moors*, from

Mezquidan, *A.* an Oration.

Meſnalty, the right of a

Meſn, the Lord of a mannour, holding of a ſuperiour Lord, alſo a writ, when the Tenant is diſtrained by the ſuperiour for ſervice due to the mean Lord.

Meſnagery, *-rie*, *f.* [the practice of] Husbandry or Huſwifry.

Meſopotamia, *Apamia*, *Adiabene*, (*Aram Naharaim*, *h.* *Syria* of the rivers) a large Country of *Aſia*, between the Rivers *Tigris* and *Euphrates*.

Meſozeugma, the figure *Zeugma* with the verb in the midle.

Meſſagery, a diligence in doing a meſſage.

Meſſalians, *Maſſil-*, Hereticks holding that the ſacraments did neither good nor harm, &c.

Meſſilana, the Luxurious Wife of *Claudius* the Emperour.

Meſſana, *-ſina*, the chief city of *Sicily*.

Meſſapia, *Meſſa-*, part of *Italy*, conteining *Apuglia* and *Calabria*.

Meſſarius, a mower or harveſter.

Meſſenij, the people of

Meſſene, a City of *Greece*, which held out long againſt the *Spartans*, but at laſt was reduced to abſolute ſlavery.

Meſſengers of the Exchequer, Four Purſuivants attending the Lord Treaſurer.

Meſſiah, *-as*, *h.* Chriſt or Anointed.

Meſſile, as *Miſſile*, (in the laſt ſenſe.)

Meſſina, the beſt port-town in *Sicily*.

Meſſor, *l.* a reaper or mower.

Meſſorious, *l.* belonging

to

to reaping or harvest.

Mestilo, Messin, Mascorn, Wheat and Rye mixt.

Mestizos, Sp. the breed of *Spaniards* by the *Americans*.

Mest, o. for *Most*.

Mestier, f. a trade, also necessity.

Mestifical, l. making heavy or sad.

Mesuage, Mess-, a dwelling-house [with Garden and all things belonging to it]

Messuagium, (in *Scotland*) the Mannor house.

Met, Mette, o. Dreamed.

Met, No. Four pecks.

Metabasis, g. a Transition or passing from one thing to another.

Metachronism, g. an errour in Chronology or reckoning of time.

Metacism, l. a fault in pronouncing.

Metaleptick, belonging to

Metalepsis, g. a participating, the continuation of a trope in one word through a Succession of significations.

Metal, Mettle, the breech of a Great Gun.

Under-Mettle, with her mouth lower than the breech.

Over-Mettle, with the mouth higher.

Metalliferous, l. bringing forth Metals.

Metallick, -ine, l. belonging to Metals.

Metamorphize, to transform, or change the form or shape.

Metamorphosis, g. a changing of one shape into another.

Metaphorical, belonging to or spoken by a

Metaphor, g. a borrowing of a word to express something which it doth not signifie naturally, a similitude comprehended in one word.

Metaphysical, Supernatural, belonging to

Metaphysicks, g. a Science which enquires of the form and end (as Physicks doth of the efficient and matter) of things. The highest part of it treats of God, Spirits, &c.

Metaplasm, -mus, a necessary change (of words or letters) by reason of the verse, &c.

Metaris, *Maltraith*, the washes, an arm of the Sea in *Lincolnshire*.

Metathesis, g. a transposition or change of letters.

Mete-gavel, sa. Tribute or Rent paid in Victuals, changed into money by *Hen.* 1.

Metellus, a famous Roman General, also a Priest who lost his eyes by venturing to fetch the *Palladium* out of *Vesta*'s Temple on fire.

Mete, (for Meet,) o. equal, also to deal, to yield.

Metempsychosed, passed by

Metempsychosis, g. a passing of the soul from one body to another.

Meteorologist, one that studies or is skilled in

Meterology, g. the Doctrine of

Meteors, g. apparitions on high, or bodies imperfectly mixt of vapours drawn up into the air, as Comets, Clouds, Wind, Rain, &c.

Meteoroscopie, *g.* a part of Astrology, handling the difference of sublimities and distance of Stars.

Metewand, a yard or measuring rod.

Meth, Meeth, o. the same as *Mead* or

Metheglin, (Br. Meddiglin) a Welch drink of wort, herbs, hony and spice boild together.

Methodical, belonging to

Method, g. a ready way or manner, an orderly or artificial disposing of things.

Methodist, one that so disposeth things or that treats of method.

Methodists, Galenists.

Methridate, as *Mithridate*.

Methuselah, h. (the weapons of his death) he lived 969 years.

Meticulosity, a being

Meticulous, *l.* timerous, fearful.

Metient, l. measuring.

Metiochus, the Son of *Alcibiades* (at war with *Darius*) being taken prisoner, was honourably received and enriched.

Metius Suffetius, Dictator of the *Albans*, torn in pieces by *Tullius Hostilius*'s wild horses, for not assisting him (according to Covenant) against the *Fidenates*.

Metonymical, belonging to a

Metonymie, g. a putting one name for another, as of the Cause and Subject for the Effect and Adjunct, or e contra.

Metope, the distance or space (in a pillar) between the Denticles and Triglyphs.

Metopomancy, g. Divination by the face or forehead.

Metoposcopy, g. telling mens Natures (and fortunes) by looking on their faces.

Metrenchyta, g. an instrument to inject liquid medicines into the womb.

Metrical, l. belonging to

Meeter, or verse.

Metropolis, g. the chief or Mother-City of a Province.

Metropolitan, belonging thereto, also an Arch-Bishop, who (usually) hath his seat there.

Metropolitan and Primate of England, the Arch-Bishop of *York*.

Metropolitan and Primate of all England, the Arch-Bishop of *Canterbury*.

Meve, o. for move.

Mewet, o. in secret.

Metz, a City of *Lorrain*.

Mexican, belonging to

Mexico, a famous City of *Nova Hispania*.

Meurs, a Town on the *Rhine*.

Meurte, a River in *Lorrain*.

Mezentius, a King of the *Thuscans*, who (with his Son *Lausus*) assisting *Turnus* were slain

M I

M I

slain by *Æneas*.

Mezieres, a Town in *Champagne*.

Miagrus, *Mya-*, *Myopes*, *Achor*, the God of flies.

Miasm, *g*. a defilement.

Micajah, *h*. who is like the Lord?

Michael, *h*. who is like God?

St. *Michaels Mount*, a Promontory in *Cornwall*, fortified by *John* Earl of *Oxford* against *K.Edw. 4th*.

Michal, *h*. who is perfect?

Miche, to play the truant, or hide ones self cut of the way.

Michis, white-loaves, paid sometime as a Rent.

Michleta, a kind of Confection.

Mickle, *sa*. much.

Microcosm, *g*. the little World, Man.

Microcosmical, belonging thereto.

Microcosmography, *g*. a description thereof.

Micrography, *g*. a description of minute bodies.

Micrology *g*. a speaking or treating of petty affairs.

Micropsychy, *g*. smallness of Soul, faintheartedness.

Microscope, *g*. an instrument to discern the full proportion of the smallest things.

Mictus sanguinis, *l*. a pissing of [thin, wheyish] bloud.

Midas, King of *Phrygia*, who had his desire of his guest *Bacchus*, that whatsoever he touched might be turn'd into gold, till (being almost famished) he was counselled to wash in *Pactolus*, whose sands (thereby) became golden.

Midding, *sa*. *No*. a mixen or dunghill.

Middleburg, the chief City of *Zealand*, another in *Mentz*, &c.

Middle-men, half-files, they that are in the sixth rank of ten, or the fifth of eight (but improperly.

Middleham, a Town in *York-shire*.

Midge, *No*. a gnat.

Midian, *h*. Judgement or striving.

Middleton, a Town in *Dorcetshire*, and almost 40 more.

Midriasis, *g*. the dilatation of the apple of the eye.

Middlewich, a town in *Cheshire*,

Midhurst, a Town in *Sussex*.

Midriff, as *Diaphragm*.

Migrame, as *Megrim*.

Migration, *l*. a removing or departing.

Mikel, for *Mickle*.

Mildernix, a kind of Canvas for Sail-Clothes, &c.

Mile, a thousand paces, or 1760 yards.

Dutch Mile, 4000 paces.

German Mile, 5000 paces.

Milbrook, a town in *Cornwall*.

Mildenhall, a Town in *Suffex*.

Miles, *Milo*, a mans name.

Milesij, the people of *Miletus*, *Anactoria*, *Melazzo*, the chief City of *Ionia*

Milan, *Millain*, a City in *Italy*.

Milford-haven, a large and comodious haven in *Pembrokeshire*.

Militant, *l*. fighting, combating.

Military, belonging to

Militia, *l*. warfare, Soldiery the implements and furniture for war.

Milken, *c*. a house-breaker.

Milky way, as *Via lactæa*.

Millea e, *Mil-leat*, a trench to convey water to or from a Mill.

Millefoile, the herb yarrow.

Mill, *c*. to steal.

Millenaries, *-ian*, as *Chiliast*.

Millet, *Milium*, a plant bearing a multitude of small grains.

Milliary, *l*. mile-mark a stone pillar (in *Rome*) with a brass ball, from whence all the Miles were reckoned. Such a one *London stone* is thought to have been

Million, a thousand thousand.

Milo, a *Crotonian*, who (at the Olympick games) carried an Oxe a furlong, killed him with his fist, and ate him in one day.

Mill-holms, *No*. watry places about the Mill dam.

Miloglossum, one of the four muscles of the tongue.

Miltiades, an Athenian who (with 11 thousand Greeks) overthrew 600 thousand *Persians*, yet (being accused of bribery) was forced to dye in chains.

Milton, a Town in *Kent*, and about 30 more.

Milverton, a Town in *Sommersetshire*.

Milwyn, *La*. green-fish.

Mimical, apish, belonging to a

Mime, *-mick*, *g*. a Jester, or fool in a play, also a kind of play more wanton than a Comedy.

Mimographer, a writer of such Poems.

Minacity, *-ature*, *l*. menacing or threatning.

Minchings, *o*. (*Monecha*) Nuns.

Minchin-Hampton, a town in *Glocestershire*.

Mindbruch, *sa*. a hurting of honour or Worship.

Minden, a town in *Westphalia*.

Minehead, a town in *Sommersetshire*.

Mine, *f*. as *Meen*.

Mineralist, one skill'd in

Minerals, metallick substances, dug out of

Mines, whence metals are taken, as quarries, whence stones, and pits, whence clays are dug.

Mineral Courts, to regulate the affairs of lead-mines.

Minerva, the Goddess of Wisdom and all the Arts, born of *Jupiters* brain without a Mother.

Minerval. *l*. a reward given for teaching, and (properly) a banquet before a vacation.

Ming, *No*. mention.

Minge, *o*. for mingle.

Minginator, *T*. a maker of Fretwork.

Minia-

Miniated, painted, in-laid (with gold, &c.

Miniature, a drawing of pictures in little, usually with

Minium, *l.* red lead.

Minim, half a Sembrief.

Miniments, as *Muniments*.

Minims, *Minorites*, as *Bonhommes*.

Miniographer, a painter or writer with Vermillion, or any red colour.

Minion, *Mignon*, *f.* a Darling or Favourite, also the name of a piece of Ordinance.

Minious, *l.* of a Red or Vermilion colour.

Minish, *o.* for *Diminish*.

Ministry, *l.* [Church] service.

Ministers, *o.* for Ministrels or Musicians.

Miniver, as *Meniver*.

Minning-daies (*q. Minding-daies*) *La.* Months mind or Years mind, Anniversary or Commemoration daies, when some Office was said for the soul of the Deceased.

Minor, *l.* lesser, younger.

Minor [*proposition*] the Assumption or second part of a syllogism.

Minoration, a making less.

Minorative, diminishing.

Minority, a being under age, Nonage.

Minorca, *-qua*, a Mediterranean Isle on the *Spanish* Coast.

Minors, as *Friar Minors*.

Minos, a King of *Creet*, supposed (for his justice) to be made a Judge in hell, his wife *Pasiphae* having lain with a Bull (or her man *Taurus*) brought forth the

Minotaur, a Monster (half-man, half-bull) kept in the Labyrinth made by *Dædalus*, and devoured yearly seven of the Noblest *Athenian* Youths, till (in the third year) *Theseus* slew him, and escaped by the help of *Ariadne*.

Minovery, (*q. Main-œuvre*) an Offensive handy-work in the Forest, as an Engin to catch Deer, &c.

Minster, *Sa. Monastery*.

Minstrel, (*f. Menestril*) a fidler or piper.

Mint at it, *No.* aim at it, or have a mind to it.

Mint, the place where the Kings coyn is formed, (formerly *Caleis*, now the Tower of *London*.)

Minting, (*q.* minding or coining) *Li. T.* endeavouring

Minute, the sixtieth part of an hour.

Minute, *l.* very small.

Minute-Tythes small-tythes belonging to the Vicar.

Minution, a making little.

Mirabilary, a book of wonders.

Mirach, the girdle of *Andromeda*.

Miraculous, wonderful, above the force or course of Nature.

Miradical, speaking strange things.

Mire-Court, a town in *Lorrain*.

Miriam, *h.* as *Maria*.

Mirifical, *l.* wonderfully wrought or working.

Mirmillones, *Galli*, a sort of Gladiators or Sword-fighters.

Mirour, *Mirrour*, *f.* a looking-glass.

Misagast, *Sf.* mistaken.

Misanthropy, *g.* hating of men.

Misanthropist, *g.* he that hates the Company of men.

Misadventure, *Misav-*, the killing of a man partly by negligence, partly by chance (as by careless throwing of a stone, &c.) whereby he forfeiteth his Goods.

Misbode, *o.* Wrong (by word or deed.)

Miscellaneous, *l.* mixt together without Order.

Miscellanies, Collections of several various matters.

Miscreed, *No.* descryed.

At Mischiefe, *o.* Conquered.

Miscreant, *f.* an Infidel.

Miscord, *o.* to differ

Misconisant, Ignorant, not knowing.

Miscontinuance, as *Discon-*.

Mise, *Mize*, *f.* cast or put-upon, a tax, expence or charges, also

Mise, (in a Writ of right) is the same as that which (in all other actions) is called an Issue.

Mise (in *Wales* is the customary present (of 5000 pound) to every new Prince, paid thrice in the reign of King *James*, *viz.* to himself, Prince *Henry*, and Prince *Charles*.

Mise (in the County Palatine of *Chester*) 3000 Marks paid to every new Earl

Misen-sail, between the Poop and Mainsail.

Change the Misen, bring the yard to the other side of the mast.

Miseraick, as *Meseraick*.

Miserere, *l.* (have mercy) the beginning of the Psalm of mercy, one of the penitential Psalms usually given as the Benefit of Clergy.

Miserere mei, a Disease (from an obstruction of the small guts) voiding the excrements upward.

Misericordia, Mercy, Amercement, an Arbitrary and moderate punishment.

In Misericordiâ, Amerced or at Mercy.

Misfill, *f.* (*q. Misfell*) *o.* miscarried.

Misfeasans, mis-doings, trespasses.

Mish-mash, *Ge.* a Chaos or confused heaps of things.

Mish, *Commission*, *c.* a shirt.

Mish-topper, *c.* a Coat.

Mishering, *miskering*, as *Abishersing*.

Miskenning, (misunderstanding) erroneous proceeding, also varying ones speech in Court.

Miskin, *o.* a little bag-pipe.

Mis-

Missida, a *Saxon* province.

Misnomer, a misnaming.

Misogamy, *g.* a hating of marriage.

Misogyny, *g.* hatred of women.

Misogynist, *g.* a Woman-hater.

Misprision, (*f. Mespris*) contempt, negligence or Oversight, also a Mistaking.

Misprision of Clerks, their neglect in writing or keeping Records.

Misprision of Treason or Felony, Not revealing it, when we know it commited, the first incurs imprisonment during the Kings pleasure and loss of goods, the other is only finable by the Justices before whom the party is attainted.

Misquame, *o.* to displease.

Missate, (*q. mis-sate*) *o.* became not, was misbecoming.

Miss, for *Mistress*.

Missal, *l.* a Mass-book.

Misselden, *Meseldine*, *Misselto*, *Mess*-, an excrementitious plant (with slimy white berries) growing upon trees.

Missen, as *Misen*, whereof some long ships have two, *viz.* the

Main-Missen next the main-mast, and the

Bonaventure-missen, next the poop.

Missil, *l.* a dart or any thing shot or thrown, also (in Heraldry) a mixture of several colours together.

Mission, *l.* a sending, also a Popish Commission to preach the *Roman* Faith in other Countries.

Missionaries, the Priests that are so sent, also as

Fathers of the Mission (in *France*) they go by pairs (in imitation of the Apostles) to assist the Clergy, with obedience to the Bishop.

Missive, *l.* a sending, also sent, and that which witnesseth ones being sent.

Mis-trial, a false or erroneous trial.

Mister, *o.* need, want, also as

Mistery, (*f. Mestier*,) a craft or trade.

Mis-user, an abuse of liberty or benefit.

Miswoman, *o.* a whore.

Misy, Copper (shining like gold) found in *Egypt* and *Cyprus*.

Misthrown, *o.* cast [thine eye] the wrong way.

Mistimed, *o.* Mis-spent the time.

Mites, Vermin (smaller than lice) about the heads and Nostrils of hawks.

Mitches, *o.* Manchets.

Mithridate, *Meth-*, an Antidote against infection, invented by

Mithridates, a King of *Pontus* who spake 22 Languages, rebelling and being overcome by the *Romans*, he would have poison'd himself, but could not.

Mitigate, *l.* to pacify or quiet.

Mitta, ten bushels.

Mittens, *f.* thick winter gloves [without distinction of fingers.]

Mitte, *o.* Mighty.

Mittimus (we send) a writ by which Records are transmitted from one Court to another, also a Justices warrant to a Jailor, to receive and keep an Offender.

Mittendo Manuscriptum pedis finis, a Writ for the searching and transmitting the foot of a fine from the Exchequer to the Common-pleas.

Mitral, *l.* belonging to a

Mitre, was to a Bishop, as a Crown to a King.

Mitylene, an ancient City (and now the whole Isle of *Lesbos*.)

Mixen, *S.* a Dunghill.

Mixolydian, (*q. Mixt Lydian*) Musick, lamentable, fit for Tragedies.

Mixt-tithes, of Cheese, milk, the young of beasts, &c.

Mize, as *Mise*.

Mizzy, *No.* a quagmire.

Miz-maze, as *Maze*,

Mizmor, *Sp.* a Dungeon.

Mnas, a famous *Italian* Pirate.

Mnason, (*q. Mneson*,) *g.* an Exhorter.

Mnemosyne, *g.* (Memory) the Mother of the Muses by *Jupiter*.

Mnestheus, as *Menestheus*.

Moabites, the Offspring of *Moab*, *h.* Of the Father.

Mobbi, a drink (in *Barbados*) made of Potato-roots

Mobility, *l.* moveableness, inconstancy.

Mockel, *Muckle*, *o.* Mickle.

Mockadoes, a kind of stuff.

Modality, the manner or qualification of a thing in the abstract.

Modbury, a town in *Devonshire*.

Modder, (*D. Modde*) and *Mawther*, (*Da. Moer*) *Nf.* a young girl.

Modefy, *f.* to moderate, or put into the

Mode, *f.* fashion.

Modena, the chief City of

Modenois, an *Italian* Dutchy.

Moderata Misericordia, a Writ for the abating an immoderate amerciament.

Modo et forma, *l.* in manner and form.

Moderation, *l.* temperance, discretion, government.

Moderatour, *-tor*, *l.* a Discreet Governour, and Decider of Controversies.

Modern, *l.* New, of late time.

Modiation, a measuring by the bushel.

Moder, as *Modder*.

Modicum, *l.* a small pittance.

Modificable, capable of

Modification, the act of

Modifying, qualifying, measuring, limiting.

Modus decimandi, any composition for Tithes in kind.

Modulation, *l.* an exact singing or warbling.

Modwall, a bird that destroyes bees.

Moeble, o. (*f. Meuble, Muable*) Moveable.

Mœris, an *Egyptian* King who undertook and finished the

Mœris, an admirable lake receiving the superfluity of *Nilus*, and supplying them with water in time of drought

Mognions, *f.* Arms for the shoulders.

Mogontus, an ancient *British* Idol in *Northumberland*.

Moguntine, belonging to

Moguntia, *Mentz* in *Germany*, where printing was invented, *An.* 1440.

Mohatra, *Sp.* a taking up money upon usury.

Moiety, *Moitie*, *f.* the half of any thing.

Moile, o. a dish of marrow and grated bread.

Moiles, *Mullei*, high-soald shoes anciently worn by Kings and great persons.

Moison, o. (*f. Moisson*, harvest) ripeness [of corn.]

Mokes, *Sf.* the meishes of a Net.

Mokel, *sa.* Bigness.

Molar, *l.* belonging to a mill.

Molar teeth, Cheek-teeth, Grinders, five on each side both above and beneath.

Molasses, the refuse Sirrup in boiling Sugar.

Mole, a Peer or Fense against the Sea.

Molebrute, a great grunting fish.

Molech, *h.* as *Moloch*.

Molendarious, *-dina-*, belonging to a mill.

Molendinum ad ventum, a wind-mill.

Molendinum Bladonicum, *bladum*, *de Blado*, a Com-mill.

Molestation, *l.* a vexing or troubling.

Moliminous, having, using, or requiring much strength.

Molinists, great opposers of the *Jansenists*, and followers of

Molina, a *Spanish* Jesuit, maintaining that God did not premove the will in free acts &c.

Molition, *l.* an attempting or endeavouring.

Mollificative, having power to

Mollify, *l.* to soften, or cause

Mollitude, *l.* softness, tenderness, effeminateness.

Mollock, *Meore*, o. dirt or dung.

Moloch, *Molech*. *h.* (railing, or a King) an Idol having the brazen body of a man with the head of a Calf.

Molter, *No.* Mill-toll.

Moloechite, as *Malachite*.

Molucques, *Asian* Islands.

Moly, an herb of great use (and virtue) among the Gods, whose root was supposed dangerous for mortals to dig up.

Momblishness, o. talking, muttering.

Mombelliard, a town in *Franche* County.

Mome, *-mus*, a feigned Deity (Son of *Nox* and *Somnus*) whose business was to find fault and carp at all the other Gods.

Moment, *l.* a minute, also weight or concernment.

Momentary, of short continuance.

Mompellier, a City of *Languedoc*, in *France*.

Mon, o. Might, (*q. Mun* or *Must*.)

Mon, *Mona*, *Anglesey*.

Monachal, *Monial*, belonging to

Monachism, *g.* the state and condition of a Monk.

Monadical, belonging to

Monas, *g.* unity, the number of one.

Mon amy, *f.* My friend.

Mon-Castel, a town in *Flanders*.

Monarchical, belonging to

Monarchy, *g.* Government by a

Monarch, *g.* one Man (or Woman) ruling alone.

Monasterial, belonging to *Monasteries* colledges for

Monasticks, *g.* Monks, or Solitary Religious people.

Mond, *f.* a golden globe, the Ensign of an Emperour, challenging a kind of right to the whole world.

Mone, o. (*q. Mond*) a globe.

Moneduie, *l.* a Jack-daw.

Moneresse, o. a She-Mourner [at Funerals.]

Moneth, Four weeks, or Eight and twenty daies.

Twelve-Moneth, a whole year.

Twelve moneths, to be reckoned by 28 dayes to the moneth.

Calendar Moneth, as exprest in every yearly Almanack.

Moneth of apparition, 26 daies and 12 hours, the Moon being in combustion with the Sun and disappearing the other 3 daies.

Moneth of Consecution or Progression, from one conjunction to another, 26 dayes and an half.

Medical or Decretorial Moneth, 26 dayes and 22 houres.

Moneth of Peragration, 27 dayes and 8 hours, the Moons revolution from any part of the Zodiack to the same again.

Moneths-mind, *Sa.* The 30th. day after any ones death.

Mong-corn, o. Maslin.

Monger, a small Sea-vessel for fishing.

Monger, *Mangere*, *Sa.* a Merchant.

Moniers, *Moneyors*, the Mint-men or Coyners.

Monitory, *l.* the place of

Monition, *l.* admonition, warning, the work of a

Monitor, *l.* an admonisher or Counsellour.

Monks-hood, *Consolida Regalis*, a flower.

Monmedi, a town of *Luxemburg*.

Mon-

Monmouth, a town and County in *Wales*.

Monoceros, *-rote*, *g.* an unicorn.

Monocord, *g.* having but one string

Monocular, *-lous*, one-eyed.

Monodical, belonging to a

Monody, *g.* a funeral ditty sung by one alone.

Monogamy, *g.* a marrying but one [wife or husband.]

Monogdon, *g.* an eight, or one out of eight.

Monogram, *g.* a writing or sentence of one line or verse.

Monologie, *g.* speaking alone or alwaies in the self-same tone, also a long discourse to little purpose.

Monomachy, *g.* a single combat, hand to hand.

Monologue, *-gian*, *g.* one that loves to hear himself talk

Monophagie, *g.* a feeding alone, or on one kind of meat.

Monopolize, to play the

Monopolist, he that useth or hath the grant of a

Monopoly, *g.* an ingrossing of commodities into ones hand, that none can sell or gain by them but himself.

Monops, *Bonasus*, a *Paeonian* beast, which (being pursued) casts forth ordure deadly to those it lights on.

Monoptote, *g.* [a Noun] of one only case.

Monoptick, *g.* seeing onely with one eye.

Monostick, *g.* a single verse.

Monosyllable, [a word] of one only syllable.

Monothelites, *g.* Hereticks (*Anno.* 640.) holding but one will in Christ.

Monstrable, *l.* which may be shewed or declared.

Monstrance de droit *f.* a writ of Chancery to restore one to lands or Tenements, shewn to be his Right.

Monstre, *o.* an essay or (rather) master-piece.

Monstraverunt, a writ for Tenants in ancient demesne, not to be distreined for toll or other service contrary to their liberties.

Monstrosity, *l.* a being

Monstrous, *l.* beyond the ordinary course of nature.

Mount be'gard, a Town and Earldom in *Germany*.

Montanus, an heretick who held that the Holy Ghost was not given to the Apostles, but to him and the

Montanists, his followers.

Montanous, *l.* belonging to or full of Mountains.

Montchensy, *de monte canisio*, a great surname in *Kent* and *Suffolk*.

Montferrat, an Italian Province divided between the Dukes of *Mantoua* and *Savoy*.

Mont fiasco, a rich wine from

Montefiascone, a City in *Italy*.

Montfort, a Town in *Utrecht*

Montera, *-ro*, *sp.* a Hunters or Horsemans cap.

Montgomery, *Mons Gomericus*, a City in *Wales*.

Monticulous, *l.* full of

Monticles *l.* little hills.

Montificket, *de monte fixo*, a noted name.

Montivagant, *-gous*, *l.* wandring on the Mountains.

Monts, *Mons*, the chief town of *Hainault*.

Monument, *l.* a memorial, tomb, statue, &c.

Montreali, a City in *Sicily*.

Montrose, a Marquisate of North *Scotland*.

Monychus, a Centaur that pulled up Trees by the Roots.

Monyma, complained that her Diadem was good neither in prosperity nor adversity, because it broke when she would have hang'd herself in it, after her husband *Mithridates* was overthrown.

Mony-wort, *Nummularia*, herb two pence.

Mood, *Modes* *l.* manner measure, rule, also an humour or temper of mind.

Moods of Verbs, Indicative Imperative, Subjunctive and Infinitive,

Moods in Musick, Dorick Lydian, Æolick, Phrygian and Ionick.

Moon-wort, *Lunaria*, a small plant of great virtue in curing wounds, bruises, Cancers, &c.

Moon-Curser, *c.* a link-boy.

Moor-hen, as *Coot*.

Moor the ship, lay out her anchors (at least two) most conveniently for her to ride by.

Moor a-cross or athwart, with one anchor on one side and another on the other side of the River,

Moor a-longst, with one Anchor a-head and the other a-stern.

Moor-Water-shot, quartering, between both the former.

Moor a-proviso, with one Anchor down, and her head moored with a hawser to the shore.

Moorland, a Moorish barren part of *Staffordshire*.

Moot-men, Students (in the Innes of Court and Chancery) who do

Moot, *Mote*, to plead or handle cases in Law (for an house-exercise.) see *Mote*.

Mooted, (in heraldry) torn up by the roots.

Mopsical, *l.* mop-ey'd, which cannot see well.

Moral, *l.* belonging to manners or civility, also

Morally, after the manner of men, or as the case now stands.

Morality, an exercising of the

Moral or Cardinal Vertues, Prudence, Justice, Temperance, and Fortitude.

Moralize, to give the

Moral sence of a thing, as the

Moral of a Fable, the application of it to mens lives and manners,

Moration, *l.* a tarrying.

Moravia, *Marcomannia*, part of *Bohemia*.

Moratur (or *Demoratur*) *in lege*, he demurrs or abides upon on the Judgment of the Court.

Morbidezza, *I.* tenderness, softness, effeminacy.

Morbifical, *l.* bringing sickness or diseases.

Morbulent, *l.* sickly, full of diseases.

Morbus Gallicus, *Neopolitanus*, *Hispanicus*, *Indicus*, the Great or French Pox.

Mordacity, *-ancy*, *l.* sharpness, biting, bitterness of speech.

Mordecai, *h.* bitter.

Mordicate, *l.* to bite

Mordicative, *l.* biting or stinging.

Morea, the *Peninsula Peloponnesus* in *Greece*.

Moresk-work, *Moresque*, *f.* a rude or antick, painting or carving, a wild resemblance of all things intermingled.

Mores, *No.* hills.

Moreton, a town in *Devonshire*.

Morgan, *Br.* Seaman.

Morglay, (*q. Mort-glaive*) a mortal or deadly sword.

Moriam, as *Morion*.

Morigeration, a being

Morigerous, *l.* dutiful, obedient.

Morion, *f.* a Murrian, a steel-cap or head-piece.

Moris, *Morice*, *Maurice*, *-itius*, a Martyr under *Maximianus*.

Morisco, *Sp.* a moor, also a Morrice (or moorish) dance

Morking, *-kin*, a Deer (or other beast) that dies by mischance or sickness, also as

Morling, *Mortling*, wool taken from the skin of a dead Sheep.

Mormal, *o.* a canker or Gangrene.

Morology, *g.* a foolish speaking.

Morosity, *l.* a being

Morose, *l.* froward, peevish, wayward.

Morowed, *o.* morning.

Morowning, the same.

Morpeth, a town in *Northumberland*.

Morpheus, [the God of] sleep.

Morphew, (*q. Mort-feu* a dead fire) a white scurff upon the body.

Mors-munster, as *Pfirt*.

Morsee, part of North *Juitland*.

Mort, *c.* a Woman.

Morta, *l.* one of the destinies, See *Nona*.

Mortal, *l.* deadly.

Morter, *o.* a [funeral] lamp.

Mort d' ancester, as *Assise of Mort-*.

Morgage, *f.* (dead pledge) a pawn of Lands or goods for money borrowed, to be the Creditors for ever, if the money be not repaid at the time.

Tenant in Mortgage, holding such Lands or Tenements.

Mortiferous, *l.* death-bringing.

Mortification, *l.* the action of

Mortifying, killing [of lust] punishing and subduing [the Flesh.]

Mortise, *f.* the fastening a piece of Wood (as it were by biting) into another piece.

Mortling, as *Morling*.

Mortmain, *f.* (dead hand) an alienation of Lands or Tenements (with the Kings licence of Mortmain) to a Corporation or Fraternity (and their Successors) as Bishops, Parsons, &c.

Mortress, *-eis*, *o.* a made dish of hens, crums of bread, Yolks of Eggs and Saffron boild together.

Mortuary, *l.* corps-present, a gift left by a man (at his death) to his Parish Church, for tithes not duly paid in his life-time, by custom becom'n due (*viz.* a noble, if the goods be worth between 30 and 40 pound, 10 shillings, if above, &c.) and in some places for the passage of a corps through another Parish.

Mortuum caput, the gross reliques of any thing distilled.

Mosaick, *-cal*, belonging to

Moses, *h.* drawn up [out of the water.]

Mosaique, *-ical*, *Musaique*, *-sive work*, a most curious kind of work inlaid with small pieces of stone, glass, shells, &c. sometimes in wood, called *Tarsia* or *Marquetry*.

Mosa, the River *Meuse* (or *Maes*) running through *Lorrain* and the Low Countries.

Mosco, *-ow*, the chief City in

Moscovy, *Mus-*, [the principal province of] White *Russia*.

Mosche, *-ea*, *Mosque*, as *Meskite*, a *Turkish* Church.

Moselle, a river running through *Lorrain*, &c.

Mosses, *La.* Moorish and boggy places.

Mospach, a town in the *Palatinate* of the *Rhine*.

Moss-troopers (like the *Irish* Tories, and *Italian Banditi*) that live (in the North of *England*) by Robbery and Rapine.

Mostick (*q. Malstick*, *Ge.* paint-stick) which the Painters rest upon while they are at work.

Mosul, *Nineve*.

Mote, (*sa. gemote*) a Court, Plea or Convention, also a Castle, and as moot.

Mot, *f. Motto*, *I.* a word, Emblem, Impress or Device, also a lesson which Huntsmen wind on their horn.

Mote, *o.* Must.

Motable, *l.* alwaies moving.

Motacism, *l.* the dashing out of the Letter. *m*.

Motet, *f.* a verse or stanza in Musick, a short poem.

Mother, a painfull rising of the Womb, for which all sweet smells are bad, and stinking ones good.

Motherwort, *Cardiaca*, a cleansing astringent herb.

Mother-tongues, having no affini-

affinity with one another.

Motion, *l.* a moving.

Motive, moving, also a moving cause or argument.

Moveable Feasts, which alwayes keep the day of the week, but vary in the day of the moneth:

Motred, *o.* muttered.

Mouch, *o.* to eat up all.

Mougnon, *f.* the but-end of a thing, the brawny part of the arm, also a brassel or Armour for the arm.

South Moulton, a town in *Devonshire*.

Mound (*q. Muniment*) a fence or hedge.

Mounsoun, an *East-India* wind, blowing constantly three months one way, and the next three contrary.

Mounster, an Irish Province.

Mount a piece, lay her on the Carriages, also, lay her mouth higher.

Mountabour, a town in *Westphalia*.

Mountain of Piety, a Charitable stock raised and lent (for a small consideration) to the Poor, to free them from the usury and extortion of the Jews.

Mountaunce, as *Mountenaunce*.

Mountebank, *Montimbanco*, *I. Charlatam*, *f.* Quacksalver, *D.* a wandring and jugling Physician.

Mountsorrel, a town in *Leicester-shire*.

Mountenance, *o.* (*f. Montance*) the price that any thing amounts to, the quantity.

Mourdant, *o.* the tongue [of a buckle.]

Mourning of the Chine, a disease in Horses, exulcerating the Liver, corrupting the Heart, and killing.

Mouse-ear, *Pilosella*, a binding and cleansing herb.

Mous-hole, a town in *Cornwal*.

Mow. (*f. amas*) a pile or stack) of Corn or Hay.]

Mowe, *o.* I may.

Mowlen, *o.* moulder away, or moulded.

Mower, *c.* a Cow.

Mow-heater, *c.* a drover.

Moylery, *o.* pains.

Welly Moyder'd, *Che.* almost distracted.

M S. Manuscript.

Muccilaginous, *Mucculent*, *Mucu-*, *l.* full of snot, filth or flegme.

Mucidity, *Mucour*, hoariness, filthiness, or being

Mucid, *l.* mouldy, finewed.

Muckre, *o.* to hoard up.

Muck, *Li.* moist.

Mucronated, *l.* sharp pointed.

Mudereeses, Turkish Readers, instructing Scholars in all Church duties, &c.

Muckson up to the Buckson, *Dev.* dirty up to the knuckles.

Mue, a place where Hawks are kept, while they

Mue, *f.* change [their Feathers.]

The Mues, the Kings Stables, where formerly his Hawks were kept.

Muffling-cheat, *c.* a Napkin.

Mufti, (*Tu.* Oracle or answerer of doubts) the chief Priest among the Turks, created by the Emperour himself.

Mugient, *l.* lowing or bellowing.

Mugwet, as *Gatherbag*.

Mugwort, *Artemisia*, an herb which (they say) removes weariness.

Mulatto, *Sp.* one whose Father or Mother only was a black.

Mulberg, a town in *Misnia*.

Mulcible, *l.* which may be appeased.

Mulct, *l.* a fine or amerciament.

Mulito, *I.* a moil or great mule, used to carry sumpters.

Mulhausen, a town in *Alsatia*.

Mulheim, a town of *Berg* in *Germany*.

Muliebrity, *l.* womanliness, delicateness.

Mulierosity, unlawful lust after Women.

Mulier, *l.* a woman that hath known man, also a wife.

Mulirtie, *Mulerie*, the being or condition of a

Mulier, (*q. Meilleur*, *f* better) *filius mulieratus*, the lawful Issue, preferred before an Elder Brother born out of Matrimony.

Mullar, (*f. Mouleur*,) the upper stone, which Painters grind their colours with, upon the grinding stone.

Mulled sack, (*Mollitum*) burnt and Sugar'd.

Mullock, *No.* dirt or rubbish.

Mullet, a barbel, also (in Heraldry) a starlike spot falling with five ends signifying a third brother, also a Chirurgeons small pincer-like instrument.

Mulse, *l.* honeyed wine.

Mulsulmans, *Muss-*, *A.* (faithful people) Mahometans so called among themselves.

Multa (or *Multura*) Episcopi, a fine paid by the Bishops to the King, for power to make their own wills and have the probate of other mens.

Multatitious, *Mult-*, *l.* gotten by fine or forfeit.

Multifarious, *l.* of divers sorts, or divided many ways.

Multiferous, *l.* bearing much.

Multifidous *l.* having many clefts.

Multiformity, a being

Multiform, *l.* having many forms or shapes.

Multiloquent, *-quous*, *l.* full of words.

Multinominal, *l.* having many names.

Multiparous, *l.* bringing forth many [at a birth.]

Multiplicity, a being
Multiplicious, l. manifold.
Multiplicable, capable of
Multiplication, augmenting, making much or many.
Multiplication of Gold or Silver, forbidden 5. *H.* 4.
Multipotent, l. able to do much.
Multiscious, l. knowing much.
Multisonant, l. sounding much.
Multitudinous, having many, or belonging to a
Multitude, (by some) ten persons at least, others leave it to the discretion of the Judge.
Multivious, l. having many wayes.
Multivagant, l. wandring much.
Multivolent, l. of many minds, mutable.
Multure, f. the grist, also the Millers toll.
Mum, a kind of Physical Beer made (originally) at *Brunswick* in *Germany*, with husks of walnuts infused.
Mummery, f. a personating others in a mask or antick habit.
Mumpers, c. gentile beggars.
Mumps, a swelling of the chaps.
Mumial, belonging to
Mumy, *Mummy*, l. *Pissasphaltum*, *Pici-bitumen*, a pitchy substance, either from bodies embalmed in *Arabia*, or made of Jews lime and bitumen.
Muncer, the Ring-leader of the
Muncerians, a sort of rebellious Anabaptists in *Germany*.
Mundane, l. worldly.
Mundanity, worldliness.
Mundatory, as Purificatory.
Mundbrech, sa. a breach of mounds or fences.
Mundick, a hard stony substance found in the Tin-ore.
Mundificative, belonging to
Mundification, l. the act of

M V

Mundifying, purifying, cleansing.
Mundivagant, l. wandring about the world.
Munerate, l. to reward or recompense.
Munger, as *Monger*.
Municipal, -pial, l. enjoying, or belonging to the freedom of a City.
Munick, the chief City of *Bavaria*.
Muniferous, l. gift-bearing.
Munificence, l. liberality, a being
Munificent, -cal, bountiful.
Muniment, l. a fence or Fort.
Muniment-house, a little strong room for the keeping of plate and
Muniments, *Min-*, Charters, evidences, &c.
Munite, l. to fortifie, also as
Munited, armed, fenced.
Munster, a Province in *Ireland*, and a City in *Westphalia*.
Munk-seam, the strongest way of sewing sails, with the edge of one canvas over the edge of the other.
Muns, c. the face.
Murage, a toll taken of every laden Cart or Horse, toward the building or repairing the walls of that City or Town.
Mural, l. belonging to a wall.
Mural Crown, given to him that first scaled the walls of an Enemies City.
Murcia, part of *Spain*.
Murcid, l. cowardly, slothful.
Murder, a wilful killing of a man upon premeditated malice.
Murderers, small canon, carrying
Murdering-shot, to clear the Decks, when men enter.
Murengers, yearly Officers in *Westchester*, who keep the walls in repair.
Muret, a Town of *Gascoigne* in *France*.

M V

Muricide, l. a Mouse-killer.
Muriel, a womans name.
Muring, the raising of walls.
Murk, *No.* dark.
Murklins, *No.* in the dark.
Murnival, (f. *Mornifle* a trick) four [cards of a kind.]
Murrain, a kind of disease or rot among Cattel.
Murray, *Moravia*, part of North *Scotland*.
Murrey, (*Maurus*,) a dusky or dun-colour.
A Muith of Corn, *No.* abundance.
Musach cassa a chest in the Temple at *Jerusalem*, whereinto the Kings were wont to cast their Offerings.
Musæus, a famous Greek Poet, contemporary with *Orpheus*.
Musahib Alloh, *Tu.* (a talker with God) *Moses*.
Musaph, a book of all the Turkish Laws.
Musard, f. a loyterer.
Muscadel, -dine, f. Wine (brought from *Candy*) having the flavour of Musk.
Muschamp, a name (in *Northumberland*) formerly of great note.
Muschetto, (*Moschetta*, l. a little fly) a kind of gnat.
Musculous, belonging to, or full of
Muscles, l. fleshy parts of the body, serving for instruments of motion.
Musculous vein, the first branch of the flank-veins, communicating it self with divers muscles about the belly and loins.
Muscovites, people of
Muscovy, *Russia*, bordering on *Tartary*.
Muscosity, abundance of Mice, also a being
Muscous, l. mossy.
Musen, when a Stag or Male Deer casts his head.
Muses, (*Calliope*, *Clio*, *Erato*, *Thalia*, *Melpomene*, *Terpsichore*, *Polyhymnia*, *Urania*) Daughters of *Jupiter* and *Mnemosyne*, Goddesses of Poetry and Musick.

Muse, *-set*, *f.* the place through which the hare goes to relief.

Musive, as *Mosdique*.

Musk, *Pat*, a perfume growing in a little bag or bladder within an *Indian* beast like a Roe or Wild Goat.

Musket, the Tassel or Male of a Sparrow-hawk.

Muskin, (*q. Mouskin*) a Finch, or Titmouse.

Musmon, a certain beast, resembling partly a sheep, partly a goat.

Musrol, *f.* an iron ring to put about a horses nose.

Mussack, a drink much used by the *Chineses*.

Mussitation, *l.* a muttering.

Mussulmans, as *Mulsulmans*

Must, *l.* New-prest wine.

Mustachio, *-che*, *f. -chos*, *Sp. g.* the beard upon the upper-lip.

Mustaphis, *-pheis*, *Turkish* Doctors or Prophets.

Mustelline, *l.* belonging to a Weasel.

Muster of Peacocks, an old (but Elegant) word for a company of them together.

Mustered of Record, enrolled among the Kings Soldiers.

Muster-master General, Master of the Kings Musters.

Mustriche, *Mous-*, *o.* (*Mustricula*) a shoemakers last.

Mustulent, *l.* new, fresh, sweet as *Must*.

Mutability, a being

Mutable, *l.* changeable, inconstant.

Mutation, *l.* a change.

Mutations, the places where Strangers (as they journeyed) did change their Post-horses, &c.

Mute, *l.* dumb, or (in Law) not answering directly; also any Consonant except the Liquids, also (*Sc.*) as *Mote* or *Moot*.

Mutes, certain [dumb] executioners among the *Turks*.

Muteth, [the hawk] dungeth.

Mutilate, *l.* to maim, curtail, or diminish.

Mutiny, *f.* [to raise] a sedition, especially among Soldiers.

Quintus Mutius Scævola, burnt his right hand for killing a Courtier instead of *Porsenna* (King of the *Hetrusci*) warring against *Rome*.

Mutual, *l.* interchangeable, from one to another.

Muzrole, as *Musrol*.

Muzzle-ring, the greatest cirle about the mouth of a great gun.

Mycterism, *g.* a wiping ones nose, a closer kind of Sarcasm.

Mydias, the reputed Authour of Coats of Mail.

Mynnyng daies, as *Minning*.

Mynt, *c.* Gold.

Myriarch, *g.* a Captain of a

Myriad, *g.* ten thousand.

Myrmice, a maid who (for contemning *Ceres*) was turn'd into an Ant.

Myrmidon, an ancient King of *Thessaly*, and Son of *Jupiter*.

Myrmidons, *Thessalians* that went with *Achilles* to *Troy*.

Myrobalanes, *Egyptian* Nuts or Acorns, of five kinds, *viz. Bellerick*, *Chebule*, *Citrine*, *Emblick* and *Indian*.

Myropolist, *g.* a seller of sweet ointments or perfumes.

Myrrha, Mother of *Adonis* by her Father *Cynaras* (King of *Cyprus*) who (when he knew it) would have slain her, but flying into *Arabia* she is said to be turn'd into a tree of that name.

Myrrhine, *-rhean*, belonging to

Myrrh, an *Arabian* gum (between white and red) of an opening, cleansing and dissolving nature.

Myrsus, King of *Lydia*, Father of

Myrsilus, *Candaules*, the last of the race of the *Heraclidæ*.

Myrtilus, the son of *Mercury*, drowned (instead of being rewarded) by *Pelops*, for whom (at a race) he left the Chariot-wheel loose and brake the neck of his Master *Oenomaus*.

Myrtle, a low, tender and fragrant tree, sacred to *Venus*, worn garland-wise by those that triumphed after Victories obtain'd without slaughter of men.

Mysia, part of *Asia* the less.

Mystagogical, belonging to a

Mystagogue, *g.* he that interprets Mysteries, that hath the keeping of Church-reliques and shewing them to strangers.

Mysteriarch, *g.* a Chief prelate or master of sacred mysteries.

Mystical, Mysterious, secret, obscure.

Mythologist, he that doth

Mythologize, or practise

Mythology, *g.* an expounding of Fables.

N.

N*Aam*, *sa.* a distreining of a mans goods.

Naaman, *h.* Comely.

Nab, *c.* a head.

Nab-girder, *c.* a bridle.

Nab-cheat, *c.* a hat.

Nabal, *h.* a fool or mad.

Nacre, *f.* Mother of pearl.

Nad, (*q. Ne bad*) *o.* had not.

Nadab, *h.* a Prince.

Nadir, *A.* the point of heaven directly under our feet, and opposite to *Zenith*.

Næniæ, Funeral songs.

Naiades, *g.* Nymphs (or feigned Goddesses) of Rivers and Fountains.

Nail of beef, *Sf.* Eight pound.

Naiant, (*f. Nageant*) swimming.

Naif, *f.* natural, lively.

Naifstone, perfect in all its properties, or found so naturally, as if it had been artificially cut.

Nakoners, o. brasen horns.

Nal, o. Ale-house.

Nam, o. for *Am not*.

Namation, a distreining, or (in *Scotland*) an impounding.

Namaz, the *Turkish* Common prayer.

Name, o. took.

Namur, one of the *Neatherlands*.

Nantwich, a town in *Cheshire*.

Nancy, the chief City of *Lorrain*, surrendred to the *French*, 1633.

Nantes, a City on the *Loire* in *Britany*.

Nap, the tufted superficies of Cloth, also a fit of sleep.

Nap, c. to cheat at Dice.

Napeæ, g. Nymphs of the Woods and Mountains.

Napper of Naps, c. a sheep-stealer.

Napery, f. linnen-clothery, or Table-linnen.

Naphthe, -*tha*, Median Oil, *Babylonish* Bitumen, a kind of Marle, which being fired, is more incensed by water.

Napkin, T. a pocket handkerchief.

Naples, a *Spanish* Kingdom in *Italy*, tributary to the Pope.

Narbone, a City of *Languedoc*.

Narcissine, belonging to

Narcissus, a beautiful youth, who (slighting Eccho, and falling in love with his own shadow in the water) pined away to a white Daffadill, also a Bishop of *Jerusalem*, who (they say) by his prayers turned Water into Oyl to supply the Church lamps.

Narcotic, (or *Narcotique*) medicines, making senseless, stupifying any member.

Nard, Spikenard, an *Indian* and *Syrian* plant.

Narelles, o. Little

Nares, the nostrils or holes in a hawks beak.

Narrative, l. declarative, expressing, also as

Narration, a report or relation

Nart, o. Art not.

Nas, o. was not.

Narses, an Eunuch, general (after *Belisarius*) of *Justinians* army against the *Goths*.

Nasal vein, between the Nostrils.

Nasicornous insects, with horns on their noses.

Nasie, c. drunken.

Naskin, c. a jail or *Bridewell*.

Natal, *Natural*, also as

Natalitious, belonging to

Nativity, a birth or birthday.

Natalitious gifts, (among the Grecians) sent by the Neighbours on the fifth day.

Natation, l. a swimming.

Nated, l. born, framed of nature.

Nathanael, h. Gods gift.

Nativo habendo, a writ for the apprehending and restoring a Lords Villain, whom he claims for his inheritance.

Natural, a fool born.

Naturalist, a natural Philosopher, skilled in the causes of natural things.

Natural Son, base born.

Naturalize, f. to admit into the number of natural subjects.

Nat wilne, o. not desire.

Naval, l. belonging to a Ship, or to a

Navy, a Fleet or company of Ships.

Navarre, a Kingdom of *Spain*.

Naucifie, l. to slight or disesteem.

Nave, that part of a wheel in which the Axel-tree runs also the largest Temple (or Room) in a Church.

Naufrage, l. shipwrack.

Navicular, l. pertaining to a small ship.

Navigable, l. Sailable, which may be sailed on.

Navigate a ship, carry or direct her at Sea.

Navigation, l. [the art of] Sailing.

Navigator, l. a Sailer.

Navity, l. diligence.

Naulage, f. the fraight or mony for passing the Water.

Naumachy, g. [the place of] a sea-fight.

Nauplius, King of *Eubœa*, to revenge the death of his Son *Palamedes* (by *Ulysses's* means) he drew the Greek Navy (by a false fire) on the Rocks.

Nauseate, l. to loath, to be ready to vomit, also to make one so.

Nauseous, -*eative*, loathsom, making one ready to vomit.

Nausicaa, she met *Ulysses* shipwrackt and naked, and brought him to the Palace of her Father *Alcinous*.

Naustible, a haven for ships.

Nautick, -*cal*, l. belonging to Ships or Sea-men.

Nautilus, a fish resembling a ship under sail.

Naxos, *Strongyle*, *Dia*, one of the *Cyclad*-Isles, where *Ariadne* (left by *Theseus*) married *Bacchus*.

Nazal, f. the nose-piece of an helmet.

Nazarene, one of

Nazareth, the place where Christ and his Parents dwelt, hence

Nazarenes, -*rites*, Christians.

Nazarite, h. (separated) one who for a while (wherein he abstained from wine, shaving, &c.) dedicated himself to God.

Ne admittas, a writ for the Plantiffe in a *quare impedit*, least the Bishop should admit the Defendants Clerk during the suit.

Nead, a beast in *Samos*, whose great bones are kept as miraculous, and whose voice

voice (they say) shakes the Earth.

Ne, o. now.

Neæra, the Mother of *Lampetia* and *Phaethusa*.

Neal-too, a deep bank or shore without *Showling*.

Neopolitan, belonging to

Neapolis, *Naples*, (*Parthenope*) in *Campania* in *Italy*.

Neap tides, (*Sa. Napte*, scarcity) the small tides which happen seven dayes after the Moons change and full.

Dead Neap, at lowest, four dayes before the full or change.

Be-Neaped, wanting water to carry her off the ground, out of a dock or barr'd harbour.

Near now, *Nf.* just now.

Nearre, *Li.* Neather.

Neat, (*D. Nieten*, to but) an Ox, Cow or Steer.

Neat-land, let out to the Yeomanry.

Neb, a Tooth.

Nebuchednezzar, *h.* the mourning of the Generation.

Nebule, (in Herald.) a representation of the Clouds.

Nebulon, *l.* a knave or Rascal.

Nebulous, *-osous*, *l.* misty or cloudy.

Necessitate, *l.* to force (as a thing of necessity.)

Necessitous, indigent, poor.

Neck-stamper, *c.* a pot-boy.

Neckabout, *Y.* any [womans] Neck-linnen.

Necromantick, belonging to a

Necromancer, one that practiseth the wicked Art of

Necromancy, *g.* Conjuration by raising the dead, or the Devil in their shape, also the black Art in general.

Necromancers, (*in a sort*) *command*, and Witches (saith K. *James*) obey the Devil.

Nectarine, a kind of Peach, also as

Nectarean, belonging to

Nectar, *g.* the drink of the feigned Gods, rendring the drinkers immortal.

Nedely, o. of necessity.

Nedes cost, *Sa.* [by temptation] of necessity.

Neders, o. adders.

Nefandous, *l.* hainous, not to be named.

Nefarious, *l.* very wicked, accursed.

Negation, *l.* a denying.

Negative, belonging thereto, also that manner of expression.

Negative pregnant, including an affirmative, when a man denies not the thing laid to his charge, but the circumstance.

Negatory, belonging to a denial.

Negotiation, *l.* a merchandizing or trafficquing, also any managing of business.

Negotious, *l.* full of business.

Negrepont, an Island in the *Archipelago*.

Negro, *I.* a Negar or Blackamore.

Nehemiah, *h.* the Lords rest.

Writ of Neifty, whereby a Lord claimed his

Neif, (*f. Naive*) a bondwoman or shee-villain.

Nieffe, *Neive*, *No.* a fist.

Ne injuste vexes, a writ forbidding the Lord to distrein, the Tenant having formerly prejudiced himself by doing or paying more than he needed.

Nemæan (*lion, games*, &c.) belonging to

Nemæa, a woody part of *Greece*, where *Hercules* slew a lion of monstrous bigness.

Neld, (*D. Naelde*) a needle.

Neme, *Staf.* Uncle.

Nemene, o. to name.

Nemesis, *Adrastia*, *Ramnusia*. the Goddess of revenge.

Nemine contradicente *l.* no man contradicting it.

Nemoral, *-rons*, *l.* woody.

Nemorivagant, *l.* wandring in the woods.

Nempne, *Nempt*, o, named.

Nenuphar, *A.* a water-lily.

Neogamist, *g.* a new-married man.

Neopolitan, as *Neapolitan*.

Neophyte, *g.* a new-set plant, also a new disciple or Convert.

Neoterique, *-ical*, *g.* of late time or new.

St. Neots, a town in *Huntington*, and another in *Cornwall*, with a Well dedicated to St. *Keyne*, whereof (they say) whether Husband or Wife drink first, they get the Mastery.

Nep, *Nepeta*. Cat-mint.

Nepe, *Heref.* a nevew or Turnip.

Nepenthe, *g.* an herb put into wine to remove sadness, by some Buglos.

Nephele, *g.* (a cloud) the Mother of *Helle* and *Phryxus* by *Athamas*.

Nephelian Crook-horn, the sign Aries, or the Ram from whose back *Helle* fell.

Nephritick, *g.* troubled with pain in the Reins of the Back.

Nepotation, *l.* riotousness, luxury.

Neptunian, belonging to the Sea, or to

Neptune, (Son of Saturn and *Ops*) the God of the Sea.

Nequient, *l.* unable.

Nere, o. (for near) untill, as far as.

Nere, o (for Ne were) were it not.

Neread, a Mermaid (whose males are *Tritons*) one of the

Nereides, Sea-Nymphs, Daughters of

Nereus, a God of the Sea.

Nerfe, o. for *Nerve*.

Nero's, Tyrants, from

Domitius Nero, a Roman Emperour, who kild his Mother, Wife, Master, St. *Paul*, &c.

Nerthes, o. Headsmen.

Nervosity, a being

Nervous, *-vy*, *l.* full of

Nerves, *l.* sinews, by which the brain gives sense and notion to the body.

Neyrs, o. Reins.

Nescience, a being

Nescient, *-ious*, l. ignorant.

Nescock, *Nescock*, a wanton fondling, that was never from home. See *Cockney*.

Nesh, *Nash*, No. tender, weak.

Nesse, *Orford* haven in *Suffolk*.

Nessus, a *Centaur* slain by *Hercules* for attempting to ravish his wife.

Nest, o. Next.

Nest of rabbets, a Company

Nestorian, belonging to

Nestor, an Eloquent *Grecian* who came with 50 ships to the *Trojan* Wars; he lived almost 300 years.

Nestorius, a *German* Bishop of *Constantinople*, his tongue rotted in his head, he was the first founder of the

Nestorians, Hereticks holding (among other things) that there were two persons (as well as Natures) in Christ.

Netherlands, Low Countries, the Dukedomes of *Limburgh*, *Luxenburgh*, *Gelderland*, *Brabant* the Marquisate of the *Holy Empire*, the Earldoms of *Flanders*, *Artois*, *Hainault*, *Namur*, *Zutphen*, *Holland*, *Zealand*, and the Baronies of *West Friezland*, *Utrecht*, *Over-Issel*, *Machlin*, *Groening*, beside the Bishopricks of *Liege* and *Cambray*.

Nethinims, Hewers of wood and Drawers of water for the Temple.

Netting-sails, laid upon the

Nettings, small ropes seised together with rope-yarns (in form of a net) to shadow the men in a close fight, &c.

Neven, o. named.

Nevin, a town in *Caernarvanshire*.

Nevers, the chief City of *Nivernois*.

Neufchasteau, a town in *Lorain*.

Nevosity, a being full of moles, warts or freckles.

Neustria, *Westrich*, *Normandy*, part of *Gallia Celtica*.

Neutrality, being

Neutral, Neuter, indifferent, belonging to neither.

Newark, (*q. New-work*) a pleasant town on the River *Trent* in *Nottinghamshire*.

Newbourg, a Dukedom in *Bavaria*.

Newberry, a town in *Berkshire*.

New-castle, a town on the River Tine in *Northumberland*.

New-castle under Lyne, in *Staffordshire*.

Newent, a town in *Gloucestershire*.

Newing, E. Yeast, barm.

New-Colledge, (in *Oxford*) built by *W. Wickham* Bishop of *Winchester*.

New-Market, a town in *Suffolk* and in *Cambridgshire*.

Newport, a town in *Flanders*, in the Isle of *Wight*, *Shropshire*, *Bucks*, &c.

Newstat, a town in the Palatinate of the *Rhine*.

New-years-gifts, offered by the *Roman* Knights (*Jan.* 1.) in the Capitol to the Emperour, whether he were there or no. In *Italy* the greatest present the meanest.

Newnham, a town in *Glocestershire*.

Newton, the name of above a hundred small towns in *England*.

Nexible, l. which may be knit or tied.

Nexility, l. pithiness, closeness and compactness [of speech]

Niaisery, f. simplicity, childishness.

Nias-hawk, taken out of the nest before she prey'd for her self.

Nicean, *Nicene*, belonging to

Nice, *-ea*, a City of *Bithynia*, famous for the Council of 318 Bishops, *An.* 314.

Niceté, f. idleness, or simplicity.

Nices, the same as

Niches, l. hollow places in walls, wherein Images are set.

Nicholaitans, Hereticks who had their wives in common, &c. from

Nicholas, (*q.* Conquerour of the People) a Deacon of *Antioch*.

Nicia, g. victorious, a womans name.

Nicias, an Athenian general, overthrown by the *Syracusians*.

Nicodemites, Hereticks in *Switzerland*, professing their Faith in private like

Nicodemus, g. Conquerour of the people.

Nicomedia, *Nicker*, a City in *Bithynia*, where *Constantine* the great died.

Nicopolis, *Gallipoly*, a City of *Epirus*, near to which *Augustus* overcame *M. Anthony* and *Cleopatra*.

Nicostrata, *Carpenta*, the mother of *Evander*.

Nicotian, Tabacco, from the Authour *John*

Nicot, Ambassadour Leiger for *France* in *Portugal*, where he made that great

Nicots Dictionary, French and Latin.

Nictation, l. a winking or twinkling with the eyes.

Nidgeries, *Nig-*, f. trifles, fooleries.

Nidifie, l. to make a

Nidifice, l. a birds-nest.

Niding, *Nithing*, *Niderling*, *Nidering*, o. a Coward, or base low-minded man.

Niddesdale, part of South-*Scotland*.

Nidor, l. brightness, also the smell of any thing burnt or roasted.

Nidulation, *Nidification*, l. the making of a nest.

Nient comprise, an exception to a petition as unjust, because the thing desired is not conteined in the Deed on which it is grounded.

Nifle, o. a toy of no value.

Nigella, the herb Gith.

Nightertale, (*q. -deal*) o. by night.

Night-

Night-Mare, (*D.Nacht-Maer*, Night-evil) as *Incubus*.

Nigh, *No.* to touch or come nigh.

Night-shade, *Uva Vulpis*, *Cuculus*, *Morella*, Dwale or Petty-morrel.

Night-spel, a prayer against the Night-Mare.

Nigg, *o.* for niggard.

Nigon, *Nigeon*, *Nigeot*, an Idiot or fool.

Nigrefaction, the action of *Nigrefying*, making black.

Nigromancy, as *Necro-*.

Nihil dicit, (he saies nothing) a failing to answer the Plaintiffs plea, so that Judgment passes, &c.

Nihil capiat per breve, the Judgment given against the Plantiff.

Nihilorum Clericus, Clerk of the

Nihils, *Nichils*, Issues which the Sheriff (being apposed) saies are illeviable and nothing worth.

Nihilifie, *l.* to slight, or account as Nothing.

Nil, *Pompholyx*, *Spodium*, the sparkles that fly from metals tried in a furnace.

Nil, (*q. Ne will*) will not.

Nil ultra, *l.* nothing farther, the inscription of *Hercules*'s pillars.

Nilling, *o.* unwilling.

Nilus, the Father of Rivers, running through *Ethiopia* and *Egypt* (almost three thousand miles) yearly overflowing and fatning the Land.

Nim, *Nem*, (*D. Nemmen*, to take) to filch or steal away.

Nimbiferous, *l.* bringing storms or Tempests.

Nimbot, *f.* a Skip-jack, Dandiprat, or dwarfe.

Nimiety, a being

Nimious, *l.* too much, excessive, superfluous.

Nimmeguen, a Town in *Gelderland*.

Nine Nations, the Commonalty of *Brussels*.

Ningid, *-guid*, *l*, Snowy.

Ninus, the Son of *Jupiter Belus*, and King of *Assyria*, who mightily enlarged the Empire, and was (at last) secretly made away by his wife *Semiramis*.

Niobe, *Tantalus*'s Daughter and *Amphion*'s Wife, while she was railing against *Juno* (who had perswaded *Apollo* to kill her children) she was carried by a whirlwind into *Asia* and turn'd into a stone.

Niphates, a hill between *Armenia* and *Assyria*, whence *Tigris* flows.

Nippers, small ropes (with a little truck, or wale-knot, at one end) to hold off the Cable from the Capstain.

Niseus, a Tyrant of *Syracuse*, who spent that little time the Augurs told him he had to live, in Luxury and Riot.

Nisi prius, a writ for the Sheriff to bring an Enquest empanel'd to *Westminster* at a certain day, or before the Judges of the next Assises.

Nisroch, *h.* flight, a Syrian idol.

Nist, (*q. Ne wist*) knew not.

Nisus, King of *Megara*, feigned to be turn'd into a Hawk.

Nithing, as *Niding*.

Nitidity, *Nitour*, a being

Nitid, *L.* bright, clean or neat.

Nittle, *No.* handy, neat.

Nitrous, full or savouring of

Nitre, *l.* a spongy salt-like substance (ruddy and white) mistaken by some for Saltpetre.

Nival, *Niveous*, *l.* snowy.

Nivernois, a Province of *France*.

Nixii, feigned Gods assisting Child-bed women.

Nixus, *Ingeniculum*, *Engonasin*, *Hercules* striking at the Serpent.

Nizie, *c.* a fool.

N. L. Non Liquet, it doth not plainly appear, the cause is difficult.

No. (*Sa. Neah*,) *o.* near.

No, *Alexandria* in *Egypt*.

Noah, *h.* ceasing, resting.

Nobilitate, *l.* to ennoble or promote.

Noblesse, *f.* Nobility (of blood or mind.)

Nocent, *l.* guilty, also as

Nocive, *l.* hurtful.

Noctem de firma, entertainment for a night.

Noctiferous, *l.* night-bringing.

Noctivagant, *l.* wandring by night.

Nocturnal, *l.* nightly, also a night-dial.

Nocturne, part of the old Church-service said in the night. The Psalms were divided (by the Fathers) into seven Nocturnes.

Nocument, *l.* hurt, dammage.

Nocuous, *l.* hurtful.

Node, *l.* a knot or hard swelling.

Nodinus, a Roman God overseeing the joints in Cornstalks.

Nodosity, *l.* a being

Nodous, *l.* knotty, difficult.

Noel, *f.* Christmas.

Noie, *o.* for annoy.

Nold, (*q. Ne would*) *o.* would not.

Noli me tangere, (touch me not) an herb whose seed spurts away as soon as touched, also a piece of flesh (in the Nostrils) growing worse for being touched, also the French disease.

Nolne, as *Nold*.

Nomades, people of *Scythia Europæa*.

Nomarchy, *g.* the Office or jurisdiction of a

Nomarch, *g.* a Major, or other Governour, having preeminence in the ministration of Laws.

Nombre de Dios, (*Sp.* Name of God) a rich town in *Castella del oro*.

Nombrel, (*f. Nombril* a navel) the third and lowest part of an Escutcheon, the other two (upward) being the Honour and Fesse points.

Nome, o. took.

Nomenclature, the office of a

Nomenclator, *l.* a cryer in Court, calling all by their names.

Nominal, *l.* belonging to a name.

Nominally, by name.

Nominalia, Roman Feast-days when they gave names to children (to females on the eighth, to Males on the ninth day.)

Nomination, *l.* a naming or appointing.

Nomographer, *g.* a writer of Laws.

Nomothetical, belonging to

Nomothesie, *g.* a making or publishing of Laws.

Nona, Decima & morta, the Latin names of the Destinies, *Clotho, Lachesis* and *Atropos*.

Non-ability, an exception against any person, why he cannot commence a suit.

Nonacris, an Arcadian mountain, at whose foot is the River *Styx*.

Nonage, a mans being under fourteen years in some cases (as marriage,) and one and twenty in others.

Non-claim, a mans not claiming within the time limited by Law, as within a year and a day, &c.

Non compos mentis, not in his right wits, *viz.* 1. An Ideot by nature. 2. By sicknes or other accident. 3. A Lunatick, having lucid intervals. 4. which (by his own act) deprives himself, as a Drunkard, but this gives no priviledge to him or his Heirs.

Non-conformist, one that doth not conform [to the Church of *England*.]

Non distringendo, a writ of divers particulars, according to divers cases.

Non implacitando, &c. a writ forbidding a Bailiff to distrein a Freeholder without the Kings writ.

Non est culpabilis, the defendants general plea to an Action of trespass, utterly denying the fact.

Non est factum, an answer to a Declaration, denying that to be his deed, upon which he is impleaded.

Non Merchandizando, for Justices of Assize, to enquire whether victuals be sold in gross or by retail, &c.

None of the day, the third quarter, from Noon to half Sunsetting.

Nones of a Moneth, the ninth day before the Ides; In March, May, July and October, the six dayes (and in other moneths the four dayes) next after the Calends or first-day.

Non liquet, it is not clear, (like our *Ignoramus*) referring the matter to another trial.

Non obstante, *l.* notwithstanding.

Non molestando, a writ for one molested contrary to the Kings protection.

Non omittas, commanding the Sherift himself to execute a Writ delivered to a Bailiff, but neglected.

Non-pareil, *f.* peerless, without fellow; also one sort of the Printing Characters.

Non-plus, *l.* (no more) the end of his Latin, [to put to] silence.

Non ponendo in assisa, to free, men (by reason of age, &c.) from serving on assises and Juries.

Non Principiate, having no beginning.

Non procedendo, &c. to stop the tryal, till the Kings pleasure be known.

Non-residency, a being

Non-resident, unlawfully absent from his [spiritual] charge.

Non residentia pro Clericis Regis, not to molest a Clerk (in the Kings service) for non-residence.

Non sanæ memoriæ, an exception against the act of any man, as being *Non compos mentis*.

Non solvendo, &c. not to take the mulct imposed on the Kings Clerk for non-residence.

Non-suit, the Plaintiffs renunciation of the suit, when the Jury is ready to give in their verdict.

Non-tenure, an exception to a Count (or declaration) by saying, he holds not the Lands contained therein.

Non sum informatus, as *Informatus non sum*.

Non-Term, time of the Kings peace, Vacation-time.

Nonupla, a quick time (of 9 Crochets) peculiar to Jigs, &c.

Nook, (*D. Een Hoeck*) a corner.

Nore, *o.* nourishing.

Nortelry, *o.* nurture.

Nory, *o.* a nurse.

Noryce, *o.* a foster-child.

Norbertins, a Religious Order called also *Præmonstratenses*.

Nor, *no.* than.

Noricum, *Bavaria* in *Germany*.

Normal, *l.* exact, according to rule or square.

Norman, belonging to

Normannia, *-andy*, a Dukedom in *France*.

Norballerton, *North-*, the cheif town of

Northallerton-shire, part of *York-shire*, where *Ralph* Bishop of *Durham* (in the battle of the Standard) overthrew David King of *Scots*.

Norrel-ware, corruptly for Lorimers.

Norrey, *Norroy*, (*q. North-Roy*) the third of the three Kings at Arms, whose Office lies on the north-side of *Trent*, as *Clarentius*'s on the South.

Norton, above 50 small towns.

Northleake, a Town in *Glocester-shire*.

Northampton, (*q. Northaventon*,) the cheif town of *Northamptonshire*, near which K. *H.6* was

was taken prisoner by *Rich. Nevil* Earl of *Warwick*.

Northwich, a town in *Cheshire*.

Northgoia, the upper *Palatinate*.

Norwegia, -*wey*, (q. *Northway*) part of *Denmark*.

Norwich, -*ck*, the chief Town of *Norfolk*.

Nosognomonick, See *Medicine*.

Nost, o. for knowest.

Nostock, the stinking tawny jelly of a fallen vapour, or (by Dr. *Charlton*) the nocturnal pollution of some plethorical and wanton star.

Not, (q. *Na wot*) know not.

Notation, l. the derivation of words.

Notted, E. shorn, polled.

Notary, l. a scribe or Scrivener, taking notes and short draughts of Contracts, &c.

Note, *Nedes*, [necessary] business.

Note, o. St. Need.

Notes, o. nuts.

Note, a hawks fetching off the oyl from her tail, to prune her-self.

Note of a fine, a brief of it (made by the Chirographer) before it be engrossed.

Notification, l. an information or advertisement.

Note, no. to push or goar with the horn.

Notion, l. knowledge or understanding, also a conceit or point delivered.

Noto, a Town in *Sicily*.

Notius, -*ios*, the Southerly part of *Pisces*.

Notorius, l. extraordinary or manifest.

Nottingham, the chief town of *Nottinghamshire*.

Nottchead, o. notcht pate.

Novæ tabulæ, new debt-books, an easement proposed in favour of debtors at *Rome*.

Novale, Land newly plowed up.

Novatians, Hereticks following

Novatus, (*Anno* 215.) he condemned second marriages received not Apostates though penitent, &c.

Novation, l. a making new.

Novator, l. a renewer.

Novel, f. new.

Novels, 168 volumes of the Civil-law, added (by *Justinian*) to the *Codex*, also little Romances.

Novel assignment, of some circumstance (in a declaration) more particularly than was in the writ.

Novempopulana, *Gascoigne* in *France*.

Novenary, l. belonging to or consisting of nine.

Novendial, l. of nine days.

Novennial, l. of nine years.

Novercal, l. belonging to a Step-mother.

Novice, a new beginner in any art or Profession.

Novitiate, l. novice-ship.

Novity, l. newness.

Nowth, *Nowth*, o. now.

Nowed, (f. *Nouée*,) tied in a knot.

Nowel, as *Noel*.

Noxious, as *Nocent*.

Nubia, a Kingdom in *Africa*.

Nubiferous, l. cloud-bearing.

Nubilous, l. cloudy.

Nab, c. the neck.

Nubbing, c. hanging.

Nubbing-cheat, c. Gallows.

Nubbing-Cove, c. hangman.

Nubbing-ken, c. Sessions-house.

Nubivagant, l. wandring among the clouds.

Nuceous, l. belonging to nuts.

Nudation, l. a making

Nude, l. bare or naked.

Nude contract, without any consideration given, whence no action can arise.

Nudils, plegets of lint or cotton, applyed to the Womb.

Nudity, l. nakedness, poverty.

Nugal, -*atory*, belonging to

Nugation, l. trifling.

Nugator, l. a trifler.

Nugipolyloquides, a great babler about trifles.

Nuisance, *Nusance*, f. annoyance or damage.

Nullifidian, l. a seeker, of no Religion or honesty.

Nullity, l. nothing, the being nothing, or of no effect.

Nullo, a Cipher standing for nothing.

Numa Pompilius, the second King of the Romans, who instituted sacred rights, by appointment (as he said) of the Goddess *Ægeria*.

Numbles, f. the entrails of a Deer.

Numeral, l. belonging to number.

Numerical, l. the same, also particular, individual.

Numeration, l. numbring, that part of Arithmetick which teaches the value of figures in their several places.

Numerist, a kind of Register, Notary, or Auditor, a Roman Officer.

Numitor, King of the *Albans*, driven out of his Kingdom by his younger brother *Amulius*.

Nunchion, an afternoons repast.

Nunnery, a Colledge of

Nunns, (f. *Nonnes*) Virgins devoted (from the World) to the service of God.

Nunciature, a report or message.

Nuncupation, l. a rehearsing or calling by name.

Nuncupative, l. called, declared by word of mouth.

Nuncupative will, made by word of mouth before sufficient witness.

Nundinal, -*ary*, l. belonging to a fair or market.

Nundination, l. a trafficking in Fairs or Markets.

Nuntio, *Nuncio*, I. the Popes [Lieger] Ambassadour.

Nuper obijt, a writ for a

Coheir deforced by her coparcener, &c.

Nuptial, *l.* belonging to weddings.

Nuptial gifts, sent before the betrothing.

Nutrialist, a bride, bridegroom, or one that makes matches.

Nurture, (*f. Nourriture*) a nourishing or bringing up [in good manners]

Nusance, as *Nuisance*.

Nutation, *l.* a nodding.

Nutritive, *-ritious*, *l.* belonging to

Nutriment, *l.* nourishment.

Nutrition, *l.* a nourishing.

Nuys, a town in the Arch-Bishoprick of *Colen*.

Nyctalops. *g.* purblind.

Nycteus, the Son of *Neptune*, *Amalthæa's* husband, and Father of

Nyctimene, having (by her Nurses help) lain with her Father, and flying from his wrath, was turn'd into an Oak.

Nye, (*f. Nid*,) a nest.

Nymphal, *-phous*, belonging to a

Nymph, *g.* a Lady or Bride.

Nymphs of the Woods, &c, Virgin-Goddesses.

Nymphet, *f.* a little Nymph.

Nysa, a City (built by *Bacchus*) in *India*.

Nysus, as *Nisus*.

Nything or *Nithing* [*of his pains*, *&c. No.* very sparing.

O.

O. for one.

O. Ni. (*Oneratur*, *nisi habeat sufficientem exonerationem*) marked upon the Sheriffs head, (when he enters into his account for Issues. &c.) whereby he becomes the Kings debtor.

Oale-gavel, as *Gavel-fester*.

Oaxis, a *Cretian* River from

Oaxis, the Son of *Apollo*, who lived there.

Oaxus, a City of *Creet*, from

Oaxus, the Son of *Acacallis* Daughter of *Minos*.

Obacerate, *l.* to stop ones mouth, that he cannot tell his tale quite out.

Obadiah, *h.* Servant of the Lord.

Obambulate, *l.* to walk abroad, about or against.

Obarmation, *l.* an arming against.

Obay, *o.* abide.

Obduction, *l.* a covering about.

Obduration, a hardning, or growing

Obdurate, *l.* hard, obstinate, unrelenting.

Obedientia, a certain ancient Rent, also an Office or the administration of it.

Obedientials, *-les*, those that have the Execution of any office under their Superiours.

Obeisance, *f.* dutiful Obedience.

Obclise, to rase or blot out.

Obelisk, *l.* one great square stone, like a Pyramid, also a stroke (in writing) signifying that somthing is amiss.

Obequitate, *l.* to ride about.

Ober-Sax, part of *Saxony*.

Oberration, *l.* a wandring about.

Obesity, *l.* fatness, grossenesss.

Obeysinge, *o.* as *Obeisance*.

Objectator, *l.* he that makes an

Objection, *l.* a casting against, a reproach or laying to one charge,

Obit, *l.* death, decay, sunsetting, also a Funeral Song or Office for the dead.

Objuration, *l.* a binding by oath.

Objurgatory, *l.* belonging to

Objurgation, *l.* a chiding or rebuking.

Oblata, old debts put to the present Sheriffs charge.

Oblat, *f.* a maimed Soldier maintained in an Abbey, also the place or maintenance it self.

Oblats of St. Jerome, an Italian Congregation of secular Priests, founded by St. *Charles Boromeus*.

Oblation, *l.* an Offering [to God, the Church, or any pious use,] also an aid or subsidy-money.

Oblatration, *l.* a barking or exclaiming against.

Oblectation, *l.* a delight, recreation or pleasure.

Oblesion, *l.* an hurting.

Obligatory, *l.* binding, also as

Obligation, *l.* a binding, a bond conteining a penalty, with a condition annexed.

Oligor, he that enters into bond.

Obligee, to whom it is made.

Oblimation, *l.* a plaistering or dawbing over.

Obliquation, a causing of

Obliquity, a being

Oblique, *l.* crooked, awry.

Oblique cases, all but the *Rectus* or Nominative.

Obliterate, *l.* to blot out.

Oblivion, forgetfulness.

Act of Oblivion, forgetting and forgiving all offences past.

Oblivious, *l.* forgetful.

Oblocutor, a back-biter.

Oblong, *l.* a four-square figure whose length exceeds its breadth, the most proper are these, 1. Sesquialtera, 2. Sesquitertia, 3. Sesquiquarta, 4. Diagonial (increased to the length of the Diagonal of the single square) 5. Superbitiens tertias, 6. Dupla, which is a double square.

Obloquy, reproach or slander.

Obmutescence, a holding ones peace.

Obnection, *l.* a knitting or tying fast.

Obnoxiety, a being

Obnoxious, subject or liable [to

to punishment, &c.]

Obnubilate, to darken with clouds.

Obnunciate, to foreshew some unlucky event.

Obnunciation of Assemblies, dissolving them, upon fore-knowledge or conjecture of ill success.

Obolata terræ, by some half an acre, by others half a perch.

Obole, a small coyn, with us an half-penny, also an half-peny weight, among Apothecaries 12 grains, among Gold-smiths 14.

Obreption, a creeping or stealing upon by craft.

Obreptitious, which hath cunningly stolen upon.

Obrizum, *Obryzum*, *g.* fine gold [of *Ophir*.]

Obrogate, to interrupt or gainsay.

Obrogate a Law, to publish a law contrary to (and for the abolishing) the former.

Obrumpent, breaking.

Obscene, *l.* filthy, smutty, unchaste.

Obscenity, ribaldry, baudery.

Obscuration, a making

Obscure, *l.* dark.

Obsecrate, earnestly to beseech.

Obsequies, funeral rites, ones last duty to the deceased.

Obsequious, dutifull.

Obseration, a locking up.

Observant, dutifull, respectfull.

Observants, *-tins*, a kind of *Franciscan* Fryers, instituted by one *Bernard* of *Siena*, 1400.

Obsession, a besieging or compassing about.

Obsest, haunted with an evil spirit.

Obsibilate, to whistle or hiss against.

Obsidian-stone, a kind of precious stone (in *Pliny*.)

Obsidional, belonging to a Siege.

Obsidional Crown, given to him who raised an extraordinary siege.

Obsigillation, a sealing up.

Obsolete, *l.* grown old, out of use or fashion.

Obstacle, an hindrance.

Obstetricate, to play the midwife.

Obstetricious, belonging to Midwives or their Office.

Obstinacy, a being

Obstinate, stubborn, self-willed.

Obstipate, to stop up.

Obstreperous, making a great noise.

Obstrigillation, a reproving or resisting.

Obstruction, a stoppage, or hindrance of passage.

Obstupify, to abash or astonish.

Obtemperation, an obeying.

Obtenebrate, to darken.

Obtestation, an obtesting, humble beseeching, or calling God to witness for any thing.

Obticence, a keeping silence.

Obtorted, wreathed or wrested.

Obtrectation, detraction, back-biting.

Obtrite, worn, bruised or trodden under foot.

Obtrition, a bruising or wearing away against any thing.

Obturation, *l.* a stopping, shutting or closing up.

Obtuse, blunt, heavy, dull.

Obtuse angle, when two lines include more than a square.

Obvallation, an encompassing with a trench.

Obvarication, a hindring ones passage.

Obvention, a meeting or coming against.

Obventions, Offerings, also [Spiritual] Revenues.

Obvert, to turn about or against.

Obviate, to meet, or to resist.

Obvious, meeting, Easie to find or understand.

Obumbrate, to over-shadow.

Obuncous, very crooked.

Obundation, a flowing against.

Obvolate, to fly against.

Obvolution, a rowling to and fro, or against.

Occæcation, *l.* a blinding.

Occidental, belonging to the

Occident, the setting of the Sun, the West, also as

Occiduous, decaying, declining, going down.

Occipital, belonging to

Occiput, *l.* the Noddle or hinder part of the head.

Occisor, *o.* a killer.

Occision, *l.* a killing or slaying.

Occlusion, a shutting up.

Occular, as *Ocular*.

Occulcation, a trampling upon.

Occult, hidden, secret.

Occultation, a hiding.

Occupation, an using, also an Employment or Trade, and (in Law) the putting a man out of his Free-hold in time of War.

Occupative, employed or possessed.

Occupant, he that first takes possession.

Occupative field, which (being deserted by its proper owner) is possessed by another.

Occupavit, a writ for one ejected in time of War.

Occurr, to be in the way, or offer it self.

Oceanick, *-ine*, belonging to the

Ocean, the main Sea, which encompasseth the World.

Ochlocracy, *g.* Government by the Multitude or common rout.

Ochus, a great *Phœnician* Philosoper.

Ochus, *Artaxerxes*, he buried his Sister and Mother-in Law alive, kill'd his Uncle, &c. was poisoned (at last) by his Physician *Bagoas*.

Ockham, *Okam*, Old ropes untwisted and pulled into loose flax again.

White Ockham, Tow or Fla-

Flet, to drive into the seames of the ship.

Ocious, *l.* idle.

Octangular, Eight-cornered.

Octave, an Eighth.

Octaves, *Utas*, the Eighth daies next after some Principal feasts.

Octavo, having eight leaves to a sheet.

Octennial, of eight years.

Octogon, *g.* a figure of eight angles.

Octohedrical, having eight sides.

Octonary, as *Octave*, also belonging to Eight.

Octostic, as *Ogdastic*.

Ocular, belonging to the eyes.

Oculate, full of eyes or holes, quick-sighted.

Oculate Faith, confirmed by, or representing things (as it were) to the eye-sight.

Oculist, one skild in the eyes.

Oculus Beli, a white-bodied gem with an eye-like black in the midst.

Oculus Christi, Wild Clary, an herb very good for the eyes.

Oculus Tauri, (the Bulls eye) a Constellation in *Gemini*.

Ocy, *o.* (*Obs*) I wish.

Ocypete, *g.* one of the Harpies.

Ocyroe, a prophetess who foretold her being turned into a Mare.

Oda Basbaws, Heads of the Companies of *Agiam Oglans*.

Odelet, a short or little

Ode, *g.* a song or Lyrick poem.

Odenchasteau, a town in *Lorrain*.

Oderbury, a Town on the

Oder, a river runing through *Branlenburgh*.

Oder, *o.* for *Other*.

Odible, the same as

Odious, hatefull, detestible.

Odio et atia, (or *batia*) a writ for the under-Sheriff to enquire whether a man be committed for malice or just suspicion [of murder.]

Odium, *l.* hatred, bad opinion.

Odoacer, having utterly defeated *Augustulus* (the last that usurped the title of *Roman* Emperour) proclaim'd himself King of *Italy* and *Placentia*.

Odontick, *g.* belonging to the teeth.

Odor, *-our*, *l.* a sent or smell.

Odoraminous, the same as

Odoriferous, sweet-smelling, or Spice-bearing.

Odrysian, belonging to

Odrysa, a City in *Thrace*.

Oeconomical, belonging to

Oeconomy, *g.* the government of an House or Family.

Oeconomist, such a Governour.

Oecumenical, *g.* General, belonging to the whole habitable World.

Oedastine, *g.* skilfull in weights and measures.

Oedematous, subject to, or full of

Oedeme, *-my*, *g.* a flegmatick swelling, which will retain an impression like dough.

Oedipus, he unfolded the riddle of *Sphinx*, slew his Father *Laius* King of *Thebes*, and married his Mother *Jocasta*.

Oenomaus, King of *Elis* from whom (at a race) *Pelops* won his Daughter *Hippodamia*.

Oenopolist, *g.* a Vintner.

Oesophagus, *g.* the gullet, or mouth of the Stomach.

Offembourg, the cheif town of *Ortbau* in *Alsatia*.

Offertory, an offering, or place where offerings are kept, also a particular part of the mass.

Offenbach, a town of *Brisgow* in *Schwaben*.

Official, he whom the Arch-Deacon substitutes for the executing of his Jurisdiction.

Officialis principalis, the Chancellor, to whom the Bishop commits the charge of his spiritual Jurisdiction.

Officiales Foranei, Commissaries (beside the other.)

Officiarii non faciendis, &c. a writ willing a Corporation not to chuse such or such a man

Officinator, an Artificer, a second superintendent over the under Artisans.

Officine, *l.* a shop or work-house.

Officious, *l.* dutiful.

Offing, the open Sea, or channel of a River.

Offrende, *o.* an offering.

Oft sithes, *o.* many times.

Ofton, a town in *Suffolk*, from

Offa, King of the *Mercians*.

Offuscate, to shadow, to make dark, dim or dusky.

Off-ward, to the off-ward, toward the Sea.

Og, *h.* a toste, or a mock.

Ogdastick, *g.* a Stanza of eight verses.

Ogive, *Ogee*, *f.* a circlet or round band (in Architecture.)

Ogles, *c.* eyes.

Ogresses, *f.* round black figures (in Heraldry) resembling bullets.

Ogyges, an ancient King of *Baeotia*.

Oisterloit, Bistorta, Snake-weed.

Oke, a *Turkish* measure, about our quart.

Okeham, a Town in *Rutland*.

Okehampton, a town in *Devonshire*.

Oker, a colour (of several sorts) for painting.

Oker de lace, yellow Oker.

Okingham, a town in *Barkshire*.

Okum, as *Ockham*.

Oldenburg, an Earldom in *East-Friezland*.

Oleaginous, belonging to an Olive-tree.

Old, *o.* old age.

Old Mr. Gory, c. a piece of Gold.

Old land, *Sf.* newly plowed up, having lain long untilled.

Oleander, the shrub Rosebay.

Oleity, *l.* oiliness, or [the time of] making oil.

Oleron lawes made by K. *Richard* the first, when he was at

Oleron, an Isle in the bay of *Aquitane*.

Olfact, to smell much or often.

Olfactory, belonging to smelling.

Olibanum, the true *Arabian* Frankincense.

Olicana supposed to be the same as *Ilkely* in *Yorkshire*.

Olidous, having a strong smell (good or bad.)

Oligarchy, *g.* government by a few.

Olimpiad, as *Olym-*.

Olitory, belonging to a Kitchen-garden or pot herbs.

Olivaster, a wild olive, or olive-coloured.

Oliver, peace-bringing.

Oliveres, *o.* olive-trees.

Oliviferous, olive-bearing.

Olivity, (as *Oleity*) the time of gathering olives.

Ollet, *So.* Fewel.

Olla, *Sp*: a pot to boil meat, also the meat it self.

Olla podrida, *Sp.* (*f. Bisque*) an *Olio*, or hotch-pot of several meats together.

Olmeres, (*f. Ormiers*) *o.* Elmes.

Olofernes, General of *Nebuchadnezzars* Army.

Olympia, *Pisa*, a City of *Greece*, near unto which were celebrated the

Olympick (or *Olympian*) *games*, instituted by *Hercules* in honour of *Jupiter*, and kept every

Olympiad, the space of five years, the *Grecian Epocha*.

Olympias, -p'a, *g.* heavenly, a womans name, from

Olympus, a high Hill in *Thessaly*, used (by the Poets) for Heaven.

Olynthus, a Thracian City which King *Philip* of *Macedon* won by corrupting the Soldiers.

Olysippo, *Lisbon*, the chief City of *Portugal*.

Ombrage. *f.* a shadow.

Omega, *g.* (great O) the last letter of the greek Alphabet.

Omelet, *f.* a pancake or froise.

Omen, *l.* a sign portending good or bad luck.

Omentum, *l.* the caul, or suet enwrapping the bowels.

Omer, *h.* three pints and a half, the tenth part of an Ephah (*Ezek.* 16. 36.) *Homer*, *h.* forty five gallons, ten Ephahs (*Ezek.* 4[illegible]. 11.)

Omy, *No.* mellow [land.]

Ominous, *l.* hausening, portending good or (most commonly) ill luck.

Omission, *l.* a neglecting or letting pass.

Omneity, the allness or all-being of a thing.

Omnifarious, of all sorts, or all manner of wayes.

Omniferous, all-bearing.

Omnigenous, of every kind.

Omnimode, of every fashion.

Omniparent, bringing forth all things.

Omnipercipiency, a perceiving or understanding all things.

Omnipotency, a being

Omnipotent, Almighty.

Omnipresent, every where present.

Omniregency, a ruling power over all.

Omniscient, -*ious*, all knowing

Omnitenent, containing all.

Omnitinerant, travelling all about.

Omnivagant, wandring all about.

Omnivalent, able to do all things.

Omnivolent, willing or desiring all.

Omnivorous, devouring all, eating all kind of things.

Omologie. *g.* a confession, also agreeableness or proportion.

Omoplata, the muscles of the Shoulder blade.

Omphacy, *g.* the juice of unripe grapes.

Omphale, a Queen of *Lydia*, who made *Hercules* sit and spin, while she put on his lions-skin.

Onbie, *o.* a pace.

Onagre, *g.* a wild ass, also a sling to shoot great stones.

Onde, *o.* breath. (*f.* a wave.)

One-berry, as herb *Paris*.

One-blade, an herb good in wounds of the Nerves.

Oneder, *Che.* the Afternoon.

Onerary *l.* serving for burthen or carriage.

Onerando pro rata portionis, a writ for a joint-tenant distreined for more than the proportion of his land.

Onerate, *l.* to load or overcharge.

Ones *o.* for once.

Onirocriticism, the skill of interpreting dreams.

On knew, *o.* for one knee.

Onocrotal, a bittour, or such like bird.

Onology *g.* vain babling, or talking like an Ass.

Onomantical, belonging to

Onomancy, *g.* divination by names, also the skill of repeating many names by memory.

Onomatopoeious, belonging to

Onomatopy, -*poeia*, *g.* the feigning of a name from some kind of sound.

Onpress, *o.* downward.

Onques puis lever, *f.* can I ever rise or escape?

Onslaught, *D.* the storming [of a Town, &c]

Onycha an Arabian tree, the droppings of whose juice is thought by some to congeal into the

Onyx, *g.* (the nail) a precious

cious ſtone of the colour of ones nail, by ſome called a Chalcedony.

Oaſt, *Eaſt*, *Som.* a kiln.

Opacity, a being

Opacous, *-aque*, *l.* ſhady.

Opal, *g.* a precious ſtone of divers colours mixt, yellowiſh, green and purple.

Openheim, a town in the *Palatinate* of the *Rhine*,

Openheed, *o.* bare headed.

Opera, *l.* (labour) an Italian Recitative play performed by voices, adorned with Muſick and Perſpective Scenes.

Operarious, belonging to

Operation, a working, or to an

Operator, a workman.

Operculated, cloſe-covered.

Operiment, *l.* a covering.

Operoſity, a being

Operoſe, *l.* buſie at work, laborious, alſo curiouſly wrought.

Opertaneous, *l.* done covertly, in ſecret or within doors.

Ophthalmy, *g.* an inflammation of the outermoſt skin of the eye.

Ophiogenes, *g.* generated of Serpents.

Ophites, *g.* a kind of marble, ſpeckled like a Serpent.

Ophiuchus, a Conſtellation in *Sagittary*.

Ophiuſa, a *Balearick* Iſland full of Serpents.

Ope-land, *Sf.* looſe or open, plowed up every year.

Opiate, *l.* a Confection of Opium.

Opiferous, bringing help.

Opifice, *l.* workmanſhip.

Opimous, *l.* fat, wealthy.

Opinable, *l.* capable of

Opination, thinking or ſuppoſing.

Opinator, a ſuppoſer (not a poſitive affirmer) of things.

Opinative, *Opiniative*, wedded to his own opinion or humour, full of

Opiniatrety, (*f. Opiniaſtrete*) *-ty*, *o.* Opiniativeneſs, obſtinacy, ſelf-willedneſs.

Opiparous, *l.* ſumptuous.

Opiſthograph, *g.* [a thing] written on the back or both ſides.

Opiſthographical, belonging thereto.

Opitulate, *l.* to help or aid.

Opium, *l.* the juice of black Poppy, cauſing ſleep.

Opobalſame, *-mum*, *g.* the gum diſtilling from the balm-tree.

Opoponax, *g.* the ſap of *Panax* a hot-Country plant, or (by Dr. *Wilkins*) the gummy juice of the root of *Hercules* all-heal.

Oppication, *l.* a covering with pitch.

Oppidan, *l.* a townſ-man.

Oppignorate, *l.* to pawn.

Oppilation, *l.* an Obſtruction or Stoppage [in the inward parts.]

Oppilative, obſtructive, ſtopping.

Oppletion, *l.* a filling up.

Opponent, *l.* an Antagoniſt, or contradicter, oppoſing the Reſpondent.

Oppertunely, ſeaſonably.

Oppoſite, *l.* contrary or over againſt.

Oppoſites, things oppoſed or ſet againſt one another.

Oppoſition, a reſiſting or ſetting againſt, and (in Aſtrology) the being ſix ſigns diſtant.

Opprobrious, reproachful.

Oppugn, *l.* to aſſault, beſiege or violently oppoſe.

Oppriſt, *o.* upriſen.

Ops, Daughter of *Cælus* and *Veſta*, wife and Siſter of *Saturn*.

Opſimathy, *g.* a learning late.

Opſonation, *l.* a catering.

Opſonator, *l.* a caterer, manciple.

Optable *l.* deſirable.

Optation, *l.* a wiſhing.

Optative, wiſhing or deſiring.

Optick, *-cal*, *g.* belonging to the ſight.

Optick ſinews, which bring the virtue of ſeeing to the eyes.

Optimacy, *l.* Government by the Nobles.

Optimity, *l.* profitableneſs, excellency.

Option, choice, election.

Opulency, wealth, a being

Opulent, *l.* rich, plentiful.

Opuſcule, *-cle*, *l.* a ſmall work.

Or, *o.* *Li.* for erte.

Ora, as *Ore*.

Or. f. Gold [colour.]

Orache, *-age*, Atriplex, an inſipid pot-herb.

Oracle, *l.* an anſwer or counſel given by God, a Propheſie.

Oracles of Apollo, *Jupiter*, &c.) illuſions of the Devil (in imitation of the real ones) which ceaſed upon the coming of Chriſt.

Oracular, belonging thereto.

Oral, *l.* belonging to the Mouth, Face or Voyce.

Orange, a town on the *Rhone* in *France*.

Oration, *l.* prayer, alſo a ſpeech.

Oratory, *l.* Eloquence, alſo a place of Prayer.

Oratory of St. Jerome, a place (at *Rome*) frequented by, and giving name to the

Oratorians, Fryers inſtituted by *Philip Nerius*, a *Florentine*, and confirmed by *Pope Pius*, IV. 1564.

Oratour, *l.* an Eloquent ſpeaker or pleader.

Orbation, *l.* a depriving, or taking away.

Orbiculated, *l.* made

Orbical, *-cular*, round, in the form of an

Orbe, *l.* a globe or ſphere, a body contained under one round ſuperficies.

Orbity, *l.* a want or privation [of Parents, Children, &c.]

Orbona, a Roman Goddeſs implored againſt Orbity.

Orcades, the thirty Britiſh Iſles of *Orkney*.

Orch, *Ork*, a monſtrous fiſh (the Whales enemy) called

led a whirl-pool; alſo a Butt (for Wine or Figs.)

Orchal, a ſtone (like Allum) uſed by Dyers to raiſe a red.

Orchamus, King of *Babylon*, who Buried his Daughter *Leucothoe* alive for lying with *Apollo*.

Orchanet, (*A. Alcanet*) *Anchuſa*, wild Bugloſs.

Orchel (as *Orchal*) ſeems (in ſome old Statutes) to be a kind of Cork.

Orches, a Town in *Flanders*.

Orcheſtre, *g.* the place where the Chorus danceth, or where the Muſicians ſit.

Orchis, *Satyrion*, Dogs-ſtones.

Orcus, a *Theſſalian* River (flowing out of the *Stygian* Lake) ſo thick that it floats on the River *Peneus*.

Ordael, -- *deal*, *Sa.* Judgment.

Fire Ordeal, [a purging ones ſelf from a Crime imputed by] walking blindfold and bare-foot over red-hot Plow-ſhares.

Water Ordeal, [a purgation by] putting ones Arms up to the Elbows in ſeething hot water.

Ordalian Law, ordaining the foreſaid trial, abrogated in the time of King *John*.

Orde, *Sa.* the point.

Order in Files, three foot; and the open Order ſix.

Order in Ranks, ſix foot; and the open Order twelve.

Ordinal, belonging to Orders; alſo a Book of Direction for Biſhops, or of Orders in a Colledge, &c.

Ordinal Numbers, Firſt, Second, Third, &c.

Ordinatione contra ſervientes, a Writ againſt Servants that leave their Maſters.

Ordinary, (in Civil-Law) any Judge having Power to take knowledge of cauſes in his own right (as he is Magiſtrate) and not by Deputation.

Ordinary, (in Common-Law) he that hath ordinary Juriſdiction in cauſes Eccleſiaſtical.

Ordinaries, Proper Charges belonging to the Art of Heraldry.

Ordination daies, the ſecond Sunday in Lent, *Trinity* Sunday, the Sunday following, the Wedneſday after *September* 14. and *December* 13.

Ore, the out-part of any thing, alſo an old Coin (of 16 pence) mentioned in Dooms-day book.

Oreads, *g.* Nymphs of the mountains.

Oreb, *h.* a Crow, or Pleaſant.

Oredelph, Ore lying under ground, alſo the liberty of claiming the

Ore found in a mans own ground.

Oreford, a Town in *Suffolk*.

Oreſtes, the ſon of *Agamemnon*, and Friend of *Pylades*, his body (being digged up) was found to be ſeven cubits long.

Orewell, a Haven in *Eſſex*.

Orewood, Sea-wrack, a kind of Sea-weed, which (in *Cornwall*) they manure their land with.

Orfgild, *Sa.* a reſtitution of cattel, or penalty for taking them away, or (by *Lambert*) a reſtitution made by the Hundred of any wrong done by one in pledge.

Orford, a town in *Suffolk*.

Orfraies, *f.* a frizled cloth of Gold, worn heretofore both by the Clergy and Kings themſelves.

Orgal, the lees of wine dried and uſed by Dyers to make cloth drink in their colours.

Orgallous, -*gail*-, *o.* proud.

Organ Ling, for *Orkney Ling* where the beſt is taken.

Organical, belonging to an

Organ, *g.* an inſtrument.

Organick veins, as *Illack*.

Organiſt, an Organ-player.

Organie, *Origanum*, wild Marjerom (growing much on Mountains.)

Orgeis, *Organ Ling*, the greateſt ſort of North-Sea fiſh.

Orgeis, Revels inſtituted by

Orpheus, to the honour of *Bacchus* (every third year)

Orial Colledge (in *Oxford*) built by King *Edward* the ſecond.

Orichalcum, a Copper metal like gold, and another factitious.

Orientality, the luſtre of the Eaſt, the being

Oriental, belonging to the

Orient, *l.* the Eaſt.

Orifice, the mouth, hole or entrance [of a wound, &c.]

Oriflambe, as *Auriflambe*, the holy purple ſtandard of St. *Denis*.

Original, *l.* Natural, alſo the firſt draught of a writing, alſo as

Origine, a beginning, fountain, ſtock or pedigree.

Oriol, *l.* the little waſte room next the hall, where particular perſons dine.

Orion, a Great hunter, ſtung to death by a Scorpion and both placed among the Conſtellations.

Oriſant, *o.* for *Horizon*.

Oriſmada, *P.* the Fire worſhipped by the *Perſians* as a God.

Oriſons, (*f. Oraiſons*) prayers.

Orle, a threefold line doubled, admitting a tranſparency of the field through the innermoſt ſpace.

Orloge, *o.* a Dial.

Orleans, a City on the *Loire* in *France*.

Orlop, any Deck of a ſhip, except the firſt.

Ormeschurch, a town in *Lancaſhire*.

Ormus, a *Perſian* City in an

an Isle abounding with shells that breed the fairest pearls.

Ornature, *l.* an adorning.

Orndrus, *Cu.* afternoons drinking.

Ornithology, *g.* the speaking (or a discourse) of birds.

Ornomancy, *g.* Divination by Birds.

Orontes, a river of *Cælosyria*.

Orped, *o.* gilded.

Orphanism, the state of an

Orphan, *g.* a Fatherless child.

Orphean, belonging to

Orpheus, a *Thracian* Poet, whose harp (they say) drew stones, woods, wild beasts &c.

Orpiment, *Orpin*, a soft and yellow kind of *Arsenick* or *Ratsbane*.

Orque, *l.* a hulk or huge ship, also as *Orch*.

Orrice, *Iris*, a *Flower de lice*.

Orsey, a Town and County in *Germany*.

Ortelli, (*f. Orteils*, toes) the claws of a dogs foot.

Orthodoxy, a being

Orthodox, *-xal*, *g.* of a right opinion or sound faith.

Orthogonal, *g.* having right or even corners.

Orthographist, he that doth

Orthographize, or practise

Orthography, *g.* the manner of true writing, also a perfect plat-form of a building.

Orthopnæa, *g.* shortness of breath.

Ortive, *l.* Easterly, rising.

Ortyard, a place (now for fruit-trees, but at first) for

Orts, Scraps.

Ortygia, *Delos*, one of the *Cyclad* Islands.

Orval, Clary or Cleareye.

Orythia, Daughter of *Erictheus* King of *Athens*, ravisht away by *Boreas*.

Oryen cause, *o.* Either urgent or Orient, Emergent, Occasional.

Oryx, *Orinx*, *g.* a kind of African wild goat.

Orzabow, a Town in *Podolia*.

Osanna, as *Hosanna*.

Osberf, *Sa.* light of the Family.

Osborn, *Sa.* House-child.

Oscian play, a light Roman sport pleasing the People.

Oscillation, as *Meriton*

Oscines, the Birds by whose voices the Augurs foretold things to come.

Oscitancy, *-ation*, *l.* a yawning or gaping, also idleness.

Osculation, *l.* a kissing or embracing.

Osenbridge, a Town in *Breme* in *Westphalia*.

Osiris, King of *Ægypt* and Husband of *Io* (or *Isis*) worshipped in the form of an Ox.

St. *Osith*, (formerly *Chic*) a Town in *Essex*, from

Osith, a Royal Nun, slain by Danish Pyrates.

Osmonds, Iron-stone or Oar.

Osmund, *Sa.* House-peace.

Osnabrug, a Town in *Westphalia*.

Osprey, as *Ossifrage*.

Ossendorf, a Town in *Westphalia*.

Osse, *Che.* (*audere*) to offer, intend or dare.

Ossicle, *l.* a little bone.

Ossifrage, *l.* the bonebreaking Eagle.

Ossifragant, bone-breaking.

Ossuary, *l.* a Charnelhouse or place where bones are kept.

Ostend, a Port in *Flanders*.

Ostentional, *l.* a Souldier attending the Prince at publick shews.

Osterreich, *Ostrich*, *Austrasia*, *Austria*, the extream Province of East *France*.

Ostent, a wonder or Monster; also a shewing or pointing at.

Ostentation, *l.* vain-glory, boasting.

Ostentatious, *l.* set out for shew, or vain glory.

Ostentiferous, *l.* bringing Monsters or strange sights.

Osterburg, a Town of *Brandenburgh*.

Ostiary, *l.* a Door-keeper.

Ostholme, an Isle of North *Juitland*.

Ostiology, *g.* a Discourse of bones.

Ostomachy, *g.* a playing [or fighting] with bones.

Ostracism, an *Athenian* Banishment for ten years (by delivering a shell with the Name) devised by *Clisthenes*, who was the first so Condemned.

Ostration, *g.* shelliness.

Ostriferous, *l.* Oister-bearing.

Ostringer, *Ostregere*, *o.* an Eastern [Gos-hawk] Falconer.

Oswestrey, (*Br. Croix Oswalds*) a Town in *Shropshire*, from

Oswold, *-wald* (House-ruler or Steward) a devout King of *Northumberland*, torn in pieces by *Penda* the Pagan King of the *Mercians*.

Otacousticon, *g.* an instrument to help the Hearing.

Otalgia, *g.* a pain in the Ears.

Othan, *Odinus*, *Woden*, *Mars*.

Other, *o.* for, Or.

Othes, *Otho*, *Eudo* (*Ge.Hud*, a keeper a mans name.

Othryades, the only surviver of 300 *Lacedemonians* (who had slain as many *Argives*) and writing on his shield I have overcom'n, kil'd himself also.

Otoorackes, *Tu.* (sitters down) old Janizaries no longer fit for war.

Otranto, a City of *Naples*.

Otraque, *-qua*, drink (in the *Moluccoes* and *Philippines*) coming from a Nut.

Ottadini, the ancient inhabitants of *Northumberland*.

Otter, an amphibious beast of Chase.

Otterendorp, a town of

Breme in *Westphalia*.

Otterbourn, a town in *Northumberland*.

Otus and *Ephialtes*, the Sons of *Neptune*, two of the Giants that warr'd with Heaven, reported to have grown (in nine years) the length of nine Acres.

Oval l. round like an Egg, also belonging to

Ovation, laying of Eggs, also a small triumph (for a bloodless victory) the souldiders shouting (O, O!) and a Sheep (*Ovis*) being sacrificed.

Ouch, a boss, neck-lace, or any ornament of Gold or Jewels.

Oudenard, a town in *Flanders*.

Over-blows, it blows so hard, they can bear no topsails.

Oudwater, a Town in *Holland*.

Overest, o. uppermost.

Overfret, o. overspread.

Overhipped, (for -hopped) o. leapt over.

All-Overly, o. utterly.

Overgrown-Sea, when the waves are at the higest.

Over-masted, having the masts too large or too long.

Oversamessa, *-senesse*, *-segenesse*, an ancient penalty or fine upon those that heard of a Murder or Robbery and did not pursue.

Overset, overturn and founder the Ship.

Overset the Cable, turn it over, being quoiled up.

Overwheled, o. for *Overheled*, *-veled*, or -whelmed.

Overthrown, when (being to be trimmed a-ground) she falls over on a side.

Overture, f. an opening, a proposition or conference.

Overt, (f. *Ouvert*,) open, manifest.

Overt, as *Leovr*.

Over-Wesel, a Town of *Treers*.

Over-yssel, one of the United Provinces.

Oviary, l. a flock of Sheep.

Ovil, l. a sheep-fold.

Oviparous, l. breeding by eggs or spawn.

Oulney, a town in *Buckinghamshire*.

Ounce, twenty peny weight, also a *Lynx*.

Oundel, a town in *Northamptonshire*.

Ounding, *Own-*, o. rising like waves.

Owndy and Crisp, o. sliked and curled.

Ourage, (f. *Oeuvrage*) work.

Ouster le main, (f. *Oster la main*) *Amoveas manum*, a writ which was sent to the Escheator to deliver possession out of the Kings hands to the party that sues.

Ouster le mer, (f. *Outre-*) an excuse (by being beyond Sea) for not appearing in Court.

Ousted, (f. *osté*) removed or put out.

Outfangthef, Sa. a Lords priviledge of calling a man of his Fee (taken for Felony in another place) to judgment in his own Court.

Out-law, one deprived of the benefit of Law and out of the Kings protection.

Outlawry, as *Utlary*.

Outlicker, a timber standing out from the poop, serving (in small ships) for the haling down of the Missen sheat.

Out-parters, Thieves of *Rides-dale*, taking Cattel (or other booty) without that liberty.

Outraie, o. depart, run.

Out-riders, Bailiffs errant, sent by Sheriffs to summon persons to their Courts.

Outrance, o. destruction, extremity.

Outwail, o. a very sorrowfull thing.

Owles, o. hooks (f. *houlette*, a sheep-hook.)

Owelty (or *Ouelty*) *of services*, an Equality, when the Tenant paravail owes as much to the *Mesn*, as the *Mesn* doth to the Lord Paramount.

Owhere, o. any where.

Owresby, a Town in *Lincolnshire*.

Owen, *Oen*, *Audoenus*, *Eugenius*.

Ox-eye, a large kind of daisy, also a kind of woodpecker.

Oxenford, a town of *Mentz* in *Germany*, also as

Oxford, on the river *Ouse*. The University began *An.* 806. having 3 Colledges built by K. *Alfred*.

Ox-boose, *No.* an Oxstall in Winter nights.

Oxgang of Land, *Bovata terræ*, commonly taken for 15 Acres.

Oxter, *No.* (*Axilla*) an arm-pit.

Oxycrat, a poor *Persian* drink of Water and a little Vinegar.

Oxygon, g. a triangle of 3 acute angles.

Oxymel, g. a Syrop (against Phlegmatick humours) of Honey, Vinegar, and Water.

Oxymel compositum, with Roots and Seeds boiled in it.

Oxymel Scylliticum, made of Honey, Vinegar, and the Sea-onion.

Oxymoron, g. (Subtily foolish) an Epithet of a contrary signification.

Oxyporopolist, g. he that sells meat in sharp sawce.

Oxyrrhodium, g. Oyl of Roses and Vinegar mixt.

Oyer and Terminer, (f. *Ouir-*) a Commission granted to certain persons, to hear and Determine certain causes.

Oyer de record, a petition that the Judges (for better proof sake) will please to hear or peruse a Record.

Oyes, (f. *Oiez*) Hear ye!

Oyse, a river in *France*.

Oze, *Owze*, soft muddy ground.

Ozene-

Ozena, -*na*, *g*. a stinking sore in the nose.

Ozier, a Sallow.

P.

P*Aagium*, money paid for passage through another's jurisdiction,

Pabular, *lous*, -*latory*, *l*. belonging to forage or provender.

Pacal, belonging to peace, also an *Indian* tree.

Pacation, *l*. an appeasing.

Pacator, *l*. a pacifier.

Pace, two foot (and in some places 3) and a half.

Geometrical Pace, (by which miles are measured) five foot.

Pace of Egypt and Samos, six foot.

Pace of Asses, a great company of them together.

Pace, *o*. for appease.

Pachynum, a *Sicilian* promontory, towards *Peloponnesus*.

Paciferous, *l*. peace-bringing.

Pacifique, -*ficatory*, belonging to

Pacification, *l*. peace-making.

Pack of wool, a horse-load, 17 stone and a pound.

Packers, that barrel up herrings, sworn to do it duly 15 *Car*. 2.

Packing Whites, a kind of Cloth.

Pactitious, according to a

Pact, -*tion*, a bargain or agreement, also a Truce.

Pactolus, a *Lydian* River with gold-colour'd sand, ever since *Midas* washt himself in it.

Pad, *o*. a bundle, also (*c*.) the high-way.

Paddock (*D*. *padde*) a Frog, or a Toad, also a little park.

Padelion, *Pes leonis*, great Sanicle.

Paderborne, a town in *Westphalia*.

Padnage, as *Pann*-.

Padua, a *Venetian* City and University.

Paduentage, *f*. Common of Pasture.

Paddestow, a town in *Cornwall*.

Padus, the Italian River *Po*.

Pæan, *g*. a Song to *Apollo*.

Pædagogue, *g*. a Schoolmaster.

Pædobaptism, baptism of Infants.

Pæonia, part of *Macedonia*.

Pagaments, a sort of Frize cloth.

Paganalian, belonging to

Paganals, *l*. wakes or Countrey-holidayes.

Paganical, belonging to the Countrey, or to a

Pagan, *Paynim*, Heathen.

Paganims, for *Painims*.

Paganism, heathenism, also the custom of Countreymen.

Pageant, a triumphal arch.

Paginal, belonging to a

Page, *l*. the side of a leaf.

Pagod, an Indian Idol, also their piece of gold about an Angel value.

Paico, an Indian herb against the stone in the Kidneys.

Paigles, Ox-lips.

Paillardise, *f*. Whoredom.

Pain fort & dure (*f*. *Peine*-) a being prest to death, for refusing to put themselves on the ordinary trial of God and the Country.

Painemaine, (*q*. *de matin*) *o*. white-bread.

Païsage, Landskip or Countrey-work.

Païs, *f*. a Countrey.

Paladin, *f*. a Knight of the round table.

Palamedes, Son of *Nauplius* King of *Eubœa*, having caused *Ulysses* (against his will) to go to the *Trojan* war, *Ulysses* (by a false accusation) caused him to be stoned to death.

Palasins, *o*. [Ladies] of honour.

Palastre, *o*. a combat.

Palapuntz, an Indian drink of Aqua-vitæ, Rose-water, Citrons and Sugar.

Palatical, belonging to the

Palate, *l*. the roof of the mouth, where (as in the Tongue) the sense of tasting lies, also to tast or try.

Palatine, belonging to the *Palat* or to a Princes Palace.

Count Palatine or Paladine, a supream Officer in a Soveraign Princes Palace.

Count or Prince Palatine of the Rhine, the *Palsgrave*, one of the Electoral Princes.

Palatinate, a County Palatine, a principal County or Shire, having the Authority (as it were) of a Royal Palace.

County Palatines (in *England*) *Lancaster*, *Chester*, *Durham*, and *Ely*, their Power is abridged by 27 *H*. 8.

County Palatine of Hexham, reduced (by 14 *Eliz*.) to be a part of the County of *Northumberland*.

Palatius, *Palassius*, a precious stone redder than the Carbuncle or Ruby, being the Palace or Matrix where that is begotten.

Pale, *o*. a spangle.

Pale, two perpendicular lines from the top to the bottom of the Eschuteon.

Paleated, *l*. mingled with chaff.

Palefray, *Palfray*, *f*. a stately horse with trappings.

Pale-maille, *f*. *Pell-Mell*, a game with a bowl struck with a Mallet through an iron arch at either end of an alley.

Paleous, *l*. chaffy.

Palermo, the Residence of the *Sicilian Vice-Roy*.

Pales, the Goddess of shepherds.

Palestine, part of *Syria*, containing *Judea*, *Samaria* and *Galilee*.

Palestrical, belonging to wrestling.

Palfrey, as *Palefray*.

Palici, *Palisci*, twin-Sons of *Jupiter* and *Thaleia*, the earth swallowed her up (accord-cording to the wish) and let out the Children again (when their time came) into the World.

Palilia, Feasts unto Pales.

Palilogia, *g.* a repetition of the same words.

Palindrom, *g.* a sentence the same backward as forward, as *Ablata, at alba.*

Palingenesie, *g.* regeneration or being born again.

Palingman, a merchant Denizen, born within the English pale.

Palinode, *-dy*, *g.* recantation, another [kind of] Song.

Palinurus, a Promontory of *Lucania*, where

Palinurus, the Pilot of *Æneas*, sleeping, fell into the Sea.

Palizado, *Sp. Palissade*, *f.* a defence of stakes, &c.

Pall, *l.* a long robe, also the black velvet laid over a Corps, also a narrow ornament of Lambs wool sent by the Pope to Arch-Bishops, and worn about their necks at the Altar.

Palladion, *Sp.* *-ium*, *l.* an image of *Pallas* kept by the *Trojans*, who supposed that it preserved their City.

Pallas, as *Minerva*, she is said to furnish *Perseus* with a shield and looking-glass, when he slew *Medusa*.

Pallat, the Painters thin piece of wood that holds his colours.

Palled, *f.* pale, dead.

Palle-maille, as *Pale-*.

Pallet, one half of the Pale in Heraldry.

Palletoque, *Pallecoat*, *f.* a pages Cassock or short cloak with sleeves.

Palliard, *c.* whose Father is a born begger.

Palliardize, as *Paillardize*.

Palliate, *l.* to cover [with a Cloak.]

Palliation, a cloaking.

Palliative, belonging thereto.

Palliative Cure, a wound skin'd over, healed outwardly but festering underneath.

Pallid, *l.* pale, fearful.

Pallification, *l.* piling, or strengthening the ground-work with Piles.

Palma la nova, a Fort in *Friuli*, with nine bastions and 700 pieces of Canon.

Pallor, *l.* paleness.

Pallizado, as *Palizado*.

Palmar, *l.* belonging to a

Palm, a hands breadth, 4 fingers.

Greater Palm, a span, or (by some) a shaftment.

Palmata, a handful.

Palm-Sunday, the next before Easter, when they met Christ with branches of

Palm-tree, which bears Dates, used as a token of victory, because it shoots upward (though opprest with much weight) and the leaves never fall.

Palmer, a Pilgrim visiting holy places (with a staff or boughs of Palm) also a worm with many feet (eating the Palm-tree) also as

Palmatory, a ferular, to strike the palm of the hand.

Palmester, a Diviner by

Palmestry, as *Chiromancy*.

Palmeto-tree, of whose juice (in the Isle *Mauritius*) they make a pleasant wine.

Palmetto royal, the Cabbidg-tree.

Palmiferous, palm-bearing, also victorious.

Palmipedous, whole or flat-footed, like water-fowl.

Palos, a Port of *Andalusia*.

Palpation, *l.* a stroaking or flattering.

Palpable, *l.* which may be felt.

Palpitation, *l.* a panting.

Paltsgrave, *D.* *Pfaltzgraff*, *Ge.* Count Palatine, especially the Prince Elector Palatine of the *Rhen*.

Paludament, *l.* a Coat-armour (worn by Chief Captains) also a Heralds coat of Arms.

Paludiferous, *l.* causing fens or Marshes

Palumbine, belonging to a Ring-dove or Wood culver.

Pampeluna, the Chief City of *Navarre*.

Pamphili, Great *Italian* boats of 300 oars.

Pamphlet (*D. Pampier*, paper) a little sorry book or paper.

Pamphylia, part of *Asia* the less.

Pampination, *l.* a pruning of vines.

Pampinean, belonging to vine-leaves or branches.

Pan, the God of Shepherds.

Panada, *-do*, *Sp.* meat made of Crums of bread and currants boiled.

Panage, as *Pannage*.

Panaretus, *g.* containing all vertues.

Panathenaic, belonging to

Panathenaea, *Athenian* Solemnities kept every year, and (the Greater) every fifth.

Pancart, *f.* a paper of all the rates of Customs due to the [*French*] King.

Panches, the Mats made of Synnet and fasten'd to the yards, to save them from galling.

Panchaian, *-ique*, belonging to

Panchaia, part of *Arabia*, where is much Frankincense.

Panchymagogon, *g.* purging all humours.

Pancratical, belonging to a

Pancratiast, one skild in wrestling and all feats of activity.

Pancreas, *g.* the sweet-bread.

Pandarism, the work of a

Pandar, a Pimp or bawd.

Pandects, *g.* books treating of all matters, also as Digests, a Volume of the civil Law.

Pandiculation, *l.* a gaping and stretching of one self.

Pandion, King of *Athens*, and

and Father of *Progne*.

Pandor, -*der*, (*D*. a taker of pawns) as *Pandar*.

Pandora's box, full of all miseries, opened by *Epimetheus* the Spouse of

Pandora, the first woman made by *Vulcan*, and endowed by all the Gods and Goddesses.

Pandoxatrix, an Ale-wife who also brews her self.

Pandurist, he that playes on a

Pandure, a Rebeck, or rather a *Bandore*.

Panegyrick, g. a general assembly or Solemnity, also an Oration in praise of Great Personages.

Panegyrist, g. the author thereof.

Panel, -*lla*, (f. *panne*, a skin) a roll with the names of Jurors return'd by the Sheriff to pass upon a Trial.

Pangonie, g. a precious stone with very many corners.

Panguts, (f. *Pançu*) a drossel or Gor-belly.

Panick, *Painick*, a grain like to millet.

Panick fear, sudden and distracting, inflicted (as it were) by the God Pan.

Panicle, a little leaf.

Panifice, l. a making of bread.

Pankers, for *Panters*.

Pasnage (q. *Pastinage*) *Pannage*, *Pawnage*, f. Mast for hogs, or the money taken for it.

Pannade, f. the prauncing of a lusty horse.

Pannel, the pipe next to the Fundament of a hawk.

Pannam, c. bread.

Pannicle, l. a little piece of cloth.

Fleshy Pannicle, the fourth covering of the body from head to foot.

Pannier, *Panier*, f. a bin, basket, or dosser for bread.

Pannier-man (in the Inns of Court) winds the horn to call them to dinner, provides mustard, &c.

Pannonian, belonging to

Pannonia, Hungary.

Panomphæan, g. (all-oracular) an Epithet of *Jupiter*.

Panoply, g. compleat harness, a whole suit of Armour.

Panoplique, compleatly armed.

Panpharmacon, g. a medicine for all diseases.

Pansie; *Jacea*, Hearts-ease.

Pansophy, g. wisdom in all things.

Pantagruelist, f. a good companion, imitating

Pantagruele, a feigned Giant in *Rabelais*.

Pantolone, I. an old amorous covetous Dotard.

Pantalones. -*loons*, a sort of breeches well known.

Pantarb, -*arva*, *Sp*. the stone of the Sun.

Panter, c. the heart.

Panters, o. toiles for Deer, pitfals.

Pantheology, g. the whole body of Divinity.

Panthéon, g. a *Roman* Temple dedicated to all the Gods, and since (by Pope *Boniface* 4) to the Virgin *Mary* and all Saints.

Pantherine, [spotted] like a

Panther, a female *Libard*.

Pantomime, -*imick*, g. an actor of all parts.

Pantometry, g. a measuring of all things.

Panurgie, g. skill or medling in all matters.

Papacy, l. the Popedome.

Papal, l. belonging to the

Pape, f. (*Pappas*, g. a Father) the Pope or Bishop of *Rome*.

Papality, as *Papacy*, also Popishness.

Papaverous, -*reum*, l. belonging to Chestoul or poppy.

Papelard, f. an Hypocrite.

Papelardise, f. hypocrisy.

Paphian, belonging to

Paphos, a City in *Cyprus* dedicated to *Venus* by

Paphus, the Son of *Pigmalion* (by a statue of his own making) and King of *Cyprus*.

Papian (or *Poppæan*) law (among the *Romans*) making the people heir to a single mans estate.

Papilionaceous fly, a butterfly.

Papplar, c. milk pottage.

Papulosity, l. fulness of pimples or blisters.

Papyriferous, bringing forth

Papyrus, the rush whereof paper was made.

Papyrius Cursor, a *Roman* General who overthrew the *Samnites*.

Papyropolist, g. a seller of paper.

Parabien, *Sp*. a welcoming or congratulation.

Parabolical, belonging to a

Parable g. a similitude.

Parabola, the same, also one of the crooked lines proceeding from the cutting of a Cone or Cylinder.

Paracelsian, belonging to, or following the method of

Paracelsus, a Physitian who used exceeding strong Oyls and waters extracted from the natures of things.

Parachronize, g. to mis-time [a thing.]

Paraclete, g. an Exhorter, Advocate or Comforter.

Paraclite, g. a man defamed or having an ill name.

Paracmastical, g. [the hot fit of a feaver] declining by little and little, till it totally cease.

Parade, f. a shew or appearance [of Soldiers, &c.]

Paradiastole, g. a distinction, an enlarging by interpretation.

Paradigora, g. an Example.

Paradigmatize, to exemplify.

Paradise, g. a Garden or place of pleasure.

Paradoxal, -*xical*, belonging to

Paradoxology, a speaking by

Paradoxes, g. things that seem

seem strange, absurd, and contrary to the common opinion.

Paradrome, g. an open Gallery.

Paraenetical, g. perswasive.

Parage, o. parentage, also as *Pareinerie*.

Paragogical, belonging to

Paragoge, g. an addition to the end of a word.

Paragon, f. a compeer, to compare, also a Peerless [Dame, &c.]

Paragraph, g. a Pilcrow, where the line breaks off, the Subdivision of a Section.

Paralipomenon, g. left out.

Paralipomena, the Books of the Chronicles, containing many things omitted in the Kings.

Paralepsis, the letting a thing pass (really or in pretense.)

Parallactick, belonging to

Parallax, g. the difference between the true and apparent place of a star, by reason of our beholding it from the Superficies (and not the Centre) of the earth.

Parallel, g. Equal, also to compare.

Parallelogram, a Square made of

Parallels, lines equally distant and never meeting, five Circles imagined about the Globe.

Paralogize, to make a

Paralogism, g. a fallacious syllogism.

Paralytick, belonging to or sick of the

Paralysis, g. Palsy, a resolution of the sinews.

Paraments, Robes of state

Parament, *Parement*, the red flesh between the skin and body of a Deer.

Lord Paramount, the highest Lord of a Fee, of whom the Mesn Lord holds.

Paramour, f. a Lover.

Paranymph, g. a Brideman or maid; also he that makes a speech in praise of those that are commencing Doctors, &c.

Parapegmata, g. the Tables in which Astrologers write their Art.

Parapet, f. a batlement or Brest-work on a Rampier.

Paraphe, f. a mark in the margent, also an under-signing, or the flourish that is added.

Paraphanalia (and in Civil Law

Parapoernalia) the Goods which a Wife brings her husband over and above her dowry, as Apparel, &c. which (especially in *York*) are not to be put in the Husbands Inventory.

Paraphrast, g. he that doth

Paraphrase, or write a

Paraphrase, -*stical exposition*, a short Comment.

Parasang, a *Persian* measure of Thirty Furlongs.

Paraselene, g. a Mock-moon reflected by a cloud.

Parasitical, belonging to a

Parasite, g. a flatterer or smell-feast.

Parasitical plants, that live on the stocks of others, as *Missletoe*, &c.

Parathesis, g. Apposition or putting to, also the words enclosed within *Crotchets*.

Paratragediate, to help on a tragedy, make a matter worse than it is.

Parature, l. the preparation or matter whereof a thing is made.

Tenant paravail, the lowest or immediate Tenant, having the avail or profit of the land.

Paraunter, *Per*-, o. peradventure.

Parayba, a Portugal town on the River *Domingo* in *Brasil*.

Parazone, a wood-knife or dagger.

Parboil (q. *Part-boil*) to boil in part, not fully.

Parbreak, o. to vomit.

Par unkle, a rope seised together and put double about a Cask, to hoise it by.

Parcae, l. the Destinies, *Clotho*, *Lachesis*, *Atropos*, bearing, spinning and cutting the thred of mans Life.

Parcel-maker, an Exchequer Officer making the parcels of the Escheators Accounts.

Parcel a seam, cover it with Canvas, hot Pitch and Tar.

Parceners, as *Coparceners*.

Parcinerie, their holding of land joyntly, without dividing it.

Parciloquy, l. a sparing or niggardly discourse.

Parcity, l. Frugality, Thrif

Parco fracto, a writ against him that breaks a pound, for beasts lawfully impounded.

Pard, l, a Libard or Male panther.

Parde, o. (f. *par Dieu*) by God.

Pareasse, -*as*, a serpent with a little head (but a mouth wide enough to swallow a pigeon) and making a furrow with his tail.

Parecbasis, g. a digression.

Paregmenon, g. a joyning together of words derived from one another.

Parelcon. g. the adding one word to the end of another.

Pareil, one kind of printing Character.

Parelij, g. Mock-Suns reflected by a thick cloud on each side of the Sun.

Parellelisation, or rather

Paral-, a making of

Parellels.

Parenchyma, g. the [bloody] substance of the Liver, Spleen and lights.

Pareneticks, as *Paraen*-.

Pareneticks, Fatherly (or Masterly) Admonitions.

Parent, l. obedient.

Parental, belonging to

Parents or Ancestours.

Parentation, l. a Celebrating [their] Funerals.

Parenthesis, g. the interposing something (thus) within a sentence, which nevertheless would be entire without it.

Parenticide, *l.* a killing or killer of Parents.

Parergy, *-gue*, *f.* *-gum*, *-gon*, *g.* something added by the by, beside the main business.

Parfay, (*f.* *par foy*) by faith.

Parfite, *o.* perfect.

Parget, plaister.

Parian, belonging to

Paros, one of the Cyclades, from whence they bring pure white marble.

Paritation, *l.* evenness [of accounts.]

Paricidal, belonging to a

Paricide, *l.* a killing or killer of Father, Mother, or any of near kin.

Parient, *l.* travelling with young.

Parilian, as *Palilian*.

Parility, as *Parity*.

Paris, *Alexander* the Son of *Priam*, he seduced *Helena* from *Greece*, which occasioned the *Trojan* War.

Paris, the Metropolis of *France*.

Paris-Garden, Bear Garden, the house of *Rob. de Paris* in the reign of *Rich.* 2. who proclaim'd it a receptacle of the Butchers Garbage.

Parishens, *o.* Parishioners.

Parisyllable, *l.* an Equal syllable.

Parisyllabical, having no more syllables in the Genitive than were in the Nominative.

Parity, *l.* equality.

Paritude, *-ure*, *Parture*, *l.* a breeding or bringing forth.

Park, an inclosure for deer or other wild beasts.

Park-bote, a being quit of enclosing a park.

Parley, *f.* a talking [together.

Parliament, (*f.* *Parlement*, a conference) an Assembly of the King and 3 Estates (Lords Spiritual, Temporal, and Commons) of *England*, for debating matters touching the Common-wealth, &c.

Parliamentum indoctorum, at Coventry (6 Hen. 4.) to which no Lawyer was to come.

Parliamentum insanum, at *Oxford*, 41. Hen. 3.

Parma, a City and Dukedom of *Italy*.

Parmaceti, (for *Sperma Ceti*, the Whales seed) an excellent oyntment.

Parmesan, an Inhabitant (or Cheese) of *Parma*.

Parnassian, belonging to

Parnassus, a *Grecian* Mountain sacred to *Apollo* and the

Parnassides, the Muses.

Parnel, a pretty Woman-lover.

Parochial, belonging to

Parishes, about 9284 divisions of the Land by *Honorius* Arch-Bishop of *Canterbury*, 636.

Parœmia, *g.* a proverb.

Parole, *f.* a word or promise.

Paronomous, belonging to

Paronomasia, *g.* a likeness of words.

Paros, see *Parian*.

Paroxysm, *g.* a fit.

Parrels, made of tracks, ribs and ropes (about the mast) for the sliding of the yard.

Parricide, as *Paricide*.

Parrhasius, the Painter who drew the Curtain which *Zeuxis* (thinking real) bad him draw.

Parrhesia, *g.* a freedom of speech.

Parsimonious, full of, or belonging to

Parsimony, *l.* sparing, good husbandry.

Parshor St. *Cruce*, a town in *Worcestershire*.

Parsly-hedg, *Caucalis*, an herb.

Parsly-pert, *Calculum frangens*, *Perce-pierre Anglorum*, or Break-stone.

Parson imparsonee, *Persona impersonata*, a Rector in present possession of a Parochial Church.

Partage, *f.* a parting or dividing.

Parterre, *f.* Garden-work [on the ground.]

Parters of Gold, as Finors.

Partes Finis, &c. an Exception taken against a fine levied

Parthenian, *g.* belonging to Virginity.

Parthenope, the old name of *Naples*, also one of the *Syrens*.

Parthian, belonging to

Parthia, *Arach*, in *Asia*.

Partialize, to use

Partiality, *l.* a being

Partial, inclining to one party more than another.

Partiary, *l.* one that doth

Participate, *l.* give or take part with another.

Partible, which may be parted

Participles, Adjectives derived from Verbs (with some signification of time) as loving, loved &c.

Particle, *l.* a little part, a small undeclined word.

Partit Jury, as *Medietas linguæ*.

Partile aspect, of two planets in the same number of Degrees and Minutes.

Particularize, to instance in particulars.

Partion, *l.* a breeding.

Partisan, *f.* a partaker, also a [Lieutenants] leading-staff.

Partitione facienda, a writ against a Coparcener that refuses to joyn in

Partition, *l.* a division.

Partitor, *l.* a Divider.

Partlet, an old kind of band, both for men and women, a loose collar, a womans ruff, *Che*.

Partners, the Timbers that keep the mast steddy in the step.

Partriche, *o.* a partridge.

Parturient, *l.* about to bring forth [young.]

Parture, for *Parcuere*, (*f.* *par cœur*) by heart.

Parvis, *o.* a porch.

Parvity, *l.* smalness, Nonage.

Pas à pas, *f.* step by step.

Pascal, belonging to

Pas-

Pascage, -*uage*, *f.* Pasturing or grazing.

Paschal, belonging to the

Pasche, *g.* the passover or Easter.

Paschal Rents, Synodals.

Pascuous, *l.* serving for Pasture or feeding.

Mad-pash, *Che.* Mad-brain.

Pasiphaë, the Wife of *Minos*.

Pasquil, -*in*, an old *Roman* Statue, also a Libel (wont to be fixt thereon) who's answer was affixt to *Marforeo* (another old Statue.)

Passade, *f.* Alms given a Passenger; also the manage of a Horse backward and forward.

Passagio, a Writ for the Keepers of the Ports to grant passage over Sea.

Passant, *f.* passing, going.

Passardo, a *Nepas-artua-rope*, to hale down the sheat-blocks of the main and fore-sail, when the Ship goes large.

Passau, a Town in *Bavaria*.

Passenger, *Pellerin*, a kind of small-trained Hawk.

Pass-flower, Pulsatil.

Passe-port, *f.* a pass or safe-conduct.

Passibility, a being

Passible, *l.* able to suffer.

Passion, suffering, also an affection of the mind.

Passive, suffering, or having suffered.

Pastern, *f.* the hollow of the heel,

Pastilicate, to make or use

Pastils, little rolls of Paste, Pills.

Pastinate, to dig [in a Garden.]

Paston, a Town in *Norfolk*.

Pastophories, the most Honourable *Egyptian* Priests.

Pastoral, -*ritious*, belonging to a

Pastor, *l.* a Shepherd.

Pastoral [Song] of Herdsmen.

Pasvolant, *f.* an Hireling foisted in by a Captain on Muster-days.

Patache, a small *Indian* Ship.

Patacoon, a *Spanish* piece about 4*s.* 8*d.*

Patagous, *Magellanicans*, said to be 10 foot high.

Pataque, a *Neopolitan* piece of an hundred Quadrins.

Patart, a *Dutch* Stiver, whereof five make 6 *d.*

Patavinity, the property of, or Relation to *Padua*.

Patay, a Town of *Beausse* in *France*.

Cross Patee, whose ends are broad and opened.

Patefaction, *l.* an opening or discovering.

Patelena, a Goddess of Corn, when the Cups opened.

Patelin, *f.* a flatterer.

Paten, a wooden shoe with an Iron bottom.

Patentee, to whom the King hath granted

Patents, as Letters Patent.

Patency, a being

Patent, *l.* open, uncovered.

Pater-guardian, the head of a *Franciscan* Colledg.

Paternal, Fatherly.

Paternity, *l.* ones being a Father.

Pathetical, *g.* affectionate.

Pathologick, belonging to

Pathology, *g.* a part of Physick, treating of the causes and differences of Diseases.

Pathologist, *g.* a Writer of Diseases and their Symptoms.

Pathopeia, *g.* an expression of a Passion.

Patible, *l.* sufferable.

Patibulary, *l.* belonging to a Gallows.

Patibulated, hanged on a Gibbet.

Patin, *l.* a great Platter, Charger, or Bason; also the flat plate used by Priests (with the Chalice) at Mass.

Patise, a reddish colour.

Cross Patonce, who's ends are both broad, and (as it were) three ways hooked.

Patration, *l.* a doing, perfecting or committing.

Patriarchal, belonging to a

Patriarchate, -*chy*, the Estate, Seat, or Dignity of a

Patriarch, -*ark*, *g.* a chief Father, the first Father of a Family or Nation; also a National Primate.

Patriciate, the Dignity of

Patricians, the most Noble *Romans*, descended of Senatours.

Patricide, as *Parricide*.

Patrick, a Patrician.

Patrimonial, belonging to a

Patrimony, *l.* an Inheritance left by the Father.

Patrimony of St. Peter, an *Italian* Province belonging to the Pope.

Patrizate, *g.* to resemble or imitate ones Father.

Patriot, a Benefactor or Lover of his Countrey.

Patrocinate, -*onize*, to defend or plead for.

Patronal, belonging to a

Patron, *l.* advocate, defender; also (in Civil-law) he that hath made a Servant free; and (in the Canon and Common Law) he that hath the gift of a Benefice.

Patroclus, *Achilles*'s Friend, slain in *Achilles*'s Armour.

Patronymicks, -*cal* names, derived from ones Father or Ancestors.

Patter & Pray, *o.* repeat many *Pater nosters*.

Patulicate, *l.* to be opened or widened.

Pavade, *o.* a Dagger.

Pauciloquent, *l.* using

Pauciloquy, fewness of words.

Paucity, *l.* fewness.

Paudishaw, *Tu.* an Emperour.

Pavefie, *l.* to affright.

Pavefaction, a terrifying.

Pavese, -*vice*, *l.* a large Shield covering the whole Body.

Pavia, a Great City of *Milain*.

Paviage, money towards paving.

Pavidity, a being

Pavid, l. timerous.

Pavilion, f. a Warlike Tent.

Pavin, *Pavane*, f. a kind of Dance.

Paul, h. wonderful or rest.

Paulin, f. little *Paul*.

Pannage, as *Pannage*.

Pavoisade, f. a Target-defense for Gally-slaves against small shot.

Pavonine, l. belonging to a Peacock or Hen.

Pausade, f. a pausing or resting [place.]

Pausanias, a famous *Lacedemonian* Captain; also a Youth who slew *Philip* of *Macedon*, because he had no redress for being Ravished.

Paw', a short Iron fastened to the Deck to keep the Capstain from recoiling.

Ut-pawl the capstain, let it go back.

Pawme, o. palm [of the hand.]

Pax, l. peace, also the *Pix* or Box (*Sp. Paz.*) where the Popish Sacrament is put.

Pay the seams, lay on hot pitch.

Pay the Ship, lay on the stuff (in Graving.)

Payed, when (in a tack) the Sails are flat against the shrowds and she cannot fall back.

Peace of God and the Church, vacation-time.

Peak, c. lace.

Peal, No. cool [the pot.]

Pean, *Erminois*, or yellow Ermine (in Heraldry.)

Pearch, *Perche* a Rod, Pole, a measure of 16 foot and a half, in some places above 20.

Pearl a Gem bred in shell-fish; also the least Printing Character (except the Diamond)

Pease, o. (q. appease or pause) to stay.

Pease-holt, E. Pease-straw.

Peccadillo, Sp. a small fault,

Peccaminous, l. full of sin.

Peccant, l. sinning, offending.

Peccator, l. a sinner.

Peccavi, l. I have offended.

Peck, *-kidg*, c. meat.

Pecorous, l. full of Cattel

Pectinals, l. Fish who's bones are streight like combs (as Soals, &c.)

Pectination, l. a combing, also raking of Corn.

Pectoral, l. belonging to, good for the Breast and Lungs; also a Breast-plate or Stomacher.

Pecuarious, l. belonging to Cattel.

Peculator, he that commits

Peculation, l. robbing the Prince or Common-wealth.

Peculiar, l. particular, private, proper.

Court of Peculiars, dealing in

Peculiars, Parishes exempt from other Ordinaries, and peculiarly belonging to the See of *Canterbury*.

Regal Peculiar. the Kings Chappel, under the immediate Jurisdiction of the Supream Ordinary (the King.)

Peculiate, l. to punish a mans purse, take away his goods; also to enrich.

Pecuniary, l. belonging to

Pecunia, l. money, and (anciently) Cattel or other substance.

Pedage, l. money given for passage.

Pedagogism, the office of a

Pedagogue, as *Pædag*--

Pedal, l. of a Foot.

Pedality, measuring by, or able going on foot.

Pedaneous, l. going on foot.

Pedantism, the office of a

Pedant, f. an Ordinary School-Master.

Pedanteries, f. Pedantick humours, Ink-horn terms.

Pedation, l. a propping of vines.

Pedature, l. the proportion of feet assign'd to workmen.

Pedee, a [Commanders] foot-boy.

Pederasty, *Pæd*-, g. a lusting after boyes.

Pedestal, f. a foot-stool, the foot of a pillar.

Pedestrial, belonging to a Footman.

Pedicle, l. a little foot, also a stalk of fruit.

Pediculous, l. lousy

Pedler, a Scotch or wandring Merchant.

Pedobaptism, as *Pædob*-.

Pedomancy, Divination by the lines at the soles of the feet.

Pedor, l. filthiness [of prisons]

Pedotribe, g. an instructor of Children to exercise their bodies.

Peek, the room in a ships hold, from the bits to the stem.

Heave a Peek, heave the ships hawse right over the Anchor.

Ride a peek, with the main-yard and fore-yard sloped into a St. *Andrews* Cross (lest another ship come foul of them.)

Peeper, c. a looking-glass.

Peeping, c. sleepy, drowsy.

Peel-town, in Man Isle.

Peed, No. blind of one eye.

He pees, No. He looks with one eye.

Peevish, No. witty.

Peere, o. for appear.

Peer, f. a work raised against the force of the Sea.

Peers, (f. *Pairs*) Equals, Jury-men, also Lords.

Peerage, the condition of Peers of the Realm, also an imposition for maintaining a Sea-peer.

Peery, c. fearfull.

Peeter, c. a portmantle.

Pegasean, like or belonging to

Pegasus, the flying horse of *Perseus*.

Pegnin, the Metropolis of *China*.

Pejerate, l. to forswear.

Pejorate, l. to make or grow worse.

Peitrel, *Poi*-, *ral*, f. the brest-leather of a horse.

Pekois,

Pekois, *o.* a pickax.

Pelagians, Hereticks, followers of *Pelagius*. he denied Original sin, held that man of himself might keep the Commandments, &c.

Pelagick, belonging to the Sea.

Pelasgi, *Grecians* inhabitants of

Pelasgia, part of *Peloponnesus*.

Pelf, Pill, the broken remains of a fowl, after the hawk is relieved.

Pelias, Brother of *Æson* King of *Thessaly*, slain by his own Daughters.

Pelion, a *Thessalian* Mountain laid upon *Ossa* by the Giants in their war with Heaven.

Pell, *o.* a house.

Pellican, a bird said to feed her young ones with her bloud.

Pellicle, *l.* a thin skin or rinde.

Pelliculation, the practice of a

Pelliculator, *l.* a deceiver with fair words.

Pellucid, *l.* clear, to be seen thorow.

Pel-mel, *f.* Confusedly.

Pelopæa, the mother of *Ægisthus* by her own Father *Thyestes*.

Peloponnesus, *Moréa* (in *Greece*) on the Adriatick Sea.

Pelops. being killed by his Father *Tantalus* and set before the gods, *Ceres* ate his shoulder, but *Jupiter* reviv'd him and made him an ivory one.

Pelota, *f.* the ball of the foot.

Pelt (in Falconry) the dismembred body of a dead fowl.

Peltiferous, bearing a

Pelt, *l.* a target of skins like a half-moon.

Pelt-wool, pulled off the

Pelt, the skin [of a dead Sheep.]

Pelure, rich fur.

Pelusian, belonging to

Pelusium, *Damiata*, one of the 7 mouths of *Nilus*.

Pembridg, a town in *Herefordshire*.

Pen, *Br.* a head.

Penarious, *l.* belonging to victuals.

Penates, *l.* Houshold gods.

Penbrock, a town in *Wales*.

Penbauk, *No.* a Beggers can.

Pendent, *l.* hanging.

Pendents, Ear-jewels.

Pendants, small streamers, hung out to adorn the ship, also short ropes fasten'd to all the yard arms (except the missen) into which the braces are reeved.

Pendiloches, *f.* the lowest and dangling parts of Jewels.

Pendulosity, *l.* a being

Pendulous, *l.* hanging, ropy, also doubtfull.

Pendulum, a Regulator, exactly proportioning the time in watches, &c.

Peneian Vale, *Tempe*, on the banks of

Peneus, a River in *Thessaly*.

Penelope, the Constant wife of *Ulysses*, who to deceive her Suiters (promising her respite till that piece of work she had in hand was ended) undid by night whatsoever she did by day.

Penetrability, a power to pierce, or a being

Penetrable, which may be

Penetrated, pierced thorow.

Penetral, *l.* the inward open part of a house.

Penible, *f.* painfull.

Peninsule, *Penisle*, *l.* almost an Island.

Penistons, a coarse wollen cloth.

Penitential, penitent, belonging to sorrow or repentance.

Penitentiary, a place (in *Rome*) where the Priests hear Confessions and enjoyn pennance, also as

Penitentier, the Priest that enjoyns it.

Pennant, as *Pendant*.

Pennigerous, *l.* winged, feathered.

Pennipotent, *l.* strong of wing.

Pennes fele, *o.* many pence.

Pennocrucium, *Peneridge* in *Staffordshire*.

Penny, Catyledon, Navelwort.

Pennyroyal, Organy, puddingrass.

Penny-weight, twenty four grains, whereof one makes 20 Mites, and one Mite 24 droits.

Peny, was our ancient currant silver.

Penoncels, little

Penons (*f. Pennons*) flags, streamers.

Penreth, a town in *Cumberland*.

Penses, (*f. pensée*) pansies.

Pensiculation, -*ita*-, *l.* a weighing or diligent considering.

Pensford, a town in *Somerset*.

Pension, *l.* a yearly stipend or paiment, also (in *Grayes Inn*) a Parliament, Council or Assembly of the members of that Society.

Pension-writ, against those (in *Greys Inn*) that are in arrear for Pensions, &c.

Pensioners, the more noble sort of Guard to the Kings person.

Pensive, *f.* thoughtfull.

Pentagamist, having had 5 wives.

Pentahedrical, *g.* of 5 sides.

Pentaglottical, *g.* skild in 5 tongues.

Pentagonal, *g.* of 5 corners.

Pentameter, *g.* of 5 feet.

Pentaptotes, Nouns of 5 cases.

Pentarch, a Captain of five.

Pentasium, a lake deadly to serpents, wholsom to men.

Pentasticks, Stanza's of 5 verses, porches of 5 rows of Pillars.

Pentateuch, *g.* the 5 Books of *Moses*.

Pentecontarch, g. a Captain of 50.

Pentecost, g. the fiftieth day [from Christs resurrection] Whitsunday.

Pentecostals, Whitson farthings, pious Oblations at that Feast.

Penthesilea, Queen of the *Amazons*, slain by *Achilles*.

Pentheus, torn insunder for despising *Bacchus's* rites.

Penulator, l. a Furrier.

Pentireme, a Galley of 5 oars in a seat.

Penurie, l. want.

Penurious, l. very poor.

Pepin, King of *France* and Father to Charles the great.

Pepire, o. a Love-potion.

Peplography, g. a description of the

Peple, -*lum*, l. a hood [for women at their Churching.]

Pepperwort, *Lepidium*, of a sharp and cleansing nature.

Peptick, g. concoctive.

Pepyns, *Pepins*, f. Kernels.

Peracter, as Circumferentor.

Peraction, l. a finishing.

Peragration, l. a wandring about

Perambulation, l. a walking about, or surveying.

Perambulatione faciendâ, a writ for the Sheriff to distinguish the bounds of Mannors.

Perangust, l. very narrow.

Perarate, l. to plow thorowly.

Percase, o. by chance.

Percepiere, f. Break-stone, an herb in *Somerset-shire*.

Perceptible, l. perceivable.

Perchemyne, o. Parchment.

Perch stone, found in the head of a Peareh.

Percolation, l. a straining thorow.

Percontation, -*cunct*- l. a diligent enquiring.

Pererruciate. l. greatly to torment.

Percussion, l. a striking.

Perevillis, one of the Pursivants at Arms.

Perdiccas, one of *Alexanders* Commanders.

Perdition, l. loss, destruction.

Perdix, being thrown from a high Tower by his Uncle *Dædalus* (for inventing the Saw) he was changed into a Partridge.

Perdonatio Utlagariæ, the pardon of an Out-law (upon yielding himself.)

Perduction, l. a leading through.

Perdu f. lost.

Perdues, Companies chosen for the most desperate Services, forlorn-hopes.

Perduellion, -*ism*, l. an open Act of Hostility.

Perduration, l. a continuing.

Peregrine, l. Outlandish, a kind of Falcon.

Peregrination, l. a Travelling; also a Planets being in a Sign, wherein he is altogether a stranger.

Peremptory, l. absolute.

Perendination, l. a putting off from day to day.

Perennity, l. long continuance.

Perenticide, l. a Cut-purse.

Pererration, l. a wandring about.

Perflation, l. a blowing through.

Perfidy, l. Treachery.

Perforation, l. a boring through.

Perfretation, l. a passing through, or over Sea.

Perfriction, l. a shivering for cold; also as

Perfrication, l. a rubbing thorowly.

Perfunction, a finishing or discharging.

Perfunctory, slight.

Perfusion, a pouring upon.

Pergamus, a City of *Natolia*, where Parchment was invented.

Pergamenous, belonging thereto.

Pergraphical, g. very artificial.

Periander, a *Corinthian* Tyrant, one of the 7 wise men.

Pericardian, belonging to the

Pericard, g. the heart-purse.

Pericardick vein, a branch of the main ascendant branches of the hollow vein.

Periclitation, -*ancy*, l. an endangering.

Pericrany, -*ion*, g. the skin covering the skull.

Perjenet, o. (f. *Poir jeunet*) a young pear-tree.

Perigee, the place wherein a star is nearest the Centre of the Earth.

Perihelium, g. the point wherein the Earth (or any planet) is nearest the Sun.

Perimeter, the outmost line of any solid body; also a verse that hath a syllable too much.

Perinde Valere, a dispensation to a Clerk who (though incapable, yet) is *de facto* admitted.

Perioch, g. the Argument or Contents of a Discourse.

Periodical, belonging to a

Period, g. a certain or full term of time or sence.

Periœci, -*oici*, g. those that inhabit the same Climate.

Peripateticks, g. followers of *Aristotle*.

Peripherie, g. Circumference.

Periphrastical, spoken by a

Periphrase, -*sis*, g. a circumlocution.

Peripneumonical, sick of a

Peripneumony, g, an inflammation of lungs and shortness of breath.

Perisciians, g. whose shadows are cast round about them.

Perissology, g. a superfluity of speech.

Peristaltic motion, the quibling motion of the guts, to squeeze out the Excrements.

Peristatick, g. having or belonging to circumstances.

Perit, Twenty four blanks, or the twentieth part of a Droit.

Peritonæum, g. the Cawl.

Perjury, l. a being

Perjured, forsworn in a Judicial proceeding.

Periwig, as *Perwick*.

Perkin, q. Peterkin, little *Peter*.

Permagles, little *Turkiſh* boats.

Per my & per tout, [ſeiſed, as a Joint-tenant] by every parcel and by the whole.

Permanent, *l.* durable.

Permeation, *l.* a paſſing through.

Permiſcible, which may be mingled.

Permiſſible, which may be permitted

Permiſſion, l. leave.

Permiſtion, *l.* a mingling together.

Permutation, *l.* an exchanging.

Permutatione &c. a writ for the admiſſion of a Clerk upon Exchange.

Pernicious, *-ciable*, *l.* dangerous, deſtructive.

Pernicity, *l.* ſwiftneſs.

Pernoctation, *l.* a tarrying all night.

Pernancy, a taking or receiving.

Pernour, (*f. Preneur*) a taker.

Peroration, *l.* a concluding.

Perpend, *l.* to examine or weigh.

Perpenders, Perpent-ſtones, fitted to the thickneſs of a wall.

Perpendicle, *l.* a plumbline.

Perpendicular, directly down.

Perpenſion, *-ſation*, *l.* a diligent weighing or conſidering.

Perpeſſion, *l.* an enduring.

Perpetrate, *l.* to commit.

Perpetuate, *l.* to cauſe

Perpetuity, *l.* everlaſtingneſs.

Perplexable, full of

Perplexity, *l.* doubtfulneſs, trouble.

Perplication, *l.* a folding to and fro.

Perquiſite, not left by Anceſtors but gained of ones ſelf.

Perquiſites, *l.* profits ariſing by the by.

Perquiſition, *l.* a diligent Enquiring.

Perre, *o.* (*q. pierrée*) a monument.

Perry-wright, *o.* embroidered with precious ſtones.

Perquiſitor, *l.* a ſearcher.

Perſcrutation, *l.* a thorow ſearch.

Perreptation, a creeping through.

Perſe, *f.* sky-coloured.

Perſcribe, *l.* write out to the end.

Perſant, *o.* piercing.

Perſecution, a following hard after.

Perſeverance, *l.* conſtant continuance.

Perſia, a famous Eaſtern Kingdom.

Perſide, to ſit ſtill

Perſiſt, *l.* to continue.

Perſonable, enabled to hold plea in Court.

Perſonality, *-lty*, a being

Perſonal, belonging to a perſon.

Perſonal tithes, of profits by Labour, Merchandize, &c.

Perſonate, *l.* to repreſent ones perſon; alſo to ſound aloud.

Perſons ne Præbendaries, &c. a writ for ſpiritual perſons diſtrained for taxes.

Perſpective, *l.* the Art of helping the ſight by Glaſſes, &c.

Perſpicacity, *l.* quickneſs of apprehenſion.

Perſpicience, *l.* perfect knowledge.

Perſpicil, *l.* a looking or perſpective glaſs,

Perſpicuity, a being

Perſpicuous, *l.* clear, plain.

Perſpirable, capable of

Perſpiration, *l.* a breathing thorow.

Perſtringe, *l.* to wring or touch hard upon.

Perterebrate, *l.* to bore thorow.

Perth, *-thia*, part of North *Scotland*.

Pertical, belonging to a perch or pole.

Perticata terræ, the fourth part of an acre.

Perticulas, certain Alms or School-Commons. See *Pittance*.

Pertinacy, *-city*, a being

Pertinacious, *l.* obſtinate.

Perinens, a Kinſman or Woman.

Pertinent, to the purpoſe.

Pertingency, a reaching to.

Pertingent, *l.* extending or joyning to.

Æ. *Pertinax*, a *Roman* Emperour, who obſtinately refuſed the Empire for a while.

Per quæ ſervitia, a Writ for a Cognizee of a Mannor, &c. to compel the Tenant (at the time of the Note of the Fine levied) to attturn to him.

Perturbation, *l.* a troubling.

Pervade, to paſs into, thorow and over all.

Pervagation, *l.* a wandring through, or up and down.

Perverſity, *l.* a being

Perverſe, *l.* froward, Croſs.

Pervert, *l.* to overthwart or overthrow; alſo turned from good to evil.

Perveſtigation, *l.* a finding out by diligent ſearch.

Pervicacy, *l.* a being

Pervicacious, *l.* obſtinate.

Pervigilation, *l.* a watching all night.

Pervink, the herb

Pervinkle, or *Periwinkle*.

Pervious, which may be paſſed through.

Perviſe, *Parviſe*, Mooting, an afternoons Exerciſe.

Peruvians, the people of

Peru, a large province in the Weſt-Indies.

Perwick, *-wig*, *Perruque*, *f.* a cap of falſe hair.

Pery, *o.* a Peartree.

Peritory, *o.* for *Pellitory*.

Peſame, *Sp.* a condoling.

Peſage, *f.* cuſtom for weighing.

Peſſary, *l.* a ſuppoſitory of ſoft wooll.

Peſſonæ tempus, Shacking-time, *Nf.*

Peſſone, Maſt.

Peſſun-

Pessundate, l. to tread or cast under foot, to destroy.

Pesterable wares, troublesome and taking up much room in a Ship

Pestiferous, l. bringing the *Pestilence* or Plague.

Petalism. a *Syracusian* Banishment (for five years) by writing the Names on Olive-leaves.

Petard, -*arre*, f. a Mortar-like Engine to break open Gates, &c.

Petarrade, f. [a Horses yerking out behind, accompanied with] farting.

Petauristick, belonging to a

Petaurist, g. a dancer on the Ropes.

Petches, a Town in *Essex*.

Peterburgh, a Town in *Northampton-shire*.

Peter, g. a stone or Rock.

Peter-corn, given by King *Athelstane* to the See of *York*.

Peter-pence, Rome-fee, Rome-scot, Rome-penning, a penny for every Chimney, given by *Ina* King of the West-*Saxons*, towards the maintenance of a *Saxon* School.

Petersfield, a Town in *Hantshire*.

Peters-post, a famous Quarry in *York-shire*, whose stones built St. Peters Church in *York*.

Petherton, a Town in *Somerset-shire*.

Petit, f. little.

Petit Sergeantry, a holding Lands of the King by some small Service.

Petit Treason, when a Servant kills his Master, a Wife her Husband, or a Clerk his Ordinary.

Petitory, belonging to a

Petition, a Request to a Superiour.

Petous. o. for Piteous.

Petra lana, a stone of wool.

Petrary, as *Mangonel*.

Petreius & Juba, being overthrown by *Cæsar*, consented to kill one another.

Petrification, l. the action of,

Petrifying, turning into stone.

Petrobusians, Hereticks that denyed the keeping of Feasts.

Petrol, a kind of Bitumen or Naphtha.

Petronel, f. a Horsemans Piece, hanging or aiming at the breast.

Petropolitan, belonging to

Petropolis, *Rome*; also

Peterborow in *Northampton-shire*.

Pettifogger, a silly Atorney, Trouble-town, without Law or Conscience.

Petty Tally, a Competent proportion of Victuals in a Ship.

Petulancy, a being

Petulant, l. sawcy, wanton.

Petworth, a Town in *Sussex*.

Pexity, l. the nap or roughness of the Web.

Pey, o. (f. *Paix*) Security.

Peysen, o. for appease

Pfirt, *Mors-Munster* in *Alsatia*.

Pfullendorf, a City of *Schwaben*.

Phædra, Daughter of *Minos*, and Wife of *Theseus*.

Phæmone, the first Priestess of *Apollo* at *Delphos*, and inventress of Heroick verse.

Phænomena, g. appearances.

Phaeton, Guiding the Chariot of the Sun (for a day) set the World on fire.

Phaetontiades, his Sisters.

Phagedenick, g. troubled with a Cancer, eating the flesh.

Phalangeary, -*ean*, belonging to a *Phalanx*, a Squadron of 8000 Foot-men, set in array.

Phalangarians, those Soldiers.

Phalaris, a *Sicilian* Tyrant, who burnt *Perillus* in the Brazen Bull, which he had made for the tormenting of others.

Phalerated, l. adorned with Trappings.

Phaleucian, -*eusick Verse*, of a Spondee, Dactyl, and three Trochees.

Phanatick, as *Fanatick*.

Phantasie, g. Imagination, Fancy.

Phantasm, g. a Vision or Apparition.

Phao, a *Lesbian* Youth made beautiful by an Oyntment given him of *Venus*.

Pharaohsh, (a making bare) the General Title of the Kings of *Egypt*.

Phare, -*ros*, g. a Watch-Tower or Beacon by the Sea.

Pharetriferous, l. bearing a Quiver of Arrows.

Pharisaical, belonging to

Pharisaism, the Profession of

Pharisees, Jewish Separatists, pretending extraordinary Holiness.

Pharmaceutick, -*cal*, -*matical*, belonging to

Pharmacy, -*ceuty*, g. the Art of Selecting, preparing, and mixing Medicines.

Pharmacopolist, g. an Apothecary.

Pharnaces, the Son of *Mithridates*, overthrown by *Cæsar*.

Pharsalian, belonging to

Pharsalus, a Town of *Thessaly*, on the Banks of *Enipeus*.

Phasm, g. a terrible Vision.

Pheer, o. a Companion.

Pheon, an Arrow-head (in *Her.*)

Phenicia, a Province of *Asia*.

Phial, as *Vial*.

Philadelphia, g. Brotherly love; a City of *Mysia* in *Asia* the less.

Philadelphians, g. lovers of Brothers or Sisters.

Philanthropal, full of

Philanthropy, g. love to man.

Philargyrous, full of

Philargyry, g. love of Silver.

Philantry, g. self-love.

Philibert, *Ge.* famously bright.

Philippe-ville, a Town in *Hainault*.

Philip, g. a lover of Horses.

Philippick, belonging to

Philippopolis, a City of *Macedon*.

Philippicks, *Demosthenes's* Invectives against

Philippus, King of *Macedon*, *Alexanders* Father; also a Gold Coin of 3 shillings, and a Silver one of 4.

Philips-Norton, a Town in *Somerset-shire*.

Philipsbourgh, a Key of *Germany*, in the lower *Palatinate*.

Phillis, g. lovely.

Philoctetes, the Companion of *Hercules*, who left him his Bow and poysoned Arrows.

Philodespot, g. a lover of his Master.

Philologer, one given to

Philology, g. the study of speech & Discourse; also as

Philomathy, love of Learning.

Philomel, a Nightingale, made of

Philomela, flying from *Tereus* who had Ravish'd her, and cut her Tongue out.

Philomusus, g. a lover of the Muses.

Philonomia, the Mother (by *Mars*) of the twins *Lycastus* and *Parrhasius* Kings of *Arcadia*.

Philopolite, g. a lover of his City.

Philosophical, belonging to a

Philosopher, a studier of

Philosophy, g. the study of wisdom, or knowledge in things Rational, Natural and Moral.

Philostorgy, g. Parents love to Children.

Philotimy, g. love of honour.

Philtre, the hollow in the upper lip.

Philtre charmed, enchanted with

Philtres, g. love-potions, or medicines.

Philyrian Scout, *Sagittarius*, the Centaur *Chiron*, Son of *Saturn* and

Philyra, the Daughter of *Oceanus*.

Phinehas, h. a bold countenance.

Phineus, a King of *Thrace* slain by *Hercules*.

Phlebotomy g. letting bloud (by opening a vein.)

Phlegeton, g. a flaming river of hell.

Phlegmatick, full of

Phlegme, the cold and moist humour of the body.

Phlegmone, g. a swelling with an inflammation of the bloud.

Phlegræan fields, in *Thessaly* where the Gods and Giants fought.

Phlegyas, King of the *Lapithæans*, set under a great stone (in Hell) ready to fall on his head, for burning the Temple of *Apollo* who had ravisht his Daughter *Coronis*.

Phœbe, *Diana*, the Moon.

Phœbus, *Apollo*, the Sun.

Phœnix, an *Arabian* bird, said to live alone above 5 or 600 years and then to burn her self in a nest of spice, from which ashes springs a young one.

Phorbas, the Son of *Priam*, slain by *Menelaus*.

Phorcys, King of *Corsica*, Father of *Medusa*.

Phosphor, g. the Morning-star.

Phraseology, a Discourse of

Phrases, g. proper forms of speech.

Phrenetick, frantick, troubled with a

Phrensie, -nzy, g. madness

Phrygians, the careless, wanton inhabitants of the Greater

Phrygia, part of *Asia*.

Phrygian Garment, of Needle work.

Phrygian Wisdom, After-wit.

Phthisick, g. a Consumption Cough of the Lungs.

Phylacist, g. a Jailor.

Phylacterians, Sorcerers condemned *Anno* 62.

Phylactery, g. a preservative or Charm.

Phylacteries, Scrolls of parchment (with some parts of the Law) worn by the Jews, to mind them of keeping Gods Commands, *Exod.* 13. 9.

Phylarch, g. the Governour of a Tribe or Family.

Phillis, hang'd her self for *Demophoon*, and was turn'd into an Almond-tree.

Physiarch, g. the Governour of Nature.

Physick, g. Medicine

Physicks, g. Natural Philosophy.

Physician, one skil'd in both.

Physiognomer, -*mist*, a professour of

Physiognomy, g. a discovering mens natures by their looks, also contracted to

Physnomy, the feature of the face.

Physiologer, a practiser of

Physiology, g. a reasoning or searching of Natural things.

Piacle, l. [a Sacrifice to purge] some great Offence.

Piacular, -*lous*, belonging thereto.

Pia Mater, the inmost skin enclosing the brain.

Pian Piano, I. by little and little, soft and fair.

Piaster, an *Italian* coyn about a Crown.

Piation, l. a purging by Sacrifice.

Piazza, I. a broad open place, as a Market-place, &c. also (corruptly) the walks about it set with pillars, &c.

Pica, l. longing, also a printing Character.

Picards, a kind of Adamites, also great boats used on the *Severne*.

Picardize, to imitate the

Picards, *-dits*, people of

Picardy, a Province of *Gallia Belgica* the Grainary of *France*.

Piccage, money paid at Fairs for breaking the ground to set up booths.

Pickadilly, a famous Ordinary at St. *James's* built by one *Higgins* a Taylor who made

Pickadils, (*D. Pickedillekins*) the round hems , or several divisions set together about the skirt of a Garment or collar much in fashion the last age.

Pickeer, (*I. Picare*) to skirmish.

Pickering, a town in *Yorkshire*.

Pickigni, *f.* a word used (like *Shibboleth*) to distinguish Aliens from the native French as Bread and Cheese did the English and Flemings in *Wat Tylers* rebellion.

Pickage, as *Piccage*.

Picle, *Pitle*, *Pightel*, (*I. Piccolo*, small) a smale Close.

Pickeron, as *Piqueron*.

Pictor, *l.* a Painter.

Pictural, *-torian*, *-rial*, *l.* belonging to a picture,

Piedmont, part of *Italy* under the Duke of *Savoy*.

Pie-powder-Court, *Curia pedis pulverizati*, to redress all disorders at Fairs.

Pigel, *o.* for pickle.

Piger Henricus, a very slow distilling Instrument.

Pight, *o.* pitched, propped.

Pigment, *l.* paint.

Pignerate, *l.* to [take in] pawn.

Pigneratitious, pawned, or belonging to pawning.

Pike, *o.* peep.

Pike on the bean, *c.* run for it.

Pigritude, *l.* sloth.

Piladion, a song or dance of

Pilades, a notable Comedian.

Pilaster, a small pillar, also the swelling of the Uvula.

Pilch, (*Pellicea*) a woollen or fur-garment, also a Childs flannel clout.

Pilcrow, as *Paragraph*.

Pille of Foddray, (*pilla*) a pile or Fort on a Sea-Creek in *Lancashire*.

Pile, a two fold line (in Heraldry) like a wedge.

Pilgrim, (*I. Peligrino*) a devout traveller to some holy place, a Palmer is a general and perpetual Pilgrim.

Pillaw, a Turkish dish of Rice and Mutton-fat boil'd.

Pillow, the timber which the Boltsprit rests on.

Pillours, (*f. -eurs*) *o.* robbers,

Pilores, *o.* the same.

Pilosity, *l.* hairiness.

Pilotage, the office of a

Pilot, a Steersman.

Piment, (*q. Pigment*) *o.* a drink of Wine and Honey.

Pimplean, belonging to

Pimplea, a Mountain of *Macedon*, with a Fountain sacred to the

Pimpleiades, the Muses.

Pimpompet, *f.* an antick dance of three kicking each others bum.

Pin-col, *No.* a pin-cushion.]

Nick the Pin, drink just to the pin placed about the middle of a wooden cup. This caused so much debauchery that Priests were forbidden to drink at or to the pins.

Pine, *o.* a pit, also (*No.*) difficult.

Pingles, *Pingres*, *f.* a (womanish) play with Ivory balls.

Pingle, *No.* as *Picle*.

Pinguedinous, *l.* fat.

Pinguedinize, the same as

Pinguefie, *l.* to make fat.

Piniferous, *l.* pine-bearing,

Pinipinichi, an Indian milky juice purging Choler.

Pinnace, a kind of small Ship.

Pinnigerous, *l.* having fins.

Pinne, a humour in a hawks foot.

Pinsor, *l.* a Baker.

Pintel, an iron pin that keeps the gun from recoiling, also the Rudder-pins hanging it to the Sternpost.

Pintle-pantle, *Pintledy-pantledy*, *Li.* (*Panteler*, *f.* to pant) trembling for fear, or frequent beating [of the heart.]

Pinules, *l.* the sights of the *Albidada*.

Pioneers, *-nors*, (*f. Pionniers*) underminers and diggers in an army.

Pip, a white scale on the top of the tongue in poultry.

Pipation, *l.* a crying or weeping.

Pipe, the Great Roll in the Exchequer.

Pipe [*of wine*, &c.] 26 gallons, or half a tun.

Pipperidges, *E. Sf.* barberries.

Piquant, *f.* pricking.

Pique, *f.* a quarrel.

Piqueron, *f.* a Dart or Javelin.

Piramid, as *Pyramid*.

Pirate, *o.* perry.

Piratical, belonging to

Piracy, the trade of a

Pirate, *l.* a Sea-Robber, (formerly any Sea-Soldier, or the Overseer of a pira or Haven-peer.)

Pirenean, belonging to

Pirene, a fountain made by *Pegasus* dashing his foot against the rock.

Pisa, a City of *Tuscany*.

Piscaria, *-ry*, a liberty to fish in another mans water.

Piscary, *l.* a place for fish.

Piscation, *l.* a fishing.

Pisces, the 12th sign of the Zodiack.

Piscicle, *l.* a little fish.

Piscinal, belonging to a fish-pond.

Pisculent, *l.* fishy, or which may be fished.

Pissasphalt, *g.* Pitch and the Lime *Bitumen* mixt.

Pissuppress, the suppression of a horses Urine.

Pistachoes, small, Physical, *Syrian*, Pistack-nuts.

Pistick,

Pistick, *l.* pressed, bruised.

Pistillation, *l.* a pounding in a Morter.

Pistolado, *l.* a Pistol-shot.

Pistorian, *-ical*, belonging to a baker or baking.

Pistrine, *l.* a mill, prison, or bake-house.

Pit-a-pat, as *Pintle-Pantle.*

Pitching-pence, paid (in fairs and markets) for every bag of Corn, &c.

Pithian, as *Pythian.*

Pittance, (*f. pitance*, *q. pietance*) the small portion of victuals given the Monks in Colledges, a small repast.

Pittacus, one of the 7 Wise men of *Greece.*

Pituitous, *l.* Flegmatick.

Pix, as *Pyx.*

Placability, a being

Placable, *l.* easily appeased.

Placaert, *D.* a proclamation.

Placard, *-quard*, *f.* a Bill posted up, a Table of Laws, Orders, &c.

Placard (in our Law) a licence to use (otherwise) unlawfull games.

Placence, the Palace at *Greenwich.*

Placeta, (in some old deeds) a place or parcel.

Placidity, a being

Placid, *l.* mild, peaceable.

Placit, *l.* an opinion, also a Decree.

Plagiarian Law, against

Plagiaries, *l.* stealers of Mankind, or of other mens writings.

Plagues, (*D. Plagghe*, a Clout) *o.* parts.

Plain Table, for the surveying of Land.

Plaintiff, he that makes a

Plaint, Complaint, the exhibiting (in writing) any action personal or real.

Plan, *l.* a large compass or circle.

Planetary, a Caster of Nativities, also as

Planetick, belonging to the

Planets, *g.* the 7 wandring stars, *Saturn*, *Jupiter*, *Mars*, the *Sun*, *Venus*, *Mercury*, and the *Moon.*

Planiloquent, *l.* using

Planiloquy, plain speech.

Planimetry, *g.* a measuring of plains or flat things.

Planisphere, *l.* a plain Sphere, as an *Astrolabe.*

Plank upon plank, a kind of furring, by laying another plank on the ships-side after she is built.

Plantar, belonging to the sole of the foot.

Plantar Arteries, two branches of the thigh-arterie.

Plantation, *l.* a planting, also a Colony placed in a foreign country.

Plant, *c.* to lay, place, or hide.

Plantigerous, bearing plants.

Plasmator, a Potter.

Plasmature, a making of earthen ware.

Plastick, belonging to

Plastique, *g.* Sculpture, the Art of forming things [of Earth.]

Plastography, *g.* a counterfeit writing.

Plat, *g.* flat.

Of Platthan edge, *o.* [More] of Ease than Grief, of the flat than the edge of Fortunes sword.

Platanine, belonging to a

Platane, *l.* a Plane-tree.

Plateasm, *g.* a speaking over-broad.

Plate, a hoy.

Platonist, a follower of

Plato, the Divine Philosopher Cheif of the Academicks.

Platonick love, a contemplative Idæa, abstracted from all gross sensuality.

Platonick year, the 36 thousandth, when all things must return (forsooth) to their present state.

Plats, flat ropes to save the Cabel in the hawse from galling.

Plaudite, *l.* Clap your hands for joy, also a clapping, &c.

Plausible, acceptable, seeming very fair.

Plausidical, speaking plausibly and Eloquently.

Plausor, *l.* he that claps his hands, praiseth or encourageth.

Play, *o.* to ply or Go often.

Playing hot, *So.* boyling hot.

Plea, that which either party alledges for himself in Court.

Pleas of the Crown, Suits in the Kings name for Offences against his Crown and Dignity.

Pleas of the Sword, were to the Earl of *Chester*, as Pleas of the Crown to the King.

Common-pleas, agitated between Common persons.

Plebeian, vulgar, belonging to the

Plebeity, the Commonalty.

Plebicolist, a favourer of the Commons.

Plebiscite, a decree of the people.

Pleck, *Y.* a place.

Pledge, *f.* a surety.

I'll Pledge you, I'll look that you receive no hurt [from the *Danes*] while you drink, but now 'tis used in another sense.

Plegiis acquietandis, a writ for the surety against the other, if he pay not the money duly.

Pleget, *Spl-*, a long plaister of Leather or Linnen.

Pleiades, *g.* 7 Daughters of *Atlas*, turn'd into the 7 stars.

Pleide, *o.* for plied.

Plenary, *l.* full.

Plenarty, a [Benefices] being full. (Institution is a good plenarty against a Common person, but not against the King without Induction.)

Plenere, *o*. fully.
Plenilunary, belonging to the
Plenilune, *l*. the full moon.
Plenipotentiaries, Ambassadours with full power to treat and conclude upon all things contained in their Commission.
Plenitude, *-ty*, *l*. fulness.
Pleonasmick, belonging to a
Pleonasm, *g*. an adding of something superfluous.
Plerophory, *g*. a fulness or perfection.
Plesaunces, *o*. pleasures.
Pleskow, a Town in *Muscovy*.
Plethorick, *-cal*, troubled with a
Plethora, *-ry*, *g*. an abundance of humours, also the headach occasioned thereby.
Plevin, as *Replevin*.
Pleuritick, subject to the
Pleurisie, an inflammation of the
Pleura, *g*. (the side) the inward skin of the ribs.
Pliant, *-able*, *f*. flexible.
Plicature, *l*. a folding.
Plight, *o*. plucked.
Plimouth, a famous port Town on the mouth of
Plim, a River in *Devonshire*.
Plinth, *g*. the square bottom of a pillar.
Ploce, *g*. (a binding together) an emphatical repetition of a word, connoting its quality.
Plonkets, course woollen clothes.
Plores (*f*. *pleurez*) weep.
Plottons, (*f*. *ploton* a botton of thread) divisions of Soldiers with 8 in front.
Plott, a Sea-card.
Plow-alms, a penny anciently paid the Church for every
Plow land, as Hide, &c.
Plow Munday, next after Twelfth-day, when our Northern Plow-men beg Plow-money to drink, and in some places if the Plow-man (after that daies work) come with his whip to the kitchin-hatch and cry Cock in the pot, before the maid saies Cock on the Dunghill, he gains a Cock for Shrove-Tuesday.
Plumage, *f*. feathers, also as
Plumassary, a bunch of Feathers.
Plumbagin, *l*. silver mingled with lead oar; also lead which was put into a Furnace with Gold or Silver-Oar, to make them melt the sooner.
Plumbean, *-eous*, *l*. like lead.
Plume, the colour of a hawks feathers.
Pluming, dressing up the Feathers, or pulling them off.
Plume-striker, a Parasite, brushing the Feathers from your cloathes.
Plumiferous, *l*. feather-bearing.
Plumtuous, *o*. for plenteous.
Plumosity, *l*. fulness of Feathers.
Plunder, *D*. to rob or spoil (as Soldiers) first used 1642.
Plural, *-litive*, containing many.
Plurality, *l*. Moreness, the having more than one.
Pluries, the third Writ issued after the *Original Capias* and *Sicut alias*.
Plurifarious, *l*. of divers fashions.
Plus ne pourroye, *f*. I could do no more.
Plutarch, a famous Philosopher of *Chronea*.
Pluto, the God of Hell and Riches, who (they say) first taught the use of money.
Pluto's helmet makes men invisible.
Pluvial, a Priests Vestment or Cope, also as
Pluvious, *l*. rainy.
Ply, *So*. to boil (as a pot.)
Plymouth, as *Pliminouth*.
Plymton Maries, a town in *Devonshire*.
Pneumatical, *g*. belonging to wind or spirits.
Pneumaticks, books of
Pneumology, *g*. a Discourse of Winds or Spirits.
Pnigitis, a kind of black Earth.
Po, the largest river of *Italy*.
Pocillator, *l*. a Cupbearer.
Pocklington, a town in *Yorkshire*.
Pocket of wool, half a Sack.
Poco a poco, *Sp*. by little and little.
Poculent, *l*. drinkable.
Podagrical, gouty-footed.
Podarge, a swift Mare, on which *Zephyrus* begat *Achilles*'s horses.
Podesta, *I*. a *Venetian* Governour of Cities.
Podimetry, *g*. a measuring by the foot.
Podolia, a Province in *Poland*.
Poësie, *g*. Poetry, a Poets work.
Poëm, *g*. a Copy of verses.
Poetaster, a sorry Poet.
Poile, *o*. *Apulia* in *Italy*.
Poinard, *f*. a Dagger.
Point, *f*. the plight one is in, also rich needle-work.
Point-blank, punctually, hitting the white or nail on the head.
At Point devise, *o*. exactly.
Point of Land, the sharpness of any head-land at Sea.
Points of the Compass, 32 divisions of the wind.
Point the Cable, undo the end and lay it over again with synnet, marling, &c.
Pointel, *o*. a writing pen, or pencil.
Poitrel, *f*. as *Pectoral*.
Polein, picks set in the forepart of shooes and tied up to the knees with Silver or Gold chains, forbidden by *Edw*. 4th.
Poles, *o*. for *Pauls*.
Poland, see *Polonians*.

Polarity, a being

Polar, *-ry*, belonging to the

Poles, *l.* the (North and South) ends of the imagin'd axel-tree whereon the heavens move; also heaven.

Polaquia, a Province of *Poland*.

Polemark, *g.* an *Athenian* Lord Marshal in the Field.

Polemical, *g.* warlike, also controverted.

Polemicks, treatises of war, also disputations.

Policies of assurance or ens-, *Assecurationes*, Instruments between the Merchant-Adventurer and him that (upon certain considerations) Ensurers the safe arrival of Ship or goods.

Politicks, Treatises of

Polity, *-cy*, *g.* Government (of Church or state.)

Political, belonging thereto.

Politician, a Statesman.

Polive, *o.* a pulley.

Politure, *l.* polishing, neatness.

Deed Poll, a single deed unindented.

Pollard, an old coyn forbidden, a Codfish, a Stag (having musen'd or cast his head) a sort of fine bran, also as

Pollenger, a tree that hath been usually topt.

Poll, *o.* a head.

Pollicar, *l.* belonging to a thumb or Inch.

Pollicitation, *l.* a free promising.

Pollinarious, *l.* belonging to meal or fine flower.

Pollinctor, *l.* an embalmer.

Pollincture, an embalming.

Polonians, *Polanders*, *Poles*, the people of

Poland, a Kingdom bordering on Turky.

Poltron, *f.* a rascal or Coward.

Polverine, *Rochetta*, Levant ashes for the making of glasses.

Polychrests, *g.* things of a various use.

Polychreston, *g.* a medicine of much use.

Polycrates, a Tyrant of *Samos*, who found his ring (let fall into the Sea the day before) in the belly of a fish; crucified at last by *Orontes* the Persian.

Polydamas, Son of *Antenor* who with (*Æneas*) betrayed *Troy* to the Greeks.

Polygamy, *g.* a being married to many at the same time.

Polygarchy, *g.* a Government by many.

Polyglot, *g.* of many languages.

Polygony, the herb Knotgrass, also a being

Polygone, *g.* of many corners.

Polygraphy, *g.* a writing in divers manners.

Polyhistor, *g.* he that knows and describes many things.

Polyhymnia, *-lymnia*, one of the Muses.

Polyloquent, speaking much.

Polymathists, *g.* men skil'd in (or treatises of) many disciplines.

Polymorphean, *g.* having many shapes or forms.

Polyphagian, *g.* a great eater.

Polypharmacal, *g.* having many medicines.

Polypheme, *-mus*, a giant with one eye, which *Ulysses* put out.

Polyphon, *g.* [an instrument with] a multiplicity of sounds.

Polypragmon, *g.* one that is

Polypragmatick, very pragmatical.

Polyptote, *g.* having many cases or terminations.

Polypus, the fish Pourcontrel or many-feet, also a *Noli me tangere* in the Nose.

Polysyllable, *-bical*, *g.* having many syllables.

Polysyndeton, *g.* a superfluity of conjunctions.

Pomace, pugs, must, the dross of Cyder-pressings.

Pomada, see *Pommade*.

Pomander, (*q. Pomamber*, *D.*) a ball of perfumes.

Pomarious, belonging to a

Pomary, *l.* an Orchard or apple-loft.

Pomatum, *l.* Cyder.

Pomegranate, a shell-fruit (chiefly of *Granata* in *Spain*) full of grains or kernels.

Pomel, *o.* round [as an apple.]

Pomelygrise, *o.* (*f. Gris pommill*) dapple-gray.

Pome-paradise, a *John*-apple.

Pomerania, between *Sweden* and *Brandenburgh*.

Pomerellia, part of *Poland*.

Pomeridian, *Postm-*, afternoon.

Pomey, a green apple (in Heraldry) Consecrate to *Venus*.

Pomfret, *Pontfract*, *Kirby* (in *Yorkshire*) whose bridge brake with the multitudes accompanying *William* Archbishop of *York*, at his return from *Rome*.

Pomiferous, *l.* bearing

Pomes, *l.* apples, pears, plums, &c.

Pommade, *f. Pomatum*, *-te*, a sweet ointment, also as

Pomada, a trick in vaulting.

Pomery, *l.* the precincts without the town-walls.

Pomona, the Goddess of Orchards.

Pompatick, done with

Pomp, *l.* state or solemnity.

Pompets, *f.* Printers Ink-balls or Ball-stocks.

Pompey, a brave *Roman* General, put to flight by *Cæsar* (in the Civil wars) at *Pharsalia*.

Pompous, *l.* stately.

Pomum Adami, *Adams* *lit*, the protuberance of the Throat.

Ponderize, to ponder or weigh.

Ponde-

Ponderity, *-rosity*, a being

Ponderous, *l.* heavy, weighty.

Pone, a Writ to remove a cause from an inferiour Court to the Common Bench.

Pone per vadium, a writ willing the Sheriff to take surety for ones appearance.

Ponendis in assisis, a writ directing the Sheriff what kind of persons ought to be empanneld.

Ponendum in Balliam, a writ for a Prisoner to be bailed.

Ponendum sigillum ad exceptionem, a writ willing the Justices to set their seals to exceptions brought by Defendants.

Pont à Mouson, a town in *Lorrain*.

Pont du Gard, three bridges (on the river *Gardon*) one over another.

Pontage, a Contribution (or Toll) towards the maintaining or rebuilding of bridges.

Pontibus reparandis, a writ commanding the repair of a bridge

Pontick, belonging to

Pontus, a part of *Asia*.

Pontick nuts small-nuts.

Pontifical, *-cial*, belonging to a

Pontif, *-fex*, *l.* a Bishop or Prelate.

In his Pontificalibus, Episcopal Ornaments, richest attire.

Pool, a town in *Dorcetshire*.

Poil, *o.* *Poland* (plain-land.)

Pool-evil, a swelling between the Ears and Nape of the [horses] neck.

Poop, the uppermost part a-stern of the Ships hull.

Poops, *No.* Gulps (in drinking.)

Popelot, *-lote*, *o.* a puppet or young Wench.

Popelin, *f.* a little finical darling.

Popere, *o.* a bodkin.

Popinal, *l.* belonging to

Popination, a haunting the

Popina, *l.* a Victualling-house or Tavern.

Popingey, a greenish parret, also *Symphonia*, an herb of that colour.

Poplemans, Hobgoblins, from

Popleman, (or *Popielus*) a *Polonian* Tyrant.

Poplitick, belonging to the ham.

Poplitick vein, the Garter-vein.

Poppæan Law (among the *Romans*) against a single life.

Popped, *o.* drest fine.

Populace, *f.* the same as

Populacy, the vulgar or meaner sort of people.

Populeon, *g.* an ointment of Poplar.

Popularity, a being

Popular, *l.* [beloved] of the common people.

Population, *l.* a wasting or unpeopling.

Populiferous, *l.* bearing poplar-trees.

Populosity, a being

Populous, *l.* full of people.

Porcary, *l.* a Swine-sty.

Porcelane, the Chalky earth (beaten and steep'd in water) of which they make the China-dishes.

Poraile, *o.* base, beggerly.

Porcine, *l.* hoggish.

Porculation, *l.* a fatning of hogs.

Porcupine, a beast that shoots her bristles at the dogs.

Porosity, a being

Porose, *-rous*, *l.* full of

Pores, *l.* very little holes.

Porpoise, *Phocæna*, a duskish fish foretelling storms by approaching the shore.

Porphyratick, belonging to purple, or to

Porphyry, a fine streak'd Marble, of which is made the

Porphyry-Chair, wherein the Pope is inaugurated.

Porrection, *l.* a stretching out.

Port, put the helm to Larboard or the left side.

Port-vein, the carrying vein seated in the liver.

Portable, *l.* which may be carried.

Portate, *l.* a bearing or bringing.

Portcullis, *f.* a Gate made to fall or slip down.

Portegue, *-tugaise*, *f.* a gold coyn worth 3 pound, 10 s.

Portemote, *Sa.* a Court held in Port-towns.

Portend, *l.* to betoken.

Portentifical, working wonders.

Portentous, *l.* monstrous, betokening some ill event.

Porters of the Verge, Vergers, bearing white wands before the Judges.

Portglaive, *f.* a Sword-bearer.

Portgreve, *Sa.* the Governour of a Port-town, and of *London* before the Two Bailiffs who preceeded the Maior granted by King *John*.

Portguidon, *f.* the Troops Cornet.

Portioners, *-narii*, the several Ministers that serve one Parsonage alternately.

Portmanteau, *f.* a Cloak-bag. But our *Portmantleis* of leather.

Portmen, Inhabitants of the Cinque ports, also the 12 Burgesses of *Ipswich*.

Porto, a town that gave name to

Portugal, a Kingdom bounded with *Spain* and the Western Ocean.

Porto bello, St. *Philip*, a strong town in *America*.

Portos, *Porthose*, *o.* a Breviary or service-book.

Portpain, *f.* a towel carrying bread for the Table at Court.

Portsale, the sale of fish so soon as it arrives in the haven,

ven; also a publick sale of things to them that bid most.

Portsouth, *o. Southwark*.

Portsmouth, a town in *Hantshire*.

Posade, *f.* the lighting down of Birds, also any resting or resting place.

Pose, *o.* for suppose.

Pose, a rheum stopping the nose and hindring the speech.

Position, *l.* a foundation [upon which an argument is built.]

Posna, a City of lower *Poland*.

Possessive, *-sory*, *l.* belonging to

Possession, *l.* property, or actual enjoyment.

Possed, *o.* tossed, pushed.

Possown, an Indian beast receiving her young ones (on occasion) into a bag under her belly.

Possibility, a being

Possible, *l.* able to be done.

Post diem, the Sheriffs penalty (4d. to the *Custos brevium*) for returning a writ after the day assigned.

Post disseisin, a writ for him that had recovered Lands, &c. and is disseised again.

Post fine, a duty belonging to the King, for a fine formerly acknowledged.

Post term, 20 d. taken by the *Custos brevium* of the Court of Common Pleas, for filing any writ after the Term.

Poste o Power.

Postea, a Record of the proceedings upon a trial by *Nisi prius*.

Posteriority, a being or coming after. He that holds of two Lords, holds of the first by priority, of the last by Posteriority.

Posteriors, *l.* the back-parts.

Posthumian, belonging to a

Posthume, *l.* a Child born after the Fathers death.

Posthume (*or Posthumous*) *works*, published after the Authors death.

Postick, *l.* being behind

Postile, (*q. appostile*, *f.* a small addition to a greater discourse) a short exposition on the Gospel.

Postillon, *f.* a guide or Post-boy; also he that rides one of the first Coach-horses.

Postliminious, belonging to

Postliminie, *-niage*, *l.* the return of one thought to be dead, restored to his house by a hole through the wall.

Postmeridian, *l.* done in the afternoon.

Postnate, *l.* born after.

Postome, *o.* Impostume.

Postpone, *-pose*, *l.* to set behind, to slight.

Postposure, a setting behind or esteeming less.

Postriduan, *l.* done the next day after.

Post-script, an addition at the end of a writing.

Postvene, *l.* to come after.

Postventional, coming after.

Postulatory, belonging to a

Postulate, *l.* a request or demand.

Postulata, Fondamental principles (in any science) taken for granted.

Pot, a head-piece.

Potable, *l.* fit to drink.

Pot-ashes, made of the best wood ashes (for Sope.)

Pottacco, *Sp.* a small Sea-vessel.

Potation, *l.* a drinking.

Pote, *No.* to push or put out.

Pote the clothes off, *No.* kick them off.

Potatoes, Indian roots of great vertue.

Potent (in Heraldry) the top of a croutch.

Potent, *-ntial*, powerful.

Potentials, things apt to give power or strength.

Potentates, *Potest-*, men in authority and power.

Potosi, a town in *Peru*, having the best Silver Mines.

Potorious, *l.* drinky.

Potton, a town in *Bedfordshire*.

Potulent, *l.* drinkable.

Pouches small bulk-heads in the hold (to keep up Corn &c.)

Poul, *Sf.* a boil or ulcer.

Pouldavis, *Ouldernes*, *Medrinacles*, course Canvas.

Pounce, *sp.* to jag or cut in and out.

Pounces, Hawks claws.

Poundage, a subsidy granted the King (of twelve-pence in the pound) of all merchandize imported or exported.

Pour fair proclamre, &c. a writ commanding the Maior &c. to proclaim that none cast filth into ditches or other places adjoining.

Pourcontrel, as *Polypus*.

Pourmenade, *f.* a walk.

Pourpartie, the division of Parceners Land.

Pourpresture, an encroachment, or any thing done to the Nusance of the Kings Tenants.

Poursuivant, *f.* a follower, also a Kings messenger on special occasions.

Poursuivants at arms, Blewmantle, Rouge-cross, Rouge-dragon and Percullis, attending (and commonly succeeding) the Heralds.

Pourtraicture, the drawing a

Pourtract, *-ict*. *f.* a draught, picture or resemblance of any thing.

Pourveyance, the work of a

Pourveyor, an Officer providing Corn and victuals [for the Kings house.]

Powk, *o.* for pug.

Powre, *o.* stare, pore.

Power of the County, *posse Comitatûs*, the aid and attendance of all above the age of 15 (that are capable of bearing Arms) when any force is used in opposition to the execution of justice.

Poynaunte, o. pricking.

Poynings Law, an Act of Parliament in *Ireland*, 10. *H. 7*. (Sir *Edw. Poynings* being Lieutenant) making all English Statutes (to that time, but none made since) of force in *Ireland*.

Præ-, is (in English) most commonly written *Pre-*.

Practick, *-cal*, belonging to

Practice, or actual exercise.

Pragmatic, *Sp.* a Proclamation; also an agreement between a secular Prince and a Bishop.

Pragmatical, *g.* expert in law business, or (as now tis used) busie about other mens affairs.

Prague, the Metropolis of *Bohemia*.

Prancer, *c.* a horse.

Prandicle, *l.* a break-fast or little dinner.

Pransorious, *l.* belonging to dinner.

Prattily, *No.* softly.

Prats, *c.* Thighs.

Pratical, belonging to

Pratique, *I.* practice, also a licence to traffick.

Prating-cheat, *c.* a tongue.

Pratum falcabile, Meadow-grounds.

Pravity, *l.* naughtiness.

Preamble, a tedious preface.

Prebendary, an Assistant to the Bishop, he that receives a

Prebend, *l.* a portion allowed the Members of a Cathedral Church, also the place.

Prebendal, belonging thereto.

Prebition, *l.* a giving or offering.

Precaution, *l.* fore-warning, fore-sight or being aware.

Precariæ, bind-daies (for bidden daies) dayes works which some Tenants are to give the Lord in harvest.

Precarious, granted by entreaty, only so long as the other pleaseth.

Precedential, belonging to

Precedence, a going before, an excelling.

Precedent, foregoing.

Précedent, an Example.

Precellence, *-cy*, Excellency.

Precention, the flourish or Entrance of a Song.

Precentor, the Chantor, that begins the tune.

Prece partium, the continuance of a Sute by the consent of both parties.

Preceptive, belonging to precepts.

Preceptor, a Schoolmaster.

Preceptories, benefices that were held by the better sort of Templars.

Precidaneous, going, Cut or killed before.

Precincts, bounds.

Precipice, a down-right descent.

Precipitate, to cast down headlong, do a thing rashly, also Red Mercury, a corroding powder.

Precocity, a being too early [in ripening.]

Precognition, fore-knowledge.

Preconious, belonging to commendation, or the Common Cryer.

Preconsultors, Preadvisers, a Colledge at *Venice*.

Precontract, a former bargain.

Precursor, a fore-runner.

Predatory, belonging to

Predation, robbing.

Preddy [*ship*, Ordinance, &c.] ready [for fight.]

Predecessours, Ancestors.

Predestination, fore-appointment.

Predial, *-itory*, belonging to Lands, Farms or Mannors.

Predial tithes, of things growing from the ground.

Prediator, a Lawyer expert in Actions real or concerning Lands.

Predicables, *Porphyries* 5 terms, Attributes of all things, *Genus*, *Species*, *Differentia*, *Proprium* and *Accidens*.

Predicaments, Ten General places, in which every limited Nature is disposed, *viz.* Substance, Quantity, Quality, Relation, Action, Passion, Where, When, Situation and Habit.

Predicate, *l.* to publish or preach, also that which is

Predicated, spoken or affirmed of the Subject.

Prediction, *l.* a foretelling.

Predominant, bearing rule.

Preëminence, right of excellency.

Preëmption, the first buying.

Prees, a town in *Shropshire*.

Preëxistence, a being before.

Preëxistent, being before.

Preface, a speech preparatory to the Discourse.

Prefe, *o.* for proof.

Prefecture, the Office or jurisdiction of a

Prefect, a Governour of a City or Province.

Preference, advancement.

Prefigurate, to foreshew by signs.

Prefinition, a fore-determination.

Prefix, to fasten before, also to appoint [a time.]

Prefract, obstinate.

Pregnancy, a being

Pregnant big with child, also full, copious, ripe.

Pregression, a going before.

Pregustation, a tasting before.

Preignotary, as *Pronotary*

Prejudicate, fore-judged.

Prejudice, rash judgment before trial, also harm.

Prejudicial, hurtfull.

Prelal, belonging to the Printers press.

Prelation, a setting before.

Prelature, the same, also a Prelateship.

Prelate,

Prelate, the Governour of a [Cathedral] Church.

Prelections, Lectures.

Preliminary, as *Liminary*.

Prelude, *-dium*, a proem or Entrance, and (in Musick) a Voluntary or flourish before a song or lesson.

Prelusion, the same.

Premature, too soon ripe.

Premeditate, think beforehand.

Premious, rich in gifts.

Premise, to speak something by way of Preface or principle.

Premisses, things spoken before.

Premission, a sending before.

Premium, a reward [at School.] the money given for ensuring a ship, &c.

Premonstrate, foreshew.

Premunire, (*q. præmonere*) imprisonment and loss of goods,

Premonition, a fore-warning.

Premunition, a fore-arming.

Prender, (*f. Prendre*) the power of taking a thing before 'tis offered.

Prender de Baron, an Exception disabling a Woman from pursuing an appeal of Murder against the killer of her former husband.

Prenomination, a forenaming.

Prenotion, a fore-knowing.

Prenuncious, foretelling.

Prenuntiate, to foreshew.

Preoccupate, prevented, taken afore-hand.

Preominate, to presage.

Preordain, to ordain before.

Preordinate, fore-ordained.

Prepensed, *f.* forethought.

Preponderate, *l.* to weigh more or before.

Prepose, to set before.

Preposition, a part of speech set before other parts.

Preposterous, contrary to order.

Preproperous, over-hasty.

Prepuce, the fore-skin.

Prerogative, a peculiar Authority or *Preëminence*.

Prerogative Court [*of Canterbury*] wherein are proved the wills of those who had goods of any considerable value (usually 5 *l.*) out of the Diocess wherein they died. In *York* 'tis called th' Exchequer.

Presage, to Guess or foretell.

Presbyterian, belonging to

Presbytery, Government of the Church by

Presbyters, *g.* Priests, Elders.

Prescience, *l.* fore-knowledge.

Prescind, to cut before, to divide or break first.

Prescribe, to appoint or limit.

Prescription, appointing, limiting, also a long customary course or use of a thing.

Presen,o. to tread on.

Presentaneous, present, effectual.

Presentation, the Patrons offering a Clerk to the Bishop to be instituted in a Benefice of his gift.

Presentee, the Clerk presented.

Presentment, a meer denunciation of the Jurors or other Officers (without information) of an offence inquirable in that Court.

Preside, to be over or oversee.

Presidial, belonging to a

President, an Overseer, and sometime as *Precedent*.

Presidary, as *Presidial*, also belonging to a

Presidy, a Garrison or Succour.

Pressure, an oppression or grief.

Prest (*f.* ready) a duty paid by the Sheriff upon his account in the Exchequer.

Prest-money, as *Imprest*.

Presteign, a Town in *Radnorshire*.

Prestation-Money, paid by Arch-Deacons yearly to the Bishop,

Prestiges, delusions, impostures.

Prestigiation, a jugling.

Prestigious, Jugler-like.

Preston, a town in *Lancashire*, and about fourty more.

Presto, *Sp*, quickly.

Presumption, arrogance, also cause of judging so or so.

Presuppose, to suppose before-hand.

Pretence, *-text*, an excuse.

Pretensed, pretended.

Pretension, a laying claim.

Pretention, a passing by.

Pretermission, an omitting.

Preternatural, besides nature.

Pretorian, belonging to a

Pretor, a General, Chief Justice, Consul or Maior.

Pretorian guard, Ten thousand, who were to the Emperour, as the *Janizaries* to the *Turk*, and *Mamalukes* to the *Sultan* of *Egypt*.

Prevalency, a being

Prevalent, prevailing, powerfull.

Prevarication, double-dealing.

Prevaricator in *Cambridg* (as *Terræ filius* at *Oxford*) makes an ingenious Satyrical commencement speech.

Prevenient, *-ventional*, coming before.

Previd, *o.* hardy.

Previdence, a foreseeing.

Previous, going before.

Prevy, *o.* came.

Priam, *-mus*, the Son of *Laomedon*, King of *Troy*, in whose time the City was sackt by the *Greeks*.

Priapism, *-mus*, Erection without lust, from

Priapus, the lascivious God of Gardens.

Prich, *No.* thin drink.

Pricker, a Huntsman on horse-back.

Pricket, a brocket, spitter or Male Deer a full year old.

Pricking, a hares footing in the dirt.

Prickfoure, *o.* a rank rider.

Prick-timber, *Euonymus*, Spindle-tree.

Pridian, *l.* of the day before.

Prid (for *Lamprid*) *gavel*, a Rent paid the Lord of *Rodeley* in *Glocester-shire*, for fishing for Lampreys in *Severn*.

Pridwen, King *Arthurs* shield, with the picture of the Virgin *Mary*.

Prigging, *c.* riding.

Prigs, *o.* Thieves.

Prig-napper, *c.* a horse-stealer.

Prig-star, *c.* a rival in Love.

Priket, *o.* a small wax-Candle.

Prill, *o.* (*q. prickle*) to gore.

Primacy, *f.* the dignity of a

Primate, *l.*, a Metropolitan.

Primage, the Sailers due at the loading and going out of a Ship from any Haven.

Prime, *l.* first, chief, large, also the first hour of the day, and one of the Roman Canonical hours (from 6 to nine,) also the Golden Number, and (in surveying) 19 inches and 54 parts of an inch.

Primer, the Office of the blessed Virgin, divided into seven parts, 1. Matines and Laudes. 2. The Prime. 3d. 5th. None (or ninth hour) 6. Vespers (or Evensong) 7. the Compline.

Primero and *Primavista*, *I.* two old games at Cards.

Primevous, *l.* of the first age.

Primices, *l.* first-fruits.

Primier Seisin, was a branch of the Kings Prerogative whereby he had the first possession of all Lands and Tenements holden of him in chief.

Primigenious, *l.* coming naturally or originally of it self.

Priming, the first ground colour [in painting the Ship.

Priming-Iron, to pierce the Carthrage, through the touch-hole.

Primitial, belonging to first-fruits.

Primitive, *l.* first, ancient, not derived of others.

Primogeniture, *l.* the first birth.

Primordial, [belonging to] the first beginning.

Primum Mobile, *l* the first mover, the tenth Orb.

Lord Prince, the Kings eldest Son, now called

Prince of Wales, since *Edward* 2d. who was born at *Carnarvan*.

Principality, Sovereignty.

Prindle, as *Croft*.

Princock, *No.* (*q. praecox* or *cockrel*,) a youngster too soon ripe-headed, a pert and forward fellow.

Priors Aliens, French Governours of Religious houses erected here for Outlandishmen, supprest by *Hen.* 5.

Priority, *l.* a being before.

Prioress, the Governess of a Nunnery.

Prisage, *f.* a prising, also the Kings custom or share of lawful prizes (usually $\frac{1}{10}$)

Prisage of Wines, as *Butlerage*.

Priscilla, little *Prisca* (*l.* old.)

Priscillianists, Hereticks (*An.* 388.) who followed

Priscillianus, he held a good and an evil God Creators of all things, denied the Trinity, &c.

Prise, that which is taken of the Kings Subjects by the Purveyors.

Prism, *g.* any saw-dust, also a solid triangle, hence

Prismatical glasses, representing variety of colours.

Pristine, *l.* ancient, accustomed.

Pristis, *l.* a long and slender fish, also such a Ship.

Privado, *Sp.* a favourite or private friend.

Privation, *l.* a depriving or taking away.

Privative, depriving, &c.

Priviledge, *l.* a liberty granted besides the Course of Common Law.

Privity, *f.* private familiarity.

Privy, (in Law) a partaker, or he that hath an interest in any action or thing.

Privy to, acquainted with.

Privy Artery, passing from the descendent branch of the great Artery, and bestowing it self among the privities.

Privy-Seal, used after the Privy signet and before the Great Seal (and in some smaller things that do not pass the Great Seal at all.)

Prize, that which is taken by conquest, letters of Marque, Robbery, &c. any kind of booty; as also the Combat or contention for it.

Probability, *l.* likelyhood.

Probate of Testaments, proving of Wills (in the spiritual Court) either in common form by the Executors oath, or (to avoid future debate) by witnesses also.

Probatick pond, *g.* the Sheeps pool, *Bethesda*.

Probatical, *-ional*, belonging to

Probation, *l.* a proving.

Probatine piscant, *o.* the Sheeps pool.

Probationer, a trier, also he that is to be tried or approved before he be admitted.

Probator, a prover or App-, who was to prove his allegation by battel or the Countrey, as the Appealed would.

Pro-

Probatory, *l.* the place or Instrument of proof.

Probatum est, *l.* it is approved.

Probe, (*f. curette*) an instrument to search the depth of wounds.

Probity, *l.* honesty.

Problematical, belonging to a

Probleme, *g.* a hard question.

Proboscide, *g.* the Elephants trunk.

Procacity, *l.* Malepertness.

Procatarick cause, foregoing or causing another cause.

Procedendo, a Writ sending a suit back to the Inferiour Court whence it had been called.

Procerity, a being

Procere, *l.* tall.

Procers, Irons hooked at the ends used by Glass-makers.

Process, all proceeding at law, and particularly that by which a Man is called into any Temporal Court.

Procession, a going forward, also a visiting the bounds of the parish in Rogation-week.

Processional, belonging to process or proceeding.

Processum continuando, a writ for the continuing of a process, after the death of the Chief Justice, &c.

Prochein amay, *f.* he that is next of kin to a Child in his Nonage.

Prochronism, *g.* a setting down too much in computing of time.

Procbyta, a *Tyrrbene* Isle arising (they say) from a Mountain of the Isle *Inarime* thrown into the sea by an Earthquake.

Prociduous, belonging to

Procidence, *l.* a falling down.

Procinct, *l.* readiness.

Proclivity, a being

Proclive, *l.* easy, apt, enclining.

Proconsul, *l.* a Deputy Consul.

Procrastinate, *l.* to delay.

Procreate, *l.* to beget.

Pro confesso, for granted, as a bill is taken after a fourth insufficient answer.

Proctors, soliciting other mens business, gathering their tithes, &c.

Proctors of the Clergy, chosen and appointed to sit in the Convocation house in time of Parliament.

Proctors of the University, two chosen yearly to see goods Orders kept.

Proculcation, *l.* a trampling under foot.

Procurations, proxies, paid the Bishop or Arch-deacon yearly, in respect of Visitation.

Procurator, *l.* a Proctor, and (at *Venice*) the second person in dignity.

Procyon, *g.* the lesser dog-star.

Prodigality, *l.* a being

Prodigal, wastfull, riotous.

Prodigence, *l.* unthriftiness.

Prodigious. belonging to a

Prodigy, *l.* a monstrous, wonderfull and strange sight.

Proditorious, *l.* Traitor-like.

Prodrome, *g.* a fore-runner.

Product, -*cate*, brought forth out of another.

Production, *l.* a bringing forth or lengthening.

Proecthesis, the producing a reason to clear or defend himself.

Proeme. *g.* a preface.

Prof, *Prove*, an Enquest.

Profectitious, belonging to

Profection. *l.* a going.

Profer. the time appointed for the Accompts of Sheriffs (and other Officers) in the Exchequer, twice a year.

Profession, the entering into any Religious Order.

Professour, *l.* a publick Reader.

Proficient, *l.* profiting, or one that hath profited.

Profile, *I.* the picture of a thing drawn sidewaies.

Profligate, to put to flight, also debauched.

Profluence, *l.* an abundance.

Profundure, *f.* -*dity*, *l.* a being

Profound, *l.* very deep.

Profuse, *l.* lavishing.

Profusion, a pouring out lavishly.

Progenitors, Forefathers.

Progeny, *l.* an Off-spring.

Progne, *Philomela's* Sister.

Prognosticate, *l.* to foretell.

Prognosticks, boding signs.

Progression, *l.* a going on.

Progressional, belonging thereto.

Prohibition, a forbidding or hindering.

Prohibitio de vasto, &c. a writ forbidding the waste of land in controversy.

Prohibitory, -*tive*, forbidding.

Projection, *l.* a casting forward, or a contriving.

Projectitious, *l.* exposed, cast out.

Pro indiviso, the possession of Coparceners before partition.

Projecture, *l.* the jutting out of buildings.

Prolation, *l.* a pronouncing.

Prolatation, *l.* a deferring.

Proleptical, belonging to

Prolepsis, -*sie*, *g.* a conceiving in the mind before hand, a preventing what another thought to alledge.

Proletaneous, -*arian*, -*ious*, *l.* having many Children and little to maintain them, vulgar.

Prolification, a making

Prolifical, *l.* fruitfull.

Prolixity, *l.* a being

Prolix, liberal, tedious.

Prologue. *g.* the speech before a play.

Proloquutor, *l.* The Speaker [of either Convocation House.]

Prolusion, *l.* as *Preludium*.

Prolyte, *g.* a Licentiate that hath studied the Law 4 years.

Promenade, *f.* as *Pournenade*.

Promesse, *f.* a promise.

Prometheus, Son to *Japetus*, stealing fire from heaven to put life in his Image, was chain'd to *Caucasus*, where a Vulture gnaw'd his liver.

Prominence, a being

Prominent, *l.* jutting out or over others.

Promiscuous, *l.* mingled.

Promissary, to whom a promise is made.

Promissory, *l.* belonging to a promise.

Promontory, *l.* a hill butting into the sea.

Promoters, -*mooters*, who (for reward) complain of Offenders.

Promptitude, a being

Prompt, *l.* ready, quick.

Promptuary, *l.* a buttery.

Promulgation, *l.* a publishing.

Prone, *l.* with face downward.

Pronephew, *l.* a Nephews son.

Pronotary, as *Protono*-.

Proem, as *Proeme*.

Propagate, *l.* to spread abroad, or plant young vines.

Pro partibus liberandis, a writ for the partition of Lands between Co-heirs.

Propelled, thrust forward.

Propension, -*ity*, *l.* a being.

Propense, heavy, inclined.

Properate, *l.* to make hast.

Property, the highest right a man can have to a thing, also a natural quality.

Properties, the Accoutrements of Actors.

Prophecies (in Law) Wizzardly foretellings.

Prophetize, to prophesy, or foretell things to come.

Prophetical, belonging thereto.

Prophylactic, *g.* preservative.

Propination, *l.* a drinking to one.

Propinquity, *l.* nearness.

Propitiate, *l.* to appease by Sacrifice.

Propitiation, atonement.

Propitiatory, belonging thereto, also the Mercy-seat or place where God was

Propitious, favourable.

Propontis, the sea from the streights of Hellespont to *Thracian* Bosphorus.

Proportion, *l.* answerableness.

Proposition, *l.* a sentence or matter propounded.

Propounders, seems to be *Monopolists* or else *Projectors*.

Propretor a Deputy *Pretor*.

Proprietary, -*tor*, *f.* the owner, whose the Propriety is.

Propudious, *l.* shamefull.

Propugnacle, *l.* a fortress.

Propugnator, *l.* a stiff maintainer.

Propulsation, *l.* a driving back.

Propulsory, serving thereto.

Proreption, *l.* a creeping on

Prorex, *l.* a Vice-Roy.

Proritate, *l.* to stir up.

Proroked himself, *o.* hid himself in a Rock.

Prorogued, *l.* put off for some time, but not ended.

By Prorogation (in open Court) there is a Session, and then such Bills as had not Royal assent, must (the next assembly) begin again: But in Adjournment (or Continuance) there is no Session, and therefore all things continue in their former state. For every several Session of Parliament is (in Law) a several Parliament.

Prosaick, *l.* being in or belonging to

Prose, not verse.

Proscision, *l.* a cutting up.

Proscription, a making one

Proscript, *l.* an Outlaw, exposed to every mans sword.

Prosecutor, who follows a Cause in anothers name.

Proselyte, *g.* a stranger converted to our Religion (formerly to the Jewish.)

Proserpine, the Daughter of *Jupiter* and *Ceres*, ravisht to hell by *Pluto*.

Prosimetrical, *g.* part prose and part verse.

Prosodian, one skil'd in

Prosody, *g.* the Art of accenting aright.

Prosopopœia, *g.* a feigning of a person to speak.

Prospect, *l.* a view afar off.

Prospicuous, *l.* fair to behold.

Prospicience, *l.* foresight.

Prosternation, *l.* a laying flat.

Prosthesis, *g.* an addition to the beginning of a word.

Prostitute, *l.* to let out the use of her body.

Prostrate, *l.* to lay (or lying) flat along.

Prosyllogism, *g.* an auxiliary syllogism, to help the main one.

Protatick, belonging to

Protasis, *g.* a proposition; also the first part of a Comedy.

Protection, *l.* a guarding or being guarded.

Protelation, *l.* a driving away.

Protend, *l.* to stretch forth.

Protervity, *l.* frowardness.

Protesilaus, going to the *Trojan* war (contrary to the Oracles advice) was slain by *Hector*.

Protest a bill of Exchange, declare (on the Exchange) that you are not satisfied by his Factor, and the Law of Merchants allows you satisfaction out of his goods, if he have any in the Realm.

Protestants, so called at *Spires* in *Germany* (1529) from their

Protestation, *l.* an open declaration of ones mind, also a form of pleading when one doth not directly affirm or deny the thing alledged.

Proteus, a Sea-God who (they say) turn'd himself into all kind of shapes.

Prothonotary, as *Proto-*.

Protocol, *g.* the first draught of a Deed, &c. also the upper title-part of a leaf.

Protofole, *g.* the first leaf.

Proto-Forestarius, was the Chief Justice of *Windsor* Forest.

Protolicia, supposed to be *Prudhow Castle* in *Northumberland*.

Protologie, *g.* a preface.

Protomartyr, *g.* the first [Gospel] Martyr, St. *Stephen*.

Protonotary, a chief Clerk, (three in the Common-Pleas and one in the Upper-Bench.)

Protoplast, *g.* the first formed, *Adam*.

Prototype, *g.* the first pattern.

Prototypographer, *g.* the chief Printer.

Protozeugma, *Zeugma* with the verb in the beginning.

Protraction, *l.* a deferring.

Protractor, *l.* a prolonger; also a surveying instrument.

Protreptick, *g.* Doctrinal.

Protrude, *l.* to thrust forward,

Protrusion, a thrusting, &c.

Protuberant, *l.* swelling out

Protype, *g.* a pattern for moulds.

Provango, a whale-bone-instrument, to cleanse the Stomach.

Proveditores, *l.* the Venetian Overseers join'd to the general.

Provedore, -*vid*- the Governour of *Zant* Isle.

Prover, as *Approver*.

Provence, a large French Province.

Proverbial, belonging to a

Proverb, *l.* an old pithy saying.

Provident, *l.* wary.

Provincial, belonging to a

Province, the Arch-Bishops jurisdiction.

United Provinces, *Gelderland*, *Holland*, *Zealand*, *Zutphen*, *West-friezland*, (*Utrecht*) *Over-Yssel*, *Groening*.

Provincial (among Fryers) the chief of their Order in such or such a Province.

Provining, *f.* laying a branch (of a vine, &c.) to take root.

Provision, providing one with a Benefice.

Provisional, for a season, by way of foresight or

Proviso, *l.* a caveat or condition.

Provisor, a pourveyor.

Provocation, *l.* a stirring up or challenging.

Provocative, apt to provoke.

Prowl, to pilfer by night.

Provost Marshal, an Officer in the Navy, having charge of the Prisoners taken at Sea.

Provostal, belonging to a

Provost, (*f. prevost*) the President of a Colledge and several other Officers in *France*.

Prow, the fore-part of a ship, or any jutting like it; also (*o.*) honour, and profit.

Prowess, *f.* courage.

Proxie, a Proctors warrant from his Client, also any deputy.

Proxies, as *Procurations*.

Proximity, *l.* the greatest nearness.

Proyns, *o.* as Prunes.

Pruce, *o.* *Borussia*, *Prussland*, *Spruceland*.

Prudentiality, [an aptness to breed] prudence.

Pruinous, *l.* frosty.

Prunel, fickle-wort.

Prunella's, a restorative fruit, like small figs.

Prunes, [the hawk] picks and annoils her self.

Prurient, *l.* itching.

Pruriginous, *l.* itchy.

Prussia, part of *Poland*.

Prutenicks, Mathematical tables, dedicated to *Albertus* Marquis of *Brandenburgh* and Duke of *Prussia*, 1551.

Pry, *o.* for pray.

Psallocitharist, *g.* a singer to the harp.

Psalm, *g.* a Divine Song.

Psalmist, the composer of it.

Psalmody, *g.* a singing of Psalms.

Psalmography, *g.* a writing of Psalms.

Psaltery, *g.* a shalm, (like a harp) with 10 strings.

Psephism, *g.* a Decree.

Pseudodox, *g.* false glory, or falsely glorious.

Pseudography, *g.* false writing.

Pseudologer, a practiser of

Pseudologie, *g.* lying.

Pseudomancy, *g.* false divination.

Pseudomartyr, *g.* a false Martyr or witness.

Pseudonymal, *g.* having a false name.

Pseudoprophet, *g.* a false Prophet.

Psorophthalmy, *g.* an itching scurf on the eye-brows.

Psychomachy, *g.* a war of the soul [and body.]

Ptisane, *l.* barley-broth.

Ptolomæus, the name of several Egyptian Kings.

Puberty, *l* [the signs of] ripe age.

Pubescent, growing to ripe age.

Publick Faith, on which the Parliament rais'd money to to carry on the war.

Publican, *l.* a farmer of publick Rents or Revenues.

Publication, *l.* a making common.

Pucelage, *l.* Virginity.

Puckets, *Sf.* nests of Caterpillars.

Pucle-Church, a town in *Glocestershire*.

Puddings, ropes nail'd to the ends of the yard-arms, to save the Robbins from galling.

Pudhepec, (for *Wu-*) *Sa.* a felling

felling of Wood [in the Park, Forest, &c.]

Pudibund, *-dous*, *l.* bashfull.

Pudicity, *l.* Chastity.

Pudor, *l.* shamefac'dness.

Pudzeld, as Woodgeld.

Puerility, *l.* childishness.

Puerperous *l.* Child-bearing.

Pugil, *l.* half a handfull.

Pugillation, the exercise of

Pugils, *l.* Champions, fist-fighters.

Pugnacity, *l.* a desire of fighting.

Pugnatory, *l.* belonging to a fighter.

Puisné, *f.* Younger, born after, puny.

Puissance, *f.* power.

Pulchritude, *l.* comeliness.

Pulicine, *l.* belonging to a flea.

Pulicosity, *l.* a being

Pulicous, full of fleas.

Pullail, (*f. poulaille*) wild-fowl.

Pullation, *l.* a breeding Chickens.

Pullulate, *l.* to bud.

Pullhely, a town in *Carnarvanshire.*

Pulmentarious, *l.* belonging to water-gruel.

Pulmonarious, *l.* diseased in the lungs.

Pulmonary, *l.* Lung-wort.

Pulmonical, belonging to the lungs.

Pulp, *l.* the substantial part of any thing, also a Cuttle-fish.

Pulsation, *l.* a beating upon.

Pulsator, *l.* a striker.

Pultifical, *l.* serving to make pottage or pap.

Pultrie, *o.* for poultry.

Pulverisation, *-izing*, *l.* a reducing to pouder.

Pulverulent, *-rous*, *l.* Dusty.

Pumicate, *l.* to smooth with a

Pumice stone, a spungy stone, the scum of *Etna* and other burning hills.

Pump-brake, the handle.

Pump-dale, in which the water runs to the Scupper-holes.

Pumpet-ball, as *Pompet.*

Punch, a mixture of Brandy, Water, Limons and Sugar.

Punchion of wine, (*f. poinson*) 80. gallons.

Punctilio, *I.* a little

Puncto, *I.* a point.

Punctual, *l.* exactly, to a hairs breadth.

Pundonnore (*f. point d' honore*) a bravado.

Pundbrech, *Sa.* a breaking open the pound.

Pungency, *l.* a pricking.

Punick, Carthaginian.

Punick faith, falshood.

Puny, as *Puisné.*

Punition, *l.* a punishment.

Pupil, *l.* the apple of the eye, also an Orphan under age and tuition, also a Disciple of a Colledg-Tutor.

Purbeck, a demy-Island on which stands *Crof* Castle in *Dorsetshire.*

Purchasing, the getting a rope in by haling, &c. It is easier (though longer) purchasing upon a block of three sheevers than two.

Purfle, (*f. pourfile*) a border or fringe.

Purflew (in Heraldry) all Furs used in Borders.

Purgation, the clearing one self of a crime.

Purgatory, *l.* the Papists place of cleansing (by fire) between Death and Heaven.

Purgative, purging.

Purification, *l.* a cleansing.

Purificatory, the little linnen cloth that wipes the Chalice.

Purification of the Virgin Mary, Candlemas, *February*, 2.

Purim, *P.* the feast of Lots kept for deliverance from *Haman.*

Puritans, a Nick-name of *Calvinists.*

Purlue, (*f. pur lieu*) all that space that is severed by perambulations from the antient forest.

Purlieu-man, who (being able to spend 40 shillings *per annum* of free hold) is licensed to hunt on his own ground within the *Purlieu.*

Purloin, *f.* to pilfer.

Purport, the true meaning.

Purpurean, *l.* of purple.

Purpresture, as *Pour-.*

Purprisum, an enclosure.

Purrel, a list ordered (35 *Eliz.*) to be made at the end of Kersies.

Pursivant, as *Pour-.*

Purtrey, *o.* for *Pourtray.*

Purveyour, as *Pour-*

Purveu, (*f.* a patent) the body of the Act, beginning with Be it enacted-.

Purulent, *l.* filthy, mattery.

Pusillanimity, *l.* a being

Pusillanimous, faint-hearted.

Pustulous, *l.* full of

Pustules, blisters, pushes.

Putage, *f.* Fornication [on the womans part.]

Putative, *l.* supposed.

Putatory, belonging to

Putation, *l.* pruning.

Puteal, *l.* of a well.

Putid, *l.* stinking.

Putor, *l.* a stink.

Putre. (*f. puterie*) Fornication.

Putrescence, a rotting.

Putrid, *l.* rotten, corrupt.

Putrifaction, *l.* rottenness.

Puts over, [the Hawk] removes her meat from her Gorge into her Bowels.

Puttocks, small shrowds from the main to the top-mast-shrowds, for the Easie going into the top.

Putty, a powder of calcin'd tin) used by Artificers.

Putura, (*q. potura*) a Custom claimed by some Keepers and Bailiffs, to take Mansmeat, horse-meat and Dogs meat *gratis*, within the

the perambulation of the Forest or hundred.

Pycar, Piker, a kind of ship mentioned 31 *Edw*. 3.

Pygmachy, *g*. a fighting with clubs or hurlbats.

Pygmies, Mountainous *Indian* dwarfs, said to have perpetual war with the Cranes.

Pyladium, as *Piladion*.

Pynanto,*o*. a starveling.

Pyramidal, -*dical*, like a

Pyramid, *g*. an *Egyptian* building like a Spire-Steeple.

Pyramidography, *g*. a treatise concerning it.

Pyrate, as *Pirate*.

Pyre, *g*. a pile of wood, to burn the corps.

Pyrenæan hills, dividing *France* and *Spain*.

Pyrites, *g*. the fire-stone.

Pyromancy, *g*. divination by fire.

Pyroticks, *g*. burning medicines.

Pyrotechny, *g*. a making of fire-works.

Pyrrhonian, belonging to

Pyrrho, a *Greek* Sceptick who thought nothing certain.

Pyrrhonism, that Philosophy.

Pyrrhus, King of *Epirus*, slain (at the taking of *Argos*) by the fall of a Tile.

Pythagorical, belonging to

Pythagoricism, the Tenet of

Pythagoras, Authour of the *Metempsychosis*.

Pythian games, in the honour of *Apollo*, who slew

Python, a monstrous serpent, also a prophecying spirit, and one possest therewith.

Pythoness, a She-Python or Prophetess.

Pythonical, belonging to or practising

Pythonism, the art of prophesying by a Devilish spirit.

Pyx, *l*. the vessel containing the *Roman Hoste*, also an antient yearly solemn weighing of Gold in the Star-Chamber.

Q.

Q. *Quintus*, the fifth.

q. *quasi*, as if it were.

Quab, a Water-weasel or Eel-pout.

Quack, *D*. Frivolous, trifling.

Quacking cheat, *c*. a duck.

Quick salver, *D*. a Mountebank.

Quad, *D*. Bad.

Quadragenarious, of 40 years.

Quadragesimal, belonging to lent or to

Quadragesima [*Sunday*] the first in Lent (being about 40 daies before Easter.)

Quadran, *f*. a Sun-dial.

Quadrain, *f*. a staff of 4 verses.

Quadrangular, like a

Quadrangle, *l*. a 4 square figure.

Quadrant, *l*. a quarter of a circle or of any measure.

Quadrantal, 4 fingers thick, also a figure like a die.

Quadrantata terræ, as Farding-deal.

Quadrat, *l*. a square (to take the distance or height of a place.

Quadrate, -*tick*, [made] 4 square.

Quadrature, *l*. a squaring.

Quadricornous, *l*. with 4 horns.

Quadriennial, of 4 years.

Quadrigamist, one four times married.

Quadrigarious, belonging to a Coach (or Coachman) with 4 horses.

Quadrigenarious, of fourty.

Quadrilateral, of 4 sides.

Quadrin, *f*. *Liard*, a small coyn, about a farthing.

Quadringenarious, of four hundred.

Quadripartite, *l*. divided into 4.

Quadrireme, *l*. a Gally of 4 oars on a seat, or 4 men to an oar.

Quadrisyllable, of 4 syllables.

Quadrivial, *l*. having 4 waies or turnings.

Quadrugata terræ, a Teemland, tilled with 4 horses.

Quadrupedal, *l*. with 4 feet.

Quadrupedant, going on 4 feet.

Quadrupedian [*Signs*] representing four footed beasts

Quadruple, *l*. 4 fold.

Quadruplation, a doubling 4 times.

Quadruplicate, to fold or repeat a thing 4 times.

Quæ plura, was a writ to enquire what land there was more than was found by th'Escheators inquisition.

Quakenburg, a Town in *Westphalia*.

Quakers, Friends, a sort of modern Enthusiasts.

Quaint gires, *o*. strange fits.

Quale jus, a writ for the Escheator to enquire (between Judgment and Execution) whether the Clerk have right to recover, and there be no Collusion to defraud the true Lord.

Qualify, *l*. to make fit or quiet.

Qualifications, Conditions.

Qualm, *o*. calmness, also the cry of Ravens.

Quamdiu se bene gesserit, a formal clause in the grant of Offices; and is no more than the Law implies, if the Office were granted for life.

Quantum meruit, an Action of the Case, grounded on a promise of paying a man so much as he should deserve.

Quandary, (*Qu'en dirai-je*? *f*. what shall I say to't?) a study or doubt what to do.

Quap, o. for quake.

Quaplod, a town in *Lincolnshire*.

Quarantain, f. Lent, or any space of 40 daies (of prayers, cessation of arms, or carrying on Ship-bord when you come from a place infected.)

Quarainty, *Sp.* fourty [days.]

Quardecue, *Quart d' ecu*, *f.* the fourth part of a [French] Crown.

Quare ejecit infra terminum, a writ for a Lessee cast out before his time is expired.

Quare impedit, a writ for one disturbed in the right of his purchased Advowzon.

Quare incumbravit, a writ against the Bishop conferring a Benefice (within six months) whilest others are contending for the right of presenting.

Quare intrusit, *&c.* a writ that lay against a Ward, marrying and entering on his Lands without the consent of his Lord and Guardian.

Quarels, *Querels*, *l.* complaints, all Actions personal and real.

Quare non permittit, a writ for one that has right (for a turn) to present.

Quare non admisit, a writ against the Bishop refusing to admit his Clerk who has recovered in a plea of Advowzen.

Quare obstruxit, a writ for him who cannot have his right in passing through his Neighbours ground.

Quarentena habenda, a writ for a widow to enjoy her

Quarentene, *-tine*, 40 days continuance in the chief Mansion-house of her deceased husband.

Quareria, a stone-quarrey.

Quarrels, *o.* arrow-heads.

Quarril, *f.* 1d. ob. the fourth part of a Spanish Royal.

Quarron, c. a body.

Quarry, the fowl that is flown at and slain, also the Hounds reward after hunting, and the Venison it self

Quartane [*Ague*,] returning every fourth day.

Quartary, the 4th. part of a Sextary, also a quarter of a pound.

Quartation, a separation into 4 parts.

Quarter, 8 striked bushels, also a piece of timber 4 square and 4 inches thick.

Quarter-Sessions, a Court held (every quarter) by the Justices of Peace in every County.

Ships-Quarter, from the Steeridge to the Transom or fashion-piece.

Quarter-bullet, quartered in to four parts.

Quarter-Deck, over the Steeridg, as far as the Masters Cabin.

Quarter pierced, (in Heraldry) a square hole in the middle of a Cross.

Quartering, sailing with

Quarter-winds, coming in abaft the Main-mast shrowds just with the quarter, when all sails may draw together.

Quartile aspect, the distance of 3 (a quarter of 12) Signs.

Quarto, with four leaves in a sheet.

Quartz, a kind of flint, with lead and Silver in't.

Quash, to annul or overthrow.

Quassation, *l.* a shaking.

Quater Cosins, *f.* fourth or last Cosins, good friends.

Quaternary, belonging to

Quaternion, *-ity*, the number of four, by which the *Pythagoreans* swore, because of the Elements and name of God which in most languages consisteth of 4 letters.

Quaviver, (*q. aqua-*) a Sea-Dragon.

Quaver (in Musick,) half a Crochet.

Queach, *o.* a quickset.

Quecbord, (perhaps shovel bord) a game prohibited, 17 *Edward* 4th.

Queen-Gold, a duty belonging to every Queen-Consort, upon divers grants of the King.

Queens Colledge (in *Oxford*) built by *Philip* the wife of *Edward* 3d. who (in honour of her) built

Queenborough, a town in *Kent*.

Queed, (*q. Quade*) *o.* the Devil.

Queest, *o.* as *Culver*.

Que estate, which estate.

Que est le mesme, *f.* which is the same thing.

Queint, *o.* quenched, also strange.

Quem redditum reddat, a writ to cause a Tenant to atturn, &c.

Quercine, *-culane*, *l.* Oken.

Querela coram Rege et Consilio, a writ calling one to justifie a Complaint made before the King and Council

Querimonious, *l.* complaining.

Queintises, *o.* devises.

Queme, *Sa.* to please.

Querrour, *o.* a stone-miner.

Quercy, a *French* Province.

Quern, *D.* a hand-mill.

Querpo, as *Cuerpo*

Querulous, full of complaint.

Query, (*quaere*) a Question.

Quest, Inquest, inquiry into misdemeanours (in the Ward.)

Quest-men, who are chosen and meet about Christmas to that purpose.

Questor, *l.* a Publick Treasurer, also a Judge.

Questuary, *-rious*, exercising a trade to gain thereby.

Questus est Nobis, a writ against him to whom the thing is alienated which causeth the Nusance.

Qui bien aime tard oublie, *f.* he that loves well, forgets late.

Qui est la ? f. who is there ?

Quia improvide, a superfedeas granted where a writ is erroniously sued out, &c.

Quick-silver, a slimy water mixt with pure white earth.

Quiddity, the essence of a thing, also a Quirk or Subtile question.

Quiddanet, a Confection between a Syrup and Marmalade.

Quidditative, essential.

Quid juris clamat, a writ for the Grantee of a reversion, when the particular Tenant will not atturn.

Quid pro quo, Συνάλλαγμα, one for another, a mutual performance of Contracts.

Quiescent, *l.* resting, not sounding.

Quietancia, as *Acquiet-*.

Quietus [*est*,] an acquittance given Accountants in the Exchequer.

Quietus est granted the Sheriff, discharges him of all accounts due to the King.

Quilibet quippe, the proportion every Bencher (of the Inner Temple) payes at the Terms end for Battles or Exceedings.

Quimpercorintin, a City of lower *Britany*.

Quinary, *l.* of five.

Quincuncial, belonging to

Quincunx, *l.* five ounces, also five trees (or more) so set together, that a regular angularity and thorow prospect is left on every side.

Quincupedal, of 5 foot.

Quindecimvir, one of the 15 Joint-Governours of a Common-wealth.

Quingenarious, of 500.

Quinible, (*q.* whinable) a treble.

Quinquagesima Sunday, Shrove-Sunday (being about 50 dayes before Easter.)

Quinquangle, 5 cornered.

Quinque-libral, of five pound.

Quinquennal, *-nial*, of 5 years.

Quinquepartite, divided into 5.

Quinque portus, the Cinque ports.

Quinquereme, a ship of 5 oars on a side, also a Galley of 5 men to an oar.

Quinquevir, one of 5 in Joint-authority.

Quinquiplicate, to make it 5 times double.

Quinsieme, *Quinzime*, *f.* the 15th day after any feast; also the 15th part of every town in *England*, an ancient tax, but not levied now without the Parliament.

Quintage, [the laying out] a fifth part (for younger Brethren)

Quintain, *f.* a wedding-sport (in *Shropshire*, &c.) running a-tilt with poles against a

Quintin, a thick plank set fast in the high-way, &c.

Quintal, as *Kintal*.

Quintessential, belonging to

Quintessence, *l.* the virtue or purest substance extracted out of any thing.

Quint-exact, *Quinto exactus*, the last call of a Defendant, when if he appear not, he is returned Outlawed.

Quintile, July, the 5th [Month] from *March*.

Quintuple, *l.* five-fold.

Quinzain, *f.* fifteen dayes, or a staff of 15 verses.

Quire, *Queer*, *c.* base, roguish.

Quirinal, belonging to

Quirinus, Romulus.

Quirister, as *Corister*.

Quiritation, a complaining or calling for help.

Quirites, Romanes.

Quistron, *o.* a beggar.

Quite-claim, a quitting of ones Claim or Title.

Quit-Rent, White-Rent, a small Rent of acknowledgment.

Quitter, the dross of tin.

Quod Clerici non eligantur, a writ for a Clerk who (by reason of his land) is like to be made Bailiff, &c.

Quod Clerici beneficiati, a writ exempting a Clerk of the Chancery from contributing towards the Proctors of the Clergy in Parliament.

Quod ei deforceat, a writ against him (or his heir) that took away land recovered by a Tenant in Tail, Dower, or for Life.

Quod, *o.* for quoth, saith.

Quodlibetical, belonging to

Quodlibets, Quirks or Quiddities, School-Questions.

Quodlibitaries, that follow their own fancies.

Quod permittat, a writ for his heir that is disseised of his Common of pasture, against the heir of the Disseisor.

Quod persona nec prebendarij, &c. a writ for Clerks distrained for their fifteenths.

Quo Jure, a writ to compel one to shew by what right he challenges Common of pasture.

Quo minus, a writ against the Grantor making such wast in his woods that the Grantee cannot enjoy his grant of House-bote and Hay-bote; or for any (that paies the King a fee-farm Rent) against another for debt or damage.

Quorum, Of which [Justices, He is to be one.]

Quotidian, *l.* daily.

Quotient, (*Quoties*, *l.* how often ?) the number arising out of any Division.

Quotted. *Sf.* Cloy'd, glutted.

Quo Warranto, a writ against him that usurps a Franchise of the Kings; or him that intrudes as heir.

Quoyl, a rope laid round, one take over another.

Quyn, a wedg-like-piece of timber, to put under Ordnance in mounting them.

Cantick-Quoyns, short three-edged ones to put between Cask, &c.

Quyke, o. a quick(or living beast.

Quyre of a Boar, the hounds fee, (perhaps from *Coeur*, f. the heart.)

Quyssben, o. a Cushion.

R.

R*Aa*, o. a Roe.

Raab, *Javarin*, a Hungarian Fortress.

Rabates, [the hawk] recovers the bearers fist.

Rabbeting, a close kind of joining boards (by laying them over) to keep out wind or dust, also the letting in of the planks to the Ships keel.

Rabbinical, belonging to the

Rabbies, *-bins*, h. the Jewish Masters or Doctors.

Rabbinist, one skil'd in their works, also a dunce.

Rabdomancy, g. divination by rods.

Rabid, l. raging, mad.

Racemation, l. grape-gleaning.

Racemiferous, cluster-bearing.

Racha, *Raca*, h. rascal, a term of reproach.

Rachel, h. a sheep or lamb.

Rachetum, *-bat-*, Thiefbote, the compensation or redemption of a Thief.

Racine, f. a root.

Rack, the Duke of *Exeter's* Daughter, an Engin to extort Confessions, brought into the Tower by him (being Constable, 16 *H. 6.*) intending to bring in the whole Civil Law.

Rack, *Rek*, *No.* to take thought or care.

Rackel, *Rakil*, o. hasty.

Rack Vintage, a second voyage of our Merchants into *France*, for

Rack'd wines, cleansed and drawn from the Lees.

Rad Knights, as *Rod K-*.

Radamant, as *Rhada-*.

Rhadegund, *sa.* favourable Counsel.

Rade vore, *sa.* Tapestry.

Radgondes, o. a kind of Ulcer.

Radiant, l. shining.

Radiation, l. a casting forth bright beams.

Radicality, a being

Radical, belonging to the root, nature or life.

Radical question, propounded when the Lord of the Ascendant and of the Hour, are of one nature and triplicity.

Radicate, l. to take root.

Radial artery, a branch of the arm-hole artery bestowing it self on the

Radius, the upper and greater bone of the arm, also a line from the Center to the circumference.

Radlings, *No.* windings of the wall.

Raffinage, f. refinement or quintessence.

Raffle, f. a trying to throw most on three dice, also rifling, o.

Raft, a timber float-boat.

Rafull of knaves, o. a Rabble.

Raft, o. (q. *reft*) rent.

Rag (or *Rake*) *of Colts*, a great company of them, (q. *Race*)

Ragery, o. (perhaps) Roguery.

Raght, *Raught*, reached.

Ragman, o. (q. *ragement*) madness.

Rageman, a statute of Justices assigned by *Edw.* 1. to hear all complaints of injuries done 5 years before.

Ragot, a cunning French begger, who wrote all his subtilties and died very rich.

Ragounces, *sa.* a kind of precious stone.

Raguset, a City in *Dalmatia*.

Ragwort, a bitter, cleansing herb.

Railighe, a town in *Essex*.

Railed, *Rei-*, (q. *rolled*) o. ran.

Raillery, f. jesting, merriment.

Raimund, *ge.* quiet.

Rains, fine linnen of

Rains, *Rennes*, a City of *Britanny* in *France*.

Rain-deer, a northern Hart with large Antlers.

Raised [*in Flesh*,] grown fat, spoken of a hawk.

Rake, so much of the Ships hull as over-hangs both ends of the keel.

Rakestele, o. the handle of a rake.

Ralphe, *Radulph*, g. helpful Council.

Rally, f. to reunite [dispersed Companies.]

Ramagious, belonging to

Ramage, f. boughes.

Ramage hawk, wild.

Rame, *No.* to reach.

Ramberge, f. a long swift Ship.

Ramboozе, *-buzze*, a drink of Eggs and Ale (or in summer, Milk and Rose-water) with Wine and Sugar.

Ramkin, a Fort (in the Isle *Waleberen* in *Zeland*) called the key of the *Netherlands*.

Rament, l. a scraping or remnant.

Ram-head, a great block with 3 sheevers, for the main and fore-Halliards.

Ramist, a follower of

Ramus, a modern Abridger of many Arts.

Rammo, a Haven in *Zeland*.

Ramosity, l. fulness of boughs.

Rampant, rearing up his fore-feet.

Rampier, *-part*, f. a fortress-wall or Bulwark.

Ram-

Rampick, *o.* [an old tree] beginning to decay at top.

Rampions, *Rapunculus*, an herb.

Ramsey, a famous Abbey in *Huntingtonshire*, and other small Towns

Ramsey-town, in Man Isle.

Ramsons, *Allium ursinum*, an herb.

Ran, *s.t.* an open rapine.

Rancidity, a being

Rancid, *l.* mouldy, musty.

Rancor, *-our*, *l.* rottenness, also malice or spight.

Rank as *Roke*, *o.* hoarse as a rook.

Randal, *Ranulph*, *sa.* pure help.

Ranges, pieces of timber (with wooden pins) to belay the ropes to.

Ranger, *Rainger*, as *Raunger*.

Ransome, *f.* to redeem, also [the price of] Redemption.

Ranters, of the Family of Love.

Ranula, *l.* a swelling under the tongue.

Ranular vein, the first branch of the outward throat vein ascending to the tongue.

Rap an *Ren*, *l.* and *sa.* snatch and catch (or else rend.)

Rapacity, *l.* a being

Rapacious, ravenous.

Rape, the ravishing a woman, also (in *Sussex*) a sixth part of that Country.

Rape, *o.* (*q. Rapid*,) haste, quickly.

Rape wine, a small wine, of water and the Mother of prest grapes.

Raphael, *h.* Physick of God.

Rapidity, *l.* a being

Rapid, *l.* swift, violent.

Rapine, *l.* an open violent robbery.

Rapinous, ravenous.

Rapport, *f.* a report, relation or resemblance.

Rapsodist, the Authour of a

Rapsody, *g.* a confused collection,

Raptu hæredis, a writ for the taking away an heir.

Rapture, *l.* a taking away by violence, also an Extasy.

Rarefaction, *-fying*, or causing

Rarity, *l.* a being

Rare, thin, who's quantity is more and substance less.

Rase, a measure of Corn, disused.

Rasion, *-sure*, *l.* a shaving.

Rascal of Boies, *o.* a great Company.

Raskail, *o.* trash.

Rasp, *-patory*, a grosser kind of File.

Market-Rasen, a Town in *Lincoln-shire*.

Ras algeuse, a Star in *Gemini*.

Rate, *o.* counselled, also the milt, *f.*

Rate tythe, for cattel kept in a parish less than a year.

Rathe, *Sa. Sf.* Early.

Ratifie, *l.* to confirm.

Ratiocinative, pertaining to

Ratiocination, *l.* reasoning.

Rationabili parte bonorum, a writ for the Widow (or children) claiming the Thirds.

Rationabilibus divisis, for the rectifying the bounds of 2 seigneuries.

Rationale, a book shewing

Rationality, a being

Rational, *l.* reasonable, also the High Priests Breastplate.

Rationary, belonging to account or reckoning.

Ratisbone, a City of *Bavaria*.

Ratle, *Crista galli*, the herb Coxcomb.

Ratles, [the Goat] cries.

Ratling-Cove, *c.* a Coachman.

Ratling-Mumpers, *c.* beggers at Coaches.

Ratlings, the steps of the ship-shrouds.

Ratton, *o.* a little rat.

Ratzenburgh, a Town in *Mecklenburg*.

Ravage, *f.* Spoil, havock.

Raucity, *l.* hoarsness.

Ravenglas, a Town in *Cumberland*.

Ravenna, a City of *Italy*.

Ravisable, *o.* Ravenous.

Ravensperg, a County in *Westphalia*.

Ravishment, *f.* an unlawfull taking away [of a Woman or Heir,] also as *Rape*.

Raundon, *o.* (*f. à la randon*) at random.

Raunge, *Range*, the Office of a

Raunger, *Ranger*, who conducts the straying wild beasts to the Forest.

Raunson, *o.* for Ransom.

Ray, *f.* a beam [of the Sun.]

Ray [*cloth*,] never coloured.

Rayes, *Reies*, *o.* Roundelaies, Songs.

Raynous, *o.* (*q. Roigneux*) Scabbed.

Re, an Isle near *Rochelle*.

Reach, the distance of two points of land which bear in a right line to one another.

Read, *Rede*, *o.* Counsel.

Reading, the chief town in *Barkshire*.

Reäfforested, made Forest again.

Reäl, *Sp.* a coyn worth 6d.

Reälize, to cause

Reälity, a being real.

Realty, opposed to *Personalty*.

Ream, (*Rieme*, *Ge.* a string) twenty quires, also a Realm.

Realti, *o.* for *Royalty*.

Rear, *o.* thin.

Reasonable aid, was a duty claimed by the Lord, to marry his Daughter or Knight his eldest son.

Reässume, *l.* to take again.

Reathen, *o.* soon.

Reättachment, a second attachment.

Rebate, as *Chamfer*, also to allow (what the interest would have com'n to) for antepaiment.

Rebaptization, a baptizing again.

Rebecca, *h.* fat and full.

Rebeck, a 3 ſtring'd fidle. alſo (*o.*) an old Trot.

Rebesk, as *Arabeſque*.

Rebus, *f.* a Name (or other conceit) expreſt in picture, (with an equivocal Motto)

Rebutter, *f.* a repelling the Heir by a Warranty from the Donour.

Recalcitrate, *l.* to kick backwards.

Recant, *l.* revoke, unſay.

Recapitulation, *l.* a brief repeating the heads.

Recaption, *l.* [a writ for one that ſuffers] a ſecond diſtreſs for the ſame cauſe.

Recargaiſon, *f.* a backfraught.

Recede, *l.* to go back.

Recent, *l.* freſh, new.

Recenſion, -*ſement*, *f.* a reckoning.

Receptacle, *l.* a ſtorehouſe.

Receptary, *f.* a note of Receipts.

Reception, two Planets being in each others dignity.

Receptitious, *l.* received.

Receptivity, a being

Receptive, apt to receive.

Receſs, *l.* a going back or aſide, a by-place.

Rechabites, ſons of *Rechab*, *Jer.* 35.

Reche, a Town in *Cambridg.*

Recheat, a Hunters leſſon, when they loſe the game &c.

Recidivation, *l.* a relapſe.

Recidivous, *l.* falling back.

Reciprocal, *l.* mutual.

Reciprocation, an interchanging.

Reciſion, *l.* a cutting off.

Recitation, a rehearſing.

Recitative, rehearſed [in *Operaes*.]

Reck, *Ret* *h.* *o.* care.

Reclaim, to tame [a hawk.]

Reclamation, *l.* a crying out againſt.

Recluſe, *l.* one cloiſter'd up,

R E

Recogitate, to ponder upon.

Recognition, a review, conſidering, or acknowledgement.

Recognitors, *l.* the Jurymen.

Recognitione adnullanda &c. a writ for the diſannulling a forced recogniſance.

Recognize, to conſider again.

Recognizee, to whom is made a

Recognizance, a bond of record from the

Recognizor, who acknowledges the Debt in Court, &c.

Recognizance, is alſo the Verdict of the Jury.

Recollect, *l.* to call to mind.

Recollects, a ſort of *Franciſcans*.

Reconvention, a contrary Action (in Civil Law) brought by the Defendant.

Record, an Act committed to writing in any of the Kings Courts, and is (when that Term is ended) uncontroulable.

Recordation, a remembering.

Recordare (or *Recordari*) *facias*, a writ for the Sheriff to remove a cauſe from an inferiour Court, to the Kings Bench or Common-Pleas.

Recorder, whom the Magiſtrate of any Town (having a Court of Record) aſſociates to himſelf for direction in Law.

Recordo et Proceſſu Mittendis, calling a Record (and the whole proceſs) from an Inferiour to the Kings Court.

Recovery, the obtaining a thing by Trial of Law.

Recoupe, *f.* to defalk or diſcount.

Recourſe, *l.* refuge, retreat.

Recoyl, *f.* to draw back [the tail.]

Recreance, *o*, againſt hope,

R E

Recreandiſe, *o.* Infidelity

Recreant, *f.* eating his words.

Recreantiſe, *f.* Cowardiſe.

Recreation, *l.* a refreſhment.

Recrementitious, full of

Recrement, *l.* droſs, dregs.

Recrimination, *l.* the returning a reproach or accuſation.

Recruit, ſupply, fill up.

Rectangle, *l.* an even angle.

Rectangled, having right angles or corners.

Rectification, *l.* a rectifying or making ſtreight.

Rectilineal, of right lines.

Recto, a writ of right, trying both for poſſeſſion and property, and if the Cauſe be loſt, there is no remedy.

Recto de dote, whereby a woman demands her whole Dower.

Recto de dote unde nihil habet, whereby (having no Dower aſſured) ſhe demands her Thirds.

Recto de rationabili parte, for a Coparcener &c. to recover his ſhare.

Recto de advocatione Eccleſiæ, for him that claims the Advowſen to himſelf and his Heirs in fee.

Recto de cuſtodiâ terræ et hæredis, for a Guardian in ſoçage, or appointed by the Anceſtors will.

Recto quando dominus remiſit, when the Lord (in whole Seigneury the Lan lies) remits the Cauſe to the Kings Court.

Recto ſur diſclaimer, when the Lord avows upon the Tenant, who diſclaims to hold of him.

Rectorial, belonging to a

Rector, *l.* a Governour.

Rector Eccleſiæ Parochialis, A Parſon [with a Vicaridge.]

Rectory, a Parſonage (with all the appurtenances.)

Rectitude, *l*, uprightneſs.

Rectus in Curiâ, he that stands at the Bar, and has nothing brought against him

Reculade, *f.* a recoyling.

Reculver, a Town in Kent.

Recuperatory, belonging to

Recuperation, *l.* a recovering.

Recure, *o.* recover.

Recurrent, *l.* running back

Recursion, *l.* a running back.

Recurvate, *l.* to bend back

Recusants, *Romanists*, or any that refuse to come to Church.

Red, *o.* meaning.

Red-Sea, the *Long-Sea*, dividing *Africa* and *Asia*.

Redacted, *l.* forced back.

Redamancy, -*mation*, *l.* a loving them that love us.

Redargue, to re- (or dis-) prove.

Redarguation, a controlling.

Redborn, a Town in *Hertfordshire*.

Reddendum, the reservation of Rent to the Lessor.

Redditive, belonging to

Reddition, *l.* a restoring or yielding; (in Law) an acknowledgment that the thing belongs not to himself.

Reddour, *o.* (*q. roideur*) violence.

Rede, *o.* advise, help.

Redeless, *o.* helpless.

Redford, a Town in *Nottinghamshire*.

Redemptions, *l.* Ransomes.

Redevable, *f.* obliged.

Redhibition, a forcing one to take that again which he sold.

Rediculus, a certain God, worshipt for frighting *Hannibal* from *Rome*.

Redient, *l.* returning, new.

Redintegration, *l* a renewing.

Redisseisin, a second *disseisin*.

Redition, *l.* a returning.

Redituaries, a sort of *Franciscans* having Lands, &c.

Redolent, *l.* sweet-smelling.

Redonate, *l.* to restore.

Redoubted, reverenced.

Redoubt, [the jutting out of the corners of] a Fort.

Redound, *l.* to abound.

Redowr, (*q. redoubleur*) *o.* turning, doubling.

Redowbting, *o.* praising.

Red shanks, *Irish Scots*.

Redstert, a red-taild-bird.

Redubbers, *Ad-*, they that buy stolen cloth and turn it to some other form or colour.

Reduction, *l.* a bringing back.

Redversies, *de Riparijs*, the family of the *Riverses* in *Cornwal*.

Redulcerate, *l.* to renew a wound.

Redundancy, *l.* a being

Redundant, overflowing, having too much.

Reduplicate, *l.* to double again.

Reduplication, as *Anadiplosis*.

Reduplicative, which doubles (or may be doubled) often.

Reed, *o.* red.

Reem, *La.* to cry.

Reëntery, the resuming a possession we had lately forgone.

Reer-County, as *Rier-*.

Reeve, *Reve*, *Greve*, *Sa.* a Governour, the Bailiff of a Franchise or Mannour.

Reeve the rope in the block, put it through.

Reevo, (Sp. *arriva*) up.

Reëxtent, a second extent upon Lands or Tenements.

Refection, *l.* a refreshing.

Refectory, -*tuary*, a Hall or dining-room.

Refel, *l.* to disprove.

Referendaries, *Rapporteurs*, Officers under the Masters of Requests (in *Germany* and *France*.)

Reflection, *l.* a bending or beating back.

Reflux, *l.* the flowing back.

Refocillate, *l* to cherish.

Reformado, *Sp.* an Officer who (having lost his men) is either cashier'd or put lower.

Reforms, [the hawk] prunes her feathers.

Refracted, *l.* weakned.

Refraction, *l.* a breaking open or a rebounding.

Refreide, *o.* refrain [for fear.]

Refractory, *l.* stubborn.

Refranation, a Planets becoming retrograde, while he is applying to another.

Refret, (*f. refrain*) the burden of a song.

Refrete, *o.* full [fraught.]

Refrigerate, *l.* to cool, refresh.

Refroiden, *o.* to cool.

Refrynyd [*hawk*,] *o.* neezing and casting water through her nostrils.

Refuge, *l.* a place of succour.

Refulgent, *l.* glistering.

Refund, *l.* to melt again, pour or pay back.

Refuite, -*use*, *o.* refuge.

Refusion, *l.* a pouring back.

Refute, *l.* to disprove.

Regal, *l.* Royal, Kinglike.

Regal of France, a costly ring offered by a King of *France* to St. *Thomas* of *Canterbury*, worn afterwards by King *Henry VIII*.

Regal Fishes, Whales and Sturgeons.

Regale, *f.* to feast like a King.

Regalia, *l.* the rights of a King.

Regality, *l.* Kingship.

Regalo, *Sp.* a Royal dainty.

Regardant, *f.* looking back or to.

Regard, the Office and jurisdiction of the

Regarder, the Overseer of all other Forest-Officers.

Regards, *f.* observations.

Regency, rule, government.

Regeneration, *l.* a being

Regenerate, -*ted*, born again.

Regenspurg, a town of lower *Bavaria*.

Regent, *l.* ruling.

Regerminate, *l.* to spring again.

Regi-

Regible, l. that may be ruled.

Regicide, l. a King-killer.

Regifical l. Royal, stately.

Regifugium, l. a feast kept (*Feb.* 23.) for the banishment of *Tarquin*.

Regio assensu, the writ of the Royal Assent to chuse a Bishop.

Regiment, l. Government, also the command of a Colonel, about ten Companies.

Register, a Record, or Recorder.

Registry, his Office and Books.

Reglutinate, l. to unglue or glue again.

Regnardise, to practise

Regnardism, the subtilty of

Regnard, f. a Fox.

Regius Professor, reader of Divinity, Hebrew, Greek, Law or Physick, founded by *Hen.* VIII. in each University.

Regrate, o. courtesie, estimation.

Regrator, formerly he that bought by the great and sold by retail, now he that buys and sells again in the same market or within 4 miles thereof, a Huckster.

Regratulate, to rejoyce (or give thanks) again.

Regress, *-sion*, l. a returning.

Regret, f. sorrow, an ill-will.

Regularity, l. a being

Regular, orderly.

Regulars, regular Priests, Monks under some particular rule.

M. Atil. Regulus, a Roman taken prisoner by the *Carthaginians*, and having liberty upon his parole, return'd accordingly and was put to death.

Regurgitate, l. swallow again.

†*Rehoboam*, h. breath of the people.

Rejection, l. a casting off.

Reif away, sc. snatch away.

[*Reiglement*, f. a ruling.

Reight, o. reached.

Regnous, o. ruinous.

Reimboscee, Sp. return to the wood, lye in ambush again.

Rehabilitation, the Popes bull for reinabling a Clergyman.

Rein, o. run.

Rejourn, *Readj-*, to adjourn again.

Rejoynder, (in Civil Law Duplication) an exception or answer to a Replication.

Reinforce, f. to strengthen again.

Reister, (*D. Ruyter*) a horsman.

Reit, o. a Sea-weed.

Reiterate, l. repeat again.

Reive, as *Reif*.

Rejumble, Li. to rise [in ones Stomack.]

Rekelness, o. rashness.

Reken, o. reckon.

Reking, a high copped hill in *Shropshire*.

Relaies and Limers, o. standers at advantage with darts to kill Deer.

Relapse, l. fall back.

Relatist, a reporter.

Relative, l. having relation to another thing.

Relaxate, l. loosen, release.

Relay, f. a setting on more hounds when the Deer and the rest are past by.

Release, an instrument whereby Estates, &c. are extinguished, enlarged, &c.

Relief, a certain paiment to the Lord at the entrance of some Tenants.

Relegation, a banishment [for a certain time.]

Relent, l. to grow soft or pitiful.

Relevant, relieving.

Relevate, l. to raise again.

Releeved up, o. rais'd my self up.

Relict, l. a widow, or any thing that is left.

Religate, l. to tye fast.

Relinquish, l. to forsake.

Reliquary, f. a place for

Reliques, l. what is left [of the Cloaths or bodies of Sts. deceased.]

Reliquator, l. he that hath the arrears of another in his hand.

Reluctance, *-ation*, l. a striving against.

Remede, Li. to remove, also a reward, and (in *T.*) a good colour [in the face.]

Remainder, an estate limited in Lands, &c. to be enjoy'd after the estate of another expired *e. g.* a man may grant land to one for term of his life, the Remainder to another for term of his life.

Remand, f. to command back again.

Remancipate, l. to sell or return a commodity into his hands that first sold it us.

Reme, o. take away, deny.

Remansion, l. a remaining.

Remersel, a town in *Zeland*.

Remembrancers, of the Exchequer, three, *viz.*

The Kings Remembrancer, who enters all Recognizances, &c.

The Lord Treasurers Remembrancer, he makes process against all Sheriffs, &c.

Remembrancer of the first Fruits, takes all compositions for first Fruits and Tenths.

Remes, o. for Realms.

Remew, o. to refuse.

Remigation, l. a rowing.

Remigration, l. a returning.

Reminiscence, l. a calling to mind.

Remiss, l. slack, careless.

Remissible, pardonable.

Remissionary, f. who is pardoned.

Remitter, restoring a man to his best and most ancient Title.

Remonstrance, a shewing of reasons; also an Instrument (of silver or gold) wherein the Sacrament is exposed on the Altar.

Remonstrants, *Arminians*.

Remora, l. a Sea-Lamprey which (they say) stops the course of a ship.

Remord, o. To cause.

Remorse, l. the biting or sting

Ring of Conscience.

Remote, *l.* far off, distant,

Remuable, *o.* moveable, ready.

Remunerate, *l.* to recompense.

Remus, Brother to *Romulus*.

Renably, *-ally*; *o.* ready.

Renal, *l.* belonging to the Kidneys.

Renardism, as *Regnar.-*

Renavigation, a sayling back.

Rencontre, *-cunter*, *f.* a sudden adventure or meeting

Rendevous, *Rendez-vous*, *f.* (Render your selves at) the place of Muster.

Rendlesham, *-lis-*, a town in *Suffolk*.

Reneez, *f.* Apostates.

Renegado, *Sp.* he that deserts his colours or Religion.

Renege, *l.* to refuse.

Renged, *o.* compassed about.

Reniant, *f.* a revolter.

Renimed, running Mead (in *Middlesex*) where the Barons assembled to claim their Liberties of King *John*.

Renitence, *-cy*, *l.* a resistance, or a shining.

Renks, *o.* for ranks.

Ren radder, *o.* run readily.

Rennes, a City in *France*.

Rents resolute, payable to the Crown out of Abbey-Lands.

Renodate, *l.* to unty.

Renomie, *o.* renown.

Renovate, *l.* to renew.

Renovelances, *o.* renewings.

Renversed, *f.* over-turned.

Renue, *o.* to pull or get.

Renumerate, *l.* to pay back.

Renunciate, *l.* to bring word again.

Renvoy, *f.* a sending back.

Reny her lay, *o.* deny her law.

Repairs, the Hares haunts.

Repandous, *l.* bent back.

Reparation, *l.* a mending.

Reparatione facienda, when one Joint-Tenant is willing to repair, and the other not.

Reparty, *f.* a subdivision also a reply.

Repast, *f.* a meal.

Repe, *o.* to pluck up, also to care.

Repastinate, *l.* to dig again about vines.

Repe and Renne, *o.* for rap and rend.

Repeham, a town in *Norfolk*.

Repatriate, *l.* to return to ones own Country.

Repellance, a repealing or disanulling.

Repensation, *l.* a recompensing.

Repentine, *l.* sudden.

Repercussion, *l.* a beating back.

Repercussive, belonging thereto, also a medicine driving the pain from that place.

Repertible, to be found.

Repertitious, *l.* found.

Repertory, *l.* an Inventory.

Repignerate, *l.* to redeem a pawn.

Repleader, to plead again.

Replete, *l.* full, filled.

Repletion, *l.* a filling.

Replegiare, to replevy or redeem a distress by putting in legal sureties.

Replegiare de averiis, a writ to release Cattle distrain'd, upon surety to answer the suit.

Replegiari facias, another to the same purpose.

Replevie, *-vin*, the bringing that writ, and releasing Cattel on that condition, also the bailing of a man.

Replevish, to let go upon bail.

Replication, *l.* an unfolding, also the Plaintiffs reply to the Defendants answer in Chancery.

Report, a relation or repetition of a case debated.

Reportator, *l.* he that carries back.

Repose, *l.* to lay upon, to rest.

Reposition, *l.* a setling again.

Reposition of the Forest, an Act whereby certain forest-grounds made purlieu, were (by a second view) laid to the Forest again.

Repossede, *l.* to possess again.

Repository, *l.* a storehouse.

Represe, *-rise*, *o.* reproof.

Reprehend, *l.* to reprove.

Reprehension, *l.* a reproving.

Representation, a likeness.

Representative, in the room of another, or he that supplies his place.

Repress, *l.* to keep down.

Reprimende, *f.* a reproof.

Reprisal, as Law of *Marque*.

Reprises, Yearly deductions out of a Mannour, as Pensions, &c.

Reprive, a respiting the Execution of the Law.

Reprobate, *l.* cast out of favour.

Reptile, *-itious*, *l.* creeping.

Repton, a Town in *Darbishire*.

Republique, *l.* a Commonwealth.

Repudiable, which may be

Repudiated, put away, divorced.

Repudious, *l.* villanous, hatefull.

Repugnancy, a being

Repugnant, *l.* contrary.

Repugne, *l.* to resist.

Repullulate, *l.* to burgen and spring again.

Repumicate, *l.* to smooth with a pumice-stone.

Reputation, *l.* credit.

Requests, *f.* Petitions.

Requiem, *l.* rest, Mass for the Dead, from

Requiem æternam dona eis Domine, part thereof.

Rere-County, See *Rier-*

Rere-ward, the hindmost part of the Army.

Resagor, *o.* Rats-bane.

Reseit, an admission of a third person to plead his right in a cause commenced between other two; also a bare admittance of plea.

Rescind, *l.* to cut asunder.

Rescissory, *-rian*, belonging to

Rescission, a disanulling or undoing.

Rescous,

Reſcous, f. a reſcue of a diſtreſs, or perſon arreſted.

Reſcuſſor, the Reſcuer.

Reſcribendary, a *Roman* Officer, who taxed Supplications.

Reſcript, l. a written anſwer to a Letter, petition, Writ, &c.

Reſearch, f. a continuance [of Services, &c.]

Reſentment, *Reſſentiment*, f. a true and ſenſible apprehenſion.

Reſeration, l. an unlocking.

Reſervation, l. a keeping back in ſtore; alſo as

Reſervedneſs, a being

Reſerved, cloſe, not free in diſcourſe.

Reſiance, *-idence*, a being

Reſiant, *-ident*, f. continually dwelling or abiding in a place.

Reſidentiary, he that reſides, or the place of abode.

Reſiduum, l. the reſt.

Reſignation, l. an unſealing; alſo reſigning [a benefice.]

Reſilience, *-liment*, *-ition*, l. a rebounding or ſtarting back.

Reſinous, *-naceous*, of Roſin.

Reſipiſcence, l. repentance.

Reſolution, l. untying, full purpoſe and intention.

Reſonant, l. ſounding again.

Reſort, *Reſſ-*, f. the authority or juriſdiction of a Court.

Reſource, f. as *Reſſource*.

Reſpiration, l. a taking breath.

Reſpectu computi Vicecomitis habendo, a writ for the reſpiting the Sheriffs account.

Reſpectful, giving reſpect.

Reſpective, according to ſeveral reſpects or relations.

Reſpite of homage, was a ſmall ſumme paid every fifth term for the forbearance of homage till the Prince were at leaſure to take it.

Reſplendent, l. gliſtering.

Reſpondent, l. he that anſwers the Opponent in diſputations or Interrogatories.

Reſpondeat Superior, Let the Mayor and Commons [of *London*] anſwer [for the Sheriffs inſufficiency.]

Reſponſalis, he that appears in Court for another.

Reſponſe, f. an anſwer.

Reſponſible, liable or able to anſwer or give account.

Reſponſion, ſurety.

Reſponſions, certain accounts made to the Knights of St. *John* of Jeruſalem.

Reſponſory, l. anſwering.

Reſport, o. reſpect or care.

Reſſide, o. ruſty.

Reſſource, f. a new ſpring or riſing again.

Reſtagnant, l. over-flowing.

Reſtagnation, a bubling up.

Reſtauration, l. a reſtoring or repairing.

Reſtible, l. tilled (or bearing) every year.

Reſtipulation, l. an engaging to anſwer an Action at Law.

Reſtitutione extracti ab Eccleſia, to reſtore one to the Church which he had recovered for Sanctuary.

Reſtitutione temporalium, for a Biſhop to recover his Temporalities and Barony.

Reſtitution, l. a reſtoring [one unlawfully diſſeiſed.]

Reſtiveneſs, a being

Reſtive, *-ty*, (f. *reſtif*) ſtubborn, drawing back.

Reſtriction, l. a reſtraint, or ſtraitening.

Reſtrict (or diſcriminal) line, ſeparating the hand from the arm.

Reſudation, l. a ſweating.

Reſvery, f. a raving, madneſs.

Reſul Alloh, Tu. (the Meſſenger of God) Mahomet.

Reſult, f. concluſion, iſſue, alſo as

Reſultancy, rebounding.

Reſummons, a ſecond ſummons.

Reſumption, l. a taking again [into the Kings hands, what he had (upon falſe ſuggeſtion) granted.]

Reſupination, l. a lying with the face upward.

Reſurrection, l. a riſing again.

Reſuſcitate, l. to raiſe again.

Retail, f. a cutting (or ſelling) in ſmall parcels.

Retainer, *Retei-*, a ſervant wearing the Livery and attending only upon ſpecial Occaſions.

Retaliate, l. to do like for like.

Retard, l. to ſtop or hinder.

Retchleſneſs, o. careleſneſs.

Retenementum, (in old deeds) a with-holding.

Retent, l. holden back, alſo unbent.

Retention, l. a retaining.

Retentive faculty, duly keeping the nouriſhment within the body.

Retiary, l. the Net-bearer [in fighting, &c.]

Reticence, l. ſilence, concealment.

Reticle, l. a ſmall net or caul.

Retinacle, l. a ſtay or hold.

Retinue f. a train of attendants.

Retort, f. a crooked body, a Lymbeck of glaſs, alſo to twiſt or turn back.

Retour, f. a return.

Retract, l. to revoke or draw back.

Retraction, l. a drawing back.

Retractation, a recanting.

Retraxit, an exception againſt one that had withdrawn his Action, ſaying (in open Court) He will proceed no further.

Retreat, f. a retiring [place.]

Retribution, l. a recompenſing.

Retriment, l. droſs or dregs.

Retrieve, (f. *retrouver*) to find again, to ſpring partridges again.

Retroaction, l. a driving back.

Retroactive, driving back.

Retrocede, l. to go back.

Retrocession, a retreating.

Retrocopulation, a coupling backward.

Retroduction, a bringing back.

Retrograde, l. to go (or going) back (contrary to the succession of the Signs.)

Retrogradation, a going back.

Retrogression, -ition, the same.

Retromingency, a staling backward.

Retromingents, Animals that piss backward.

Retrospection, l. a looking back.

Return, a Certificate of what is done in the Execution of writs &c.

Returns, Daies in Bank, allotted for the several sorts of proceedings in every term: wherein

Crastino, signifies the morrow after the day annexed;

Octabis, 8 daies after (inclusive)

Quindena, 15 daies after;

Tres, three weeks after;

Mense, that day moneth;

Quinque, that day 5 weeks.

Returno habendo, a writ for the return of Cattel (distrein'd and replevied) to him that has proved his distress lawfull.

Returnum Averiorum, for the return of the Cattel to the Defendant, when the Plaintiff doth not declare.

Returnum Irreplegiabile, for the final restitution of Cattel to the owner, found by the Jury to be unjustly distreined.

Reuben, h. Son of vision.

Reuda, an *Irish* Captain who seated himself in *Scotland*.

Reve, o. (q. bereave) spoil.

Reve, as *Reeve*.

Revelation, l. a discovering.

Master of the Revels, who hath the Ordering of the

Revels, f. Night-sports of dancing &c. in the Innes of Court, &c.

Revene, l. to return.

Revenue, f. yearly rent.

Reverberate, l. to reflect or beat back.

Reverberation (in Chymistry) the calcining of bodies by fire in a

Reverbitory, -beratory, l. a Lymbeck or Furnace.

Revere, l. to fear and honour.

Reverential, with reverence and aw.

Reverse, f. a back-blow, also the back-side.

Reversed, l. turned backward or upside down.

Reversion, l. a returning [of a possession to the former owner or his heirs.]

Revery, as *Resvery*.

Revert, l. to return.

Reverticle, l. a place to return unto.

Reves, o. Rents, Tythes.

Revestiary, *Revestry*, the Vestry, where Church-Vestments are kept.

Review, -vise, f. look over again.

Bill of Review, exhibited by leave of the Court when some errour appears after the Decree (in Chancery) is signed and enrolled.

Revivistion, l. a coming to life again.

Reviving, the same, also a renewing or bringing to life again.

Bill of Revivor, (in Chancery) when one party dies, to revive and finally determine the former Cause.

Reuks, o. for *Rooks*.

Reunite l. to joyn together again.

Revocable, l. capable of

Revocation, l. a calling back.

Revolt, f. to fall away.

Revolve, l. to toss up and down.

Revolution, l. a turning round to the first point.

Revulsion, l. a pulling up or away, also a forcing of humours to contrary parts.

Rew, o. to take pity.

Rewet, (f. rouette) the lock of a harquebuse.

Rewis, o. (f. rues) streets.

Rewish [pigeon] D. earnest in copulation.

Rewey [cloth] unevenly wrought, or full of rews.

Reygate, a Town in *Surrey*.

Reyne, o. [clean] water.

Rhabdomancy, g. Divination by a rod or staff.

Rhadamant, -thus, *Æacus* and *Minos*, the 3 feigned Judges in hell.

Rhagides, g. the third skin encompassing the eye.

Rhætia, higher and lower (*Grisons* and *Boidrij*) bordering on *Helvetia*.

Rhapsody, as *Rapsody*.

Rhedarious, l. belonging to a Charret, Waggon or Coach.

Rheggio, a City of *Naples*.

Rheimes, a City of *Champagne* in *France*.

Rhenish, belonging to the

Rhene, *Rhine*, a *German* river.

Rhenen, a town in *Utrecht* and *Westphalia*.

Rhesus, a King of *Thrace* slain in his aid of *Troy*.

Rhetorical, belonging to a

Rhetor, -rician, he that useth or teacheth

Rhetorick, g. the Art of speaking Eloquently, or well and wisely.

Rhinfield, a town of *Schwaben*.

Rhineberg, or *Berck*, a town of *Colen*.

Rhinoceros, -rote, g. an *Indian* beast with a horn on his nose.

Rhode le Duché, a town of *Limburgh*.

Rhodomel, g. honey of Roses.

Rhodus, *Rhodes*, a Mediterranean Island where (they say)

ſay, the Sun (to whom 'tis conſecrate) ſhines every day in the year.

Rhomb, Rhumb, g. a ſpinning wheel, alſo a figure of equal ſides but unequal angles, as a quarry of glaſs.

Rhombs, the points of the Mariners compaſs.

Rhomboidal, belonging to a rhomb or to a

Rhomboides, g. a romb whereof 2 ſides are longer than the other two, alſo a muſcle in the ſhoulder-blade.

Rhonchiſonant, l. imitating (by way of jeer) the noiſe of ſnorting.

Rhoſne, a river in *France*.

Rhubarb, a plant (for its wholeſomeneſs) called the Friend, Life, Heart, and Treacle of the Liver.

Rhyparographer, g. a writer (or painter) of baſe trifles.

Rhythmical, made in or belonging to

Rhythm, g. ryme, meeter, harmony, proportion.

Rial, o. for Royal.

Rialto, a Marble bridge at *Venice*, where the Merchants meet.

Rib, the diviſion between the feathers in a quill, alſo the ſide timber of a Ship.

Ribadavia, a mild White-wine made at

Ribadavia, a town of *Gallicia*.

Riband, (in Heraldry) the 8th. part of a Bend.

Riband, f. a baud.

Ribaldrie, f. roguery, whoredom.

Ribib, o. for ribaud.

Ribible, o. a rebeck or fidle.

Riballa, ſtrong *Zant* wines.

Riche-Cour, a town in *Lorrain*.

Richard, ſt. of a ſtrong nature.

Richmond, (q *Rich Mount*) a town in *Surrey*, alſo the Chief Town of

Richmondſhire, part of *Yorkſhire*.

Riches of Marterns (or *ſables*,) a great company of them.

Rickmansworth, a town in *Hertfordſhire* and *Buckinghamſhire*.

Riddeled, o. plaited, wrinkled.

Riddle-cakes, *La.* thick ſour-cakes.

Ricture, l. a grinning.

Rides, [the ſhip] is holden faſt with the anchors.

Ride a croſs, with the yards hoiſed up to the hounds.

Ride a good (or great) road (and ſtreſs,] where the Wind and Sea had much power.

Riddle, ſ. an oblong ſieve (to ſeparate the ſeed from the Corn.)

Riders, great timbers bolted on weak places of the Ship.

Ridg-cully, c. a Goldſmith.

Ridgil, which hath loſt but one ſtone.

Ridiculous, l. to be laughed at.

Riding Clerk, one of the ſix Clerks of the Chancery.

Ridings, the Eaſt, Weſt and North diviſions of *Yorkſhire*.

Riens, f. nothing.

Rier County, a place appointed by the Sheriff (after his Court ended) for the receipt of the Kings money.

Rife, o. for rifle.

Rifts, a corruption of the horſes Palate.

Rigation, l. a watering.

Ridge, *Rudg*, o. the back.

Rigging, the ropes belonging to the Maſts or yards.

Rigel, Orions left foot.

Rightwiſe, *Sa.* Righteous.

Rigidity, l. a being

Rigid, l. ſtiff, ſurly, ſevere.

Right the helm, keep it upright.

Rigols, o. a claricord [inſtrument.]

Rigorous, l. full of

Rigour, hardneſs, ſeverity.

Rimmon, h. a Pomegranat.

Rimoſity, a being

Rimoſe, *-ſous*, l. full of Chinks.

Rimpeled, o. for rumpled.

Rine, *No.* to touch.

Ringelenſtein, a town in *Weſtphalia*.

Riner, *Che.* a very good caſt.

Ring-bolts, for the tackle of the Ordnance.

Ring-head, an engin to ſtretch woollen.

Ring-tail, a Kite with a whitiſh tail.

Ring-walk, a hunters round walk.

Ring-wood, a town in *Hantſhire*.

Rio de la hacha, a ſmall *Weſt India* Province.

Rining, o. for raining, dropping.

Rintelin, a town in *Weſtphalia*.

Riot, the forcible doing an unlawful act by 3 (or more) aſſembled therefore.

Riparious, l. belonging to water-banks.

Ripariæ, the water within the bank.

Ripen, a town in North-*Jutland*.

Riphæan-hills, *Hyperboræan* Mountains of *Scythia*.

Ripley, a town in *Yorkſhire*.

Rippon, in *York-ſhire*.

Riple the flax, *No.* wipe off the veſſels.

Ripper, *Sſ.* a pedder, dorſer, or badger.

Ripiers, that bring fiſh from the Sea-coaſt to the In-land.

Riſe, o. beauty.

Riſhe, o. for ruſh.

Riſible, l. capable of

Riſion, l. laughing.

Riſingham, a town in *Northumberland*.

Riſing-timbers, the hooks placed on the keel.

Riſings, the thick planks on which the timbers of the decks do bear at boths ends.

Riſque, f. danger, hazard.

Ritual, belonging to

Rites, l. Cuſtomes, Ceremonies.

Rituals, books containing the Rites of the Roman Church.
Rivage, *f.* the water-side.
Rivality, the envie of
Rivals, Corrivals, two fetching water from the same river, in love with the same thing, &c.
Riveling, *o.* turning in and out.
Rivulet, *l.* a small river.
Rixation, *l.* a wrangling.
Rizons, a City of *Illyria*.
Road, a place near the Land for a Ships riding.
Wild Road, with little land on any side.
Roader, a Ship riding at anchor in a road.
Roan, a dark horse-colour.
Roan, a town in *France*.
Robert, *Ge.* famous counsel.
Robertines, a religious order erected by
Robert Flower, whose Father *Took Flower* was twice Maior of *York*.
Roberdsmen, Mighty thieves, like Robin-hood.
Robigalia, May-feasts in honour of
Robigus, a Roman God preserving Corn from being
Robiginous, *l.* blasted.
Robins, the small lines that make fast the Sails to the yards.
Roboration, *l.* a strengthening.
Roboreau, *l.* of Oak.
Roburnean, *l.* the same.
Robur, a place in Roman Prisons whence men were thrown head long.
Robusteous, *l.* strong as Oak.
Roch, *o.* as *Rock*.
Rochelle, a town in *France*.
Rochester, a City in *Kent*.
Roche de Marche, a Town in *Luxemburgh*.
Rochet, *f.* a frock, also a Bishops Vestment.
Rochetta, as *Polverine*.
Rocket, an herb smelling like milk burnt-to.
Rod, a Pearch, or Pole.

Rodage, *f.* a toll exacted by some French Lords of Carts passing by their Lordships.
Rode, *Rud*, *o.* Complexion.
Rod (or Rad) Knights, certain Servitors, who held their Land by serving their Lords on horse-back.
Rodnet, a net for blackbirds or Wood-cocks.
Rodomond, *f.* one that useth
Rodomontades, *l.* the boastings of
Rodomonte, a vapouring Hector in *Orlando Furioso*.
Rofe, *o.* did rend and rive.
Rofe-tyle, creast or ridge-tyle.
Roe, a kind of Deer.
Rogal, *-lion*, belonging to
Rogus, a great [funeral] fire.
Rogation, a desire, prayer.
Rogation-week, *Gang-week*, *Grass-week*, the next week but one (of prayers, processions and abstinence) before Whitsunday.
Rogatists, the moderate sort of Donatists.
Roggeth, *o.* for rocketh.
Roger, *q.* *Ruger*, *D.* quiet, or
Rodgar, strong Counsel.
Roger, *c.* a Cloak-bag.
Rogitate, *l.* to ask [often.]
Roignous, *o.* ruinous.
Roile, *o.* to range.
Roin, *o.* a skar.
Roiston, a town in *Hertfordshire*.
Rider-roll, a Schedule added to a roll or record.
Rolls, *Domus Conversorum*, the place where the Chancery Rolls are kept.
In Rolls, with rolls of gold on the edges of the Covers.
Rollo, a Danish Captain, who seated himself in *Normandy*.
Roman Indiction, 15 or 3 five years, at the end of which the *Romans* exacted their several Tributes, 1. Of Gold. 2. Silver. 3. Brass and Iron.
Romancist, *sp.* a composer of

Romances, feigned histories.
Romanize, to imitate the
Romans, people of *Rome*.
Romanists, Papists.
Romant, the most eloquent French, or (in *Lorrain* and the borders of *Germany*) that language which is not *German*.
Romford, a town in *Essex*.
Romney, a Town in *Kent*.
Romer, *o.* wider.
Romberville, a town in *Lorrain*.
Romboyld, *c.* with a warrant.
Rome-feoh, and
Romescot, as Peterpence.
Rome, the cheif City of *Italy*, built by
Romulus, Grand-son of *Numitor* (King of *Albans*) by his Daughter *Sylvia* and *Mars*, who being exposed on the bank of *Tiber*, was nourished (they say) by a Wolf, and (at last) was hurried away in a Whirlwind.
Roncevale, *Roscida vallis*, a town of *Navar*.
Rondacher, he that bears a
Rondache, *f.* a round target.
Rondel, *o.* as *Roundelay*.
Ronges (*q.* *Ranges*) *o.* the sides of a ladder.
Rondelier, *f.* an user or maker of such targets.
Rood of Land, a quarter of an Acre.
Rood-loft, between the Church and Chancel, where was placed the
Rood, *sa.* a Crucifix, or the Image of Christ upon the Cross.
Roof-trees, small timbers (from the half-deck to the forecastle) to bear up the gratings and ledges wherein the Nettings lye.
Roop, *No.* hoarsness.
Rooper, an *East India* Coin, about 2 s. 9 d.
Rope-yarnes, the yarns of any rope untwisted.
Rore, *o.* uproar.
Ropen, *o.* to reap.
Roral, *-rid*, *-rulent*, dewy.

Roriferous, *l.* dew-bringing.
Rosere, *o.* a Rose-plat.
Rosial, *o.* Red.
Rosimunda, (*Sa.* Rose of peace) she was forced by *Herminges* to drink the poison which she offered him, by whom she had procured the death of her Husband *Alboinus* (King of the *Lombards*) because he drank a health to her in a cup made of her Fathers skull.
Rosary, *l.* a bed or garland of roses, a rose-water-still, also Fifteens, a pair of beads (of 15 Pater-nosters and 150 Aves) much used by the
Arch-confraternity of the *Rosary*, instituted by St. *Dominick*.
Rosid, *l.* dewy.
Roses, a port town in *Catalonia*.
Roseoman, an *Irish* County.
Rose, the flower of *Venus*, consecrated by *Cupid* to *Harpocrates* the God of silence.
Under the Rose, among private Lovers, not to be divulged.
Rosi-Crucians, Chymists, Brothers of the Rosy-Cross.
Rosion, *l.* a gnawing.
Rosse, a *Scotish* County, also a town in *Hereford*.
Rostration, *l.* a putting in the beak or bill.
Rostoc, a Town of *Mecbleburg*.
Rot, a file or 6 Soldiers.
Rotal, like a wheel.
Cropping of the Rotan, *c.* the Carts tail.
Rotation, *l.* a wheeling.
By Rote, (*f. par rotine*) roundly, as a wheel runs.
Rotheram, a town in *Yorkshire*.
Rotherfoil, the dung of
Rother-beasts, *No.* horned-.
Rotterdam, a town in *Holland*.
Rotulus Wintoniæ, Domesday book.
Rotundity, *l.* roundness.
Rou, *o.* ugly, froward.
Rove, the little iron plate to which the Clinch-nails are clinched; also (*o.*) did rive.
Rouge, *f.* red.
Rouge-Cross, and
Rouge-Dragon, two pursuivants at arms.
Rought, *o.* cared.
Rouncevals, Pease that came from
Ronceval, a place at the foot of the *Pyreneans*.
Roundel, a ball (in Heraldry) also as
Roundelay, *f.* a shepherds song or dance.
Roundlet, an uncertain measure from 3 to 20 Gallons.
Round-house, the uppermost room of a ships stern.
Round-in (or *aft*) let rise the Main or fore-tack, &c. when the wind larges upon them.
Roune, *o.* to cease.
Rounds, the fragments of Statues.
Rout, *f.* an assembly of 3 (or more) to commit an unlawfull act.
Routeth, *o.* snorteth.
Rowland, *Rolland*, *Rodland*, *Ge.* Land-Counsel, (*I. Orlando.*)
Rowle, the round piece wherein the whip-staff goes.
Rowney, *o.* a Cart-horse.
Rounge, *o.* to gnaw.
Rowning, *o.* silence, whispering in the ear.
Rowpand, *o.* Calling.
Rowse, raise [a hart.]
Rowses, [the hawk] shakes her self.
Rowse-in the cable, hale-in so much as lies slack.
Rowt, *Rawt*, *No.* to bellow.
Rowt, a Company [of Wolves.]
Colour de Roy, *f.* the King of France's colour, Violet.
Royal, *f.* Kingly.
Royal Society, a Fellowship of Noble and Ingenious men (founded 14 *Car.* 2.) for the improvement of Natural Knowledge.
Royalist, *f.* a lover of the King.
Royalty, *f.* the Kings Prerogative.
Royston, a town in *Cambridgshire*.
R. P. Res-publica, the Common-Wealth, also as
Regius Professor.
Rubace, *-cel*, a yellowish precious-stone.
Rubefaction, *l.* a rubefying or making red.
Rubet, *l.* a toad-stone.
Rubicon, the large *Italian* river *Runcone*.
Rubicund, *-dous*, *l.* bloud-red.
Rubid, *l.* ruddy.
Rubie, *l.* a red precious-stone.
Rubiginous, rusty. See *Rob-*.
Rubor, *l.* redness.
Rubricate, *l.* to make red.
Rubrick, *l.* a Title, Rule or Sentence in Red, a Calendar of Saints and Festivals.
Rubrificative, [a strong plaister] making the place look red.
Rucking, *o.* lurking.
Ructation, *l.* a belching.
Rudg-washt Kersey, made of fleece-wooll, washt only on the Sheeps back.
Rudge-bone, *o.* *Os sacrum*, the rump-bone.
Rudheath (in *Cheshire*) was a Sanctuary (for a year and a day) to Offenders.
Rudiments, *l.* Principles or first plain instructions.
Rue, *Dev.* to sift.
Ruel-bone, *o.* the whirl-bone of the knee.
Ruff, Pope, a fish like a small pearch.
Ruffin, *c.* the Devil.
Ruffler, *c.* a notorious Rogue.
Ruff-peck, *c.* bacon.
Ruffians-hall, Smithfield, where trials of skill were plaid by Ruffianly people.
Rugby, a Town in *Warwickshire*.

Ruzen, an Iſland of *Pomerania*.

Rugoſity, *l.* a being

Rugoſe, *-ſous*, full of wrinkles.

Ruinous, *l.* falling to decay.

Rum, Kill-devil, a *Barbado's* drink ſtronger than brandy.

Rum, *c.* gallant.

Rum boozing welts, *c.* bunches of grapes.

Rumboyl. *c.* the Watch.

Rum-Cully, *c.* a rich fool.

Rum dropper, *c.* a Vintner.

Rum-gutlers, *c.* Canary.

Rum-hopper, *c.* a drawer.

Rum-padders, *c.* brave high-way men.

Rum-vile, *c.* London.

Rumb, as *Rhomb*.

Rumbeg, *Tu.* Lord of Rome, the Pope.

Rumia, the Goddeſs of ſucking.

Rumidg (or *Rummage*) the hold, clear it of lumber, for the ſtowing of goods.

Rumiforate, *-ize-*, *l.* to report abroad.

Ruminate, *l.* to chew the Cud, alſo to ponder.

Ruminus, [*Jupiter*] beflowing teats or breaſts.

Rumſey, two towns in *Hamſhire*.

Rumſchab, *P.* the King of Rome, the Pope.

Runcinus, a load-horſe, or Cart-horſe.

Runcina, the Goddeſs of

Runcation, *l.* weeding.

Run, that part of the ſhips hull under water, which comes lanker by degrees from the floor-timber to the ſtern-poſt.

Rune, Somerſet. a water-courſe.

Runge, *No.* a ſlacker.

Rung-heads, the ends of the

Rungs, the ground-timbers which give the floor of the ſhip.

Runlet, as *Roundlet*.

Runnel, *No.* Pollard-wood.

Runner, a rope uſed in the hoiſing of heavy things.

Over-hale the Runner, pull down that end with a hook in it, to hitch into the ſlings &c,

Rupelmond, a Town in *Flanders*.

Ruption, *l.* a breaking.

Ruptor, *l.* a breaker.

Ruptory, *f.* a Corroſive, or that which hath power to break.

Rupture wort, an herb good for a

Rupture, *l.* a burſtneſs.

Rural, *l.* of the Countrey.

Rural Deanry, the Juriſdiction of a

Rural Dean, an Officer under the Arch-Deacon, for diſpatch of buſineſs.

Ruremond, a town in *Gelderland*.

Rurigene, *l.* born in the Country.

Ruſca apum, a hive of bees.

Ruſh-grown, as *Bob-tail* (in Archery.)

Ruſhin-Caſtle, in Man Iſle.

Ruſſia [*alba*] Muſcovy.

Ruſſia nigra, a Province in *Poland*.

Ruſtication, *l.* a dwelling in the Country.

Ruſticity, *l.* a being

Ruſtick, *-cal*, clowniſh.

Rut, Copulation of Deer, alſo the daſhing of the ſea againſt any thing.

He Rutes it, *Che.* cries fiercely.

Ruth, *h.* watered or filled.

Rutilant, *l.* gliſtering like gold.

Rutilate, *l.* to ſhine or make bright.

Ruttier, (*f. Routier*) a direction to find out Courſes (by Sea or Land,) alſo an old beaten Soldier (that knows all the places.)

Ry, *o.* a ſwelling about the hawks head.

Ryal, *o.* for Royal.

Rye, a Sea-town in *Suſſex*.

Ryparographer, as *Rhypa-*.

Ryfelere, *o.* a hawk that only rifles the feathers of a Fowl.

Rynt ye, *Che.* By your leave, ſtand handſomly.

S.

S*Abaoth*, *h.* Hoſts, Armies.

Sabatons, *o.* Soldiers boots.

Sabbath, *h.* [Day of] Reſt.

Sabatarians, Obſervers of the *Jewiſh* Sabbath.

Sabbatical [*year*] the Seaventh, when the Jews reſted from Tillage, &c.

Sabbatiſm, a keeping of the Sabbath.

Sabellians, Hereticks that followed one

Sabellius, he held but One Perſon in the Godhead, under 3 names, &c.

Sable, *f.* black (in Heral.) alſo a rich fur of a little *Tartarian* beaſt.

Sabrina, the Severn River.

Sabulous, *l.* Sandy, Gravelly.

Saburrate, *l.* to balaſt a ſhip.

Saccharine, *l.* of Sugar.

Sac, *Sacha*, (*Sa.* Cauſe) the Royalty which the Lord of a Mannor claims, of holding plea in Cauſes of debate among his Tenants.

Sacaburth, *-bere*, he that is robbed.

Saccus cum brochia, was a Tenure by finding a Sack and a broach for the uſe of the Kings army.

Sacerborgh, *Sicker-*, a ſufficient pledge or Cautioner.

Sacerdotal, *l.* Prieſtly.

Sachem, a Prince or Ruler among the Weſt-*Indians*.

Sacksfettes, *o.* Either feat or fat (full) ſacks.

Sackleſs, *No.* Innocent.

Sackbut, *Sp.* a drawing trumpet.

Sack of wool, 26 stone of 14 pound. in *Scotland* 24 stone of 16 pound.

Sacrafield Rent, paid by some Tenants of *Cuton* Manor in *Sommerset*.

Sacramental, *l.* belonging to a

Sacrament or Oath.

Sacramentaries, Calvinists in the Doctrine of the Sacrament.

Sacrary, *l.* a Sextry or Vestry.

Sacre, *l.* to hallow or dedicate

Sacred Artery, descending to the marrow of *Os Sacrum*.

Sacred vein, a branch of the flank vein running thither.

Sacred Majesty, the Kings inviolable person.

Sacriferous, bearing holy things.

Sacrificial, belonging to

Sacrifices, holy offerings.

Sacrilegious, *l.* committing

Sacrilege, *l.* the robbing of God, a Church, &c.

Sacristy, *l.* a vestry.

Sacrist, *-stan*, a Sexton or Vestry-keeper.

Sadducism, the doctrine of the

Sadduces a Jewish Sect, who received only the Pentateuch, believed no Spirit, &c.

Safe-conduct, a security gien by the Prince (under the broad Seal) to a stranger, for his quiet coming in and passing out of the Realm.

Safe-pledge, a surety for a mans appearance.

Sagacity, *l.* a being

Sagacious, quick of apprehension.

Sagamore, an Indian King.

Sagapenum, the gum of the plant *Ferula* or Fenel-giant.

Sagibaro, *Sachbaro*, *sa.* a Justice.

Saginate, *l.* to cram.

Sagittal, *l.* of an arrow, also he streight seam upon the ead.

Sagittary, *-rius*, the Archer (or Centaure) in the Zodiack.

Sagittiferous, *l.* shaft-bearing.

Sagittipotent, a cunning Archer.

Saguntine, balonging to

Saguntus, a City of *Valencia* in *Spain*.

Saie, (*Sp. Saietta*) a kind of stuff.

Sailen, *o.* for Assail.

Sailors, Seamen, also (*o.*) dauncers.

Sain alse, *o.* for seen also.

Saint Anthonies fire, a hot Cholerick blood rising to a tetter.

St. Andrews, a City in *Scotland*.

St. Denis, the Patron of *France*.

St. Die, a town in *Lorrain*.

St. Domingo, the cheif town of *Hispaniola*.

St. Helene, the *Sea-Inne*, an Isle (in the way to the Indies) where they take in much water.

St. Hippolyte, a town in *Lorrain*.

St. Hubert, a City in *Luxemburgh*.

St. Laurence, as *Madagascar*.

St. Malo, a Port of *Britany*.

Mont St. Michel, a town on a Rock in the Sea between *Britany* and *Normandy*.

St. Miel, a town in *Lorrain*.

St. Nicholas, a town in *Muscovy* and *Lorrain*.

St. Omer, a town in *Artois*.

St. Patrick, the Patron of *Ireland*.

St. Quentin, a town in *Picardy*.

Saint-foin, *f.* holy-grass, *Medic-fodder*, Spanish Trefoyl, Snail (or horned) Clover-grass.

Saint John to borow, *o.* with good speed (he undertaking for you.)

Saint Piarre, a Palsey and cramp together.

Saintwary, *o.* Sanctuary.

Saker, (*f. Sacre*) a kind of hawk, and peice of Ordnance.

Salacia, the Goddess of water.

Salacious, *l.* full of

Salacity, lust, wantonness.

Salad, as *Salet*.

Salamanca, an University of *Leon*.

Salamander, *l.* a beast (like a lizard) that will live (for a while) in the flames.

Salarian, *l.* of Salt.

Salarian verse, sung by the Priests of *Mars*.

Salariated, having a

Salary, *l.* a stipend or wages, (as needful as Salt.)

Salarium, Salt-Custom.

Salebrity, *l.* a being

Salebrous, rugged, uneven.

Salenæ, *Salndy* (or *Sandy*) in *Bedfordshire*.

Salet, *-lade*, *f.* a head-piece.

Salew, *o.* for salute, honour.

Saliant, *l.* (in Heraldry) leaping.

Saligots, *f.* Water-nuts or water-Caltrops.

Salgemma, a clear *Hungarian* Salt like Cristal.

Salij, the 12 Priests of *Mars*.

Solene, a Salt-pit, vate or house.

Saline of the Levant, hard Salt extracted from sea-froth.

Salinous, *l.* of Salt or Salt-pits.

Salique Land, *France*, or the Land about

Sala, a River in *Misnia*.

Salique Law, that no Woman shall reign or Inherit Land. *De terra salica nulla portio hæreditatis mulieri veniat*, *&c.*

Salisbury, *Sarum*, the chief City of *Wiltshire*, whose Cathedral hath Gates, Windows and Pillars answering the Months, Daies and hours in a Year.

Salivarious, like spittle.

Salivation, a fluxing by spittle.

Sallow, the Goats willow.

Sally, *Sp.* to issue out [upon the besiegers.]

Salmacian, *-idan*, belonging to

Salmacis, a Fountain in *Caria* where the Nymph *Salmacis* and *Hermaphroditus* became one, and is said to effeminate all that drink or bath in it.

Salmagundi, *I.* a dish of cold Turky and other things.

Salmon-pipe, an engine to catch them in.

Salmon sewse, the issue or young fry.

Salmoneus, King of *Elis*, struck to hell with a thunderbolt, as he was thundering with his Chariot over a bridge of Brass.

Salomon, *c.* the Mass.

Salomon, *Sol-*, *h.* peaceable.

Salow, *o.* white (*D. Saligh*, happy) contrary to the present use.

Salsamentarious, *l.* belonging to Salt things.

Salsipotent, *l.* ruling the Sea.

Salsure, *l.* a salting.

Saltatory, *l.* belonging to

Saltation, *l.* a leaping.

Saltatorium, a Deer-leap.

Saltimbanco, *I.* a Montebank.

Saltuary, *l.* a forester.

Salture, *l.* a leaping.

Saltkot, a town in *Lincolnshire*.

Salvage-money, allowed (by the Civil Law) to the Ship that saves another from enemies.

Salva guardia, the Kings protection to a stranger fearing violence for seeking his right at Law.

Salvatel vein, runs through the wrist into the hand to the division of the third and little fingers.

Salubrity, wholsomness, also healthfulness.

Salve, *l.* God save you.

Salvediction, a salting.

Salver, a broad plate (with a foot) used in giving Beer, &c. to save the Carpet or Cloaths.

Salus, a gold Crown coyn'd by *Hen.* 5th. in *France*.

Salutary, *l.* wholesome.

Salutatory, *l.* where people stand to salute a Prince.

Salutiferous, *l.* bringing health, Salvation, or safety.

Salutigerous, *l.* bringing commendations from one.

Salzbourg, a City in *Bavaria*.

Samaritans, people of *Samaria*, part of *Syria*.

Sambenito, *San* (*or Santo*) *Benito*, *sp.* a Sack-cloth in which Penitents are reconciled to the Church.

Sambre, a river of *Hainault*.

Sambuke, *l.* a dulcimer, also an engine of war.

Sameile, *sc.* as much.

Samian, belonging to

Samos, an Isle where were good earthen pots and whetstones.

Samet, *Sammet*, *D.* Sattin or Velvet.

Samoners, *o.* for summoners.

Samogitia, a Province of *Poland*.

Samonds, *de sancto Amando*, an ancient family in *Wilts*.

Samothracia, *Dardania*, an Ægæan Isle.

Samplar, (Exemplar) a pattern [of needle-work] or rather (for Sarpliar) the Canvas on which the Scholars work.

Sampson, *h.* there the second time.

Samuel, *h.* heard (or placed) of God.

Sanable, *l* curable.

Sanative, *l.* healing.

Sanballat, *h.* a bramble hid in secret.

Sance-bell, *Sanctus bell*, wont to be rung when the Priest said, *Sanctus*, *Sanctus*, *Sanctus*, *Dominus*, *Deus Sabaoth*.

Sanchia, *Sancta*, a womans name.

Sanctification, *l.* a making holy.

Sanctiloquent, speaking holily.

Sanctimony, *-ity*, *l.* holiness.

Sanction, *l.* a decree.

Sanctuary, *l.* a holy place, a refuge for Offenders.

Sanctum Sanctorum, the most holy part of the Temple.

Sand, *o.* sending.

Sandal, *h.* an old-fashion'd open shoe; also as

Sanders, *Saunders*, a precious physical *Indian* wood, of 3 sorts, Red, white and yellow.

Sandapile, *l.* a bier.

Sandarack, *l.* Red Arsenick or Orpine (for paint.)

Sand-bag, on which the Graver turns his plate.

Sandwich, a port-town in *Kent*.

Sandever, *Suin-*, *f.* (the fat of glass) a very white salt easily dissolving.

Sandon-Castle, in *Wight-Isle*.

Sandwich, a Town in *Kent*.

Sand-gavel, a payment for liberty to dig sand.

Sanglant, *f.* bloudy.

Sanglier, *f.* a wild boar.

Sanguin, *-nary*, *-neous*, *-nolent*, *l.* bloudy.

Sanguis draconis, the red gum of the Dragon-tree.

Sanhedrim, *-in*, *h.* the supream Court or Council of the Jews, *viz.* the High-Priest and 70 Elders.

Sanjacks, *Sangiacks*, Turkish Governours of Cities, Next (in Dignity) to *Bashaws*.

Sanicle, *l.* a healing herb.

Sanity, *l.* health, soundness.

Sankfin, *Sang-fin*, *f.* the final end of a lineage.

Santalum, Sanders.

Santon, a Town in *Cleveland*.

Santo, *-on*, *Sp.* a great Saint.

Saphen (or *Saphana*) *vein*, the Mother vein, the first branch of the thigh vein.

Saphick (or *Sapphique*) *verse*,

verse, of a Trochee, Spondee, Dactyl, and two Trochees invented by

Sapho, *Sappho*, a Poetress of *Mitylene*.

Saphire, an *Indian* azure stone.

Sap-green, the Juice of the Rhamnus (or Christs thorn) berry (for dying and paint.)

Sapidity, *-por*, *l.* a being

Sapid, *l.* Savory.

Sapientipotent, mighty in

Sapience, *l.* wisdom.

Sar, a river in *Lorrain*.

Saraband, *I.* a kind of quick air in Musick.

Sarah, *h.* Lady or Mistress.

Sarbrucken, a town of *Triers*.

Sarcasm, *g.* a biting taunt.

Sarcastical, belonging thereto.

Sarcel, a hawks pinnion.

Sarcenet, a kind of thin Taffata.

Sarcinate, *l.* to load with packs.

Sarcinarious, belonging to packs.

Sarcling-time, *f.* weeding-.

Sarcocolla, *g.* a healing *Persian* gum.

Sarcoma, *g.* a bunch of flesh growing on the nose.

Sarcophage, *g.* Eat-flesh, a stone wherein bodies enclosed do quickly consume, also any tomb.

Sarcotick, *g.* breeding new or superfluous flesh.

Sarculate, *l.* to weed.

Sardanapalus, a very luxurious King (the last) of *Assyria*, who (in the rebellion) burnt himself and all his wealth.

Sardeleben, a town in *Brandenburg*.

Sardinia, a *Spanish* Isle in the *Mediterranean*.

Sardel, *-dine*, *l.* a pilcher.

Sardonyx, *Sardonian* (or *Sardine*) stone, a *Corneol*, found in

Sardinia, a *Ligustick* (or *Libyan*) Island.

Sardon, a venemous herb (like smallage) causing a

Sardonick laughter, immoderate and deadly.

Sare, *o.* for *sorex*

Sarentine, a town in *Mechlenburgh*.

Sarlinish, *o.* a kind of *Sarcenet*.

Sarmatia, a large Countrey, part in *Europe*, part in *Asia*.

Sarmentitious, *l.* of twigs.

Sarpedon, King of *Lycia*, kild at *Troy* by *Patroclus*.

Sarplesis, *-eris*, *o.* packs.

Sarpliar, (*f.* *Sarpillere*) a piece of Canvas &c. to wrap wares in.

Sarplar (or *Pocket*) *of wool*, (in *Scotland*, *Serpliathe*) half a Sack or 80 stone. *Cow.*

Sarve the rope, lay on synnet, yarn, canvas, &c.

Sarse, a hair-sieve.

Sarsaparilla, Prickly-bindweed.

Sartor, *l.* a Botcher.

Sarum, Salisbury.

Sased, *o.* stuffed.

Sassafras, Ague-tree of *Florida*, the bark is sweet in smell and very Physical.

Sasse, a Floud-gate, Lock, Turn-pike, Sluce.

Sassinate, as *Assassinate*.

Satanical, belonging to

Satan, *Sathan*, *h.* an Adversary, the Devil.

Sate me sore, *o.* toucht me greatly.

Satellite, *l.* a Sergeant or Yeoman of the guard.

Satiate, *l.* to satisfy or cloy.

Satiety, *l.* fulness.

Sation, *l.* sowing, planting.

Satisdation, *l.* a putting in of Surety.

Satisfaction, *l.* amends, content.

Satorious, of sowing or sowed.

Satournade, *o.* yellow, or rather leaden and livid.

Satrap, *g.* the Governour of a [*Persian*] Province.

Saturate, to chuse

Saturity, *l.* fulness, plenty.

Saturnals, *-lian feasts*, celebrated (about the midle of *December*) in honour of

Saturn, an old heathen Deity, Son of *Cælus* and *Vesta*, deposed by his Son *Jupiter*, also the dullest of the Planets, also (in Chymistry) Lead, and (in Heraldry) Sable.

Saturnia, the line of Saturn, (from the palm toward the midle finger.)

Saturnian, *-ine*, barren, Dull, Melancholy, Unlucky.

Satyre, an hairy Monster, like a horned man with Goats feet; also an invective poem.

Satyrical, belonging thereto.

Satyrist, such a writer.

Satyriasis, as *Priapismus*.

Satyrion, *g.* Rag-wort, Standle-wort.

Saverden, a town in *Lorrain*.

Sauciate, *l.* to wound.

Bolonia Saucidge, made of chopt Beef, Bacon, Pepper, ginger and salt in an Ox gut.

Save, *o.* (*I.* *Savio*) Sage, Wise.

Saver default, to excuse a default.

Savine, a shrub like *Tamarisk*.

Saul, *h.* desired.

Sault, *o.* for *Assault*.

Saults, *f.* jumps.

Saultoir, (in Heraldry) St. *Andrews* Cross.

Saunce dout, (*f.* *Sans doute*) without doubt.

Savoy, a Dutchy between *France* and *Switzerland*.

Saunders, as *Sanders*.

Saunkefin, as *Sankfin*.

Sautry, *o.* for *Psaltery*.

Sawsfleme, *o.* red-faced.

Saws, *Saughs*, *o.* sayings.

Saur-pool, *No.* a stinking puddle.

Sax. Saxony, part of Germany,

many, the Country of the *Saxons*, (wearing Seaxes or crooked swords) who (next to the *Romans*) conquered *Britain*.

Saxifical, *l.* turning (or turned) to stone.

Saxifrage, an herb that breaks the stone in the Kidneys.

Saxifragant, *l.* breaking (or broken against) stones.

Saxmondham, a town in *Suffolk*.

Say of it, *Sf.* taste of it.

Scabious, *l* Scabby, also an herb.

Scabrous, *l.* rough, uneven.

Scævity, *l.* a being left-handed, or unlucky.

Scævola, as *Mutius Scæ-*.

Scalado, *Sp.* the scaling of a town.

Scalar, *-ry*, belonging to a *Scale*, *l.* a ladder.

Scale of miles, a measure of them proportionable to the Draught.

Scale of musick, the Gammut.

Scale, a place in *Zant*, where (after 14 daies) one stands and publickly cites offenders.

Scalæ Gemoniæ, as *Gemony*.

Scaldis, the river *Scheldt* in the low Countries.

Scallop, *Shallop*, *Sp.* a Ship-boat.

Scalp, the skin covering the skull.

Scalper, *-ping yron*, a Chirurgeons scraping Instrument.

Scammony, purging bindweed.

Scandalize, *g.* to slander, also to give one occasion (by example) to sin or be offended.

Scandalous, *l.* giving offense.

Scandalum Magnatum, [a writ to recover damage upon] a wrong done to any high Personage, by false reports &c.

Scanderbeg, (*Tu.* Lord *Alexander*) *George Castriot* Prince of *Epirus*, who is said to have slain 3000 *Turks* with his own hands.

Scandia, *-inavia*, *Scanzia*, *Basilia*, *Baltia*, a large *Peninsula* containing part of *Denmark*, and the greatest part of *Sweden*.

Scandular, *l.* of Shingles or wooden tiles.

Scania, *Schonen*, part of *Scandia*.

Scansion, *l.* the scanning or proving of a verse.

Scantilone, *o.* (for Scantling) a measure.

Scapular, *l.* belonging to the shoulder, also as

Scapulary, the upper narrow cloth worn by Friers, down to their feet on both sides.

Scar, *o.* a steep rock.

Scarabee, *l.* a beetle.

Scaramouche, an *Italian Zani* (or Player) who lately acted in *London*.

Scarborough, a town in *Yorkshire*.

Scarcebeed, *o.* for *Scarcity*.

Scarkalla, some old prohibited fishing tool.

Scarfing, letting the end of one timber into the end of another, wood and wood, or very close and even.

Scarification, *-fying*, a cutting or lancing.

Scariole, broad-leaved *Endive*.

Scarpe, the slopeness of a wall, also (in Heraldry) a Commanders Scarfe.

Scarre, *No.* a naked rock.

Scathe, *D.* to hurt.

Scathless, *o.* indemnified.

Scatinian law, against preposterous venery.

Scaturiginous, *l.* Overflowing.

Scavage, *Schevage*, *Schewage*, *Scheauwing*, *Sceawing*, *Scewinga*, *Sa.* a toll exacted of Merchant Strangers for Wares shewed or offered to sale; forbidden by 19 *Henry* 7.

Scavengers, (*D. Schaven* to shave) two yearly Officers in every Parish about *London*, who hire Rakers and Carts to cleanse the streets.

Scedasus, a *Bœotian* who kill'd himself for his daughters being ravisht & drowned in his absence.

Scelestique, *l.* wicked.

Sceleton, *g.* an anatomy, or frame of dry bones.

Scellum, *Schel-*, *D.* a rogue.

Scenical, belonging to a

Scene, *l.* the changing of persons on a Stage, also the forepart thereof.

Scenker, *Skinker*, *Sa.* he that fills the cup.

Scenography, *g.* the presenting a work with its shadows, according to perspective.

Sceptical, belonging to

Scepticism, the Opinion of

Scepticks, *g.* Philosophers contemplating things and leaving them in suspense, professing they knew nothing.

Sceptriferous, *l.* Scepter-bearing.

Scevity, as *Scævity*.

Scevola, as *Scævola*.

Schamlat, a town in *Westphalia*.

Schammatha, *h.* as *Maranatha*, an Excommunication to death.

Scharp, a river in *Flanders*.

Schediasm, *g.* an extempore work.

Schedule, *l.* a little scroll.

Schelt, a River in *Flanders*.

Schelink, a town in *Westfrizeland*.

Scheme, *g.* a figure or outward fashion.

Schene, 5 miles, and in some places 7 and an half.

Schenk, a Fort in *Gelderland*.

Schiff, a Ship-boat.

Schirius, a hard swelling without pain.

Schismatical, belonging to a

Schismatick, one guilty of

Schism, g. a separation or division [in the Church.]

Schlesie, *Silesia*.

Schelstad, a town in upper *Alsace*.

Scholastica, a womans name.

Scholastick, g. Scholar-like.

Scholay, o. [School] exhibition.

Scholiast, a writer of a

Scholy, *-lion*, g. a short and critical exposition.

Schoonhoven, a town in *Holland*.

Schwerin, the chief town of *Mecklenbourg*.

Sciagraph, g. a platform or description of a building.

Sciamachy, g. a counterfeit fighting, or with shadows.

Sciater, l. an instrument to design a situation.

Sciatherical, belonging to a sun-dial.

Sciatick vein, seated above the outward ankle, usually opened for the

Sciatica, l. the hip-gout.

Science, l. skill, knowledge.

Liberal Sciences, Grammar, Logick, Rhetorick, Musick, Arithmetick, Geometry, Astronomy.

Scientifical, l. filling or filled with skill.

Scilcester, a town in *Northumberland*.

Sciled, o. (q. *Seiled*) closed.

Schmitar, as *Scymitar*.

Scintillation, l. a sparkling.

Sciolous, belonging to a

Sciolist, l. a smatterer.

Sciomantie, g. divining by shadows.

Scion, a graff, or young shoot.

Scipper, *Sch-*, *Sk-*, D. the Master of a Ship, also (with us) any Sea-man.

Scipio, a name of sundry famous Romans.

Scire facias, a writ calling one to shew why Judgment (passed at least a year before) should not be executed.

Sciron, a Pirate of *Megara*.

Scirpean, l. of bulrushes.

Scirrhous, belonging to

Scirrhus, as *Schirrus*.

Scissile, *-sible*, l. to be cut.

Scissure, l. a cleft or division.

Scitament, l. a pleasant dish or discourse.

Scite, l. a decree or statute.

Scitturn, *Hamp.* a shrewd-turn.

Sclavonia, *Widishmark*, westward on the Adriatick.

Scluse, a town in *Flanders*.

Scolion, as *Scho-*.

Scoll, o. a shole of fish.

Scolopendra, g. a venemous worm with many feet, also a fish that frees himself of the hook by casting out his bowels.

Scom, g. a scoff or jeer.

Sconce, (in *Oxford*) to set a mulct upon ones

Sconce, a head, a block-house or fortress.

Scopelism, g. rockiness.

Scopticks, g. Jeers, flouts.

Scopulous, l. full of rocks.

Scorbutic, *-cal*, of or subject to the

Scorbute, l. the Scurvy.

Scordium, Water-Germander.

Scorning, o. (f. *Escorner* to unhorn) changing.

Scorpion, a seven-footed Serpent with a sting in his tail, also an engine to shoot arrows.

Scorpion-grass, resisting the poison of vipers.

Scortator, l. a whoremonger.

Scot and Lot, a customary contribution laid on all subjects, according to their ability.

Scot-Ale, *Ale-shot*, a drinking at the Foresters for fear of his displeasure.

Scotists, followers of

Scotus, *John Duns*, or subtile Doctor opposer of the *Thomists*.

Scotomatical, troubled with a

Scotomy, g. a Vertigo or dizziness in the head.

Scottering, a wad of pease burnt and parcht by the boyes in *Herefordshire*, at the end of harvest.

Scottish-waith, Sc. the Picts wall.

Scovel, l a Malkin.

Scoundrel, I. a base fellow.

Scoure, c. to wear.

Scout, c. a watch.

Scout, D. a discoverer.

Scowen, an Isle in *Zeland*.

Scrat, a kind of Hermaphrodite.

Screable, l. which may be spat out.

Screation, l. a spitting.

Screkingham, a town in *Lincolnshire*.

Scribes, l. Writers, and (among the Jews) expounders of the Law.

Scriesten, a town in the *Palatinate*.

Scribender, a Scribe.

Scrip, c. [a piece of] paper.

Scriptorian, l. belonging to writing.

Scrivenish, o. (q. *Scrivnerish*) subtilely.

Scrofulous, *Scroph-*, belonging to the

Scrofula, l. the Kings-evil.

Scrudland, *Sa.* Land allotted for buying Apparel.

Scruff, sorry fuel gathered by poor folk by the *Thames* side.

Scrupular, belonging to a

Scruple, l. seven grains and a half.

Scrupulosity, a being

Scrupulous, full of

Scruples, l. doubtings.

Scrutable, capable of

Scrutation, l. searching.

Scrutiny, a search, a perusal of suffrages or Votes.

Sery [*of fowl*,] a great flock.

Sculk of Frerys, o. a Company of Fryers or Brethren.

Sculk of Foxes, a great many.

Sculpter, l. a Carver.

Sculpture, a graving.

Scumber, a Foxes dung.

Scuppers, the holes through which the water runs off the Deck.

Scur-

Scurrility, a being
Scurrile, *-lous*, *l.* basely abusive, saucily scoffing.
Scut, a hares tail.
Scutage, a subsidy granted *H.* 3. for his voyage to the Holy Land.
Scutagio habendo, a writ against him that held by Knights service.
Scute, *o.* 3 Shill. 4 Pence.
Scutcheon, as *Escutcheon*; also a bud for inoculation.
Scutiferous, *l.* Shield-bearing.
Scutiform, like a Scutcheon or Shield.
Scuttle, a square hole to go down through the Deck.
Scutum armorum, a Coat of arms.
Scyld, *Sa.* debt or default.
Scylla, the Rock over against *Charybdis*, between *Sicily* and *Italy*.
Scylas, *-llis*, a skilfull diver who regain'd much shipwrackt wealth.
Scymitar, *l.* a crooked *Persian* sword.
Scyre-gemot, *Sa.* was a Court held (twice a year) by the Bishop and Sheriffs, giving in Charge both the Ecclesiastical and Temporal laws.
Scytale, *l.* a field-mouse, also a staff which the *Lacedemonians* wrote secret letters on.
Scythick, *-ian*, belonging to
Scythia, a large Northern Countrey.
God him Se, *o.* look upon him, or bless him.
Sea-lamprey, as *Remora*,
Sea-lungs, Sea-froth.
Seal, a Sea-calf.
Seam, as *Seme*,
Sean-fish, taken with a
Sean, *Li* a great long net.
Sea rover, a Pirate.
Seasing, binding ropes fast with rope-yarn.
The boats Seasing, the rope that fastens it to the ships side.
Seasnaple, a kind of shel-fish.
Seater, a Saxon idol.
Seax, a crooked *Saxon* sword.
Sebacean, *l.* of tallow.
Sebastian, *g.* honourable.
St. Sebastians, a town in *Brasil* built by the *Portingals*.
Sebasto-crator, the third man in the *Constantinople*-Empire, the second being *Despot*.
Sebesten, *Myxaria*, an *Assyrian* plum.
Secament, *l.* a chip, &c.
Secandunum, *Seckington* in *Warwickshire*.
Secant, a line from the Centre through one extream of an Arch, meeting the tangent rais'd from the Diameter at the other.
Secation, *l.* a cutting.
Secern, *l.* to sever (by sifting.
Secession, *l.* a departing.
Seclude, *l.* to shut out or apart.
Seclusion, a shutting out.
Seclusory, *l.* a place where a thing is shut up apart.
Second, the sixtieth part of a minute.
Second deliverance, a writ for a second replevying of Cattel upon security, &c.
Secondary, next to the Chief Officer.
Secondine, the Heam (in Beasts) or after-birth (in Women.)
Secta ad Curiam, a writ against him that refuses to perform his Sute.
Secta facienda, &c. a writ to compel the heir that has the elders part of the Coheirs, to perform service for all the Coparceners.
Secta Molendini or *ad Molendinum*, against him that forsakes the mill he used to frequent; or against a tenant holding by making sute to the Lords mill.
Secta ad justitiam faciendam, a service to which a man is bound by his fee.
Secta unica, &c. for the heir distrained to more sutes than one.
Sectis non faciendis, for a woman, who (for her dower) owes no Sute of Court.
Sectary, *l.* the follower of a
Sect, a party [divided from the Church.]
Section, *l.* a division [of a Chapter.]
Sective, *l.* [to be] cut.
Sector, two right lines with an angle at the Centre, and the Circumference assumed by them, also an Instrument with all variety of angles &c.
Secular, belonging to an age or the World.
Secular plaies, (to *Apollo* & *Diana*) once in 100 years.
Secular Priests, conversing in the World, not tyed to a Monastick life.
Secunda superoneratione pasturie, a writ against him who (after an admeasurement made) surcharges the Common again.
Secundary, as *Secondary*.
Secundate, *l.* to cause to prosper.
Secundine, as *Secondine*.
Securiferous, *l.* ax-bearing.
Securitatem inveniendi, &c. a writ to stop one from going out of the Kingdom without licence.
Securitate pacis, against him that threatens another with death or danger.
Sedation, *l.* a rendering one
Sedate, *l.* quiet, appeased.
Se defendendo, a Plea for killing one in his own defence, yet must he procure his pardon from the Lord Chancellor, and forfeits his goods to the King.
Sedentary, *l.* sitting much.
Sediment, *l.* setling, dregs,
Seditiary, one that is
Seditious, given to

Sedition, *l.* faction, mutiny.

Sedan, a town and province by *Champagne* and *Luxemburg*.

Seduce, *l.* to lead aside.

Seduction, a mis-leading.

Sedulity, *l.* diligence.

Sedulous, *l.* diligent.

Seed-leap or *lib*, *E.* a basket for seed-corn on the arm.

See, *o.* a Seat.

Seeling, a sudain heeling, forced by the motion of the Sea or Wind.

Seel, *Seal*, *E.* time, season.

Seem (or *Seam*) of glass, 120 pound.

Seer, *Sere*, *o.* dry.

Segador, *Sp.* a harvest-man.

Sege of herons or *bittours*, a great company.

Segge, *D.* Say.

Segges, *Sa.* Soldiers.

Segmentation, a cutting into

Segments, *l.* pieces, parcels.

Segnity, *l.* slothfulness.

Segregate, *l.* to separate [from the flock.]

Sejant, *Seisant*, *Seant*, *f.* sitting upright (in Heraldry.)

Sejan-horse, of a wonderfull bigness and composure, first backt by

Sejanus, a great favourite of *Tiberius*, whose pride brought him to a miserable end.

Seignorage, the Kings challenging an allowance for Gold and Silver brought in the Mass to be coyned.

Seignory, the Jurisdiction of a

Seignor, *-nier*, *-neur*, *f.* a Lord.

Seimour, *de Sancto Mauro*, an Ancient and Noble Family.

Seinde, *o.* for singed [Bacon.]

Seint, *o.* (*f. Ceinte*) a gir-

Seisina habenda. &c. to deliver lands to the Lord (convict of Felony) after the King hath had the Year, day and Waste.

Seisin, *f.* possession.

Primier Seisin, the first, &c.

Seising, taking hold of.

Sejugate, *l.* to separate.

Sejunction, a putting asunder.

Seke, *o.* for Sick.

Seker, *o.* in like manner, truly.

Selah, *h.* a note of resting or of observation.

Selbie, a town in *Yorkshire*.

Selde, *o.* for Seldom.

Selda, *Sa.* a seat, window, shop, &c.

Sele-graving, in steel or copper, as flat-stich is in wood.

Seland, the greatest Island in the Baltick Sea.

Selenite, *g.* a stone with a white spot encreasing and decreasing with the moon, also a Moon-Dweller.

Selenography, *g.* a description of the Moon.

Seleucus, one of *Alexanders* Captains, King of *Syria*.

Self-heal, a wound-herb.

Sell, *No.* Self.

Sellander, a Scab in the bend of a horses hinder ham.

Selkougth, *Sa.* Seldom known.

Selle, a River in *Lorrain*.

Selimus, the *Turk* that added *Ægypt* and *Arabia* to his Empire.

Selion, *Seillon*, *f.* a Ridge of land between two furrows; also a Land (of uncertain quantity.)

Sellary, *l.* a place of benches.

Selt, *Che.* a Chance.

Selvage, the margin of linnen cloth.

Selve momet, *o.* the same moment.

Sely, *o.* for silly, also (*D. Salig*) happy.

Seltz, a Town in lower *Alsace*.

Sem, *Shem*, *h.* a Name.

Seme, *E.* a horse-load, 8 bushels.

Semblable, *f.* alike.

Semblance, *f.* likeness, a seeming.

Semblaunt, *o.* a look.

Semibrief, a full time (in Musick.)

Semde, *o.* for *Seemed*.

Semele, the Mother of *Bacchus*.

Semelihede, *o.* Comliness.

Sementation, *l.* a seeding.

Sementine, belonging to sowing or seed-time.

Sementing, *o.* (for *Cementing*) dawbing.

Semicastration, *l.* half-gelding.

Semicircular, *l.* like half a Circle.

Semicolon, half a Colon (;)

Semicope, *o.* a short cloak.

Semicupe, *-pium*, a half-bath up to the navel.

Semidiameter, half a Diameter, from the Circumference to the Centre.

Semidole, a pipe, half a Tun.

Semiferous, half wild.

Semihore, half an hour.

Semimarine, half marine.

Seminality, a being

Seminal, *l.* belonging to seed.

Seminary, *l.* a seed-plot or Nursery [of plants, learning &c.

Seminate, *l.* to sow or breed.

Semination, a sowing &c.

Seminifical, *l.* producing seed.

Semipedal, *l.* of half a foot.

Semipelagians, holding Grace necessary to the perseverance, but not the beginning of good works.

Semiquadrat, an aspect of 45 degrees.

Semiquaver, half a quaver.

Semiquintil, an aspect of 36 degrees.

Semi-

Semiramis, Wife to *Ninus* whom she made-away and succeeded in the Kingdom of *Assyria*.

Semitar, as *Scymitar*.

Semitate, *l.* to make paths.

Semivowels. *l.* the liquids.

Seminstulated, half-burnt.

Sempiternal, *l.* everlasting.

Sempt, *o.* for seemed.

Semuncial, of half an ounce.

Sena, a purging plant of *Syria* and *Arabia*.

Senacherib, *h.* bramble of destruction.

Senary, *l.* belonging to 6. a verse of 6 feet, the sixth daies work.

Senatorian, belonging to a

Senator, an Alderman, or one of the

Senate, *l.* the supream Council.

Sendal, *f.* fine linnen, also a kind of *Cyprus* Silk.

Seneca, Tutor to *Nero*, who caused him to bleed to death.

Sends much, [the Ship] falls deep (a-stern or a-head) into the trough of the Sea.

Seneschal, -*shal*, *f.* a steward.

Senesce, *l.* to be

Senescent, growing old.

Senencia, Widow-hood.

Senfy, *Nor.* likelyhood.

Sengle, *f.* a girth.

Sengreen, housleek.

Senhusen, a town of *Brandenburgh*.

Senie, as *Sena*.

Seniority, a being

Senior, *l.* elder.

Sensation, a perceiving by sense.

Sensiferous, *l.* sense-bringing.

Sensine, *Gu.* since then.

Sensory, *l.* an Organ of the

Senses, Hearing, Seeing, Smelling, Tasting, Feeling.

Sensible, *l.* apt to perceive or be perceived.

Sensitive, having sense.

Sensuality, *l.* a pleasing or indulging of the Senses.

Sentement, as Sentiment, a thought.

Senten, *o.* for sent.

Sententiosity, a being

Sententious, *l.* full of

Sentences, wise sayings.

Sentiment, *f.* a feeling apprehension.

Sentinel, *f.* a sentry standing to watch.

Senvie, (*f.* *Senevé*) the mustard plant.

Separation, a setting apart, dividing.

Separatist, one that withdraws himself from the Church.

Separatory, an instrument to pick out splinters of bones.

Sepiment, *l.* a sense or hedge.

Seplasiary, -*iator*, *l.* a maker or user of sweet oyntments.

Seposition, *l.* a setting apart.

Sept, *l.* an enclosure.

Septs, the multitudes of the same name in *Ireland*.

Septangle, *l.* a figure which is

Septangular, of seven corners.

Septemfluous, of 7 streams.

Septempedal, *l.* of 7 foot.

Septemvirate, *l.* the authority of

Septemviri, 7 co-equal Officers.

Septenary, a seven, also as

Septemarious, belonging to seven.

Septennial, of seven years.

Septentrional, Northern.

Septical, *l.* making rotten or ripe (as matter in a sore.)

Septifarious, of seven fashions.

Septifluous, as *Septemfl.*

Septimane, *l.* a week, also falling out on the seventh [day, week, &c.

Septimarians, weekly Officers in Monasteries.

Septimestre, of seven months.

Septuagenary, of 70.

Septuagesimal, the same, also belonging to

Septuagesima [*Sunday*,] the next but one before Shrove-Sunday.

Septuagint, *l.* the Greek translation of the Bible (at the request of *Ptolomy* King of *Egypt*) by the

Septuagints, the seventy (or 72) interpreters, Jewish Elders.

Septuary, a week, or any thing composed of seven.

Septuncial, of 7 ounces.

Sepulchral, *l.* of the grave.

Sepulchred, buried.

Sepulture, *l.* a burying.

Sequacious, *l.* easily following.

Sequedrie, as *Surquedrie*.

Sequatur sub suo periculo, a summons, when one appears not at an alias and a pluries.

Sequela curiæ, suit of Court.

Sequele, *l.* a consequence, a retinue.

Sequence, *l.* a following of things in order.

Sequences, verses answering one another

Sequentially, in Order.

Sequestrator, he that doth

Sequester, -*trate*, to separate a thing in Controversie from the possession of both parties, also to seize on the rents of Delinquents estates.

Sequestration, is also the Ordinaries disposing the goods of one deceased, whose estate no man will meddle with, also the gathering the fruits of a void benefice for the use of the next incumbent.

Sequestro habendo, a writ for the dissolving the Bishops sequestration of the fruits of a Benefice, &c.

Seraglio, the Turks Palace.

Serain, *f.* the evening fresh air, also the damp vapour then falling.

Seraph, a Turkish gold coyn about a Crown.

Seraphick, -*cal*, like the

Seraphim, *h.* (shining or flaming) the highest order of Angels.

Seraphis, -*pis*, an Egyptian Idol.

Sercil feathers, a hawks pinions.

Sere, the yellow between the hawks beak and eyes.

Sere, *sc.* for sore.

Sered pokettes, *o.* lockt up.

Serenade, *f.* evening musick under his Mistresses window.

Serene, *l.* without clouds.

Serenity, *l.* clearness.

Sergeant at Law or of the Coif, *Serjeant Countor*, the highest degree in the Profession of the Common Law.

Sergeanty, service due to the King by his Tenants tenure.

Grand Serjeanty, to be performed in person.

Petit Serjeanty, yielding some small thing toward his wars, as a Sword, &c.

Sergreant, a Griffin (in *Heraldry*.

Sericated, *l.* clad in Silk.

Series, *l.* an Order or succession.

Sermocinate, *l.* to discourse.

Serosity, the wheyish part of blood.

Serous, *l.* wheyish, waterish.

Serotine, *-nous*, *l.* late in the Evening.

Serpentary, Vipers-grass.

Serpentine, belonging to

Serpents, *l.* all creeping things.

Serpentine verses, beginning and ending with the same word.

Serpentine, as *Basilisco*.

Serpet, *o.* a kind of basket.

Serred f. joined close.

Sertorius, a Roman, general of the *Lusitanians* against the *Romans*, slain at supper. *Diana* was said to attend him in the form of a Hart.

Servable, that may be kept.

Servage, *o.* slavery.

Servet, as *Sherbet*.

Servile, *l.* slavish.

Serviotis, *fe.* (*f. Serviettes*) Napkins.

Servitor, *f.* a Servant, a poor Scholar waiting on another.

Servitors of bills, now the Tipstaffs of the Kings Bench.

Servitude, *l.* slavery.

Serys, *o.* the skin of the hawks feet (*f. Serres*, pounces)

Seseli, *f.* Hart-wort.

Sesostris, a King of *Egypt*.

Sesquialteral, containing one and a half.

Sesquiquarta, when a fourth part is added.

Sesquitertian, having a 3d part more than another.

Session, *l.* a sitting.

Sessions, the quarterly sitting of Justices in Court.

Sesterce, *-tie*, *H. S.* (for *IIS.* or *L L S.*) a fourth part of the Roman *Denarius*, two As's and a half, almost twopence.

Sestine, *f.* a staff of 6 verses.

Set [*a land, Ship, &c.*] observe by the compass upon what point they bear.

Set-bolts, Irons forcing the works and planks of the Ship together.

Sethim, *Setim*, *Sittim*, *Shittim*, a tree of *Judæa*, whose timber never rots.

Setle the Deck, lay it lower.

Setigerous, *l.* bristle-bearing.

Settle, a town in *York-shire*.

Setron, *o.* (*q Citron*) bright of hue.

Settles, *o.* grafts.

Setfoil, Tormentile.

Setwall, *Valerian*.

Severance, the singling of those that joyn in one writ.

Sevenock, a town in *Kent*.

Seven-shale, a town in *Northumberland*.

Severians, Hereticks following

Severus, he condemned marriage, Flesh, Wine, &c.

Severn, a famous River by *Shrewsbury*, *Worcester*, *Gloecester* and *Bristol*.

Sevidical, speaking cruelly.

Sevil, as *Sivil*.

Sevocation, *l.* a calling aside.

Sew, *Sewen*, *o.* for sown.

Sewed [*ship*,] when (the water being gone) she lies dry.

Goes Sew, *Sf.* [the Cow] goes dry.

Sewer, he that ushers up and places the meat of a great Personage; also a passage for water into a River (corruptly called the [common] shore.

Sewel, a thing set to keep out Deer.

Sewing, *o.* placed, following.

Sewis, (*f. Suivre*) to follow.

Sexagesima [*Sunday*,] next before Shrove-Sunday and the sixth before Passion-Sunday.

Sexennial, of 6 years.

Sextant, a very small coyn, or the sixt part of any thing divided into twelve.

Sextantary, belonging thereto.

Sextary, a pint (or pound) and a half.

Sexte, part of the Canon-Law added to the decretals.

Sexten, as *Sacristan*.

Sextery, as *Sacrary*.

Sextile, *l.* an Aspect of 60 Degrees, also as

Sextilian [*Moneth*] August.

Sextule, a dram and a scruple.

Sextuple, *l.* containing six.

Sey, *o.* seen, saw.

Sfachia, a town in *Candia*.

Shack, *Nf.* a general common for Hogs, from the end of harvest till seed-time.

To go at Shack, to go at large.

Shack-bolt, a shackle or fetter.

Shad, *o.* parted.

Shadrach, *h.* a little tender dug.

Shackles, oblong ship-rings for the shutting of the Ports, &c.

Shaft, an arrow, and (in *Darbyshire*) a digging like a Well.

Shafman, *No.* the same as

Shaft-met, *-ent*, *Sa.* the measure of the fist, with the thumb set up, half a foot.

Shaftsbury, a town in *Dorset-shire*.

Shallop, *Se-*, *Ch-*, *f.* a small sea-vessel, also a shel-fish.

Shamgar, *h.* desolation of the stranger.

Shamois, as *Chamois*.

Shamsheer, a Persian sword more crooked than a Scymiter.

Shan, *Li.* shamefacedness.

Shank, the longest part [of the Anchor,

Shank-

Shank-painter, a ſhort chain (by the Ships ſide) on which reſts all the weight of the anchors after-part.

Shap, o. fate, deſtiny.

Shapely, o. likely.

Shapournet, a reſemblance, (in Heraldry) of the Chaperon or French-hood.

Sharmbude, o. a Beetle.

Sharping-corn, given at Chriſtmas (by ſome Farmers) to their Smith, for ſharping plough-irons, &c.

Shaſh, the whole piece of linnen (Telbent) whereof the Turbant (or rather *Sharuck*) is made, or which is tied about the midle.

Shavaldries, o. feats of Chivalry.

Shaw, o. ſhadow, tuft of trees, a wood round a cloſe, *Sſ.*

Shaw, P. a King.

Shaw-zawdeh, P. the Grand Seignors Son.

Shawl, *Sſ.* a winnowing ſhovel.

Shead, *La.* to diſtinguiſh.

Shearing, when the ſhip goes in and out, and is not ſteered ſteddily, alſo (*No.*) reaping.

Sheer-hooks, moſt unuſeful irons ſet into the yard-arms (to cut the enemies ſhrowds, &c.)

Sheat-anchor, the biggeſt.

Sheats, ropes bent to the clew of all Sails, alſo the planks (under water) which come along the run of the Ship and are cloſed to the ſtern-poſt.

Sheath a Ship, caſe it (under water) with thin boards over hair and tar, to keep out the Southern Worms.

No Shed, *No.* No difference between things.

Shed, *Che.* to ſtrike off a piece.

Shede, o. to de]part.

Sheen, *Shene*, o. ſhining.

Sheep-ſhanks, two maſts (or yards) ſet up and ſeaſed acroſs one another near the top.

Sheers, two poles ſo ſet up.

Sheevers, which run round in the pullies and blocks.

Sheffield, a town in *Yorkſhire*.

Shefford, a town in *Bedfordſhire*.

Shekle, as *Sicle*.

Sheldaple, a Chaffinch.

Sheld, *Sſ.* flecked, party-coloured.

Shem, as *Sem*.

Shemmering, o. glimmering.

Shend, o. to blame, or ſpoil.

Shent, o. a barrow-pig.

Shepen, o. ſimple, fearfull.

Shepens, o. Sheep-coats.

Shepſter, o. Shepherd.

Shepton-mallet, a town in *Somerſet-ſhire*.

Sherbet, a pleaſant drink (of Limons, Sugar, Amber, &c. or Violets, Honey, juice of Raiſins, &c.) of great requeſt among the Turks and *Perſians*.

Sherborn, a town in *Yorkſhire*, *Dorcet-ſhire*, and other places.

Shermans-craft, the ſhearing of Cloth (at *Norwich*.)

Sherry, (*Sp. Xeres*) a Sea-town of *Corduba* in *Spain*.

Shetland, a Northern Iſle.

Shete, o. ſat, or ſhoot.

Shetten, o. ſhut in.

Shibboleth, h. an ear of Corn.

Shield, *ſa.* to defend.

Shift, o. to beſtow.

Shildes, o. French Crowns.

Shilling, *ſa.* was but five pence.

Shilo, -*oh*, h. ſent.

Shimper, *Sſ.* to ſhine.

Shingle, a lath.

Shingled, o. for ſingled, or made of Shingles.

Shingles, a heat ariſing in the body, if it get round, it kills.

Ship-money, an impoſition (1635.) for the providing Ships for the Kings ſervice, &c. declared unlawful by Stat. 17. *Car.* 1.

Shippen, *No.* a Cow-houſe.

Shipton, a town in *Shropſhire*, *Worceſter-ſhire*, and about a dozen more.

Shire, *ſa.* a diviſion or County.

Shirif, -*ref*, *Shire-reve*, *ſa.* the cheif yearly Officer (under the King) of a Shire.

Shirifalty, the time of ones being Sheriff.

Shire-Clerk, the under-ſheriff or his deputy.

Shirtband, *T.* a band.

Shoad, the Tin-ſtones in *Cornwal*.

Shoars, props.

Shode, o. a buſh of hair.

Shoder, o. for ſhoulder.

Shope me, o. ſhoved or thruſt my ſelf.

Shoplift, o. one that pretends to cheapen, and ſteals wares.

Shore, o. a cleft or cranny.

Shoreſhode, o. for Sheriffdom.

Shoreham, (old and new) in *Suſſex*.

Shorling, a fell after the Fleece is ſhorn off, alſo a ſhorn Sheep.

Shot of Cable, two cables ſpliced together.

Shoud, a Turkiſh Juſtice.

Shoulderd head, an arrow head (with a ſhoulder) between blunt and ſharp.

Shoulder-pight, when the pitch or point of the horſes ſhoulder is diſplaced.

Showl, ſhallow at Sea.

Good Showling, growing ſhallow by degrees.

Shraping, o. ſcraping.

Shrew, a kind of Field-mouſe very miſchievous to Cattel.

Shrewsbury, *Shroes-*, *Salop*, the chief town of *Shropſhire*.

Shrift, -*iving*, *ſa.* auricular confeſſion.

Shright, o. a ſhriking or crying out.

Shrine, (*Scrinium*, a cheſt) that which contains the body of a Saint.

Shrowds, the ropes that come from either ſide of all the Maſts.

Shrove-tide, Confeſſion-time.

Shrove-

Shrove-tuesday, the first tuesday after the first new-moon that happens after *January*.

Shuck, *so.* a husk.

Shullen, *o.* for *Shall*.

Shun, *Sf.* to shove.

Shymar, a short vest, formerly a Bishops long robe.

Sialoquent, *l.* spitting in his speech.

Sib, *sa.* kindred.

No sole Sib'd, *No.* Nothing akin.

No more Sib'd than sieve and riddle, that grew both in a wood together, *Che.*

Sibberidg, *-red*, *Sf.* banes of Matrimony.

Sibilation, *l.* a hissing.

Sibils, as *Sybils*.

Siccaneous, *l.* dry, without springs.

Siccifical, *l.* causing

Siccity, *l.* drieness.

Sich, *Sike*, *No.* a little water-course, dry in summer.

Sicilian, belonging to

Sicily, an Isle by *Italy*.

Sickerly, *No.* surely.

Sicle, *Shekel*, *h.* half an ounce, half a Crown.

Siclike, *o.* such like.

Sicut alias, a second writ when the first was not executed.

Side-laies, when dogs are let slip at a deer as he passes.

Side-men, Assistants to the Church-wardens.

Side, *No.* long, also proud.

Si douset et la margarete, (*Si doucette est la marguerite*, *f.*) so sweet is the daisy.

Siderated, *l.* planet-struck.

Sideral, *-real*, *-an*, Star-like.

Siderite, *g.* an Iron-like stone, or the loadstone drawing iron.

Sidon, a City of *Phœnicia*, plentifull in fish.

Sidy, *Sf.* surly, moody.

Sie, *o.* to fall, also as

Sigallion, as *Harpocrates*.

Sigele, *Sa.* a Neck-lace.

Sigh, *Seigh*, *o.* for *Saw*.

Sigillar, *l.* belonging to a seal.

Sigillative, apt to seal or be sealed.

Sigillum Hermetis, an extraordinary way of luting glasses.

Sigismund, *Sa.* victorious peace.

Sigles, *g.* Cyphers, initial letters put for the whole words.

Signacle, *l.* a sign or seal.

Signatory, *l.* sealing.

Signature, *l.* a mark.

Signaturist, a marker.

Signet, one of the Kings seals wherewith his private letters are sealed.

Signiferous, *l.* Ensign-bearing.

Significavit, a writ for the imprisoning him that stands obstinately excommunicate 40 dayes; also in other Cases.

Sike mister men, *o.* such like men.

Sikerd, *o.* allied.

Silentiary, *l.* he that sees good rule and silence kept.

Sile down, *No.* Sink down.

Sile, *So.* filth.

Sile, *o.* for *Exile*.

Silery, as *Cilery*.

Siliceous, *l.* flinty.

Siligineous, *l.* of fine flower.

Sillinder, *Cylinder*, the bore of a piece.

Sillogism, as *Syll-*.

Sillographer, *g.* a writer of scoffs.

Siliquous, *l.* of the husk.

Silk-thrower or *throwster*, a trade that winds, twists and spins (or throwes) silk.

Silvestrous, as *Syl-*.

Silures, people of *South-Wales*.

Silurist, one of *South-Wales*.

Silver-spoon-head, a kind of arrow-head.

Simeon, *Shi-*, as *Simon*.

Similar, *-ry*, *l.* like, of the same substance.

Similitude, *l.* likeness.

Simmeren, a town in the lower Palatinate.

Simon, *h.* hearing, obedient.

Simoniacal, belonging to

Simony, buying or selling of spiritual things, from

Simon Magus, a *Samaritan* Sorcerer, who would have bought the power of giving the Holy Ghost.

Simoniacks, followers of *Simon* (in that or any Heresy.)

Simon Islip, the first Erector of a printing press in *England* 1471.

Simonides, a Lyrick poet of *Thessaly*.

Simous, *l.* flat-nosed.

Simpler, *-list*, he that studies

Simples, plants and drugs.

Simpson, *E. Sf.* Groundsel.

Simulacre, *l.* an Image.

Simulation, *l.* a counterfeiting.

Simultaneous, *l.* bearing a private grudge.

Sin, *o.* for *Since*.

Sinai, *Horeb*, a Mountain of *Arabia*.

Sinapism, *l.* a medicine of mustard (to raise blisters, &c.)

Sincerity, *l.* a being

Sincere, *l.* pure (as honey without wax.)

Sindic, as *Syndic*.

Sindon, *g.* very fine linnen.

Sine, a perpendicular from one extream of an Arch to the other.

Sine assensu Capituli, a writ aginst him that alienates Lands without consent of his Chapter or Covent.

Sine die, without day, dismist the Court.

Sing-cantor, as *Succentor*.

Singeries, *f.* apish tricks.

Single, the tail of a Deer.

Singularity, a being

Singular, *l.* without fellow.

Sinisterity, a being

Sinister, *l.* left-sided, unlucky.

Sinister base point, under the sinister point, in the lower

lower part of an Escutcheon.

Sinnet, Rope-yarns platted together and beaten smooth (to sarve ropes, &c.)

Si non omnes, a permission for some Commissioners (when all cannot meet) to finish a business.

Sinon, a crafty *Grecian* who (by *Virgil*) betrayed *Troy*.

Sinopical, belonging to

Sinoper, -*ple*, *Cinnabar*, Ruddle.

Sinus, a gulph or large bay.

Sion, as *Scion*.

Siphak, *A*. the Inner rim of the belly, joyn'd to the Cawl.

Si-quis (If any one &c.) a bill set up for something lost.

Sir, (*f. Sieur* or *Seigneur*) prefixt to the Christen-Names of Knights, and Surnames of Bachelors of Art.

Sire, spoken (now) only to the king of France.

Si recognoscat a writ against the Debtor having acknowledg'd the debt before the Sheriff.

Syren, as *Mermaid*.

Sirenical, belonging thereto.

Sirenize, to allure like them.

Sirickzed, a town in *Zeland*.

Siringe, *g*. a Chirurgeons Squirt.

Sirius, the Dog-star.

Sirocco, *I*. a noxious South-East wind.

Sisamnes, a Judge whom *Cambyses* flea'd for bribery.

Sisley, as *Cicely*.

Sysiphus, a Robber slain by *Theseus*, in hell he is said to roll a stone up hill, which returns and makes his labour endless.

Sitarch, *g*. a Pourveyor.

Site, *Situation*, *l*. the seat or standing of a place.

Sithcundman, *sa*. the Gentleman who was to lead the men of his parish.

Sithness, *o*. seeing that.

Sitient, *l*. thirsting.

Sitomagus, *Thetford* in *Norfolk*.

Sittim, as *Sethim*.

Sittenborn, a Town in *Kent*.

Sivil, *Sevil*, the Chief City of *Andaluzia* in *Spain*.

Sixain, *f*. a sixth, also as *Sestine*.

Size, a farthing [bread, &c.] noted with an S. in the buttery-book at *Cambridge*, where

To Size, is the same as to battel at *Oxford*, and

Sizer, as *Servitor*, or *Batteler*.

Sizygy, as *Syz*-.

Sizzing, *Sf*. Yeast, barm.

Scaddle, *Scathy*, *Sf*. Ravenous, Mischievous.

Skarfing, as *Scarfing*

Skarmoch, *o*. Skirmish.

Skathe, *No*. loss, harm. One doth the Skath, another has the scorn.

Skegg, that little inconvenient part of the keel, which is cut flaunting and left a little without the stern-post.

Skeer the Esse, *Che*. separate the dead ashes from the Embers.

Skeeling, *Sf*. an Isle or bay of a barn.

Skeleton, as *Seel*-.

Skellum, as *Seel*-.

Skere, *o*. a fray.

Skew, *c*. a dish.

Skeyn, an *Irish* dagger.

Skid the wheel, *K*. keep it steddy (with an iron hook) upon a descent.

Skiff, *Scph*, *Sch*-, a ship-boat.

Skink, strong Scotch pottage of knuckles and sinews of beef.

Skinker, as *Scen*-.

Skiret, a dainty, strengthening root like a Parsnip.

Sklcir, *o*. a scarf.

Sklendre, *o*. slender.

Skleren, *o*. to cover.

Skorchlith, *o*. Scorcheth.

Look Skrow, *Sf*. sowrly.

Skry Sc. to Cry.

Skupper, as *Scupper*.

Skypton, a town in *Yorkshire*.

Slape-ale, *Li*. plain ale (not medicated.)

Skappel, *Sf*. a piece or part.

Slay, (*D. Slagen*, to strike) a Weavers instrument with teeth like a Comb.

Slat on, *No*. cast on, or dash against.

Slatch, the midle part of a rope hanging slack without the Ship; also a small interval of fair weather.

Slat, *c*. a sheet.

Sleasie Holland, Vulgarly all sleight Holland, but properly that which comes from

Slesia, *Schlesie*, *Silesia*, part of *Germany*.

Sleak out the tongue, *Ch*. put it out in derision.

Sleck, *No*. small pit-coal; also to slack or quench.

Sleech, *No* take up [water.]

Sleepers, the timbers fore and aft the bottom (on either side the Keelson) which describe the narrowing of the ships floor.

Sleford, a town in *Lincolnshire*.

Slego, an *Irish* County.

Sleswick, a Dutchy of South *Juitland*.

Slete, *No*. to now or set on [a dog.]

Slew fyre, *Sc*. struck fire.

Slewth of beerys, *o*. Slouth of bears.

Sliding of corage, *o*. Easily daunted.

Slidder, *o*. slippery, falling.

Slight a Fort, demolish it.

Slim, *Li*. crafty, naughty.

Sliming, a hawks muting long-waies entirely without dropping.

Sling, to fasten Cask &c, in a pair of slings.

Slive, *Li*. to creep.

Sliverly, *Li.* crafty.

Sliver, *o.* a piece or parcel.

Slo, *o.* for flay.

Slockster, *Slocker*, *D.* he that enticeth away mens servants.

Slot, the print of a Stags-foot.

Slot the door, *Li.* shut it.

Slough, a damp, also a ditch, and (in Hunting) the place where a Bore lies.

Slouth of Bears, a great Company of them.

Slug, a Ship that Sails ill and heavily.

Sloutelich, *o.* slovenly.

Smacking-Cove, *c.* Coachman.

Smalt, a kind of blue paint, or enamel.

Smaragdin, like a

Smaragd, *l.* an Emerald.

Smartle away, *No.* waste away.

Smittle, *No.* to infect.

Smear of Curyousss, *o.* a Company.

Smec, a contraction of

Smectymnuus, the initial letters of five Co-authors of one Book, viz. *Stephen Marshal*, *Edm. Calamy*, *Tho. Young*, *Mat. Newcomen*, and *W. Spurstow*.

Smegmatick, *g.* like a wash-ball.

Smelling-cheat, *c.* a garden or nosegay.

Smelting, the melting of metal in the Oar.

Smeth, *Smothery*, an ointment to take away hair.

Smilax, a virgin who (for *Crocus's* love) pined into a Kidney-bean.

Smired, *St.* anointed.

Smiter, *c.* an arm.

Smiting-line, fastened to the Missen yard-arm.

Smite the Missen, pull that rope, to break the fartheling rope-yarn, and let the sail come down.

Smoke-silver -penny, paid many Ministers, either in lieu of Tithe wood, or the old Rome-scote.

Smopple, *No.* [short and fat] Py-crust.

Smuterlich, *o.* snout-fair.

Smuglers, Stealers of Custom.

Smutty, obscene.

Smylting, *Sa.* a mixture of Gold and Silver, a Soldering.

Smyrna, a City of *Ionia.*

Snag, *Sf.* a snail.

Snake weed, Adders wort.

Snap-dragon, a Hob-goblin; also a plant.

Snap haunse, a fire-lock.

Snatch-block, a great block with a sheever, and a notch through one cheek, by which they reeve any rope into it.

Snathe, a Town in *Yorkshire.*

Snee, *Sny*, *No.* to abound or swarm.

Snees-wort, an herb causing to sneeze.

Snete, the fat of Deer.

Snettersham, A Town in *No folk.*

Snever-spawt, *No.* a slender stripling.

Snock the door, *No.* latch it.

Snitch, *Snitchel*, *c.* a fillip.

Snilches, *c.* sees or eyes you.

Snite, *No.* wipe [your nose.

Snithe-wind, *Li.* a cutting wind.

Snudg, *c.* one that hides himself in a house to do mischief.

Snurl, *Sf.* a pose or cold in the head.

Snytyth, *o.* [the hawk] snites or wipes her beak.

Soar, to fly up aloft.

Sobriquet, *f.* a nick-name or by-word.

Soc, *Soke*, *Soken*, *sa.* a power to Minister Justice, also that Jurisdiction. Hence

Soca, a Lordship endow'd with liberty of keeping a Court of

Socagers, *Sockmen*, Tenants whose tenure is

Socage, *Soccage*, (*f. Soc.* a plough-share) a tenure by some husbandry-service to the Lord of the fee.

Sociality, *Society*, *l.* fellowship, Company.

Socinianism, the doctrine of the

Socinians, followers of *Lælius* the Uncle and his Nephew *Faustus*

Socinus, *Sozzo* of *Sienna* (1555.) he denied Christs eternal Divinity, &c.

Socna, *sa.* a privilege or liberty.

Sockets, holes for the pintels of the rudder, murderers, &c.

Socome, a Custom of grinding at the Lords mill.

Bond-Socome, to which they are bound.

Love-Socome, when done freely.

Socord, *l.* Idle or Idleness.

Socratick, belonging to

Socrates, a famous Athenian Philosopher, called (by the oracle) the wisest man.

Sodalicious, belonging to

Sodality, *l.* a fellowship.

Sodor, a town in *Sura*, (one of the *Hebrides*) where are interred 60 Kings.

Sodomitical, belonging to a

Sodomite, he that commits

Sodomy, buggery, the sin of

Sodom, *h.* their secret or lime.

Soest, a Town of *Mark* in *Germany.*

Sofees, Turkish Pharisees.

Soget, *o.* (*I. Soggetto*) subject.

Soil (*or Sile*) *the milk*, *No.* strain it.

Soigne, *Soin*, *f.* care.

Sojour, *f*, tarrying, dwelling.

Soken, *o.* trade, dealing.

Sokemans, as *Socagers.*

Sol, *l.* the Sun, or gold.

Solace, *l.* comfort.

Solar, *l.* of the Sun, also an upper room.

Solary, the same, also a Sundial, a pension for living retired from business, or for building upon the Common-Wealths soil.

Solda, as *Selda*, a shop or shed.

Soldado, *sp.* *Soldat*, *f.* a Soldier.

Soldan, *Sould-*, as *Sultan*.

Soldin, a town of *Brandenburg*.

Soldures, Gauls that vowed friendship and to share in the good and bad fortunes of any.

Soleated, *l*. shod [with iron.

Solecism, as *Solæcism*.

Solein, *o*. only.

Solegrave, *-reve*, *o*. February.

Solemnity, [yearly] pomp.

Solemnize, to celebrate.

Solennial, Solemn, done publickly every year.

Solent, the sea between the Isle of *Wight* and *Hampshire*.

Sole tenant holding in his own right, without his wife (or any other) joyned.

Solevation, *Sp*. a lifting up.

Solfe, *o*. to sing *Sol*, *Fa*.

Solicitation, stirring in a business.

Solicitor, one employ'd to take care of suits depending.

Solicitous, full of

Solicitude, *l*. care.

Solidata, as Fardingdeal, also a soldiers pay.

Solidation, *l*. a making whole.

Solids, regular bodies or figures, *viz*. a Circle, Cube, Pyramid, Cylinder, and *Dodecaëdron*.

Solifidian, holding faith only necessary to salvation.

Solifuge, *l*. a venemous creature found in the silver Mines of *Sardinia*.

Soliloquy, *l*. talk alone

Solinus terræ, two plowlands and almost an half.

Soliped, *l*. whose foot is whole.

Solisequious, following the sun.

Solistime, *l*. divination by the dancing of bread thrown to chickens.

Solitaneous, *-ary*, without company.

Solitude, *l*. loneliness.

Solivagant, *l*. wandering alone.

Soller, as *Solar*, a Chamber.

Solæcismical, belonging to

Solæcism, *g*. a speaking contrary to grammar.

Solomon, *h*. peaceable.

Solon, one of the seven wise men of *Greece*.

Solstitial, belonging to

Solstice, Sun-stead, when the Sun is highest and lowest (about the midle of June and December.)

Solwedel, a town of *Brandenburg*.

Soluble, *l*. which one may

Solve, *l*. loosen, unty.

Solute, *-tive*, loosed or loosening.

Solution, a dissolving or undoing.

Solutione feodi Militis Parl. a writ for a Knight of the Shires allowance.

Sol. feo. Burgen. Parl. for a Burgess.

Sombwilne, *o*. some one.

Sommer, as *Summer*.

Sommerton, a town in *Somersetshire*.

Somniculous, *l*. sleepy; also as

Somniferous, bringing sleep.

Somnolency, a being

Somnolent, *l*. drowsy.

Somnus, *l*. [the God of] Sleep.

Sond, *o*. Will, Commandment, also sand and messenger.

Sondbache, a town in *Cheshire*.

Soncesse, *o*. a noise.

Songal, *-gle*, *Heref*. a handful of gleaned corn.

Sontircls, *o*. Sunny (shining) tresses of hair.

Sonnenberg, *Sunn-*, a town of *Brandenburg*.

Sonorous, *l*. loud, shrill.

Sontage, a tax of 40 shilling upon every Knights fee, also coarse cloth for bagging, &c.

Sontick, *l*. hurtful.

Sontick disease, continual, hindring ones business.

Sontina, a Town of *Colen*.

A-Soon, *No*. at even.

Soot, *Sote*, *o*. sweet.

Sophia, *g*. wisdome.

Sophism, *g*. a deceitful sentence.

Sophist, *-ter*, a crafty Caviller.

Sophistical, deceitful.

Sophisticate, *l*. to falsify.

Sophistry, circumvention by false arguments.

Sophronia, *g*. prudent, temperate.

Sophy, the King of *Persia*.

Sopited, *l*. laid to sleep.

Sopition, *-porat-*, a laying or being laid to sleep.

Soporiferous, *l*. causing sleep.

Sorb, *l*. a service-berry.

Sorbition, *l*. a supping.

Sorbonists, Divines of the

Sorbonne, a Colledge in *Paris* founded (1264) by *Robert de Sorbonne*, an Almoner and Preacher of St. *Lewis* 9.

Sorcery, *-elery*, *-llage*, *f*. Witchcraft.

Sord, *o*. sorrel-coloured.

Sorde (or *Sute*) *of Mallards*, *o*. a great company.

Sordet, *-dine*, *f*. the little pipe in the mouth of a trumpet.

Sordidate to make

Sordid, *l*. foul, base.

Sore a cale, *o*. very cold.

Sore, a male fallow deer 4 year old.

Sorel, one of 3 years old.

Sore-age, the first year of a hawk.

Sore-hawk, till she has mewed.

Sorites, *g*. an argument of divers propositions heaped, wherein the Predicate of the former is the subject of the latter, and the last predicate attributed to the first subject.

Soritical, belonging thereto.

Sorlinges, many small Islands on the West of *England*.

Sororiation, a becoming

Sororiant, *l*. whose breast

begin to shew.

Sororicide, *l.* a Sister-killer.

Sorority, Sister-hood.

Sortilegy, *l.* lottery, divination by lots.

Sortition, *l.* a casting lots.

Sortitor, *l.* a caster, &c.

Sospital, *l.* safe, wholsom.

Sospitation, *l.* a keeping safe.

Sotel, *o.* for *Subtle*.

Sote *o.* sweet.

Sothale, as Scotale or Filctale

Sothfast, *sa.* Faithfull.

Soukle, *o.* wretched.

Soulack, a *Turkish* Officer.

Soudan, *o.* for *Souldan*.

Soul Mass-Cakes, still given (in some places) to the poor on All-souls day.

Souid, *o.* inspired [with a new soul.

Soul-scot, money paid the Priest at the opening of the grave.

Sound, any great in-draught of the Sea (between two head-lands) where there is no passage through; particularly a famous Eastern Sea.

Sounding-lead, about 7 *l.* weight, and 12 inches long.

Sounding line, about 20 fadom, markt at 3 with a black leather, at 5 with a white rag, at 7 red, at 10 and 15 with leather.

A deep sea-line is sometimes 200 fadom.

Source, *f.* a spring.

Sourd, *f.* deaf; also as

Sounder, a Company [of Swine or wild boars.

Sourdet, as *Serdet*.

Sourd, *o.* to arise, proceed.

Sou, *Sol*, *f.* a penny.

Sous-claviere artery, the ascendent branch of the great artery.

South-Hampton, the chief town of *Hamtshire*.

South-Vicont, the Under-Sheriff

Southam, a town in *Warwickshire*.

Southcast, a town in *Hantshire*.

Southold, a Town in *Suffolk*.

Southwark, a town in *Surry*.

Southwell, a town in *Nottingham*.

Southsaws *o.* true speeches.

Sow and plite, *o.* Seal and fold.

Sower, (for *sore*) a deer. *o.*

Sowgh, *o.* to sound.

Sowl, *Sool*, *No.* any thing eaten with bread.

Sowl him by the ears, *Li.* worry him (as a dog does the Sow.)

Sown, *o.* for Swoon and Sound.

Sown, (*f. Souvenu*) remembred.

Estreats that Sown, such as the Sheriff can gather.

Sowned, *o.* ordained (publisht with sound of Trumpet.)

Sowter, *o.* (Sutor) a Shoemaker.

Sozzo, *l.* Socinus.

Anti-Sozzo, a Treatise against Socinianism.

Spa, as *Spaw*.

Spacht, *No.* apt to learn.

Spade, *l.* one gelded (man or beast.)

Spadiards, Labourers [with spades] in the *Cornish* tin-mines.

Spadiceous, *l.* of a bright bay.

Spagyrical, belonging to a

Spagyrick, *l.* an Alchymist.

Spahy, (*P. Spawhee*) a *Turkish* horsman compleatly armed.

Spaid, a red male deer 3 year old.

Spaidairs, White-friers, with 2 red swords on their habits.

Spalding, a town in *Lincolnshire*.

Spannishing, *o.* full breadth.

Spancel, *No.* a rope to ty a Cows hin-legs.

Spane, *No.* wean [the Child.

Spar, *Speir*, *Spir*, *No.* to enquire or cry at the market.

Spar the door an [illegible] be come, *Nf.* shut it lest he come in.

Spars, Gem-like stones found in lead-mines.

Sparsion, *l.* a sprinkling.

Sparadrap, a linnen rag dipt in melted plaister.

Sparsedly, scatteringly.

Spartans, the people of

Sparta, Lacedæmon, a famous City of *Peloponnesus*.

Sparth, *o.* a double ax or spear.

Spasmatical, belonging to a

Spasm, *g.* the Cramp.

Spat, the spawn of Oisters.

Spat, *-tter*, *-tule*, *l.* a splatter or slice to spread plaisters.

Spatiate, *l.* to walk abroad.

Spaw, *Spa*, a town in *Liege*, famous for medicinal Waters.

Spawhawn, *Spaan*, *Spahan*, *Jespaa*, *Hispahan*, *Dura*, *Hecatompylos*, the Chief City of *Persia*, called (by them) Half the World.

Spayad, *o.* as *Spaid*.

Lord Speaker, of the house of Peers.

Mr. Speaker, of the house of Commons.

Speal, *Spell*, *No.* a Splinter.

Spearmen, as *Pensioners*.

Speces, *o.* parts or pieces.

Specialty, a bond, bill, or such like Instrument.

Specifical, belonging to or constituting a

Species, *l.* the different kind or form of a thing.

Specify, to shew or signify in particular.

Specification, a signifying, &c.

Specimen, *l.* a proof or trial.

Specious, *l.* fair in shew.

Spectable, *l.* to be lookt on.

Spectacle, *l.* a publick shew.

Spectative, speculative, contemplative.

Specta-

Spectatour, *l.* a beholder.
Spectre, *l.* an apparition.
Specular, belonging to or helping the sight.
Speculate, *l.* to watch on high.
Speculatory, belonging to
Speculation, *l.* espial, watching, observing.
Speculum oris, an instrument to skrew open the mouth.
Speeks, long nails.
Speek the missen, put the yard right up and down by the mast.
Speedwell, the herb *Fluellin*.
Speer, *Che.* the Chimney-post.
Spell, *Sa.* a word, also a charm.
Give him a Spel, row or pump in his turn or stead.
Spell the missen, let go the sheat and speek it up.
Spelt, *Zea*, a kind of wheat in *Italy*, *France* and *Flanders*.
Spelter, *Zink*, a modern metal.
Spend a Mast, &c. lose them by foul weather.
Spenen, *o.* for spending.
Spending their mouth. is the same in hounds, as Opening in Grey-hounds, questing in Spaniels, and barking in other Dogs.
Spene, *K.* a Cows pappe.
Sper, *o.* open, manifest.
Sperid, *o.* asked.
Sperable, *l.* to be hoped.
Sperage, Asparagus.
Sperkel, *o.* wandring.
Spermatical, belonging to
Sperm, *g.* natural seed or spawn.
Sperma Ceti, as *Parma Ceti.*
Spermatize, to cast forth Sperm,
Spermatique artery, goes from the body of the *Aorta* to the Testicles, and there joyns the vein governing those parts.
Spermatick vein, the third branch of the trunk descendant of the hollow vein.
Spoustick, *g.* done in haste.

Sphacelism, *g.* an ulcerating in the Brain.
Spherable, which may be made
Spherical, round, like a
Spere, *g.* a globe or circle.
Sphericity, such a roundness.
Spheromachy, *g.* playing at ball or at bowls.
Sphincter, *g.* the muscle of the Fundament.
Sphinx, a kind of Baboon; (in Poets) a Monster near *Thebes*, destroying all that could not unfold her ridles, but *Oedipus* doing it, she brake her own neck.
Spicate, *l.* eared as corn.
Spice, *T.* Raisins, Figs, &c.
Spice, *o.* a kind.
Spiciferous, bearing corn-ears.
Spicilegy, *l.* a gleaning of Corn.
Spiculator, *l.* a spearman of a guard.
Sea-spider, a Carvel, casting out many strings for small Fish.
Spignel, mew, Baldmony, Bearwort.
Spigurnels, was the Sealers of the Kings writs.
Spikenard, an Indian odoriferous plant.
Spillisby, a town in *Lincolnshire.*
Spinal, belonging to a
Spine, *l.* a thorn or sting, also the back-bone.
Spindle, the smallest part of the Capstern between the 2 Decks.
Spingard, an old kind of Chamber-gun.
Spinge, *o.* to sprinkle.
Spiniferous, *l.* thorny.
Spinosity, *l.* thorniness.
Spinster, the title of all unmarried women, from the Viscounts Daughter downward.
Spintrian, *l.* belonging to new inventions of lust.
Spiracle, *l.* a breathing hole.
Spiral, rowling in several circles one about another.
Spirarch, *g.* a Captain.
Spiration, *l.* a breathing.
Spirlinga, a small *Sicilian* town that conspired not in their Vespers.

Spiritualities [*of a Bishop*,] the profits he receives as Bishop, and not as Baron of Parliament.
Spiritualization, (in Chymistry) a changing the whole body into spirit.
Spiritual Electors, the Bishops of *Colen*, *Mentz* and *Triers.*
Spiss, *l.* thick, gross, firm.
Spissity, *-tude*, *l.* thickness.
Spitter, as *Brocket.*
Spittle, (*I. Spedale*) an hospital.
Splattyd, *o.* drest, dight.
Splay, *o.* for display.
Splaying, the parting of a horses shoulder from the breast, (occasion'd by some slip, &c.)
Spleen-wort, Ceterach, Milt-wast.
Spleget, as *Pleget.*
Splendent, *-did*, *l.* bright, brave.
Splendor, *l.* brightness, &c.
Splenetick, troubled in the
Splene, the milt under the left short-ribs, purging the Liver of superfluous Melancholy bloud.
Splenitique artery, the greatest branch of the Cœliaque ending in the Spleen.
Splenetick vein, a main branch of the port-vein, ending (in four parts) in the Spleen.
Splice the ropes, make fast their ends into one another.
Spodium, footy dregs of dross in the meking of Brass.
Spoliation, *l.* a spoiling or robbing, also a writ for one incumbent against another (of the same Church and Patron.)
Spondalion, *g.* a heathen hymn sung at the burning of the incense.
Spondee, *g.* two long syllables.
Spondyles, *g.* the chine-bones.
Spongious, *l.* like to

Sponge,

Sponge, Spunge, *l.* a kind of plant-animal growing only under the Sea-rocks of *Samos.*

Sponſal, -litious, *l.* belonging to a Spouſe or to marriage.

Sponſion, *l.* a [mutual] promiſe.

Spontal, -ane, -eous, *l.* free, voluntary, without conſtraint.

Spontaneity, voluntarineſs.

Spoom the ſhip, put her right before the wind and Sea (without any Sail.)

Sporades, ſcattered *Carpathian* Iſles.

Sport, *l.* a hand-basket or panier.

Sport, *o.* deportment.

Spouſe, *f.* a Bride-groom or Bride.

Spouſage, betrothing.

Spouſail, *o.* the ſame.

Spout, (at Sea) a little river running out of the clouds.

S. P. Q. R. Senatus Populuſque Romanus, the Senate and people of *Rome.*

S. P. Q. L. -Londinenſis, of London.

Spraints, Otters dung.

Spray, *o.* a bough or ſprig.

Sprent, *o.* ſpringed, leapt.

Sprent, *o.* ſprinkled.

Spretion, *l.* a deſpiſing.

Spretor, *l.* a ſcorner.

Sprights, ſhort arrows with wooden heads (ſhot out of muskets) which would pierce a ſhips ſides.

Spring a maſt, to have it crackt.

Springolds, *o.* for ſpringals.

Springal, *D.* a ſtripling.

Spruntlit, *o.* ſpotted.

Spring-tides, three daies after the full and change of the moon.

Spullers of yarn, Triers if it be well ſpun and fit for the loom.

Spume, *l.* foam, froth, ſcum.

Spumid, *l.* frothy.

Spumiferous, froth-bearing.

Spunge, as *Sponge*, alſo a ſtaff (with a piece of Lamb-skin) to ſcoure a gun.

Spunk, an excreſcence on the ſides of trees, alſo half-rotten [aſh] wood.

Spun-yarn, rope-yarn ſcraped thin to make caburn, &c.

Spurcidical, *l.* ſpeaking ſmuttily.

Spurious, *l.* baſe-born, counterfeit.

Spurkets, the holes or ſpaces between the futtocks (or the rungs) by the ſhips-ſides.

Spurrey, *Spergula*, an herb.

Sputative, *l.* ſpitting much.

Squadron, *f.* a ſquare body of Soldiers.

Squaimus, *o.* for ſqueamiſh.

Squames, *o.* Scales.

Squalid, *l.* filthy, naſty.

Squamigerous, *l.* ſcale-bearing.

Squat, *Sſ.* bruiſe by falling.

Squeeker, *c.* a bar-boy.

Squill, *l.* the Sea-Onion.

Squinant, *-th*, *g.* the ſweet ruſh, Camels meat, an Arabian plant.

Squincy, *-nancy*, *l.* a ſwelling in the Throat.

Squireth, *o.* waiteth upon.

Squobled, when (between ſetting and impoſing) ſome lines (in a form) fall out of Order.

S. S. Sacroſanctus, (or *Sancti*) holy; *Spiritus Sanctus*, the Holy Ghoſt, or *Sacra Scriptura*, the holy Scripture.

Stability, *l.* firmneſs.

Stable-ſtand, a ſtanding one (with his bow bent) ready to ſhoot at Deer, or his dog ready to ſlip, &c.

Stabulate, *l.* to keep or be kept up as Cattel in a ſtall.

Stacker, *Li.* ſtagger.

Stack of wood, (in *Eſſex*) 14 foot in length, 3 in heighth and breadth.

Stacte, the gum of the Myrh-tree.

Stad, (*q. beſted*) *o.* encumbred.

Stade, *l.* a furlong.

Stade, *Stode*, a town of *Breme* in *Weſtphalia.*

Staffanger, a Port-town of *Norway.*

Staffier, (*I. Staffa*, a ſtirrup) a lacquey.

Stafford, the cheif town of *Stafford ſhire.*

Stael, a town in *Gelderland.*

Stag, a red male Deer five years old.

Staggard, one four years old.

Come a-ſtages or a-back-ſtages, with the ſails driven back againſt the ſhrowds, as the ſhip muſt before ſhe can tack.

Stagirite, *Ariſtotle*, born at *Stagira*, a town in *Macedonia.*

Stagnarium, for *Stann-*, a tin-mine.

Stagnes, *l.* ponds.

Stainard colours (in Heraldry) tawny and murrey.

Staindrop, a town of *Durham.*

Stallage, (*ſc. ſtallange*) *Siliquaticum*,

Stall-money in Fairs, &c.

Stall-whimper, *c.* a baſtard.

Stalling-ken, *c.* a brokers, or any houſe that receives ſtolen goods.

Stalboat, a kind of Fiſhers boat.

Stalkers, a kind of nets.

Stallion, *l.* a horſe kept for Mares.

Stamineous, *l.* of hemp or flax.

Stamps, *c.* legs.

Stampers, *c.* ſhoes or carriers.

Stam-fleſh, *c.* to cant.

Stamwood, *Sſ.* the root of trees ſtub'd up.

Stanbol, *Tu.* *Conſtantinople.*

Stanch [*hound*,] old, experienced.

Standard, *Eſt-*, *f.* the chief enſign of an army, alſo the ſtanding meaſure, to which all others are framed.

Standel, a young ſtore-oak, whereof 12 muſt be left ſtanding at the felling-an acre of wood.

Stanes, a town in *Middleſex.*

Stanford, a town in *Northampton-ſhire*, alſo another in

in *Lincoln* (where an Academy was (only) begun, in the reign of *Edw.* 3d.) and ſeveral other ſmall towns.

Stang, No. a Cowl-ſtaff, alſo to make one ride thereon.

Stannar, the mother of metals, a ſecret fume whereof they are made.

Stank, o. weary, faint.

Stannaries, l. the Corniſh Tin-works.

Stanza, I. a ſtaff [of verſes.

Staple, f. a publick Mart, whither Engliſh Merchants (by common order) were to carry their wares for whole-Sale.

Staple Inne, (by *Holbourn* bars) an Inne of Chancery, formerly for Staple-merchants.

Star-board, ſa. the right ſide of a ſhip.

Starfe, o. died.

Star-chamber, a Court at *Weſtminſter* put down by 17 *Car.* 1.

Stark, No. ſtiff, weary.

Star of Bethlehem, *Ornithogalum*, a kind of herb.

Stargard, a town in lower *Pomeren*.

Starrulet, a little ſtar.

Start, No. a tail or handle.

Start, put up [a hare.

Starwort, *Bubonium*, *Aſter Atticus*, a cooling and drying herb.

Startling, o. for ſparkling.

Staſiarch, g. the chief rebel.

Stater, g. in Silver 2 s. 6 d. in Gold, 17 s. 6d.

Staveſaker, an herb whoſe ſeed is uſed to kill lice and the itch.

Staticks, g. the ſcience of weights and meaſures.

Station, l. a ſtanding-place, a bay or road for Ships.

Station-ſtaff, a ſurveying-pole.

Stationary, ſetled in any place.

Stationers Company, takes in Bookſellers, -Binders, and *Stationers* (properly ſo called) ſell Paper, Ink, Wax, &c.

Stative, l. ſtanding, pitched.

Statuary, l. a ſtone-cutter.

Statuminate, l. to underprop.

Statute, l. Act of Parliament.

Statute-Merchant, and

Statute Staple, Bonds made and acknowledged in manner directed by the Statutes.

Statutes, Statute (or petit) Seſſions, kept yearly for the diſpoſing of Servants.

Statuto Stapulæ, a writ for the body and goods of him that forfeits the Statute-Staple.

Statutum Mercatorium, againſt him that forfeits Statute-Merchant.

Statutum de Laborariis, againſt Labourers that refuſe to work.

Staw'd, No. (for ſtowed) ſet.

Steccado, ſp. the liſts rail'd in for a combat, alſo a pale or fence before trenches.

Stechfelt, (for *Steffens felt*) a town in lower *Alſatia*.

Stechados, a beautiful and opening herb.

Stede, o. a place.

Stedſhip, o. firmneſs.

Steel, the body of an arrow.

Steel yard, as *Stil-yard*.

Steer, to govern a ſhip with the helm.

Steerage, -idge, the place where the ſteers-man ſtands.

Stee, No. a ladder.

Stem, No. to beſpeak a thing.

Stein, *Steven*, the ſame.

Steindel, a town in *Brandenburg*.

Steke or ſteick the dure, No. ſhut the door.

Steganography, g. a diſcourſe of covering buildings.

Stellar, l. ſtarry.

Stellation, l. adorning with ſtars, alſo blaſting.

Stele So. a ſtalk or handle.

Stelletto, *Stiletto*, I. a dagger.

Stelliferous, l. ſtar-bearing.

Stellion, l. a ſpotted lizzard, that caſts his skin (a Soveraign remedy for the falling ſickneſs) and enviouſly devours it every half year.

Stellionate, l. deceit in Merchandize.

Stelt, a town of *Berg* in *Germany*.

Stem, a ſtalk, ſtock or lineage, alſo the great timber coming up compaſſing from the keel before the forecaſtle.

Stem for Stem, right with their heads one againſt another.

Give her the Stem, the ſame as *Go Stemming aboard her*, run right upon her with the ſtem.

Stennery, as *Stannary*.

Stenais, a town in *Lorrain*.

Stenning, a town in *Suſſex*.

Stenten, o. to ſtay (ſtint.)

Stenography, g. ſhort-writing.

Stentorian, like unto

Stentor, a Grecian whoſe voice was louder than 50 mens together.

Stephen, g. a Crown.

Step, the timber wherein a maſt is placed.

Step-mother, Mother-in-law

Sterbrech, *Streb-ſa*, an obſtruction of a way, or a turning it out of the way.

Stercorean, -*orarious*, l. belonging to dung.

Stercoration, l. a dunging.

Stered, o. dealt withal.

Stereleſs, o. without a ſtern.

Sterelich, o. earneſtly.

Stereometry, g. the meaſuring of ſolid bodies.

Sterile, l. barren.

Sterility, l. barrenneſs.

Sterling, as *Eaſterling*, alſo part of South-*Scotland*.

Sterling-money, *nummi Eſterlingi*, brought to perfection by the Eaſterlings under *Rich.* 1.

Stern, the aftermoſt part of a ſhip, alſo the tail of a Grey-hound or Wolf.

Sternberg, a town of *Mecklenburg*.

Sternfaſt, a rope faſten'd to the ſtern, to keep it firm.

Sterne, o. to lay down (*ſternere*.)

Sternon, g. the breast-bone.

Sternutatory, a powder to cause

Sternutation, l. sneezing.

Sterquilinous, -nious, belonging to a dung-hill.

Sterve o. to dy.

Stesimbrotus, a Theban Captain, put to death (by his Father Epaminondas) for fighting the enemy without orders.

Stetin, the chief town of Pomerania.

Steves, [the bolt-sprit or beak head] stands too upright.

Steving of Cotton, Stowing it.

Stevon, o. a Sound.

Stews, Hot (or Whore) houses; also little fish-ponds, So.

Sthenobæa, receiving a repulse from Bellerophon, accused him falsly to her Husband.

Stibes, -ez, Thebes in Greece.

Stibium, Antimony, from the Darby-shire mines, &c.

Stich-wort, an herb good against stiches and pains in the side.

Stiff-gale, a strong wind.

Stife quean, No lusty.

Stigian, as Stygian.

Stighed, o. ascended.

Stigmatick, -cal, one that is

Stigmatized, g. branded with a hot iron.

Stigonomancy, g. divination by writing on the bark of trees.

Stillatory, l. a still, or distilling.

Stilletto, as Stelletto.

Stillicide, l. Eaves-dropping.

Stillicidous, -latitious, dropping.

Stillyard, Steelyard, Guilda Teutonicorum, where the Hanse and Almain Merchants used to reside.

Stimulate, l. to prick or provoke.

Stipation, l. a guarding about.

Stipendial, l. belonging to wages.

Stipendary, l. taking wages, or paying tribute.

Stipendious, l. having often served for wages (in war.)

Stipone, a sweet compound summer-drink.

Stipticity, a being

Stiptick, -cal, g. of a binding nature.

Stipulate, l. to make a

Stipulation, l. a solemn and formal Covenant or promise.

Stiria, Stiermark, part of Austria.

Stiricide, l. the dropping of icicles.

Stirious, l. belonging to icicles.

Stirps, l. a stalk, stock or kinred.

Stithe, No. strong, stiff.

Stithy, No. an anvil.

Stoage, for Stowage.

Stoaked [pump or ship] when the water cannot come to the well.

Stoccado, Sp. a thrust or stab.

Stockbridg, a town in Hamshire.

Stockholm, the chief town in Swedeland.

Stock-drawers, c. stockings.

Stocks, posts framed to build a ship or boat upon.

Stocked, o. cast [into prison.

Stode of maarys, o. a company of Mares.

Stoical, belonging to

Stoicism, the doctrine of the

Stoicks, g. Porch-Disciples of Zeno at Athens, who held a fatal necessity, freedom (in a wise man) from all passions &c.

Stoikesomaticks, g. the makers of certain Chaldean figures or Images.

Stoke, above 50 small towns.

Stoly [house] Sf. dirty, cluttered.

Stole, l. a long robe, also the Ornament about the Priests neck and cross his breast, denoting the yoke of Christ and the cord that bound him; a tippet.

Stolidity, l. a being

Stolid, l. foolish, fond, lewd.

Stomachick, that cannot keep the meat in his stomach.

Stomachick vien, ends (in 2 branches) in the hollow of the ventricle.

Stomachosity, l. a being

Stomachous, angry, disdainfull.

Stomatick, g. with a sore mouth.

Stone, a town in Staffordshire, and about a dozen more.

Stone of wool, ought to be 14 li.

Stone of beef, 8 pound, in Heref. 12.

Stone-falcon, building in rocks.

Stone-fly, a May-fly.

Stone-henge, a wonderfull pile of stones on Salisbury-plain.

Stont, o. for stood.

Stony-stratford, a town in Bucks.

Stook of corn, 12 sheaves.

Stooming of wine, with bags of herbs (and other infusions) to make Rochelle &c. pass for Bacbrag.

Stooping, the hawks bending down to strike a fowl.

Stopford. a town in Cheshire.

Stoppers, peeces of rope to stop the Cables from going out too fast.

Storax, a fragrant Syrian gum.

Stork, D. a bird famous for piety to his parent, feeding him when old and impotent.

Storks-bill, as Crows-bill.

Stormaria, part of Holstein.

Storming, assaulting a place.

Stot, *No.* a young horse or bullock.
Stotal, for *Scotale*.
Stovene, as *Zuche*.
Stover, *E.* fodder.
Stowk, *No.* as stook, also a pail-handle.
Stow your whids, *c.* speak warily.
Stowage, the place or money paid for
Stowing, laying goods in a Ships hold or ware-house.
Stownds, *o.* sorrows, dumps.
Stound, *Sf.* a little while, also (*No.*) a wooden small-beer-vessel.
Stound-meal, *o.* of small continuance.
Stowrs, *o.* shocks, brunts.
Stowr, *No.* a hedge-stake or ladder round.
Strabism, *l.* a looking asquint.
Straelsonde, a Port-town in *Pomerania*.
Strage, *l.* a great slaughter, felling of trees, &c.
Strake, *o.* to pass.
Strake, the iron about the fellies of a wheel, also the seam between two ship-planks.
Straits, *Streits*, course narrow cloth or kersey.
Stranded, run upon the
Strand, *sa.* the bank or shore.
Strand, *Sf.* a twist of a line.
Straineth, [the hawk] snatcheth.
Strangury, *-ullion*, *g.* a making water by drops and great pain.
Strappado, *I.* an engine to punish soldiers by drawing them up and letting them drop.
Strasbourg, a town in *Alsace*, with a tower of 630 steps up.
Stratagemical, full of
Stratagems, *g.* subtle [warlike] inventions.
Stratford upon Avon, in *Warwick shire*.
Stratification, a strewing corroding powder on metals
Stratiotick, *g.* warlike.
Straton, a town in *Cornwal*.
Stratocracy, *g.* government by an army.
Stratuminate, *l.* to pave.
Stream-anchor and cable, used in Rivers and fair weather.
Straught, *o.* for stretched.
Streight, *Straight*, a narrow sea-passage between two lands.
Street-gavel, two shillings paid yearly by the Tenants to the Lord of *Cholington* in *Sussex*, for going out and returning into it.
Streme-works, following the veins of Tin by trenching, as Lode-work is by digging shafts in higher places.
Stre, *We.* straw.
Strene, *Streen*, *o.* kinred.
Strenuity, *l.* a being
Strenuous, valiant, hardy.
Strepe, *o.* for strip.
Streperous, *l.* hoarse, jarring.
Strepitate, *l.* to make a noise.
Stretch forward, deliver it along into the mens hands to hale by.
Strictive, *l.* gathered, cropped.
Stricture, a gathering, also a spark from a red hot iron.
Strident, *-dulous*, making a
Stridor, *l.* a crashing noise.
Strig, *Sf.* the stalk of Fruit.
Strigilate, *l.* to curry [a horse.
Strigment, *l.* filth rub'd off.
Strike, *No.* a bushel.
Strike sail, pull them down
Strikle, *-er*, stritchel, that which strikes off the over-measure.
Strip, *Strop*, destruction or mutilation.
Stripe, *o.* kinred.
Strocal, a long iron instrument (like a fire-shovel) in glasse-making.
Strom, *No.* an instrument to keep the Malt in the fat.
Stromatick, *g.* belonging to strewings.
Stromaticks, books of several scattered subjects.
Strond, as *Strand*.
Strophes, *g.* subtilties in arguing.
Stroud, a town in *Glocester-shire*.
Strushings, *No.* Orts.
Structure, *l.* building.
Strumatick, troubled with
Strume, *-ma*, *l.* a wen or swelling in the neck, &c.
Strunt, *No.* a tail or rump.
Stuckling, *Sf.* an apple-pasty.
Stude (*or Stode*) *of Mares*, a great company, a stock of breeding Mares.
Studious, *l.* careful.
Study of Oxford, &c. University.
Stull, *E.* a luncheon [of Bread, &c.
Stultiloquy, *l.* foolish talk.
Stum, the flower of fermenting wine put up in vessels with iron hoops.
Stunt, *Li.* stubborn, angry
Stupefaction, *l.* astonishing.
Stupendious, *b.* wonderful.
Stupid, *l.* dismaid, senseless.
Stupidity, dulness.
Stupor, *l.* amazement.
Stupration, *l.* a deflowring.
Stuprous, *l.* adulterous.
Sturbridge, a town in *Worcester-shire*.
Sturmister, a town in *Dorcet-shire*.
Sturk, *no.* a Bullock or Heifer.
Sturrup, a piece patcht to the keel with an iron like a stirrup.
Sturt, *o.* to straggle.
Stusnet, *Sf.* a posnet, skillet.
Stut, *Somers.* a gnat.
Stygian, hellish, belonging to
Styx, *g.* a poisonous fountain of *Arcadia*, feigned to be a River in Hell by which the Gods swore, and he that swore falsly was banished from Heaven and Nectar for 1000 years.
Stylo novo, after the new

Gregorian Account.

Stylo veteri, after the old Julian account.

Styptick, as *Stiptick*.

Suada, the Roman Goddeſs of Eloquence.

Suaſory, *l.* perſwading, exhorting.

Suaviation, *l.* an amorous kiſſing.

Suaviloquent, *l.* ſweet-ſpoken.

Suaviloquy, ſweet ſpeech.

Suavity, *l.* ſweetneſs.

Sub-, *l.* under, ſomewhat.

Subaction, a bringing under.

Subagitation, a driving to and fro, a ſoliciting. &c.

Subalbid, whitiſh.

Subalpine, under the Alps.

Subaltern, taking turns alſo under another.

Subalter and Sept, *o.* for *Gibralter and Septa* (now *Ceuta*.)

Subaquaneous, under water

Subaudition, hearing a little

Subcineritious, under aſhes.

Subclavian, under lock and key.

Subclavicular vein, a main aſcendant branch of the hollow vein.

Subcutaneous, under the skin.

Subdial, being

Sub dio, in the open air.

Subdititious, in anothers room.

Subdolous, deceitful.

Subduct, to draw back or away.

Subduction, a bringing under, a reckoning or an allowance.

Subgette, *o.* for ſubject.

Subhaſtation, an out-cry, portſale, ſelling confiſcate goods under a ſpear.

Subhumerate, to undergo a burden.

Subject, to put under.

Subject, one under another, the matter treated of, the ſubſtance to which qualities adhere.

Subingreſſion, a ſubtle entring,

Subitaneous, *-ary*, ſudden.

Subjugate, to ſubdue or bring

Sub-jugum, under the yoke, or ſpears ſet like a gallows.

Subjunction, a joyning under.

Subjunctive, under-ſetting.

Subjunctive mood, which depends on another verb or a conjunction.

Sublapſarians, hold that God (in his reprobating of men) did conſider them as faln (but without reſpect to their final impenitence.)

Sublation, a taking away.

Sublevate, to lift up, or help.

Subligate, to bind underneath.

Sublimation, a carrying aloft, alſo (in Chymiſtry) the ſticking of dry exhalations to the ſides of the Alembick.

Sublimatum, white *Mercury*, a corroſive powder.

Sublimatory, an inſtrument (or veſſel) of ſublimation.

Sublime, lofty.

Sublimity, height.

Sublition, an under-daubing, graſing or laying the ground colour under the perfect.

Sublunary, under the Moon.

Submarine, under-ſea.

Submerſion, plunging, drowning.

Submiſſion, a yielding.

Subordination, a being

Subordinate, ſet under another.

Suborn, to prepare or procure [falſe witneſs, &c.]

Subpedaneous, *Supp-*, ſet under foot, as a foot-ſtool.

Sub-pœna, (under the penalty [of 100 pounds, &c.) a writ to call a man into the Chancery; alſo as a witneſs, into any Court.

Subreptitious, as *Surrept-*.

Subriguous, moiſt underneath.

Subriſion, a ſmiling.

Subrogation, as *Surro-*.

Subſannate, to mock or jeer,

Subſcription, an underwriting.

Subſecive, cut off [from other buſineſs] done at times.

Subſequent, immediately following.

Subſervient, helping, in order to.

Subſidence, a ſinking down.

Subſidiary, auxiliary.

Subſidy, aid, alſo a tribute Aſſeſſed by Parliament.

Subſiſtence, abiding, continuance.

Subſortition, a chuſing by lot after others have choſen.

Subſtantial, real.

Subſtantive, a word that ſignifies the ſubſtance or being of a thing.

Subſtitute, to put in the room of another, alſo a Deputy.

Subſtitutive, appointed in anothers place, alſo conditional.

Subſtraction, a taking a leſſer number from the greater.

Subſtruction, an underpinning, groundſelling, or laying the foundation of a houſe.

Subſult, to leap under or about.

Subſultation, ſuch a leaping.

Subſultory, leaping under.

Subtegulaneous, under the houſe-eaves or roof.

Subtenſe, chord, a right line from one extream of an arch to the other, like the ſtring of a bent bow.

Subterduction, a private leading away or ſtealing.

Subterfluous, flowing under.

Subterfuge, an evaſion or cunning ſhift.

Subterranity, the being

Subterrany, *-neous*, underground.

Subtiliation, the turning a body into liquor or fine powder.

Subtilties, quirks, cunning sayings.

Subtract, as *Substract*.

Subventaneous, under the wind.

Subversion, an overthrowing.

Subvert, to overthrow.

Suburbian, belonging to

Suburbs, the out-part of a Town or City.

Suburbicarian, within the Jurisdiction of the City [*Rome*.

Subvulturian, like a vulture, living by rapine.

Suc, *f.* Juice.

Succedaneous, *l.* succeeding another.

Succedaneous medicament, instead of one that cannot be got.

Succedent houses, 2d, 5th, 9th, 11th.

Succentor, *l.* a [bass or under] singing-man.

Succenturiate, *l.* to fill up the [Soldiers] vacant places.

Succernate, *l.* to sift meal.

Succiduous, *l.* ready to fall.

Succinct, *l.* girt up, also brief.

Succineous, belonging to

Succinum, *l.* amber.

Succisive, as *Subsecive*.

Succollation, *l.* a beating on the shoulders.

Succubus, a she-devil said to ly with men.

Succulency, a being

Succulent, *l.* juicy, plump.

Succumbents, *l.* excommunicate penitents kneeling behind the Quire or Pulpit.

Succussion, *sation*, a violent shaking, trotting or jolting.

Suction, *l.* a sucking.

Sudation, *l.* a sweating.

Sudatory, belonging thereto; also a hot-house.

Sudbury, a Town in *Suffolk*.

Sudorifick, causing sweat.

Sudorous, sweaty.

Suecia, Swedeland, a Kingdom North of *Germany*.

Sueth, *r.* wipeth (*f. Essu-*

Suffarcinate, *l.* to stuff up.

Suffarraneous, *Subf-*, *l.* under another servant; also carrying meal to sell.

Suffection, Substituting.

Suffition, *l.* a perfuming (on hot coals.)

Sufflamen, *l.* a trigger, to

Sufflaminate, to scatch or scotch a wheel.

Sufflation, *l.* a puffing up.

Suffocate, *l.* to strangle or choak.

Suffossion, *l.* an undermining.

Suffragan, *l.* a Bishops Vicegerent.

Suffragation, a giving ones

Suffrage, *l.* a vote or voice in electing.

Suffraginous, *l.* having the scratches or spaven.

Suffraunt *o.* a sufferer.

Suffricate, *l.* to rub off or under.

Suffumigation, *l.* a conveying smoke up [into the body.

Suffusion, *l.* a spreading or pouring upon; also a pin or web in the eye.

Suggestion, *l.* a prompting.

Sugillation, *l.* a beating (or being) black and blew, also a slander.

Subit, See *Gazul*.

Suicide, *l.* Self-murder.

Suist, a selfish man.

Suit of the Kings peace, the pursuing a man for breach of the Kings peace.

Sulcation, a making furrows,

Sulphureous, like or full of

Sulphur, *l.* brimstone.

Sul, *We.* a plough.

Sul-paddle, a plough-staff

Sultan, *Soldan*, (*P.* an Earl) a King or Soveraign, particularly the Turk; also as

Sultanin, a Turkish gold coin, near 8 shillings.

Sultana, the Empress.

Sulzbach, a town in *Bavaria*.

Sumach, *-ak*, *-aque*, a rank black-berry'd plant used by Diers.

Sumage, a toll for carriage on hors-back.

Summary, a brief Epitome.

Summ'd, [a hawk] having her feathers complete.

Summer, the main beam (in building.)

Summit, *-ty*, *l.* the top or height.

Summist, *-mulist*, an abridger.

Summons in terra petita, made upon the land which the party sues for.

Summons ad Warrantizandum, the process whereby the Vouchee is called.

Sumner, a Summoner.

Sumpter-horse, carrying necessaries for a journey.

Sumptify, *l.* to be at great expences.

Sumptuary laws, against excess in apparel, &c.

Sumptuous, *l.* costly, stately.

Sunamite, *Shu-*, *h.* sleeping.

Sund, *Sond*, *Sa.* a streight.

Sundew, Lustwort, Moorgrass, Redrot.

Sungow, the South part of *Alsatia*.

Super-, *l.* Over, upon.

Superable, to be overcom'n.

Superabound, to abound very much.

Superaffusion, a pouring upon.

Superannate, *-nuate*, to outlive, or grow out of date.

Superbiloquence, proud speech.

Superbiloquent, *l.* speaking proudly.

Superbipartiens-tertias, (*q. super bis tertias*) an oblong whose length is encreased by 2 thirds.

Supercbery, *f.* superfluity; also an injury or sudden assault.

Supercilious, *l.* proud, haughty.

Supereminence, *l.* an excellency above others.

Supererogatory, belonging to

Supererogation, laying out more

more than one has received, doing more than our duty.

Superfetation, a conceiving with young upon young.

Superficiary, he that pays quit-rent for a house built on anothers ground; also as

Superficial, belonging to a

Superficies, *l.* Surface, outside.

Superficialize, to do a thing

Superficially, slightly, Overly.

Superfluity, *-ance*, excess.

Superfluous, more than needs.

Superjection, a casting upon.

Superinduce, to bring or draw one thing over another.

Super-institution, one upon another.

Superintendent, an Overseer.

Superintendents, were Scotch Presbyterian Bishops.

Superiority, a being

Superiour, above others.

Superiour Planets, above the Sun.

Superlative, highest of all.

Superlative degree, ending in *-est*, or having most prefixt.

Supermeate, to pass over.

Supernal, from above.

Supernatation, a swimming upon.

Supernumerary, above the ordinary (or full) number.

Supernatural, above nature

Superoneratione Pasturæ, against him that over-burdens the common.

Super Prærogativa Regis, against the Kings widow, for marrying without his Licence.

Supersaliency, a leaping upon.

Superscription, a writing over or on the out-side.

Supersede, to omit, or cease.

Supersedeas, a writ to stop the doing what otherwise ought to be done.

Supersession, a surceasing or leaving off.

Superstitious, full of

Superstition, too much scrupulousness, giving too much to ceremonies.

Super Statuto Edw. 3. against him that keeps another mans Servants departed against Law.

Super statuto de York, against him that uses Victualling during the time he is Mayor.

Super statuto facto pour Seneschal, against the Kings Steward or Marshal, for holding plea in his Court of Freeholds or for trespass not made within the Houshold.

Super Statuto de Articulis Cleri, against distreining in the Kings high-way or in the Glebeland.

Supervacuous, *-caneous*, needless.

Supervene, to come upon.

Supervisor, a Surveyor.

Supervive as *Survive*; also to recover from peril of death.

Supinity, a being

Supine, *l.* with the face upward, careless.

Supines, the Accusative and Ablative cases of Verbal Nouns.

Suppedaneous, as *Subpe-*.

Sppeditate, *l.* to supply [with foot forces.

Suppellecticarious, *Supell-*, *l.* belonging to houshold-stuff.

Suppilation, *l.* a pilfering.

Supplant, *l.* to trip up, to beguile; also to prop up a plant, &c.

Supplement, *l.* a supply.

Suppliant, *f.* humble; also a Petitioner.

Supplicate, *l.* to beseech.

Supplice, *l.* punishment, also prayer and Sacrifice.

Supplicn, *o.* to make Supplication.

Supplosion, *l.* a stamping noise

Suppositious as *Subdititious*.

Suppository, any solid thing put up into the body to make it soluble (usually boild honey [and egge.]

Supposted, *l.* underset or suborned.

Suppress, *o.* to keep down.

Supprise, *l.* to overcome.

Suppuration, *l.* a mattering, the ripening of a bile, &c.

Supputation, *l.* pruning or reckoning.

Supramundane, *l.* above the world.

Supralapsarians, holding that God, in his reprobating of men, did consider them before their fall.

Supremacy, *l.* a being

Supreme, highest in power.

Supremity, *l.* the state of men after death, the last and highest action of a thing

Sural, belonging to the calf of the leg.

Surannation, *f.* a growing out of date, above a year old

Surate, an *Indian* Port-town of *Cambaia*.

Surbating, *f.* a galling or over-heating the soles of the feet.

Surcease, *f.* to give over.

Surcharge, *f.* Charge upon charge.

Surcharge the Forest, to put in more beasts than he has right to Common.

Surcingle, *f.* an upper girth or girdle.

Surcle, a young graff or twig.

Surcoat, *f.* an upper garment, a Coat of Arms over Armour.

Surcrew, *Surcroit*, *f.* vantage, overgrowing.

Surculate, *l.* to prune or cut off young shoots.

Surculous, *l.* full of sprigs.

Surdity, *l.* a being

Surd, deaf, also dumb.

Sureby, a port in *Yorkshire*,

Surface, as *Superficies*.

Surges, [the cable] slips back at the capstain.

Surge, a wave.

Surkney, *Suckney* *f.* a frock.

Surmount, *f.* to excell.

Surpass, *f.* the same.

Surplice, *Surpilch*, the Ministers white vestment.

Surplusage, *f.* superfluity, adding more than needs.

Sur-

Surpriſal, *f.* a ſudden aſſault.

Surquedry, *o.* pride, preſumption.

Surrebutter, a ſecond Rebutter.

Surrejoynder, *f* the Plaintiffs oppoſition to the Defendants rejoinder (in civil Law, Triplication.

Surrender, a Tenants yielding up his land, &c. to him that has the next remainder or reverſion.

Surreptitious, *l.* done by ſtealth.

Surrey, *o.* Syria.

Surrogation, the ſubſtituting a

Surrogate, a [Biſhops] deputy.

Surround, compaſs about.

Surſanure, a ſore skin'd over.

Surſengle, *f.* a long uppergirth.

Surſiſe, penalties (in *Dover*-Caſtle) laid on thoſe that do not duly pay their duties for Caſtleward.

Survive, *f.* to out-live.

Surviver, the longer-liver of two joynt-tenants.

Suryal [horns] more than royal, *o.*

Suſan, *nna*, *h.* a lilly or roſe.

Suſception, *l.* an undertaking.

Suſceptible, *l.* apt to take impreſſion.

Suſceptor, *l.* an undertaker, a Godfather.

Suſcitation, *l.* a raiſing or ſtirring up.

Suskins, a coyn prohibited 3 *Hen.* 5.

Suſpend, *l.* to hang up, defer, ſtay, keep in doubt.

Suſpenſion, a hanging up, doubting, alſo a temporal ſtop of a mans right.

Suſpenſories, *f.* cords hanging down for a ſick man (in bed) to eaſe or remove himſelf by.

Suſpiral, *f.* a breathing-hole; alſo a ſpring paſſing under-ground to a conduit.

Suſpiration, *l.* a ſighing.

Suſter, *o.* for ſiſter.

Suſtentation, a maintaining.

Suſurration, *l.* a whiſpering.

Sute-ſilver, paid to excuſe the Free-holders of *Clun* Manor in *Shropſhire*, from appearing at Court Barons.

Sutherland, part of North-*Scotland*.

Sutler, *Suttler*. (*D. Seeteler*, a Scullion or Huckſter) one that follows an army, to ſell meat, drink, &c.

Sutorious, belonging to a *Sutor*, *l.* a Shoomaker.

Sutton, about 60 ſmall Towns.

Sutton Cofield, in *Warwickſhire*.

Suture, *l.* a ſeam, or any thing like it.

Suzan, *P.* a needle.

Swa. *ſa.* ſo.

Swabber, a ſmall Officer who cleans the ſhip, &c.

Swaben, or *Schwaben* [land] *Suevia*, a German Province.

Swad, *no.* a pea-ſhell, alſo a ſhallow-pate.

Swag, *c.* a ſhop.

Swaffham, a town in *Norfolk*.

Swain, *ſa.* a Countrey-bumkin, alſo a Bockland-man or Freeholder.

Swainmote, *Swanimote*, *ſa.* a Court of Forreſt-Free-holders kept thrice a year.

Swale, *o.* ſwelled.

Swale, *no.* windy, bleak, alſo to ſinge, burn or blaze away.

Swallow-tail, a ſtrong forked faſtening together two pieces of timber.

Swan, a Conſtellation.

Swapt-down, *o.* ſquatted down.

Swarth, *Cu.* the Ghoſt of a dying man.

Swarthy *D.* blackiſh, tawny

Swart-Ruyter, *D.* a horſeman with black arms.

Bartholdus *Swartz*, the German Fryer that invented Gun-powder.

Swaſh-buckler, a bragging Hector.

Swathe, *No.* Calm.

Swatch, *No.* a tally.

Sweal, *Sſ.* to ſinge.

Sweb, *No.* to ſwoon.

Sweden, *Swethland*, a Northern Kingdom.

Sweeps, [the hawk] wipes her beak.

Swegh, *o.* force, noiſe.

Swelwen, *o.* to ſwallow.

Swepe, *Swipe*, an inſtrument (with croſs beams) to draw water, alſo as

Swepage, the crop of hay got in a Meadow.

Swere, *ſa.* a column or neck.

Sweren, a town of *Mecklenburg*.

Sweven, *o.* a dream.

Swift, a martlet, with feet ſo ſhort that he cannot riſe from the ground.

Swift the maſts, eaſe and ſtrengthen them with

Swifters, ropes belonging to the main and fore-maſts, to keep them ſtiff and ſuccour the ſhrowds.

Swill, *No.* a three-footed keeler to waſh in.

Swilk, *ſa.* ſuch.

Swilker ore, to daſh over.

Swilpough, a dilling.

Swinbull, *Swine-crue*, *No.* a hog-ſty.

Swink, *ſa.* labour.

Swinker, a labourer.

Swipper, *o.* nimble.

Swithin, (*Sa.* very high) a pious Biſhop of *Winchester*, *Anno* 860.

Swith, *Switch*, *o.* quickly.

Switzerland, a warlike nation (by the *Alpes*) divided into 13 Cantons or Republicks.

Swole-hot, *o.* ſultry-hot.

Swoling (*or Suling*) *of land*, *Carucata terra*, as much as one plough can till in a year.

Swoll, a town in *Over Yſſel*.

Sword-ſleiper, *ſa.* a Sword-cutler in the North of *England*.

Swerle, *Sſ.* to ſnarle.

Swote, *o.* ſweet.

Swough, *o.* a ſound, or a ſwooning.

Sybbe and Som, *ſa.* Peace and ſafety.

Syba-

Sybaritical, like the

Sybarites a very effeminate and luxurious people of

Sybaris, a town of *Calabria* in *Italy*.

Sybil, *g.* divine doctrine or Counsel.

Sybilline, belonging to the

Sybils, 10 heathen women who (they say) prophesied of Christ.

Sybillianists, a heathen Nick-name for Christians.

Sycomanty, *g.* divination by a Fig or a

Sycamore, a fair tree of *Egypt*, *Rhodes*, &c. between a Fig and Mulberry, whose Fruit (like a wild seedless fig) grows on the very body of the tree.

Sycophantize, to play the

Sycophant, *g.* a Parasite, properly an Athenian informer of Figs (and other goods) exported.

Syderation, *l.* Tree-plague, a blasting, also the benumming of a limb.

Syderosous, *l.* full of stars, also planet-struck.

Sye, *o.* as *Sile-down*.

Sylla, a famous Roman general and Dictator, who (at last) retired to *Puteoli*.

Syllabical, belonging to or consisting of a

Syllable, *g.* a compleat sound.

Syllabize, to make syllables or syllabus.

Syllabary, a book treating of

Syllables, also as

Syllabus, *l.* the Index of a book.

Syllepsis, one verb plural with two Nominatives singular, &c.

Syllogistical, belonging to a

Syllogism, *g.* a Conclusion drawn from two premisses, *viz.* the proposition or Major, and the Assumption or Minor.

Syllogize, to argue by Syllogisms.

Sylva Cædua, Coppice-wood.

Sylvanectum, *Sentis*, in *Pycardy*.

Sylvanus, the God of woods.

Sylvan, a wild-man.

Sylvatical, *-vestrick*, *-ious*, *l.* woody.

Sylvigerous, *l.* bearing wood.

Symbolical, belonging to a

Symbol, *g.* a sign or badge, a secret note or sentence, a shot (in paying) also the Creed.

Symbolize, to concur in opinion or humour, to joyn purses, to signifie by signs, &c.

Symbolography, *g.* a description of

Symboles', also of instruments or Presidents.

Symmachy, *g.* confederacy in War.

Symmetrist, *-ian*, one skil'd in

Symmetry, *g.* a due proportion of parts.

Symmist, *g.* a Privy-Counsellor, or Colleague in a [sacred] profession.

Sympathetical, belonging to

Sympathy, *g.* natural agreement in affection or passion.

Sympathize, to have a mutual affection or fellow-feeling.

Symphoniacal, belonging to

Symphony, *g.* harmony, consent.

Symphonist, *g.* a Songster.

Symploce, *g.* a giving the same beginning and ending to several clauses.

Symposiaques, Treatises of Feasts.

Symposiast, *g.* Master of the Feast.

Symptomatical, belonging to a

Symptome, *g.* a sign, accident or effect of a disease.

Synæresis, *g.* a contracting [two syllables into one.

Synagogical, belonging to a

Synagogue, *g.* an assembly, Jewish Church.

Synalæpha, *g.* the cutting off a final vowel before an initial one.

Synaxis, *g.* the holy Communion.

Syncategorematical, *g.* which hath no predicamental or self-signification, but (being added to another) makes it differ from what it was (as all, none, &c.)

Syncentrick, *g.* having the same centre.

Synchondrosis, *g.* a joyning together by a gristle.

Synchronism, *g.* a being

Synchronical, *g.* contemporary, done at the same time.

Synchoresis, *g.* a concession, granting or yielding.

Synchrism, *g.* a thin spreading ointment.

Syncopate, *-pize*, to contract, cut away, or to swoon.

Syncopation, when the striking of time falls in the midst of a note, notes driven till the time falls even again.

Syncope, *g.* the taking a letter or syllable from the midle, also a sudden decay of the spirits.

Syncretism, *g.* the joyning of two enemies against a third person.

Syncrisis, *g.* comparison.

Syndic, *g.* a censor or Controller.

Syndiques of Geneva, the 4 chief of their 200 Common-Council men.

Syndicable, subject to censure.

Syndicat, a Syndicks office.

Syndrome, *g.* a concourse or running together.

Synecdochical, belonging to

Synecdoche, *g.* the putting a part for the whole, or *e contra*.

Synedrium, *-ion*, *g.* a Council.

Synerize, to contract by the figure.

Syneresis, as *Synær-*.

Syngulter, *o.* a Boar (above four years old) leaving his founder.

Syngraph, *g.* a bond or bill.

Syno-

Synodale, a tribute paid the Bishop or Arch-Deacon (by the inferiour Clergy) at Easter Visitation.

Synodal, *-dical*, belonging to a

Synod, *g.* a Convocation or Ecclesiastical Assembly.

Synoicciosis, *g.* a reconciling, attributing contraries to the same thing.

Synonimize, to make use of

Synonyma's, words that are

Synonymal, *-mous*, *g.* of the same signification.

Synoper, *l.* red-lead.

Synople, *f.* (in Heraldry) green.

Synopsis, *-sy*, *g.* a short view.

Syntagm, *g.* a Treatise, Ordinance or placing things together.

Syntax, *g.* the same; also the joyning of words into sentences.

Syntectical, *g.* weak, often swouning.

Synteresy, *g.* the pure part of Conscience, accusing or excusing.

Syntheme, *g.* a watch-word, also a riddle, and as *Diploma*.

Synthetical, belonging to

Synthesis, *g.* an agreement in sence, not in word.

Syntomy, *g.* conciseness, brevity.

Syracuse, a City in *Sicily*.

Syren, as *Siren*.

Syria, part of *Asia*.

Syrinx, a Nymph (flying from *Pan*) turn'd into a reed, which he made his pipes of.

Syrtes, [African] Quick-sands.

Sysor, *o.* one of the Assise or Jury.

Systatique, *g.* placing together.

System, *g.* the compass of a song, the body of any Art or Science.

Systole, *g.* a Contraction.

Syzygy, *g.* a Conjunction [of the Sun and Moon.

T.

T. The brand of one convict (of any Felony save murder) and having the benefit of Clergy.

Taas, *o.* (*f. Tas*) a heap.

Tab, *No.* the latchet [of a shoe.

Tabacco, *Tob-*, brought from an Indian Isle (of the same name) by Sir *Francis Drake*, 1585.

Tabard, as *Taberd*.

Tabs, St. Ebbes, *Ebbechester*, a town of *Durham*.

Tabefaction, *l.* a corrupting.

Tabefy, to melt or consume.

Tabellarious, belonging to a

Tabellary, an Auditor or letter carrier.

Tabellion, *l.* a publick Notary.

Taberd, *-ard*, a sleeveless coat, also a Heralds Coat of arms in service.

Tabern, *No.* a Cellar.

Tabernacle, *l.* a booth or Tent, also a little vessel in which the Popish Sacrament is put on the altar.

Feast of Tabernacles, kept in remembrance of their living in Tents when they came out of *Egypt*.

Tabernarious, *l.* belonging to Taverns or shops.

Tabid, *l.* wasting away.

Tabifical, *l.* causing a Consumption.

Tabitha, *h.* a Roe-buck.

Table of Apelles, representing the excellency of sobriety (on one side) and the deformity of intemperance) (on the other.)

Twelve Tables (*of Brass*) Roman laws brought (by the *Decemviri*) from *Athens*.

Tabling of fines, making a Table with the Contents of every Fine (past in any one term) for every County where the Kings writ runs.

Tabouret, *f.* a pin-case, also a Childs low stool.

Privilege of the Tabouret, *f.* for some great Ladies to sit in the Queens presence.

Tabular, *-rious*, *l.* belonging to Tables or Writings.

Tabulary, *l.* a place where publick writings are kept.

Tabulate, *l.* to floor or board.

Taces, armour for the thighs (tackt with straps to the Corslet.)

Tacamachacca, a sweet gum used for the Teeth and head.

Taches, *o.* pranks.

Tachos, a king of *Egypt*, whose jeering at *Agesilaus's* shortness, broke their league and lost him his Kingdom.

Tachygraphy, *g.* Swift-writing.

Tacoy *o.* to pluck-to.

Tacit, *l.* silent.

Taciturnity, *l.* silence.

Tacks, great ropes (seased into the clew of the sail, reeved into the Chestree and comn in at the ship-side) to carry forward the clew and keep the sail close by a wind.

Tack the ship, bring her head about, to ly quite the other way.

Tackle, small ropes (running in 3 parts) to heave in goods, &c.

Tacticks, *g.* military books or Officers.

Taction, *l.* a touching.

Taddy, an Indian drink issuing from a tree.

Tagge, *Sf.* a sheep of the first year.

Tagliacotius, a Chirurgeon of *Bononia* who made a new nose (of another mans flesh) for one of *Brussels*.

Tagliacotian, belonging thereto.

Tagus, the gold-sanded river

Taio, between *Castile* and *Portugal*.

Tail, (*f.* cut or divided) a fee

fee (opposite to fee-simple) not in a mans free power to dispose of.

Tail general, limited to a man and his Issue by any Wife.

Tail special, limited to a man and his Wife, and the Heirs of their particular bodies.

Tail, is also the same as

Talley, a cleft piece of wood to notch an account upon.

Tails of Kentish men, a feigned punishment for their cutting off the tail of St. *Tho.* of *Canterbury's* horse.

Tailagiers, *o.* gatherers of

Tailage, Tall-, a tax.

Tainct, a small red spider infesting Cattle in Summer.

Taint, conviction, or one convict of Felony, &c.

Takel, *o.* an arrow or feather.

Talaries, *l.* *Mercuries* winged shoes.

Talassion, as *Thalassion*.

Talcum, *Talk*, a *Sussex* Mineral transparent as Chrystal (but not so fine as the *Venetian*) of which they make a curious white wash.

Talent of Silver, (among the Jews) about 375 pounds.

Of Gold, 4500 pounds.

Tales, (*l.* such) a book (in the Kings-Bench office) of such Jury-men as were of the

Tales [*de circumstantibus*] a supply of Jury-men for them that appear not, or are challenged by either party.

Taleshide, as *Talwood*.

Taley, *Tally*, see *Tail*.

Talion, *lex talionis*, a punishment like the offence.

Talismanical, belonging to

Talismans, *A.* Artificial magical images or figures made under certain constellations.

Tally aft the sheats, hale them aft.

Talmudical, belonging to the

Talmud, *Thalmud* (*h.* discipline) a Collection of the Jewish Ceremonies, and superstitious traditions.

Talmudist, a student therein.

Talpicide, *l.* a killing or killer of Moles.

Talus, slain by his Uncle *Dedalus* envying his ingenious inventions of the Saw, Potters wheel, &c.

Talwood, *Talshide*, Firewood cut into billets of a certain length.

Tamadua, the Ant-bear in *Brasile*, feeding on ants.

Tamarinds, an Indian, Physical, opening and cooling Fruit.

Tamarisk, a shrub of two sorts whereof the less boild in Wine (and a little Vinegar) greatly helps the Spleen

Tambour, *f.* a Drum.

Tamburine, an old kind of instrument disused.

Tamerlane, a Scythian who led *Bajazeth* the Turk about in an iron cage.

Tamesis, the *Thames* compounded of *Tame* and *Isis*.

Tampoon, *Tamkin*, the wooden stopple of a Canon.

Tampoy, a pleasant *Molucca*-drink (of a kind of Gilliflowers.

Tamworth, a town part in *Warwick* and part in *Staffordshire*.

Tanacles, *I.* torturing pincers.

Tanais, a river between *Europe* and *Asia*.

Tanet, *Tha-*, a Kentish Isle.

Tangent, a right line perpendicular to the Diameter, drawn by one extream of an Arch and terminated by the secant, drawn from the center through the other extream of the said arch.

Tangibility, a being

Tangible, *l.* touchable.

Tangier, an English town of the Kingdom of *Fesse* in *Barbary*.

Tanistry, an Irish custom, whereby the most powerful and worthy did inherit the principality.

Tank, a small pool.

Tanquam, (*l.* as) a Fellows fellow (in the University.)

Tant me fait mal departir de ma dame, *f.* so much it grieves me to part with my Mistress.

Tant que je puis, as much as I can.

Tantalized, in the Condition of

Tantalus, feign'd to stand up to the chin in water with pleasant Apples at his mouth, yet unable to compass either.

Tantamount, *I.* equivalent, of the same price.

Taps or Beats, [the hare or coney] makes a noise.

Taper bored, [a piece] wider at the mouth than breech.

Tapinage, *f.* a secret lurking.

Tapis, *-sant*, lurking, squatting.

Tapite, *o.* Tapistry.

Taprobane, *Sumatra*, an Indian Island 1000 Miles long and above 600 broad.

Tarantarize, to sound

Tarantara, *Taratan-*, the sound of Trumpets (to battel.)

Tarantula, a most venemous spider, or a fly whose sting (they say) is only cured by Musick, from

Tarantum, a City of *Naples* where they abound.

Tardy, *l.* slow, also guilty.

Tardigrade, *l.* slow-paced.

Tardiloquent, *l.* of slow speech.

Tardity, *l.* slowness.

Tare and Tret, [allowance for] the weight of box, bag, &c. and waste in emptying, &c.

Tares, [wild] vetches.

Targe, *o.* for Target.

Tarn, *No.* a lake.

Tarky, *Sf.* dark.

Tarnish, to lose the gloss or splendour.

Tarpawling, *-paulin*, a tar'd canvass laid on the deck, to keep

keep the rain out.

Tarpeia, a maid that betray'd the Capital to the *Sabines* for their bracelets, who (adding their shields too) prest her to death.

Tarquinius superbus, last King of *Rome*, Father of

Tarquinius Sextus, ravishing *Lucretia*, caused the extirpation of Kingly Government.

Tarracon, a City of *Arragon*.

Tarragon, a Sallet-herb.

Tarraß, as *Terrasse*.

Tarshish, *h.* the Ocean or main Sea.

Tarsus, a City of *Cilicia*.

Tartar, *Argal*, hard lees sticking to the sides of wine-vessels.

Tartarean, *-rine*, belonging to

Tartarus, *l.* hell.

Tartaria, a large part of *Asia*.

Tasck, *Br.* a tribute.

Tasels, Cloth-workers burs.

Tasse, *f.* a heap.

Tassay, *o.* for to assay.

Tassel, *Tiersel*. (*f. Tiercelet*) the male Hawk, less (by a third) than the female.

Tasses, as *Taces*.

Tast, *No*, smell.

Tatch, *Tetch*, *o.* craft.

Titus Tatius, a Sabine Captain, (after long wars) made a sharer in the Roman Government.

Tattershall, a town in *Lincolnshire*.

Tatterways, *o.* for tatterags.

Tave, *Li.* to rage.

Taudrey, for St. *Audry* (*Ethelred*.)

Taudrey-lace, bought at *Audry* fair in *Cambridgeshire*.

Tavistoke, *Teav-*, a town in *Devonshire*.

Taunt-mast, too high for the Ship.

Taunton, *Thonton*, a town on the River *Thone* in *Sommerset-shire*.

Taught the rope, set it stiff.

Taurean, *-rine*, *l.* of a Bull.

Tauricorneus, *l.* horned like a Bull.

Tauriferous, *l.* nourishing or bearing Bulls.

Taurinum, the City *Turin* in *Piedmont*.

Taurus, the largest hill in *Asia*, also the Zodiack bull.

Tautological, belonging to

Tautology, *g.* a repeating the same thing [in other words.

Tawn, *No.* to swoon.

Taxatio bladorum, an imposition on corn.

Taxers, two yearly Officers (at *Cambridge*) who gage all weights and measures (they formerly rated houses.)

Taximagulus, a King of *Kent*, who opposed *Julius Cæsar*.

Tay, a River dividing *Scotland* into North and South.

Taygetus, a steep hill near *Sparta*.

Tea, an Indian drink made with the leaf of a shrub, &c.

Team, *Theam*, *Tem*, *Theme*, a Royalty granted the Lord of a Mannour to have and judge Bond-men, &c.

Team, *Teem*, *No.* poure out.

Teamfull, *No.* brim-full.

Tech, *o.* for touch.

Technical, *g.* artificial.

Technology, *g.* a treating of arts or workmanship.

Tectonick, *g.* of building.

Tectorian, *l.* of covering or pargetting.

Tedder, *D.* [a rope] to tye a beast that he may graze no farther.

Tediferous, *l.* torch-bearing.

Teen, *No.* angry.

Good or few Teen, *Che.* good or foul taking.

Tegment, *l.* a covering.

Teisdale, part of South-*Scotland*.

Teine, a Hawks pursiveness, being quickly weary.

Teirse, as *Tierse*.

Tell no store, *o.* account as nothing.

Telary spiders, as weave webs.

Telephus, exposed in the woods and brought up by a Hart, becoming King of *Mysia*, was wounded and cured by *Achilles* dart.

Telescope, *g.* a large prospective-glass.

Teliferous, *l.* dart-bearing.

Telisman, as *Talisman*.

Tellers, (in the Exchequer) four Officers, receiving all money, &c.

Tellus, *l.* [the Goddess of] the Earth.

Teme, *o.* for (*Theme*) argument.

Temen, *o.* to bind or lay.

Temerarious, *l.* rash.

Temerity, *l.* fool-hardiness.

Tempe, *g.* pleasant Fields at the foot of *Hæmus* in *Thessaly*.

Temperamental, belonging to

Temperament, *l.* a due proportion [of the four humors.

Temperance, *l.* Moderation [in diet and desires.

Temperature, *l.* as *Temperament*.

Tempestivity, *l.* seasonableness.

Templars-Inne, (in *Fleet-street*) built by the

Templaries, as Knights of the Temple.

Temporal vein, the Temple vein opened for the Megrim, &c.

Temporal augment, an encreasing the quantity of a vowel.

Temporalties, (*-alities*,) of Bishops, their Revenues, as Barons of Parliament.

Temporal, *-raneous*, *-ary*, *-reous*, *l.* belonging to (or continuing for) a time.

Temporize, to observe or comply with the times.

Temporizer, a time-server.

Temse, *No.* a fine small sieve.

Temulency, *l.* drunkenness.

Temulent, -*tine*, *l.* drunken.

Temse-bread, sifted.

Tenacies l. apple stalks.

Tenable, holdable.

Tenacity, *l.* a being

Tenatious, *l.* holding or sticking fast, stiff-necked.

Tenancies, Tenements.

Tend, *l.* to bend, stretch out, shew forth.

Very Tenant, immediate.

Tendency, an extending, a making towards.

Tender, to offer.

Tenderlings, the soft tops of Deers horns in bloud.

Tendons, *l.* instruments of motion at the top of muscles, knitting them to the bones.

Tendrels, -*rons*, *f.* the same, also little sprigs (of Vines, &c.)

Tene, *o.* sorrow.

Tenebres, *f.* (darkness) the Roman service (on Wednesday, Thursday and Fryday before Easter) representing Christs apprehension in the Garden, when at the end of every Psalm they put out a Candle, till all the 15 are out, and he left friendless and under the power of darkness.

Tenebrion, *l.* a Night-walker.

Tenebrosity, a being

Tenebrous, *l.* dark, obscure.

Tenedos, an Egean Isle, whither the Greeks retired for a while.

Tenementis legatis, a writ for a Corporation to hear controversies touching Tenements devised by Will.

Tenentibus in assisa non onerandis, a writ for him to whom a deffeisor hath alienated land (whereof he deffeised another) that he be not molested for damages awarded, &c.

Tenerity, *l.* tenderness.

Tenesmus, *Tenas-*, *g.* a continual (but vain) desire of going to stool.

Tenne, (in Heraldry) an Orange or tawny colour.

Tenon, that part of the timber that is put into the mortise-hole.

Tenor, *l.* an order, fashion, state, content or substance, also that part (in Musick) next the Bass.

Tenore indictamenti mittendo, a writ calling the record of an inditement (and process) into the Chancery.

Tenses, the different endings of Verbs to signifie difference of time, *viz.* (in Latin) the Present, Preterim perfect, Preterperfect, Preterpluperfect and Future.

Tensile, *l.* to be bent or stretched out.

Tensity, *l.* stiffness or tightness.

Tent, Mastick and Turpentine which Jewellers put under Table-Diamonds, when they set them in work.

Tent wine, *Vino tinto*, *Sp.* all Wines (in *Spain*) except white.

Tent, *Che*, to look to.

Tentation, *l.* a trying.

Tentative, *l.* a posing or poser of those that are to commence.

Tenths, the Kings yearly portion of Ecclesiastical livings.

Tentor, a stretcher (used by Clothiers) prohibited.

Tentorean, *l.* belonging to a *Tent* or Pavilion [in war.

Tentife, *o.* (*q.* attentive) careful.

Tenuate, *l.* to cause

Tenuity, *l.* a being

Tenuious, -*ous*, thin, lean, slender weak.

Tenure, the manner whereby lands are held.

Tepefaction, -*fying*, *l.* a warming.

Tephramantie, *g.* Divination by ashes thrown in the Air.

Tepedity, a being.

Tepid, *l.* lukewarm.

Teraphim, *h.* images [for private use.

Teratology, *g.* a discourse of wonders.

Tercel, as *Tassel*.

Tercel-gentle, a Male Faulcon.

Tercera, a Western Isle.

Terebellum, *l.* a kind of Crows-bill.

Terebinthine, belonging to

Terebinth, *l.* Turpentine.

Terebrate, *l.* to bore, or thirl.

Terebration, *l.* a boring, &c.

Tergeminous, *l.* three-fold, or three born at a time.

Tergiductor, *l.* a bringer-up.

Tergiment, *l.* that which is put into the scales to make weight.

Tergiversation, *l.* a turning the back, a non-suit.

Term, *l.* a bound or limit, also the time when places of judgment are open for all Law-suits.

Hillary-Term, begins *Jan.* 23. (except it be Sunday) and ends *Feb.* 12.

Easter-Term, begins the Wednesday fortnight after Easter day, and ends the Munday after Ascension day.

Trinity-Term, begins the Friday after Trinity Sunday, and ends the Wednesday fortnight after.

Michaelmas-Term, begins *Oct.* 23. (except it be Sunday) and ends *Nov.* 28.

Tarmagant, thrice (or very) great.

Termentine, *l.* Turpentine.

Terminals, feasts (*Feb.* 22.) in honour of

Terminus, the Roman God of bounds, deciding controversies of Husbandmen.

Termonland, Glebeland.

Termor, he that holds for term of years or Life.

Terminate, *l.* to limit.

Termination, a bounding or ending.

Ternary, -*rious*, belonging to

Ternion, *l.* the number three.

Terns, *No.* large ponds.

Terra extendenda, a writ for

for the Eſcheator to find the true yearly value of Land, &c.

Terra excultabilis, land that may be tilled.

Terra fruſca or *friſca*, freſh land, not lately plowed.

Terra giliforata, held by paying a Gilly-flower.

Terra Lemnia, red aſtringent Earth of *Lemnos*.

Terra lucrabilis, that may be gained from the Sea (or a waſte) to particular uſe.

Terra ſigillata, Earth (ſent from *Lemnos*) ſealed, againſt wounds, Fluxes, Poiſons, &c.

Terra veſtita, (in old Charters) ſown with corn.

Terræ-filius, *l.* the bondrol at the *Oxford* Act, See *Prævaricator*.

Terraqueous, *l.* of Earth and water mixt.

Terrar, *-rer*, a ſurvey of all the acres (and their bounds) in an eſtate.

There is a *Terrar* in the Exchequer of all Glebe-lands in *England*.

Terraſſe, *Tar-*, *f.* a bank of Earth, alſo an open walk or gallery.

Terreſtrifie, to cauſe

Terreſtricty, a being

Terrene, *-reſtrial*, *l.* Earthly.

Terre-Tenant, *f.* he that hath the actual poſſeſſion of the Land.

Terricrepant, *l.* rebuking terribly.

Terrier, a Catalogue of all the Lords Tenants, &c.

Terring, a town in *Sſ.*

Terris, bonis et Catallis, &c. for a Clerk to recover his lands, &c. having clear'd himſelf.

Terris et Catallis, &c. to reſtore to the debtor diſtreined above the debt.

Terriſonant, *l.* ſounding terribly.

Territory, *l.* the land within the bounds of any place.

Terrulent, *l.* full of Earth.

Terry, an Indian liquor drawn from the Palm-tree.

Terſe, *l.* neat, polite.

Tertian, the third part of a tun, 84 gallons.

Tertian, *-ary*, *l.* belonging to the third.

Tertian ague, returning every other day (taking in the extreams.)

Tertiate, *l.* to till ground (or do any thing) a third time.

Tertiation, a dividing into three.

Tervin, a town in *Cheſhire*.

Teſſerarius, belonging to a

Teſſera, *l.* a die, or any ſuch ſquare, a token, watchword, &c.

Teſt, a broad inſtrument (made of maribone-aſhes) hoop'd with iron, on which they refine gold and ſilver.

Teſtaceous, *l.* of tile or brick.

Teſtaceous Animals, having ſhels.

Teſtamentarious, belonging to a

Teſtament, *l.* ones laſt will [having an Executor expreſt.

Teſtatum, a writ (after *Capias*) when a man is not found in the County where the action is laid.

Teſtation, *l.* a witneſſing.

Teſtator, *l.* He-, and

Teſtatrix, *l.* She that makes a will.

Teſter, ſix-pence, See *Teſton*.

Teſters, *o.* ſculls, ſallets, head pieces.

Teſticular, belonging to

Teſticles, *l.* the Stones.

Teſtif, *o.* (*q. Teſty.*) wild-brained.

Teſtification, as *Teſtation*.

Teſton, *f.* an old ſilver coin formerly worth 12 pence, ſinking by degrees to gilt braſs and ſixpence.

Teſtudinous, belonging to or like a

Teſtudo, *l.* a Tortoiſe ſhell, or Target-fence in war.

Tetanical, having a crick in the neck.

Tetbury, a town in *Gloceſterſhire*.

Tethys, a Goddeſs of the Sea.

Tetch, *o.* a faſhion, alſo a ſtain.

Tetches, *o.* forwardneſs.

Tetrachord, *g.* an inſtrument of 4 ſtrings, a forth in the Gamut.

Tetrade, *f.* a meſs of 4.

Tetraeterie, *g.* four years.

Tetraedron, *g.* a figure of four ſides.

Tetraglottical, *g.* of four Tongues.

Tetragonal, belonging to a

Tetragon, *g.* a quadrangle.

Tetragrammaton, *g.* the Name of 4 letters (almoſt in every language) *viz. Jehovah*.

Tetralogy, *g.* a diſcourſe in four parts.

Tetrameter, *g.* a verſe of 4 feet.

Tetraptote, *g.* a noun of 4 caſes.

Tetrarch, *g.* a Governour of the 4th. part.

Tetrarchy, *g.* a Government by four.

Tetraſtick, *g.* 4 verſes.

Tetraſyllabical, *g.* of four ſyllables.

Tetricity, *-ritude*, *l.* ſourneſs of countenance.

Tetrick, *l.* ſoure, crabbed.

Tetronymal, *g.* of 4 names.

Teverton, a town in *Devonſhire*.

Teutonick, belonging to the

Teutches, *Almains*, *Germans* (in the largeſt ſence.)

Tewksbury, a town in *Gloceſterſhire*, famous for woollen cloth and Muſtard.

Texel, *o.* a Chimney.

Texel, a Bay and Port in *Holland*.

Textele, *o.* (*q. textuel*, *f.*) well verſt in the text.

Textile, *l.* woven, embroidered.

Textorian, belonging to

Texture, *l.* a weaving.

Teynted, *o.* for tainted, dipt.

Thaborites, the followers of *John Ziſka* a Bohemian rebel

(1426) from *Tabor*, a hill so called by him, which he took from a Noble-man.

Thack-tile, plain or side-tile.

Thack, o. for *Thwack*.

Thalassiarch, g. an Admiral.

Thalassical, g. Sea-green or blewish.

Thalassion, l. a Nuptial song among the old *Romans*.

Thales, one of the 7 wise men of *Greece*.

Thalestris, an Amazon-Queen, who went 30 daies journey to meet *Alexander*.

Thalia, one of the Muses.

Thalmud, as *Talmud*.

Thame, a town in *Oxfordshire*.

Thane, Sa. a Noble-man, Freeman, &c. but properly an Officer of the King.

Thankeheld, o. thank-worthy.

Thare, o. needeth.

Thascry, o. Outcry.

Tharcakes, La. as *Bannocks*.

Tharm, Li. Guts prepared for puddings.

Thavies Inn (in *Holborn*) one of the Innes of Chancery, formerly the house of *John Thavie* an Armourer.

Thaxted, a town in *Essex*.

The, *Thee*, o. thrive.

Theatral -rical, belonging to a

Theater, -tre, g. a stage.

Theatral Law, punishing those that presumed to sit in the Knights seats.

Theatins, *Thietins*, a Religious Order instituted by *John Peter-Caraff*, who (before he was Pope *Paul* 3.) was Bishop of

Theate, *Thiette*, a City of *Naples*.

Theave, E. an Ew of the first year.

Thebæ, *Thebes*, *Stibes* in *Ægypt*, another in *Bæotia*.

Thbes, Nf. Goos-berries.

Thech, *Theich*, o. plain, smooth.

Thedome, o. thriving.

Theifthe, o. Theevish.

Theke, o. such.

Theft-bote, the receiving goods from a thief, to favour and maintain him; the punishment is ransom and imprisonment.

Thelemite, g. a Libertine.

Thelonium, a writ to free Citizens from toll, according to their Charter or Prescription.

Theme, g. an argument to discourse on.

Themis, a Goddess of Justice.

Themistocles, a banished *Athenian*, who (being entertained by *Xerxes* and made General against his Country-men) poisoned himself.

Thence, o. to get or find.

Thenne, o. for thence.

Theos, g. God.

Theobald, *Tibald*, Sa. Bold among the people, or soon virtuous.

Theocracy, g. Gods Government.

Theoderic, *Deric*, *Terrey*, Sa. Rich in people.

Theodolite, a Surveying instrument.

Theodom, Sa. Servitude.

Theodore, *Tydder*, g. Gods gift.

Theodosia, the feminine of

Theodosius, g. as *Theodore*.

Theogony, g. the generation of the Gods.

Theologaster, a pitiful

Theologue, -ger. g. a Divine.

Theological, belonging to

Theology, g. Divinity.

Theologige, to play the Divine.

Theomachy, g. a fighting against God or the Gods.

Theomagical, g. belonging to Divine wisdom.

Theomancy, g. Divination by abusing the Names of God

Theominy, the wrath of God.

Theonville, a town of *Luxemburgh*.

Theophilus, g. lover of God.

Theorba, I. a large Lute.

Theorematick, belonging to a

Theoreme, g. a Principle in any Art; but chiefly respecting contemplation, as Probleme doth practice.

Theoremist, a Professor of *Theorems* or undoubted truths.

Theoretick, belonging to

Theory, g. the speculative part of any Science without practice.

Theosophical, g. Divinely-wise.

Therapeutick, g. healing.

Theraphim, as *Teraphim*, humane images.

Theriacal, g. of treacle, of a viper or other wild beast.

Thermesy, to heat [with over-eating hot things.

Thermid, o. therewith.

Thermometer, g. a Weather-glass.

Thermopolist, g. a seller of hot things.

Thermopolæ, a long ridge of Mountains in *Greece*.

Thesaurer, g. a Treasurer.

Thesaurize, to heap or hoard up treasure.

Theseus, by *Ariadnes* help slew the *Cretian Minotaur*.

Thesiphon, as *Tysiphone*.

Thesis, g. a general argument or position.

Thessalonica, *Salonique*, in *Macedonia*.

Thessalia, -ly, part of *Greece* between *Bæotia* and *Macedon*.

Thetick, belonging to

Theta, (the first letter of Θάνατος Death) a note of Condemnation.

Thetford, a town in *Norfolk*.

Thetis, [a Nymph of] the Sea.

Theu, o. though.

Theryt, o. Doves.

Thew'd, No. towardly.

Thewes, o. qualities.

Thight, o. well compacted.

Thight-

Thight ship, staunch, making but little water.
Thilk, o. such, or this.
Thiller, the horse that bears up the
Thills, the fore-part of a Wagon or Cart.
Thingus, a Thane.
Thirdborow, as *Headborow*.
Thirdings, the third part of Corn on the ground, &c.
Third-night-awn-hynd, a guest lying the third night in an Inne was accounted a domestick, and the Host answerable for his offences, *Forman night uncuth*, *Twa night geste*, *Third night awn hynde*.
Thirl, Li. to bore.
Thivel, *Thible*, No. a stirring-stick.
Tho, o. then and those.
Thokes, broken bellied fish.
Thola, l. the Scutchin or knot in the midst of a timber vault, a pinacle, Tabernacle, and the place (in Temples) where gifts are hung up; also to stay, brook or endure, *Der*.
Thomas, h. a twin.
Thomists, followers of
Thomas Aquinas, a School-Divine called (by Papists) Angelical Doctor.
Thomyris, Queen of *Scythia*, who threw the head of *Cyrus* into a tub of blood, saying
-- *Satia te sanguine, Cyre*
Thone, *Thong*, No. damp.
Thong-Castle, *Castor*, in *Lincolnshire*.
Thor, *Jupiter*, a Saxon Idol giving name to Thursday.
Thore, o. before.
Thoracique, g. belonging to the breast.
Thornbury, a town in *Glocestershire*.
Thornton, about 30 small towns.
Thorow-toll, paid formerly at *Bough* in *York-shire*.
Thorp, *sa*. a Village, the name of above 50.
Thorruck, o. a heap
Thoughts, the rowers seats in a boat.
Tholouse, a City in *Languedoc*.
Thourgy, as *Turgy*.
Thowls, the pins which the Oars bear against.
Thrages, o. busie matters.
Thracia, part of *Europe* East of *Macedon*.
Thrapston, a town in *Northamptonshire*.
Thraskites, followers of *John*
Thrask, a broacher of Judaical opinions in *England*, 1618.
Thrasonical, like unto
Thraso, g. a great boaster.
Thrasybulus, an Athenian exile, who freed them from the 30 Tyrants.
Thrave, two stooks or 24 sheaves, also a bevy of quails, and (in *Li*.) to urge.
Threke, o. thrust.
Thremot, (q. *terræ mot*) o the blast of a horn.
Threne, g. a lamentation [song.
Threnetick, g. mournful.
Threnody, g. the singing of a funeral song.
Threpe, *sa*. to affirm confidently, also to call, rebuke and impose, or heap, *No*.
Threst, o. to oppress.
In a Threw, (q. throw,) o. quickly.
Thrie, o. for thrive.
Thrilled, *Thirled*, *sa*. killed.
Thridborow, as *Third*-.
Thrippa, *Che*. to beat.
Thrimsa, three shillings, or rather the 3d. part of a shilling.
Thring, o. to thrust.
Trithing, a Court of three or four hundreds.
Throb, *sa*. to pant or beat.
Thrones, the third rank in the Celestial Hierarchy.
Throppie, *Y*. to strangle, also the wind-pipe.
Thrope, o. for Thorp.
Throsshers, o. quails.
Throw, No. to turn as Turners, also anger, haste, o.
Thrutch, *Che*. thrust.
Thrusk, a town in *Yorkshire*.
Thucydides, an eloquent Greek Historian.
Thule, a Northern Isle.
Thummim, h. perfections.
Thuriferous, l. bearing frankincense.
Thursday, *Thorsday*, *Da*. *Dondersdagh*, D. See *Thor*.
Thwart-ships, a-cross the ship.
Thwite, No to whittle.
Thy, *sa*. therefore.
Thyatira, a City of *Lydia*.
Thyland, part of North *Juitland*.
Thymelical, of Players.
Thymick vein, the first branch of the *Subclavicular* going to the kernel under the Canel-bone.
Thymomancy, g. a presaging from ones own hopes or fears.
Thymous, l. full of thyme.
Thyrse, g. a stalk, also *Bacchus's* Javelin wrapt with ivy.
Tiara, l. a Turbant.
Tib of the buttery, c. a goose.
Tiber, a River by *Rome* as the *Thames* by *London*.
Tibial, l. belonging to pipes.
Tibicinate, l. to pipe.
Tiching, *Der*. drying turves in the Sun.
Tickrum, c. a licence.
Ticktack, f. trictrac, at touch and take, a game at Tables.
Tid, o. hapned.
Tiddeswell, a town in *Darbyshire*.
Tide, D. time.
Tide-gate, where the tide runs strongest.
Lee-ward Tide, running with the wind.
Wind-ward Tide, against Wind.
Tides-men, Officers attending ships till the Custom be paid.
Tiel, a town in *Gelderland*.
Tierce, *Tiers*, f. the third part of a pipe, 42 Gallons.
Tiercel, *Tercel*, as *Tassel*
Tiercet, f. a staff of 3 verses.

Ties,

Ties, the ropes by which the yards hang.

Tiflers, *Tyffelers*, *o*. for *Triflers*.

Tigh, *Teage*, *Sa*. a Close.

Tigillum, *l*. a crucible.

Tigrine, *l*. like a Tiger.

Tiliden, *o*. they tilled.

Tillemont, a town in *Brabant*.

Tiller, in a boat, is the same as Helme in a Ship.

Tils, a tent or canopy.

Tilts, as *Tournaments*.

Timariots, Turks who hold the parts of conquered Lands by a kind of Knights service.

Timber of skins, fourty.

Timbers of Ermine, the rews of Ermine in the Robes.

Timbesteres, *o*. timbrel-players.

Timbres, *f*. little bells.

Timbrel, (*D. Trommel*) a Taber.

Timerous, fearfull.

Timidity, *l*. fearfulness.

Timocracy, *g*. government by the richest.

Timon, a soure *Athenian* hating all company.

Timotheus, *-thy*, *g*. an honourer of God.

Timpany, as *Tympany*.

Tincel, (*f*. *Estincelle*, a spark) a glistering stuff (of silk and copper, &c.)

Tincture, *l*. a stain, colour, touch, or taste.

Tineman, *Tienman*, an old Forest Night-Officer.

Tine the door, *No*. shut it.

Tine (tin) the candle, *So*. light it.

Tingible, *l*. that may be stained or died.

Tinkeled, *o*. for *Twinkled*.

Tinniment, *l*. a tinkling.

Tinsel, as *Tincel*.

Tint-wine, as *Tent-*.

Tintamar, *f*. a clashing or jingling noise.

Tintinnation, *l*. a ringing.

Tiny, small, slender.

Tip the cole to Adam Tiler, *c*. give the [stoln] money to to your [running] Comrade.

Tip staff, one of the Warden of the Fleets men.

Tipocosmy, *Typ-*, *g*. a type or figure of the World.

Tiren, *o*. tear.

Tire of Ordnance, a set fore and aft.

Cable-Tire, the row in the midle of a coyld cable.

Tiresias, a blind *Theban* Prophet.

Tirconnel, an *Irish* County.

Tiromancy, *Tyr-*, *g*. Divination by cheese.

Tirol, *Ty-*, part of *Austria*.

Tissue, *f*. woven, plaited.

Cloth of Tissue, silk and silver or gold.

Titanick, belonging to

Titan, (Poet.) the Sun.

Tite, *o*. befalleth.

Tithing-man, the Chief of a

Tithing, a Society of ten families bound for one anothers good behaviour.

Tithonus, ravisht by *Aurora* into *Æthiopia*, and turn'd at last into a Grasshopper.

Tithymal, Milkthistle, Sea-lettice or Wolfs-milk.

Titillation, *l*. a tickling.

Titter, *Tidder*, *Tider*, *No*, soon, quickly.

Titulation, *l*. a stumbling.

Titular, *l*. having only a title.

Tmesis, *g*. a separating the parts of a compound word.

Tmolus, a *Lydian* Mountain, whence the river *Pactolus* flows.

Tobacco, as *Tabacco*.

Tobiah, *-as*, *h*. the Lord is good.

Tod of wool, Two stone, 28 pound.

Todder, *o*. for the other.

Toftman, the owner of a

Toft, a place where a messuage hath stood.

Tofet, as *Tovet*.

Toforn, *o*. before.

Togedir, *o*. for together.

Toils, hunters nets.

Tol, *l*. to take away.

Toll, liberty to buy and sell within the precincts of a Mannor; also Custom for passage, buying, &c.

Tolbuyth, *-booth*, a Custom-house; also the chief prison at *Edenburgh*.

Toletum, *Toledo*, the chief City of New-Castile, who's wall hath 150 Towers.

Tole, *o*. a clout or toy.

Tolen, a town in *Zealand*.

Tolerable, which one may

Tolerate, *l*. endure.

Toleration, an indulgence.

Told no tale, *o*. never reckoned upon it, slighted it.

Tolsey, *Toldsey*, the Exchange at *Bristol*.

Tolestale, the Town-hall of *Dublin*.

Tolt, a writ removing a cause from a Court Baron to the County Court.

Tolutation, *l*. an ambling.

Tolutiloquence, smooth speaking.

Toman, a *Persian* coyn of 3 *l*. 6 *s*.

Tomblesterers, *-listeres*, *o*. tumblers, dancers.

Tome, *g*. a division or volume.

Tomboy, *sa*. a girl that tumbles about like a boy.

Tomentitious, *l*. of flocks.

Tomin, *f*. the weight of a Spanish Real, also (among Jewellers) 3 Carrats.

Tomine, *o*. for to mind or mean.

Tomkin, as *Tamkin*.

Tonical, belonging to a

Tone, *l*. tune, note, accent.

Tone, *o*. toes, claws.

Tonge, a town in *Shropshire*.

Tongres, a town of *Liege*.

Tonne, as *Tun*.

Tonitruate, *l*. to thunder.

Tonnage, a Custom for goods brought or carried in Tuns or such like vessels.

Tonnage and Poundage, began 45 *Edw*. 3.

Tonnellers, those Seamen that fill the casks with water.

Tonsils, *l*. kernels at the root of the tongue, subject to inflammations, &c.

Tonsorious, belonging to a
Tonsor, *l.* a Barber.
Tonsure, *l.* a clipping.
Toucan, *No.* to wonder or muse.
Too-too, *No.* very well or good.
Toom, *Tume*, *No.* empty.
Toothing, the working-in of bricks in a party-wall.
Toparch, *g.* one having
Toparchie, *g.* the Government of a place.
Top-armors, cloaths tied (for shew) about the tops of the Masts, to hide men in fight, &c.
Topaze, a precious stone, one gold-coloured, another Saffron.
Tophet, *h.* a place near *Jerusalem* where they burnt their Children to *Moloch*.
Topiary, *l.* of Arbors.
Topos, *g.* a place.
Topical, belonging to
Topicks, *g.* common-places of invention for arguments.
Topography, *g.* the descripti-on of particular places.
Topping-cheat, *c.* the gallows.
Topping-Cove, *c.* the hangman.
Top-rope, wherewith they strike the main and fore top-mast.
Topsy-turvy, for th' up-side th' other way.
Tor, *sa.* a tower or high rock.
Torcencious, *o.* using extortion.
Torcular vein, a branch of the throat-vein ascending to (and moistning) the brain.
Torce, (in Heraldry) a wreath.
Torch-royal, the start in a stages-head, next above the Royal.
Torcularious, of a wine-press.
Tories, Irish Out-laws.
Tormentick, setfoil.
Torminous troubled with
Tormins, *l.* gripings in the guts.
Tornado, *Sp.* a sudden violent storm at Sea.
Tornatil, *l.* turned or made with a wheel.
Tornus, a town of *Burgundy*.
Torosity, *l.* brawniness.
Torpedo, *l.* cramp-fish, benumming ones hands (though toucht with a pole.)
Torpidity, a being
Torpid, *l.* benummed, astonied.
Torpor, *l.* a drowzy dullness.
Torquated, *l.* wearing a collar or chain.
Ti. Man. Torquatus, beheaded his Son for fighting against his command, though victorious.
Torrefaction, *-fying*, rosting, scorching, parching.
Torrent, *l.* a violent landflood.
Torrets, *o.* rings.
Torrentine, belonging thereto.
Torrington, a town in *Devon-shire*.
Torrid, *l.* scorching-hot.
Torsion, *l.* a wringing.
Tortfeasor, a trespasser.
Tort, *f.* injury, extortion.
Torteauxes, *f.* wastels, round coloured figures like cakes (in Heraldry.)
Tortile, *l.* bent, writhen.
Tortiloquy, *l.* crooked discourse.
Tortive, *l.* squeezed, wrung out.
Tortuosity, *l.* a being
Tortuous, winding in and out.
Torvid, *l.* cruel, stern.
Torvity, sourness, grimness.
Toscany, as *Tuscany*.
Totage, *f.* the same as
Totality, *l.* the total or whole summe or substance.
Toties quoties, *l.* as often as.
Totilas, a King of the *Goths*, who overcame the Romans.
Totnes, a town in *Devonshire*.
Toteth, *o.* looketh.
Totoler, *o.* (*q.* tatler) prating.
Totted, markt in the Exchecquer (with the word *Tot*) as a good debt to the King.
Totteray, was 4 pence for every bushel and half of Corn sold at *Maldon* in *Essex*.
Tottie, *o.* wavering.
Totty, *o.* dizzy.
Tovet, *Tofet*, *K.* two pecks.
Touked, *o.* ducked.
Tought, *o.* for tough or taught.
Tour, *f.* a tower or turn.
Tournet, *o.* for turret.
Tour-frizette, *f.* curls for womens foreheads.
Tournement, *f.* a turning, also justing or tilting.
Tournois, belonging to
Tournay, a town in *Flanders*
Livre Tournois, &c. the tenth part of a pound sterling.
Tout, *f.* whole.
Tout temps prest & encore est, *f.* (alway ready and is so now) a plea of defence for one sued for any debt or duty.
Touting-ken, *c.* tavern-bar.
Tout, *c.* to look out or upon.
Towage, the towing or dragging any thing at the stern.
Towgher, *Cu.* a dowry.
Towel, (*q.* tewel) a tail.
Towcester, a town in *Northamptonshire*.
Towton, a town in *Yorkshire*, where (1461) 30 thousand were slain in a battle between *York* and *Lancaster*.
Toxie, *l.* venemous.
Toylet, *f.* a bag for night-cloathes, also a cloth richly wrought.
Trabal, *l.* belonging to a beam.
Tracas, *-sserie*, *f.* a restless needless hurrying up and down.
Track, *c.* to go.
Traces, the foot-steps of wild beasts.
Trachean, (*-chian*) artery, the pipe of the Lungs.
Tract, *l.* a line (or discourse) at length, also the footing of a Boat, and (in the Mass) the Versicles between the

Epistle and the Gospel.

Tractable, l. easie to be handled.

Tractate, l. a treatise.

Tractations, l. handling.

Tradition, l. a delivery [of doctrine].

Traditive, delivered by word of mouth.

Traduce, l. to slander.

Traduction, l. a defaming, also a translating.

Trafine, the Chirurgions best Trapan.

Tragacanth, g. (Goats-thorn) a gum from a shrub of the same name.

Tragecomedy, between a tragedy and comedy.

Tragedian, a Tragick-Actor, also as

Tragediographer, g. a writer of

Tragedies, lofty plaies, treating of Great and Bloudy exploits.

Tragelaph, g. a stone buck, Deer-goat, or Goat-hart, got between a Buck-goat and Hind.

Tragematopolist, g. a Confectioner.

Tragick, *-cal*, belonging to Tragedies; cruel.

Trajection, l. a passing over.

Trajectitious, carried over-sea.

Trail, o. an arbour.

Trail-bastan, see Justices of, &c.

Traiterous position, of taking arms by the Kings authority against his person or those commissioned by him.

Tralatitious, l. borrowed, vulgar.

Tralucency, a shining thorow.

Tramontane, Northern, beyond the *Alps* (from *Italy*.)

Trammel, E. a Chimney-iron whereon to hang pots, &c.

Trancilers, o. husbandmen.

Tranquillize, to cause

Tranquillity, l. quietness.

Transaction, l. a dispatching of business.

Transalpine, l. beyond the *Alps*.

Transcendent, surpassing [the predicaments.

Transcolate, to strain thorow.

Transcript, that which is

Transcribed, written from the Original.

Transcripto recognitionis, &c. a writ for the certifying a recognisance into Chancery.

Transcripto pedis finis, &c. a writ for the certifying (into Chancery) the foot of a fine levied before Justices in Eyre, &c.

Transcurrence, a running over.

Transduction, l. a leading over.

Transection, *-exion*, a turning from one sex to another.

Transeminate, to pass from Woman to man.

Transfer, to carry over.

Trasfiguration, a changing from one form to another.

Transfix, to run one through

Transfretation, passing over-sea.

' *Transfume*, to smoak through.

Transfusion, a pouring from one thing to another.

Transgression, a passing the bounds.

Transgression, a writ or Action of Trespass.

Transire, a Custom-house Warrant or Let-pass.

Transjection, a casting over.

Transition, l. a passing from one thing to another.

Transitory, soon passing, and (in Law) opposed to Local.

Translation, a changing from one thing, place or language to another.

Translucid, thorow-bright.

Transmarine, beyond-sea.

Transmeable, which one may

Transmeate, pass through or beyond.

Transmew, o. to change.

Transmigration, a flitting or passing from one place (or body) to another.

Transmission, *-mitting*, conveying from one to another.

Transmotion, a removing the cause of a thing from ones self.

Transmute, to change from one form to another.

Transmutation, such a change.

Transnomination, a changing name.

Transome, a brow-post or over-thwart beam; the timber athwart the ships stern.

Transpare, to appear through

Transparency, a being

Transparent, to be seen through.

Transpass, to pass beyond.

Transpeciate, to change kind or form.

Transpierce, to pierce through.

Transpiration, a breathing forth (through the skin.)

Transplant, to plant in another place.

Transport, to carry over-sea.

Transport, a rapture of mind.

Transpose, to change the order.

Transposition, a mis-placing.

Transprose, to turn out of verse into prose.

Transubstantiation, a change of one Substance into another, as of the bread into the body of Christ (according to the Papists.)

Transvasation, a pouring from vessel to vessel.

Transude, to sweat through

Transvection, a carrying over.

Transverse, a-thwart.

Transversion, a turning or going a-cross.

Transult, to leap over.

Transumption, a taking from one to another.

Transvolation, a flying over.

Transylvania, *Silemburghen*, part of *Dacia*.

Tra-

Trapan, as *Trepan*.

Trantery, money arising by amercements of Ale-sellers, &c.

Trapezium, g. a figure of 4 unequal sides and oblique angles.

Traames, the unseen acti-ons of Spirits and Ghosts.

Thrashed, o. deceived.

Trasonings, the doublings of a Roe-buck before the Hounds.

Traskites, as *Thraskites*.

Travado's, *Portug.* whirl-winds at Sea.

Trave, f. a trevise or little room to shooe unruly horses in.

Trate, o. an old trot.

Traverse, f. to cross or deny, also the Ships way.

Traverses, turnings and windings, troubles.

Traverse-board, with all the points of the compass on it, and holes for the Steersman to skore how many glasses they go upon them.

Travested, -ti, f. drest in another mans cloathes.

Traulismus, g. a stammering.

Traumatick, g. belonging to wounds.

Trasoun, o. for Treasure.

High Treason, an offence against the security of the King or Common-wealth.

Petit Treason, when a servant, wife or Priest, kill their Master, Husband or Ordinary.

Treasure trove, *Tresor trouvé*, f. Treasure found, which not being owned, belongs (by the Civil Law to the finder, but by the Common-Law) to the King.

Treat, f. taken out, withdrawn.

Treated, f. handled or entertained.

Treatise, o. attractive.

Treble, three fold, also the highest part in Musick.

Trebuchet, *Tribuch*, *Terbichetum*, a Tumbrel, Cokestole, Cuckingstole or Goging-stole.

Trecentene, l. of three hundred.

Treachour, o. treacherous.

Trectes, o. straightway.

Tree-nalls, oak-pins to fasten the ship-planks.

Treen-ware, No. Earthen.

Bread of Treet, made of fine Wheat.

Trefoil, three-leav'd grass, of several sorts.

Tregoney, a town in *Cornwall*.

Tregetor, o. a Jugler.

Tregit, o. deceit.

Trellis, *Treilliffe*, f. a lattice.

Trellized, cross-barred.

Tremendous, l. to be feared,

Tremor, l. a trembling.

Tremulous, quaking.

Tren, f. a Sea-instrument to strike fish withal.

Trenchant, f. cutting.

Trench the ballast, divide it.

Trene, (for *treves*, f.) a truce.

Trental, f. a thirty [masses for the dead.

Trepan, *Trappan*, (*I. Trappare*) to catch in a trap, also as

Trepandiron, an instrument used about broken sculls.

Trepeget, o. a battering-ram.

Trepidate, l. to quake for fear.

Trepedation, a trembling.

Trespass, any transgression of the Law, except felony or treason.

Tressel-trees, lying (along st-Ships) cross the cross-trees.

Trespassants, f. Passengers.

Tressis-agaso, l. a pitiful half-peny groom.

Tresses, locks of hair.

Trestle, a 3 footed stool.

Tres-wins, c. three-pence.

Triacle, an antidote against poison.

Tretes, o. is streightened.

Triad, g. a trey or three.

Trew, o. for truce.

Treves, the same as

Triers, a City in *Germany*.

Triangle, a figure which is

Triangular, l. of 3 corners.

Triarchy, g. a government by three

Triarch, g. a Master of a ship with three tops or three rows of Oars.

Triarians, the stout Roman Soldiers in the reer.

Tribe, a kindred or company dwelling together in the same Ward or Liberty.

Tribes, the posterity of *Jacobs* twelve Sons.

Triblesees, a town in upper *Pomerania*.

Tribunal, l. a Judgment-seat.

Tribunitial, belonging to a

Tribune, a chief Roman Officer.

Tribune of the [*Common*] *People*, to defend their rights against the Nobles.

Tribune of the Soldiers, to see them well armed and ordered.

Tributary, l. paying

Tribute. l. money exacted out of mens Estates.

Trica, the hair of *Berenice* (a Constellation.)

Trice, o. to convey.

Tricenarious, l. of thirty.

Trichlich, o. richly, or neatly (with fine tricks.)

Tricennial, l. of 30 years.

Trieliniarch, g. the usher of the dining-room.

Tricliniary, l. belonging to a

Triclinium, l. a dining-room.

Tricornous, l. with 3 horns.

Tricoterie, f. cheating [in law suites.

Tricotomy, g. a dividing into three.

Tridentiferous, l. bearing a

Trident, l. a 3 forked mace.

Tridentine, belonging to

Trent, a City in the North of *Italy*.

Triduan, l. of three daies.

Triennial, l. of 3 years.

Triental, l. an half pint.

Trierarch, g. the Master of a Ship.

Trieterick, g. of every third year.

Trifallow, Her. to plow land the 3d time (for the same crop.

Trifarious, *l*. of three manner of waies.

Triferous, *l*. bearing thrice a year.

Trifistulary, *l*. of three pipes.

Trifole, *-lie*, *l*. three leaved grass.

Triform, *l*. of three forms.

Trifurcous, *l*. three forked.

Trigamist, *g*. having three wives.

Trigeminous, *l*. threefold [twins.

Triglyphs, *g*. borders graven like three furrows.

Trigonal, like a

Trigon, *g*. a triangle, also as *Triplicity*.

Trigonometry, *g*. a measuring of Triangles.

Trihing, as *Trithing*.

Trill, *-lo*, *I*. a quavering grace in singing.

Trill, *o*. to turn or drill.

Trilogy, *g*. a discourse in 3 parts.

Trim of a ship, that way which she goes best.

Trimenstruous, *l*. of three Moneths.

Trimodial, *l*. of 3 bushels.

Trinacrian, belonging to *Trinacria*, *Sicily*.

Trine, *c*. Tyburn, or to hang.

Trine, *l*. belonging to 3.

Trine aspect, the distance of 4 signs (a 3d part of the Zodiack.)

Tring, a town in *Hertfordshire*.

Trinitarians, as *Mathurins*; also New *Arrians*, denying the Trinity, and blaspheming it with the name of Infernal *Cerberus*.

Trinity, *l*. the number of three.

Trinity-house (at *Deptford*) belongs to a Company of Sea-men, who (by the Kings Charter) take care of things belonging to Navigation.

Trink, an old kind of fish-engine.

Trinobantes, the *Britains* of *Midlesex* (in *Cæsar*.)

Trinoctial, *l*. of 3 nights.

Trinodal, *l*. of 3 knots.

Trinominal, *l*. of 3 names.

Trinquet, *f*. the top-gallant sail, also any gay trifle.

Triobolar, *l*. of three halfpence.

Triours, chosen by the Court to try if the Challenge against a Jurour be just.

Trip, *o*. a small piece.

Trip of sheep Nf. a few.

Trip of goats, a great Company.

Tripartite, *l*. divided into three.

Tripedal, *-aneous*, *l*. of 3 foot.

Triperie, *f*. a tripe-market.

Triplication, a making

Triple, *l*. threefold.

Triplicity, 3 of the signs.

Fiery Triplicity, Aries, Leo, Sagittarius.

Aëry, Tri-, Gemini, Libra, Aquarius.

Watry Tri-, Cancer, Scorpio, Pisces.

Earthly Tri-, Taurus, Virgo, Capricorn.

Tripedical, like a

Tripode, *g*. a three footed stool.

Tripoly, the plant Turbith or blew Cammomel, also a stone with whose powder they polish jewels, also a town in *Barbary*.

Tripontium, Torcester in *Northamptonshire*.

Triptote, *g*. a noun of three cases.

Tripudiary divination, by the rebounding of crums thrown to chickens.

Tripudiate, *l*. to dance.

Tripudiation, a tripping on the toe.

Triquet, *-trous*, *l*. Triangular.

Trireme, *l*. a gally of three Oars on a side, or three men to an Oar.

Trise-up, hale by a dead-rope not running in a block.

Trisagion, *g*. Holy, Holy, Holy.

Hermes (or *Mercurius*) *Trismegistus*, an *Egyptian* Philosopher, Priest and King.

Trist, *o*. a mark.

Trista, *-tis*, *-tris*, a Mans immunity from attendance on the Lord of a Forest in his hunting.

Tristifical, *l*. which doth

Tristitiate, or make

Tristful, sad, sorrowfull.

Trisulk, *l*. three-furrowed.

Trisyllabical, *g*. of three syllables.

Trite, *l*. thred-bare.

Tritheites, *g*. Hereticks holding three distinct Godheads.

Trithing, the third part of a shire, also the Court now called Court-Leet (between a Court Baron and a County Court.)

Triticean, *l*. of wheat.

Triton, a Sea-god (*Neptunes* Trumpeter) also a Weathercock.

Triturable, capable of

Trituration, *l*. a threshing.

Trivial, *l*. common, belonging to the high-way.

Triumphal, *-ant*, belonging to a

Triumph, *l*. a solemn shew, at the return of a General from Noted Victories

Triumvirate, the office of the

Triumviri, three in Equal authority.

Troce, *o*. a wreath or withy.

Trochee, a foot of the first syllable long and the other short.

Trochings, the many small branches on the top of the Deers head:

Trochisk, *g*. a little wheel, also a Cake of medicinal things.

Trode, *o*. a path.

Troglodites, Wild *Africans*.

Trompe, *f*. a trumpet.

Tromperie, *f*. deceit.

Trona, a weigh-beam.

Tronage,

Tronage, custom for weighing wool.

Tronator, a *London*-Officer weighing wool.

Tronum, cœlestial dew.

Tropical, belonging to a

Trope, *g*. the turning a word from its proper signification. (Figure respects the sentence.)

Trophy, *g*. any thing set up in token of victory.

Tropicks, two Circles imagined for the bounds of the Suns course.

Tropological, belonging to

Tropology, *g*. a discourse of or by Tropes and Figures

Trosque, as *Trochisk*.

Trover, *f*. an action against him that refuses (upon demand) to deliver the goods he found.

Trough, the space between two waves.

In the Trough of the Sea, under the Sea, with her broadside to the Sea.

Trou-madam, *f*. Troll-madam, or Pigeon holes.

Trousonyd, *o*. [an eel] drest.

Trouth, *o*. for Truth.

Troy-weight, 12 ounces to the pound, by which they weigh Bread, Gold, Silver, Pearls, precious stones and Medicines.

Truand, *f*. a vagabond, or common beggar.

Trubridge, a town in *Wilts*.

Truchman, *f*. an Interpreter.

Trucidation, *l*. a murdering.

Trucks, the entire wheels of carriages, also the wooden balls belonging to the Parrels.

Truculent, *l*. cruel, bloudy.

Truets, *Trew*- *Sf*. pattens.

True-love, herb-*Paris*.

True-day, the day of parley at the

True-place, a place of conference, in *Northumberland*.

Trug, *o*. three trugs make two bushels.

Trug-corn, paid the Vicar of *Lemster*, for officiating at some Chappels of ease.

Trug, *Sf*. a tray for Milk, &c.

Trull, *l*. a vile harlot, also to trundle, *Sf*.

Trullissation, *l*. a plaistering.

Truncation, *l*. a cutting short.

Trunk, *l*. the body of a tree or man (without head, arms and legs.)

Trundlers, *c*. Peas.

Trundle shot, cast upon the midle of an Iron sharp at both ends.

Truphat, the occult virtue of Minerals preferring every metal.

Trunnions, the two knobs on the sides of Ordnance.

Trusses, ropes fasten'd to the parrel of the yards (to bind them to the Mast or hale them down.)

Truro, a town in *Cornwal*.

Trutinate, *l*. to weigh, examine. &c.

Try, to have no more sail forth but the main-sail.

Tryppe of gette, *o*. for trip of Goats.

Tuant, *f*. killing.

Tubal, *h*. worldly.

Tubal-Cain, *h*. worldly possession.

Tube, *l*. a long pipe[through which runs the chine-marrow.

Tubercula, *Montes*, the risings at the roots of the fingers.

Tuberous, *l*. full of bunches.

Tubicinate, *l*. to trumpet.

Tubulation, *l*. a making hollow like pipes.

Tuck, the gathering-up of the Ships quarter under water.

Tuddinton, a town in *Bedfordshire*.

Tudiculate, to work with hammers.

Tufa, *o*. a banner.

Tuel, the fundament of a beast.

Tuilleries, *f*. (where tiles were made) a stately Fabrick near the *Louvre*.

Tuition, *l*. a protecting.

Tul, *o*. to allure, also a tile.

Tulipant, an Indian head-shash.

Tullianum, a Roman dungeon.

Tullus Hostilius, a warlike Roman King, struck dead with a thunderbolt.

Tully, *Mar. Tullius Cicero*, the Roman Orator.

Tumbler, *c*. a Cart.

Tumbrel, a Cucking-stool, also a dung-cart.

Tumefaction, -*fying*, a making

Tumid, *l*. swoln, puft up.

Tumor, *l*. a swelling, pride.

Tumulate, *l*. to entomb.

Tumultuary, *l*. done in haste.

Tumultuous, *l*. full of trouble.

Tunals, trees of *Nova Hispania*, in whose leaves are bred the costly worms called Cocheneile.

Tun, a measure of 252 gallons, a weight of 20 hundred.

Tun of Timber, 40 solid feet.

Tunbridge, a town in *Kent*.

Tun-greve, *Villæ præpositus*, a Reeve or Bailiff.

Tunick, -*cat*, *l*. a [sleeveless] Coat, also as

Tunicle, *l*. a little coat or skin.

Tunis, a City in *Barbary*.

Turban, an innumerable company of stars, also a presage from all four Elements.

Turbant, a Turkish hat.

Turbary, a right of digging turves on anothers ground.

Turbervils, *de turbida villa*, an ancient Family of *Dorcetshire*.

Turbination, *l*. the making a thing like a top.

Turbinous, *l*. belonging to a storm or whirl-wind.

Turbith, the herb Tripoly.

Turbith mineral, a red powder used in the French disease.

Turbulent, *l*. troublesome.

Turckeim, a town in upper *Alsace*

Turgescence, *l*. a being

Turgent, -*gid*, puft up.

Turgy, *Theurgie*, *g.* white Magick, a pretended conference with good Angels.

Turin, the chief town of *Piedmont*.

Turingia, part of *Saxony*.

Turmeric, a yellow root for the yellow jaundice.

Turn, the Sheriffs Court, kept twice a year.

Turneament, *Tournement*, Justing, Tilting, a Martial Exercise on Horse-back.

Tourney, the same.

Turno Vicecomitum, a writ calling men (out of their own hundred) to the Sheriffs Turn.

Turnsole, the Heliotrope.

Turpentine, a clear moist Rosin from the Larch and other trees.

Turpifie, *l.* to make unclean.

Turpitude, *l.* filthyness.

Turquise, a blew precious stone.

Turwin, a town in *Artois*.

Turtle-dove, a small kind of mournful Pigeon, living alway single after the Mates Death.

Turriferous, *l.* bearing towers.

Tuscan-work, a plain, massy, rural sort of Pillar.

Tuscia, -*any*, a Dukedom in *Italy*.

Tusky'd, *o.* [a Barbel] dight.

Tusinz, a Baltick Island.

Tut, an Imperial Ensign (of a Globe with a golden cross on it.)

Tutelar, -*ry*, belonging to

Tutele, *l.* wardship, protection.

Tutelina, a goddess protecting Corn.

Tutia, a Vestal Virgin, who (to clear her self) carried water in a sieve.

Tutie, a white Physical substance, bred of the sparkles of brazen furnaces.

Tut-mouthed, whose chin and nether jaw stand out too far.

Tutor, *l.* a Guardian or instructer.

Tutsan, (*q. tout sain*) Park-leaves, a good wound-herb.

Tuysco, the particular Idol of the *Duytsch* or old *Germans*, giving name both to them and our Tuesday.

Tuway, *o.* for two.

Twait, Wood-ground turn'd to arable.

Twa-nights-geste, answerable himself for what harm he doth.

Twelfth-day, Epiphany-Feast.

Twelve-men, the Jury or Enquest, but a grand Enquest consists of 16 at the least.

Twibel, *D.* an instrument to make mortoise-holes.

Twilight, Cock-shoot time, between day and night.

Twettle, *o.* for to whitle.

Twin, *o.* to divide in two.

Twist, *o.* a bough.

Twight, *o*, twitched, pulled.

Twinters, *Bedf.* Cattel two winters old.

Twitter, *No.* to tremble.

Twy, or *Thry*, *o.* twice or thrice.

Twyfold, *o.* two-fold.

Twyst, *o.* thrust, pinched.

Twytten, *o.* (*q.* whitled) carved.

Tyberiade, a draught of a place, from that name of *Bartholus*, a Lawyers book, first graced with such figures.

Tybur, *Tivoli*, near *Rome*.

Tydder, as *Theodore*.

Tye-top, *No.* a garland.

Tygendis of Pies, a flock of them.

Tymariots, as *Tima*-.

Tymber of skins, as *Tim*-.

Timpane, *g.* a drum, also the Parchment-instrument on which a sheet is printed.

Tympanism, a Jewish beating to death.

Tympanize, to play the

Tympanist, a drummer, also one that is

Tympanitical, troubled with or curing the

Tympany, a hard Swelling of the belly with wind, &c.

Tynt, *o.* shut up.

Typical, belonging to a

Type, *g.* an example, figure or shadow of a thing.

Typocosmy, *g.* a figure of the World.

Typographer, *g.* a Printer.

Typographical, belonging to

Typography, Printing.

Tyrannicide, the killing a

Tyrant, *g.* a cruel Governour.

Tyrconel, an Irish County.

Tyrian, belonging to

Tyre, a City of *Phœnicia*.

Tyrianthine, of purple.

Tyro, *l.* a fresh-water Soldier.

Tyrociny, *l.* an apprenticeship.

Tyrol, as *Tirol*.

Tyromancy, *g.* Cheese-divination.

Tyrone, *l.* a Novice.

Tyrrhene, of *Tuscany*.

Tyryd, *o.* [an egge] drest or poacht

Tysiphone, one of the Furies.

Tyte, *Sc.* for quite.

V.

V-, (in the West) generally used instead of F-.

Vacancy, a being

Vacant, *l.* void, empty, at leisure.

Vacation, *l.* as *Vacancy*, also the time between Term and Term.

Vacary, *Vachary*, *La.* a Cow-house or pasture.

Vachoris, an Egyptian King, who retired to a private austerity.

Vacillation, *l.* a tottering.

Vacive, *l.* void, empty.

Vacuity, *l.* emptiness.

Vacuna, Goddess of rest.

Vacuum, *l.* an empty place.

Vadelet, -*lect*, *Valect*, -*et*, *f.* (a Servant) a Benchers

Clerk

Clerk of the Inner Temple, corruptly cal'd Varlet.

Vadimony, *l.* Suretiship or day of appearance.

Vafrous, *l.* crafty, Subtle

Vagabond, *l.* an idle wanderer.

Vagation, *l.* a wandering.

Pure Vageour, *o.* poor begger.

Vagination, *l.* a sheathing.

Vaginipennous, *l.* having their wings in sheaths or cases.

Vail-bonnet, strike sail, put off the hat, &c.

Vaire, a fur composed of Argent, Gules, Or and Sable.

Vaivode, as *Vayvode*.

Valadolid, the old seat of the *Spanish* Kings.

Valasca, an *Amazonian* Queen of *Bohemia*.

Val d'ombre, *Val ombreux*, a shady vale in the Appenine, where *John Gualbert* a *Florentine* began a Religious Order (1040.)

Valdo, Author of the *Waldenses* in *Piedmont*.

Vale, *l.* Farewell.

Valect, as *Vadelet* or *Valet*.

Valence, *-tia*, a town in *Spain*, *France*, and *Milan*.

Valenciennes, *-chi-*, a town in *Hainault*.

Valencourt, a town of *Namur*.

Valentine, a *Roman* Bishop whose feast is kept Feb. 14. about which time birds chuse their Mates.

Valentines, Saints chosen for special patrons for that year, or (among us) men and women chosen for special loving friends.

Valentinians, hereticks following

Valentinianus, who held that Christ received not flesh of the *Virgin Mary*.

Valerian, a plant good against the Plague, &c.

Valerian law, whereby one might kill him that usurp'd Magistracy without the peoples consent.

Valet, *f.* a mean servant, anciently any young Gentleman under 18.

Valet de Chambre, *f.* a groom of the Chamber.

Valetudinary, *l.* sickly, also an Hospital.

Validation, a causing

Validity, *l.* a being.

Valid, strong, firm.

Valkenburgh, a town of *Limburgh* and other places.

Valor of Marriage, was a writ for the Lord to recover the value of a Marriage profer'd to the Infant and refus'd.

Valtorts, *de valle torta*, a Noble Family in *Cornwal*.

Valtoline, a province of *Switzerland*.

Valves, *l.* folding-doors.

Vambrace, *Vanb-*, *f.* a gauntlet.

Vamp, *-py*, *-pay*, *o.* a sock.

Van, *Vanguard*, (*f. Avant-*) the fore-part of an army.

Vancurriers, *f.* fore-runners.

Vandalia, *Burglave*, a Diocess in North *Juitland*.

Vandelbiria, suppos'ed to be *Wandlesbury* in *Cambridgshire*.

Vang, *Som.* to take or undertake.

Vang to him, answer for him.

Vaniloquence, *l.* vain-babling.

At the Vant, at the Font.

Vantarius, the Kings fore-foot-man.

Vantchemise, *f.* a fore-shirt.

Vapid, *l.* stinking.

Vaporation, a casting forth

Vapors, *l.* fumes, steams, easily resolved into water.

Vaporiferous, raising vapours.

Vapulation, *l.* a being beaten.

Variable, subject to

Variance, *-ation*, *l.* alteration.

Variegation, an adorning with divers colours.

Varlets, was used (20 *Richard* 2) for yeomen-servants.

Varry, *Virry*, *f.* argent and azure mixt.

Varvels *f.* small silver rings at the hawks legs, with the owners name.

Vasiferous, *l.* vessel-bearing.

Vassalage, *f.* the duty or condition of a

Vassal, a slave; also a tenant in fee.

Vassow, a town in *Podolia*.

Vastation, *l.* a destroying.

Vastity, *l.* hugeness.

Vasto, a writ against a Tenant making waste.

Vatican, a hill in *Rome*, where was built (by *Sixtus* 4) the

Vatican, or Palatine, a famous Library.

Viticinate, *l.* to prophecy.

Vaticinian, belonging to

Vaticiny, *l.* a foretelling.

Vatinian, belonging to

Vatinius, a Roman whom all men hated.

Vavasorie, lands held by a

Vavasour, *Valv-*, one in dignity next a Baron.

Vaucolcur, and

Vaudemont, a town in *Lorrain*.

Vandeville, *Virelay*, a Countrey ballad, or common proverb.

Vaumur, *f.* a bulwark.

Vaunt courers, as *Vancurriers*.

Vauntlay, setting hounds in a readiness where the chase will pass.

Vaward, as *Vanguard*.

Vayvode, a Governour in *Transilvania*, *Walachia*, &c.

U-hatch, as *Tu-hatch*.

Uberate, *l.* to make

Uberous, having

Uberty, plenty fertility.

Ubication, a things being in a place.

Ubiquitarians, holding that Christs body is every where.

Ubiquitary, belonging to

Ubiquity, a being in all places at a time.

Veal-money, Veal-noble-money, paid the Marquess of *Winchester* yearly by some Tenants.

Vechons, *o.* hedg-hogs.

Veckc, *o.* an old woman.

Vecordy, *l.* dotage, stupidity.
Vectarious, of a Carriage.
Vectible, carriable.
Vectigal, *l.* [paying] tribute.
Vection, *l.* a carrying.
Vectitation, a carrying often.
Vectorian, apt to carry.
Veer more cable, let it run out.
The Wind Veers and hulls, goes in and out suddenly.
Veering, with the sheat veered out.
Vegetal, *-able*, *l.* living and growing as
Vegetables, Plants.
Vegetation, a refreshing.
Vegetive, *l.* lively, strong.
Vehemence, *-cy*, earnestness.
Vehicular, belonging to
Vehicles, *l.* any carriages.
Vejours, as *Viewers*.
Veil, *l.* to cover, also that which covers.
Veliferous, *l.* bearing Sail.
Velifical, displaied (as with Sails.)
Velification, a hoising or making Sail.
Velitation, *l.* a skirmishing.
Velites, *l.* light-arm'd Soldiers.
Velivolent, *l.* flying [with full Sail.
Velleity, a wishing and woulding.
Vellicate, *l.* to pull, detract.
Vellication, a twitching, &c.
Velling, *We.* plowing up turf to burn.
Velocity, *l.* swiftness.
Velvet-flower, as *Floramor*.
Velume, fine Parchment of Calves-skin.
Venalitious, belonging to
Venality, *l.* a being
Venal, to be sold or bribed
Vena Porta, as Port-vein.
Venarie, the sport of Hunting.
Venatick, *-torious*, belonging to
Venation, *l.* hunting, or to
Venator, a hunts-man.
Vendible, which one may
Vend, *l.* put off, sell.

Vendicate, *l.* claim, challenge.
Venditation, *l.* a vain boasting
Vendition, *l.* a selling.
Venditioni exponas, a writ for the Under-Sheriff to sell goods formerly taken for the satisfying a Judgement.
Venedocia, North-Wales.
Venefick, *-cal*, *-cial*, *-cious*, *l.* belonging to
Venefice, *l.* poisoning or Witchcraft.
Venenous, *-niferous*, poisonous.
Venerate, *l.* to shew
Veneration, reverence.
Venereal, *-reous*, given to
Venery, *l.* carnal lust, also hunting, *o.*
Venereal disease, French.
Venice, a famous City of *Italy*, built (421.) upon 60 Islands.
Venie, a touch in the body with a weapon.
Venew, as *Venue*.
Venged, *o.* for avenged.
Venial, *-able*, *l.* pardonable
Venial sins, (among Papists) whose guilt the bare confession doth expiate.
Venire facias, a writ for the Sheriff to cause 12 men of the same County to say the Truth upon an issue taken.
Venous, *l.* full of veins.
Venous Artery, a principal one (the other being *Porta* and *Trachea*) carrying blood from the hearts left ventricle to the Lungs.
Venloe, a town in *Gelderland*.
Venire facias tot Matronas, the same as
Ventre inspiciendo, for the search of one that sayes she is with child and withholds land from the next heir at Law.
Vent, *l.* a wind, a report, a breathing-hole.
Venta Belgarum, *Winchester*.
Venta Icenorum, *Caster* in *Nf.*
Venta Silurum, *Caerwent* in *Monmouthshire*.
Vensilia, *Wensyssel*, *-slie*, part of North *Jutland*.

Ventelet, *f.* a small gale.
Ventiduct, *l.* a conveyance of wind.
Ventilate, *l.* to fan or winnow.
Ventosing, *o.* cupping.
Ventosity, *l.* windiness.
Ventoy, *f.* a fan.
Ventricle, *l.* the Stomach, also any round concavity in the body.
Bloudy Ventricle, the right side of the heart containing the natural blood.
Spiritual Ventricle, the left side containing the Arterial blood.
Ventriloquist, one that useth
Ventriloquy, *l.* a speaking (as it were) out of the belly.
Ventripotent, *l.* big-bellied.
Venue, *Venew*, *Visne*, the place next to that where the thing in trial is supposed to be done.
Venundate, *l.* to buy and sell.
Venus, [the Goddess of] lust, also the morning-star (for 9 moneths) and Evening-star (for 9 more.)
Venus Esquage, Knights service to Ladies.
Venus Navel-wort, Kidney-wort, Wall-peny-wort.
Venustate, *l.* to beautifie.
Vepricosous, *l.* full of brambles,
Ver, *l.* the Spring.
Veracity, *l.* a speaking truth.
Verament, *o.* truly.
Veray, *o.* (*q vray*) very.
Verbality, a being
Verbal, *l.* belonging to words or
Verbs, the principal words, without which (exprest or understood) no sentence can be, they signifie Being, as I Am, I read or Am reading, &c.
Verbatim, *l.* word for word.
Verberable, worthy or capable of
Verberation, *l.* a beating.
Verbigerate, *l.* to noise abroad.
Verbosity, a being
Verbose, *l.* full of words.
Verdant, *f.* green, fresh.

Verde,

Verde, *-dea*, white *Florentine* wine.

Verderor, *Viridarius*, a Judicial Officer of the Forest, who receives attachments of all trespasses, &c.

Verd-grease, *Vert-greece*, *Verdig-*, the green rust of brass or copper hang'd over strong vinegar.

Verdict, *Vere-dictum*, the answer of the Jury upon any Cause.

Verditure, one sort of green paint, the other being green-Bice, Vert Greece, and Sap-green.

Verdoy, a bordure charged with leaves, fruits, &c.

Verdure, *-deur*, *f.* greenness.

Verdun, a City in *Lorrain*.

Verecund, *-dous*, *l.* bashfull.

Verge, *f.* a wand, a Sergeants Mace, also the compass of the Kings Court (12 miles) bounding the jurisdiction of the Lord Steward of the Kings houshold.

Verger, *f.* he that bears a *Verge* before a Magistrate.

Vergere, *o.* an Orchard.

Vergobert, a Magistrate (with power of Life and Death) among the *Hedui* (in *France*.)

Veridical, *l.* telling truth.

Veriloquent, *l.* the same.

Verify, *l.* to prove.

Verilaies, as *Vire-*.

Veriloquy, *l.* a speaking truth, or the true Etymologie and meaning of a word

Verisimility, *l.* likely-hood.

Veritrate, *o.* for *Very Trot*.

Vermiculated, *l.* worm-eaten; also wrought with divers colours.

Vermail, *-mell*, *o.* the same as

Vermilion, *f.* a ruddy colour (of Brimstone and Quicksilver.)

Vermination, *l.* a breeding of worms.

Vermiparous, *l.* bringing forth worms.

Vernacia, a kind of Malmsey drunk much at *Rome*.

Vernacle, the Cloth of St. *Veronica*, wherewith Christ wiped his face, and (if you'll believe the Papists) left his picture on it.

Vernaculous, *l.* of ones own countrey.

Vernage, *o.* sweet wine.

Vernal. *l.* of the spring.

Vernant, *l.* green, springing.

Vernility, *l.* slavish behaviour, flattery.

Verona, a *Venetian* City in *Italy*.

Verre, *f.* glass.

Verrey, as *Varry*.

Verrucous, *l.* full of warts.

Versable, *-atile*, capable of

Versation, *l.* turning, winding.

Versicle, *l.* a little verse.

Versify, *l.* to make verses.

Version, *l.* a translation.

Versutiloquent, *l.* speaking craftily.

Vert, (*f.* Green) any Greens (in the Forest) apt to cover Deer.

Vert-greece, as *Verdigreece*.

Vertebræ, Chine-bones.

Verteræ, Burgh under *Stanmore* in *Westmorland*.

Vertible, which one may turn.

Verticality, a being

Vertical, *l.* right over ones head, also wavering.

Verticillate, *l.* knit together as a joynt, also apt to turn.

Verticity, the top of a thing, or aptnesse to turn.

Vertiginous, *-ginous*, troubled with the

Vertigo, *l.* a dizzinesse in the head.

Vertumnals, Feasts unto

Vertumnus, a God of all shapes, governing mens minds.

Vertuoso, as *Virt-*.

Vervain, Holy herb, Pigeons grasse, *Juno's* tears.

Vervecean, *-cine*, of a weather.

Vervels, as *Varv-*.

Vervise, as *Plonkets*.

Verulam, a City of *Hertfordshire*, whose ruines still appear.

Very Lord and Tenant, Immediate.

Vesanous, *l.* mad, outragious.

Vesculent, *l.* Eatable.

Vesicatory, *l.* a cupping-glass, or plaister to raise

Vesicles, *l.* little bladders, blisters.

Vesperal, *l.* Western.

Vespers, *-ra's*, Evening prayers.

Sicilian Vespers, a General Massacre of the *French* by those Islanders (1582.)

Vesperies, [the Sorbonists] evening exercises.

Vespertine, *l.* of the Evening.

Vespilone, *l.* a Night bearer of Corpses in Plague-time, &c.

Vesses, Set-cloaths, commonly made in *Suffolk*.

Vest, a long-skirted doublet.

Vestry-men, a select number of Parishioners who yearly choose Officers.

Vestal Virgins, consecrated (for 30 years) to the service of

Vesta, a *Roman* Goddess, in whose temple if the fire went out, it was to be renewed by the Sun-beams.

Vestiary, a Vestry or Wardrobe.

Vestible, *l.* a porch.

Vestigate, *l.* to seek by the

Vestiges, *l.* foot-steps.

Vestitor, *l.* a Tailor.

Vestment, *l.* (*f. Chasuble*) the Mass-priests upper garment, also as

Vesture, any cloathing; also [admittance to] a possession, and the profit of it.

Vetation, *l.* a forbidding.

Veteran, *l.* [one] old in Office.

Veteratorian, experienced, crafty.

Veteravia, as *Weteraw*.

Veterinarian, belonging to or dealing in Horses

Veterine, *l.* belonging to burdens or carriages.

Vetitum Namium, a distress which the Lord forbids his Bailiff

Bailiff to deliver to the Sheriff who would replevy it.

Vetust, l. old, ancient.

Vexillary, l. [belonging to] an Ensign.

Vexillation, l. a Company under one standard.

Uffa, the first King of the East-Angles.

Ufkins, His Successors.

Uffers, *Usfers*, certain great Ships.

Ugsumness, o. terribleness.

Via combusta, (the burnt-way) the last 15 degrees of *Libra*, and first of *Scorpio*.

Via lactea, the milky-way.

Via solis, a line from the ring-finger toward the hollow of the hand.

Viage, o. for *Voiage*.

Vial, a pot or glass with a wide mouth; all plate serving for wine or water.

Viands, f. victuals [of Flesh.

Viary, l. of the way.

Viatick, l. of a journey.

Viaticum, l. provision for a journey.

Viatorian, l. belonging to

Viator, l. a traveller, also one contra-distinguish'd to comprehensor (who has attain'd the sight of God.)

Vibration, l. a brandishing.

Vibrissation, l. a quavering [in singing.

Vicario deliberando, &c. a writ for a Clerk imprison'd (on forfeiture of a recognisance) without the Kings writ.

Vicarious, l. belonging to a

Vicar, one in anothers stead.

Vice-versa, on the contrary way.

Vicenals, solemn games and vows for 20 years.

Vicennarious, -esime, -mal, l. belonging to the twentieth.

Vice-Chamberlain, next to the Lord-Chamberlain.

Vicegerent, a Deputy.

Vice-roy, f. a Deputy-King.

Vicinage, as *Voisinage*.

Vicinal, belonging to

Vicinity, l. Neighbour-hood.

Vicis & venellis mundandis, a writ against a Mayor, &c. for not cleansing their streets.

Vicissity, -tude, l. a changing by turns.

Vicount, *Visc-*, a Sheriff, also a Noble-man next an Earl;

Writs Vicountiel, triable in the Sheriffs Court.

Vicountiels, Ferms which the Sheriff rents of the King.

Victimate, l. to offer a

Victime, l. a sacrifice.

Victor, l. a Conquerour.

Vidame, *Vice-dominus*, an honour in *France*, (the first of their *Seigneurs Mediocres*) and was at first the same to a Bishop (in his temporal jurisdiction) as a Vicount to an Earl.

Videlicet, *viz.* to wit, that is.

Viduation, l. a depriving or causing.

Viduity, l. widow-hood.

Vie, a town in *Lorrain*.

Viemalim, a small *American* bird feeding on dew and the juice of flowers, and therefore sleeps all the winter.

Viended, o. having plenty of meat.

Vienna, *Wien*, the seat of the German Empire.

Vies, *Devises*, a Castle in *Wilts*.

Vietor, l. a Cooper.

View, the print of a Fallow-Deers foot.

Viewers, sent by the Court to view any place or person.

View of Frank-pledge, the Sheriffs or Bailiffs looking to the Kings peace, and seeing that every man be in some pledge.

Vigesimal, l. of the twentieth.

Vigil, l. a watching, also the Eve of solemn Feasts.

Vigilance, a being

Vigilant, l. watchful.

Vigintivirate, the Office of the

Viginti viri, 20 men in co-equal authority.

Vigone, f. [a Spanish Sheep whose wool makes] a Demi-caster.

Vigorous, l. full of

Vigour, l. strength, courage.

Vi laica removendo, a writ to remove a forcible possession of a benefice by laymen.

Vilify, l. the same as

Vilipend, l. to disesteem.

Vility, l. baseness, cheapness.

Vill, a Mannor, Parish, or part thereof.

Villication, l. the rule of husbandry, under the Master of a Mannor.

Villain, f. a bond-servant.

Villanis Regis subtractis, &c. was a writ for the bringing back the Kings Bondmen taken out of his Mannors.

Villanous Judgment, casting the reproach of Villany on a man, as for Conspiracy, Perjury, &c.

Villein Fleeces, bad ones, shorn from scabbed Sheep.

Villenage, a tenure by doing servile work for the Lord.

Vilna, the chief town and University of *Lithuania* in *Poland*.

Viminal, -neous, l. of Osiers.

Vina Chia, Wines of *Chios* or *Scio*, the best Greek wines.

Vinari envermailed, o. a Vineyard made red.

Vinarious, belonging to Wines.

Vinatorian, of a Vine-dresser.

Vincent, l. Victorious.

Vincible, l. to be overcomn.

Vincture, l. a binding.

Vindemial, -atory, belonging to

Vintage or *Vine-harvest*.

Vindemiate, to gather Grapes, or other ripe Fruits.

Vindication, l. a revenging, also a clearing or delivering.

Vin-

Vindicative, *-ttive*, revengefull.

Vindonum, *Silecester* in *Hantshire*.

Vineatick, *l.* of Vines.

Vincrous, *No.* hard to please.

Vinipote, *l.* a wine-bibber.

Vinitorian, belonging to vines or vine-yards.

Vinnet, a bordure with which Printers garnish their leaves

Vinolent, *l.* full of wine.

Vinosity, a fulnesse of wine.

Vintage, Grape-gathering.

Violate, *l.* corrupt, defile or transgresse.

Viol, an instrument of six strings.

Violin, *f.* (a small Viol) with four.

Base Violin, with four, as the treble.

Viol, a hawser (at the Jeer-capstain) fastened with nippers to the cable (at the Main capstain) for more help in weighing anchor.

Viperine, belonging to a

Viper, a yellowish hot-Countrey-serpent, with a short tail, grating as he goes.

Vipseys, certain springs near *Flamborough* in *Yorkshire*.

Viragin, *-go*, *l.* a manly Woman.

Virason, a Cool Sea-gale about *Hispaniola*, &c.

Vire, *f.* a quarrel or Cross-bow arrow.

Virelay, *f.* a Roundelay.

Virgate of land, a yard-land.

Virge, the raies obliquely striking through a cloud.

Virger, *as Verger*.

Virginal, *l.* virgin-like.

Virginals, a Maidenly Instrument, with keys as the Organ and Harpsicon.

Virginia, part of *America*.

Virgo, *l.* the Zodiack-maid.

Virgula divinatoria, a hazel rod, whereby they pretend to discover mines.

Virgult, *l.* a company of young shoots together.

Viriatus, a *Portingal* Robber, who at last became a great Commander.

Viridario eligendo, for the choice of a *Verderor*.

Viridate, *l.* to cause

Viridity, greennesse, strength

Virility, *l.* Manhood.

Viripotent, [a maid] marriageable.

Virtuoso, *I.* an accomplisht, virtuous and ingenious person.

Virulency, *l.* a being

Virulent, *l.* very venemous.

Viscated, *l.* drest (or caught) with bird-lime.

Visceral, *l.* of the bowels.

Visceration, *l.* a dole of raw flesh; or the garbage given the hounds.

Viscidity, *-cosity*, a being

Viscid, *-cous*, *l.* clammy.

Visel, a town of *Cleves*.

Visibility, *l.* a being

Visible, apt to be seen.

Visier, a prime Officer and Statesman in *Turky*.

Vision, *l.* a sight.

Bishops Visitation, every 3 years.

Arch-Deacons Vis-, every year.

Visitation of manners, the Regarders Office.

Visne, as *Venew*.

Visor, *l.* a spy.

Visu franciplegii, to exempt him from the view of frank-pledge who is not resident in the Hundred.

Visual, belonging to the sight.

Vital, belonging to life.

Vitality, *l.* livelinesse, the spirit of life.

Vitation, *l.* an avoiding

Vitelline, *l.* like the yolk.

Vitemberga, *Wittemberg* in *Germany*.

Vitiate, *l.* to corrupt, debauch.

Vitiferous, *l.* Vine-bearing.

Vitilitigate, *l.* to raise quarrels.

Vitiosity, *l.* a being

Vitious, full of vice.

Vitrean, *-rine*, *-ical*, *l.* of glasse.

Vitrificable, capable of

Vitrification, *l.* a change into glass.

Vitriolous, belonging to

Vitriol, *l.* Copperas, between a stone and metal.

Vituline, *l.* of a Calf.

Vituperable, worthy of

Vituperation, *l.* a blaming.

St. Vitus's dance, a kind of madness, from a malignant humour of kin to the *Tarantula*.

Viva pecunia, live cattel.

Vivâ voce, by word of mouth

Vivacity, livelinesse, vigour.

Vivary, *l.* a place to keep living birds, beasts or fish.

Vivency, a living.

Vivian, (a mans name) lively.

Vivifical, *-cent*, *l.* which doth

Vivify, quicken, or make

Vivid, *l.* lively, strong.

Vivification, an enlivening.

Viviparous, *l.* bringing forth young ones alive.

Vixen, *Fixen*, a little Fox or Vexer.

Vizier, as *Visier*.

Ukrain, part of *Poland*.

Ulcerate, to break out into an

Ulcer, *l.* a running sore, full of putrid virulent matter.

Ulcerous, full of Ulcers.

Ule, *Yule*, *Yeule*, *Yool*, (*Sa. Gehul*) Christmas.

Uliginous, *l.* wet, plashy.

Ulme, a City of North-*Schwaben*.

Ulophone, *g.* venemous glue of *Misleto*, also *Vervilago*, the black or Camelion thistle.

Ulster, an Irish Province.

Ultimity, a being

Ultime, *-mate*, *l.* last, utmost.

Ultima basia, the last kisses (or touches) of the pencil.

Ultion, *l.* a revenging.

Ultra marine, *l.* from beyond-sea.

Ultra mundane, *l.* beyond the [visible] world.

Ultroneous, *l.* with a free-will.

Ulverton, a town in *Lancashire*.

Vlulate, l. to howl.

Vlysses, a subtle Greek, Prince of *Ithaca*, who did great service at the *Trojan* wars.

Vmbel, l. a bone-grace.

Vmbelliferous, bearing.

Vmbels, the round seedy heads of Fennel,&c.

Vmber, a sad yellow paint, also a kind of mungrel-sheep and a tender mouth'd fish.

Vmbilical, l. of the Navel.

Vmbilical arteries, two from the Navel to the sides of the Bladder the first begotten in Infants.

Vnbilical vein, which nourisheth the Infant and (after birth) closeth it self, sealing the Liver to the Navel.

Vmbilicality, a being (like the Navel) in the midst.

Vmbrage, f. a shadow, also suspition.

Vmbragious, *-atical*, *-ile*, *-lous*, l. shady, obscure, private.

Vmbratiles, rotten bodies made visible again by the magical virtue of the stars.

Vmbraid, o. upbraided.

Vmbrello, l. a skreen or fan.

Vmbriferous, l. casting a shadow.

Vmbrosous, l. very shady.

Vmple, o. fine lawn, (q. *Wimple*.)

Vmstrid, No. astride, astridlands.

Vmquhill, *-ile*, o. heretofore.

Vn-, is Negative or Privative, as

Unaccessible, not to be com'n at,

Undeceive, to remove ones mistake, &c.

Unanimity, l. a being

Unanime, *-mous*, of one mind.

Unberd, (q. unbarred) o. laid open.

Unbethink, *On-*, *sc.* to bethink.

Unbreyden, o. unbraided.

Uncome, o. a Fellon.

Uncore-prist, the Defendants plea (sued for a debt) that he tendred it and is yet ready to pay.

Uncoupted, o. for uncoupled.

Uncuth, *sa.* unknown, also a Guest of one night, for whose offence the Landlord was not answerable.

Unction, l. annointing.

Vnctorian, belonging thereto.

Unctuosity, a being

Unctuous, l. oily, fat.

Uncus, l. a hook or anchor.

Undation, l. a flowing of waves.

Undee, (in Heraldry,) like waves.

Undenae, earthly Spirits.

Under-setter, an Inmate.

Undertakers, were Deputies to the Kings Purveyors.

Undercroft, a vault underground.

Underfong, o. undertake.

Undergrow, o. little of stature.

Undermeles, o. afternoons.

Undern, *-noon*, o. afternoon.

Underneme, o. (take down) Excommunicate.

Underspore, o. put under.

Undisonant, roaring like waves.

Undulate, *-ted*, made like waves.

Undulation, a moving up and down like waves.

Uneth, *Um-*, o. scarce, with difficulty.

Unganand, o. ungainly, foolish.

Ungreable, o. for unagreeable.

Unguent, l. ointment.

Unguentum armarium, weapon salve.

Unhele, o. sickness.

Unick, *-ique*, f. the only.

Unicornous, l. of one horn.

Unify, l. to make one.

Unidel, o. in vain.

Uniformity, a being

Uniform, l. of one fashion.

Union, as *Unity*, also the combining or consolidating two Churches into one.

Union-pearls, the best sort, growing alwaies in couples.

Uniparous, l. bearing one at a time.

Unison, f. the agreement of 2 notes in one.

Unition, l. a causing

Unity, l. oneness, concord.

Unity of Possession, a joint possession of 2 rights by several titles, as having a Lease of Land, and then also buying the Fee-simple of it.

Universality, l. a being

Universal, general, all.

University (in Civil Law,) a Corporation or body politick,

Universities, the Scholastick Societies in *Oxford* and *Cambridge*.

University Colledge, the most ancient in *Oxford*, founded by King *Alfred*.

Univocal, l. of one voice or word, signifying but one thing.

Univocally spoken, apply'd to more in the same signification.

Vnkennel, force [the Fox] from his hole.

Vnlage, Sa. a wicked or unjust law.

Vnlawful Assembly, of 3 (or more) with force to commit some unlawfull act; and (for the exercise of religion) 5 above those of the family.

Vnleash, let go the dogs.

Vnna, a Town of *Mark* in *Germany*.

Vnplite, o. to explain.

Vnques prist, a plea by professing ones self always ready to do what is required.

Vn sans Changer, f. one without changing, alway the same.

Vnseliness, o. unhappinesse.

Vnsperd, (q. unspard) o. unlockt.

Vnsumm'd, [hawks feathers] not at their full length.

Unſwote, o. not ſweet.
Untachyd, o. [a bittour] dreſt.
Unthewed, o. unmannerly.
Unweather, *Sa.* a ſtorm, tempeſt.
Unwemmed, o. unſpotted.
Unwiſt, o. unknown.
Unwit, o. folly.
Unwrie, o. uncover.
Unyolden, o. not yeilded.
Vocabulary, l. a ſmall Dictionary, or book of words.
Vocality, a being
Vocal, l. belonging to voice.
Vocation, l. a Calling.
Vocative, belonging to calling.
Vociferation, l. a crying out.
Voculation, the right accenting of a word.
Vogue, f. Sway, authority, clear paſſage [of a ſhip at Sea.
Voidance, *Vacatio*, the want of an Incumbent on a Benefice.
Voider, an Arch-line moderately bowing from the corner of the Chief to the Nombril of th' Eſcutcheon.
Voiders, broad diſhes (or baskets) to take away the remains at Table.
Voiding, (in Heraldry) taking away ſome part of the inward ſubſtance, ſo that the field is ſeen through the Charge.
Voitland, part of *Saxony*.
Voiſinage, f. Neighbourhood.
Volage, f. unconſtant.
Volant, f. flying.
Volary, a flying-place.
Volatility, a being
Volatical, -*il*, -*lous*, flying, not fixt, apt to evaporate.
No ens Volens whether one will or no.
Volgivagant, *Vul*-, l. like or among the Common people.
Volitate, l. to flit up and down.
Volition, a willing.
Vollow, *Sf.* fallow.
Volocity, l. a flying.

Voloy, a river in *Lorrain*.
Volta, *Lav*-, *I.* a courſe or turn [in riding, dancing, &c.
Volubility, l. a being
Voluble, l. eaſily rolled, round, nimble in ſpeech.
Volumus, (we will) the firſt word of a Clauſe in the Kings Writs of Protection and Patents.
Voluminous, of a large
Volume, the bulk or ſize of a book.
Voluntary, l. free, without force.
Volunde, o. the will.
Voluntative, proceeding from the will.
Voluper, o. a Kerchef, (*q. inveloper.*)
Voluptable l. pleaſurable, cauſing delight.
Voluptuous, l. devoted to pleaſure.
Volutation, l. a rolling.
Volutina, the Goddeſs Overſeer of the cups wherein the corn is encloſed.
Vomanus, a river in Italy.
Vomes, (*q. fomes*) o. foming.
Vomition, l. a vomiting.
Vomitory, belonging thereto.
Voor, *Sf.* a furrow.
Voracity, l. greedy devouring.
Voraginous, like a
Vorago, l. a Whirl-pool or Gulph.
Voration, l. a devouring.
Votary, l. he that binds himſelf by a vow.
Vote, l. a voice or ſuffrage.
Votive, l. vowed or deſired.
Vouch ye ſave, o. for Vouchſafe.
Voucher, f. a calling one into Court to Warrant or make good a thing, alſo to avouch, avow, affirm boldly.
Voucher, *Vocans*, he that voucheth.
Vouchee, *Warrantus*, that is vouched.
Vound-ſtone, (q. found or foundation) o. free-ſtone.

Vowels, the ſingle ſounding letters, *a*, *e*, *i*, (or *y*,) *o*, *u*.
Voyles, f. vails [for Nuns.
Upland, high-ground, not Mooriſh.
Up-ſetting-time, *T.* when the Child-bed woman gets up.
Uphap, o. (*q.* heap up) overcover.
Upplight, o. taken up.
Upriſt, o. for up-riſing
Upſwale, o. ſwelled up.
Uppingham, a town in Rutland.
Upton, (upon Severn) in *Worceſterſhire*, and about 50 more ſmall towns.
Upſal, a City and Univerſity in *Sweden*.
Vraic, Wrack, a Sea-weed uſed for fuel in *Jerſey* and *Gernſey*.
Urania, the Heavenly Muſe.
Uranoſcopy, g. a view of the Heavens.
Urbane, -*nical*, l. of a City.
Urbanity, l. Civility, Courteſy.
Urbicarian, l. of the City [*Rome*.
Ure, o. (*f. heur*) chance.
Urent, l. burning, parching.
Ureter, g. the urine-pipe from the reins to the bladder.
Urgent, l. preſſing.
Uriah, h. fire of the Lord.
Uriel, h. the fire of God.
Uriconium, the village Wrekceſter, (once a famous City) in *Shropſhire*.
Urim and Thummim, h. (lights and perfections) the bright precious ſtones in the High-Prieſts breſt-plate, *Lev.* 8.
Urinary, the urine-pipe from the bladder.
Urinator, l. a Diver.
Urith, *So.* Etherings or haſle-windings of hedges.
Urn, l. a pitcher [for the aſhes of a burnt corps;] alſo 2 gallons and a half.
Uroſcopy, g. a caſting ones water.
Urſa major, the Greater

Bear, and

Ursa minor, the Lesser Bear, Northern Constellations.

Ursine, bear-like.

Ursula, l. a little she-bear.

Urus, *Ure-ox*, a huge wild bull.

Urynes, *o.* Nets to catch Hawks.

Usance, *f.* use, usage.

At Usance, at the months end.

Double Usance, two months

User de action, the pursuing an Action in the proper County.

Ushers (in the Exchequer) 4 that attend the Chief Officers.

Usedom, an Isle of *Pomeren*

Usquebagh, *Iscobah*, *Irish* Aqua-vitæ.

Ustion, l. a burning.

Ustulate, l. to burn or sear.

Ustulation, a curling with hot irons.

Usucaption, l. prescription or long possession.

Usufructuary, l. [one] reaping the profit of that whose propriety is anothers.

Usury, l. [the taking] Interest or Use-money.

Usurpation, l. a taking against right.

Utas, the eighth day after any Term or Feast.

Utensils, *f.* houshold-stuff, things necessary for use (in house or shop.)

Uterine, l. of the womb.

Utible, that may be used.

Utility, l. profitableness.

Utinam, l. I (or a) wish.

Utfangthef, *Sa.* a Lords Privilege of punishing a Thief taken within his Fee, though he dwell (and commit the theft) out of it.

Utlagato capiendo, &c. a writ for the taking an

Utlage, *Sa.* an Out-law.

Utlary, *-awry*, the making one an Out-law, for contemptuous refusing to appear, when lawfully sought and called into Law.

Utopian, belonging to

Utopia, *g.* a feigned well-governed Countrey described by Sir *Thomas More*.

Utrecht, a City (near *Holland*) whence you may go to 30 walled towns to dinner and to 50 to bed.

Utter, Outward.

Utter Barristers, that plead without the Bar.

Utterance, *o.* extremity.

Uttoxcetor, a town in *Staffordshire*.

Uval, *Uveal*, l. of a grape.

Uvea tunica, a coat of the eye, like a grape-skin.

Uvid, l. wet, moist.

Uviferous, l. bearing grapes.

Vulcan, *Jupiters* Smith, [the God of] fire.

Vulgarity, l. a being

Vulgar, l. common, vile.

Vulgarization, a making common.

Vulgate, l. published abroad.

Vulgo, l. commonly.

Vulned, (in Heraldry) the same as

Vulnerated, l. wounded.

Vulnerary, [a curer] of wounds.

Vulnifical, l wounding.

Vulpinarinesse, craftiness.

Vulpinate, l. to play the fox.

Vulpine, l. of or like a fox.

Vulsion, l. a pulling.

Vultuosous, l. of a grave (or heavy) countenance.

Vulturine, of or like a

Vulture, l. a ravenous bird.

Vyrel, *o.* (*f. virole*) a ferril at the end of a staff.

Uvula, l. the palate.

Uvula-spoon, to blow up pepper and salt to the Uvula hanging loose.

Uxbridge, a town in *Middlesex*.

Uxellodunum, *Cadenac* in *France*.

Uxorious, l. of (or doting upon) a wife.

Uxitas, the same as

Uzita, an *African* City.

Uzziah, as *Azariah*.

Uzzielites, the Of-spring of

Uzziel, *h.* Gods He-goat.

W.

W*Aar*, *o.* as *Waier*.

Wadenborch, a town in *Westphalia*.

Wafts, signs hung up for a boat to come aboard, or that the ship is in distress.

Waftors, Frigots that convoy Merchant-men.

Waga, *Vaga*, a weigh 256 pound.

Wage, *Gage*, *f.* to put in security, to follow or prosecute.

Wager of Law, an offer to

Wage his Law, make oath (by himself and Compurgators) that he ows not the debt charged by surmize.

Wagerland, part of *Holstein*.

Waif, *Weif*, *derelictum*, what a thief had stoln and (being pursued or overcharged) leaves behind him.

Waild wine, *o.* choice wine.

Wain, (*D. wan*) want, decrease.

Wainable, tillable.

Wair of Timber, 2 yards long and one foot broad.

Waist, as *Waste*.

Waive, to forsake.

Waived (*in women*,) is the same as Outlawed (*in Men*) for contemptuous refusing to appear.

Waiviaria mulieris, is as much as *utlagatio viri*.

Wake, the smooth water which a ship makes a-stern her, and shews what way she goes.

Get her Wake, (in chasing) get as far into the Wind as she, and so go right after her.

Wakeman, the chief Magistrate of *Rippon* in *Yorkshire*.

Wake-Robin, *Arum*, Cuckow-pit, Starch-wort.

Wakes, were vvont to be kept the Sunday after that Saints day to vvhom the Church vvas dedicated.

Walburg, *sa.* Gracious.

Walcheren, an Isle of *Zeland.*

Waldeck, a Saxon County.

Wald, as *Weald.*

Waldenses, a Sect follovving.

Waldo, of *Lions* in *France*, he denied the real presence, condemned the eating of Flesh, &c.

Walwin, *ge.* a Conqueror.

Wallis, *o.* waves.

Wale, as Bend in Navigation.)

Wale-reared, not ship-shapen, but built right up (after she comes to her bearing.)

Walkers, Foresters.

Walker, *D.* a Fuller.

Walk-mill, *No.* a Fulling-mill.

Wallingford, a town in *Berks.*

Wall-Pepper, Stonecrop.

Wallen hoven, a town in *Over-Yssel.*

Walsal, a town in *Staffordshire.*

Walsham, a town in *Norfolk.*

Walsingham, (old and great) in *Norfolk.*

Walt, *No.* to overthrow, totter, or lean one way.

Walt, not having ballast enough.

Walter, *ge.* a Pilgrim or a Wood-man, also to welter, *o.*

Waltham-Abbey, in *Essex.*

Waltsome, *o.* loathsome.

Wandsdike, (*q. Wodensdike*) a wonderful long ditch in *Wiltshire.*

Want, *No.* a mole, or mouldwarp.

Wantage, a town in *Barkshire.*

Wankle, *No.* limber, fickle.

Wang, *sa.* a Field, also a jaw.

Wang-teeth, *o.* Cheek-teeth or Grinders.

Wanger, *o.* a male or bouget

Wanhope, *o.* despair.

Wantrust, *o.* mistrust.

Wantey, a surfingle for Carriers horses.)

Wanwerd, *o.* [hard] fortune.

Waped, *o.* as *Awhaped.*

Wapentake, a hundred (from delivering their weapons to the Lord, in token of subjection.)

Wapse, *&c. Sf.* for wasp, &c.

Warbling of the wings, a Hawks crossing them together over her back.

Warble, to quaver [in singing.

War and War, *No.* worse and worse.

Warch, *Wark*, *No.* to ake, to work.

Ward, the jurisdiction of an Alderman, also part of a Forest, also the heir of a Tenant holding by Knights service, during his nonage.

Warden, a Guardian or Keeper.

Wardcors, (*q. Garde-Corps*) Gard of the body.

Wardmote Court, kept in every ward of *London.*

Ward-robe, where Kings and Great Persons Garments are kept.

Wards and Liveries, a Court erected by King *Hen.* 8. taken away by 12 *Car.* 2.

Wardstaff, carrying a load of straw with 6 horses, two men in Harness, *&c.* to *Aibridge*, (by which service *Lambourn* Mannor in *Essex* is held.)

Wardwit, *-wyte*, *Warwit*, a being quit of paying for watch and ward.

Ware, a town in *Hertfordshire.*

Warectum, *terra Warecta*, land that has lain long untill'd.

Waren, a place priviledg'd by the King, to keep

Beasts and Fowl of Warén, *i. e.* Hares, Coneys, Partridges and Pheasants.

Ware your money, *No.* bestow it well.

Warham, a town in *Dorcetshire.*

Warisht, *No.* well stored, having conquer'd a disease (or difficulty) and secure for the future.

Wariangles, birds full of noise and ravening.

Warison, *o.* reward.

Warish, *o.* to save or deliver.

Warnoth, a forfeit of double rent by the Tenants of *Dover-Castle*, if they fail at the day.

Warned, *o.* denied.

Warnstore, *o.* to fortifie [with arms.

Warp, the thrid at length, into which the woof is woven.

Warp, *aw- sa.* to cast.

Warpe, a hawser (or any rope) used in the

Warping a Ship, haling her in or out of a harbour (for want of wind.)

Warrans, *o.* [wary] designs.

Warrantus, he that makes a

Warranty, a Covenant by Deed, to secure a bargain against all men.

Warrantia Chartæ, a writ for one enfeoffed with clause of Waranty and impleaded in a writ of entry, &c.

Warrantia diei, a writ to excuse ones appearance, being employ'd by the King.

Warrant of Atturney, whereby a man appoints another to do something in his name, warranting his action.

Warrington, a town in *Lancashire*, on the edge of *Cheshire.*

Warsaw, *-sovia*, a town in *Poland.*

VVarscot, a Saxon contribution towards the vvar.

Warth, *No.* a Foord.

Warwick, the chief town of *Warwick-shire.*

Wary, *La.* to curse also to lay an egge.

Wary, *Waren*, *o.* to weary, afflict, consume.

Wash of Oisters, to strike.

VVesc-

Washeringhen, a town in *Gelderland*.

Wash the Ship, by making her heel over to a side vvhen they cannot come aground to careen.)

Wash off the Shore, close by the shore.

Wassail, (*sa.* *Was-heal*)be in health.

Wassail-bowl, of Spiced Ale, on Nevv-years Eve.

Waste, spoil of houses, woods, &c. to the prejudice of the heir, &c. also as *Waste-ground*, lying as *Waste and Common*.

Waste, that part of the Ship between the Main-mast and Fore-castle.

Waste-boards, set up between the gun-wale and wast-trees, or the sides of a boat (to keep the sea out.)

VVaste-clothes, all that are round about the Cake-work of the Ships hull, the fights of a Ship.

VVastel bread, *o.* fine cimnel.

VVatche, a town in *Somersetshire*.

VVatch, (at Sea) 4 hours, also half the Ships company.

VVater-born, just a-flote.

VVaterford, an Irish Port-town.

VVatergage, a Sea-wall or bank, also a gaging instrument.

VVatergang, a trench (or trough) for a stream of water.

VVater-line, the depth that the Ship should swim in, when laden.

VVater-shot, mooring (not a-cross nor with the tide, but) quartering (between both,)

VVater-lock, a fenced watering-place.

VVater-way, a small ledge of timber close by the sides of the Ships deck.

VVatford, a town in *Hertfordshire*.

VVatweil, a town in upper *Alsatia*.

VVatlington, a town in *Oxon*.

VVatling street, *VVerlam-*, one of the Roman High-waies (whereof *Vitalian* had the oversight) from *Dover* to *Anglesey* in *VVales*, also the milky-way.

VVattles, (to fold Sheep) *So.* made of split wood in fashion of gates.

VVave-offerings, certain loaves for yearly first Fruits, *Lev.* 23.

VVavey, (in Heraldry) the resemblance of a swelling wave.

VVaving, making a sign for a Ship (or boat) to come towards (or go from) them.

VVaws, *o.* for waves.

VVax-shot, *-scot*, was paid thrice a year toward Church Candles.

VVay, *o.* to guide.

VVay of a Ship, (forward or aftward-on) the Ships rake and run.

VVay-bred, *No.* Plantain.

VVay-bit, *VVea-*, *VVee-*, *Y.* a little bit, a little more.

VVayled, *o.* grown old.

VVaymenting, *o.* lamenting.

VVaymouth, a town in *Dorcetshire*.

VVainfleet, a town in *Lincolnshire*.

VVayned, *o.* put back.

VVde, *o.* for wood.

VVeald of Kent, (*sa. wald*) the woody part thereof.

VVeanel, a young beast newly weaned.

VVeapon-salve, applyed to the weapon that made the wound.

VVear, *No.* cool [the pot.

VVeat his Head, *No.* look it.

VVeather, to go to windward of a place.

VVeather-bow, *&c.* next the weather.

VVeather-Coils, [the Ship being a-hull] lays her head the other way, without loosing any sail (only by bearing up the helm.)

VVeather-man, an Archer that diligently observes the weather.

VVeather the Hawk, set her abroad to take the air.

VVea-worth you, *No.* woe betide you.

VVebley, a town in *Herefordshire*.

VVebbe, *o.* a VVeaver.

VVed, *sa.* a pawn or pledge.

VVede, *VVeed*, *sa.* a Garment.

VVeel, *La.* a whirlpool.

VVeen, *o.* to think.

VVeet, *VVite*, *No.* nimble, swift.

VVeigh, 256 pound.

VVeild, to rule or sway [a Scepter &c.

VVeir, *VVaar*, *Northum.* Sea-wrack.

VVelked, *o.* withered.

VVelkin, *-kin*, *sa.* the sky.

VVellaneer, *No.* alas!

VVellingborough, a town in *Northampton-shire*.

VVellington, a town in *Shropshire*.

VVells, a City in *Somersetshire*.

VVeleful, *o.* wealthy.

VVell, *o.* to spring.

VVelmeth, *o.* riseth.

VVelt, *o.* (*q.* weilded,) ruled.

VVelsh, *VValsh*, *VVallish*, Gallish.

VVem, *E.* a small blemish [in cloth.

VVend, *No.* to go.

VVenlock, (little and great) in *Shropshire*.

VVeald, *VVold*, *sa.* a Forest.

VVere-wolf, *sa.* a Man-wolf, or German Sorcerer (by an enchanted girdle, &c) turn'd wolf and worrying humane Creatures.

VVere, *VVair*, *so.* a pond.

VVere, *o.* a maze or doubt, also to defend.

VVerb, a town of *Brandenburgh*.

VVerden, a town in *Mark* in *Germany*.

VVerkington, a town in *Cumberland*.

VVerne, *o.* to deny or put off.

VVeroance,

VVeroance, a West-Indian Lord.

VVerre, VVere, VVergeld, -gild, *sa.* a mulct for killing of a man.

The VVergild of an Archbishop (or Earl) was 15 thousand thrimsas.

VVeregelt-thef, a thief that might be redeemed.

VVerre, *o.* grief.

VVerry, *o.* to destroy.

VVerryed, *o.* banished.

VVerth, *o.* for worth.

VVesel, a town in *Cleveland.*

VVestbury, a town in *VVilt-shire.*

VVeston, a town in *Sommerset-shire*, and above 50 more.

VVestloe, a town in *Cornwall.*

VVestphalen, part of

VVestphalia, a large German Province, stored with Chesnuts and good bacon.

VVestern, *o.* to draw toward west.

VVestreth, *o.* setteth at the west.

VVesty, *No.* dizzy, giddy.

VVest-friezland, one of the Neatherlands, feeding the best horses and Cattel in *Europe.*

VVest-Saxonlage, the law of the west-Saxons.

VVestminster, (the Monastery westward of *London*) vvas the ancient seat of our Kings.

VVete, VVit, VViff, *o.* to knovv.

VVeteraw, a German Province.

VVetherby, a tovvn in *York-shire.*

VVhapple-way, *so.* a horse (but not a cart) vvay.

VVharfinger, the keeper of a

VVharfe, a broad place (near the shore) to lay vvares upon.

VVharfage, the fee for landing things there.

VVharre, *Che.* Crabs, as soure as vvharre.

VVheedle, (*Br.* a story) a subtle dravving of one in, also he that doth so.

VVheam, VVheem, *Che.* so close that no vvind can enter it, also convenient.

VVheamow, *No.* Nimble.

VVheden, *we.* a simple fellovv.

VVheen-cat, *No.* a she-cat.

VVheen (or Queen) fugol, *sa.* a Hen-Fovvl.

VVheint lad, *Che.* (*q. Queint*) a fine lad (ironically.)

VVhelps, like brackets set to the body of the Capstain.

VVhere, *o.* a maze.

VVhicket for *VVhacket*, *Quittee* for *Quattee*, *K. Quid pro quo.*

VVhiche, *o.* on ark or chest.

VVhids, *c.* vvords.

VVhilk, *o.* vvhich.

VVhilom, *o.* heretofore.

VVhines, [the Otter] cries.

VVhins, Furs, Fursbushes.

VVhip, *-staff*, vvith vvhich the steers-man turns the helm.

VVhirkened, *No.* choaked.

VVhirlbat, as *VVhorl-*.

VVhirlbone, upon the knee.

VVhisket, *No.* a basket or shallovv ped.

VVhit, *c.* Nevv-gate.

VVhite, *Che.* to requite, also to blame.

Lean the VVhite off your sell, *No.* remove the blame from your self.

VVhite-hall, *York-Place*, taken from Cardinal *VVolsey* by King *Hen.* 8.

VVhite-hart Forest, Blackmore-.

VVhite-hart Silver, imposed on *Tho. de la Linde* (by King *Hen.* 3) for kiling a beautiful vvhite hart, and is still paid.

VVhite-spurs, a sort of Esquires.

VVhitby, a tovvn in *York-shire.*

VVhit-Church, a tovvn in *Hant. Shropshire*, and several others.

VVhitmister, a tovvn in *Glocestershire.*

VVhite straites, a course kind of *Devonshire* cloth.

VVhitle, to make vvhite [by cutting.

Whittle, *we.* a doubled blanket worn over Womens Shoulders.

Whitlow-grass, Nailwort, good against

Whitlows, or Fellons.

Whitsontide, the time about

Whitsunday, (*Sa.* Wied, sacred) when the Holy Ghost descended on the Apostles in the form of fiery tongues, and when there was wont to be a General Baptism in white.

Whoave, *Che.* to cover or whelm over.

Whole case boots, large hunting or riding boots.

Who whiskin, *Che.* a Whole drinking black pot.

Wholsom ship, as *Howlsom.*

Whoodings, the planks fastened alongst the Ships side into the stem.

Whookt, *Che.* shook [every joynt.

Whorlbats, straps (with leaden plummets) used in Roman exercises.

VVhorts, the same as

VVhortle-berries, Bilberries.

VViborch, a City in North *Juitland.*

VViche, a town in *Utrecht.*

VVick, *o.* stinking, counterfeit.

VVicket, *c.* a casement.

VVickham, a town in *Bucks.*

VVickliviſts, *-vians*, followers of

VVicklif, Curate of *Lutterworth* in *Leicestershire*, (1380.)

VVickware, a town in *Glocestershire.*

VVidows-bench, *Sf.* a share of their husbands Estate which they enjoy beside their jointure.

VViegh, VVaagh, *No.* a leaver or wedge.

VVieres, *o.* Witches, Destinies.

VVigan, a town in *Lancashire.*

VVight, an Isle on the South of *England.*

VVight, *o.* swift.

VVighton, a town in *York-shire.*

VVigor-

VVigornia, Worcester.

VVigreve, *Sa.* a Wood-ward.

VVild-fire, invented by the *Grecians*, (about 717.)

VVildeshusen, a town in *Westphalia*.

VVild-water-cresses, Ladies smock, Cuckow-flower.

VVilfred, *Sa.* Much peace.

St. Wilfrids needle, a hole (in a vault under *Rippon* Church) through which Chaste Woman might pass, others not.

Wilk, *VVhilk*, *No.* a peri-winkle or Sea-Snail.

Last will, a Testament. But a Testament properly has an Executor exprest.

VVill of the wisp, Ignis fa-tuus.

VVillern, *No.* Wilfull, pee-vish.

VVilliam, (*Ge. VVilhelm*) Much defence, or (*Guild-helm*) having a gilt helmet.

VVillow-weed, *-herb*, loose-strife.

VVilton-house, the Seat of the Earls of *Pembroke*, near

VVilton, a town in *VVilt-shire*.

VVily, full of wile or craft.

VVimple, a plaited linnen about the necks of Nuns; also a flag or streamer.

VVimborn-minster, in *Dor-cetshire*.

VVimund, *Sa.* sacred peace.

VVinne, *o.* to complain.

VVincaunton, a town in *Som-merfetshire*.

VVinch, a pulling (or screw-ing) Engine.

VVinchcomb, a town in *Glo-cestershire*.

VVinchelsey, a town in *Sus-sex*.

VVinchester, a town in *Hantshire*, another in *North-umberland*.

VVind-berry, *No.* bill-ber-ry.

VVind the ship, bring her head about (with the boat or oars at the stern-ports.)

How winds the ship? On what point of the compass lies her head?

VVinder, *o.* to trim [the hair.

VVinding-tackle, for the hoysing-in of goods.

VVindlass, the beam which (with hand-speeks) winds-in the Cables.

VVind-row, Hay (or grass) raked in rews, to be cockt.

VVindsore, *VVindleshore*, a town in *Barkshire*, another in *Cornwall*.

VVind-taught, [too much rigging, &c.] holding wind stiffly aloft.

VVine Ape, *o.* Apianum, Muscadel.

VViners, *o.* Vine-branches.

VVinfrid, *Sa.* Win-peace, a mans name.

VVinifred, *-nef-*, a *British* Virgin-Saint, revived by *Bruno* the Priest, after *Cradacus* had cut off her head, in a place where sprang up

St. VVinfreds well, in *Flint-shire*.

VVinly, *No.* quietly.

VVinslow, a town in *Bucks*.

VVinter-heyning, from *Nov.* 11. to *Aril* 23. No common-ing (that while) in Dean-forest.

VVinter-rigg, to fallow land in winter.

VVisard, *VViz-*, (*Sa. VVite-ga*, a prophet) a cunning-man.

VVise-acre, (*D. VVaer-seg-her*) Tom Tell-troth, a fool.

VVise-men of Greece, 7 viz. *Solon*, *Chilo*, *Cleobulus*, *Thales*, *Bias*, *Pittacus*, and *Perian-der*.

VVisbbich, a town in *Cam-bridgshire*.

VVishippers, *o.* Astrolo-gers.

VVish, *o.* to wash.

VVisket, as *VVhisket*.

VVisly, *o.* even.

VVismar, a Hans town in *Meklenbourg*.

VVist, *o.* to advise, to save or secure.

VVist, *Sa.* known.

VVitcher, *c.* silver.

VVitcher-bubber, *c.* a silver-bowl.

VVitcher-cully, *c.* a silver-smith.

VVitcher tilter, *c.* a silver-hilted-sword.

VVitfree, a priviledge from

VVite, *Sa.* a penalty or fine; also to blame, *No.*

VVitterden, *-red*, *VVin-terd-*, a West-Saxon tax im-posed by the publick Coun-cel of the Kingdom.

VVithernam, *Sa.* the driv-ing away a distress, so that the Sheriff (upon the Re plevin) cannot deliver it to the party distreined.

Withers, the extream part of a horses neck, near the saddle bow.

Withsey, *o.* to deny.

Withsit, *o.* to withstand.

Witney, a town in *Oxon*.

Wittal, *-ol*, *Sa.* one that knows himself a Cuckold

Wittemberg, the seat of the Saxon Electors.

Witten Witterly, *o.* to know certainly.

Wivescomb, a town in *Som-metsetshire*.

Wiver, as *Wyver*.

Wlate, *Sa.* to hate or loath.

Woad, (*I Guado*) an herb (like plantain) used in dying blew.

VVoadmell, a hairy course stuff, made of Island vvool.

VVoborn, a tovvn in *Bed-fordshire*, another in *Bucks*.

VVoddeth, *o.* grovvs mad.

VVoden, *Sa.* (fire or furi-ous) an Idol giving name to Wednesday.

VVodensburgh, a village in *VViltshire*.

VVogh, *La.* a vvall.

VVolds, *Sa.* plain vvood-less hills.

VVolgast, a tovvn in *Po-merania*.

VVollin, an Isl and of *Po-merania*.

VVolves teeth, a (in a hor-ses upper javv) that hinder his chevving.

VVol-

Wolverhampton, a town in *Stafford*.

Won, o. ftore,plenty.

Wone, o. a dwelling place.

Wonde, o. to turn back.

Wonders of the world 7. *viz*. 1. The Pyramids. 2. *Mausolæum*. 3. The Temple of Ephefus. 4 Walls of *Babylon*. 5. *Coloffus* of *Rhodes*. 6. Statue of *Jupiter Olympicus*. 7. The *Egyptian Pharus*.

Wong, *Sa*. a field.

Wonne, *D*. to dwell; alfo (*q. Wont*) a fafhion or cuftom, and a remedy, o.

Wood, *Wod*, *Sa*. mad.

Woodbinde, Honey-fuckle.

Woodcock-foil, *So*. of a woodcock colour, not good.

Woodgeld, cutting wood in the foreft, alfo [a freedom from paying]money for the fame.

Woodmote Court, the Foreft Court of Attachments.

Wood-plea Court, held (twice a year) in the Foreft of *Clun* in *Salop*.

Woodfhaw, o. wood-fide or fhadow.

Woodftock, a town in *Oxon*.

Woodftock tower, a Labyrinth built by King *Hen*. 2. for *Rofamund Clifford* (utterly defaced.)

Wood-wants, *No*. holes in a poft or piece of Timber.

Woodward, a Foreft-Officer (walking with a foreft-bill) prefenting all offences, &c.

Woodwofe, a wild-man or Satyr.

Wood and Wood, letting 2 fhip-timbers clofe into one another.

Woof, the thred weaved crofs the warp.

Wool-drivers, they buy wool of fheep-mafters, and carry it on horfback to Markets.

Wolfefhead, as *Wulves*-.

Wooldbridge, a town in *Suffolk*.

Woolpit, another.

Wool-ftaple, the Town where wool was fold.

Wool winders, that wind or bundle up the fleeces, (fworn to do it truly between the owner and buyer.)

Wopen, o. for wept.

Woor, the fame as

Wore, *K*. Sea-Wrack.

Worcefter, the City of that fhire.

Worch-bracco, *Che*. (Work-brittle) intent upon ones work.

Workesworth, a town in *Darbyfhire*.

Wormatia, the City

Wormes, in *Germany*.

Worm, an iron at a ftaffs end to draw fhot out of a piece.

Worm the cable, ftrengthen it by laying a fmall rope alongft it between the ftrands

Worried, *No* choakt.

Worfop, a town in *Nottingham*.

Worftead, a town in *Norfolk*.

Wort, as *Wart*.

Worth, o. to be.

Worth up, o. to afcend.

Woft, o. knoweft.

Wotton, above 30 fmall towns.

Wotton-baffet, in *Wilts*.

Wotten underedge, in *Glocefterfhire*.

Would the maft, &c. bind it with a rope to keep on the fifh (or fomewhat to ftrengthen it.)

Wouldings of the bolt-fprit, the ropes that lafh it faft down from rifing off the pillow.

Wowe, o. a field or wood.

Sea-Wrack, a Sea-weed.

Wrake and Wreche, o. wrath and revenge.

Wranglands, mifgrown trees that will never prove timber.

Wrathed, o. moved to anger.

Wrawnes (*q*. Wrothnefs or roughnefs) o. frowardnefs.

Wray, *Wrey*, o. to bewray, difcover.

Wreath, a Boars tail, alfo a Torce (between the Mantle and the Creft.)

Wreck, (*f. Varech*) the perifhing of a fhip and every perfon in it. What part of it is caft afhore belongs to the King, but if man, dog, or cat efcape, the goods are the owners ftill (if claim'd within a year and day.)

Wreedt, *D*. Wroth.

Wreke, *D*. to revenge.

Wrenches, o. traps, cheats.

Wreken, -*kyn*, as *Reking*.

Wreme, o. to compafs about.

Wright, *Wyrhta*, *Sa*. a workman.

Writ, (*breve*, *actio*, *formula*) the Kings precept whereby any thing is commanded to be done touching a Sute or Action.

Original Writs, fent out of the high Court of Chancery to begin the fute.

Judicial Writs, from the Court where the Caufe depends, after the Sute is begun.

Wro, o. Wrath, grief.

Wroken, o. revenged.

Wrot, o. forrowful.

Wrotham, a town in *Kent*.

Wry, *Wryne*, *Wrene*, o. to cover.

Wryen, o. to change, alfo as

Wrygh, o. covered.

Wryeth, o. getteth, worketh.

Wrytheth, o. cafteth out.

Wulfer, *Sa*. helper.

Wulfrune, a devout Woman who enriched

Wulfrunes Hampton, *Wolver-hampton* in *Staffordfhire*.

Wulvesheved, -*head*, *Sa*. the condition of an Outlaw, whofe head was accounted as a Wolfs.

Wun, *No*. as *Wonne*.

Wurtsberg, *Wir*-, Herbipolis, a City in Germany, whofe hills abounded with

Warts, *Worts*, *fa*. Herbs.

Wyke, a farm or little village.

VVyte, as *VVit*.

VVych-house, the house in which the salt is boiled.

VVyuer, (*q. Viper*,) *o.* a kind of Serpent.

VVye, a town in *Kent*.

VVymondham, a town in *Norfolk*.

VVynsing, *o* a sweet singer.

VVyntrea *o.* wrinkled.

VVyse. *o.* a Proverb.

VVyshe, *o.* [he] washed.

VVyten, *o.* to keep [from falling, &c.

VVyttes, *o.* the Senses.

X.

X*Aintogne*, *Sain-*, a Province of *France*.

Xangti, (among the *Chinois*) the supreme Govern of Heaven and Earth.

Xanthi, a People of *Asia*.

Xantippe, the froward wife of *Socrates*, who said he kept her to exercise his patience.

Xantho, one of the Sea-Nymphs.

Xanthus, *Scamander*, a River by *Troy*.

Xativa, a town of *Valentia* in *Spain*.

Xenocrates, a severe *Chalcedonian* Philosopher.

Xenodochy, *g*, an Inne or Hospital.

Xenophon, a famous *Athenian* Philosopher and general.

Xensi, a principal Province of *China*.

Xeres [*de la frontera*,] a town of *Andaluzia* in *Spain*.

Xeriff, the title of some *Barbarian* Princes.

Xerophagy, *g.* the eating of dry Meats.

Xerophthalmy, *g.* a dry red itching of the eyes.

Xerxes, Son of *Darius* and King of *Persia*, whose Army of seventeen hundred thousand men was beat by fourty thousand Greeks.

Xilinous, *l.* of Cotton.

Xyloaloes, as *Lignum Aloes*.

Xylobalsamum, *g.* the sweet wood that produceth Balm.

Xylopolist, *g.* a VVood-monger.

Y.

Y*A. D.* yea, *Y.*

Yacht, a Dutch pleasure-boat.

Yall, *o.* to go (*f.* Aller.)

Yape, *o.* to jest.

Yard, three foot, settled (saies Sir *Richard Baker*) by *Hen.* 1. according to the length of his own arm.

Yard, the timber (cross the mast) at which the sail hangs.

Main-yard, five 6 parts of the keels length, &c.

Top the Yards, make them hang even.

Yard-*land*, Verge of land an uncertain quantity from 15 to 40 acres.

Yare, *No.* Covetous.

Yare, *Sf.* nimble, smart.

Yare, *o.* ready.

Yark, *No.* prepare.

Yarmouth, a Port of *Norfolk*, also another in *Wight*.

Yarn, *o.* to study.

Yarrow, *o.* faint-hearted, also an herb that stops bleeding.

Yarum, a town in *Yorkshire*.

Yate, Yatt, a Country Gate.

Yave, Yafe, *o.* gave, regarded.

Yaws, [the Ship] goes in and out with her head.

Ybe, *o.* for been.

Ybet, *o.* made shetter.

Yblent, *o*, blinded.

Ybourded, *o* jested.

Ycast (for *Y cast*) *o.* left.

Ychaped with silver, *o.* having a silver handle.

Ycleaped, *sc.* called.

Yclenched, *o.* covered, crossbar'd.

Yclothed, *o.* for clothed.

Ycorven, *o.* cut.

Ycrased, *o.* broken.

Ydo, *o.* stayed or (for *Ydon*) done.

Ydraw, *o.* for draw.

Year, *Day* and *Waste*, the King has the profits of their Lands & Tenements that are attainted of Petit-Treason and Felony for a Year and a Day, and also may (except the Lord of the Fee agree with him for it) destroy the houses, root up woods, &c.

Lunar Year, twelve revolutions of the Moon, three hundred fifty four daies.

Solar Year, three hundred sixty five daies and six hours.

Yearn, to bark as Beagles at their prey.

Yearn, *o.* shrill.

Yedding, *o.* brawling and cadding.

Yede, as *Yewed*.

Yeeld, *o.* to reward.

Yeender, *Eender*, *Der.* the forenoon.

Yeander, *No.* yonder.

Yeepsen- *Yaspen*, *E.* as much as can be taken up in both hands together.

Yef, *o.* for If.

Yefts, *o.* for Gifts.

Yeld-hall, *o.* for Guild-hall.

Yelding, *o* for yeelding.

Yellow-goulds *o.* Marigolds.

Yeme, (*q. Hyeme*) Winter.

Yeman, *Yeoman*, (*q. Young man*, or *Geman*, *sa.* a married man or common, or else *Guma*, *sa.* a painful man) *Ingenuus*, the next in order a Gentleman.

Yeoman, an Officer in the Kings house between the Serjeant and the Groom.

Yeogmen, for *Yeomen* in 33 *Hen.* 8.

Yene, *o.* nigh, or as in

Afore Yene, *o.* over against.

Yerd, *o.* rod, plague, Government.

Yern, *o.* (for earn) to deserve

ſerve or deſire, alſo earneſtly.

Yepely, o. cunningly, vviſely.

Yeſts, (q. heſts,) o. precepts.

Yetten, o. to get, lay up.

Yeve, o. for Give.

Yeven, Yeoven, o. for Given, Dated.

Yewd, No. VVent.

Yewing, o. going.

Yex, to Hick-cough or Hick up.

Yfrounſed, o. frovvning.

Yfor this, o. even as.

Yhed, o. on high.

Yhold, o. held, accounted.

Ykleped, o. named.

Yle, (q. idle) o. vain, empty.

Ynde, (q. Indian) o. black.

Ynow, o. enough.

Yod, as Yewd.

Yoke, a double rope (from the helm to the ſhip-ſides) to help the ſteering (vvhen their hands are too vveak.)

Yolden, o. yielded.

Yoman, See Yeman.

Yonker, D. a Gentleman.

Yonkers, the young foremaſt-men vvho take in top-ſails, &c.

Of Yore, o. heretofore.

Yorely, o. ancient.

York, the City of that ſhire.

Youghall, an Iriſh Port.

Youketh, [the havvk] ſleeps.

Yoxley, a tovvn in Huntingtonſhire.

Ypiked, o. ſet forth [vvith peaks.

Ypocras, o. Hippocrates.

Ypres, Ipres, a tovvn in Flanders.

Yqueint, o. quenched.

Yreken, o. raked.

Yren o. diſpleaſure (Ira.)

Yſam, o. ſeen.

Yſlawe, o. ſlain.

Yſſelſtein, a tovvn in Holland.

Yſteppe, o. ſtepped.

Yſtorve, -en, o. dead.

Ytake, o. taken.

Ytwight, o. tvvitched.

Yuernagium, the vvinter ſeed-time.

Yuba, an Indian herb of vvhich they make bread.

Yu batch, No. a Chriſtmas batch.

Yu-block, No. the ſame as Yule-block, a Chriſtmas block.

Yu-games, No. the ſame as Yul-games, See Yle.

Yule-dag, Da. Chriſtmas day.

Yule of Auguſt, Lammas.

Yvoire, o. Ivory.

Ywoxe, o. vvaxen, grovvn.

Ywrien, o. covered.

Ywroke, o. for VVreaked, revenged.

Z.

Z-, (In the Weſt.) for S-.

Zaara, the Deſert, Lybia.

Zabern, or Elſaſz-Zavern, a tovvn in lovver Alſace.

Zabulon, Ze-, b. a dvvelling-place.

Zachary, -riah, b. mindfull of the Lord.

Zacynthus, Zante, a Venetian Iſland, VVeſt of Greece.

Zacutus Lyſitanus, a famous Jevv Phyſician in Amſterdam.

Zald, Sc. (q. Yald) yielded.

Zaleucus, a Locrian Lavvgiver vvho put out one of his ovvn eyes & one of his Sons, to fulfill his ovvn lavv againſt adultery.

Zamolſis, a Thracian Philoſopher.

Zane, I. [a ſilly] John.

Zany, I. a Tumbler vvho procures laughter by his mimick geſtures, &c.

Zanni, I. ſuch Jack-puddings.

La Zeecha, the Mint at Venice.

Zara, a Venetian City in Dalmatia.

Zecchine, I. a gold coin about 7 ſhillings 6 pence.

Zecchine, Tu. vvorth 9 ſhillings.

Zede, Sc. vvent [to vvrack.

Zedekiah, Zid-, b. the Juſtice of the Lord.

Zedoary, an Indian hot and dry plant.

Zeland, one of the united provinces, alſo a Daniſh Iſland.

Zelot, g. one that is jealous or zealous (fervent.)

Zelotypi, g. Jealouſy.

Nova Zembla, a nevv-diſcovered Northern Iſle.

Zenith, A. the point directly over our heads.

Zeno, a Greek Philoſopher Authour of the Stoicks.

Zenobia, Zebennia, Queen of Palmyrene in Syria, ſhe Uſurpt the Governement of the vvorld, but vvas overcom'n and led in triumph (by Aurelian) in golden chains.

Zephyre, -rus, g. Favonius, the Weſt-vvind.

Zereth an hebrevv meaſure of 9 inches.

Zero, ſ. the Cypher or Nought.

Zerubbabel, Zorobabel, b. repugnant to confuſion.

Zeſt, f. the peel of an Orange, &c. ſqueezed into a glaſs of vvine (to reliſh it.)

Zethus, a Muſician, tvvin-brother to Amphion.

Zeugma, (g. a joyning) making the verb (or Adjective) by ſupplement to anſvver divers ſuppoſites.

Zeuxis, a famous Greek Painter.

Zimri, b. a Song.

Zink, as Spelter.

Zodiack g. an imagined circle containing the yearly courſe of the Sun through the 12 Signs, viz. Aries, Taurus, Gemini, Cancer, Leo, Virgo, Libra, Scorpio, Sagittarius. Capricornus, Aquarius, Piſces.

Zoiliſts, men that imitate

Zoilus, Homeromaſtix, a critical carping Poet of Amphipolis vvho wrote againſt

gainst Homer.

Z. me, a River in Brabant.

Zonarious, belonging to a

Zone, g. a girdle, or purse, also a fifth part of the heavens.

Torrid Zone, between the two Tropicks of Cancer and Capricorn.

Temperate Zones, between the Tropicks and the Polar Circles.

Frigid Zones, between the Polar Circles and the very Poles.

Zonigrism, an instrument (with a long narrow neck) to convey bitter potions into the stomach.

Zonnets, fantastical bodies of the Gnomes or Pigmy-Spirits.

Zoögraphical, belonging to a

Zoögrapher, an author of

Zoögraphy, g. a description (or painting) of beasts.

Zoöphites, g, plant-animals, partaking the Nature both of plants and living creatures, as spunges, &c.

Zopyrus, he cut off his ears, &c and fled to Babylon (pretending Darius had done it) and (being made their general) betray'd it.

Zoroäster, the first King of Bactria, and Author of Persian Magick, who laught (they say) so soon as he was born.

Zorobabel, as Zerubb-.

Zubal, the Philippine Island where Megellan died.

Zube, Stovene, a withered or dry stock of wood.

Zulp, a town by Colen.

Zundel, tinder.

Zutphen, one of the United Provinces.

Zwallock, a town in Cornwall.

Zweibrucken Deux ponts, a Dukedome in the lower Palatinate.

Zygostatical, belonging to a pound of 16 ounces (or to a

Zygostate, g. the Clark of a Market.

Zythepsary g. a brew-house.

Zz, a mark (in old Physicians) for Myrrh.

FINIS.

www.ingramcontent.com/pod-product-compliance
Lightning Source LLC
Chambersburg PA
CBHW031545260326
41914CB00002B/272

* 9 7 8 1 5 8 4 7 7 5 9 5 9 *